THE ENCYCLOPEDIA OF APOCALYPTICISM

Volume 1
The Origins of Apocalypticism in
Judaism and Christianity

The Encyclopedia of Apocalypticism
Edited by Bernard McGinn,
John J. Collins, and Stephen J. Stein

Volume 1
*The Origins of Apocalypticism
in Judaism and Christianity,*
edited by John J. Collins

Volume 2
Apocalypticism in Western History and Culture,
edited by Bernard McGinn

Volume 3
*Apocalypticism in the Modern Period
and the Contemporary Age,*
edited by Stephen J. Stein

THE ENCYCLOPEDIA
OF APOCALYPTICISM

Volume 1
THE ORIGINS OF APOCALYPTICISM
IN JUDAISM AND CHRISTIANITY

Edited by
John J. Collins

Continuum New York

1998
The Continuum Publishing Company
370 Lexington Avenue
New York, NY 10017

Printed in the United States of America

Library of Congress Cataloging-in-Publication Data

The encyclopedia of apocalypticism / edited by Bernard McGinn, John J.
  Collins, and Stephen J. Stein.
        p.   cm.
  Includes bibliographical references and index.
  Contents: v. 1. The origins of apocalypticism in Judaism and
Christianity / edited by John J. Collins — v. 2. Apocalypticism in
Western history and culture / edited by Bernard McGinn — v.
3. Apocalypticism in the modern period and the contemporary age /
edited by Stephen J. Stein.
    ISBN 0-8264-1087-1 (set : hardcover). —ISBN 0-8264-1071-5 (v. 1 :
    hardcover)
      1. Apocalyptic literature—Comparative studies.   2. End of the
  world—Comparative studies.   I. McGinn, Bernard, 1937–   .
  II. Collins, John Joseph, 1946–   .   III. Stein, Stephen J., 1940–   .
  BL501.E53   1998
  291.2'3—dc21   97-46016
                                                         CIP

Contents

NB. That, unlike many many-authored volumes, this is not (just) a stimulating variety of viewpoints. It makes for (an approximate) continuity of narrative, for "a" history.

General Introduction

It is the free thinking intellect that makes history and its deep decisions roll and echo down through the centuries. In this way history is the apocalypse (that is to say, the opening) of the decision of the intellect for or against God. (Hans Urs von Balthasar, *The Glory of the Lord, IV, The Realm of Metaphysics in Antiquity* [San Francisco: Ignatius Press, 1989], 39)

AS WE APPROACH 2000–2001 C.E., THE YEAR THAT WILL MARK the beginning of the new millennium, fascination with the meaning of history and especially of historical transitions is already on the rise. Fervent expectations abound—both positive ones hoping for the emergence of an improved earthly society in the new millennium and negative ones fearing the end of the world, either the Armageddon depicted in the Bible or more secular versions of final destruction.

Apocalypticism, broadly described as the belief that God has revealed the imminent end of the ongoing struggle between good and evil in history, has been a major element in the three Western monotheistic faiths of Judaism, Christianity, and Islam. While comparable beliefs about final reward and retribution are found in religions all over the world, there are genetic and historical links in the apocalyptic traditions of these three faiths that argue for a comprehensive and collective treatment. The three volumes of the *Encyclopedia of Apocalypticism* attempt to provide such a treatment.

It is important to note at the outset what the encyclopedia intends to do and what it does not. As mentioned, these volumes will not deal with views about the meaning and end of history found in other religious traditions except insofar as these had some direct relation to the three Western faiths. Second, the format adopted is that of an "encyclopedia" in the etymological sense of a "general course of instruction" covering the essential aspects of the phenomenon, not a "dictionary" in which every possible person, place, or thing in some way considered apocalyptic is briefly treated. Therefore, each volume will comprise a relatively small number of comprehensive articles (forty-three over the three volumes) that will offer original syntheses of scholarship on central themes, periods, and issues in the history of Western apocalypticism. A third important preliminary observation, one that deserves a more detailed discussion, concerns the question of definitions.

Apocalypticism (a recent word) is derived from "apocalypse," the Greek word for revelation and the name of the last book of the Bible. Apocalypticism refers to the complex of ideas associated with the New Testament Apocalypse, especially the imminent end of history and the catastrophic events that it entails. Apocalypticism is an analogous term, and it admits of different emphases. Some material is recognized as apocalyptic because it relates to the end of history. Other material is apocalyptic insofar as it describes supernatural revelation and the activities of angelic and demonic powers. In these volumes we have not attempted to impose a strict definition, but rather to include a broad range of materials that may be regarded as apocalyptic in various senses. The reader should be aware that different contributors may use the terminology in slightly different ways. We believe, however, that there will be little confusion, and that it is amply compensated for by the wealth of material brought to the discussion.

In modern scholarship apocalypticism has also been related to other terms, especially "eschatology" (teaching about the last things), "millennialism" or "chiliasm" (belief in a coming better age on earth, such as that described in the thousand-year reign of Christ at the end of the book of Revelation), and "messianism" (hope for a heaven-sent savior who will usher in the better age). Messianism is a distinct phenomenon, insofar as it focuses on specific savior figures. "Eschatology" can be used for all sorts of human goals (e.g., national liberation) that do not necessarily qualify as apocalyptic, and millennialism is properly speaking a narrower concept that concentrates on earthly utopias. Nonetheless, all these terms overlap and are often used interchangeably. The precise nuance given to them by a given author must be inferred from the context.

Over the past thirty years, more scholarship has been devoted to apocalypticism than in the previous three hundred. This is true not only regarding the origins of apocalypticism in Judaism and early Christianity (the subject of volume 1), but also of the development of Christian apocalyptic traditions in Europe down to the modern era and the related apocalypticisms of medieval Judaism and early Islam (treated in volume 2). Even more recent has been the recognition of the importance of apocalypticism in the history of the New World and the continuing role that apocalyptic convictions, literal and revised, religious and secularized, play in contemporary society (the subject of volume 3). We believe that the time is ripe to produce a major account of apocalypticism's role in Western history and in the current world situation.

The Encyclopedia of Apocalypticism has been made possible not only by this explosion of scholarship over the past generation but also by the growing public interest in ends and beginnings that is gaining momentum as we approach the new millennium. Much of this fascination involves media-driven interests that will fade soon after the parties ushering in January 1, 2000 (though actually, the new millennium will not begin until January 1, 2001). Though not unmindful of the timeliness of the project, our conception of this multivolume effort looks beyond 2000–2001 in an attempt to provide an indispensable resource for the study of apocalypticism as an ongoing religious and cultural movement.

A glance at the history of predictions concerning the date of the end in Christianity helps relativize the importance of 2000–2001. In the sixteenth century a Protestant divine named Sheltco à Geveren adapted a talmudic passage about the six-thousand year duration of history in the following manner, as cited from the English translation of his treatise:

> Two thousand Vayne [i.e., before the Mosaic Law], two thousande Lawe, two thousand Christe. And for our sinnes which are many and marveylous, some years which are wantyng, shal not be expired.

Sheltco's expectation of an end by two thousand years after Christ (or more likely before), however, is very much the exception rather than the rule. A few other historical witnesses to fears that the end will occur around 2000 can be found, but amidst the multitude of dates that at one time or another have been put forward for the dread event many others have been far more popular than 2000 (and now mostly are in the past). Even the still-current belief that expectation of the end was more widespread around the year 1000 C.E. than at other times in the Middle Ages must also be abandoned.

The "millennial" year 2000–2001 means even less in Judaism and Islam, which depend on different calendars and predictive systems. In later Judaism, for example, the "time of the end" (ʿēt qēṣ from Dan. 2:28) was sometimes tied to the prediction of the mysterious coming of the *shiloh* in Gen. 49:10. Since the numerical equivalent of this term in Hebrew is 335, the year 335 in any millennium of the Jewish calender could be identified with the end. In early Islam, on the other hand, it was the centennium, that is, each hundred years after the founding event of Islam, the Hegira of the prophet Muhammad (622 C.E.), which was often the subject of fears regarding the end. These observations help underline why the importance of apocalypticism transcends the upcoming media aspects of the year 2000–2001. *The Encyclopedia of Apocalypticism,* therefore, has been designed to provide a lasting tool for those who wish to understand the role of apocalypticism over the past two millennia and more, as well as into the twenty-first century—and beyond.

To stress the significance of apocalypticism is not to deny its ambivalence. Most of the apocalyptic thinkers and movements studied in these three volumes adhered to literal interpretations of what they believed were divine revelations about the approach of the end and the rewards and punishments it would entail. All such prophecies have proved delusory. Recording the history of a delusion—or at least what has thus far proved to be delusion—may appear to be a peripheral endeavor. This is why the apocalyptic traditions of Judaism, Christianity, and Islam have been dismissed by many, both believers and outsiders, as remnants of mythical thinking. With their dread of an imminent end to history, one involving God's final judgment on evil, as well as their hope in a coming supreme reward for the faithful, sometimes on earth, certainly in heaven, apocalyptic beliefs seem to many today to be marginal aspects of the Western monotheistic faiths, despite the millions of literal believers in apocalypticism (though none among our authors).

Apocalyptic beliefs (at least of the literal variety) may be judged not only outmoded but also dangerous, because of their innate power to foster self-righteousness among the elect and at times violent opposition to, even persecution of, those identified as belonging to Satan's party. Apocalypticism has been the source of hope and courage for the oppressed, and—not *too* paradoxically—intransigence and savagery on the part of some oppressors. The essays in these volumes seek neither to apologize for the extravagances of apocalyptic thinkers nor to excuse the perverse actions of their followers. Rather, they strive to understand a powerful, perhaps even indispensable, element in the history of Western religions that has been the source of both good and evil.

This introduction is not the place to attempt any sketch, however brief, of a nonliteral understanding of apocalyptic beliefs that would try to show that some form of apocalypticism seems almost ineradicable from Western society and that therefore a critical retrieval of apocalypticism is a major challenge confronting contemporary religious thought: Jewish, Christian, and Muslim. Many today are taking up this task—not just theologians and philosophers but also writers, poets, and artists. We hope that the rich harvest of historical investigation presented in these three volumes will provide basic materials to further this effort in the coming millennium.

The editors wish to take this opportunity to thank all those whose efforts made the publication of the *Encyclopedia of Apocalypticism* a reality. Special gratitude is due to Werner Mark Linz, Frank Oveis, and the staff of The Continuum Publishing Group. We are also grateful for the support of Clark Gilpin, dean of the Divinity School of the University of Chicago, whose assistance was crucial in the development of the encyclopedia.

JOHN J. COLLINS   BERNARD MCGINN   STEPHEN J. STEIN

Introduction to Volume 1

APOCALYPSE IS THE GREEK WORD FOR REVELATION, but its connotation in modern parlance derives from its use in the title of the last book of the Bible, the Revelation to John of Patmos. That book contains a kind of revelation that is distinctive and memorable, which tells of battles with dragons and beasts, of the coming judgment, of the thousand-year reign (millennium) of Christ with the elect, of the end of this world and its replacement with a new heaven and a new earth. "Apocalypse," in the sense of revelation analogous to that of the biblical book, became a popular genre in early and medieval Christianity. It is also recognized retroactively in Jewish writings of the Hellenistic period, and to some extent also in Greco-Roman and Persian literature. As a literary phenomenon, apocalypse has been defined as "a genre of revelatory literature with a narrative framework, in which a revelation is mediated by an otherworldly being to a human recipient, disclosing a transcendent reality which is both temporal, insofar as it envisages eschatological salvation, and spatial insofar as it involves another, supernatural world."[1] Such writings in antiquity are typically "intended to interpret present, earthly circumstances in light of the supernatural world and of the future, and to influence both the understanding and behavior of the audience by means of divine authority,"[2] and are often associated with groups in crisis.

xiii

The major themes of the ancient apocalypses, however, are also found, in manifold variations, in other literary genres throughout the ancient world. In the present volume, we are concerned with this broader complex of themes. The genre apocalypse provides the focal point, insofar as other material is judged relevant to the discussion because of some resemblance to the apocalypses. But the focus here is on a worldview rather than on a literary genre, and the objective is to be as inclusive as possible.

Even within the literary genre apocalypse, we find two distinct types of material. One type, the "historical" apocalypse, represented vividly by the book of Revelation, is concerned with the rise and fall of nations and with the end of history and the world. The second type ("cosmic" or "mystical"), is first developed in the books of Enoch and focuses rather on the eschatology of the individual and the fate of the soul after death. These concerns are by no means incompatible; both figure prominently in the book of Revelation and in many of the ancient apocalypses. But they are not inseparable, and we sometimes find apocalypses that pay little attention to the great public events of the end of the world. These two types of apocalypses may be taken to represent two distinct tendencies in apocalyptic tradition.

The main flowering of apocalyptic writing and thinking in the Western world took place in Judaism in the Hellenistic period, and was carried on, intermittently, in Christianity, down through the Middle Ages. The roots of the phenomenon, however, lie further back. The proximate roots of Jewish and Christian apocalypticism can be found in the Hebrew prophets, especially in the oracles of judgment and predictions of the day of the Lord. But the imagery of the apocalypses of the Hellenistic age is much more full and vivid than that of the prophets. To a great extent it harks back to the ancient mythologies of the Near East, known to us now through the rediscovered Akkadian and Ugaritic literatures. The Hebrew Bible stands in a cultural continuum with these ancient Semitic mythologies, and much mythological lore that is not reflected in the Bible lived on in oral traditions down into the common era. It is possible to trace a direct line of development from the myths of the second millennium B.C.E. to the apocalypses of the Hellenistic and Roman periods. There was also, however, an independent apocalyptic tradition in ancient Persia, which may itself date back to the second millennium. This tradition exercised some influence on Judaism and Christianity, and some scholars would argue that it is the primary fountainhead of apocalypticism in the Western world.[3] Many of the characteristic themes of apocalypticism can also be found in Greek and Roman culture, although they were relatively minor themes in those cultures. We should be wary, however, of attempts to trace all of Western apocalypticism to a single source.

This volume is divided into three main parts, with a single essay in part 4 constituting an epilogue to the whole. Part 1 contains three essays on pagan antiquity. Richard Clifford traces the roots of apocalypticism in ancient Near Eastern myth, primarily in the great combat myths represented by the Akkadian *Enuma elish* and the Ugaritic Baal Cycle. In these myths we find the theme of the battle with the chaos monster, which figures prominently in such apocalyptic writings as the books of Daniel and Revelation. This is not to suggest that apocalypticism can be reduced to the combat myth. Clifford also notes the relevance of a neo-Assyrian vision of the netherworld to the theme of otherworldly journeys and the relevance of Akkadian prophecies to the apocalyptic motif of prophecy after the fact (*ex eventu*). But the combat myth undeniably provides one major motif of apocalyptic writings and is the aspect of Near Eastern myth that exercised the greatest influence on apocalyptic tradition. Anders Hultgård provides a magisterial exposition of Persian apocalypticism. Discussions of Persian literature are bedeviled by problems of dating. The Pahlevi literature that contains the most extensive Persian apocalyptic writings is admittedly late—much later than the Jewish and early Christian apocalypses. Some scholars accordingly dismiss Persian religion as a source of apocalypticism in the West. Hultgård, however, sides with those who argue for the antiquity of Persian apocalypticism and makes a strong case that the main features of the tradition were already in place in the Achaemenid period. Finally, Hubert Cancik provides an exceptional synthesis of Greco-Roman materials that relate to apocalypticism and eschatology. Running through Cancik's study is a critique of a strand of modern thought, typified by Nietzsche, that stereotypes classical thought about time and history as a myth of eternal return. Cancik demonstrates the richness and variety of classical thought, drawing on philosophers and poets as well as on inscriptional evidence for Orphism and mystery religions.

Part 2 traces the development of apocalypticism in ancient Judaism. My own essay discusses three major phases in this development. The first is located after the Babylonian Exile, in the sixth century. In the later prophetic writings we find a tendency to picture the future in cosmic terms, with less specific reference to the concrete particularities of the prophet's own situation than was the case in the earlier period. The major development, however, takes place in the Hellenistic period, when the belief in the judgment of the dead begins to find acceptance in Judaism. The hope for a blessed hereafter is one of the major factors that distinguish the eschatology of the apocalyptic writers from that of the prophets. A third phase of the development, found in apocalypses from the Roman period (about 100 C.E.) is distinguished by the attempt to synthesize different traditions and provide a more systematic exposition of future hope. New light has been shed on Jewish apocalypticism by the Dead Sea Scrolls. The evidence is presented by Florentino García Martínez. The Scrolls provide extensive reflections on the origin of evil, the periods of history, the final battle, and most distinctively, on human participation in the heavenly world. It remains a puzzle why the authors of the Scrolls make so little use of the genre apocalypse, which was well known in this period, but they undeniably give expression to an apocalyptic worldview, expressed in different genres. James VanderKam discusses the relation between apocalypticism and messianism. The earliest Jewish apocalypses do not look for messianic savior figures. The hope for the restoration of the Jewish kingship was nourished by circles different from those who wrote the first apocalypses. Later, however, the two traditions are synthesized in the Dead Sea Scrolls and in the apocalypses of the Roman period. Finally, Michael Mach discusses the connection between the Jewish apocalypses and later Jewish mysticism. Mach's focus is on the cosmic or mystical type of apocalypse, rather than the better known "historical" type. His article provides an excellent introduction to the modern debate about the nature and origin of Jewish mysticism.

Part 3 deals with early Christianity. A century ago, Albert Schweitzer revolutionized New Testament scholarship with his thesis that the teaching of Jesus was characterized by thoroughgoing eschatology. This thesis is often challenged in modern times, but is defended vigorously here by Dale Allison. Allison has little difficulty in showing the pervasiveness of apocalyptic motifs in the Jesus tradition, as preserved in the Synoptic Gospels. It is difficult to avoid the conclusion that modern resistance to the eschatological Jesus arises from the fact that such a Jesus is too strange and uncomfortable for modern tastes. Richard Horsley, however, takes a different approach to the Jesus tradition. Horsley tries to distinguish between apocalypticism, which he associates with the work of scribes, and popular prophetic eschatology. He sees the Jesus movement as a movement of peasants, interested in the restoration of the kingdom of God on earth rather than in the end of the world as conceived in the apocalypses. His essay raises important questions about the role of social setting in the formulation of eschatological hopes. Martinus de Boer deals with the writings of Paul. The thought of Paul is complex, and many factors play a part in it. De Boer shows that one major factor is the apocalyptic belief that the day of judgment and resurrection is close at hand. Adela Yarbro Collins expounds the most influential of all apocalyptic texts, the book of Revelation. Her essay deals not only with the original setting and purpose but also with major themes in the history of interpretation. A distinctive feature of this essay is a discussion of the role of female symbolism in Revelation.

Finally, David Frankfurter provides a nuanced discussion of early Christian apocalypticism after the New Testament period, with careful attention to the variation in emphases between different geographical regions.

The epilogue to the volume is provided by Bruce Lincoln, who comments on the political implications of apocalyptic thought, which he sees as a counterpoint to royal or imperial propaganda. Lincoln draws his example of royal propaganda from ancient Persia. Other examples could easily be drawn from any sector of the ancient world, from Babylon to Rome. His essay is a useful reminder that apocalypticism is not only an exercise of the religious imagination (which it surely is) but also an instrument of political agitation which has often had powerful effects in political life.

It is often said in textbooks on ancient religion that apocalypticism flourished from approximately 200 B.C.E. to 100 C.E. Such a statement is true for Judaism, although there have also been variations on Jewish apocalypticism in later periods. For Christianity, however, the period discussed in this volume is only "the dawn of apocalyptic." The themes and motifs treated here were developed and systematized in the Byzantine and medieval periods, both in the form of a theology/philosophy of history and in the tradition of the ascent of the soul that culminated in Dante's *Divine Comedy.* The story of that development and its variegated continuation down to modern times is told in the second and third volumes of this encyclopedia.

JOHN J. COLLINS

 NOTES

1. J. J. Collins, ed., *Apocalypse: The Morphology of a Genre, Semeia* 14 (1979): 9.

2. A. Yarbro Collins, ed., *Early Christian Apocalypticism: Genre and Social Settings, Semeia* 36 (1986): 7, building on suggestions by David Aune and David Hellholm.

3. See N. Cohn, *Cosmos, Chaos, and the World to Come: The Ancient Roots of Apocalyptic Faith* (New Haven: Yale University Press, 1993).

PART 1

*Apocalypticism in the
Ancient Near East and
Mediterranean World*

1

The Roots of Apocalypticism
in Near Eastern Myth

Richard J. Clifford, S.J.
Weston Jesuit School of Theology

A POCALYPTIC LITERATURE AS SUCH IS NOT FOUND IN THE period covered by this article (the third to mid-first millennia in the ancient Near East) but chiefly in the period from the third century B.C.E. to the second century C.E., and, in some Christian circles, down to the Middle Ages. The ancient roots of apocalyptic literature, however, can be traced to far earlier literature of the ancient Near East (back to the late third millennium). Its early history is not merely of antiquarian interest, but illuminates the purpose and rhetoric of mature apocalyptic works. These latter works fall within a venerable tradition of theological and philosophical reflection on divine and human governance, a kind of ancient "political theory." Read apart from their literary history, works such as the books of Daniel and Revelation, *1 Enoch,* 4 Ezra, and *2 Baruch* can appear to modern readers as bizarre in imagery and confusing in logic.

The first modern scholar to have seriously attempted to trace the roots of apocalyptic literature in ancient texts was Hermann Gunkel (1862–1932), whose *Schöpfung und Chaos in Urzeit und Endzeit: Eine religionsgeschichtliche Untersuchung über Gen 1 and Ap Joh 12* appeared in 1895. He belonged to the history-of-religions school, or *religionsgeschichtliche Schule,* which champi-

3

oned autonomous historical-critical scholarship and insisted that the Bible be seen against its environment. Gunkel argued that Genesis 1 and Revelation 12 consisted of "basically the same material, which [in Revelation] surfaces a second time, but in a different form. In the ancient instance it is the myth of *Urzeit,* which travels from Babylon to the Bible, in the new a prediction concerning the *Endzeit*" (p. 398).

His book demonstrated that Genesis 1 and Revelation 12 were not free compositions of their authors but adaptations of traditions from outside, ultimately from Babylon. He concluded that the combat myth entered Israelite literature in the monarchic period, rather than in the patriarchal era or the Babylonian Exile, the periods of borrowing suggested by earlier scholars. It is a mark of Gunkel's genius that with the little material available to him he did not simply list motifs and themes but concentrated his attention on the one *Gattung* (the combat myth) that included so much else: the *Urzeit* ("primal time") *Endzeit* ("end-time") equation, creation and new creation, the monster symbolizing evil, and divine kingship. Gunkel's pioneering work retains its usefulness despite its obvious deficiencies: he had access to only a fraction of the Akkadian texts now available and knew nothing of the combat myth in the Canaanite texts from Ugarit (first discovered in 1929); he had a romanticist tendency to overstress origins as explanation and undervalue reception and particular usage.

Later scholars have been able to make use of the Ugaritic texts, which are closely related to early Biblical Hebrew and are composed in the same poetic tradition, as well as the enormous amount of Sumerian and Akkadian literature unearthed and published since Gunkel. It is now possible to chart the history of relevant genres, motifs, and themes in a variety of works over many centuries. In particular, scholars can describe the interaction of Canaanite and early Israelite traditions and sketch the inner-biblical development that led to fully developed apocalyptic works such as Daniel and Revelation. A number of points are still under discussion. These include the way in which traditions from Mesopotamia came into Canaan as well as the date and extent of their influence and the inner-biblical sources of apocalyptic literature.

This article is selective, examining in the early literature only those genres, motifs or recurrent elements, and ideas that were important in the later mature apocalyptic works. Among the genres, the most important by far is the combat myth, for it provided not only imagery but also a conceptual framework for explaining divine rule over the world. Other genres are the *vaticinia ex eventu* ("prophecies after the fact") found in some Akkadian texts, and the dream vision (though the relevance of the specifically Akkadian form of this last genre is disputed). Among the recurrent elements are the divine assembly under the high god responding to a major threat, cosmic enemies portrayed as monsters, various heavenly beings, divine decrees or secret knowledge, and a sage-mediator of heavenly knowledge. Among the topics are explorations of the nature of evil and new creation or restoration of the original order.

ᕈ MESOPOTAMIA

History and Religion

The course of Mesopotamian history shows two impulses, one toward local rule exemplified in the city-states, and the other, more sporadic, toward large and complex political systems aimed at dominating large areas. The first period for which there is a record is the Early Dynastic (2900–2350 B.C.E.), a period when families ruled various cities. The Akkadian and Ur III dynasties at the end of the third millennium represent a shift from city-state to nation-state. The Akkadian system, in contrast to the earlier Sumerian system, featured a centralized state around king and court. Though Sumerian and Akkadian languages and populations were distinct, the culture itself was a common Mesopotamian one.

In the second millennium, Mesopotamia became divided into two geopolitical regions, Babylonia and Assyria. From the eighteenth century B.C.E. to the end of the millennium, Babylon and Assyria were the two great nation-states. Babylon and Assyria were international in ambition and contacts, and their fortunes unfolded in an international context. Northern Syria came into the picture as its coastal cities—Ugarit, Byblos, Tyre—rose to prominence. Northwest Mesopotamia became a meeting point of Mesopotamian and Levantine culture. The essentially cooperative international atmosphere was ended, however, by population movements in the last two centuries of the second millennium. The dominant empires of the first millennium were the Neo-Assyrian empire (935–612 B.C.E.) and its successor, the Persian empire (539–333 B.C.E.), both complex and vast in extent.

The chief gods in the pantheon were Anu (Sumerian An), "sky," the god of heaven and head of the older generation of gods, whose consort was Antu; Ellil (Sumerian Enlil), son of Anu, father of Ninurta, "king of all populated land," head of the younger generation of Sumerian and Akkadian gods whose consort was Ninlil or Ninhursag and whose cult center was Nippur; and Ea

(Sumerian Enki), god of water, wisdom, and incantations, whose consort was Ninmah or Damkina and whose cult center was Eridu. With the rise of the Amorites and of the city-state Babylon, the warrior-god Marduk became important, taking over titles of other gods. In Old Assyrian religion Asshur was the national god, to whom the king regularly reported his activities, especially war. After the middle of the fourteenth century B.C.E., the Assyrian pantheon became babylonized. In the Assyrian version of *Enuma elish,* Asshur took the place of Marduk.

The assembly of the gods was an important part of the organization of the divine world and the major decision-making body; all the gods were subject to its decrees. The members were of two groups, the fifty "great gods" and "the seven gods of the fates (*šīmātu*)." The divine triad of Anu, Enlil, and Ea was preeminent, with Anu presiding over the assembly. In a democratic give-and-take, the member gods made decrees affecting matters in heaven and earth and responded to various crises. Indeed, the divine assembly can be viewed as a reflection of "democratic" practices that once prevailed in Sumerian city-states. The Akkadian term is *puḫru ilāni,* "assembly of the gods." The institution is also attested in Canaan: Ugaritic *pḫr [bn] ʾlm,* Phoenician *mpḫrt ʾl,* and biblical *ʿēdâ* (Ps 82:1) and *sôd* (Jer. 23:18, 22; Job 15:8; Ps. 89:8). In Mesopotamia, the members are specifically identified and act as individuals, but in Canaan the assembly as a whole or its head, El, acts rather than individual members (Mullen 1980).

The major office of divine governance was kingship. Kingship over the gods could be won by a particular god resolving a crisis or defeating a threat to cosmic order. Human kingship is age-old in Mesopotamia and was the dominant form of government everywhere from the early second millennium forward. The Sumerian King List seeks to demonstrate that the country was always united under one king, ruling successively in different cites: "When kingship was lowered from heaven, kingship was (first) in Eridu," and so on; it existed in heaven independently of any earthly king. When kings are mentioned in creation myths, they organize the human race so it can carry out its basic task of providing for the gods. Kings were not ordinarily considered divine but had to be appointed by the gods. A supernatural aura surrounded the king, for he was the regent of the gods, represented divine order on earth, and conversely, represented the people before the gods.

A common way of resolving threats to cosmic order was force of arms. The gods were involved in the wars that kings waged on earth; war was both political and religious. The new order resulting from the war could be said to represent the will of the god or gods. War was thus a way for the gods to exercise their rule and oversee the rise and fall of kingdoms.

Literature and Themes Relevant to Apocalyptic Literature

Genres

THE COMBAT MYTH. One of the most long-lived genres in ancient literature was the so-called combat myth. It lasted as a live genre into the period of full-blown apocalyptic works and had an enormous influence on them. In fact, the genre provided ancient poets with a conceptual framework for reflecting on divine power and human kingship, and on the rise and fall of nations. Instances of the myth in Mesopotamia are *Lugal-e, Anzu,* and *Enuma elish.* In Canaan it is represented by the Baal Cycle. In early biblical poetry it is found in Yahweh's victory over Pharaoh at the sea (Exodus 15) or over the sea itself (several psalms). No ideal form of the combat myth exists, of course, but a consistent plot line can be abstracted: a force (often depicted as a monster) threatens cosmic and political order, instilling fear and confusion in the assembly of the gods; the assembly or its president, unable to find a comman-der among the older gods, turns to a young god to battle the hostile force; he successfully defeats the monster, creating the world (including human beings) or simply restoring the pre-threat order, builds a palace, and receives acclama-tion of kingship from the other gods.

There are three combat myths sufficiently preserved to be analyzed: the Sumerian *Lugal-e* of the late third millennium; the Akkadian *Anzu,* extant in an Old Babylonian and a Standard (early-first-millennium) version; and *Enuma elish,* dated variously to the eighteenth, fourteenth, or, more com-monly, the twelfth century. Each influenced its successor.

The best way of analyzing the myths is by attending to their plot rather than to their ideas, a method somewhat contrary to modern analytical habits. For us stories are usually regarded as entertainment or as illustration of a "point" derived from discursive reasoning, but for ancient Near Easterners narrative was the medium for expressing serious thought. The plots of the three combat myths will be briefly told with attention to "discourse time," the time taken in the telling.

Lugal-e tells how the young warrior-king Ninurta (god of thunderstorms and floods) defeated the mountain-dwelling monster Azag, restored the flow of the river Tigris, after which he judged the stones that had taken part in the battle, assigning them their various functions. The story begins with Sharur, Ninurta's weapon, reporting to his master that in the mountains the plants and stones have made Azag king and that the monster is planning to take over his domain. Ninurta's first foray against them, made against the advice of Sharur, is defeated by the dust storm Azag raises. Sharur now brings to Ninurta strategic advice from Enlil, Ninurta's father: send a rainstorm to put down the dust. The strategy works; Ninurta defeats Azag. Ninurta then collects the waters that had been trapped in the mountain ice and routes them to the Tigris. Ninlil, his mother, lonesome for her absent son, pays him a visit. Ninurta sends her home before exercising judgment over the stones. Each is judged according to its degree of participation in the battle against him. Ninurta returns to Nippur to receive the acclamation of his father and the other gods.

Five features of *Lugal-e* are relevant for other combat myths, including those found in apocalyptic literature. (1) The relationship of the older god (Ninurta's father, Enlil) and the younger god (Ninurta)—a common relationship in combat myth—is perennial in ancient Near Eastern palace life, as Thorkild Jacobsen points out: "Under the early political forms, which are here reflected, the king (*lugal*) was usually a young man whose task it was to lead the army in war. The supreme ruler was an older experienced administrator, here Ninurta's father, Enlil. Thus his military exploits serve to impose and maintain Enlil's authority" (Jacobsen 1987, 236 n. 4). The same relationship holds for Anu and Marduk in *Enuma elish*, El and Baal in the Ugaritic texts, the Ancient of Days and the Son of Man in Daniel 7, and the one seated on the throne and the Lamb in Revelation 4–5. (2) The "evil," or threat to order, in this story is that the water necessary to fertilize the fields of Mesopotamia is trapped in mountain ice. The victory over or defeat of the evil consists in making that water once again available to the inhabitants, thus restoring the fertility intended by the gods. The nature of the victory casts light on the meaning of divine kingship in the myth. Kingship (including its permanence) is proportional to the threat that has been put down. The more profound the threat, the more profound the victory undoing it. Yet, as Neil Forsyth recognizes, not every warrior-god's victory is a cosmogony (1987, 44–45). Marduk's victory over Tiamat in *Enuma elish* surely is cosmogonic, but Ninurta's victory in *Anzu* is not so wide-ranging, nor is Baal's victory over Mot in the Ugaritic tablets. (3) The evil is portrayed as a "natural" force (water trapped in mountain ice), but here, as in other references to nature, there is an implied historical reference, for the northern and eastern mountains were the homelands of historical invaders of the plains. A dichotomous distinction between myth and history cannot be drawn; the two domains are related. (4) Judgment of enemies (and allies as well) follows the victory, an action that occurs also in *Enuma elish* (VI 11–32) and in the apocalypses in Daniel 7 and 8–12 and Revelation 17–19. (5) The victorious god reestablishes the original order; *Urzeit* becomes *Endzeit*. Rev 21:1 is a succinct expression of the victory: "Then I saw a new heaven and a new earth; for the first heaven and the first earth had passed away, and sea was no more."

The observations just made also apply to the second of our three Mesopotamian examples of the genre of combat myth, *Anzu*. It is partially preserved in an Old Babylonian version (first half of the second millennium) and much more completely in an early-first-millennium Standard Babylonian version, originally consisting of about 720 lines on three four-column tablets. It was canonical, in "the stream of tradition," that is, copied by scribes in their training and widely distributed. It influenced *Enuma elish*.

The prologue sings of Ninurta, "the Mighty One," a title that recurs throughout the myth. The world is in a crisis: the beds of the Tigris and Euphrates have been laid out, but no water flows in them to fertilize the land of Mesopotamia. At a certain point, the fresh waters of the Apsu are released to supply the two rivers, a happy turn of the plot somehow caused by the birth of Anzu (the text is not clear). Anzu is a birdlike creature with a monstrous head, conceived by earth and born in a mountain fastness. Such a creature would make an ideal gatekeeper for the gods, thinks Anu, the head of the older generation of gods, and recommends him to Enlil, head of the younger generation of gods. Anu's judgment proves disastrous, however, for Anzu uses his post to steal from Enlil the Tablet-of-Decrees, which determines the destiny of things, the "software program of the world." To meet the crisis, the assembly of the gods meets. Anu promises to any god who can capture back the tablet a great name and recognition as mighty. Anu turns first to Adad, then Gerra, and finally Shara, but all refuse to lead the army. They know that Anzu and not Enlil possesses the Tablet that makes its possessor's commands all-powerful.

Then Belet-ili, the mother goddess, asks Ninurta, the son of Enlil, to go out against Anzu. Family honor is at stake, she explains, for Anzu rejected his father. In contrast to the verbose refusals of the three gods, Ninurta's answer is a quick yes. He loses the first battle when Anzu's authoritative word turns his arrows back. Wise Ea's advice enables him to succeed: shake feathers loose from the birdlike Anzu and in the moment when he calls his loose feathers back to his body, release your feathered arrow so that it will be caught up in the irresistible stream toward Anzu's body. Caught up in the flow, Ninurta's arrow pierces and kills Anzu. Then Ninurta drenches the mountain open stretches with water. Wind-borne feathers from Anzu's dead body signal the gods that Ninurta is victorious. The gods summon Ninurta home and, declaring that he has avenged his father Enlil, acclaim him with a series of new names.

Analysis of *Anzu* in discourse time shows what events the poet chooses to delay on:

Prologue	Water crisis and solution	Assembly: three gods refuse to go	Appointment of Ninurta	Battle and victory	Celebration grant of names
I.1–14	1.15–83	1.84–155	I.156–II.27	I.28–III.22	
14 lines	69 lines	71 lines	79 lines	ca. 144 lines	ca. 48 lines

The initial crisis (Anzu's theft of the Tablet-of-Decrees) is quickly told (69 lines). The poem dwells on the deliberations of the assembly (Anu's attempts to persuade the three gods to recapture the tablet [71 lines] and the commission of Ninurta [79 lines, the two scenes totaling 150 lines]), Ninurta's battle and victory (ca. 144 lines), and the gods granting him new names (ca. 48 lines).

Four features of the combat myth *Anzu* should be noted as relevant to later apocalyptic works. (1) The threat from the lack of water in the opening lines is resolved somehow by Anzu's birth, but this resolution leads to the much more dangerous threat from the loss of the Tablet-of-Decrees. This turn breaks up the simple plot and foreshadows the complex two-part structure of *Enuma elish*. (2) The evil here is the dissolution of political as well as cosmic order. The assembly is rendered ineffectual as a *political* body, for it is unable from its senior members to muster an army to get back the tablet. It is *family* rather than political considerations that send Ninurta into the field. His victory restores the political office of king; with Anzu out of the way, the assembly is again effective and can acclaim him king: "They assigned to you full shepherdship of the people. As king they gave (you) your name 'Guardian of the throne'" (III.129–30). (3) The fundamental issue is kingship. Ninurta takes the kingship of the other gods; Anu, the head of the older generation, proved inadequate, as did Enlil and the three gods who refused to fight. They must yield to Ninurta, who has won the title Mighty One and restored the civic and political order destroyed by the loss of the Tablet. Ninurta's restoration of political order does not seem to be cosmogonic, though one should keep in mind that political order was part of what the ancients meant by creation. (4) Relevant to later apocalyptic literature are several recurrent elements: the monster Anzu as a composite animal (lion-headed eagle, or perhaps bat-headed, as befits one born in a cave), the active role of the assembly of the gods, and the god's personified weapon. In Daniel and Revelation, evil can be symbolized by composite animals, and the heavenly assembly plays a similar role though it is much less prominent.

The third Mesopotamian example is *Enuma elish* (named after its opening line), seven tablets in length, much copied and commented on in antiquity, and recited on the fourth day of the New Year festival.

The dramatic structure of *Enuma elish* is more complex than its predecessors, being in five acts.

1. I.1–20. The first twenty lines are a theogony, in which a series of gods are born when the primordial waters Apsu and Tiamat were an undifferentiated mass and there was no land. The emergence of the gods is also the emergence of two rival dynasties: Apsu-Tiamat versus Anshar-Anu-Ea-Marduk (Goldfless 1980, 127–30). The monster Tiamat thus represents both a natural force (cosmic waters) and a political reality. "Myth" and "history" are intertwined. Another indication of the historical interest in the entire myth is the large amount of discourse time devoted to political debate in the divine assembly.

2. I.21–79. In the initial confrontation of the rival dynasties, Ea defeats Apsu and builds his palace to celebrate the victory.

3. I.79–VI.121. Foreshadowed by the first confrontation, the major conflict between the son of Ea, Marduk, and the widow of Apsu, Tiamat, is the theme of the bulk of the work. Tiamat, still angry over the death of her husband Apsu at the hands of Ea, plots an assault against the rival dynasty. When they learn of her plans, the assembly is frightened and seeks to appoint a military commander. After two gods refuse to go, Marduk agrees on the condition that the assembly make his decree supreme. He slays Tiamat in single combat and from her body builds the universe and his shrine Esagil.

4. VI.122–VII.144. The gods, grateful for Marduk's victory and obliged by their oath, give him "Anu-ship." He in turn promises them that Babylon will be their new residence and that man, a new creature, will be their servant. From the blood of the slain Kingu (Tiamat's general), Marduk forms man. The gods build Marduk a city and a temple and give him fifty names of honor.

Many of the remarks already made about *Lugal-e* and *Anzu* also apply to *Enuma elish*. As in these other myths, one god is exalted over gods and humans. In contrast to the other myths, however, in *Enuma elish* Marduk does not *reestablish* a threatened or disturbed order but forms a world that never existed before. He creates. The genre of combat myth has been expanded not only in length and complexity but conceptually as well.

What does it mean to create in the ancient Near East? The concept of creation in the ancient Near East differs from the modern Western view, shaped as the latter is by evolutionary and scientific concerns (Clifford 1994, chap. 1). Ancient accounts usually imagined creation on the model of human activity (molding clay, building a house, fighting a battle) or natural processes (life forms left by the ebbing Nile flood). What emerged from the process for the ancients was a *populated* universe, human society organized for the service of the gods with a king and culture, and not, as with modern accounts, the physical world (often only the planet earth in its solar and stellar system). Ancient accounts were often portrayed as dramas, which is not surprising in that the process was imagined as personal wills in conflict. This is far from the impersonal interaction of modern scientific accounts. Lastly, the criterion for truth in ancient accounts is dramatic plausibility in contrast to our need for one complete explanation.

In *Enuma elish,* creation of the world is possible because a hostile rival dynasty has come to an end with the death of Tiamat. A new stage has been reached with the exaltation of Marduk. As part of this settlement, Marduk builds a palace or palace-city where he can be acknowledged by the other gods as supreme. He forms the human race to work and provide for the gods. Creation is thus intimately linked to his victory. Later biblical texts link divine victory exaltation to creation and envision creation as the building of a temple or temple-city, for example, Isaiah 65–66 and Revelation 19–22.

VATICINIA EX EVENTU. Five texts from Mesopotamia, some of them formerly designated "prophecies" from their alleged resemblance to biblical literature, are now widely judged to be relevant to apocalyptic literature. They are best described as prophecies after the fact (*vaticinia ex eventu*). Sections typically begin with "a prince shall arise." No kings are named, presumably so that the vagueness will give the impression that future events are being predicted. Kings and kingdoms, however, can be identified from the historical details. Reigns are judged sweepingly as either good or bad. The surveys are very much like the historical surveys in later works such as Daniel 7, 8, and 11 and the Apocalypse of Weeks and the Animal Apocalypse in *1 Enoch*.

Whether all five texts represent a single genre is not certain, but there are two clear subcategories: prophecies in the third person (Text A, the Dynastic Prophecy, and the Uruk Prophecy), and prophecies in the first person (the Shulgi and Marduk Prophecies).

Text A, from seventh-century Asshur, is organized by the refrain "and a prince shall arise" (repeated eight times in a fragmentary tablet). The number of years in each reign is given as well as a characterization of the major events in that reign, historical, meteorological, and agricultural. The events in Text A took place in the twelfth century, five centuries before its composition, so they all are *ex eventu* by definition.

The *Uruk Prophecy*, possibly composed in the reign of Amel-Marduk (biblical Evil-Merodach, 561–560), preserved mainly on the reverse side of the tablet, narrates the rise of six kings. The fifth king is Nebuchadnezzar II (604–562). The genuine prediction comes in lines 16–19: "After him (Nebuchadnezzar II) his son will arise as king in Uruk and become master of the world. He will exercise rule and kingship in Uruk and his dynasty will be established forever. The kings of Uruk will exercise rulership like the gods." The past "predictions" are intended to lend credibility to the last statement. The course of history has been determined by the gods: Nebuchadnezzar's son is meant to rule forever.

The *Dynastic Prophecy*, a Late Babylonian text, speaks successively of the fall of Assyria, the rise and fall of Babylonia and Persia, and the rise of the Hellenistic monarchies. The victory of Alexander the Great over Darius at Issus in 333 B.C.E. is described. After this comes the genuine prophecy, a prediction of another battle, in which Darius is victorious over Alexander: "Enlil, Shamash, and [Marduk] will be at the side of his army [and] the overthrow of the army of the Nanaean (= Thracian, i.e., Alexander) he will [bring about]. He will carry off his extensive booty and [*bring (it)*] into his palace. The people who *had* [*experienced*] misfortune [*will enjoy*] well-being. The mood of the land [will be a happy one]." By its detail, length, and climactic placement of the final prediction, the text gives the impression that the gods have determined the victory of Darius over Alexander. The predicted victory, however, never took place; Darius never defeated Alexander.

In the second subcategory—prediction in the first person (by a god or king)—are two texts that were paired in scribal editions, the Shulgi Prophecy of the late second or early first millennium and the Marduk Prophecy, perhaps from the reign of Nebuchadnezzar I (1125–1104).

In the *Shulgi Prophecy*, unfortunately heavily damaged, Shulgi, a Sumerian king of the Third Dynasty of Ur (2112–2004), who was considered a god and the founder of the city of Nippur, speaks of the kings who will come after him. His successor will submit to Assyria, and Nippur will be cast down. The reign of the Babylonian king, however, will be cut short by the command of Enlil. Another king will arise, restore the shrines, and rebuild Nippur.

In the *Marduk Prophecy*, Marduk describes his (i.e., his statue's) peregrinations, which can be dated to the first millennium: the statue's journey to Hatti and back to Babylon, to Assyria and back to Babylon, and finally to Elam and back to Babylon. The god brought prosperity wherever he went, but his stay in Elam spelled disaster for Babylon. After Marduk returned from Elam to Babylon, however, "a king of Babylon will arise" (probably Nebuchadnezzar I, 1124–1103) who will make the city prosperous and punish Elam. The last part is the genuine prophecy, made credible by the post-factum "prophecies" preceding it. The text is a propaganda piece for Nebuchadnezzar.

The many similarities between the genre of "post-factum prophecy" and the historical surveys in apocalyptic literature suggest possible influence of the older literature on the younger. The most important similarity is that past events are "predicted" to lend credibility to the last-mentioned event, as in the Uruk Prophecy, the Dynastic Prophecy, and the Marduk Prophecy. Textual damage prevents us from knowing if the same is true in the other tablets. Daniel 7, 8, 9, and 11; *1 Enoch* 83–90, 91; and the *Sibylline Oracles,* likewise "predict" some events that are already past and some that are still future, the accuracy of the "predictions" making the genuine prediction at the end more believable. Further, history is seen as a sequence of kingdoms rather than, say, the dominance of a particular city, shrine, or deity. Even in the Marduk Prophecy, the emphasis falls on the king of Babylon. Persons are not named, as they are not named in apocalyptic literature. History is painted with a broad brush; details are few and conventional; reigns are either good or evil. The apocalyptic predictions in apocalyptic literature come to the speaker through revelation. The predictions in the Shulgi and Marduk prophecies come from a deity; perhaps this is true of the other tablets, but their beginnings are too poorly preserved to tell. Lastly, the language of omen texts has stamped the language of the "prophecies," a fact that should warn us against distinguishing too sharply between mantic wisdom (the science of divination) and prophecy/apocalypticism.

There are also important differences between the prophecies and apocalyptic literature. The most important is that the apocalypticists incorporated predictions of kingdoms into a new scenario. That scenario was cosmic threat, combat, and rule of the victorious god; it envisioned the end of the present world and divine judgment upon it. One text, however, already has a certain affinity to the scenario: the Uruk Prophecy predicts that after Nebuchadnezzar II, "his son will arise as king in Uruk and become master of the world. He will exercise rule and kingship in Uruk and his dynasty will be established forever. The kings of Uruk will exercise rulership like the gods [= forever]." In summary, the prophecies show that the apocalypticists were anthologists, borrowing genres such as the post-factum prediction to demonstrate that the course of history was under God's control and that in their day history as they knew it had come to an end and a new age was about to dawn.

DREAM VISION. A late-seventh-century B.C.E. Akkadian text, "The Vision of the Nether World," has been proposed as a source of the dream vision of

Daniel 7 (Kvanvig 1988, 389–555; *ANET* 1969, 109–10). In the relevant thirty-four lines on the obverse side, a visionary, Kummāya, sees in the night a vision of the netherworld: fifteen gods in hybrid form (human or animal heads, hands, and feet) standing before him, and "one man, his body was black like pitch. His face was similar to that of an Anzu bird. He was wearing a red robe. In his left hand he was holding up a bow. In his right hand he was holding a sword." The seer then sees the warrior Nergal on a throne, who, enraged, intends to put him to death because he has dishonored Ereshkigal, Nergal's wife. Ishum, Nergal's counselor, dissuades his master. A description of an ideal king follows, though the context is unclear: "This [spirit] which you saw in the netherworld, is that of the exalted shepherd: to whom my father [ ], the king of the gods, gives full responsibility. . . ." Next comes a prediction and an admonition, and the section concludes with brief reports in the first person and in the third person.

Though the text bears a general resemblance to Daniel 7, with the night dream of gods in hybrid form and the warrior-god on a throne pronouncing judgment, there are major differences. Judgment is given against the visionary himself, whereas in Daniel it is against the beasts from the sea; the ideal ruler in the *Vision* is extremely shadowy, whereas in Daniel he receives an eschatological kingdom. The *pattern of relationships* in the two texts is quite different. Finally, the texts have little in common with regard to aim. In the *Vision,* the aim is to encourage piety to the god of the netherworld; in Daniel, it is to encourage Jews to resist the hellenizing policies of the Seleucid kings (J. J. Collins 1993, 283–86). The "Vision of the Netherworld" is of interest, however, as a precedent for the tours of heaven and hell that are popular in later, especially Christian, apocalypses.

Recurrent Elements

One of the important and persistent recurrent elements in the genre of combat myth is the divine assembly, thrown into confusion yet charged with the responsibility of resisting the monster's threats. A considerable amount of discourse time is devoted to its discussions in *Anzu* and *Enuma elish.* Dramatically, the magnitude of the threat is expressed through the terror and consternation of the gods as they meet. The decrees of the assembly are powerful and binding in heaven and on earth; they are prominent in all the combat myths. Nonetheless, its decrees are not automatically effective against every cosmic threat, for they can be rendered ineffective by a monster. A warrior-god must do away with the evil before the decrees are effective. At the end of *Lugal-e* (lines 679 forward), Ninurta receives the homage of the Anunnaki gods and his father Enlil grants him new status. In *Anzu,* the victorious Ninurta receives names of honor and authority from the gods, a harbinger of the fifty names that Marduk in *Enuma elish* receives from the gods. In *Enuma elish* the assembly's decree plays an extraordinarily important role. Before he sets out, his destiny is declared supreme: "Your destiny (*šīmtu*) is unequalled, your word (has the power of)! . . . From this day forwards your command shall not be altered. Yours is the power to exalt and abase. . . . We hereby give you sovereignty over all of the whole universe" (IV.4–14). In the final tablets (end of IV to VII) Marduk constructs the universe and the assembly's earlier decree takes effect as they acclaim his fifty names.

The decree of the assembly that exalts one deity because of his victory over cosmic enemies is a theme found in a transposed form in apocalyptic literature. Though heavenly decrees in the combat myth are primarily concerned with kingship, they can also be concerned with broader questions of the divine will and human activity. In the Bible, a vestige of the decision-making assembly is found in Gen 1:26 ("Let *us* make man in our image") and 11:7 ("Let *us* go down and confuse their language"), in the designation of heavenly beings as the host or army (the literal meaning of *YHWH ṣĕbāʾôt*), and in affirmations that Yahweh is incomparable to other heavenly beings (e.g., Exod. 15:11; Deut. 3:24; 1 Kgs. 8:23; Pss. 86:8; 95:3). Apocalyptic literature in particular exploits the heavenly assembly. God is often in the assembly, surrounded by heavenly beings, messengers or angels, and there is constant reference to "destinies," and decrees (Brown 1958a; 1958v; 1959).

Related to the decree of the assembly is the Tablet-of-Decrees (*ṭuppi šīmāti*), which in Akkadian narratives only occurs in *Anzu* (where it plays a central role), *Enuma elish* (I.57; IV.121; V.69, presumably derived from *Anzu*), and *Erra* (IV.44). The tablet was worn around the neck of the god in charge, and it could be put on and taken off like a garment—for Enlil removed it to take a bath in *Anzu.* Neither English "destiny" nor "fate" is a satisfactory translation of *šīmtu,* for these English words imply inevitability, whereas the Akkadian word connotes something *decreed* but not necessarily unalterable. "Destinies" were subject to change through magic; they were usually transmitted from a higher power, from god to king, king to subject, father to child. In mythology and literature, the highest gods, usually Anu, Enlil, and Ea, decreed the destinies establishing the nature and pattern of things in heaven and on earth. *Šīmāti* were regarded as introduced at creation, for *Enuma elish* (I.8) describes pre-creation as a period when "no destines had been decreed." Other words for similar determination of things and events are Sumerian *me* or *giš.ḫur* (= Akkadian *parṣu, uṣurtu*). In later apocalypses, the seer is frequently shown heavenly visions of meteorological and natural phenomena and of future events. Such visions should be understood against the ancient Near Eastern background of "destinies"—things and events that have been determined by the divine.

Another relevant recurrent element of the genre of combat myth is the enemy as monster. Azag is a monster. Anzu's strange appearance was proverbial; his face, possibly that of a bat, inspired terror. Though Tiamat, personified Sea, is not described clearly in *Enuma elish*, scholars assume that the dragon depicted fighting a god on many seals is Tiamat; the seven-headed Hydra of some seals may have been later identified with Tiamat. The monsters are often interpreted as natural forces: for example, the storm-god's attack on the monster in the mountains reflects thundershowers sweeping into the mountain ranges. Though such a natural reference cannot be denied, there are as well historical and political dimensions to the monsters. Azag and Anzu reside in the northeastern mountains, the homeland of the enemies of the Mesopotamian plain dwellers. *Enuma elish* views Apsu, Tiamat, and Kingu as usurpers of the legitimate throne that belongs by right to Anu and Marduk. H. H. Schmid notes:

> In Mesopotamia, Ugarit, and Israel, *Chaoskampf* appears not only in cosmological contexts but just as frequently—and this was fundamentally true right from the first—in political contexts. The repulsion and the destruction of the enemy, and thereby the maintenance of political order, always constitutes one of the major dimensions of the battle against chaos. The enemies are not other than a manifestation of chaos which must be driven back. (1984, 104)

An important motif is the seer-hero who is brought into or ascends to the world of the gods to receive wisdom and knowledge about the future. It is his task to communicate this wisdom to the human race. The preeminent seer in apocalyptic literature is Enoch, the hero of the several booklets that make up *1 Enoch*. He is also the hero in other writings and is mentioned in Sirach, Wisdom of Solomon, and the New Testament. As one raised up to heaven and given special knowledge, he served as the model for Daniel, John, and Ezra. Enoch has antecedents in Mesopotamian tradition.

A key biblical text that mediated Mesopotamian lore to Levantine literature and applied it to Enoch was Gen 5:21–24. There Enoch is seventh in a ten-member genealogy of pre-flood patriarchs. The Priestly writer makes comments about Enoch that are not made about the other nine patriarchs: instead of describing his death, the Priestly writer has "he walked with 'God' (*hāʾĕlōhîm*); then he was no more because God (*ʾĕlōhîm*) took him." The Hebrew spellings noted above are significant. The prefaced definite article *hā-* in the first occurrence suggests that the correct translation is not "God" but "divine beings," the heavenly beings who lived with God. The Genesis text thus says that even while on earth Enoch associated with heavenly beings, unlike the other patriarchs. Further, the end of his stay on earth did not mean the end of his communion with heavenly beings; he was taken up into the heavens to be with God.

The Sumerian King List, a schematic history of pre-flood kings, which exists in copies ranging from ca. 1500 B.C.E. to 165 B.C.E., has long been recognized as a source of Genesis 5. The kings in the lists, like the ancestors of Genesis, are extraordinarily long-lived; in some versions of the list, there are ten kings, the last of whom is the flood hero. Some versions have in seventh place a figure like Enoch, named Enmeduranki or Enmenduranna, who ruled in Sippar, a city sacred to the sun-god. Enoch's age of 365 years, which differs so dramatically from the other pre-flood heroes in Genesis, is most naturally explained as a reflection of the solar calendar, another link to Enmeduranki of Sippar. Most important, two texts show Enmeduranki in the presence of the gods Shamash (the sun-god) and Adad. In one he is brought in to the assembly and given special wisdom.

> Shamash in Ebabbarra [appointed] Enmeduranki [king of Sippar], the beloved of Anu, Enlil [and Ea]. Shamash and Adad [brought him in] to their assembly, Shamash and Adad [honoured him], Shamash and Adad [set him] on a large throne of god, they showed him how to observe oil on water, a mystery of Anu [Enlil and Ea], they gave him the tablet of the gods, the liver, a secret of heaven and [underworld], they put in his hand the cedar-(rod), beloved of the great gods." (VanderKam 1984, 39–40; cf. Kvanvig 1988, 185–86)

Enmeduranki is brought into heaven and there is taught divination, how to read the future. He is the prototype of the biblical Enoch, who in Genesis is taken up to heaven to walk with the heavenly beings.

Further refinement to the Enmeduranki tradition has been provided by recently published texts that have made it possible to reappraise the so-called *bīt mēseri* ritual series.[1] The texts list the *apkallu*, legendary pre-flood creatures of great wisdom; seven in number, they taught the human race wisdom and craft.

Kings	*Sages*
1. Alulim	U-An
2. Alagar	U-An-dugga
3. Ammeluanna	Enmedugga
4. Ammegalanna	Enmegalamma

5. Enmešugalanna	Enmebulugga
6. Dumuzi	An-Enlilda
7. Enmeduranki	Utuabzu

They are followed after the flood by four more sages. The text gives each *apkallu* a short notice. Utuabzu, the sage of Enmeduranki, has an especially interesting notice: "Utuabzu, who was taken up into heaven, the pure *purādu* fishes, the *purādu* fishes of the sea, the seven of them, the seven Wise, who arose in the flood, who direct the plans of heaven and earth." Riekele Borger, the editor, believes that the text strengthens the possibility that Enmeduranki as predictor of the future and the seventh ruler in primordial time was the prototype of Enoch. He notes, however, that the myth of Enoch's journey to heaven comes ultimately from Enmeduranki's sage, the seventh pre-flood sage, Utuabzu.

Genesis 5:21–24 is the oldest surviving example of the Enoch tradition in the Bible. From this modest source text a mighty stream was destined to flow.

Themes

The two themes most relevant for later apocalyptic works are cosmic threat and new creation. Though the threat is undeniably prominent in the combat myth, the most important thing is the god's defeat of it and consequent exaltation to the top rank. In *Lugal-e* the evil is that the water destined to irrigate the Mesopotamian plains is trapped in the ice of the northern and eastern mountains. This is not simply a natural malfunction but the conscious strategy of the mountain-dwelling monster Azag, who has been made king by the mountain plants and stones. Azag thwarts the gods' intent that Mesopotamian fields be fertile and support human workers to care for and feed them. Azag's act is against gods and human beings. Azag and his constituency of plants and stones are not purely mythical, for the northern and eastern mountains were the homeland of the plains dwellers' historical enemies. The evil in *Lugal-e* is therefore (in modern terms) both "natural" and "historical," affecting both gods and human beings. By defeating Azag, Ninurta truly restores the cosmos as a coherent system.

In the first part of the two-part *Anzu* the evil is the same as in *Lugal-e*, that is, the failure of the mountain waters to reach the plains. How that problem was solved (at the beginning of the epic) cannot be determined from the fragmentary text. The major evil, however, is Anzu's theft of the Tablet-of-

Decrees from its rightful custodian, Enlil. The divine decision regarding all reality encoded in the tablet is in the power of a monster hostile to the divine assembly. The evil is that things will not work right because the tablet is in the wrong hands. By getting the tablet back, Ninurta ensures the survival of the world the gods have created.

Enuma elish is more complex, and so is the evil in its two sections. In the first section (I.1–79), the evil is the rival dynasty represented by Apsu, who is killed by Ea. In the second part, the evil is the rival dynasty represented by Tiamat. She is violent and irrational; the world would never have been created if she were to rule. Marduk's victory establishes the legitimate dynasty and eventuates in creation.

The three combat myths see the universe as threatened once upon a time by a monster with sufficient power to destroy it or change it for the worse. The divine assembly—that is, the gods as deciding and acting—cannot by itself resolve the problem. The evil is not simply a cosmic malfunction but is willed by a particular being. The evil plays itself out on the natural and historical planes.

Closely related to the evil is the god's victory over it. Is the victory merely a restoration of the pre-threat order, or is it new creation? At the very least, *Endzeit* becomes *Urzeit,* for the original order is renewed. This is surely true for *Lugal-e* and *Anzu. Enuma elish,* however, is a different case. It is true creation. Marduk makes the world as we know it. The world did not exist prior to Tiamat, for it is from her body that the cosmos is constructed.

⮑ CANAAN

History and Religion

By the third millennium Syria-Palestine was populated by West Semitic peoples speaking an Old Canaanite language. After 1200 B.C.E., the Old Canaanite area was divided into three areas: Palestine (the area south of Mount Hermon, later conquered by the tribes of Israel), the areas of the Aramaean city-states, and Phoenicia, the long narrow strip of land along the Mediterranean from Arvad to Mount Carmel in the south. In a Ugaritic text, "Canaanite" refers to an area distinct from the city of Ugarit, but in modern usage "Canaanite" is customary for the whole littoral.

A common literary tradition is attested for the Old Canaanite (Phoenician) culture. Religious and mythological poetic texts excavated at the Late Bronze (mostly fourteenth century B.C.E.) city of Ugarit display vocabulary, especially word pairs, recurrent elements, and techniques found also in Phoenician inscriptions and in early biblical poetry. The Ugaritic texts provide a northern sampling of literary and religious traditions shared by Canaan and Israel.

Canaanite scribes in the employ of royal courts in the major cities knew Mesopotamian literature. Canonical texts have been found at Boghasköy (ancient Hattuša) in the Hittite empire, at Ugarit, at Meskene (ancient Emar, a crossroads of east and west), and even at Megiddo in Palestine (a fragment of *Gilgamesh*). These texts were understood by Levantine scribes, for Akkadian was a diplomatic language in the late second and early first millennia. One can assume that some scribes employed in Canaanite and Israelite temples and palaces were trained in the traditional manner—by copying canonical texts. It is thus not surprising to find Mesopotamian influence on Canaanite and biblical literature. A good example of a western borrowing of an eastern literary genre is the creation-flood story. Attested in the *Sumerian Flood Story, Atrahasis, Gilgamesh XI, Berossus,* and some versions of the Sumerian King List, it is echoed in the flood story found at Ugarit, and has strongly influenced the Bible in Genesis 2–11 (Clifford 1994, 144–46).

The god lists of Ugarit, like those of Mesopotamia, list many more deities than the few who play prominent roles in myths, but we are here chiefly concerned with the executive deities. The most important mythological texts found at Ugarit (in excavations from 1929 forward) are the story of King Keret, the story of Aqhat, and the cycle concerning Baal's combat. They are written in a cuneiform adaptation of the Canaanite alphabet.

The head of the pantheon is the patriarch El, creator of heaven and earth. His consort is Asherah. There is no sacred triad in Ugarit; Mesopotamian Enlil and Ea have no real analogues. El presides over the assembly of the gods, whose members in Ugaritic texts (unlike Mesopotamia) are not precisely identified nor shown engaged in lively debate. El or the assembly *tout ensemble* speak and act. El is portrayed as old and wise, though there are hints that in olden days he was a feared warrior-god. His decree, approved by the assembly, is of extraordinary importance. Both Anat and Asherah confess: "Thou art wise, O El, and thy decree is long life." The young god Hadad (Baal) is a warrior. The assembly decrees, "Our king is Aliyan Baal, our judge above whom there is no other." His weapons are those of the storm—lightning, thunder, wind, and rains that bring fertility—and his bellicose consort is Anat. Two divine beings play significant roles as Baal's enemies: Mot (Death) and Yamm (Sea). One of the major interpretative problems of the Baal Cycle is El's relation to Baal and to Baal's enemies Yamm and Mot. Mot is called "son of El," and Yamm in *KTU* 1.1 is given a name and palace by El. Elsewhere El favors Baal and grants him permission to build his palace.

Literature and Themes Relevant to Apocalyptic Literature

Genre of Combat Myth (Baal Cycle)

The six tablets of the Baal Cycle (*KTU* 1.1–6 = *ANET* 129–42[2]) belong to the genre of combat myth, which we have singled out as having extraordinary influence on apocalyptic literature. The similarities of the Baal Cycle to the Mesopotamian combat myths are striking: (1) the enemy is Sea in *KTU* 1.1–3 = *ANET* 129–31, 135–38, recalling Tiamat in *Enuma elish;* (2) the divine assembly under its president An or El is threatened and commissions a young warrior-god to battle the foe, though in the Baal Cycle the commission must be inferred from the goddesses' quote of the decree that their king is Baal; (3) events are decided by a battle that is cosmic in scope; (4) the warrior-god's victory is symbolized by a palace and dedication feast for all the gods. Some scholars have proposed that this combat myth originated among West Semites on the grounds that the sea phenomenologically is important only in Syria-Palestine. The theory is unlikely, however, because the word "sea" in Meso-potamian myths can refer not only to the ocean but to the waters in the northern mountains, as it does in *Anzu.* It is now clear that the literary antecedent of the Marduk–Tiamat conflict in *Enuma elish* is not the West Semitic Baal–Yamm story but the native *Anzu* (Lambert 1986).

The Ugaritic combat myth is in the same poetic tradition as early biblical poetry and thus is much more pertinent to later apocalyptic literature than the Akkadian works analyzed above. Unfortunately, four of the six tablets of the Baal Cycle cannot be put in their proper sequence because of broken beginnings or ends. Hence we cannot be certain of the plots. Here the Akka-dian works are useful, for they can supply the sequence and plot only dimly discernible in the Ugaritic texts. In the Baal Cycle only tablets V (*ANET* 138–39) and VI (*ANET* 139–41) preserve the ending and the beginning that demonstrate their sequence. (Normally the last line of a tablet is repeated as the first line of the succeeding tablet.) Tablets I–III (*ANET* 129–31, 135–38) tell of the Baal–Yamm conflict and tablets IV–V (*ANET* 131–35, 138–41) of the Baal–Mot conflict. The majority of scholars assume a single cycle, which first depicts Baal's war with Yamm and then describes his war with Mot. It is more probable, however, that the two conflicts are not two acts in a single drama but variants of the same myth. There are good indications that the two stories are variants: tablets III (*ANET* 135–38) and IV (*ANET* 131–35) show an identical sequence of actions (Baal has no palace like the other gods, an embassy is sent to the goddess to ask her to intercede with El for Baal's palace, the goddess prepares for her journey and departs for El's abode, the goddess praises El's decree, El grants permission, the craftsman god is summoned to build it. Positing two versions of a single myth avoids a dramatically implausible never-ending seesaw battle between Baal and his enemies.

BAAL–YAMM. Tablets I–III (*ANET* 129–31, 135–38) are about the Baal–Yamm conflict. We do not know the original sequence of the tablets, and so any summary of the plot must be regarded as tentative. At a certain point Yamm (Sea) is given authority ("a name") by El, who charges him to drive Baal "from his royal throne, the resting place, the throne of his domination." El commands the craftsman-god Koshar wa-Hasis to build a palace for Yamm. (Throughout the cycle, the palace plays an extremely significant role as the concretization of kingship.) So commissioned, Baal sends ambassadors to the assembly presided over by El, ordering them to surrender Baal. The assembly is terrified at the approach of Yamm's messengers, and El immediately hands Baal over, "Baal is your servant, O Yamm" ("your subject" in political language). Baal tries to fight but is restrained by Anat and Ashtart, presumably because they regard the assembly's action as legally binding. After some major gaps in the tablets, Baal eventually has the opportunity to attack his enemy with Koshar wa-Hasis at his side. Koshar fashions two magic weapons against Yamm, the second of which succeeds in knocking Yamm to the ground, where Baal finishes him off. Baal is acclaimed king: "Yamm is dead! Baal reigns!"

The Baal–Yamm story is more fragmentary than the Baal–Mot story; the plot is uncertain and important matters are left unexplained. Why does El commission Yamm and give him a palace? Why does the assembly hand Baal over to Yamm, and why is Baal later able to best him in combat? A major problem in Ugaritic mythology—the unclear relationship of El to Baal, Yamm, and Mot—keeps us from fully comprehending the essential point of this myth.

BAAL–MOT. The Baal–Death combat myth is told in tablets IV–VI of the Baal Cycle (*ANET* 138–42); the extant material is greater and in surer sequence than is the case with the Baal–Yamm story. Most scholars believe that tablets IV-V-VI are the proper sequence. Tablet VI (*ANET* 139–141) immediately continues tablet V (*ANET* 138–39), since its first line repeats the last line of tablet V, but the proper placement of tablet IV (*ANET* 131–35) is far from certain. The story begins with Baal complaining that he has no palace like the other gods and must live in the home of El. Anat intercedes with Asherah, El's wife, to bring the plea to El, reminding him, "Thy decree is wise. . . . Thy decree is: Our king is Puissant Baal, our sovereign second to none; all of us must bear his gift, all of us must bear his purse." Although Baal has been given authority by the assembly, El's permission is still needed for his palace, the full sign of his kingship. El gives his permission. Baal gathers the material and Koshar wa-Hasis builds it. At its completion, Baal declares: "My house I have built of silver, my palace of gold" (*KTU* 1.4.vi = *ANET* 134–35) and invites all the gods to a dedicatory banquet. He marches triumphantly through numerous towns in the vicinity of his Mount Zaphon and from his palace proclaims his kingship in thunder as his enemies flee. In this moment of triumph, Baal instructs his messengers to proclaim his kingship to the underworld and invites Mot.

If *KTU* 1.5 (*ANET* 138–39) directly continues, as most scholars assume (though there are difficulties), then Baal's triumph is suddenly turned upside down as Mot invites, or rather commands, Baal to come to *his* underworld domain. Baal must descend with his whole entourage, and he says to Mot, "Your servant am I, and that for ever (= no set time)." Eventually messengers report back to El that "we came upon Baal fallen to the earth. Dead is Aliyan Baal, departed is Prince, Lord of the earth!" (*KTU* 1.5.vi.8–10 = *ANET* 139). El and Anat engage in mourning rites. Anat finds the body and brings it for burial to Mount Zaphon (*KTU* 1.6.i = *ANET* 139). El is unable to find among his and Asherah's children a suitable replacement for Baal, which makes dramatically clear that Baal is irreplaceable (*KTU* 1.6.i.132–67). Afterward the bereaved Anat encounters Mot, who callously tells her he consumed Baal "like a lamb in his mouth." Later, she seizes him in rage, cuts him up and sows him far and wide (*KTU* 1.6.ii.30–37). After a break of forty lines, El declares that "Aliyan Baal lives, existent is Prince, Lord of the earth," for he sees in a dream the signs of Baal's return to life: the heavens raining oil and the wadis running with honey. El's dream shows that Baal is alive; Shapshu, the sun-goddess, is asked to search for him. After a break, Baal appears, defeats rebellious sons of Asherah and takes the throne. In the seventh year of his reign, Mot comes to exact vengeance for the humiliation inflicted upon him by Anat: "Because of you, Baal, I experienced winnowing in the sea. Give me one of your brothers that I may eat." After about sixty lines of uncertain text, Mot comes to Baal on Mount Zaphon and accuses him of giving him his own brothers to eat (*KTU* 1.6.vi.14–16). Baal and Mot then fight like animals until both fall in exhaustion. At this point Shapshu intervenes and rebukes Mot: "How dare you fight with Aliyan Baal. . . . [Bull El your father] will uproot the base of your dwelling. Surely he will overturn your royal throne. Surely he will shatter your scepter of judgment" (1.6.vi.24–29). Mot stops out of fear. Baal remounts his throne and the cycle ends with a banquet of the gods. Shapshu is lauded as judge, probably for her role in settling the conflict of kingship.

The overall interpretation of the Baal Cycle is made difficult by the uncertain sequence of tablets I–IV (and columns within tablet II), many broken passages, and our ignorance of its social location. Was the cycle recited in the temple? Was it used to support the authority of the king? Several interpretations have been proposed: ritual and seasonal, cosmogonic, and rhetorical and political. Each has some validity yet no single theory does justice to all the data. Few would deny any reference to the change of seasons. Mot represents the dry summer season or dry areas, and Baal represents the fertilizing rains of the Levantine winter. An exclusively seasonal explanation, however, neglects the obvious political features of the myth. Mot and Baal act more like generals and politicians than natural forces, and Baal's kingship has to have some reference to the Ugaritic king, who, like Baal, needed military power in order to reign. Others see in the cycle a cosmogony or creation account, in which Baal creates a cosmos after defeating some form of chaos. This interpretation accounts for the life–death struggle, and the prominence of cosmic order and the palace, but in the Ugaritic texts only El and Asherah are given the title creator; the most that Baal accomplishes by his victory over sea and death is to reconstitute cosmic and political harmony. Historical interpretations see the myth as reflecting the rise and fall of the gods of different peoples; for example, the rise of Baal allegedly at the expense of El reflects the god of a new dynasty in the history of Ugarit. This interpretation is unsatisfactory, however. Baal does not replace El but is commissioned by him, and the commission of a young god by a senior god in the face of a cosmic threat is a characteristic feature of ancient palace life and of the genre of combat myth.

The best approach is to view the cycle according to its genre, the combat myth, and to reconstruct its plot by analogy with the better-known combat myths of Mesopotamia. In the typical plot, a monster threatens the cosmic order; the assembly of the gods meets amid considerable trepidation; finding no willing warrior among the senior deities, it turns to a young outsider, who successfully defeats the monster and returns to the assembly to be acclaimed king. This abstract plotline does not completely resolve several puzzles in the Baal Cycle (e.g., the relation of El to Baal, Mot, and Yamm), but it allows us to arrange the tablets in order with some confidence. It also explains the prominent role of Baal's palace, the need for El's permission, the fact that Yamm and Mot, despite their names, are portrayed not as primordial forces but as seekers of political power. Baal's royalty explains the relation of these mythic texts to the people of Ugarit, for human kingship is a reflection of divine kingship. These myths must support the authority of the Ugaritic king, whose proper rule ensures fertility, upholds family and civic order, and sees to the proper honoring of the gods.

Recurrent Elements

The assembly of the gods plays a significant role in the Baal–Yamm story.

> The gods sat to eat, / the holy ones to dine. / Baal stood before El. / When the gods saw them [the hostile messengers of Yamm], / . . . . . / the gods lowered their heads / upon their knees, / and upon their princely thrones. / Baal rebuked them. / "Why have you lowered, O Gods, / your heads upon your knees / and on your princely thrones? / I see, O gods, you are terrified / from fear of the messengers of Yamm, / the emissaries of Judge River. / Lift up your heads, O gods, / from upon your knees, / from upon your princely thrones!" (*KTU* 1.2.I.20–28)

Despite Baal's protests, the assembly surrenders him to Yamm's messengers, and their decision, even though made in fear, is binding.

In biblical passages such as 1 Kgs. 22:19–23; Isaiah 6; and 40:1–8; Psalm 82; and Job 1–2, the assembly plays a major role, and in apocalyptic literature it sometimes forms the context in which God acts, e.g., Daniel 7 and Revelation 4–5. The biblical emphasis on the unicity and absolute power of Yahweh reduces the members of the assembly to spectators, choristers, or messengers, but the assembly persists as part of the heavenly scene.

Sea is apparently a monster. In *KTU* 1.3.III.39–IV.3, Anat recalls the allies of Yamm, the enemies of Baal: El's river Rabbim, the dragon, the crooked serpent, Shilyat with seven heads. In *KTU* 1.5.I., Lotan is the ally of Mot. Lotan appears in the Bible under the name Leviathan in Ps. 74:13–14; Job 3:8; 26:12–13; 41:1–34; Isa. 27:1; Rev. 12:3; 17:1–14; 19:20; 21:1; 2 Esdras 6:49–52. Mot is not described but may also be a monster. To judge by their names, Yamm and Mot represent forces hostile to the human race and terrify the divine assembly. Unfortunately the precise nature of their threat is unclear.

The decree is ascribed to El. The assembly is not recorded as issuing decrees on its own. When the goddesses Anat and Asherah ask El to permit Baal to build a palace after his victory over Mot and Yamm, they praise his decree: "Your decree, O El, is wise. Your wisdom is eternal. A life of good fortune is your decree. Our king is Aliyan Baal, our judge without a peer" (*KTU* 1.3.V.30–33; 1.4.IV.41–44). The kingship of Baal needs the decree of El in order for it to be realized in a palace. In the Bible, Yahweh is acclaimed king by the denizens of heaven. Psalm 29 is the most explicit: "Give to Yahweh, O sons of El, give to Yahweh glory and might. . . . Yahweh is enthroned on Flood-dragon, Yahweh reigns as king forever!"

A recurrent element in apocalyptic literature—the use of animal names for human beings—has precedents in Ugaritic and in early biblical poetry, suggesting that it was part of the Canaanite literary repertoire. Animal names convey fleetness, ferocity, or strength. King Keret's dinner guests include "his bulls" and "his gazelles" (*KTU* 1.15.IV.6–8, 17–19), which are to be interpreted as "peers" and "barons." Baal's allies include "eight boars" (*ḫnzr* = Hebrew *ḥzr*), parallel to "seven lads" (*KTU* 1.5.V.8–9). The Bible has even more examples: *ʾabbîr* ("bull," "stallion") *ʿayil* ("ram") *kĕpîr* ("young lion") *ʿattûdîm* ("he-goats") among others (Miller 1971). Daniel 7 and 8 as well as the Animal Apocalypse in *1 Enoch* 85–90 describe human heroes under the figure of animals.

Themes

The best clue to the nature of the cosmic threats in the Ugaritic texts is their names, Death (Mot) and Sea (Yamm). Death seems to represent death and sterility, and Sea, the Mediterranean Sea bordering on and perhaps threatening to overrun the coast. In the Bible the monsters have an implicit historical and political reference, but the Ugaritic texts are silent on such references. One can probably assume that the conquests of Baal have some reflex in royal ideology: for example, the king of Ugarit has been commissioned by El and his rule continues the work of Baal.

Because the nature of the cosmic evil is unspecified, the nature of Baal's victory over it must also be uncertain. Does Baal reestablish an order or does he create? He does not seem to attain the uncontested rank among the gods that Marduk attains in *Enuma elish* or to create the world. Only El and his consort Asherah are ever called creator. In comparison with the Mesopotamian accounts, Baal's royalty seems limited. At one point in the story, his enemies are actually supported by the assembly of the gods and El, and at another point he himself declares he is Mot's servant. Baal cannot defeat Mot in *KTU* 1.6.VI until Shapshu warns that El will hear and retaliate against Mot. Baal's characteristic thunderstorm is a phenomenon of winter, a hint perhaps that it is not effective in the summer season. The evidence suggests that Baal—and probably the Ugaritic king, his regent on earth—enjoy limited kingship. The limit differs strikingly from the triumph of Ninurta in *Anzu*, Marduk (or Asshur) in *Enuma elish*, and Yahweh's victory in the Bible.

The above survey of Mesopotamian and Canaanite material prompts four observations.

1. One must be careful methodologically about describing the elements of the genre of combat myth in the ancient Near East. There is no ideal form of the myth but only diverse realizations. What is essential? Joseph Fontenrose's initial classification in *Python: A Study in Delphic Myth* (1959) was useful but relied too much on the personal qualities of the actors and too little on their function. Neil Forsyth's *The Old Enemy: Satan and the Combat Myths* adapts Vladimir Propp's description in *Morphology of the Folk Tale* to provide the following scheme (Forsyth 1987, 448–51).

> 1. Lack/   2. Hero emerges/   3. Donor/   4. Journey   5. Battle   6. Defeat   7. Enemy
>   villainy.   prepares to act.   Consul-   ascendant.
>   tation.

> 7. Hero recovers/   8. Battle rejoined.   9. Victory.   10. Enemy punished.   11. Triumph.
>   new hero.

2. Kingship and cosmic order are inextricably bound up with each other in that the god's restoration of pre-threat order (*Lugal-e, Anzu;* Baal–Mot, Baal–Yamm?) or creation of order (*Enuma elish*) is *the* great act and sign of his kingship. The kingship of the victor god is in a sense "monotheistic"; that is, *one* god is singled out at the expense of the other gods' sovereignty, usurping their supremacy in the pantheon and over the universe.

3. What modern thought distinguishes as "nature" and "history" is not clearly distinguished in ancient thought. Natural forces are described as historical enemies. Monsters engage in political activities (stealing the Tablet-of-Decrees), lead armies, and conduct campaigns.

4. Do the texts look forward to a permanent final state? Norman Cohn concludes that Mesopotamian, Canaanite, and early biblical faith views were essentially "static yet anxious" (Cohn 1993, 227) and that Zoroastrianism introduced hope for a permanent phase of absolute peace. One can argue, however, that the combat myth, even outside the Bible, already contains a hope for a permanent kingdom, or, better stated, the unimpeded rule of a single deity. One god became supreme over all the other gods and over a particular cosmic evil. People presumably hoped for the abiding order, though

perhaps they were not surprised when fresh cosmic threats arose. But endless repetition, eternal return, is not the *message* in the combat myths considered above.

⇒ THE BIBLE

History and Religion

By ca. 1200 B.C.E., a group of tribes occupied part of Palestine and formed a league of tribes known as Israel, which shared a common story. Yahweh their God had rescued them from Egypt, made a covenant, and brought them into Canaan. Some poetry from this period survives.

To judge by this early poetry, Israel made use of the poetic repertory and concepts of Canaanite religious literature. The fixed pairs of words, vocabulary, and poetic syntax found in the largely fourteenth-century Ugaritic texts also occur in Hebrew poetry such as Exodus 15, Judges 5, Deuteronomy 33, and Psalm 114. The well-known animosity of the Bible to "Canaanite" religious practices should not mislead us into thinking the Israelites were a hermetically sealed enclave in Canaan. The very vehemence of the Bible shows the affinity between Canaanite and Israelite culture.

Israelite poets described Yahweh in the language used of the gods El and Baal in Canaan. The exploits of Yahweh were sometimes depicted in the genre of the combat myth. Yahweh is a storm-god using weapons of wind, rain, and lightning to defeat his foes (e.g., Pss. 18:8–20; 29; 77:12–21). Though sharing much with their neighbors, Israelite poets were distinctive in their explicit *historical* interest and reference. The poets celebrated Yahweh's victories not over other gods or monsters but over the army of Pharaoh in Egypt. Yahweh fought *Israel's* battles. These historical acts were nonetheless celebrated with mythic language and concepts, which deepened their significance and gave them a cosmic scope. The combined historical and mythic reference enabled Israel, relatively insignificant in comparison with other peoples, to reckon itself as extraordinary, the special people of the Most High God.

In the course of Israel's history, the prominence given to either the mythic or the historical dimension in religious writings varied. Early poetry generally maintained a balance between mythic and historical elements: for example, Yahweh fights on the heavenly plane for Israel (e.g., Judg. 5:4–5, 20–21), but the poem is mainly about a historical battle between Israel and a coalition of northern kings. In some works borrowed from neighboring courts and temples, Israelite scribes left mythological elements "untranslated," that is, not referred to historical events. Though some postexilic writings such as Isaiah

24–27, 65, and Zechariah 9–14 do not immediately refer mythological description to historical events, one must be cautious about making the myth–history correlation a criterion for charting the development of apocalyptic literature. Myth and history are not dichotomous concepts. Historical reference can be implicit in nonbiblical mythology, which may well have in view a historical people and dynasty (Roberts 1976). The prominence of myth or history in a literary work may depend on the genre rather than on a "worldview."

It has been argued that historical and sociological changes in the post-exilic period, particularly the end of native kingship and the related "office" of prophecy, encouraged the development of apocalyptic writing. In sixth-century literature such as Isaiah 34–35, 40–55, and the later oracles of the book of Ezekiel, a change in the character of prophecy is already discernible. New traits or patterns have emerged. One is the democratizing and eschatologizing of classical prophetic themes and forms. A second is the doctrine of two ages, an era of "old things" and an era of "new things," the beginning of a typological treatment of historical events. The significance of history was increasingly discovered in future fulfillment. A third element is the resurgent influence of myths of creation used to frame history and to lend history transcendent significance (Cross 1973, 343–46).

Literature and Themes Relevant to Apocalyptic Literature

Genre of Combat Myth

We can distinguish four stages in the use of the combat myth by Israel: (1) early poetry such as Exodus 15, (2) liturgical poetry (psalms) of the monarchic period, (3) Second Temple literature such as Isaiah 40–66 and Zechariah 9–14, and (4) fully developed apocalyptic literature such as Daniel 7 and Revelation 12. In the first stage, the old hymns celebrate a past event, Yahweh's victory, which has brought Israel into existence. Yahweh defeated threats (Pharaoh, the Red Sea) to Israel's existence enabling the people to live safely in their land. In the second stage, hymns such as Psalms 93, 96, and 114 praise the ancient past victory that brought Israel into being. In communal laments such as Psalms 74, 77, and 89, Israel is threatened by enemies. The psalmist narrates before God in liturgy ("remembers") the original combat whereby God defeated its enemies. The purpose is to persuade God to repeat the primordial victory and defeat the present threat. In the third stage, the postexilic period, Israel has been destroyed in that it has lost its land and Temple. The validity of Yahweh's past victory has been annulled. Hence the psalmist beseeches God to fight and win a victory over Israel's enemies *in the future*. In the fourth stage, exemplified in Daniel 7 and Revelation 12, a seer is told that the victory *has already taken place* in heaven; the seer is to bring the news of victory to the beleaguered faithful on earth.

The criterion for distinguishing the stages above is how the combat myth is viewed by each. In the first stage the combat-victory is a past and still valid event (the victory over Pharaoh at the Red Sea), and it is the reason for Israel's present existence. In the second stage, liturgical hymns praise the past victory as still potent. Communal laments, however, view the community as profoundly threatened to the point that the old saving event has lost its efficacy and must be renewed. In the third stage, the combat victory has been annulled, for Israel lies in ruins. Hence the community prays God to act again on the model of the ancient deed. In the fourth stage, the period of Daniel and Revelation, the combat has taken place and the victory has been won in the real or heavenly world, but only the seer (and his readers) knows it. We now turn to a representative work from each of the four stages.

1. Exodus 15 is the best known adaptation of the combat myth of the early poetry. Its early date is strongly suggested by archaic linguistic features (Cross 1973; Sáenz Badillos 1993). The first part of the poem celebrates Yahweh's defeat of Pharaoh *on* the sea (sea itself is not the enemy), and in the second part, Yahweh's leading the people to his shrine, where his kingship is acclaimed. Its genre—hymn—differs of course from the narrative realizations of the combat myth we have so far seen. The structure is not identical to Forsyth's ideal outline of the plot, which is drawn from purely narrative realizations. The first scene, "lack or villainy," occurs in v. 9, "I will purse, I will overtake, I will overtake, my desire shall have its fill of them." The assembly of gods is only vestigially preserved because of the demands of Israel's monotheistic faith. The battle is described in v. 8. Yahweh is exalted to kingship over the other gods (v. 11): "Who is like you, Yahweh, among the gods, / Who is like you, majestic in holiness, / Awesome in splendor, working wonders! You stretched out your right hand, the earth swallowed them"; (v. 18): Yahweh will reign for ever and ever!" A special emphasis is the procession of the people through Canaan to Yahweh's shrine, where his kingship will be celebrated. The narrative plot has been broken up for the sake of liturgy.

The hymn celebrates a specific historical event in the myth—Yahweh's victory over Pharaoh at the Red Sea. "Historical" here means only that the Israelites believed the exodus took place at a particular time and place. Though the extant extrabiblical combat myths did not have an explicitly historical reference, they depicted creation or reestablishment of a particular cosmic order and must have therefore had in mind a specific king and people. The Bible is, nonetheless, much more explicit about historical events and gives them much more emphasis than nonbiblical texts.

2. In liturgical poetry of the monarchic period the combat myth is discernible in some hymns, for example, Psalms 93, 96, and 114, in which it functions as in the early hymns. The combat myth functions differently, however, in communal laments such as Psalms 74, 77, and 89. In this genre Israel, threatened by enemies, recites before God ("remembers") the old combat victory at the beginning. The purpose is to persuade God to repeat the primordial victory and defeat the present threat. This use differs from the previous stage and points forward to stage 3: the victory is a past historical event but its present potency is now in doubt. People have to pray that the original deed be renewed.

Psalm 89 is a good example of how the combat myth functions in communal laments. Recent commentators rightly regard it as a literary unity (Clifford 1980). It "remembers" before Yahweh his ancient world-creating victory (in this psalm it includes the installation of the Davidic king) in order to appeal to God's *noblesse oblige:* Will you allow the king who represents your combat victory to be defeated in battle? Verses 6–19 describe that cosmic victory as a single event that includes a procession and consecration of a king.

> [10]You rule the raging Sea;
>> you still its swelling waves.
> [11]You crushed Rahab with a mortal blow;
>> your strong arm scattered your foes.
> [12]Yours are the heavens, yours the earth;
>> you founded the world and everything in it.
> [Verses 16–19 describe a triumphant procession to Yahweh's shrine, after which the Davidic king is consecrated.]
> [20]Then you spoke in a vision to your consecrated one and you said,
>> I have set (my) servant above the mighty men,
>> I have raised up a man of (my) choice from the army.
> . . . .
> [28]Yes, I make him my firstborn,
>> the highest of the kings of the earth.

3. After the capture of Jerusalem, the destruction of the Temple, and the end of the monarchy, it was understandable that Israelites concluded that God's work had come to an end. Texts such as Isa. 51:9–11 view the combat victory as no longer in effect and ask God for a new deed similar to the ancient one.

[9]Awake, awake, clothe yourself with power,
    arm of Yahweh!
Awake as in days of old,
    generations long ago.
surely it was you that hacked Rahab [sea monster] in pieces,
    that pierced the Dragon.
[10]It was you that dried up Sea
    the waters of the Great Deep,
that made the abysses of Sea
    a road for the redeemed to walk on.
[11]So let the ransomed of Yahweh return,
    let them come with shouting to Zion.

Second Isaiah imagined the ancient deed that gave birth to Israel as the exodus conquest and a cosmogonic victory (43:16–17). God is about to do something new modeled on the old (43:18–21). In the prayer of 51:9–11, the prophet asks God to do again the ancient combat victory over Sea, which will result in the return of the exiles to Zion. The ancient deed is a thing of the past; it is now projected into the future. May God bring it about!

4. In Daniel 7, written in the 160s B.C.E., vestiges of the combat myth appear. In the plot of the Mesopotamian and Canaanite examples examined earlier in this essay, the young warrior, after vanquishing the sea monster and restoring order, receives kingship from the chief god and the assembly. Though no one would argue that fourteenth-century Canaanite texts directly shaped Daniel 7, there can be little doubt that the combat myth has influenced the scene: the Son of Man coming with the clouds of heaven (v. 13) recalls the epithet of Canaanite Baal, "rider of the clouds"; the Ancient of Days (v. 9) evokes the epithet of Canaanite El, *ʾb šnm,* "Father of Years." The pattern of relationships is further proof of influence: the interaction of two god-like figures is unprecedented in the Bible but common in the Ugaritic texts; there is opposition between the sea and the cloud rider. There are, of course, major differences such as the introduction of the motif of the four kingdoms, and the beast is slain not in combat but by judicial decree (J. J. Collins 1993, 286–94). Knowledge of the Canaanite background can highlight important points in Daniel 7: the earthly kingdoms symbolized by the four beasts are agents of a more primordial evil, Sea; no battle needs to be fought, the victory is already won; Israelite monotheism has made the old warrior-god into an angelic representative of Israel.

The book of Revelation has also drawn on the combat myth. One could perhaps argue that chaps. 4–5 are a vestigial reflection of the divine assembly thrown into consternation by its inability to find within its ranks a defender of divine rule; the Lion turned Lamb would be the heavenly hero. Revelation 12 is more certain. The enemy is a seven-headed dragon, for which there is no biblical parallel but a clear one in the Ugaritic Baal cycle, "Lotan (Leviathan) the twisting serpent. . . . Shalyat with seven heads" (*KTU* 1.5.i.1–3 = *ANET* 138). The dragon's ten horns show an attempt to relate it to the fourth beast in Daniel 7. As in Daniel 7, Revelation 12 uses the combat myth (however vestigial) to show that the victory has been won (A. Y. Collins 1976). It has happened in the heavens, the real world, but is not yet displayed on earth. An event of *Urzeit* is now an event in *Endzeit*. When the beasts and the dragon will be destroyed on earth (Rev. 17:1–20:15), the new heavens will appear.

The above survey shows the various ways in which the genre of the combat myth appears in biblical literature. In many old poems and psalms the combat is past and undergirds the present order. With the exile, the present order has collapsed, and so the combat is moved to the future, with a view to restoration.

⪦ CONCLUSIONS

What can we learn about apocalyptic literature by studying its early antecedents? First of all they teach us that the imagery and themes of apocalyptic literature are not bizarre and obscurantist, as is sometimes claimed. For example, the combat myth was a customary ancient way of thinking about the world. Ancient Near Eastern "philosophical" thinking was normally done through narrative. Retelling one basic narrative in slightly different versions enabled ancients to reflect about the governance of the world and explain the course of history, especially the history of their own nation. Their era took for granted the existence and power of the gods and factored them into their reflection, as our era takes for granted and reckons with a different (and less ultimate) range of forces, for example, the power of ideas, of free trade, of energy resources. To do philosophy, theology, and political theory, modern thinkers employ the genre of the discursive essay rather than the narrative of the combat myth. Despite the differences, one should not forget that ancients and moderns share an interest in ultimate causes and both are intent on explaining the cosmos, the nature of evil, and the validity and the functions of basic institutions. Apocalyptic literature at bottom is not bizarre and opaque, but is rather a narrative way of reflecting about theology, philosophy, and history, and of inculcating a way of life.

Some of the exotic elements of apocalyptic literature, however, are intended by their authors. For example, the *post-factum* prophecies are deliberately vague, without place or personal names, to make them appear as prophecies of a future only dimly discerned. Heavenly visions are deliberately portrayed as wondrous and radically different from everyday life. Their exotic details are a narrative way of conveying the numinous quality of the heavenly world.

This article has focused on the combat myth as an important key to understanding some of the underlying issues of apocalyptic works. The genre always deals with the supremacy (kingship) of *one* god in the pantheon or heaven. Despite the mythic language, there is a "historical" perspective in all the instances of the genre because they refer to the personal and political realities of the human beings who tell them. In the Bible the historical reference is explicit, and the use of mythic language to interpret historical happenings is clear.

⌖ NOTES

1. The most important text was published by R. Borger, "Die Beschwörungsserie *bīt mēseri* und die Himmelfahrt Henochs," *JNES* 33 (1974): 183–96. Discussions are in Kvanvig 1988, 191–213; and J. C. Greenfield, "Apkallu," in *Dictionary of Deities and Demons in the Bible,* ed. K. van der Toorn and P. W. van der Horst, 134–38 (Leiden: E. J. Brill, 1995).

2. There have been several systems of reference to the Ugaritic texts, but *KTU* is now the standard text. A widely used English translation is that of H. L. Ginsberg in *ANET.* The equivalences of tablets of the Baal Cycle in *KTU* and *ANET* is as follows: *KTU* 1.1 = *ANET* VI AB iv; *KTU* 1.2 = *ANET* III AB, C, B, A; *KTU* 1.3= *ANET* V AB; *KTU* 1.4 = *ANET* II AB; *KTU* 1.5 = *ANET* I AB; *KTU* 1.6 =*ANET* I AB.

⌖ BIBLIOGRAPHY

Abbreviations

ANET   Pritchard, James B., ed. *Ancient Near Eastern Texts Relating to the Old Testament.* 3rd ed. Princeton, N.J.: Princeton University Press, 1969.

KTU   Dieterich, M., O. Loretz, and J. Sanmartín. *The Cuneiform Alphabetic Texts,* 1–28. Münster: Ugarit Verlag, 1995. The standard edition of the alphabetic cuneiform (still abbreviated *KTU* after the earlier German title).

Primary Texts
Mesopotamia
Lugal-e:
Jacobsen, Thorkild. 1987. *The Harps that Once . . . : Sumerian Poetry in Translation,* 233–72. New Haven: Yale University Press. A free translation with brief introduction and notes.
van Dijk, Jan. 1983. *LUGAL UD ME-LÁM-bi NIR-ĞÁL: Le récit épique et didactique des Travaux de Ninurta, du Déluge et de la nouvelle Création.* Leiden: E. J. Brill. A magisterial edition and commentary.

Anzu:
Dalley, Stephanie. 1991. *Myths from Mesopotamia,* 203–27. Oxford: Oxford University Press. An up-to-date translation with brief introduction and notes.
Moran, William L. "Notes on Anzu." *Archiv für Orientforschung* 35 (1988): 24–29. Authoritative discussion of new manuscripts.

Enuma elish:
Dalley 1991, 228–77. Translation and notes.
Speiser, E. A. "The Creation Epic." In *ANET,* 60–72, 501–3.

Akkadian Prophecies, Text A:
ANET, 451–52.

Akkadian Prophecies, Uruk Prophecy:
Hunger, H., and S. A. Kaufman. 1975. "A New Akkadian Prophecy Text." *Journal of the American Oriental Society* 95:371–75.

Akkadian Prophecies, Dynastic Prophecy:
Grayson, A. K. 1975. *Babylonian Historical-Literary Texts,* 24–37. Toronto: University of Toronto Press.

Akkadian Prophecies, Shulgi Prophecy, and Marduk Prophecy:
Borger, Riekele. 1971. "Gott Marduk und Gott-König Šulgi als Propheten: Zwei prophetischen Texte." *Bibliotheca Orientalis* 28:3–24.
Foster, Benjamin R. 1993. *Before the Muses: An Anthology of Akkadian Literature,* 270–72, 304–7. Bethesda, Md.: CDL.

Canaan
Baal Cycle:
del Olmo Lete, G. 1981. *Mitos y Leyendas de Canaan,* 81–233. Madrid: Ediciones Cristiandad. Richly annotated Spanish translation.
Dieterich, M., O. Loretz, and J. Sanmartín. 1995. *The Cuneiform Alphabetic Texts,* 1–28. Münster: Ugarit Verlag. The standard edition of the alphabetic cuneiform (still abbreviated *KTU* after the earlier German title).
Gibson, J. C. L. 1978. *Canaanite Myths and Legends,* 38–81. 2nd ed. Edinburgh: Clark. English translation.

Ginsberg, H. L. "Ugaritic Myths, Epics, and Legends." In *ANET,* 129–42. English translation.

Smith, M. S. 1994. *The Ugaritic Baal Cycle.* Vol. 1. Leiden: E. J. Brill. *KTU* 1.1–1.2 only, with lengthy discussion.

Secondary Studies

Batto, Bernard. 1992. *Slaying the Dragon: Mythmaking in the Biblical Tradition.* Louisville: Westminster/John Knox. A good survey of the combat myth in Mesopotamia, Ugarit, and the Bible.

Brown, R. E. 1958a. "The Pre-Christian Semitic Concept of 'Mystery.'" *Catholic Biblical Quarterly* 20:417–43.

———. 1958b. "The Semitic Background of the New Testament *Mystērion.*" *Biblica* 39:426–28; 40 (1959): 70–87.

Clifford, Richard J., S.J. 1980. "Psalm 89: A Lament over the Davidic Ruler's Continued Failure." *Harvard Theological Review* 73:35–47.

———. 1994. *Creation Accounts in the Ancient Near East and in the Bible.* CBQMS 26. Washington, D.C.: Catholic Biblical Association. A study of all the cosmogonies, some of which are combat myths, with up-to-date bibliography.

Cohn, Norman. 1993. *Cosmos, Chaos, and the World to Come: The Ancient Roots of Apocalyptic Faith.* New Haven: Yale University Press. A survey of the roots of apocalyptic thinking among the Egyptians, Mesopotamians, Vedic Indians, Zoroastrians, with attention to how belief in the end of history arose.

Collins, Adela Yarbro. 1976. *The Combat Myth in the Book of Revelation.* Harvard Dissertations in Religion 9. Missoula, Mont.: Scholars Press. Draws on the combat myth in ancient Near Eastern literature to clarify Revelation 12 and the structure of the entire book of Revelation.

Collins, John J. 1993. *Daniel: A Commentary on the Book of Daniel.* Hermeneia. Minneapolis: Fortress Press. Contains a thorough discussion of ancient Near Eastern antecedents to Daniel.

Cross, Frank Moore. 1973. *Canaanite Myth and Hebrew Epic.* Cambridge, Mass.: Harvard University Press. Contains a penetrating discussion of the Israelite borrowing of Canaanite myth with a sketch of "proto-apocalyptic" material.

Day, John. 1985. *God's Conflict with the Dragon and the Sea: Echoes of a Canaanite Myth in the Old Testament.* Cambridge: Cambridge University Press. A competent and detailed discussion of Ugaritic and biblical texts.

Fontenrose, Joseph. 1959. *Python: A Study in Delphic Myth.* Berkeley: University of California Press.

Forsyth, Neil. 1987. *The Old Enemy: Satan and the Combat Myth.* Princeton: Princeton University Press. An authoritative history of Satan from third-millennium Sumer through the Old and New Testaments, Gnosticism, up to Augustine.

Goldfless, Sanford K. 1980. "Babylonian Theogonies: Divine Origins in Ancient Mesopotamian Religion and Literature." Dissertation, Harvard University.

Kvanvig, Helge S. 1988. *Roots of Apocalyptic: The Mesopotamian Background of the*

Enoch Figure and of the Son of Man. WMANT 61. Neukirchen-Vluyn: Neukirchener Verlag. A detailed study of Mesopotamian antediluvian traditions and of Akkadian dream visions and their reuse in apocalyptic literature.

Lambert, W. G. 1986. "Ninurta Mythology in the Babylonian Epic of Creation." In *Keilschriftliche Literaturen: Ausgewählte Vorträge der XXXII Rencontre assyriologique internationale,* edited by K. Hecker and W. Sommerfeld. Berliner Beiträge zum vorderen Orient 6. Berlin: Reimer.

Miller, P. D. 1971. "Animal Names as Designations in Ugaritic and Hebrew." *Ugarit-Forschungen* 2:177–86.

Mullen, E. T., Jr. 1980. *The Assembly of the Gods in Canaanite and Early Hebrew Literature.* Harvard Semitic Monograph 24. Chico, Calif.: Scholars Press.

Propp, Vladimir. *Morphology of the Folk Tale.* Austin: University of Texas Press.

Roberts, J. J. M. 1976. "Myth *versus* History." *Catholic Biblical Quarterly* 38:1–13. A nuanced statement of the relation between myth and history in the Bible.

Rochberg-Halton, F. 1982. "Fate and Divination in Mesopotamia." *Archiv für Orientforschung* Beiheft 19:36–71.

Sáenz Badillos, A. 1993. *A History of the Hebrew Language.* Cambridge: Cambridge University Press.

Schmid, H. H. 1984. "Creation, Righteousness and Salvation: 'Creation Theology' as the Broad Horizon of Biblical Theology." In *Creation in the Old Testament,* edited by B. W. Anderson. Philadelphia: Fortress Press.

VanderKam, James C. 1984. *Enoch and the Growth of an Apocalyptic Tradition.* CBQMS 16. Washington, D.C.: Catholic Biblical Association. Thorough and reliable discussion of the sources and usage of the figure of Enoch in apocalyptic literature.

2

Persian Apocalypticism

Anders Hultgård
Uppsala University

P ERSIAN OR IRANIAN APOCALYPTICISM PRESENTS A UNIQUE
interest because of its striking similarities with the Judeo-Christian tradition, making at the same time a somewhat alien and unfamiliar impression
that is due to a different cultural background. For almost two centuries the
problem of Iranian influence on Jewish and Christian eschatology has attracted
Western scholarship and also stirred up an ardent debate. Could it be that the
entire worldview of Western apocalypticism up to the present time ultimately
derives from ancient Iran? The end and renewal of the world, the apocalyptic
time reckoning, the signs and tribulations of the end, the struggle of God and
his Messiah against evil, personified in the figure of Satan and his demons,
would thus be ideas having a foreign origin. The fact is that all these ideas are
found in Iran and, what is more, they are essential and well integrated in the
Zoroastrian religious worldview. Or—as the opposite party contends—does
Jewish and Christian apocalypticism represent a natural and continuous
development out of biblical prophecy?

The discussion is further complicated by the nature of the sources. The
origins of Persian apocalypticism are not apparent, since the older texts, the
Avesta, contain only isolated eschatological assertions or allusions to ideas
that may be interpreted in an apocalyptic framework. In fact, no coherent
apocalyptic tradition can be restored from the Avesta that has come down to

us. It is not until medieval times—that is, the early Islamic period—that we meet with full descriptions of cosmogony and eschatology that enable us to delineate a coherent apocalyptic tradition.

The purpose of this essay will be to describe and interpret the primary texts of Persian apocalypticism, to consider the historical and social context, and to address the questions of origins and influence on the Judeo-Christian tradition. By apocalypticism I here understand primarily ideas of the end and renewal of the world set in a framework of cosmic history, often transmitted in a revelatory context and particularly actualized in crisis situations. Seen in isolation from their cosmic and revelatory context, these ideas may equally well be classified as eschatological and messianic. The genre of texts describing visionary journeys to paradise and hell, like the Ardāy Wirāz Nāmag is also treated in this essay, although they are largely concerned with individual eschatology.

⌖ THE APOCALYPTIC TRADITION OF THE PAHLAVI BOOKS: AN INTERPRETIVE DESCRIPTION

The Primary Sources

For the reasons stated above it seems convenient to begin with a description and analysis of the Pahlavi texts. This is the common designation for the religious literature of the Zoroastrians compiled or written down in the late Sassanian and early Islamic periods (sixth to eleventh centuries C.E.) in the Middle Iranian literary language called Pahlavi. Being a predominantly priestly literature, it has generally a conservative character in the sense that it is largely based on authoritative tradition which was either passed on orally for generations or recorded in written form during the late Sassanian period (fifth to sixth centuries C.E.). This authoritative tradition, oral or written, is usually referred to in the texts with specific terms such as *dēn* ("the religion"), *āgāhīh* ("the knowledge"), *zand* ("the commentary of sacred texts"), and *abestāg* ("the Avesta"). The formulas introducing cosmogonical and eschatological sections normally contain such a reference combined with verbal expressions denoting the authoritative or revelatory character, for example, *pad dēn paydāg kū* ("it is revealed in the religion that . . .") or *andar dēn ōgōn nimūd ēstēd kū* ("it has been shown in the religion that . . .") (see Widengren 1983, 101–3; Hultgård 1983, 391–92 for further examples). The dating of most Pahlavi texts to the early Islamic period does thus not a priori preclude their use as sources for the history of religious ideas in centuries long before.

On the other hand, some of the materials are clearly contemporary with the compilers and authors or reflect beliefs and institutions in the Sassanian era (third to sixth centuries C.E.). The argument of the present essay, however, is that the bulk of cosmogonic and apocalyptic-eschatological traditions preserved by the Pahlavi compilers originated in earlier periods.

The fact that apocalyptic-eschatological ideas are well integrated in the general worldview of Zoroastrianism has not favored the composition of independent literary apocalypses as we find them in Judaism and Christianity. The only text that might claim the status of independant apocalyptic writing is the *Bahman Yašt* (see below). By contrast, apocalyptic-eschatological sections are a significant component in most Pahlavi writings and occur generally toward the end of the composition.

By way of introduction, the main Pahlavi books will be described in a few words and their apocalyptic-eschatological chapters briefly characterized. The huge compilation known as the *Dēnkard* (literally, "acts of the religion") was put together in the tenth century on the basis of a partly lost work from the ninth century and can be characterized as an encyclopedia of Mazdean theology and wisdom. Originally the *Dēnkard* included nine books, of which the first two are no longer extant. Besides apocalyptic allusions and fragments dispersed throughout the work, a systematic description of the apocalyptic events from the fall of the Sassanian empire up to the restoration of the world (Av. *frašokərəti*) is found in chapters 7–11 of book 7, which for the rest consists of a "Life of Zoroaster" (chapters 1–5) and of a report on "miracles" in the reign of Vištaspa (chapter 6).

The *Bundahišn* (literally, "the primal creation") is essentially a compilation on cosmogony and cosmology with important sections on general eschatology. The beginning of the work states that it conveys *zand-āgāhīh*, that is, "knowledge (derived) from the *zand*." The basic materials may have been compiled from *zand* sources already in late Sassanian times, but the final redaction of *Bundahišn* took place in the early Islamic period, since there are clear allusions to the Arab-Muslim conquest of Iran. In Western scholarship, *Bundahišn* is usually treated as consisting of two different "recensions" or "compilations," referred to by two different names—the *Indian Bundahišn* and *Greater Bundahišn* respectively—the former, which is shorter, denotes the Indian manuscript tradition, and the latter the more complete Iranian one. This is misleading terminology since in fact we have to do with a common original subsequently split into two manuscript branches. In chapter 33 an apocalyptic survey of the history of *ērān-šahr* ("the land of the Iranians") is given, as indicated by the heading *abar wizend hazārag hazārag ō ērān šahr madan* ("on the calamities to hit the land of the Iranians millennium after millennium"). Beginning with the irruption of the Evil Spirit in the creation of Ahura Mazdā, the description proceeds through the millennia of cosmic history up to the appearance of the last savior, the Saoshyant. This account is supplemented in chapter 34 with a more detailed description of the resurrection of the dead and the renewed existence: *abar ristāxēz ud tan ī pasēn* ("on the resurrection and the final body"; heading of the chapter).

A work closely akin to the *Bundahišn* is the *Wizīdagīhā ī Zādspram* (literally, "the selections of Zādspram"), which from the literary point of view is more coherent. Unlike *Bundahišn,* the *Wizīdagīhā ī Zādspram* also has an important section on the "life of Zoraster" (chapters 4–24). Its author, Zādspram, lived in the late ninth century and compiled his work from traditional sources to which he explicitly refers in some passages. Dāmdād, one of the nasks (sections) in the collection of sacred texts (cf. Dk. IX,5), is thus mentioned in 3:43 and 57 and the Spand nask in 35:18. The two last chapters of the *Wizīdagīhā ī Zādspram* (chapters 34 and 35) contain descriptions of the eschatological events presenting much original and valuable information.

The *Dādestān ī Dēnīg* was composed in the ninth century by Manuščihr, high priest of the Zoroastrians in Iran and also a brother of the above mentioned Zādspram. The composition has the form of questions and answers. No fewer than ninety-two questions (*pursišn*) are directed to Manuščihr covering a wide variety of issues. Questions 34 to 36 deal with eschatological matters, especially the resurrection of the dead and the nature of the world immediately before and after the Renovation (Phl. *frašgird*). Also cast in the form of questions and answers is the late Sassanian composition known as *Dādestān ī Mēnōg ī Xrad* (literally, "Judgments of the Spirit of Wisdom"), in which a fictive figure called Dānāg (literally, "wise, knowing") addresses questions to the Spirit of Wisdom. Scattered references to apocalyptic world history and to the events of the end-time occur throughout the book (e.g., chapters 2:93–95; 8:11–16; 27:27–31; 57: 6–7, 30–31).

The *Pahlavi Rivāyat,* a compilation of traditional materials from the early Islamic period, presents an important section on apocalypticism and eschatology (chapter 48). It deals with the two last millennia of world history, as well as the end-time and the restoration of the universe.

A short text with interesting apocalyptic materials is the one that goes under the name of *Jāmāsp Nāmag* (literally, "Book of Jāmāsp"). The text consists more precisely of some Pahlavi fragments of a more extensive writing that probably is reflected in the *Ayādgār ī Jāmaspīg* (literally, "Memoirs of Jāmasp"), a compilation of Pahlavi materials transcribed into Arabic-Persian script (= *pārsi*).

The *Bahman Yašt*, or *Zand ī Wahuman Yasn*, is not an original apocalypse, but it would more accurately be described as "a secondary compilation of apocalyptic materials of a diverse origin" (see Hultgård 1983, 388). The redaction of the materials included is minimal, and this reduces the literary quality but, on the other hand, enables the historian to get a clearer idea of the sources used. It can be divided into five different parts of unequal length:[1] (1) the vision of the four ages (I,1–5); (2) the appearance of Mazdāk and the prescription of king Xosrov Anōšurvān concerning liturgical texts (*yasna*) and their *zand* (I,6–8); (3) the vision of the seven ages and of the rich man in hell and the poor man in paradise (II,1–22); (4) the signs announcing the end of the millennium of Zoroaster (II,23–63); (5) the ultimate onslaught of enemies and demons on the lands of Iran, the liberation and the restoration of Mazdāism through Kay Wahrām and Pišyōtan, and other events of the end-time (III,1–62).

Finally there is the important text known as *Ardā Wirāz Nāmag* ("The Book of the righteous Wirāz"), which belongs to the genre of revelatory texts that purport to describe a tour of heaven and hell. In its present redaction the book must be ascribed to the ninth or tenth century but it is based on a late Sassanian version. The book presents a striking similarity with Dante's *Divina Comedia*, which it antedates by several centuries. Scholars have supposed an Oriental influence on Dante but the precise nature of this influence remains to be shown.

Forms of the Apocalyptic-Eschatological Traditions

The ideas of cosmic history and of the end and renewal of the world are embedded in a variety of forms and genres. For the evaluation of the Pahlavi texts as sources for Iranian apocalyptic beliefs in periods before the early Islamic time it is important to notice the form-historical setting of relevant passages and texts (for an attempt at form-historical analysis, see Hultgård 1983, 399–400). In many cases the determination of the forms and genres underlying the post-Sassanian compilations is difficult because citations from earlier texts are usually too short or have been reworked beyond identification.

For the tradition-historical analysis the most important genres are the *zand*-type and the *hampursagīh* form. The *zand* is an Avestan tradition that has been summarized or paraphrased into Pahlavi and enlarged with glosses and other interpolations. *Zand* texts are found especially in parts of the *Bahman Yašt* and in much of the *Dēnkard* book 7. The *hampursagīh* form ("consultation" with Ahura Mazdā) is characterized by its setting as an oracular encounter between Ahura Mazdā and Zoroaster. Extensive passages of the

Dēnkard book 7, the *Bahman Yašt,* the *Bundahišn,* and the *Wizīdagīhā ī Zādspram* are cast in the *hampursagīh* form. Some texts seem to be a mixture of *zand* and the *hampursagīh* form. The *zand* texts were composed during the Sassanian period, but the underlying traditions may well go back farther in time. The *hampursagīh* form is a genuine Avestan genre perpetuating much traditional material in the Pahlavi books.

The otherworldly journey that may serve as a frame for some of the *hampursagīh* texts constitutes a particular apocalyptic genre that is concerned with visions of heaven and hell and is well known from Jewish and Christian traditions. The ecstatic otherworldly journey seems to have been in ancient Iran an important way of receiving direct transcendent knowledge.

Cosmogony and World History: The Mythic Basis of Iranian Apocalyptic Traditions

One cannot understand Persian apocalypticism without taking into consideration its context within cosmic history. There is an inner coherence between the beginning and the end that is unique to the Iranian worldview. The creation myth gives meaning to world history at the same time that it divides its course in great periods of world ages and millennia.

In ancient Iran there seem to have been competing cosmogonies. One myth probably saw creation as a vivification of the primordial elements through a primeval sacrifice performed by the supreme deity, be it Ahura Mazdā or Mithra. This myth is alluded to in the *Fravardin yašt* of the Avesta (Yt. 13:2–3, 9–10). The oldest Avestan text, the *Gāthās,* pay homage to Ahura Mazdā as father and "creator" of the universe (Y. 44:3–5; the word *dātar* meaning here "one who sets [chaos] in order"). A myth imagining the "creation"of the world as setting up a cosmic tent may lie behind the references to Ahura Mazdā as "creator" in the *Gāthās.* The cosmogony that became prominent in Zoroastrianism certainly has roots far back in time and might have evolved out of the older myths. This cosmogonic myth with its strongly dualistic character has survived only in the Pahlavi texts, but it is attested already by Plutarch in *De Iside et Osiride* chaps. 46–47. Plutarch most probably drew on Theopompos, who wrote in the early fourth century B.C.E. It is thus possible to follow the dualistic creation myth at least back to late Achaemenian times, when it probably had replaced other myths as the standard version of Zoroastrian cosmogony.

The most complete versions of the basic cosmogony are found in *Bundahišn* (1:1–59; 1A:1–21; 4:1–28 and 6A–J) and in the *Wizīdagīhā ī Zādspram* (1:1–27; 2:1–22; 3:1–86), which both refer to earlier normative sources for their account: "In the good religion it is thus revealed that . . ." (Bd. 1:1) and "Now it is thus revealed in the religion that . . ." (WZ 1:1). There are some differences between the two accounts, but they clearly reflect the structure and contents of the same basic myth. To elucidate the intimate connection between cosmogony and eschatology we have to turn to the first part of the myth (Bd. 1:1–59; WZ 1:1–27), where the course of world history is determined. In summary it runs as follows:

In the very beginning there existed two opposed cosmic entities. One was Ohrmazd (Av. Ahura Mazdā), the supreme god who dwelt on high in omniscience and goodness. For endless time he was ever in the light. The other was Ahreman (Av. Angra Mainyu), the Evil Spirit, who had his abode down in the darkness. He was slow in knowledge but full of lust to destroy. Both powers were limitless, and there was no connection between them, since a void separated them. But they were limited at the border of the void. Ohrmazd knew in his omniscience that the Evil Spirit existed and that he would attack the realm of light, but he also knew that through creation he would be able to bring about the final defeat of Evil. Ahreman, unaware of Ohrmazd, moved around in the darkness but happened to catch a glimpse of the realm of light. Eager to destroy it, he rose up from the depths to the border and rushed forward. Ohrmazd went against him for battle, but the Evil Spirit fled back to the darkness. Now Ohrmazd created in spiritual form (*mēnōg*) the main elements of the world to come, and they remained with him in the *mēnōg* state for three thousand years. Ahreman on his side brought forward a terrible counter-creation in that he fashioned a multitude of destructive demons and evil spirits, and toward the end of the first period of three thousand years he reappeared with his host of demons at the border and threatened to destroy the creation of light. Ohrmazd foresaw that it was necessary to fix a time for battle against Ahreman, otherwise the Evil Spirit would never desist from aggression. He therefore offered him peace and proposed a treaty, knowing that thereby he would make the Evil Spirit powerless in the end. To that purpose Ohrmazd created out of eternal boundless Time historical time, which was to be limited in extension (also called "time of long dominion"). The decisive battle would be postponed for nine thousand years, and during that limited time the sovereignty would be shared between Ohrmazd and Ahreman in the way stated in *Bundahišn* 1:28:

> This too Ohrmazd knew in his omniscience that within these nine thousand years, three thousand years would pass entirely according to the will of Ohrmazd, three thousand years in the period of mixture according to the will of both Ohrmazd and Ahreman and that in the last battle it would be possible to

make the Evil Spirit powerless and that he (Ohrmazd) would (thus) prevent aggression against the created world.

The Evil Spirit agreed to the terms of the treaty, being unable to foresee the end. Ohrmazd then chanted the *Ahunawar* (a text in the *Gāthās* that became the most sacred prayer of the Zoroastrians), thereby revealing to the Evil Spirit his ultimate defeat. When Ahreman became aware of this he fell stupefied back into the darkness, where he remained in torpidity for three thousand years. During this period Ohrmazd gave material form (*gētīg*) to his first creation, which had been in the *mēnōg* state. Now the sky, the water, the earth, the primordial plant, the beneficent animal, the primordial man (*Gayō-mard*) and the fire took visible shape. The world was in a state of perfection and purity. The three thousand years completed, Ahreman rose from his torpidity, took his host of demons, and made an assault on the creation of Ohrmazd. He succeeded in penetrating into the world which was ravaged and defiled by the evil powers, and it became thus the mixture of good and evil (*gumēzišn*) that it still is. After his initial success Ahreman met resistance from the primordial elements trying to counteract him each in its own way. The Sky hardened itself and closed the passage through which Ahreman and his demons had entered to keep him captured within the world. With the help of the star Tištar and the Wind, clouds and raindrops emerged out of the Water; the rains while drowning many of Ahreman's noxious creatures gave rise to oceans, lakes, and rivers. The Earth shook upon the attack of the Evil Spirit and from that shaking mountains, hills, and valleys were produced where water could stream and plants grow. The primordial Plant withered and died from Ahreman's poisonous breath but its seeds, which contained thousands of species, were saved by Amurdād, divine guardian of plants, and spread with the rain all over the earth to be used by mankind for cure of the diseases sent by Ahreman. The beneficent Animal and the primordial Man were both struck with deadly diseases by Ahreman. The light in the semen of the beneficent Animal was saved by divine intervention and purified by the Moon, and from it came the species of animals. When the primordial Man died, he emitted his semen on the ground and after forty years the first humans, man and woman, grew up from the soil in plant form and then evolved to human shape. From them all humankind is descended.

The significance of this great cosmogonic myth is twofold. First, creation is a long process, which begins with the fashioning of spiritual prototypes by the supreme god and ends with the assault of Evil on the material primordial creation. The good creation counteracts the irruption of Evil through differentiation of the physical universe and through multiplication of the vegetative, animal, and human prototypes, and by this final stage the creation process is completed. The purpose of creation is also to entrap evil and finally to eliminate it. The basic tenets of the Zoroastrian worldview are thus determined by the cosmogonic myth.

Second, the cosmogonic myth sets the course of world history at nine thousand years and divides it in three large periods of three thousand years, which may be termed world ages, each having its own characteristics. History thus begins with the prototypical material creation, which remains in light and purity for three thousand years, and continues with a period of three thousand years in the mixed state, the beginning of which also signifies the fulfillment of the last stage in creation. At the completion of the last period of three thousand years, history ends when evil is eliminated, the dead are resurrected, and the world is restored to its original purity and perfection.

It has been argued that in Zoroastrianism world history comprises twelve thousand years divided into four world ages. This number is arrived at by including the first three thousand years, when creation was in the *mēnōg* state. Yet the Pahlavi tradition is quite clear on the point that history begins with the creation of the world in its material form, the *gētīg* state. If the twelve-thousand-year scheme was the original one, it is difficult to explain why the Pahlavi texts insist on nine thousand years as a determined traditional number (see further Hultgård 1995, 85–101). In fact, the number twelve thousand for the world's history occurs only in Arabic and Neo-Persian sources from the Islamic period (see Zaehner 1972, 97).

The cosmogonic myth provided a world history in outline which could be elaborated in further detail. It is difficult to say with certainty whether the more detailed apocalyptic schemes of the Pahlavi books constitute developments during the Sassanian period or whether they reflect yet more ancient traditions transmitted orally in Hellenistic and Parthian times. These problems will be dealt with in the second section of this essay.

The most important elaboration in the Pahlavi texts is the division of the last period of three thousand years into three millennia with similar characteristics. This period begins with the appearance of Zoroaster, and the first millennium is consequently named after him. As to the two remaining millennia, each one starts with the manifestation of a savior figure: the first is called in Pahlavi Ušēdar and the second Ušēdarmāh. Together with the last savior, Sōšāns, they are considered Zoroaster's descendants (see for this mythical complex, see Hultgård 1995, 130–49). When the third millennium of the last world age comes to an end, the final messianic figure appears, the Sōšāns (Av.

saošyant). He is really a world savior because he ushers in the restoration (*fraš-gird*) and the state of eternal bliss, which lies outside history.

The Expectation of the End

As pointed out above, the last period of three thousand years is subdivided into three different millennia, and the end of each millennium is character-ized by tribulations and disasters presaging the coming of the new savior. The coming of the first messianic figure initiates a gradual amelioration of human conditions, of moral standards, and of nature itself, which continues through the last millennium, that of Ušēdarmāh. This idea may be seen as an anticipa-tion of some elements belonging to the ultimate world restoration (Phl. *fraš-gird*). The post-Sassanian Pahlavi books all presuppose this traditional scheme, which has the appearance, however, of being a later development of an earlier and simpler scheme (see below). Without deviating from the main scheme of cosmic history, more detailed divisions of particular periods are sometimes found in the sources. The *Bundahišn* presents in chapter 33 a world history of six millennia over which mythical and historical events are distributed, from the irruption of Ahreman in the first millennium of the mixed period to the coming of Sōšāns at the end of the sixth millennium. *Bahman Yašt* divides the millennium of Zoroaster according to a quite differ-ent scheme, which sees history as a gradual deterioration. This scheme, which occurs in two variants—one with four ages and one with seven—begins with the appearance of Zoroaster (the golden age) and ends with the calamities that will affect the Iranian lands at the close of the millennium (the age of mixed iron). The ages are characterized by different metals and are represented sym-bolically as branches of a tree. This scheme, where history during different periods declines from a golden age to a last evil one, is paralleled in the Greek myth of the five succeeding races (*genos*) of humans (Hesiod, *Works and Days* 109–201) and in the Indian doctrine of the four world ages (e.g., *Mahā-bhārata* III,186–89).

THE APOCALYPTIC SIGNS AND TRIBULATIONS. The apocalyptic woes are described in most detail for the end of Zoroaster's millennium, which was the first eschatological time to come. Analysis of the Pahlavi texts shows that there is a wide variety of signs and tribulations announcing the end-time. There are nevertheless so many correspondences in motifs and details that we have to assume a basic tradition which the authors and compilers had at their dis-posal, elaborating it differently according to the particular purposes they set themselves. At the same time fresh details were added to make the allusions to contemporary events clearer. In presenting the signs of the end, their character and function, the traditional scheme of a subdivision of the last three-thousand-year period into three millennia is here followed, although it is not always clear from the texts to which particular millennium the signs described originally belonged.

The most extensive descriptions are found in the *Bahman Yašt,* the *Dēnkard* book 7, and the *Jāmāsp Nāmag* and refer to the millennium of Zoroaster. In the analysis of the apocalyptic sign tradition these descriptions will serve as the basic source material. The tribulations and disorders to come are termed "signs," and they are explicitly seen as phenomena that inevitably announce the coming of an evil time and the end of the millennium. The signs do not happen by chance, but they are part of world history, which is determined by divine will. When Zoroaster asks what sign will announce the end of his millennium, Ahura Mazdā answers: "The sign of the end of thy millennium and of the coming of the lowest [i.e. 'worst'] time is that . . ." (BYt. II,24). The *Dēnkard* introduces the account of the tribulations preceding the destruction of the reign and religion of the Iranians in the following way: "On the signs of the coming of those who shall destroy . . ." (Dk. VII,7: 29).

The motifs that make up the textual body of the signs of the end may be grouped in different categories. There are signs pertaining (a) to family, society, country, religion, and culture, (b) to subsistence and property, (c) to cosmos and nature, and (d) to biological aspects of human life. A prominent mark of the evil time to come is the inversion of values and social order. Paradoxical statements and the use of rhetorical figures are characteristic features of the style. The catalogues of apocalyptic tribulations may also be interpreted as a mirror of the traditional values and ideas that shape the worldview of a given society and religion.

THE MILLENNIUM OF ZOROASTER. The drawing near of the end begins to be seen in the dissolution of society and religion. Lawlessness, deceit, and falsehood will spread. As it is said in *Jāmāsp Nāmag:* "By night one with another they will eat bread and drink wine, and walk in friendship, and next day they will plot one against the life of the other and plan evil" (JN 13, trans. H. W. Bailey). Families will split in hatred, the son will strike the father, and brother will fight against brother. Traditional ideals and values will be abandoned and foreign customs adopted. The social order will be dissolved and also reversed. Men from the lower classes will marry the daughters of the nobles and the priests (BYt. II,38). Slaves will walk in the path of nobles; the horseman will become a man on foot; and the man on foot a horseman (JN 35–36). Religious duties will be neglected; apostasy will abound; the rituals will hardly be performed; and the sacred fires will no longer be upheld. In hyperbolic statements this is described in *Bahman Yašt* II,37: "Of hundred, of thousand, of ten thousand, only one will believe in this religion, and even this one believer will not do what is a religious duty. And the Wahrām-fire will be destroyed and disgrace will be brought on it, a thousand fires will be reduced to one only and this one fire will not be properly cared for."

There will also be physical changes in the cosmos and in nature that will announce the coming end. The sun will become smaller and will be less visible; months, weeks, and days will become shorter (BYt. II,31). Clouds will darken the whole sky; hot and cold winds will blow at the same time and carry off all fruits and grains of corn (BYt. II,42; JN 26–27). The rain will not fall at its due time, and when it falls, it will rain more noxious creatures than water (BYt. II,42). The earth will contract; crops will not yield seed; and plants, bushes, and trees will be small. This general corruption of the cosmos, which manifests itself as a diminution and deterioration of both astral and earthly phenomena will also affect humans and animals. The consequences are described in the *Bahman Yašt* as follows: "Horses, cattle and sheep will be born smaller and have bad ability, they take little burden, their hair will be shorter, their skin thinner. Their milk will not increase and they will have little fat" (BYt. II,43). A similar degeneration affects humans. They will be born smaller and have less strength (BYt. II,32) and the young will look like the old (Dk. VII,8:12).

The disasters to follow are indicated by presages. The sun darkens; in the moon different colors become visible; various portents can be seen in the sky; dark clouds spread over the earth; and storms and earthquakes ravage the world. Then men will know that the end is imminent. A heavy onslaught of enemies and demonic forces will come upon the lands of the Iranian peoples. The invasion occurs in waves that carry each time new demonic figures and hosts of enemies. In the words of *Bahman Yašt* II,24–25:

> Hundreds, thousands and ten thousands of kinds of demons (*dēw*) with parted hair, descendants of Fury (*hēšm*), the basest race, will appear from the direction of the East and rush into the land of the Iranians (*ērān šahr*). They have raised banners and carry black weapons, their hair is parted falling down on the back. They are small, the basest of servants, but powerful and most skilled in smiting.

In similar wording, the *Bundahišn* mentions hostile invasions: "Thereafter Chionites and Turks in large numbers and with many banners will rush into the land of the Iranians; they will devastate this prosperous sweet-smelling land of the Iranians" (Bd. 33:26).

The *Jāmāsp Nāmag* speaks of attacks by the *Tāzigs,* who will "daily grow stronger and seize district after district" and correlates these attacks with the disintegration of social and moral order in the Iranian lands. The Tāzigs may here denote the pre-Islamic Arabs, as in early Armenian tradition, but this usage is not exclusive. The confusion of demonic hosts and human armies is characteristic of the whole Zoroastrian tradition. The political enemies of the Iranians will take joint action with the demons of Ahreman in destroying the world.

When the woes are at their height, apocalyptic expectation sees salvation to be near. Two messianic figures will appear who are thought of as both forerunners and co-helpers of the first future savior, Ušēdar. The appearance of these two messianic figures marks the turning point of history. One of them is Kay Wahrām, whose epithet indicates that he is thought of as a reappearance of one of the early mythic rulers of Iran (Av. *kavi,* MIr *kay*). It is told that "on the night when the Kay is born, a token will come to the world: a star will fall from the sky" (BYt. III,15). Kay Wahrām will gather a multitude of victorious men, and from the East they will storm forward with uplifted white banners to the Iranian lands. They will slay enemies and demons in large numbers and liberate land and people from their oppressors. As Ohrmazd tells Zoroaster in the form of a simile: "When the end-time comes, Spitaman Zardušt, these enemies will be destroyed like a tree upon which the night of a cold winter comes and throws off the leaves" (BYt. III,23). The legend of Kay Wahrām is told only in the *Bundahišn* (33:27) and in the *Bahman Yašt* (III,14–23). The other messianic figure, called Pišyōtan, is mentioned in several Pahlavi texts which devote to his coming rather elaborate descriptions (BYt. III,25–42; Bd. 33:28; JN 99–103; Dk. VII,8:45–48). Together with his retinue of 150 holy warriors, the immortal Pišyōtan will leave Kangdiz, the stronghold of the Kayanians, the early mythic rulers of the Iranian lands, and restore the worship of Ohrmazd and purify the holy places that have been desecrated (on Kangdiz, see further Boyce, 1984). Pišyōtan clearly appears as the hidden hero who in a secluded place awaits the end-time when he will go forth with his followers and defeat the enemies. The very end of Zoroaster's millennium is thus already colored by the shift from an evil time to a new happier era. This expectation is condensed in a saying that concludes the descriptions of the millennium in both *Bahman Yašt* and the *Jāmāsp Nāmag:* "The time of the wolves will pass away, and the time of the sheep will arrive" (BYt III,40, JN 105).

THE MILLENNIA OF UŠĒDAR AND UŠĒDARMĀH AND THE COMING OF SŌŠĀNS. The manifestation of Ušēdar, the first of Zoroaster's three mythical sons, is then the confirmation of the beginning of a new era that has in fact been ushered in by his immediate forerunners. The legend of Ušēdar's conception, which takes place in the same miraculous way as that of the other coming saviors, is briefly told in *Dēnkard* VIII,55–57 and in *Bundahišn* 33:36–38 and 35:60 in slightly different versions. When only thirty winters remain of the millennium, a virgin of noble descent goes down to a lake. She walks out in the water, drinks some, and becomes pregnant from the semen of Zoroaster that has been preserved there in the form of his shining glory (Phl. *xwarrah*) protected by the goddess Anāhīd (Av. Anāhita). The *Bundahišn* adds that one can see at night the glory of Zoroaster as three lights shimmering deep down in the water. When time is ripe, each light in turn will rise to the surface and join with a young woman.

In a sense Kay Wahrām and Pišyōtan have already anticipated the task of the first savior. Ušēdar is not primarily described as the one who saves the Iranian lands from enemies and demons but rather as the spiritual figure under whose authority the world begins slowly to be transformed toward its final perfection in the *frašgird* state. The religion of the Mazdā worshipers will be revealed to him, just as it once was to Zoroaster. Nature is being recovered and the conditions of humankind are ameliorating. The Pahlavi texts speak of this progress in much similar terms: Water will fill rivers and lakes. Plants and trees will be green for three years. Famine, distress, and misery will disappear. Peace and nonviolence will increase all over the world, as also generosity. The compiler of *Dēnkard* book 7 cites a saying of Ohrmazd taken from sacred tradition (the *dēn*): "In this way, O Zardušt, when the one who receives is less distinguished than the one who gives, then generosity and giving will remain among the living beings" (Dk.VII,9:6). The demonic powers will lose strength, but an outbreak of evil will come with the appearance of the demon Malkūs, who will let loose terrible winters with heavy rains and snowfall during several years (Dk. VII,9:3; PR 48:10–17; Bd. 33:30; AJ 17:4). According to some texts this will happen in the fifth century of the millennium (so Dk. VII,9:3; PR 48:10), but the *Bundahišn* (33:30) places the calamity toward the end of the millennium, which seems more in accordance with the original apocalyptic scheme. Malkūs will be vanquished, however, and the subterranean *war* (literally, "enclosure," Av. *vara*) of Yima, where people and cattle had taken refuge, will be opened and the earth will flourish again and be repopulated. The tradition of the demon Malkūs and of the opening of the *war* draws clearly on the Avestan myth of Yima (Vd. chapter 2), the chief figure in Persian primordial history. This myth tells of how Yima is warned by Ahura Mazdā that bad winters will come. Therefore he is instructed to build a large subterranean refuge for humans and animals where they will be able to survive the winters. The narrative, which belongs to the same category of such myths as the flood stories of the ancient Near East (e.g., Genesis 6), is set in a mythic past but has been transferred to an eschatological context in the Pahlavi texts. An eschatological motif that may seem strange from a Western Judeo-Christian viewpoint is the appearance of wild animals from mountains and plains after the winters of Malkūs have come to an end (Dk. VII,9:8–12; PR 48:19–21). They seek refuge with the Mazdeans, thinking that "they will treat us like their own children." Then Ašawahišt, one of the lesser divinities, cries out from heaven: "Do not kill these beneficent animals any more as you used to do!" The Mazdeans will kill and eat an animal only upon its own request before it dwindles away: "Oh Mazdeans, eat me while I am still in vigour before reptiles and serpents shall devour me" (Dk. VII,9:9 in a citation from sacred tradition). The text then goes on to say that the Mazdeans will be satisfied to slaughter and to eat, and the animals to be slaughtered and eaten. In the afterlife—presumably at the resurrection—Mazdeans and animals will come together in friendship as it is said in the *Dēnkard:* "When they take on spiritual form those who slaughtered will meet those who were slaughtered, those who cut those who were cut, those who ate those who were eaten" (Dk, VII,9:12). This eschatological motif should be understood in the light of the sacrificial ideology of Zoroastrianism. In sacrifice the soul of the victim is sent to Ahura Mazdā and to the Spirit of the animals (Phl. *Gōšurwan*). The souls of both humans and beneficent animals will enjoy divine protection beyond death. This testifies to the care for animals taken by Zoroastrians.

The shift to the last millennium, that of Usēdarmāh, is not marked by apocalyptic tribulations if we do not follow the *Bundahišn* in placing the appearance of Malkūs and the bad winters at the end of that millennium. The birth of Usēdarmāh is believed to have happened in the same miraculous way as that of Usēdar. His reign is characterized by further progress toward the final transfiguration of the world. The savior will make one cow give milk to a thousand persons (Dk. VII,10:2). Hunger and thirst will be less strong (Dk. VII,10:2; Bd. 34:2). Plants will now be green for six years (Bd. 33:32; PR 48:24). Humankind will not eat meat any more; first they will feed on milk and plants, toward the end only on water and plants (Dk. VII,10:8–9). They will not die except when their allotted time is come or when they happen to be killed by the sword (Dk. VII,10:7; BYt. III,53). Part of the demons and noxious creatures will be vanquished and made powerless (PR 48:26–29; Bd. 33:32; BYt. III,52). Joy, peace, and generosity will increase in the world (Dk. VII,10:3). When the millennium is near its end, there will happen a disastrous event. The dragon Azdahāg (Av. *Aži Dahāka*), who up to this time has been fettered in the mountain Dumawand will come loose and together with the demons he will devour one third of humankind and one third of the animals. Upon the complaint of water, fire, and plants that have suffered hard from his violent dominion, Ohrmazd and the Amahraspand "the Bounteous Immortals" (Av. Aməša Spənta) will appear on earth and wake up the hero Karsāsp (Av. Kərəsāspa) who will slay the dragon (Bd. 33:33; BYt. III,55–59; PR 48:30–36; Dk. VII,10:10; AJ 17:5–7).

Now the final savior Sōšāns (Av. Saošyant) will appear. The description of his birth, the miracles accompanying his reaching thirty years of age, and his coming into consultation with Ahura Mazdā follow the same basic pattern as found in the legends of the two preceding saviors. The preeminence of the last savior in this legend is indicated by the fact that the sun will stand still for thirty days. At the appearance of Ušēdarmāh this miracle lasted twenty days and for Ušēdar ten days. The fifty-seven years assigned to his activity of restoring the world are mentioned in several texts (Dk VII,11:1, 4 and 7; PR 48:49; WZ 34:46) and have a symbolic meaning because they correspond to the fifty-seven years during which the religion of the Mazdā worshipers once was propagated all over the seven continents of Zoroastrian mythical geography (WZ 34:47–48).

THE ULTIMATE CONFRONTATION OF GOOD AND EVIL. The final apocalyptic events will then follow closely upon one another. The texts present roughly the same events and motifs, but have arranged them somewhat differently. The evil powers will be ultimately vanquished in a great eschatological battle (WZ 34:53) fought by Ohrmazd, the Amahraspand, Sōšāns and his fellow heroes. Some texts talk about the elimination of evil in more vague terms, but it seems nevertheless clear that the tradition of the great battle in one way or another lies in the background. The final struggle takes place in different stages. First, Sōšāns will muster an army and make a holy war against the demon of perverted truth. They will defeat the demon primarily by ritual means, since their chief weapon will be the performance of a *yasna* ceremony (PR 48:73–85). Other demons will also be vanquished by the aid of divine ritual (PR 48:89). The decisive moment is the combat between the chief deities and their demon enemies. Ohrmazd and the other divinities will appear on earth, and they will choose each his own adversary. The *Bundahišn* and the *Wizīdagīhā ī Zātspram* present this idea in the form of a systematic opposition between Ohrmazd and the Amahraspand on one side, and Ahreman and his principal demons on the other:

> Thereafter Ohrmazd will take the Evil Spirit, Wahuman will take Akōman, Ašwahišt will take Indar, Šahrewar will take Sāwal, Spandarmad will take Tarōmad, that is Nanghayt, Hordād and Amurdād will take Tayriz and Zayriz,

Truthful Speech will take False Speech, the righteous Srōš will take Hēšm with the bloody club. (Bd 34:27; so also with slight variations WZ 35:37)

Other texts give a less detailed scheme of paired opponents but concentrate on the chief adversaries: "Ohrmazd and Ahriman, Srōš and Az, will appear on earth. Ohrmazd will smite Ahriman" (WZ 34:44; see also PR 48:94–95; MX 8:10). There is also a tradition that emphasizes the role played by the god Mihr (Av. Mithra) in the end-time struggle. According to the *Bahman Yašt,* Mihr discloses to the Evil Spirit that the nine thousand years have already passed and that the demonic powers have held sway for a thousand years more than stipulated by the treaty concluded in the beginning of world history. When the Evil Spirit hears this, he will become stupefied just as he was in the primordial time when Ohrmazd revealed his own future victory at the end of time. Mihr then smites the demon Hēšm (Av. Aēšma), who becomes powerless (BYt. III,33–35). The same tradition is reflected in *Jāmāsp Nāmag* 77, which states that Mihr and Hēšm will fight against each other in an eschatological encounter. Both *Bahman Yašt* and *Jāmāsp Nāmag* place this mythologoumenon vaguely within the context of the shift from Zoroaster's millennium to that of Ušēdar, but this is most probably a secondary development.

The eschatological confrontation is clearly considered a duel between divine beings and figures of evil on the model of the first hostile encounter between Ohrmazd and Ahreman described in the cosmogony. Here it is told that the decisive confrontation was postponed for nine thousand years but when these had elapsed Ohrmazd and the Evil Spirit would meet in a final battle. According to the myth, this was agreed upon by both parties, and the narrator of the myth adds the simile: "in the same way as two men who shall fight a duel fix a time saying: let us do battle on the so-and-so day until night" (Bd. 1:13).

All traditions are unanimous in emphasizing the belief that Ahreman and evil will be eliminated from the world to come. The way commonly used to express that fact is the statement that the Evil Spirit will be made powerless and incapable of doing any more harm. This is the significance of the Pahlavi term *agār,* which frequently occurs in the texts dealing with this motif (e.g., MX 8:10; PR 48:96). In the cosmogonic myth the end of evil after the completion of the nine thousand years was already foreseen: "He [Ohrmazd] knew that by fixing a time the Evil Spirit would be made powerless" (*agār;* Bd. 1:26–28). The details concerning the elimination of evil vary but a distinctive idea is that Ohrmazd and the other divinities will chase Ahreman and the surviving evil powers out of the world and push them back to the depths of darkness whence they came (Bd. 34:30–32; PR 48:94–96).

The disappearance of evil is hastened, according to some texts, by internal dissolution and enmity within the realm of Ahreman. In this "civil war" the female arch-demon Az (Concupiscence, Greed) figures prominently. The cosmogonic myth, in one version, tells that if Ahreman during the allotted time of nine thousand years did not succeed in converting humankind to hate Ohrmazd and to love himself, the demon Az would start to devour the other evil beings, because she would no longer be able to find food from the creatures of Ohrmazd. This prediction comes true in the very end-time. Az begins to starve and turns her greed toward the demons and even toward the Evil Spirit himself, whom she deserts and even threatens to devour. In the eschatological battle she will be overcome first and then the Evil Spirit will be weakened and easier to defeat (WZ 34:34–45; PR 48:90–93).

THE RESTORATION OF THE WORLD, THE FRAŠGIRD. After the coming of Sōšāns, all people living at that time will not die. Those who are dead will be raised to life in a great act of general resurrection called *ristāxēz* in Pahlavi ("raising of the dead"). This is usually thought of as taking place after the elimination of evil. In some traditions the resurrection is thought to be performed by Sōšāns with the help of other eschatological figures (Bd. 34:3, 7–8; PR 48:54), in others it is Ahura Mazdā himself who recreates the body of the dead (Bd. 34:5–6; WZ 34:19–20). In three texts the resurrection is described in more detail, and these accounts, taken from sacred tradition, reflect the concern of explaining an idea that might have encountered questions and doubts (Bd. 34:4–9; WZ 34:1–20; 35:18–30; PR 48:53–65). These questions are put in the mouth of Zoroaster and addressed to Ohrmazd. How is it possible that those who are long dead can receive a new body? The answer is through a reference to creation:

> When I [Ohrmazd] set the sun, the moon and the stars in motion to be shining bodies in the sky [literally, "the atmosphere"], when I created seed to be thrown on the ground, to come up and grow and to bear fruit in abundance, when I gave color to the plants according to the diversity of their species, when I gave fire to plants and other things so as not to be consumed by it, when I formed a child [literally, "son"] in its mother's womb, preserved it and fashioned forth separately hair, skin, nails, blood, fat, eyes and ears. . . . then all these things were more difficult for me to create than the raising of the dead. Because at resurrection I am helped by things that once were in existence but at that time [i.e., the creation] did not exist. (Bd. 34:5; cf. WZ 34:20)

This assertion is based on the idea that in death the different parts of the human person are received by the elements of nature, whence, on divine command, they are carried back and recreated at the time of resurrection. Flesh and bones from the earth, blood from the waters, hair from the plants, the spirit of life from the wind (Bd. 34:5; WZ 34:7; PR 48:55).

The resurrection of the dead includes both righteous and wicked, Iranians and non-Iranians. It is conceived of as a ritual process enacted by Sōšāns and his helpers. Through the celebration of successive *yasna* ceremonies, all humankind will be raised in five stages, the primordial man Gayōmard and the first couple of humans, Māšē and Māšēnē, having been resurrected first (Bd. 34:6; WZ 34:18–19; 35:19–30; PR 48:56).

The question of the wicked and their destiny seems to have preoccupied the Zoroastrians in a particular way. While the belief in the separation of the souls after death, the righteous coming to paradise (Phl. *garōdmān*) and the wicked to hell (Phl. *dušox*) is uncontroversial and firmly rooted in ancient Iran, the fate of the wicked in resurrection did pose a problem, and diverging solutions are reflected in the Pahlavi books (see, e.g., PR 48:66–68). The general idea of an elimination of evil and a purification of the world and of humankind did, however, favor the belief that even the wicked could not be punished by eternal damnation but had to be purified and included in the new community of the restored world. The idea of a temporary punishment of the wicked after their souls and bodies had been reunited at resurrection imposed itself as the most satisfying solution.

The restoration of humankind to the new state of perfection is resumed in the idea of the "future body" and is believed to take place in successive moments in which also the purification of the wicked is included. Although the themes and the moments are the same in the underlying tradition, their precise order of realization does not emerge clearly from the texts, and the confusion that one senses may be due both to redactional incongruences and to different opinions recorded in the basic Sassanian sources or expressed at the time of compilation in the early Islamic period. The moments of the restoration are here described in the order in which they are presented in the *Bundahišn*.

After the raising of the dead, all people will come together in a great assembly which recalls the judgment scenes of Jewish, Christian, and Islamic eschatologies. In the Pahlavi books it is called "the assembly of Isadvāstar" so named after the eldest son of Zoroaster. In that gathering every person will recognize those whom he or she knew during life: "this is my father, this is my mother, this is my brother, this my wife and this is someone in my family"

(Bd. 34:9; cf. also PR 48:57). The wicked are already by outward appearance distinguished from the righteous like "black horses from white horses" (WZ 35:32), and the *Bundahišn* explains this by saying that the deeds of everyone will be made manifest: "at that assembly every person will behold the good deeds and the evil deeds that he or she did; the righteous shall be visible among the wicked like white sheep among black sheep" (Bd. 34:11).

Punishment and reward will be distributed. The wicked will be thrown back again to hell for three days and three nights, where they suffer much pain in body and soul, whereas the righteous are taken to paradise (Bd. 34:13–14; WZ 35:40–45). The separation is vividly depicted: "they will cause every person to pass before his own deeds, a righteous person will weep over a wicked, a wicked will weep over himself, there will be a time when a father is righteous and a son is wicked . . ." (Bd. 34:15), or "at that moment all humankind will lament together and shed tears on the ground, because the father shall see his son be thrown into hell, the son his father, the wife her husband, the husband his wife, the friend his friend" (WZ 35:41).

After punishment has been inflicted on the wicked for the three days, they are brought back to the earth and finally cleansed from their evil in streams of fire. This cleansing process is part of the universal renovation (Phl. *frašgird*) which may be seen as a purification of the world which once had been contaminated through the irruption of Ahreman and the evil powers. The metal of all the mountains will be caused to melt and to flow over the earth and burn away the stench and impurity that still are left from the evil (Bd. 34:31). All humankind must pass through these streams of molten metal. For the righteous it will be like walking through warm milk, but for the wicked it will be the real pain of passing through molten metal (Bd. 34:18–19; PR 48:70–72). The tradition behind the *Wizīdagīhā ī Zādspram* does not speak about the molten metal but of a universal conflagration that is clearly conceived of as a means of eliminating evil but also serves the purpose of separating the righteous from the wicked. The great fire is likened to a huge human figure holding in his hand a tree with the branches above and the roots below. The branches will take the righteous and bring them to paradise; the roots will seize the wicked and drop them in hell (WZ 35:40, 44). The world conflagration is seen in this tradition as part of the great eschatological battle and is compared to the primordial battle when creation offered resistance to the attack of Ahreman and the rains drowned the noxious creatures: "But as the great battle in the beginning was with the raining of water and the wind driving it, so in the end it will be with the heat of burning fire and the hard wind that makes the fire to blaze" (WZ 34:53).

The renovation of the world also implies that it is made eternal and humankind immortal. As it is said in the *Dēnkard,* translating a lost Avestan passage: "Then I who am Ohrmazd shall restore the world according to my will (to exist as) eternal, for ever prospering and powerful" (Dk. VII,11:11). For humankind the *frašgird* means immortalization and an everlasting experience of bliss and divine goodness. The ritual impact on the eschatological ideas appears also in the description of the last moments of the renovation. According to the *Bundahišn* and some other texts, Sōšāns and his followers will perform a sacrifice by slaughtering the bull Hadayōš in order to prepare the elixir of life: "From the fat of that bull and the white sacred juice (Phl. *hōm ī spēd*) they will prepare the beverage of immortality and give all humankind to drink. All humans will be immortal for ever and ever" (Bd. 34:23; cf. WZ 35:60).

The Pahlavi *Rivāyat* tells that in the *frašgird* the earth will rise toward the sky through successive acts of worship so that there will be one and the same place for the divine beings and humankind (PR 48:98–99). Despite statements on the limited nature of human knowledge of the world to come (e.g., PR 48:102) the traditions on the renovation sometimes convey rather detailed views on what life in the renewed world will look like. Besides the assertion that humankind shall behold and praise Ohrmazd and the other divinities—just as in Jewish and Christian descriptions of paradise the righteous are said to behold and praise God—other ideas are presented that reflect the Zoroastrian attachment to what is good in life. Adults will be restored to the age of forty and youth and children to the age of fifteen. Those who in life had no woman will be given one. Men and women will continue to have desire for each other, and they will be joined in love without there being any births from them (Bd. 34:24; PR 48:101, 107; cf. WZ 35:52). Plants and beneficent animals will be restored, and they will not diminish any more (PR 48:103, 107). The earth will be extended without steep mountains and hills, and it will flourish like a garden (PR 48:61; Bd. 34:33).

The significance of the renovation is strongly emphasized in the Pahlavi tradition although its details are described only in a limited number of passages. One may best sense the impact of the idea of the *frašgird* on the minds of the Zoroastrians from the short similes about its appearance that were circulated among the Persians down to the compilation of the Pahlavi books. The *Wizīdagīhā ī Zādspram* have preserved some of them: "And again the Renovation is like unto a dark night when the night draws towards its end and the sun rises over the three boundaries of the world and completes its course having returned to its proper place. Then it comes to shine anew and smites darkness and gloom" (WZ 34:25), or "The resurrection of the dead is like unto dry trees and shrubs from which new leaves shoot forth and buds open" (WZ 34:28).

THE OTHERWORDLY JOURNEY AND ESCHATOLOGY. The main Pahlavi text describing an otherworldly journey is the *Ardā Wirāz Nāmag*. The immediate reason for the otherworldly journey of Wirāz is that the Mazdeans were in doubt about the utility of their prayers and religious ceremonies, and to get divine guidance they decided to send a pious man to the heavenly world. Wirāz was chosen, and he was taken to a fire temple where he prepared his ecstatic journey by drinking wine mixed with henbane. When he fell asleep, his soul left the body and passed by the Činwad bridge into paradise. On the seventh day the soul of Wirāz returned and he rose up "as from a pleasant sleep, happy and with dreamful thoughts" (AWN 3:3). After having taken food and drink and performed a religious ceremonial, Wirāz ordered that a learned scribe be brought to him and the scribe "sat in front <of him> and everything that Wirāz said, he wrote down correctly, clearly and in detail" (3:24). On his journey to the other world Wirāz was accompanied by two heavenly figures—Srōš, the guardian angel of the Zoroastrian community, and Adur, the divinity of fire—and they function as guides and "interpreting angels." Srōš and Adur declare that they will show him the splendor and bliss of paradise, the reward of the righteous, and the darkness and torments of hell, the abode of the sinners (AWN 5). Wirāz is led along the same path on which the souls of the righteous travel after death. First Wirāz comes to a place where he sees "the souls of a number of people standing together (at an equal height)" and he asks his divine guides: "Who are they? Why are they standing here? The righteous Srōš and the god Adur said: this place is called *hammista-gān* and these souls are standing in this place until the day of bodily resurrection and they are the souls of those persons whose good deeds and sins were equal" (AWN 6:3–7).

Here one of the characteristic teachings of Persian individual eschatology is presented. The *hammistagān* literally means "raised together (to an equal height)" but generally denotes the place for those souls whose merits and sins weighed on the balance of the divinity Rašn turned out to be equal. The *hammistagān* is a place similar to the purgatory of Dante, but it does not seem to have any purifying function.

Wirāz is then led by his divine guides into the first of the three heavens, to "the station of the stars," where those righteous dwell who did not observe the religious practices and had no leading position; yet they were righteous through their other good deeds. In the second heaven Wirāz comes to the station of the moon, which curiously holds the same kind of righteous people as in the "station of the stars" except that no mention of their social position is made. The text seems here incomplete or clumsily redacted and there are other passages that show the same lack of coherence (see also Gignoux 1984, 16). Having entered the third heaven Wirāz sees in the "station of the sun" the righteous sitting on golden thrones and carpets. These are those who in life exercised "good sovereignty, rulership, and authority." The Pahlavi terms indicate a stratified leadership with "sovereignty" coming at the top. Finally Wirāz arrives in paradise itself (garōdmān), where he is introduced by the god Wahuman (Av. Vohu Manah) to the supreme deity and the beneficent immortals (amahraspandān):

> This is Ohrmazd, Wahuman said. I wished to prostrate myself in front of Him but He said: "be welcome, truthful Wirāz, you have come safely from the world of troubles to this pure and radiant place." And he ordered righteous Srōš and god Adur saying: "take pious Wirāz and show him the places and the rewards of the righteous and also the punishments of the wicked." (AWN 11:3–6)

Up to this moment Wirāz has followed the path of the souls of the righteous dead, and he has been greeted by Ohrmazd with the same words with which the souls of the dead are greeted after having achieved their heavenly journey. After having visited the other places where different groups of righteous souls dwell (chapters 12–15), Wirāz is brought back to the Činwad bridge. From here he is led by his guides along the path that the wicked souls take leading them through three stations down to hell. In accordance with the strict dualistic thinking of Zoroastrianism the road to hell is described as the inversion of that to heaven. Wirāz then tours the many different places in hell and sees the punishments inflicted on the souls of the wicked. Finally he gets a short view of the Evil Spirit himself who is constantly pouring scorn on the damned in hell. The touring of hell occupies the main part of the book (chapters 18–100); in this respect Zoroastrianism does not differ from other religions—for example, Christianity, Islam, and Buddhism, in which the descriptions of the punishments in hell are far more extensive and detailed than those of the heavenly pleasures. After the tour of hell Wirāz returns to paradise, where once more he is addressed by Ohrmazd and charged with the task of telling the Mazdeans what he saw and enjoining on them to follow "the one way of righteousness, the way of the primal teachings, because the other ways are no ways" (AWN 101:7). Ohrmazd then bids him farewell saying that all purifications and ablutions performed by the Mazdeans in concord and in mind of the divinities have verily come to his knowledge.

The purpose of Wirāz's otherwordly journey has thus been fulfilled; the community is reassured of the effectiveness of their rituals; and confidence in the normative tradition of "the primal teachings"of Mazdāism is restored.

By comparing the way in which Wirāz prepares his ecstatic journey and the details of the path he follows to enter the other world with descriptions in Middle Iranian texts of similar visionary journeys, a pattern emerges that suggests a well-established tradition in ancient Iran of mystical and visionary experience. This experience is associated with prominent figures of ancient Zoroastrian legend such as Zoroaster, Vištāspa, Jāmāspa, and historical persons from the early Sassanian period, the high priest Kirdīr being the most well-known example. The *Bahman Yašt* has recorded two dream visions of Zoroaster (I,1–6 and II,4–22) that are but two variants of the same legend. It is told that Zoroaster prayed Ohrmazd to make him immortal. Ohrmazd refused for reasons not immediately disclosed but which he intended to show by conferring on Zoroaster the quality of divine omniscience (see for this theme Hultgård 1995, 139–49) :

> Ohrmazd . . . put the wisdom of omniscience in the form of water in the hands of Zardušt and said: "Drink." Zardušt drank from it, and he [Ohrmazd] mingled his wisdom of omniscience with Zardušt. For seven days and nights Zardušt remained in the wisdom of Ohrmazd. (BYt. II,5–6)

On the seventh day Ohrmazd takes away the omniscience from Zoroaster, who awakes from the vision as from a pleasant sleep. Ohrmazd asks him what he saw in his sleep, and Zoroaster relates how he saw a rich man in hell and a poor man in paradise and a huge tree with seven ("four" in the first variant) branches each representing a different metal. Ohrmazd explains the vision of the tree to Zoroaster: "The tree that you saw is the world created by me Ohrmazd. The seven branches that you saw are the seven ages to come" (BYt II,15). These are then described and characterized in the following passage (II,16–22). In all probability the vision and its explanation by the deity are thought to take place during an otherworldly journey. After having consumed the "wisdom of omniscience," Zoroaster sees the seven world continents and he is able to distinguish the finest details of humans, cattle, and plants. This is best explained on the assumption of a movement in space. In fact, we find a reference to an otherworldly journey undertaken by Zoroaster in a short citation from sacred tradition preserved in the *Dēnkard*. Ohrmazd and the beneficent immortals address Zoroaster with the following words: "You have come to paradise (*garōdmān*); now you know the actions that are done in the corporeal world and those that will be done, even in secret" (Dk IX,28:2).

An otherworldly journey was, according to the *Dēnkard,* the chief instigation for Vištāsp to embrace the religion preached by Zoroaster (Dk. VII,4:84–86). In a citation from a *zand* text we learn that Ohrmazd sent a messenger to the beneficent immortal Ardvahišt telling him to give to Vištāsp a beverage consisting of the sacred juice (*hōm*) and henbane (*mang*). Vištāsp drank it and afterwards he lay as "a dead corpse." Having regained conscious-ness he immediately called upon Zoroaster that he might teach him "the reli-gion of Ohrmazd and Zardušt." The introduction to this *zand* quotation summarizes the rewards promised to Vištāsp if he accepted the religion: vic-tory over the enemies, lasting power, richness, and divine glory (*xwarrah*). The *Dēnkard* text does not explicitly mention an otherworldly journey, but the parallel passage in *Pahlavi Rivāyat* 47:15–19 shows that this was the case: "when he [Vištāspa] had consumed the drink he fell unconscious on the spot and they led his soul to paradise (*garōdmān*)."

The Pahlavi texts show that the trance preparing the mystical experience is induced by a specific technique performed in a ritual context. The drinking of a cup with sacred juice and henbane seems to have been the usual means of achieving the trance state. The expression "in the form of water" in the *Bah-man Yašt* to denote the drink Zoroaster consumed before his vision does not mean that it was water but only that it was a liquid.

Toward the end of the third century C.E. Kirdīr, the chief Magus of three succeeding Sassanian kings, had four inscriptions set up to commemorate his achievements. In two of them there is mention of an otherworldly journey that the Magus undertook to assure himself and his compatriots of the verac-ity of his religious mission. Although the text of the inscriptions has some lacunae, the main content is clear and its eschatological bearing is likewise apparent. Kirdīr wants to know whether he belongs to the righteous and shares in their afterlife in paradise or to the damned, who will end up in hell. Having induced a trance—the text runs "I made myself like dead"—Kirdīr, represented by his spiritual person (denoted in the text as "the one having the same form as Kirdīr"), proceeds along the same path as the souls of the dead. He is met by a beautiful woman, the *daēna*, who takes the hand of Kirdīr; they walk together along a path "radiant of light." Before arriving at the Čin-wad bridge they get a glimpse of suffering souls in hell. Crossing the bridge and still walking in the direction of the East, they come to a heavenly palace of incomparable beauty and brilliance into which they enter. Unfortunately the text becomes fragmentary at this point, but there is clearly mention of a golden throne, of bread, flesh, and wine that are being distributed. A divine figure then smiles on Kirdīr. Here a short lacuna follows after which the vision has come to an end. The concluding part of the inscriptions emphasizes the importance of Kirdīr's vision, that the Mazdean beliefs in the afterlife, in heaven and hell, are true, and that Kirdīr by the journey into the other world has received divine confirmation of his own mission.

The significance of Kirdīr's inscriptions is that they attest the tradition of ecstatic otherworldly journeys for a date of more than five hundred years before the compilation of the Pahlavi books. The descriptions of the otherworldly journeys in the *Dēnkard* and the *Bahman Yašt* are based on *zand* texts which in turn go back to Avestan texts. It is important to notice that the "Oracles of Hystaspes" were said to derive from "a wonderful dream vision" (*admirabile somnium*) which Hystaspes (= Vištāspa) received and which was interpreted by a prophesying child.

The tradition of visionary otherworldly journeys performed in a state of trance is characteristic of Iranian culture and is intimately bound up with eschatological and apocalyptic teachings.

QUESTIONS OF ORIGIN, HISTORICAL DEVELOPMENTS, AND INFLUENCE

The Avestan Background of the Pahlavi Apocalyptic Traditions

The Pahlavi books of the early Islamic period usually refer their apocalyptic ideas to an earlier authoritative tradition which we have every reason to place in the fifth and sixth centuries of the Sassanian era. By that time the Avestan script had been invented in order to record the sacred texts—in the first place those that were recited in the Zoroastrian liturgies. Only a few written copies of the complete Avesta could have been in circulation, and oral transmission had still to be relied on, be it Avestan texts or religious traditions in Middle-Iranian language. The process of translating Avestan texts into Middle-Iranian language is likely to have begun in the same period. There is evidence pointing to an authoritative collection of Avestan traditions with Pahlavi translations in the late Sassanian period to which also mythic and legendary traditions were added. There emerged then a body of texts in Pahlavi which constituted basically a translation of Avestan traditions but was to a large extent also a reinterpretation. These texts, which were transmitted both in oral and written form, came to be the main source for the compilers of the Pahlavi books with respect to eschatological and apocalyptic beliefs.

How far back in time can we follow the apocalyptic eschatology of the late Sassanian period? If we assume that the main ideas of that eschatology were based on Avestan texts composed when Avestan was still a living language—that is, before the early third century B.C.E.—we would have a useful criterion for dating these traditions. The problem is, however, that we do not know to what extent the Zoroastrian priests composed new texts in Avestan during the Parthian and Sassanian periods. Being an Old Iranian language, Avestan as a living spoken language would have been replaced by Middle-Iranian long before the Sassanian era, but it lived on as a ritual language of Zoroastrianism as it still does today. Some texts in the heterogeneous Younger Avesta present an epigonic character with a defective use of Old Iranian, which shows that the authors no longer mastered Avestan. Texts may have been composed in an imperfect Avestan all along the Sassanian period; however, for one category—namely, the Avestan traditions on which the Pahlavi *zand* texts were based—we have to assume that they were genuine and had a pre-Sassanian origin (see also Shaked 1994, 29–30). It would otherwise be hard to imagine that Sassanian priests first composed texts in Avestan which they then commented on in Pahlavi (see further Hultgård 1995, 80; Widengren 1983, 153–54). The linguistic argument is, however, intricate and not always applicable. In the first place we will, therefore, turn to other evidence for the continuity of apocalyptic-eschatological traditions in ancient Iran up to the ninth- and tenth-century Pahlavi books. This evidence can adequately be grouped in two categories: (1) native Iranian traditions contained in the Avesta, and (2) information preserved by Greco-Roman authors.

THE AVESTA AND ITS TRANSMISSION. The term *Avesta* (from Middle Iranian *abēstag*) refers to a collection of primarily ritual texts that came to be considered sacred scriptures of Zoroastrianism in the late Sassanian and early Islamic periods. The impact of the "book religions" of the ancient Middle East (Judaism, Christianity, Manicheism, and Islam) inspired the formation of a Zoroastrian canon, which had the invention of the Avestan script as its prerequisite. According to the summary in *Dēnkard* book 7, the normative traditions of Mazdāism in the late Sassanian period were divided into twenty-one minor collections called *nasks* (literally, "bundles, branches"). Comparing the present Avesta with the summary found in the *Dēnkard*, scholars have concluded that approximately three-fourths of the Sassanian Avesta were lost in the turmoils following the Arab-Islamic conquest. There is, however, uncertainty concerning the extent of a *written* Avesta in the Sassanian period, and the summary in the *Dēnkard* may partly refer to oral texts. What survived of written Avestan traditions were texts used in post-Sassanian rituals, and in these only scattered references to apocalyptic teachings occur.

The Avesta is a heterogeneous body of texts in which the *Gāthās* together with the short text called the "Yasna of Seven Chapters" stand out as having been composed in a slightly different and presumably older dialect termed Old Avestan. Linguistic evidence suggests a date around 1000 B.C.E. for the

Old Avestan texts. The other parts form what is called the Younger Avesta, which contains texts of different age and origin.

THE GĀTHĀS AND ESCHATOLOGY. The *Gāthās*, which are composed in a complicated poetic style, are allusive in character and to modern interpreters still obscure in much of their contents. The worldview and rituals presupposed by the *Gāthās* are unknown to us. Using the Younger Avesta and the Pahlavi books as keys of interpretation we may in many passages discover ideas that are typical of classical Mazdāism. We cannot be sure, however, that these passages originally conveyed precisely the meaning they had for later Mazdāism. In some cases concepts and beliefs undoubtedly changed and acquired a different and sometimes more fixed and narrow content, as, for example, with the term *saošyant* (see Hinze 1995). One thing is evident, however. Later Avestan texts, as well as the Pahlavi books, associated the apocalyptic-eschatological beliefs with words and expressions found in the *Gāthās*, although their original meaning might have been different.

The *Gāthās* are pervaded by dual oppositions on several levels. There is a cosmic dualism between the good ordering of the universe, the Truth, and a bad ordering, the Deceit or Lie, coupled with the opposition day and light against night and darkness. Correspondingly, there are on the human level two opposing groups: "the truthful" and the "deceitful." In the divine world good deities (*ahuras*) confront bad deities (*daēuuas*). On the ritual level, there are good sacrifices and bad sacrifices. A fundamental opposition exists also between two "spirits" (*mainiiu-*), be they conceived of as mental attitudes within the human person or supernatural spiritual entities. The more developed dualism on cosmic and human levels characteristic of the Younger Avesta and the Pahlavi books is certainly in line with the Old Avestan ideas.

A "final turning point" is alluded to in some passages (Y. 43:5 and 51:6), and here the context suggests an eschatological interpretation, since at that "turning point" recompense for the individual's actions will be given, "evil to the evil one, (but) a good reward to the good one" (trans. Humbach 1991). A key passage is Yasna 44:14–15, which may allude to the ultimate confrontation between Truth and Lie. In stanza 14 the antagonism of Truth and Lie is proclaimed and the reciter prays Ahura Mazdā to "bring his impetuous weapon (down) upon the deceitful (and) bring ill and harm over them" (trans. Humbach 1991). In the following stanza there is mention of two opposing armies that will confront each other, and the reciter asks Mazdā rhetorically: "to which side of the two (sides), to whom wilt Thou assign victory?" (trans.

Humbach 1991). To Zoroastrian tradition this was—probably rightly so—a clear allusion to the great eschatological battle between Good and Evil.

An important notion in the *Gāthās* is *ahu-* ("existence"), which seems to have several connotations. Qualified by *astuuant-* ("of bone") it means the corporeal existence of humans and animals; and, linked with *mainiiu-*, it denotes their spiritual existence. It may also refer to different forms of existence, ritual as well as human in general. The term *ahu-* may further denote individual existence, "life," and universal existence, "world."

The belief in the afterlife of the human person represented by the "soul" (Av. *uruuan*) is a prominent element in the *Gāthās*, the presence of which seems undisputed among modern interpreters. One may see in this eschatologization of the sacrifice one of the main innovations of the *Gāthās* (Kellens and Pirart 1988, 35). The final destiny of the truthful will be with Ahura Mazdā in the "house of Good Thought" (Y. 32:15), whereas the deceitful will in the end come to "the house of Lie" (Y. 51:14) or "the house of Worst Thought"(Y. 32:13). To arrive in paradise the truthful cross a bridge called *cinuuatō pərətuš* (Y. 46:10), meaning "the account-keeper's bridge" (Humbach, 1991), "the bridge of the Judge," or "the bridge of the mason" (Kellens and Pirart 1988). The souls of the deceitful will recoil from them, when they reach the bridge, and they will "be guests for ever in the house of Lie" (Y. 46:11; see also Y. 51:13).

Eschatological reward and punishment, which both seem to be realized through an ordeal of divine fire, are promised in *Yasna* 43:4 and 47:6 (possibly also in Y. 31:3). In *Yasna* 43, stanza 5 sets the distribution of reward and punishment to "the final turning point of creation." In *Yasna* 51:9 this eschatological recompense through fire is linked to (or specified as) an ordeal of molten metal (see aslo Y. 32:7). Several other passages seem also to include allusions to the different postmortem existence of the individuals although they may at the same time refer to divine rewards and punishments to be distributed during their earthly life (Y. 30:4; 34:13; 43:12; 44:19; 47:5).

The idea of a perfection of the world may underlie the references to making or creating the existence "brilliant," "blissful," or "abundant" in *Yasna* 30:9 and 34:15. The mention in 30:9, which is set in the context of a defeat and punishment of Deceit, expresses the wish of the Gāthic community to be among those who help to bring about this perfection. The other mention is a prayer to Ahura Mazdā to make the existence "brilliant." The claim for a continuity of beliefs between the *Gāthās* and the Pahlavi texts is also supported by the fact that *Yašt* 19 predicts the renovation of the world through the final savior in close similarity with the contents of the Gāthic stanzas (Yt. 19:89).

The otherworldly journey as a means of acquiring divine knowledge, which is characteristic of Iranian visionary experience as attested in the Pahlavi apocalypses *Ardā Wirāz Nāmag* and *Bahman Yašt,* may well have its origin far back in time. The *Gāthās* include some passages that can be interpreted as reflecting such visionary journeys. In *Yasna* 33:5 there is mention of "the straight paths on which Mazdā Ahura dwells" (or, according to Kellens and Pirart, "at the end of which, O Mazdā, the [or: an] Ahura dwells") and which are attained by the reciter. Similarly in *Yasna* 43:3 we find the wish that a particular man should teach the community "the straight paths of benefit" which can be compared to the prayer in *Yasna* 34:12 addressed to Ahura Mazdā: "Show us with Truth the paths of Good Thought, easy to travel." *Yasna* 34:13 prays Ahura Mazdā to teach the path on which "the *daēnas* of the *saošyants*" walk toward the recompense. The above passages mentioning the divine paths may refer to the good ritual behavior which bestows on the sacrificer an eschatological reward, but they may also contain allusions to the paths of divine vision. Two other passages allude to a journey undertaken by the soul (*uruuan*) or by a named person. In *Yasna* 44:8 the reciter asks along which road his soul may proceed to attain the things to come and in *Yasna* 51:16 Vištāspa is said to proceed along the paths of Good Thought to the insight (*cisti-*) conceived by Ahura Mazdā. The journey mentioned in these two passages seems to refer in the first place to the ascent of the soul after death to paradise, but may also allude to otherworldly journeys to acquire divine insight (note the word *cisti*). As we have seen, the path on which the soul after death will reach paradise in classical Zoroastrian tradition is the same along which the visionary proceeds, and the goal is also the same—namely, the encounter with the supreme deity. The description of the ecstatic vision of Vištāspa in the *Dēnkard* (Dk. VII,4:84–86) is explicitly described as a journey to paradise in the parallel account in the *Pahlavi Rivāyat* (47:30). Here the connection with *Yasna* 51:16 is obvious and implies an early interpretation of that stanza as an otherworldly journey made by Vištāspa in his lifetime.

THE RESTORATION OF THE WORLD ACCORDING TO THE YOUNGER AVESTA. The most important text in the Younger Avesta dealing with the final battle between Good and Evil and the renovation of the world is *Yašt* 19, composed most probably in the sixth century B.C.E. In stanzas 88–94 a unique eschatological prediction has been preserved which presents the basic themes of the apocalyptic eschatology as it is found in the Pahlavi books. *Yašt* 19 is dedicated to the divine glory and enumerates the heroes and figures whom the "glory" has accompanied in the past to help them fulfill their renowned actions. For the last figure the scene is set in the future and depicts the appearance and mission of Astvat.ərəta, who is characterized as a *saošiiant;* the *Yašt* thus takes up a concept from the *Gāthās* and applies it to an individual eschatological savior (see for this development Hinze 1995). The myth of the Saošyant's birth is alluded to when stanza 92 tells us that he will appear from the waters of Kansaoya and that his mother is named Vīspa.taurvairī. He is the final and most victorious among the group of *saošyants* in which the *Gāthās* also included the truthful believers who through their good thoughts, words, and actions have a part in the perfection of the existence (Y. 34:13; 46:3; and 48:12). The final battle between Good and Evil is clearly announced. Astvat.ərəta will carry the victorious weapon which the divine hero Thraētona had when he slew the dragon Aži Dahāka. He will overcome the great enemy, "the evil Lie of evil roots and born of darkness" (stanza 95). Lie will be expelled from the world of Truth. The followers of Astvat.ərəta described as a retinue of truthful, religious, and morally outstanding men, will drive away the destructive Aēšma (the demon Hēšm of the Pahlavi books). Some of the divine beings and entities surrounding Ahura Mazdā will choose each his own adversary: Vohu Manah ("Good Thought") will defeat Aka Manah ("Evil Thought"), the Truly Spoken Word will overcome the Falsely Spoken Word, "Immortality" and "Integrity" will overcome Hunger and Thirst, and Angra Mainyu ("the Evil Spirit") will flee bereft of his power (stanza 96). The theme of eschatological duels between divinities and demons found in the Pahlavi texts is thus already present in the Zoroastrianism of the early Achaemenian period. It seems to be an Indo-European motif, as it is characteristic of Old Scandinavian eschatology (the *Ragnarok* tradition) and ancient Indian epic mythology (the great battle in Mahābhārata).

The belief in the resurrection of the dead and in the renovation of the world is clearly set out in *Yašt* 19. Astavt.ərəta will make the world "perfect" a belief that we have seen is in line with Old Avestan ideas (Y. 30:9; 34:15). The world will be "non-aging, immortal, non-fading, non-decaying, forever living, forever prospering" (Yt. 19:89). The dead will rise when the Saošyant "who restores life" appears and the living beings who exist at that time will not die (stanzas 89–90). The renovation is conceived of as a gazing with spiritual power, and through the eyes of the Saošyant the whole material world will be made undying (stanza 94).

Scattered allusions to this coherent picture of the end-time are found in other passages of the Younger Avesta. The final Saošyant is mentioned in several passages and is there always associated with the epithet "victorious" (Yt.

13:129 and 145; Vd. 19:5; Y. 26:10; and 59:28). In Yt. 13:129 his two names are explained: Saošyant insofar as he will make the entire corporeal existence prosper, and Astvat.ərəta "insofar as being corporeal (and) living he will provide corporeal freedom from danger" (trans. Hinze 1995, 92). The course of world history is summarized in the expression "from the primordial man (*gaya marətan*, Phl. *gayōmard*) to the victorious Saošyant" (Yt. 13:145; Y. 26:10). The myth of his birth is alluded to in *Vidēvdād* 19:5: "until the victorious Saošyant will be born out of Lake Kansaoya." The renovation as a desired goal is prayed for in Yt. 13:58 (see also Y. 62:3; Vd. 18:51). The hope for the resurrection of the dead is expressed in Yt. 19:11: "when the dead will rise, the one who restores life, the Undying (i.e., the Saošyant) will come" and in Y. 54: "The dead will rise in their lifeless bodies."

Greek Authors on Persian Apocalypticism

The Avestan evidence is, with the exception of *Yašt* 19:88–96, both scarce and allusive in character and contrasts sharply with the rich picture of the end-time that the Pahlavi books depict. Were it not for the testimony of Greek authors, the argument for a continuity of Iranian apocalypticism from the Avesta down to the Pahlavi books of the early Islamic period would be less convincing.

Among these testimonies the one given by Plutarch, writing in the decades around 100 C.E., stands out as the most decisive. In his treatise *De Iside et Osiride* chaps. 46–47 he gives a short but rather detailed picture of Zoroastrian cosmogony and eschatology. In this part of the treatise Plutarch intends to illustrate a general opinion "held by most people and the wisest men" concerning the two incompatible principles of good and evil both having, however, their source and origin in Nature itself. To this purpose the Persian doctrine of two opposing cosmic powers presented itself as a very appropriate example. From the literary point of view his account is not uniform, and Plutarch seems to draw on different sources and informants. He thus gives two variants of the primordial state of the cosmos in which the content is the same but the terminology different (see Hultgård 1995, 96–98).

In the first place, Plutarch clearly attests the basic cosmogonic myth that we otherwise only know from the Pahlavi texts. Several points show a surprising correspondence in details, which emphasizes the reliability of the oral transmission of that myth through centuries.

The initial state of the cosmos, with Good and Evil as two opposing entities from the beginning, is described with almost identical wording to what we find in the opening of the first chapter of the *Bundahišn* and the *Wizīdā-*

gīha ī Zādspram. The good deity, says Plutarch, is called Oromazes and the evil one is called Areimanios; the former is of all things perceptible to the senses to be compared with light, the latter by contrast with darkness and ignorance (first variant in chapter 46). The wording of the second variant (chapter 47) is slightly different in that Oromazes is said to be born out of the purest light and Areimanios out of darkness. In the first variant there is also a mention of the intermediary space that separates the two cosmic powers: "midway between the two is Mithras." This should be compared with the opening of the myth in *Bundahišn* 1:1–3: "Ohrmazd was on high in omniscience and goodness, for endless time he was ever in the light. . . . Ahreman was deep down in the darkness, ignorant and full of lust to smite. Midway between them was the void" (similarly also WZ 1:1–2).

In *Bundahišn* 1:3 a variant tradition is recorded in which the "void" appears as *way* ("wind, atmosphere") at the same time considered as a deity (Av. Vayu) of the same dignity as Mithra. Plutarch adds that Oromazes and Areimanios "are at war with one another," and he then goes on to describe briefly the work of creation, how the former fashions forth six divinities who clearly correspond to the group of the Aməša Spəntas, the "Beneficent Immortals" (Bd. 1:53). Areimanios responds by creating six opposing entities, just as Ahreman brings forth the archdemons as an anti-creation according to the Pahlavi myth (Bd. 1:47–49, 55). Oromazes adorned the sky with luminaries, and "one star he set before all others as a guardian and watchman, the Sirius" (*De Isid. et Osir.* 47). The first assertion recalls the wording of *Bundahišn* 2:1: "Ohrmazd fashioned forth the luminaries between the sky and the earth." The line on Sirius appears to be virtually a citation in Greek of a passage from the Avestan *yašt* dedicated to the stargod Tištriya, who is the equivalent of Sirius: "The bright and glorious star Tištriya we worship whom Ahura Mazdā set as lord and watchman over all the stars" (Yt. 8:44).

Twenty-four other divinities are created by Oromazes and placed within the cosmic egg. A countercreation by Areimanios follows again, and he produces twenty-four demons. Areimanios and his demons then pierce the cosmic egg, and in this way, says Plutarch, was the mixture between good and evil brought about. Here the allusion to the irruption of Ahreman into the creation of Ohrmazd and as a result the emergence of the present world as a "mixed state" of good and evil is obvious.

Plutarch then passes directly to the eschatological era: "A destined time will come when as decreed Areimanios having brought on pestilence and famine will be entirely destroyed by these and made to disappear." Plutarch's emphasis on what has been decreed tallies well with the idea that the ultimate defeat of Ahreman was determined by Ohrmazd already at creation. The tribulations of the end-time are also alluded to by the words "pestilence and famine," and the idea that they are produced by Ahreman but also will cause his destruction is in accordance with the Pahlavi tradition on the deadly internal strife within the camp of the demons. When the end draws near, a heightened activity of evil is expected, as stated in the *Bahman Yašt:* "when the moment of his destruction is close, the deceitful Evil Spirit will be more oppressive and his regime worse" (BYt. II,54).

The bliss of the renovation is also touched upon by Plutarch: "the earth will become a level plain, and there shall be one manner of life and one form of government for a blessed humankind who all speak the same tongue." These ideas can be shown to have their background in the Pahlavi texts' description of the renovation. For the first statement a clear parallel is found in *Bundahišn* in a citation from sacred tradition: "This earth will become a plain, level without slopes, and there will be no hollows, hills, and peaks, no up and down" (Bd. 34:33). The other assertions can likewise be understood in the light of the *frašgird* tradition. Scholars have pointed to *Bundahišn* 34:21, where it is said that when the soul is reunited with the body "humankind will altogether be of the same voice and loudly bring praise to Ohrmazd and the Beneficent Immortals" (Bidez-Cumont 1938, 2:77; Widengren 1983, 132). It is, however, not clear if this is the meaning that should be attributed to the statement of Plutarch. The eschatological unity in manner of life and form of government alluded to in the Greek text and to which good parallels so far have not been adduced (see Widengren 1983, 132), can in fact be interpreted in the light of some Pahlavi passages concerning the renovation. In the *Dēnkard* it is said: "All humankind will gather around the religion of Ohrmazd in one community" (Dk. VII,11:6). The unity in thinking, speech, and action that exists among the Aməša Spəntas will also characterize humankind after the renovation, as is expressed in the following statement proclaimed by the Beneficent Immortals: "being of the same thought, the same speech and the same action you will be without aging, without sickness and without corruption as we the Amahraspand are" (WZ 35:2).

In the last part of his account Plutarch mentions explicitly an earlier source from which he gives a brief citation—the historian Theopompos of Chios, writing in the fourth century B.C.E., whose work unfortunately survives only in fragments. It is of great importance that the Persian periodization of world history here appears as it is told in the basic cosmogonic myth of the Pahlavi texts, although with a somewhat different distribution of the sovereignty between Ohrmazd and Ahreman. In referring explicitly to the Magi, Theopompos says that each deity in turn will rule for three thousand years and that during another period of three thousand years they will fight and make war and undo the work of the other. World history consists of nine thousand years and is subdivided into three periods of three thousand years each with its own characteristics. The final destruction of evil and the bliss of the renewed world is also briefly touched on. Areimanios (here called Hades) will perish and all humankind will be blessed and happy "without having need of food and without casting any shadow." These strange details are in accordance with Persian eschatological tradition. The *Bundahišn* and the *Dēnkard* predict that humankind will gradually feel less need of food when the end-time approaches. First one meal will be sufficient for three days. Then people will desist from eating meat and will nourish themselves with milk and vegetables and: "Thereupon they desist from drinking the milk, then they renounce the vegetables and drink only water. Ten years before the coming of Sōšans they will be entirely without food and drink and they shall not die" (Bd. 34:3; Dk. VII,10:8–9; WZ 34:38–41).

This process is the inverse of that which the first human couple underwent who began by drinking water, then added vegetables, milk, and finally also meat (Bd. 34:1). For the idea of the blessed casting no shadow, similar beliefs were propagated also by the Pythagoreans, who said that "the souls of the dead do not cast a shadow" (Plutarch *Quaest. Graecae* 39). The Iranian background may be found in the Avesta as suggested by Bidez-Cumont (1938, 2:78), and it has been plausibly argued that the idea is also related to the renouncing of food (Widengren 1983, 132). The citation from Theopompos concludes with the curious statement that the god (Oromazes) who had brought about the final bliss for humankind now "will have quiet and repose for a time." This may be explained from the idea that Ohrmazd having achieved the renovation, does not have to perform any action (PR 48:101; see also Bd. 34:22).

The detailed concordances between the account of Plutarch and the Pahlavi texts show that Plutarch and his source Theopompos were well informed on Iranian ideas of cosmogony and eschatology and suggest in addition that this knowledge derived directly from Persian informants. Through the testimony of Theopompos we further know that the basic cosmogonic myth, with its apocalyptic-eschatological implications, was in circulation in the late Achaemenian period and probably also in the fifth century B.C.E.

The belief in the resurrection of the dead is not explicitly mentioned in the account of Plutarch but is certainly implicit in what he says of the blissful state of humankind after the disappearance of evil. Other Greek writers refer to Theopompos as their chief source in attributing the resurrection of the dead to teachings of the Magi and Zoroaster. So does Diogenes Laertius in his Proemium: "who [Theopompos] says that according to the Magi humankind will become alive again and be immortal. That is also told by Eudemos of Rhodes." Eudemos is another fourth-century B.C.E. author who apparently knew about Persian beliefs but whose works have not survived. Aenas of Gaza (sixth century C.E., excerpt in Bidez-Cumont 1939, 2:70) also refers to Theopompos for the idea of resurrection: "Zoroaster predicts that there shall be a time when a resurrection of all the dead will come. Theopompos knows what I say and he teaches also the other (writers)."

The "Oracles of Hystaspes"

The diffusion of Iranian apocalyptic beliefs in antiquity is not only echoed among Greco-Roman writers but can also be seen in the emergence of apocalyptic compilations with a more or less strong Iranian influence. These texts related to the Sibylline tradition were usually attributed to Hystaspes, being the Greek form of the Iranian Vištāspa, and propagated in different versions and by different groups during the Hellenistic period and the first centuries of our era (see Colpe 1991). The "Oracles of Hystaspes" owed their origin to a milieu where Iranian apocalyptic ideas were used to maintain spiritual and political resistance against Macedonian and Seleucid rule in western Asia. The Oracles were reused among various groups during subsequent centuries now with an anti-Roman tendency. The opposition against Roman imperial rule rallied Iranians with Syrians, Jews, and other Oriental peoples and the "Oracles of Hystaspes" enjoyed a wide popularity as an apocalyptic pamphlet. No original version of a Hystaspes text has survived; we know their content only through incomplete paraphrases and summaries given by Lactantius mainly in his *Divine Institutions,* written in the beginning of the fourth century C.E. Although Lactantius was a Christian, his knowledge of the Bible seems to have been limited. On the other hand, he was well versed in Greek and Latin literature and the source for his paraphrasing extracts was most probably an intermediate Hystaspes text compiled from a Greco-Persian prophecy. It has been suggested that this intermediate text was a compilation in Greek produced by Jews in Asia Minor before the destruction of the temple in Jerusalem (so Flusser 1982). The Iranian substratum of that version of the Oracles, as condensed and reworked by Lactantius, is not easily distinguished from the Hellenistic Jewish layer. The problem is that we do not find many characteristic details that can be unambiguously associated solely with Zoroastrian apocalyptic ideas, as is the case, for example, with the account of Plutarch. As scholars have long noticed, the description of the apocalyptic signs in the Lactantius paraphrase recalls strikingly those found in the Pahlavi texts, in particular the *Bahman Yašt*. On the other hand, the similarities with Jewish and early Christian apocalypses are equally apparent, a fact that may be explained by the universal content of these signs and by cross-cultural influences. This makes the separation of genuine Iranian ideas from Jewish and Christian traditions an intricate matter. The changes in cosmos and nature announcing the end-time predicted in Lactantius, *Inst. Div.* 7.16.6–11 present unmistakable affinities with *Bahman Yašt* II,31–32 as also with the prophecy of the Astronomical Book 80:2–8 in the Jewish Enoch collection (*1 Enoch*) and the predictions in 4 Ezra 5:1–12 and 6:20–25. There is a closer correspondence in formulation, however, between the *Divine Institutions* and the *Bahman Yašt.* Lactantius says, for example, that "the year will be shortened and the month diminished and the day contracted into a short space" (16:10). The parallel predictions of *1 Enoch* 80:2: "And in the days of the sinners the years shall be shortened and the crops delayed in their land and fields"; and the one in 4 Ezra, "The sun will suddenly begin to shine in the middle of the night, and the moon in the day-time" (5:4) certainly attest the dissolution of cosmic order. However, only *Bahman Yašt* gives the precise equivalent: "The sun will be less visible and smaller, year and month and day shorter" (BYt. II,31). Rhetorical statements of the type: "from the place where a thousand had gone forth, scarcely a hundred will go forth" (*Div. Inst.* 7.16.14) are characteristic of the Iranian apocalyptic tradition but rarely occur in Jewish and Christian apocalypses. The eschatological fire described by Lactantius (*Div. Inst.* 7.21.3–7) corresponds by its function clearly to the Iranian concept and not to the Judeo-Christian one. The "Oracles" emphasize that the divine fire will burn both the righteous and the wicked, and that the wicked will be tried by the divine fire but it will not hurt the righteous: "but they whom full justice and maturity of virtue have imbued will not perceive that fire" whereas it will affect the wicked "with a sense of pain" but not destroy them. The fire "will both burn the wicked and will form them again, and will replace as much as it shall consume of their bodies." This is precisely the character of the eschatological fire that is described in the Iranian apocalyptic texts.

The scenario of the end-time in the "Oracles" resembles much the one found in Jewish and Christian "historical" apocalypses, but there are details and formulations that reveal the original Persian background. When the eschatological tribulations are at their height, the righteous will separate themselves from the wicked and flee to a mountain. The evil king who dominates the world is filled with wrath on hearing this, and he will encircle the mountain with a great army. The faithful shall implore God for help; they will be heard and God will send them a savior from heaven who with his followers shall rescue the righteous and destroy the wicked. The expectation of the coming savior in the "Oracles of Hystaspes" originally meant a Persian savior figure be it Mithra (e.g., Bidez-Cumont 1938; Widengren 1983), the final Saošyant (so Hinnells) or Darius *redivivus* (so Colpe 1991). The savior is called the "great king" (*rex magnus*), an obvious allusion to Iranian kingship terminology, and in another passage Lactantius mentions "the leader of the holy retinue" (*dux sanctae militiae*), which clearly alludes to the followers of the Saošyant, and perhaps their "leader" is none other than Pišyōtan. The scenery with the mountain is best explained from Persian customs of worshiping on the top of hills as described by Herodotus (*Hist.* 1.131–32). The righteous are called "followers of the truth" (*sectatores veritatis*), which recalls the Zoroastrian emphasis on Truth and the believers as the truthful. In an explicit reference to the prophecy of Hystaspes (*Div. Inst.* 7.18) Lactantius reproduces more directly the wording of the Oracles in saying that the faithful besieged on the mountain will implore Jupiter for help and "Jupiter will look to the earth and hear the voices of the humans and he will exterminate the wicked" (cf. the wording in the summary above from *Div. Inst.* 7.17). Jupiter here stands for Zeus, which was the established Greek name for Ahura Mazdā. It is improbable that Christians or Jews would have used Zeus in their own writings instead of the general Greek term *theos*. Lactantius is aware of this in his comment following the citation: "All this is true except one thing, namely, that he [Hystaspes] said that Jupiter shall fulfill what God shall do" (*Div. Inst.* 7.18.2).

The Iranian background of Lactantius's paraphrase of the "Oracles of Hystaspes" is thus ascertained (cf. also Shaked 1994, 31), and it seems, therefore, reasonable to conclude that the passages in the "Oracles" that show similarities of equal pertinence both with the Iranian tradition and the Jewish-Christian apocalypses should in the first place be interpreted as Persian elements. The "Oracles of Hystaspes" is undeniably an important testimony to the impact of Persian apocalyptic ideas on the western Greco-Roman world.

Historical Developments, Social and Political Settings

Eschatology, both individual and universal, is from the very beginning strongly integrated in the Iranian worldview. The *Gāthās* and the Younger Avesta show these beliefs to be deeply rooted in the sacrificial cult. As in ancient India sacrifice nourished cosmic speculation, so the Old Iranian sacrificial worship also inspired meditation on the creation and history of the world. These reflections were given concrete expression in sacral poetry, memorized and transmitted by the priests who administered the cult. They became the chief tradents of apocalyptic and eschatological ideas, but these were not kept as esoteric teachings and we may assume that beliefs in the afterlife and the ultimate victory of Good over Evil were known to wider circles of the Iranian society, the aristocracy as well as the common people.

There is a basic continuity in the Persian expectation of the end from the time of the *Gāthās* (ca. 1000 B.C.E.) down to the early Islamic period (seventh to tenth centuries C.E.). In the course of time, however, new versions of the apocalyptic eschatology evolved as a result of changing cultural and historical situations but keeping the fundamental ideas intact. The most striking innovation appears to be the triplication of the end-time and its eschatological events. This innovation seems to be the result of "deliberate scholastic developments" (Boyce 1984, 68–69). The last period of world history was subdivided into three millennia, each having its own key figure. The first millennium, that of Zoroaster, has already begun and draws to its end, but before the final restoration of the world two further savior figures are expected whose appearance ushers in each a new millennium. At the shift of the millennia broadly similar events occur characterized first by deterioration and then by improvement. The original apocalyptic tradition appearing in *Yašt* 19 and still current in early Hellenistic times as appears from Theopompos and the "Oracles of Hystaspes" was reinterpreted and its themes distributed over three "end-times." Traces of the rearrangement of traditions can still be found in the incongruences and blurrings found in some apocalyptic passages of the Pahlavi books. We may take as an example Pišyōtan and the tradition linked to him. Originally one of the comrades of the final savior Astvatarta, Pišyōtan and the tradition linked to him were later transferred to the end of Zoroaster's millennium, where he and his followers appear as forerunners of Ušēdar, the first savior to come. In the *Bahman Yašt* it is said that Ahura Mazdā and the Beneficent Immortals will manifest themselves on earth and summon Pišyōtan to restore the Mazdean religion (BYt. III,25–31). According to the *Dēnkard*, Pišyōtan will smite the Evil Spirit and the demons (Dk. 7.8.47). Both the *Bahman Yašt* and the *Dēnkard* place these events at the turn of Zoroaster's and Ušēdar's millennia. However, the appearance of the supreme deity and his "archangels" on earth and the defeat of Ahreman clearly are expected at the end of world history and these ideas were originally connected with the *frašgird* tradition.

Since eschatological beliefs were at the center of ancient Mazdāism, they could easily be actualized in times of crisis and take on new formulations. It seems that in the wake of Alexander's conquest of the Achaemenian empire apocalypticism received a fresh stimulus. New prophecies resembling the genre of Sibylline predictions were promulgated among the Iranians to encourage resistance and to give hope for a future salvation. The Iranian prophecies served the interests of a more widespread anti-Macedonian and subsequently anti-Roman movement in the eastern provinces. The late Avestan traditions underlying the present *Bahman Yašt*, the *Jāmāsp Nāmag* and the "Oracles of Hystaspes" most probably took shape in the early Hellenistic period. These traditions were faithfully preserved and presumably reused down to the Sassanian period, during which further reinterpretations were added.

The downfall of the Sassanian kingdom and the Arab-Muslim conquest of Iran profoundly affected the Zoroastrian communities. From the position as the most favored religion, Mazdāism became in a couple of centuries an oppressed minority religion. These dramatic changes gave new impetus to apocalyptic expectations, which have left their traces on the eschatological strands of the Pahlavi books. New prophecies were added, and the Sassanian apocalyptic tradition was subjected to a general reinterpretation. *Bundahišn* chapter 33 outlines the history of "the Iranian lands" according to a millennial scheme which is retrospective down to the early Islamic period mentioning the defeat of the Iranians by the Tāzīgs, the death of Yazdagird and the flight of his son into Xorasan to raise an army. Then it turns into eschatology, giving predictions of coming events leading up to the advent of Pišyōtan and the beginning of Ušēdar's millennium. The Tāzīgs have here become the Muslim Arabs, and their wicked rule is briefly described. The impact of this national disaster on the Zoroastrians is clearly stated: "From the primal creation until the present day no evil greater than this has come" (Bd. 33:22).

Movements of resistance and insurgence against the rule of the Caliphate emerged in various parts of the Iranian territories. They were led by persons who legitimated their activity by associating themselves with traditional Zoroastrian salvation hopes. In the *Jāmāsp Nāmag* a number of oracles have been preserved that partly are events after the fact and testify to the apocalyptic effervescence of the first troubled centuries of Islamic expansion (see Kippenberg 1978).

In conclusion it must be emphasized that apocalyptic eschatology is one of the prominent elements of Zoroastrianism and all along its history the expectation of the end has been transmitted as a living doctrine. Zoroastrians were thus spiritually prepared to deal with major crisis situations that came upon the "religion of the Mazdā worshipers," the Macedonian conquest of Iran through Alexander and the Arab-Muslim destruction of the Sassanian kingdom nearly a thousand years later being the most spectacular.

The Problem of Iranian Influence
on Jewish and Christian Apocalypticism

The degree and extension of Iranian influence on early Judaism and indirectly on Christianity have long been a controversial issue. The adherents of the *religionsgeschichtliche Schule* in the first three decades of the twentieth century (e.g., Wilhelm Bousset, Richard Reitzenstein, and Eduard Meyer) suggested a thoroughgoing influence from Iranian traditions especially on Jewish and Christian apocalypticism, messianism, and eschatology. The criticism leveled by Carsten Colpe (1950) against the results of the *religionsgeschichtliche Schule* did not have the general impact it aimed at. The discovery of the Qumran texts gave fresh impetus to the discussion of the Iranian impact on early Jewish religion, especially the dualistic ideas professed by the Qumran community. In modern scholarship the controversy goes on, but it seems that the tendency to admit Iranian influence prevails to varying degrees. Recent advocates for a decisive influence are Mary Boyce from the Iranist side and Norman Cohn from the side of cultural historians (Boyce 1991; Cohn 1993). Conversely, critical voices are heard that emphasize the difficulty in proving Iranian influences usually with a reference to the late date of the Pahlavi writings. Arguments for inner-Jewish developments as a sufficient explanation for the emergence of new eschatological beliefs have frequently been presented. In addition, there is a growing tendency to argue that Hellenistic, Jewish, and Gnostic ideas have influenced anthropological, cosmological, and apocalyptic ideas of the Pahlavi books. The description of the world ages symbolized by different metals in the *Bahman Yašt* is thus, according to some scholars, dependent on the book of Daniel (Duchesne-Guillemin 1982; Gignoux 1984). The microcosmos–macrocosmos speculations in some Pahlavi texts have been adduced as another example influence from late antiquity on Iranian thinking.

The issue of religious influence with respect to ideas and doctrines is delicate to handle since the evidence is seldom clear-cut and also open to different interpretations. Before an influence from one religion on another can be assessed properly two basic preconditions must be fulfilled. First, the priority in time for a particular idea in one of the religions subject to comparison; second, the possibility of religious and cultural contacts between the religions involved. Both these preconditions are present in the case of Persian influence on Judaism and Christianity.

As pointed out above an apocalyptic eschatology is firmly attested in Zoroastrianism already in the sixth century B.C.E. and is in addition well integrated in the general Iranian worldview. Jews and Persians were in close geographical contact from the Achaemenian period down to the fall of the

Sassanian empire. Palestine was under Achaemenian rule for two hundred years, from 538 B.C.E. to the Macedonian conquest. The large Jewish population in Mesopotamia remained under Iranian sovereignty also in the Parthian and Sassanian periods. Iran proper included important Jewish communities within its territory from the Hellenistic period onwards; subsequently Christians too became numerous. In Asia Minor, Iranians and Jews had likewise good opportunities for cultural and personal contacts since both groups were represented by important local communities, for the Iranians already from the Achaemenian period. From the liberation of the exiled Jews by Cyrus—hailed as a Messiah in Deutero-Isaiah—down through the centuries there were strong bonds of political sympathy between Jews and Persians. As shown by Greek and Roman writers Iranian beliefs were well known in antiquity and could not have gone unnoticed in the Hellenistic Jewish milieu as indicated by Philo of Alexandria. One may also point to religious and social affinities between the priestly classes of Jews and Persians in the Hellenistic period. The Zadokites among the Jews fulfilled the same religious functions and occupied the same position in society as the Magi among the Persians. These common interests would have facilitated contacts on both personal and official levels, and it is in fact possible to distinguish a particular strand of Iranian influenced ideas in the pre-Essene Zadokite writings (see Hultgård 1988).

The core of the question must briefly be addressed: How much does the Judeo-Christian tradition owe to Persian apocalypticism? There was no direct and general borrowing of the Iranian apocalyptic eschatology as such by Judaism and Christianity. Instead, the influence exerted itself in an indirect way but was of no less importance. The encounter with Iranian religion produced the necessary stimulus for the full development of ideas that were slowly under way within Judaism. The personification of evil in the form of figures like Satan, Belial, or the Devil, the increasing importance of the dual opposition between Good and Evil as well as their eschatological confrontation are ideas that are unlikely to have emerged without external influence. The doctrine of the two Spirits as professed by the Qumran community provides a striking example of Persian religious impact that had wider and long-lasting effects on Jewish and Christian traditions (see Philonenko 1995). This is also the case with the belief in the resurrection of the dead, which can be shown to have some Israelite antecedents in the exilic period but was not fully developed until Hellenistic-Roman times, and in addition was not accepted by all Jews. The Persian impact is also shown by many details in Jewish and Christian eschatology, both universal and individual, that appear to be Iranian borrowings (see further Hultgård 1978; Boyce 1991).

As a conclusion one may say that the emergence of an apocalyptic eschatology among Jews and Christians in the Hellenistic and Roman periods was propelled by the fruitful encounter with a religion deeply concerned with the struggle of good and evil and firmly assured of the ultimate restoration of the world.

NOTES

1. The *Bahman Yašt* is here cited according to the division of chapters and paragraphs found in the translation of E. W. West in *The Sacred Books of the East, Pahlavi Texts Part I* (Oxford, 1880).

BIBLIOGRAPHY

Abbreviations

AWN	*Ardāy Wīrāz Nāmag*	MIr	Middle Iranian
AJ	*Ayādgār ī Jāmāspīg*	MX	*Mēnōg ī Xrad*
Av.	Avestan	Phl.	Pahlavi
Bd.	*Bundahišn*	PR	*Pahlavi Rivāyat* accompanying the *Dādestān ī Dēnīg*
BYt.	*Bahman Yašt*	WZ	*Wizīdagīhā ī Zādspram*
DD	*Dādestān ī Dēnīg*	Vd.	*Vidēvdāt* (*Vendidād*)
Dk.	*Dēnkard*	Y.	*Yasna*
JN	*Jāmāsp Nāmag*	Yt.	*Yašt*

Primary Texts

Anklesaria, B. T. 1956. *Zand-Akāsīh: Iranian or Greater Bundahišn.* Bombay: Bode.

Cereti, C. G. 1995. *The Zand ī Wahman Yasn: A Zoroastrian Apocalypse.* Rome Oriental Series 75. Rome: Istituto italiano per il medio ed estremo oriente.

Gignoux, P. 1984. *Le Livre d'Ardā Vīrāz: Translittération, transcription et traduction du texte pehlevi.* Paris: Editions Recherche sur les Civilisations.

Gignoux, P., and A. Tafazzoli. 1993. *The Wizīdagīhā ī Zādspram: Anthologie de Zādspram.* Studia Iranica—Cahier 13. Paris: Association pour l'avancement des études iraniennes.

Humbach H., J. Elfenbein, and P. O. Skjærvø. 1991. *The Gāthās of Zarathushtra and the Other Old Avestan Texts.* Part I, *Introduction—Text and Translation.* Part II, *Commentary.* Heidelberg: Carl Winter. The most important English translation of the *Gāthās* and the *Yasna Haptanghaiti.*

Kellens, J., and E. Pirart. 1988, 1990, 1991. *Les textes vieil-avestiques.* Vol. I, *Introduction, texte et traduction.* Vol. II, *Répertoires grammaticaux et lexique.* Vol. III, *Commentaire.* Wiesbaden: Ludwig Reichert. A comprehensive study with a new interpretation of the *Gāthās.*

Molé, M. 1967. *La légende de Zoroastre selon les textes pehlevis.* Travaux de l'Institut d'Etudes Iraniennes de l'Université de Paris 3. Paris: C. Klincksieck.

Wahman, F. 1986. *Ardā Wirāz Nāmag: The Iranian 'Divina Commedia.'* Copenhagen: Curzon Press.

Williams, A. V. 1990. *The Pahlavi Rivāyat Accompanying the Dādestān ī Dēnīg.* 2 vols. The Royal Danish Academy of Sciences and Letters, Hist.-filosof. Meddelelser 60:2. Copenhagen: Munksgard.

Secondary Studies

Bidez, J., and F. Cumont. 1938. *Les mages hellénisés. I–II.* Paris: Société d'éditions "Les Belles lettres." A collection of Greek, Latin, and Syriac texts on Persian religion with useful comments and interpretations.

Boyce, M. 1984. "On the antiquity of Zoroastrian apocalyptic." *Bulletin of the School of Oriental and African Studies* 47:57–75. A short but penetrating survey of the development of Persian apocalypticism.

Boyce, M., and F. Grenet. 1991. *A History of Zoroastrianism. III, Zoroastrianism under Macedonian and Roman Rule.* Leiden: E. J. Brill. Deals with Zoroastrianism outside Iran proper during the Hellenistic period; includes important considerations of the question of Iranian influence on Judaism and Christianity as well as on Greco-Roman religions.

Cohn, N. 1993. *Cosmos, Chaos and the World to Come: The Ancient Roots of Apocalyptic Faith.* New Haven/London: Yale University Press. A broad account of the ancient Near Eastern roots of apocalyptic ideas, including Zoroastrianism.

Colpe, C. 1994. "Hystaspes." In *Reallexikon für Antike und Christentum,* 16:1057–82. Stuttgart: Hiersemann. Analyses in a lucid manner the intricate tradition-historical development of the Hystaspes texts.

de Jong, A. 1997. *Traditions of the Magi: Zoroastrianism in Greek and Latin Literature.* New York: E. J. Brill. Deals with the same topic as Bidez and Cumont but is more comprehensive with respect to Iranian traditions.

Duchesne-Guillemin, J. 1982. "Apocalypse juive et apocalypse iranienne." In *La Soteriologia dei Culti Orientali nell' Impero Romano,* edited by U. Bianchi and M. Vermaseren, 753–59. Leiden: E. J. Brill. Argues that the *Bahman Yašt* depends on the book of Daniel.

Flusser, D. 1982. "Hystaspes and John of Patmos." In *Irano-Judaica: Studies Relating to Jewish Contacts with Persian Culture throughout the Ages,* edited by Shaul Shaked, 12–75. Jerusalem: The Ben-Zvi Institute. A penetrating study of the "Oracles of Hystaspes" and its influence on the book of Revelation.

Hinnells, J. 1973. "The Zoroastrian Doctrine of Salvation in the Roman World: A Study of the Oracles of Hystaspes." In *Man and His Salvation,* edited by E. Sharpe and J. R. Hinnells, 125–48. Manchester: Manchester University Press. Argues that the savior figure of the Oracles is the Zoroastrian *saošyant.*

Hinze, A. 1995. "The Rise of the Saviour in the Avesta." In *Iran und Turfan: Beiträge Berliner Wissenschaftler, Werner Sundermann zum 60. Geburtstag gewidmet,* edited by Ch. Reck and P. Zieme, 77–98. Wiesbaden: Harrassowitz. Traces the development of the *saošyant* concept from the *Gāthās* to the Younger Avesta.

Hultgård, A. 1979. "Das Judentum in der hellenistisch-römischen Zeit und die iranische Religion—ein religionsgeschichtliches Problem." In *Aufstieg und Niedergang der römischen Welt* 19,1, edited by W. Haase, 512–90. Berlin/New York: de Gruyter. A detailed study of the question of Iranian influence on Judaism.

———. 1983. "Forms and Origins of Iranian Apocalypticism." In *Apocalypticism in the Mediterranean World and the Near East*, edited by D. Hellholm, 387–411. Tübingen: Mohr-Siebeck. Analyzes the forms in which Iranian apocalyptic materials are transmitted.

———. 1988. "Prêtres juifs et mages zoroastriens—influences religieuses à l'époque hellénistique." *Revue d'historie et de philosophie religieuses* 68:415–28. Points out the similarities between Jewish priesthood and the Magi, and traces Iranian influence in Jewish Zadokite writings.

———. 1995. "Mythe et histoire dans l'Iran ancien: Étude de quelques thèmes dans le Bahman Yašt." In *Apocalyptique iranienne et dualisme qoumrânien*, edited by G. Widengren, A. Hultgård, and M. Philonenko, 63–162. Paris: Maisonneuve. The study deals with apocalyptic and mythic themes in Zoroastrian tradition with an emphasis on the *Bahman Yašt*.

Kippenberg, H. G. 1978. "Die Geschichte der mittelpersischen apokalyptischen Traditionen." *Studia Iranica* 7:49–80. A useful survey with emphasis on the interaction of apocalypticism and sociopolitical history in the late Sassanian and early Islamic periods.

Philonenko, M. 1995. "La doctrine qoumrânienne des deux Esprits: Ses origines iranniennes et ses prolongements dans le judaïsme essénien et le christianisme antique." In *Apocalyptique iranienne et dualisme qoumrânien*, edited by G. Widengren, A. Hultgård, and M. Philonenko, 163–212. Paris: Maisonneuve. A comprehensive study of the influence of Persian dualism on Jewish and Christian traditions.

Shaked, S. 1994. *Dualism in Transformation: Varieties of Religion in Sasanian Iran*. London: School of Oriental and African Studies. Includes an important chapter of Zoroastrian eschatology in the Sassanian period.

Widengren, G. 1983. "Leitende Ideen und Quellen der iranischen Apokalyptik." In *Apocalypticism in the Mediterranean World and the Near East*, edited by D. Hellholm, 77–162. Tübingen: Mohr-Siebeck. A detailed account of Persian apocalyptic ideas that emphasizes their historical continuity.

Zaehner, R. C. 1972. *Zurvan: A Zoroastrian Dilemma, with a New Introduction by the Author*. New York: Biblo and Tannen. A comprehensive discussion of Zurvanism with edition and translation of important passages in the Pahlavi books.

3

The End of the World, of History, and of the Individual in Greek and Roman Antiquity

Hubert Cancik
University of Tübingen

THE TOPICS OF THE FOLLOWING ESSAY ARE THE ESCHATOLOGY and apocalypticism of the Greeks and Romans in classical antiquity. Their eschatology includes ideas (a) concerning the end of the individual and his/her continuation after death, (b) concerning the end of people, cities, kingdoms, humanity, and the possibility of their renaissance, and (c) concerning the eternity of the world or its annihilation through fire or water and possibly its renewal. The subject of this essay, then, includes cosmology, psychology (the doctrine of souls), and speculation about history from the flood of Deukalion down to the renewal of the world purified through fire (the Stoic *apokatastasis*).

These eschatological ideas appear in various forms and genres: as theories of physics, as mythical or historical narrative, as treatises *Concerning Death* or *Concerning the Soul,* in consolation writings *Concerning Sadness,* as philosophy of history, in collections of oracles, visionary accounts, as journeys to heaven or Hades, in teaching at initiation into mysteries. The symbolic teaching at initiation, the imagined journey to the moon, the accounts of those who had returned to life from a state of apparent death, reveal secrets that lie outside our experience and satisfy our curious fantasies and provide comfort when other tested methods fail to attain sure knowledge, or they give rise to fear and obedience.

This study thus concerns the most important eschatological materials and apocalyptic forms of Greek and Roman culture from Homer until the end of eternal Rome. In the process, not only those subjects, arguments, images, and schemata that would be incorporated into Christianity, mediated in part through Hellenistic Judaism, will be introduced but also those analogous and compensatory ideas that have been brought forward in politics and history apart from mythology and religion, and also the alternative concepts of the indestructibility of the world, the unending duration of history, and the divinity of the soul.

Texts concerning destruction, decline, and passing away are abundant in the fine literature of the Greeks—their epics, their wisdom, and their natural philosophy. With Homer, the end of Troy (*Iliou persis*) becomes a paradigm for the downfall of a state, people, or dynasty. Hesiod imagines a history of humanity; he portrays it as a decline from a golden race and prophesies the iron generation. The oldest sentence in western European "philosophy" establishes the theme "rise" and "fall" (*genesis, phthora*) with the help of the terms "necessity, justice, order, and time":

> And the source of coming-to-be for existing things is that into which destruction, too, happens, according to necessity; for they pay penalty and retribution to each other for their injustice according to the assessment of Time. (Anaximander [ca. 550 B.C.E.] A9 DK = 110 KRS)

Each of the three texts is radical in its own way. They became paradigms of Greek culture and have had their effect down into our own time. The concept *phthora* (*corruptio, interitus, finis*) is defined by Aristotle as a change into non-being (*hē eis to mē on metabolē*);[1] it is handed down through the cosmology of all schools until the end of antiquity and is taken up by Christians and Muslims, theologians and philosophers. Hesiod's teaching of the metal generations becomes in Ovid a sequence of world ages and the beginning of a "universal history." The sibyl who heralded the downfall of Troy, that "the day will be . . . ," was continued in the prediction of the downfall of Rome in the sibylline books of the Jews and Christians, although Virgil had already proclaimed the realm of Augustus to be "dominion without end" (*imperium sine fine*).

The eschatological material and apocalyptic forms were also included in the systematics of ancient theology. In the sixteen books of his *Theological Antiquities* Varro wrote about the "official (state) religion" of the Romans. The political theology (*theologia politikē*) is only one part of the threefold theology. The natural theology (*theologia physikē*) forms the philosophical basis of the exposition (book 1; Varro, *Antiquitates rerum divinarum*, frag. 6). Here he entertains the question whether the world is created or uncreated, whether it will pass away or endure, whether the gods came into being at a certain time or always existed, whether the soul is divine and eternal or is dissolved after death (Varro, *Ant.*, frag. 8; cf. frag. 23 §18; frag. 19). If the soul's fire leaves a person, he/she dies; thus also will the world die, if its fire passes out of it through lightning (*mundus emoritur*, "the world dies"; Varro, *Ant.*, frag. 23; frag. 29; cf. Tertullian, *Apologeticum* 38; *De anima*, frags. 773, 791 SVF). Thus, cosmological and individual eschatology explain each other.

These speculations of *theologia naturalis* are taken up in various places of the *theologia civilis*. In the teaching on the gods at the end of the work, inquiry is made as to the appropriate gods for birth, marriage, sickness, and death. Among those is Viduus, who separates souls from their bodies; Libitina, the goddess of death; and Nenia: "in her care are those whose extreme (final) time is at hand" (Varro, *Ant.*, frag. 158ff., frag. 162 [in Arnobius]). The grave and cult of the dead are also handled (book 7: *de locis religiosis*). Orcus is mentioned here, Ceres and Proserpina and the Eleusinian mysteries, which communicate "a better hope for death."[2]

Varro rejects mythical theology (*theologia fabularis*). It remains noteworthy, however, that he handles theogony (frags. 8, 19) but that he never—as far as the few fragments and paraphrases of later tradition allow us to see—discusses an end of the gods. Varro feared "that the gods would perish," but he attributed this not to the destruction of Rome or the demise of the cosmos but rather to the irreligiosity of the citizens (Varro, *Ant.*, I.2, in Augustine: *se timere ne pereant [dei], non incursu hostili, sed civium negligentia*).

Greek mythology developed no twilight of the gods. The succession of the gods ended with Zeus (see Hesiod, *Theogony*; see pp. 103–4 below). He, with the help of Prometheus, assured that the order Uranos–Kronos–Zeus could not be extended. A rebellion of disempowered deities, the escape of the giants from the underworld was imagined, but not as an episode of a mythological eschatology.[3] There was no analogy to the Antichrist, to a battle of the angels. The chaos dragon, which rises again from the abyss, is an age-old mythical monster, but he has no place at the end of Greek myth. Therefore there is no analogy to the returning Elijah or to a suffering or warring Messiah, despite the cult of the emperor and a certain ruler mysticism.

Correspondingly, among the Greek and Roman philosophers there are indeed impressive texts that relate cosmic eschatology and the death of the individual (Seneca, *Ad Marciam*; see pp. 115–16 below). To my knowledge, however, the Greeks and Romans have not suggested a dramatic scenario like the one with which Augustine introduced the last things in the last books of his *Civitas Dei*. A full systematic exposition regarding the end of the world, resurrection, judgment, damnation, and salvation, such as is developed in the supplement to the third part of *Summa Theologiae* of Aquinas (questions 69–99), is not imaginable in Varro's *Summa* of Roman theology.

⪥THE BASIC CONCEPTS

Eschatology and History of Philosophy, Divination and Apocalypticism

The concepts with which the facts and texts of classical antiquity shall be comprehended here have been developed in modernity, predominantly by Christian theologians. Their applicability to classical and non-Christian phenomena must be considered. The word "eschatology" is a creation of Protestant theology (Philipp H. Friedlieb, *Eschatologia* [1644] and Abraham Calov, *Systema* [1655–1677]). The words "apocalypticism" (F. Lücke [1791–1855]) and "theology of history" (beginning of the twentieth century) are later (Cancik 1990, 2:491–500). The word "eschatology" will be used here as a collective term for the ideas that Greeks and Romans developed concerning the death and life to come of individuals, the world, people, and states. Eschatology can be more or less mythical, scientific, philosophical, or religious. Cosmological eschatology is the counterpart of cosmogony, whose motifs it often takes up. It is striking, particularly because of their fabulous creativity, that the Greeks lack a mythical eschatology.

The word "apocalypticism" is used here for a secret or revelatory literature. The contents of this literature and its use ("spiritual opposition," political propaganda, legitimization of rulership, education) are not determined by the expression "apocalypticism." The identity of the revealer figure is specific to the culture (muses, gods, Charon, Hermes, sibyl).

The types of revelation are manifold: epiphanies of muses or gods; consultation of the dead; dream and vision; the short oracle of Pythia or the longer sayings of the sibyl. They are described with the ancient collective name "divination" (mantic art). This religio-scientific term includes everything that is undertaken to clarify the near or further future or to reveal the secrets from the past: all natural and technical divination, from lot and dream to oracle and prophecy. "Divination literature" is the technical, professional writing and, in a broader sense, like apocalyptic literature, the "fine" literature that employs the themes and motifs of divination as a framework or subject to an especially high degree.

Among the classical historical writers and philosophers there are general sayings about time, about social activities of people, about the basis and possibilities of human societies, and about history. It is known that the quality of the historical process itself and the way in which humanity is aware of its history have greatly changed in modernity and through the influence of Christianity. Nevertheless, the modern expressions "philosophy of history" and "theology of history" can be properly employed to describe what we find in antiquity.[4] In this essay the terms represent the speculative, interpretative presentation of historical events or sequences of events by means of religion and/or philosophy and science. The philosophy and theology of history tend toward general claims; they recognize and establish "meaning, value, goals." Theology of history is therefore not identical with eschatology, but eschatology, or its negation, can be part of a theology of history. Ideas such as promise, the will of the gods, fate, guidance by the gods, fulfillment, mission (*dux fatalis*), trial, progress/decline/goal are in principle possible without an explicit theological or mythological eschatology.

The End as Boundary

In antiquity, as opposed to modern times, the absolute end of a person, group, or cosmos is seldom imagined. Usually the end is imagined as a boundary and consists of a crossing over into an "otherworld," which is qualitatively, "ontologically," a "wholly other." Death is an end or a transition: *finis aut transitus.* At the least, the "shadow" of a person remains in the underworld. A realm, a city, or an army will be destroyed "from the ground up," "with the root," and "extinguished," but usually something is left over, out of which a new beginning arises. The sons of Priam are dead, but Aeneas escapes; Troy is destroyed, but Rome is its continuation (*Troia rediviva*), and from Troy there remains "immortal fame for future generations" (*Sibylline Oracles* 3.418). Catastrophic floods repeatedly annihilate the Greek culture, but a few Greeks remain up in the mountains and they begin again. This cosmos will soon be burned down in a purifying fire: but a divine element will remain and a new cosmos can come into being. These eschatologies are "relative"; they seek a "balance" between "being" and "movement," "stability" (*identitas*) and change (development, progress).

Assertions about an eternal return of the same identical thing are rare, playful experiments in thought. Assertions about the absolute end in "nothing" are rare and mostly negated. Epicurus and his school thought through this argument about individual eschatology in an exceptionally radical way: "If death is present, then we are no longer" (Epicurus, *Epistles* 3 [Diogenes

Laertius 124]; cf. Lucretius 3.840). Neither spirit nor soul is immortal; there is no underworld; the myths about judgment and punishment after death should be taken allegorically as referring to life (Lucretius 3.978ff.). But even Lucretius fights against the fear of death insofar as he proves the eternity of the atom and suppresses the end of the person (Lucretius 1.215ff.). The formula of the atomists—"nothing passes into nothing" (*nihil ad nihilum interit* [cf. 1.216])—shows that an absolute end could be fundamentally and radically conceived in antiquity. The fact that Lucretius presents this reflection in many verses and at the very beginning of his teaching, even before the introduction to atoms (1.215–64), shows how important this principle is to him, although it cannot help to comfort one about the end of the person either emotionally or logically (cf. Epicurus, frag. 297 [Usener] in Cicero, *De divinatione* 2.50.103).

MODERN INTEREST IN THE SUBJECT

Already in the nineteenth century, classical philologists studied how revelations concerning the last things among the Greeks and Romans were developed and transmitted. W. S. Teuffel wrote about "Homeric Theology and Eschatology" in 1848 (see Teuffel 1871, 1–44); Erwin Rohde about "Psyche" in 1890–94 (Rohde 1925); A. Dieterich his *Nekyia* in 1893; Eduard Norden on the classical antecedents of the *Apocalypse of Peter* (1893) and "The Eschatology of the Sixth Book [of Virgil's *Aeneid*] and Its Sources" (1903).[5] Yet it was the historians of religion and nonconformist theologians who provided a new clarity and political relevance for the subject, beyond that of general folkloric and humanistic interest. Franz Overbeck (1837–1905) researched early Christian eschatology in order to undermine the optimism of progress to which the "culture Protestants" and members of the educated class of his time had fallen prey (Overbeck 1919). His friend Friedrich Nietzsche (1844–1900), professor of classical philology in Basel, created the opposite construct for the same purpose: the teaching of an "eternal return of the same." This construct was indeed stimulated by motifs of Greek cosmology, yet it was certainly in no way the quintessence of Greek spiritual life. A comparison between Jewish and Greek religion and philosophy that proceeds from this construct necessarily leads to distortion. The favorite image used in this kind of comparison, line and circle—"goal-oriented thought, history, eschatology" versus "static idea of being, nature, eternal return"—misrepresents the historical facts on both sides (Cancik 1995, chap. 8).

It was the emigrants from old Europe, victims of the political and racist policies of the Third Reich, who especially experienced and reflected on the catastrophic form of history, its fundamental discontinuity, and its asynchronism (Walter Benjamin, Ernst Bloch, Karl Löwith, Jacob Taubes). "Break" and "rift" are their images for history, the "extension period" that still might be given before annihilation, the "postponement" of catastrophe (W. Benjamin [1892–1940]). They found an attentive public among the losers in their homeland, who crawled out of the rubble of their cities or returned home severely injured. In this country, destined to become the battlefield of a threatening nuclear war, the question, at least, of what comes after the annihilation, what is "apocalypse," was very plausible.

The questions, observations, and theses that philosophy and theology since Overbeck and Nietzsche have presented about time, the eschaton, and history in Judaism and Christianity have also influenced the image of classical antiquity. The "Occidental eschatology" (*Abendländische Eschatologie*) of Jacob Taubes (1923–1987), a highly ambitious and, because of the historical backdrop, influential book, is a good example of this. Taubes's assertions about antiquity repeat the common clichés: Greece is "the eye of the world," Israel "the ear of the world." History is denied to the old cultures on the Nile and in Mesopotamia: they are numb, petrified; their life fulfills itself in the "eternal return of the same." This picture of the Orient and antiquity is shaped by the influence of Nietzsche, both direct and mediated (perhaps through Franz Rosenzweig). Only the evaluation is controverted. Repetition and circularity, a life spellbound in nature and myth, nature defined as "blood and soil": this is how the land of the Greeks seemed to him. Taubes denies antiquity the consciousness of time (*chronos, kairos, aiōn*) and history (*pragmata, historia, mnemosynē*), mind (*logos, nous*), and justice (*dikē*); he reduces its culture to magic, eros, and nature mysticism. To him, the Greek religion shrinks to only nature gods; and these, again following Nietzsche, to Dionysus. This can then be easily refuted, for Dionysus is only "the most sacred of the Baal gods" (Taubes 1991, 11, 15; the same holds true for his assertions about Rome and late antiquity). The relationship between "Israel" and "Greece" is frozen into a sterile antithesis.

Against that type of polarization and reductionism, this study will present the most important eschatological material and its articulation through divination. It will point out the analogies and genetic relationships to Christianity and sketch the compensatory and alternative ideas that were developed in the Greek and Roman culture.

Divination

Signs

The gods care for humans (*cura deorum*); they have plans, wills, and foresight (*boulē, consilium, pronoia, providentia*); they send signs (*sēmeia, signa*), that admonish, warn, or announce inevitable disaster. The signs are in various forms and are not easy to interpret; they are like riddles (*ainigma*) and multivalent (*ambiguitas*). The truth is hidden (*kryptesthai, abditus, occultus*); the oracle gives only hints (*sēmainei;* cf. Heraclitus 204, 208, 244, 245 KRS). The god gives the prophetess "a light in the soul directed toward the future." But the words, the meter, the expressions are of a mortal woman (Plutarch, *De Pythiae Oraculis* 397C). Thus, humans retain the possibility of interpretation, freedom, and error. The revelations are either given by gods or sought actively by humans. The interpreters work in cult centers or travel as "wandering laborers." Some, like the sibyls, dispense their sayings unsolicited. The subjects of the questions are everyday problems (Will my runaway slave return?), the founding of cities or cults, the outcome of a war (You will destroy a great kingdom; Herodotus 1.53.3), and the nature of God, soul, and world.

The proliferation of signs of misfortune gives rise to fear that "eternal night" will darken the world and the hope for a savior: "do not prevent this young man from coming to the aid of the overthrown world" (Virgil, *Georgica* 1.500f., 468ff., 493). In the schema of question and answer and with an instruction discourse, Apollo answers the question whether the soul endures after death or is dissolved.[6] The visionary women of Dodona, as the first women, say: "Zeus was, Zeus is, Zeus will be, O great Zeus!" (Pausanias 10.12.5).

The secrets of nature (*secreta naturae*) and the future are also revealed in dreams. Scipio experiences the downfall of Carthage in a dream as if from an oracle. The dream is at the same time a "vision," for he sees the heavenly places (Macrobius, *Commentary on Somnium Scipionis* 1.3). All forms of divination, often fictionalized, are incorporated into higher literature: at the end of a philosophical *logos* comes the dream or myth; historical narrative is replete with a series of signs and oracles (Antisthenes of Rhodes); Pausanias not only describes the oracle of Trophonius as an eyewitness but reports the descent into the cave as personal witness from his own experience (9.39); the messenger report of the prophecies of Cassandra on the downfall of Troy and the rise of Rome fills an entire scroll. (For an overview of the forms of Roman revelatory literature, see Cancik 1983, §4.)

Fate

The will of the gods (*boulēsis, boulē, ethelein, voluntas*) makes decisions by which they themselves are bound. Once a god decides freely by himself, then he must always obey: *semper paret, semel iussit* (Seneca, *De providentia* 5.8). The order of the world must be fixed and predictable, but the freedom of humanity demands small exceptions. The divine signs were used in order to guard against destruction or to ward it off through sacrifice (*avertere* [Macrobius, *Comm.* 1.7.1f.]). According to Etruscan-Roman tradition, the Fates wrote Roman history on metal tablets, long before the founding of Rome (Ovid, *Metamorphoses* 15.807–15; see Cancik 1983, §3.2). No one can change this preexisting history, not even Jupiter. But there were already many opinions about the relationship between Zeus/Jupiter and Necessity, the Fates, and the *fatum* (Servius, on Virgil, *Aeneid* 1.39, 258, 398). Nevertheless there would be continual attempts to change the words of fate; the compromise between the desire for hard certainty and for a little more freedom is the teaching of "postponement." The "Etruscan books" teach that a delay (*dilatio*) of imminent evil can be solicited from Jupiter and destiny. There were rituals through which destiny (*fata*) could be "postponed" (*differri*) for ten years, but could not be changed. Thus Lucretius (5.107) can ask for a postponement of the world fire: "that the guiding fortune deflect it far away from us."

The Otherworld: Katabasis and Necromancy

The surest way to secure news from the otherworld (heaven or netherworld) is a journey there or a report from the dead who return. The journey into the otherworld, whether under or over the earth, can be real or mythic or fictive-fantastic. In the classical world, numerous caves provide an entrance into the netherworld: Plutonia, Acherontica, Charoneia in Acharaka (Asia Minor), Ephyra and Lebadeia (Greece), and Lake Averno (Italy). Souls ascend, as in Homer's conjuration of the dead (Nekyia: *Odyssey* book 11); heroes descend (*kata-basis*), like Orpheus, Hercules, and Theseus. Believers seeking help either go themselves into oracular caves or are represented vicariously by priests. The "Mythology of Hades" (Diodorus 1.2) describes the topography of the netherworld, the judgment, the Elysium, the penitents, the "infernal spirits," king and queen in the realm of the dead. In addition, there is often teaching about morality, the structure of the world, the nature of the soul and in some cases their rebirth (*palin-genesia*) as well as about the use of mystery initiations, which promise the initiates a better lot in the hereafter. All the motifs of "Hades mythology" are already represented in pre-Hellenistic Greek literature. Only a little of it has survived, often transformed, in the genres of higher literature (Aeschylus, *Telephos;* Aristophanes, *The Frogs;* Plato, *Phaedo*). The rich and allusive parodies of Lucian of Samosata provide the critical reader with a good introduction into this tradition (Lucian, *Verae Historiae, Kataplous, Nekyomantia, Icaromenippus, Dialogi Mortuorum*).

The netherworldly oracle of Trophonius at Lebadeia (Boeotia) is active from ancient times down to the Roman Empire. Three extensive testimonials of higher literature allow a reconstruction of the site, the time needed for a consultation, and the various rites, which were evidently not without danger, as well as an examination of various kinds of texts that were composed in and for this cult. The three witnesses, Plutarch (*De genio Socratis* 590B–592E), Pausanias (9.39), and Philostratus (*Vita Apollonii* 4.24; 8.19f.) are in different ways also personally involved (see Betz 1983, 577–97). Pausanias made use of the cult himself; Plutarch's brother Lamprias was a priest in Lebadeia (Plutarch, *De defectu oraculorum* 431C); Philostratus wrote the biography of Apollonius of Tyana (beginning of the third century C.E.) commissioned by Queen Iulia Domna for education and the promotion of the Pythagorean life. Trophonius confirmed the Pythagorean teaching for Apollonius, in that he gave him a book that included this teaching. The oracle teaches about souls and demons, gives visions of the otherworld and prophecies of the future (*ta mellonta*) and the life of believers. The teaching is presented as a lecture and in the schema of question and answer. After ascending from the underground chamber, the believer is set on the "throne of Mnemosyne" and questioned by the priests. He is still in shock, does not recognize either himself or his environment and must be taken care of by his relatives. The written recording of the revelation on a tablet is an important part of the ritual (Pausanias 39.14). Pausanias (39.13) assures us that even laughter returns to the believer who performs everything correctly.

In addition to these impressive accounts, there are almost contemporary, honest reflections of enlightened philosophers and the confessions of experienced politicians. They believe that the "Hades mythology" is a "fiction," whether detrimental (so the Epicureans) or supportive of piety and justice (Diodorus 1.2.2). Polybius, the politician and historian, praises the extravagance and pomp with which the Roman nobles pursue their cult of the dead and their religion overall (6.56): they do this "for the sake of the masses." For the state does not consist of sages; rather, the masses are thoughtless, unlawful, irrational, violent. One must "hold them together with vague fear and theater of this kind." For this reason the elders introduced into the masses the ideas of gods and "ideas about things in Hades." But Cicero already considered the opinion that in the netherworld punishments were prepared for the impious as merely "probable" (*De inventione rhetorica* 1.46). Hardly one old woman still "believes" (*credere*), as before, in the monsters down under (Cicero, *De natura deorum* 2.5); only small children "believe" in the spirits of the dead and the realm of the king of the netherworld (Juvenal 3.149ff.).

The Sibyl(s)

According to the etymology of the ancients, the name "sibyl" means, "advice or will of God" (*theoboulē*) and denotes a certain type of ecstatic divination with the following characteristics: (a) The sibyls are historical or fictitious free women (Varro assembled a "canon" of ten sibyls [*Ant.,* book 4, cf. Lactantius, *Divine Institutes* 1.6]). (b) Unlike the Pythia from Delphi, they have no firm connection to a cult center. (c) Their visions and sayings, inspired by Apollo, are spontaneous, not given by request, and are thus, so to speak, a "free prophecy." (d) The context of their messages is often disaster and "ending," the outbreak of war, natural catastrophes, demise of rulers and realms, the sequence of epochs: "the last era has already come" (Virgil, *Fourth Eclogue*). (e) In comparison to the often very short answers of the cultic oracles (*responsa*), their sayings or songs (*logoi, carmina*) are comparatively long; they are written in dactylic hexameters, collected in books and handed down. The Cumean sibyl, according to Varro (*Ant.,* frag. 56c; cf. Tibullus 2.5) offered nine "books" to King Tarquinius Priscus (206 B.C.E.) "in which there were sayings of destiny (*fata*) and remedies (*remedia*)," that is, rituals, which avert the wrath of the gods by "placating" them, or at least "delay" the destiny (see p. 92 above).

The earliest certain witness to the Sibyl (Heraclitus [ca. 500 B.C.E.]) names the most important characteristics of this type: "The Sibyl with raving mouth, uttering things mirthless, unadorned and unperfumed; reaches over a thousand years with her voice, through the god" (245 KRS).[7] Heraclitus recognizes her inspiration through Apollo, the ecstatic enthusiasm, the negative character ("un-") and the macrohistorical, "millennial" orientation of her prophecy. The scolding of the audience (readers), the threat even against people in high station, the far-reaching overview of history, the legitimation through the god and the "darkness" of her works in keeping with her holy mania, are all set forms and topics of the later sibyls as well.

Heraclitus's source is probably the self-representation of the (Ephesian?)

sibyl, as she is also known through later sibylline sayings. In the famous form of "I am" predication, the sibyl of Marpessos (Troy) reveals her special nature: "I am an intermediate being, from a mortal and a goddess" (Pausanias 10.12.1). Also the Delphic sibyl legitimizes herself as a mediator of revelations in a self-portrayal of more than twenty verses. In a hymn to herself she predicts her own death: she will not cease to prophesy, however, but will change herself into air and the call of the bird, into the grass eaten by the sacrificial animals out of whose innards "the future will be revealed" to humanity (Phlegon, *Makrobioi,* FGH 257 F37; Plutarch, *De pyth. or.* 9, 398C–D). The sibyl, who must predict the suffering (*pathē*) of others without finding credence, will be "freed" from a life that was painful enough only after ten generations. The change into a general mantic capability is, on the one hand, Stoic natural mysticism, and, on the other hand, a continuation of her unfortunate existence.

The sibyl's view of history is a sequence of catastrophes: the invasion of the barbarian army, destruction and resettlement of cities, fall of rulers and realms (Plutarch, *De pyth. or.* 9). She was already supposed to have predicted the destruction of Troy and the destruction that Helen would bring to Asia and Europe (Pausanias 10.12.2; Apollodorus, FGH 422 F1; *Sib. Or.* 3.205–6, 401ff.). These sayings, which span centuries and continents, would later be set forth in the Judeo-Christian sibyls with prophecies about the "Orient and Occident." In addition to general and mythical statements there are concrete references to specific natural catastrophes, wars, and rulers: the temple of Apollo in Delphi will be destroyed; Vesuvius will erupt; the king will die (with reference to Titus, who died in 81 C.E.; see Parke 1988, 110, 112f., 119).

These prophecies hardly differ from the oracles of the muses or Pythia (see Pausanias 10.9; Plutarch, *De pyth. or.* 6–9). Often they are part of direct political propaganda or spiritual resistance. The prophecies about the end of dynasties are of longer term. Out of these develop macrohistorical overviews about the sequence of kingdoms. Thus, the sibyls were said to have predicted the end of the Lydian kingdom (Parke 1988, 60–61) and the end of the Macedonian dynasty (Pausanias 7.8.5). Their successors were the Persians and the Romans. The Julian-Claudian dynasty ended with Nero; the sibyl had predicted: "As the last of the Aeneads a matricide will reign" (Cassius Dio 62.18). After three times three hundred years a civil war would annihilate the Romans (Cassius Dio 57.18; 62.16). Animosity against Rome elicited a wealth of prophecies already in the Seleucid period. These were taken over and furthered in part by Jewish sibyls (Fuchs 1938). A leader would come from the east, from Asia (here the "Orient" is not meant, but the Seleucid Greeks). He would lead a fight between Asia and Italy—a continuation of the ancient battle of the continents (Asia/Europe; Orient/Occident); then the "end of Roman rule" would come (Antisthenes of Rhodes, FGH 257 F 35).

An accident of transmission preserved one of the *Sibylline Oracles* on the Roman side which promised "eternal" rule to the Romans. The sibyl invites the Romans to celebrate the *saeculum* celebration (*sacrum saeculare*) in 17 B.C.E. and specifies the required rites in many verses. At the end it reads: "These things must always remain in your senses and memory, then the entire Italian land and the entire land of the Latins will always bear the yoke on their neck under your scepter" (Zosimus, *Historia nova* 2.6). Augustus began the celebration and thus secured the Roman rule for a further 110 years.

Cults

Death, Afterlife, Mysteries

The last things of a person's life were regulated in ancient burial rites and in the cult of the dead (Kurtz and Boardman 1971; Toynbee 1971). They were anticipated by the mourners as their own future and mimetically reflected in the mourning rituals. Through the funerary symbolism of graves and through the stories about the netherworld and its horrors, joys, punishments, ghosts, and demons, the afterlife becomes vivid, anthropomorphic: a distant, mythic land. Urns and sarcophagi were decorated with plants and blossoms; sea creatures in turbulent water pointed to the boundary of this life and to other forms of life beyond: "Thus richness overwhelms death."[8] Pre- and paraphilosophical speculations consider the characteristics of the soul, the manner of its continuance: Is it a "shadow" without memory or consciousness or a particle of indestructible divine substance? Can it reincarnate itself in descendants or does it dissolve into the All?

Many Greeks and not a few Romans could acquire pictorial and emotional preparation for the last things through the mystery cults. According to Cicero, who indeed was himself initiated, in the Eleusinian mysteries "we truly have recognized the foundations (the beginnings) of life and not only received a reason to live with joy, but also to die with a better hope" (*De legibus* 2.14.36):

> illis mysteriis . . . re vera principia vitae cognovimus neque solum cum laetitia vivendi rationem accepimus sed etiam cum spe meliore moriendi.

In the mysteries, the last things become a part of a comprehensive, richly symbolic teaching of "life" which mediates "knowledge." This knowledge is "fundamental" and "universal," for the mysteries of Eleusis are, as part of the Demeter religion, "a *religio* common to all people" (Cicero, *In Verrem* 2.4.114f.).

The rites and speeches, symbols and myths which brought knowledge, joy, and hope to the participants are handed down in only a few fragments (Burkert 1987a). For Eleusis, the symbolism of sowing and harvest, the experience of fasting and plenty, darkness and light is attested for certain. Eschatology is also contained in the myth of the rape of the Kore. The daughter of Demeter and Zeus was led into the netherworld, long sought by her mother, and finally released for a half year into the upper world by the god of the dead. Musaeus or his son Eumolpus, progenitor of the Eumolpids, the priests of Eleusis, or Orpheus, serve as "mediators of revelation" in the mysteries (Graf 1974, 18f., 28ff.). They are the ultimate authors of this poetry of the descent of a goddess into the world of the dead (*kat-hodos*) and her return (*an-hodos*). Even before the Trojan War, according to Hellenistic scholars, this poem was known.[9]

The mysteries are—next to the cult of the dead and necromancy—the most important means for the formation and transmission of ideas about the netherworld in institutionalized Greek religion. A passage in Plutarch clarifies this connection between death, netherworld, and initiation into the mysteries:

> Here (on earth) it (that is, the soul) is ignorant, unless it is already at the point of death. Then, however, it has an experience like those who are initiated into the great mysteries; therefore, the word is similar to the word and the thing is similar to the thing: *teleutân-teleísthai,* die—be initiated. First a wandering in error, an arduous running around, a fearful walking in the dark, which finds no goal; then before the end itself, all the monstrosity, shudders, trembling, sweat, and astonishment. After this a wonderful light comes to meet (them), pure places and meadows receive them with voices and dances and the celebration of holy sounds and venerable apparitions: amidst this moves the already perfected and initiated, having been freed and released. Crowned, he celebrates the rites and mingles with holy, pure men; from there he looks at the uninitiated, impure crowd of those living here, which, in much mud and fog are trodden underfoot and pushed together, and in the fear of death cling to their ills since they do not believe in the good things of the afterlife. (Plutarch, frag. 178, in Stobaeus)

Bacchic Eschatology

Our knowledge of Bacchic eschatology was greatly enriched by a text on two gold plates found a few years ago in a sarcophagus of Pelinna (Thessaly).[10] "Now you have died and now you have come into being, O thrice happy one, on this same day": With this paradoxical blessing (*makarismos*) the text begins. The normal valuation is turned around; life begins after death. "On this same day"—that is, the day of the real death. The day would be anticipated in the initiation of the participants.

In the netherworld the dead should say to Persephone, as it says on the gold plates: "that Bacchius himself has freed you." The statement is meant to influence the judgment of the Queen of the Dead. From what had the Bacchic Dionysus Lysius freed his participants, who could bear the name of their god "Bacchius"? The Orphic anthropology answers: from the transgression of the Titans, our sinful forefathers. They had killed, divided, and eaten the child Dionysus; Zeus had burned them with lightning and formed humanity out of their remains.[11] The Titans' heinous crime against Dionysus was their "original sin," a "primal guilt," from which the mystery initiation in the name of this very Dionysus freed them: therefore he is called "Dionysus the liberator (Liber)." The dead person awaits a transformation into a god (gold plate A4 from Thurioi); he will partake in a symposium of the blessed.

The eschatological expectations and their anthropological and theological assumptions are developed in many genres and forms of "Orphic" literature, in hymns and testaments (*diathēkē*), in epics concerning the descent of Orpheus into the underworld (*katabasis*) and concerning the genesis of the gods (*theogony;* West 1983, 1ff.). These kinds of texts would be read to the initiates (LSAM 84). The new tablets from Pelinna show how close the connection was between this teaching and the cult that was practiced in the mystery communities. Doctrine and initiation reach their goal in burial rites: a gold plate with a summary of their belief was laid in the grave with the dead. This is the *Sitz im Leben* for Bacchic eschatology. (For the eschatology of other mystery cults, see Burkert 1987a).

Epochs and Rituals

NEW TIME. The history of great periods of time, the succession of rule in heaven and the epochs of humanity, schemata of rise and fall of people, kingdoms, and cities were all prophesied by the sibyls, poeticized in theogonies and anthropogonies, told by historians in their universal histories, or pressed into chronological schemata ("the four-kingdom motif"). The founding of cities was also remembered in the cult and connected with prayers for continuance. At the new year the vows for the past year were released and new ones were made for the coming year (Alföldi 1965–66, 53–87). The downfall of the old, the transition to the new year, to a new ruler and a new dynasty took place with the help of manifold rites of passage. In addition, greater periods of time were structured ritually: the *lustrum,* a five-year period, the round periods of rulers (*quinquennalia, decennalia, vicennalia*) (M. Graf 1950). In the transition "between times" there is a chaotic moment, when, in special moments, time stops and history makes an *ep-oché:* then the "new time" truly begins. This had happened, as was later shown, at the birth of the emperor Augustus.

The cities of the province of Asia decided in the year 9 C.E. to begin a new era, backdated to the birth of Augustus (63 B.C.E.).[12] His birthday (September 23 or 24) became the beginning of the new year. The first month received the name "Caesar." The resolution was written on a stele of white stone and set up in the temple of the "Goddess Roma and Augustus" and in the sanctuaries dedicated to Caesar in the individual cities. The basis for the resolution connects cosmic, theological, and political aspects. The cosmos would have been annihilated if the Caesar had not been born; this occurred because of divine will and providence. He put an end to war and brought freedom; he surpasses all earlier and future benefactors: he is the "savior" (*sōtēr*). The birthday of this god was the beginning of the good news (*euangelia*) for the cosmos. The fears to which the demise of the Roman republic had given rise were overcome by Augustus.[13]

Through so many rites and vows at the New Year, at the beginning of a new half-decade (five years) or a *saeculum,* protected against the "end of the dominion," Rome in the year 248 C.E. finally looked back to a thousand-year rule. The "birthday of the city" (*natalis urbis*) was commemorated on the feast of Parilia (April 21; Ovid, *Fasti* 4.721ff.; 807ff.). Since 121 C.E. it was connected to the cult of "Rome and Venus," which Hadrian set up in the enormous temple on the Velia over the Roman forum. On his gold coins were printed *saeculum aureum* and, in an oval frame, *Aion,* the divine fullness of time; he held the zodiac in his right hand and the phoenix in his left (British Museum Catalogue [=BMC] Emp. III p. 278 no. 312). The accumulation of cosmic and mythic symbolism denotes not "the end of dominion" but "eternal Rome" (*Roma aeterna*).[14] Its cult was attached to Hadrian's temple and recalled the "birth" of the city, the "founder" (*conditor*) Romulus, and the rituals at the founding of the city. The thousand-year celebration of eternal Rome by the emperor Philippus Arabs (244–249) again proclaimed a "new epoch" (*saeculum novum*) in a highly uncertain period (CIL VI 6221.10.20). Other calculations, however, show exactly how ominously a "tenth" epoch could be interpreted.

THE FESTIVAL OF THE SAECULUM AND THE FALL OF ROME. The teaching of the "natural" and "civil" epochs (*saecula*) was developed by the Etruscans in their *libri rituales* and taken over by the Romans (Censorinus, *De die natali,* chapter 17). A natural *saeculum* is the highest age that a human can attain (a hundred years according to Varro *De lingua latina* 6.11). A civil *saeculum* begins with the founding of a city or a state; it lasts as long as one member of the founding generation lives. Then the new epoch begins.

Because one cannot always unequivocally determine the end of a *saeculum,* gods send signs. The Etruscans observed these signs and wrote them down. The Etruscan historians (*Tuscae historiae*) knew how many *saecula* were given to a people and how many had already passed. Thus they could calculate ahead of time the end of their own people. Ten *saecula* were given to the Etruscan people.

The middle of the first century B.C.E. corresponded to the eighth *saeculum;* the ninth and tenth ages were yet to come: "If they were exhausted, it would be the end of the Etruscan name." The comet that appeared after Caesar's murder was interpreted by the *haruspex* Volcatius as a sign for the end of the ninth and the beginning of the tenth age (Servius on Virgil, *Eclogue* 9.47).

These speculations are the context for the theological history in and behind Virgil's *Fourth Eclogue* (compiled 40 B.C.E.). A "last age" has come (*ultima aetas*): it is the tenth, says the ancient commentator Servius. It should not be the end of the "Roman name," but the beginning of the Apollonian time, a "dominion without end" (*imperium sine fine*). The triumphalist sound in this promise of an imperialism qualified by justice and piety resounds against the fear that the downfall of the Roman republic engendered. In his celebration of the *saeculum,* Caesar Augustus ritually represented this theology of history.

These were, according to an ancient calculation, the fifth games; they took place in the 737th year after the founding of the city. In the middle of the third century C.E., the tenth *saeculum* was reached (Censorinus, *De die natali* 17.15), an ominously round figure. It was, however, not clear or not known how many *saecula* were allotted to the Roman people. The methods for calculating were countless and contradictory. But behind each calculation stands the question of the "postponement."[15] Varro passed on the method according to which a famous augur, Vettius, had calculated the end of the dominion: Romulus saw twelve vultures during the founding of the city; the realm would remain twelve hundred years (Censorinus, *De die natali* 17.15). In the fifth century of Christian time, therefore, the end of Roman rule must occur. This end is not the end of history overall and not part of a general downfall of the world: for the fullness of time (*aevum*) is immeasurable, the past has no beginning, the future has no end: *praeteritum initio caret, exitu futurum* (Censorinus, *De die natali* 16.4).

Paradoxically, the Greek historian Zosimus at the end of the fifth century C.E. based the downfall of the Roman Empire in his time on the fact that the *saeculum* games had not been celebrated by the emperors Licinius and Constantine, although in their third consulate (313 C.E.) "the time of 110 years was fulfilled" (Zosimus, *Historia nova* 2.7).[16] This would be, after all, a fixed symbolic date for the end of the Roman Empire. The last games, according to this calculation, had been initiated by Emperor Septimius Severus (204 C.E.).

Because Constantine and Licinius had founded no "new *saeculum*," Goths, Huns, and Persians had overrun the empire; it was shattered "in a short time, through their own folly" (Zosimus 1.57.1). This history of the fall from the pen of a Roman official educated in Homer and Herodotus, Thucydides and Polybius is marked by the symbolic date of 313 C.E. and a long history-of-religion excursus (2.1–7). Here (1) the origin, (2) the history, and (3) the ritual of the *saeculum* games are portrayed, a noteworthy specimen of ancient writing of the history of religion.

The *saeculum* festival (*sacrum saeculare*) prays for "dominion forever" (a saying of the sibyl). As long as the Romans conducted it properly, according to Zosimus (2.7.1; cf. 2.5.5), their rule was assured. They had, so to speak, the entire inhabited world under them: "But when the celebration was neglected . . . , in a short time the empire was flooded with barbarians and disappeared for the most part . . . ." The historian Zosimus tried to show how that happened. That he—after ca. 480/500 C.E.—can give a ritual offense in the ancient Roman religion as the reason for the downfall of the empire is noteworthy enough. He rightly observed that the doctrine of the *saecula* and the Roman *saeculum festival* always anticipated "the end of the Roman name" and postponed it. Horace gave this doctrine classical expression in his *carmen saeculare*: Apollo extends (*prorogat*) the Roman rule to further epochs and into the fullness of better and better times because of the rites performed by Augustus.

THE ESCHATON IN MYTH, HISTORY, AND PHILOSOPHY

Homer: "The day will be" (*Iliad* 6.448)

At the beginning of Greek literature, as far as it is known and datable to us, and at the center of all later education, are the epics concerning the "Wrath of

Achilles" and the "Return of Odysseus." One narrates the wandering to the end of the world and "into the house of Hades" (*Odyssey,* book 10: *Nekyia*); the other, a segment from the ten-year war in Troy. Homer does not begin his *Iliad* with the beginning of the war; neither does he conclude with the capture of the city. The *Iliad* is not "The Destruction of Troy" (*Iliou persis*), as this part of the myth is called in antiquity. An epic version of the material is attributed to Arctinos . Rather, the reconciliation of Achilles and Priam, the military and the political representatives of the two parties forms the poetic conclusion of Homer's narrative. The destruction of the city, the heroic death of the youthful Achilles, and the wretched slaughter of the aged king in his palace remain in the future, after this conciliatory conclusion. The reconciliation only achieves a postponement: the "will (plan) of Zeus" will achieve its goal (*Iliad* 1.5). The expected downfall is frequently prophesied and anticipated through allusions, foreshadowing, substitutions like the destruction of the camp of the Greeks (instead of Troy) or the burial of Patroclus (instead of Achilles).

The early epic uses the myth as medium of enlightenment: as the ancients conceived it, the history of Troy is a "historical myth," the story of a unique, datable action of humans and gods. Its specific narrative structure is the *expected* downfall. It is not carried out in the narrative but remains the imminent future after the end of the narrative. Homer's public knew the continuation: death of Achilles, of Priam, of Paris, of Polyxena in front of Troy, and the ignominious return of the victorious general. Agamemnon will be done away with by his wife and her lover in the bath of his palace in Mycenae. At the end of Homer's *Iliad* all of these events are still in the future.

The myth of the violent taking of a city in Asia (Minor) through a broad coalition of Greek tribes stands at the beginning of our history of Greek literature (eighth century B.C.E.). The event becomes so important that it will be construed as a threshold between mythic and historical epochs. Here begins, after the "uncertain" and "mythic" time, the "span of historical time" (*spatium historicum*). It is established, for the most part, by the refugees of the destroyed city and the wandering victors. The ruling families of Troy are extinguished; the population of the city is done away with or sold. But Antenor, Anchises, Aeneas, and his son succeed in escaping to Italy.

Also the bravest defender of the city knew for a long time the oracle about its downfall: "The day will be when sacred Troy perishes / and Priam and the people of Priam, armed with good ashen spear" (*Iliad* 6.448f.; cf. 22.60ff.; 24.728 ff.). Later authors handed down the sayings (*chrēsmoi*) and even the name of the sibyl, who "previously revealed" (*pro-edēlōsen*) the disaster before the Trojan War. Helen would "bring death over Asia and Europe"; because of her, Troy would be taken by the Greeks. Herophile or the

Erythrean sibyl was named as the author of the sayings. Further, the Delphic sibyl claimed that Homer inserted many verses from her sayings into his poetry, and she says in advance that Homer would not tell the truth (Pausanias 10.12.2; Varro in Lactantius 1.6.9). The most renowned are the warnings of Cassandra, which no one wants to hear. Thus Apollo, the god who inspired her, ordained it. The tragic reshaping of the myth sharpens these configurations (Aeschylus, *Agamemnon* 1081f.). While Agamemnon triumphs, she laments her city: "Apollo, Apollo, leader who destroys me [Greek *ap-ollōn*]: / you have now destroyed me a second time." A Hellenistic poet (second century B.C.E.) allowed her to prophesy a world history: the battle between Asia and Europe would be ended by Rome (Lycophron, *Alexandra* 1446ff.). The primordial forms of threatening oracles and laments for cities are continued in the Jewish sibyls—with the new use of Oriental and Greek traditions (3.414ff.): "Ilion, I lament for you." Troy is for Greeks and Romans the paradigm for the destruction of a city, a dynasty, a people (*Odyssey* 1.2; Herodotus 2.120.5). Scipio looks mournfully at burning Carthage (Polybius 38.22). Troy comes to his mind and the sequence of world kingdoms, which like it are gone: Assyrians, Medes, Persians, Macedonians. The god destroys people and cities—also Rome, Polybius has Scipio say, in fear and hope. It was the Homeric epic that established this paradigm of history and eschatology at the beginning of Greek history.

Hesiod: "What will be" (*Theogony* 32)

The Poem about the Origins of Gods and Humans (Theogony)

For the history of ancient apocalypticism and eschatology, Hesiod (ca. 700 B.C.E.) does not offer a broader development of the theme of (collective) downfall or of the netherworld[17] but brings a personal call, a revelation through mediating muses, and also the complicated schema according to which the succession and genealogies of gods and humans are ordered into a unified world history. This history reaches from the chaos "which first arose" until Hesiod's own time and only a little further.

Hesiod was "the teacher of most" (Heraclitus, frag. 57 DK) but he himself was taught by the muses (*Theog.* 31f.): "They breathed into me a divine voice in order to celebrate what will be and what was before." Hesiod's poetic teaching repeats the song of the muses. They only sing, however, about what already was; from the beginning and the first human being until the establishment of our world (vv. 45, 100, 108, 115f.).

Through the order of genealogies, the marking of a sequence through "but thereafter" (116f., 132, 820, 886, 901) and occasional numbering (306ff., 886ff.), a broadly structured temporal schema develops. Hesiod or his source took the schema of the succession of the three great father gods (Uranos, Kronos, Zeus) and the rebellion of the defeated Titans from ancient eastern tradition. The succession of three world ages of nine years each, is attested among the Hittites (fourteenth century B.C.E.): a succession of the great gods Alalu, Anu, Kumarbi, Tessup; and against these Hedammu, Ullikummi, and Silver Demon rebel.[18] The pattern of succession, rebellion, and construction of a "last" legitimate rule (Zeus/Tessup) points to later historiographical speculation about the sequence of empires.

The vanquished rebels were not annihilated or damned; they do not become an anti-world. The Titans are bound in the netherworld (*Theog.* 718f.) behind bronze doors, watched by hundred-armed guards. Mount Aetna is laid on top of the snake-headed Typhon (Pherecydes in Scholion to Homer II. 2.783; KRS 72 ff.). In the battle of the gods against Typhon, Titans, giants, or Typhoeus (*Theog.* 820ff.), the end of the world seems imminent: the earth burns, it melts like tin, the sea dries up, even the netherworld trembles (*Theog.* 689ff.; 850ff.; 861). The possibility of a cosmic fire (*ekpyrosis*) is broached in the myth. But there is no Greek twilight of the gods, no Ragnarök or Muspilli. Hesiod's gods "exist forever" (*aien eontes*), deathless (*athanatoi*), ageless, but not "fateless" (*Theog.* 21). The rule of Zeus is no longer threatened; with him the series of usurpations breaks off. He rules with Reason (*Mētis*), which he has incorporated (*Theog.* 886–90), and with his spouse *Themis* (Law), who bore him Good Statutes (*Eunomia*), Justice (*Dikē*) and Peace (*Eirēnē*) (*Theog.* 901ff.).

The Poem about Work (Erga kai Hēmerai—Works and Days)

The history of the metal ages also came to Hesiod from Oriental tradition (Gatz 1967). It is a *logos* whose parts can be counted. Therefore Hesiod, as one of many arrangers of this material,[19] enumerates five phases (*Works* 109–76):

> First the immortals made a golden race . . . but they made the second race much worse, a silver one. . . . The third race Zeus made from bronze. . . . The fourth Zeus made fairer and better, the divine race of heroes. . . . I would not want to sojourn with the fifth, but either die before it or live after it.

This story is wisdom and is intended for education. It is universal because it concerns all people. Like the *Theogony*, it begins with a "first" (109) and leads into an open future. The five ages follow chronologically after one another, but they do not arise from one another. The sequence is not a uniform, steady descent but a diverse alteration of different kinds of phases. The golden age stands in sharp contrast to the silver, which is bad, violent, impious; the bronze age, on the other hand, is the mortal counterpart to the Titans of the *Theogony,* one of the numerous points of contact between the two texts. The race of heroes stands on a higher level than the bronze race; the fall into the iron age is especially deep.

The sequence of world ages is no chain of necessity; Hesiod removed possible astrological regularities in his sources. Each age was made new by the gods or Zeus; the "plans" of Zeus guide everything (122): there is no "development" from the golden to the silver age. The topic of an idealized time and space is set forth in the portrait of the golden age, of life under the rule of Kronos, and "on the islands of the blessed," at the "ends of the earth." Humans live and celebrate like the gods and with them, without cares, work, laments, or aging; death comes like sleep; earth produces fruit richly "from itself" (*automatē*). These images return in countless utopias of antiquity.

The iron age is "now"; nevertheless, Hesiod describes it in the future, as a coming time in which he would no longer like to live, but either before, in the time of heroes or "after." What "after" is, however, is not said. That which is portrayed in the threatening future of apocalyptic prophecy is the state of the present world: "They never rest from labor and misery, neither by day nor by night, perishing. . . . Zeus will also destroy this race of mortal people" (*Works* 176–80). The topic of decadence follows: the children are born with grey temples (cf. *Sib. Or.* 2.155); between the father and his children there are no similarities; among guests, companions, and brothers there is no trust; the parents are treated with disrespect; perjury, pride, deception, and envy reign (cf. Mark 13:12; *Sib. Or.* 8.95). And then finally Shame (Conscience) and Nemesis leave the world of wide streets for Olympus. Suffering remains with humanity: "and there will be no help against the evil" (201).

Thus ends the story of the ages of humans according to Hesiod. Not one word indicates that the golden age will return: the first witness for this idea is Virgil (*Fourth Eclogue*). That Hesiod should be named as an example of the "cyclical thought" must certainly go back to the latent influence that Nietzsche exercised with his so-called classical teaching of the eternal return. Hesiod, however, emphasizes a linear sequence ("first," "then," the numbering): "Hesiod leaves the prospect open. . . . Nobody can tell what comes after the present generation" (Rosenmeyer 1957). Thus Hesiod takes his place at the beginning of Greek philosophy of history.

Historiography: Epochs, Succession, and (No) End

Epochs

The most comprehensive nonmythic organization of history in Western antiquity was developed by Greek chronographers (third to first centuries B.C.E.)—Eratosthenes, Apollodorus, Castor of Rhodes—and handed down by M. Terentius Varro (116–27 B.C.E.), Censorinus, and Augustine.[20] They differentiate three great "spans" (*spatium, intervallum*) of world history: (1) *spatium incertum* (Greek *adēlon*): from the Ogygian until the Deukalion flood; (2) *spatium fabulosum* (Greek *mythikon*): up to the Trojan War, which is estimated at about 1194/1184, or until the first Olympiad (776 B.C.E.); (3) *spatium historicum* (Greek *historikon*): after the Trojan War or the first Olympiad.

In Varro the intervals last seven generations (each 9 x 7 = 63 years), that is, roughly 440 years or four *saecula* of 110 years. From this premise he deduces—of necessity, as it were—the date of the foundation of Rome, which is the beginning of a new era: seven generations after the beginning of the Trojan War (1193/753 B.C.E.).

The speculative power that constructs a world history, symbolically and arithmetically, can only be admired. The numerical system creates order and symmetry in history, gives the impression of meaning, provides orientation and, on the basis of calculability, also a measure of certainty. It is noteworthy that the depth of the historical consciousness is modest: the first "interval" extended from 2073 until 1633. It is not recorded that the ancient chronographers had asked themselves the question whether the historical epoch was also only one "interval." The end of the era of Rome, however, was calculated in many ways.

This symbolic and arithmetic construction of world history was widespread among Greeks (Plutarch), Romans (Ovid, *Metamorphoses*) and Christians (Arnobius, Eusebius, Augustine). There are also other constructions, which are more biomorphic or more astrological (Demandt 1978, esp. 37ff.). The state is born, has a childhood, grows up and becomes old: but a "second childhood" (*altera infantia*) is not impossible. After "blossoming" and "breakdown" there is a "resurrection" (Velleius Paterculus 1.7: *florere–concidere–resurgere*). Cicero (*De re publica* 2.3; 2.21; 3.34; cf. 6.27) uses the metaphor of a lifetime for Roman history, but there is no "natural death" (*naturalis interitus*) for a city, as there is for humans. On the one hand, everything that is created perishes; whatever grows, ages (Sallust, *Jugurtha* 2.3); on the other hand, the state is protected against the threat of naturalistic metaphors: "the rulers are mortal, the city is eternal" (Tiberius in Tacitus, *Annals* 3.6.3). Rome learned the "logic of rebirth": "growth comes from misfortune" (Rutilius Namatianus 1.139f.).

In myths and astronomical speculation, great spans of time are measured out. The punishment of Prometheus was to last thirty thousand years (Aeschylus, *Prometheus* 94, with scholion); the wandering of the defiled Daimon lasts just as long: according to Empedocles (fifth century B.C.E.), he must wander around in different forms far from the gods for thirty thousand years, until he may return to them. If the stars are returned to the position in which they were at creation, a "great year" is completed (so still Thomas Aquinas, *Supplement,* question 77, art. 3). How this is to be reckoned is debated by ancient scholars. Above all, there are other scholars who think that time is unending and will never cycle back on itself (Censorinus, *De die natali* 18.11).

The Succession of World Empires

The biomorphic, astronomical, or arithmetic division of the epochs is based on general principles. They lay claim to universality, just like Hesiod's teachings of the succession of gods and the races of humanity. Greek and Roman political historiography, which for the most part recounts specific histories of wars, peoples, or cities, also developed universal models in order to record "the common actions of the inhabited world" (Polybius 39.8). For Polybius, who had the history of all peoples converge in the "sole rule" of the Romans, such a model is the succession of world empires (38.22): Assyrians, Medes, Persians, Macedonians, and then Rome, which has perhaps already passed its high point (*akmē*) with the destruction of Carthage (146 B.C.E.).

The succession of the Eastern empires is well attested in Western antiquity (Swain 1940; Momigliano 1987; Flusser 1972). Early witnesses are Herodotus (1.95) and Ktesias, a Greek doctor and historiographer at the court of Artaxerxes II (405/404–359 B.C.E.; Diodorus 2.1.37; cf. 2.22.2). Aemilius Sura (first half of the second century B.C.E.) calculates the genealogy of Roman rule (Velleius Paterculus 1.6.6): from the Assyrians, who were the first people to rule a world empire, to the Medes, then to the Persians, then the Macedonians, and finally to the Roman people. In Sura, the division and even the calculability of great periods of history, perhaps even the consciousness of a historical epoch, become clear, but not an eschatology or an anticipation of an end-time ruler: "Between my time and the beginning of Ninus, the king of the Assyrians, who was the first world ruler, lie 1995 years." The occasion for his calculations was the Roman victory over the Seleucids and the Macedonians (189 and 171/169 B.C.E.). The rule of Alexander and his Diadochoi was "transferred" to Rome (Velleius 1.16; cf. Justin, *Epitome* 1.3).

This was different from what the author of the book of Daniel (164/163 B.C.E.) had hoped. In Daniel (chap. 2) a myth of metal ages (cf. Hesiod, *Works*) is combined with a schema of four kingdoms. This combination is not found in the Greek and Roman tradition.

The End within History

The Greeks had ample opportunity to experience, imagine, and write history "from the end backward." The great epochs of their history were set by violent natural catastrophes. They could not become adults, because their cultural development was continually violently interrupted (cf. Plato's *Timaeus*). At the beginning of their historical and literary tradition is the epic of the fall of Troy and the many stories of the downfall of the victors. So many states were remembered as destroyed in the collective memory. As Pausanias (born ca. 111/115 C.E.) beholds the ruins of Megalopolis ("Great-city") in Arcadia, he is overcome for a whole chapter (8.33) by the memory of Mycenae and Nineveh, which was once the royal capital of Assyria, and also of Thebes in Boeotia: these cities are now abandoned and thoroughly destroyed. Megalopolis become a by-word for a city that was definitively laid waste: "the great city is a great desert" (Strabo 8.388; cf. the taunt songs about Tiryns and Babylon). Kleomenes destroyed it, "so that no one could even hope that it would be resettled" (Polybius 2.55). Pausanias carefully mixes cultures and epochs: he names the Egyptian Thebes and the Minyan Orchomenos and Delos, once the common trade center of the Greeks, now uninhabited. From Babylon only the sanctuary of Bel remains and the wall, and it was certainly once the greatest city under the sun, just like Tiryns in the Argolis: "God annihilated these" (*tauta men epoiēsen ho daimōn einai to mēden*). This catalogue of ruined cities is scarcely balanced during the rise of others (cf. the catalogue of cities destroyed and cursed by the Romans in Macrobius, *Saturnalia* 3.9.13). Pausanias reflects on this reversal of fortune and realizes that there is never any certainty.

For the destruction of Carthage (146 B.C.E.) we have an eyewitness account. The city burned for seventeen days; then it was plowed up, and salt strewn over it; a curse was laid upon it and any settlement forever forbidden (Appian 8.1.2). Carthage was a colony of Tyre, founded fifty years before the capture of Troy (so Appian), capital of a great empire in Africa and Spain. The Romans destroyed it because they wanted the five thousand square miles of good land for themselves (*Cambridge Ancient History*, 8:484). Two friends, Polybius and Scipio, the Greek author of universal history and the Roman victor, viewed the ruins of the city, "which was then fully at an end, completely and totally ruined" (Appian 8.19.132).[21] Scipio wept over the enemy and recognized that god must overthrow cities, people, and all dominions, just like individual people. Troy, once a happy city, had suffered that. The empires of the Assyrians, Medes, and Persians had suffered that, and just recently the power of the Macedonians; then the words of the poets escape Scipio's lips: "the day will be when sacred Troy perishes, / and Priam and the people of Priam, armed with good ashen spear" (*Iliad* 6.448f.; cf. Polybius 29.21).

Polybius asked his student and friend what he meant by this citation. With that Scipio openly named his own fatherland, for which he feared in regard to the human condition: "And Polybius, who heard it himself, reported this" (Appian 8.20.133).

The following elements make this account a paradigm of collective eschatology: the ritual annihilation after the military one; the sequence of the four world kingdoms with an eye to the downfall of the fifth; the reference to the Greek archetype, the oracle of destruction against Troy, and the city's demise; and the theology-of-history generalization to "all" people and rulers.

The end that they had prepared for others was in the historical consciousness of the Romans of the late Republic, and so was the possibility of their own end. The Etruscan culture, whose kings had built the religious center on the capitol, was dying out in the first century. Their end was prophesied: two *saecula* were left, "then the end of the Etruscan name would occur"—*finem fore nominis Etrusci* (Servius on Virgil, *Ecl.* 9.47). In the middle of the fourth century B.C.E., the Romans had defeated the "peoples" of Latium who were related to them. They debated "whether Latium should exist thereafter or whether it shouldn't"—*sit Latium deinde an non sit* (Livy 8.13f.). Mercifully they then granted a limited existence to vanquished Latium. Nonetheless, fifty-three peoples in Latium disappeared from history. A Roman historian and an observant natural historian marveled that they were destroyed without a trace left behind: *interiere sine vestigiis* (Pliny, *Natural History* 3.68–70). Livy of Padua formulated the situation programmatically and not uncritically, with reference to the first great Roman work of destruction: "Rome is growing meanwhile from the ruins of Alba"—*Roma crescit interim Albae ruinis* (1.30.1; cf. 1.31.1; see Cancik 1995b).

Only seldom do those who are dying, who are to exist no longer, who can leave behind no traces but ruins at most, leave behind documents of their consciousness of dying. The apocalypse in *Corpus Hermeticum* (Asclepius, chapters 24–27), which laments the downfall of the Egyptian world, is therefore an especially useful witness.[22] The Egyptian religion is persecuted by

Greeks or already by Christians; "there will be a time" when the gods abandon Egypt; the seer raises the lament: "O Egypt, Egypt." The holy land is full of corpses, the river full of blood: the city and the people, the culture and the Egyptian land are destroyed. The collective eschatology takes on cosmic proportions: Egypt is indeed "an image of heaven" (*imago caeli*). The world itself is already old (*senectus mundi*); it will be destroyed and thereby purified. This Egyptian apocalypse uses Stoic eschatology in order to formulate a hope: *apokatastasis* in the Coptic text, *reformatio* and *restitutio* in the Latin translation (chapter 26). Even the return of the gods is promised.

Political and spiritual resistance to Rome expressed itself in innumerable prophecies of doom (Fuchs 1938). Antisthenes of Rhodes (second century B.C.E.) artfully assembled various kinds of signs and texts in prose and in verse in his historical work (FGH no. 508). His work is directed against Roman aggression in the Aegean, which definitively shattered the rule of the Seleucids in the First Syrian War (191–88 B.C.E.). A longer part is preserved, taken out of context and reworked, in the writing of Phlegon of Tralles' *Concerning Miracles* (FGH no. 257; second century C.E.). In three increasingly dramatic passages, signs and prophecies are communicated that were to occur in the Roman army after they had slain the Greeks at Thermopylae. These texts move from everyday political divination to a collective eschatology. They pile up the topics of the threatening oracle, announce retaliation for the defeat and the wrath of Zeus and Athena. They promise to the Romans "the end of dominion" (FGH no. 257 F 36), indeed complete "downfall," slavery, death, blood, destruction. Hate elevates the conflict with the military imperialists from the West to a conflict of the continents, Asia versus Italy:

> For there will come a very strong army, bold,
> from afar from Asia, where the sun rises . . . .

Asia and the Orient here are the Greeks and their allies in Europe and in the East. Apparently, the cliché "East versus West" is rather complex and not evident at all: the horrible barbarians are here the westerners. Roman counter-propaganda and self-criticism absorbed and contradicted anti-Roman apocalypticism: the "King from the East" whom the sibyl and Jewish and Asian oracles have predicted,[23] is not a Persian king, Mithridates, or a Jewish Messiah but a Roman general who has just conquered the Jews and who will establish the Flavian dynasty. "The East will again gain strength," it says (Tacitus, *Historiae* 5.13.2), "and those who come from Judea will attain dominion." Tacitus explains in his history of the Jews (*Hist.*, book 5), a classic text for educated anti-Semites, that this oracle paradoxically legitimates the rule of

Rome over the Orient. There is no revenge of Asia on Rome; the power will return not to Asia but to "eternal Rome"—*Roma aeterna.*[24]

Philosophy: Origin, Destruction, Renewal

The Presocratic Cosmologies

THE ORDER OF TIME. The oldest sentence in Greek philosophy, the wording of which can be approximated, sets up the theme of "rise" and "fall" of the cosmos with the help of the concepts "necessity" and "justice" (Anaximander [ca. 550 B.C.E.]). The process runs "according to the assessment of Time" (*kata tēn tou chronou taxin*):[25] the regularity, duration, and the "just" balance reached between contrasting principles form the structure of this cosmos. "Over and above" this process—or "outside" or "beyond"—is "the indefinite/infinite" (*a-peiron, infinitum*), from which the unending sequence of worlds goes forth in succession (Anaximander, A1 DK, in Diogenes Laertius 2.1–2 = 94 KRS). The "indefinite/infinite" itself is, like the Homeric gods, "ageless and eternal" (Theophrastus in Hippolytus, *Refutation* 1.6.1–2 = A11 DK = 101B KRS; cf. A15 DK). In this cosmological model each end is a boundary, each eschatology relative; there is no absolute end of the cosmos in the world of Anaximander.

"THUNDERBOLT STEERS ALL THINGS" (HERACLITUS). In the model of the world of Heraclitus from Ephesus (who flourished about 504/501 B.C.E.), fire is the source of everything; it condenses and dissolves; everything ends in fire (A1 DK). "The turnings (*tropai*) of fire" first bring about the sea, from the sea earth and sweltering heat (B31 DK = 218 KRS). As goods are exchanged for gold and gold for goods, thus "all things are an equal exchange for fire and fire for all things" (B90 DK = 219 KRS). Exchange and change result not in a cycle but in an oscillating process and changes, rhythms (*metra*) of the "everliving fire" (B30 DK = 217 KRS; cf. the context in Clement, *Stromateis* 5.104, 105, 115; 6.17 etc.). The eternal fire is concentrated in pure *aether,* in the stars, and above all in the sun. As lightning, it "steers" everything (B64 DK in Hippolytus, *Refut.* 9.10.7 = 220 KRS). A Christian interpreter explains: "According to Heraclitus, this fire is rational and the basis for the administration of the whole."

The human soul is a "spark" (*scintilla*) from the eternal substance of fire (A15 DK). It must remain "dry," must not become moist as if drunk (B117 DK = 231 KRS). If the person dies not from sickness but in battle, the soul is "purer" (more fiery; B136 DK = 237 KRS). It ascends to the *aether* and the stars. Thus cosmology and individual eschatology are bound together. The Stoic teaching about fire, reason, providence, and the soul draws on Heraclitus. This already shows that the teaching developed by the Stoics regarding the conflagration (*ek-pyrosis*) is more than a hypothesis about the physical universe.

"LOVE WAS QUEEN" (EMPEDOCLES). In his didactic poems, Empedocles from Akragas (ca. 495–435 B.C.E.) developed in very personal ways a wealth of apocalyptic and eschatological motifs. His relationships to the Sicilian local tradition, to Pythagorean and Orphic teaching, to the rhetoric and topic of revelatory speeches and the mysteries, have been clarified through new discoveries and research (Zuntz 1971; Wright 1981; Riedweg 1995).

In Empedocles the word "cycle" (*kyklos*) is used for the first time in an authentic text of substantial length, though with an uncertain meaning. His cosmological model works with four "roots" (elements) and two opposing powers: Strife (*Neikos*) and Love (*Philia,* Aphrodite). The cosmos is in the process of continuous change. It moves sometimes toward a separation of all parts, at other times toward unity (B17 DK = 348 and 349 KRS; 364 KRS). The "mingling" and "continual interchange" never cease; "thus far they exist always changeless in the cycle." If all parts are joined by the works of *Philia,* then the cosmos is a sphere (*sphairos*), equal to itself: a unique nonanthropomorphic divinity (B27, B31, B35 DK = 357, 358, 360 KRS).

In the history of humanity, this temporally limited situation of the cosmos corresponds to the kingdom of the Cyprian Aphrodite. Explicitly correcting Hesiod's teaching about life under Kronos and about the golden age of humanity, Empedocles asserts (B128 DK = 411 KRS): "Among them not Ares (i.e., the war god) was god nor Kydoimos (i.e., the battle-cry),/ nor was Zeus king nor Kronos nor Poseidon,/ but Kypris (i.e. Aphrodite) was queen." She was worshiped not with bloody sacrifices but with pictures, painted animals, myrrh, incense, honey. The animals were tame and lived in friendship with humans (B130 DK = 412 KRS). That Empedocles wants to reform the Greek religion is clear, but nothing is reported about a "return" of the kingdom of Aphrodite.

The "reformer" and "teacher" Empedocles was also legitimated by his personal fate. Because he had put his trust in "raving Strife" (*Neikos*), he was banned from the realm of the gods; for thirty thousand years he had to wander through various forms of mortal beings (B115DK = 401 KRS). The earth is the place of his banishment, the body is an "alien garment" (B126 DK = 407 KRS); as in the Platonic tradition the body is called "prison" or "grave" of the soul. In a description of the netherworld the fallen god laments (B118 and 121 DK = 402 KRS): "I wept and wailed, when I saw the unfamiliar place/ where Murder and Anger and tribes of other Deaths / . . . / They wander in darkness over the meadow of Doom."

The allusion to the Homeric Nekyia shows, as does the correction of Hesiod, the firm relation to the eschatological tradition. Empedocles in turn is developed in Virgil's *Katabasis* (Zuntz [1971, 201ff.] compares *Aeneid* 6.73ff., 709). The god who was banished from the divine bliss into the mortal world became plant, bird, fish, boy, and girl (B117 DK = 417 KRS); after this sequence of changes—which is never called a "circle"—he becomes then a poet, seer, and teacher and comes to be regarded "as an immortal god " (B112 DK = 399 KRS). He thus escapes the compulsion of further reincarnation. A gold tablet (A 1; Zuntz 1971, 320ff.) states: "I have flown from the sorrowful cycle (*kyklos*)." The "cycle"—whatever it means: the rhythm of human life or a series of reincarnations—can thus be left behind. So can Empedocles, after his punishment is served, return to the divine sphere. There is no indication that a new offense would be followed by a further fall.

Plato's Philosophy of History and Psychology

ELEMENTS OF A NEW DISCOURSE. The mythic, theological, and (meta-)physical models of death, soul, underworld, reincarnation, and origin, end, or eternity of the cosmos are summed up by Plato (428/427–349/348) and transformed into a new complex, through dialectic, mathematics, and the theory of forms (ideas). On the one hand, these models are criticized and rationalized; on the other hand, secondarily remythicized in new "stories." The forms of revelatory speech drawn from divination or the mysteries are in part eliminated and in part aesthetically elevated through irony and literary perfection (cf. the myth of Er in book 10 of Plato's *Republic*). From this broad Presocratic tradition about the world, humanity, and the soul, and in continuation of the old myths about Hephaistus, Athene, and Prometheus, and sophistic theories about the origin and development of human technology and culture, Plato developed a new special discourse, which since Voltaire has been called "philosophy of history."[26] Since then all religious, mythic, and theological eschatology is measured by philosophical rationality and criticism. For this reason the "quest for the eschatological roots of the philosophy of history" cannot ignore Plato and his school (Jaeschke 1986).

The discourse developed by Plato contains general terms and propositions about time and eternity, movement and change, the acting of humans and states. This discourse is neither ethics, although it contains sayings about justice and virtue, nor physics, although it contains statements about the origin of the cosmos and the movement of the stars, which, after a Great Year, find themselves back in the constellation in which they stood at the time of creation. Neither is this discourse historical research, although Mnemosyne is summoned and the history of Ur-Athens and the fabulous Atlantis is told in a style characteristic of historiography with many dates (von Wilamowitz-Moellendorff 1948, 468): "about three thousand years ago there was the flood of Deukalion, more than nine thousand years ago there was a war between Ur-Athens and Atlantis" (*Critias* 108d–e; 111a). The tendency to universality, the speculation with large, round, symbolic numbers, the interest in complicated courses of movement, the construction of simultaneity for rise and fall, the attention paid to the catastrophes of Greek history: all of these can justify the designation "philosophy of history" for this discourse. In this connection it is immaterial which of these specific answers Plato found for the questions of an absolute or relative end of time, history, or cosmos.

"THE MESSENGER FROM THE OTHERWORLD" (*REPUBLIC* 10.619b). Most of Plato's dialogues contain eschatological material, differing in form ("Acts" of the death of Socrates, Katabasis, similes) and in importance in relation to the central teaching of Socrates and Plato. These intellectually and literarily sophisticated texts have had an enormous effect on Greeks (e.g., Plutarch), Romans (e.g., Cicero), Jews (e.g., Philo) and Christians like Justin, who adopted not only the Platonic concept of God but also the literary form of the dialogue (Andresen 1952–53). Therefore a short overview, limited to individual eschatology, is useful, even if it must dispense with completeness, chronological differentiation, and systematization.

The soul of the individual human being, according to Platonic teaching, is immortal but also "uncreated" (*a-genētos*; *Phaedrus* 245c–e; *Republic* 10.611b). This is a clear difference from (orthodox) Christian teaching, according to which the soul is created. It is the "origin of movement" in humans; "it moves itself" and is "constantly moved"—thus eternal (cf. Macrobius, commentary on Cicero's *Somnium Scipionis* 2.13–16 [ca. 400 C.E.]: *anima semper movetur*). It shares in the ideal forms, grasps unchangeable being by its own power, not through the senses. Thus Plato combined the teaching about souls with the teaching about being and reason in a highly speculative way (*Theaetetus* 185d). The divinization of the soul is bought with the devaluation of the body. The body can soil the soul, entirely corrupt it; it is a grave (*sōma–sēma*) and a prison. Therefore the soul must separate itself from the body as far as possible (*Phaedo* 67c; 81c; 83d).

After death, a purification is necessary. How this takes place is narrated in poetic detail in the Myth of Er at the end of the great work about the state (*Republic* 10.614b–621). The Pamphylian Er, because he was only seemingly dead, is sent back out of the netherworld as "messenger from the afterlife." He reports the judgment of the dead and gruesome punishments; the three Fates who sing what was, what is, and what will come (Atropos); the (free) choice of lifestyle by the soul; and the reincarnation.

Plato teaches the eternity of the individual soul. His soul is therefore not only a life principle and passing constellation of Logos-material, which a certain time after death passes into the divine *aether*-fire. If the person has become truly "pure" through a philosophical life, his/her soul frees itself more quickly from the realm of the senses: only three times in a thousand years must it be reincarnated; then it is forever free from the body and enters "the race of the gods." The circle of births is broken (*Phaedrus* 248c–249a; *Phaedo* 65a, 82d, 84b, 114c). Plato's arguments and myths were particularly fascinating because they could be related to various mysteries (Orphism in *Gorgias* 493a; *Phaedo* 107d ff.) and because the death of Socrates (399 B.C.E.) provides a historical example that henceforth showed the ancients the right way for philosophers to die. Death is a recovery; Socrates reminds his companions to sacrifice a rooster to the healing god Asclepius, as one does after overcoming sickness (*Phaedo* 118). Philosophy and its consolations thus become a new area of consciousness for individual eschatology.

"End or Transition": Mors quid est? aut finis aut transitus.
(Seneca, *Epist.* 65.24)

"PURIFICATION THROUGH FIRE" AND "RENEWAL OF THE WORLD." In contrast to Platonic dualism, the Stoics stand for the unity of the world (monism) and, in contrast to the atomists (Epicurus, Lucretius), the unity of reason in everything that is: in the order of crystals, in the principle of life that has self-consciousness (*sensus sui*) and seeks to preserve itself, in human reason and in divine providence, which has made and guides the world for humanity. This reason is fire, in different states. The connection to the cosmology of Heraclitus is obvious (SVF I frag. 102 [Zeno]; I.519 [Cleanthes]; II frag. 617 [Chrysippus]). In contrast to Heraclitus, the Stoics postulate a destruction of the world, through floods or a "purification through fire" (*hē dia pyros katharsis;* SVF II frag. 617, 630 [from Clement of Alexandria, who blurs the difference between the Stoics and Heraclitus]; cf. SVF II frags. 589, 606). Therein all evil is destroyed (SVF II frag. 606). The soul of the cosmos perishes in this world fire (*ek-pyrosis*); the cosmos itself remains (SVF II frag. 397).

The cosmic conflagration effects a catharsis but is not bound up with a (second) judgment and punishment or reward of the souls. Details of the conflagration and the resulting "renewal of the world" are debated even among the Stoics.[28] Panaetius (second century B.C.E.) rejects the teaching of the cosmic conflagration and *palingenesia:* the cosmos is indestructible. The endless return of the worlds enticed others to paradox and experiments in thought. Thus, some Stoics say: "I will be the same person again in the *palingenesia*" (SVF II frag. 624) and ask "whether I am one in number then and now, because I am the same in substance, or whether I differ from myself" as a result of the succession of different worlds (frag. 627). Others assume (frag. 625) that some gods are not destroyed in the cosmic conflagration but survive it. Therefore they always know what will happen, for everything, even the smallest detail, will happen again—an ingenious basis for divination. With the gods the memory of human history at least is preserved through the cosmic conflagration. The philosophical interest in these attempts concerns the concept of infinity of space and time, the uniqueness of the particular individual, the eternity of history, the essential goodness of the substance of the world.

"DAILY WE DIE" (SENECA). L. Annaeus Seneca (d. 65 C.E.) often described the destruction of the world by water (*diluvium*) and fire (*conflagratio*) in prose and poetry and with dramatic intensity. A father reveals a brief Stoic eschatology to his daughter at the end of the *Consolation to Marcia* (*Ad Marciam* 26):[29] "When the time comes at which the world extinguishes itself in order to renew itself again, the elements will shatter through their own power, and stars collide with stars, and when all matter burns, what now shines disposed in distinct places will burn with one single fire."

In his natural history Seneca deals with the purification through water (*Quaestiones Naturales* 3.26) and adds the end of the world by water (3.27) and, following Berossus, the end by fire (3.29). The restoration of the "old order," the return of the blessed souls "into the old elements" form the end of the portrayal, which is scarcely comforting.

It is the fear of one's own demise that creates this cosmic scenario.[30] In Seneca death is always present: "Daily we die" (*Epist.* 24.20; *Ad Polybium* 4.3). Our death begins with birth. "One must learn to die one's whole life" (*De brevitate vitae* 7.3): whoever understands this maxim is a free man. Time is, for Seneca, death in life (Seneca, *Epist.* 1; see Cancik 1983, 276–81). His anthropology is thus far a present, individual eschatology. He clearly conceived time and humanity from the perspective of death and would not be hindered by the Stoic dogmas of the divinity of the soul and the return of the "old order."

Venturum Saeculum (Virgil, *Eclogue* 4.52)

The Song of the Cumean Sibyl

The poems of P. Vergilius Maro (70–19 B.C.E.) collect the eschatological tradition of antiquity, both Roman and Greek, and pass them on to Christians and Western Europe.[31] The late antique commentator Servius noted: "Virgil says much about history, much through the deep knowledge of philosophers, theologians, Egyptians" (commentary on Virgil's *Aeneid,* book 6, preface). Virgil presents Orpheus and his descent into the netherworld (*Georg.* 4.453–527; cf. *Ecl.* 4.55; *Aen.* 6.645ff.); Hesiod's ages of humanity, cosmological speculation in the song of Silenus (*Ecl.* 6) and in the teaching of Anchises (*Aen.* 6.724ff.), the golden age and the rule of Saturn, the Sibyl and her Cumean song: the so-called "messianic" poem.[32]

The *Fourth Eclogue* is a pastoral poem; it celebrates the assumption of office of C. Asinius Pollio as consul of the year 40 B.C.E. and the birth of a child. The motif of these three themes (bucolic, panegyric, birth poem) complement and overlap one another artfully and not without tension, since it remains unclear who the child is: the personification of the new age (cf. 4.10f.), a son of the consul Asinius Pollio or of Octavian, or a successful "revolutionary" of the popular "party" who would call himself Emperor Caesar Augustus directly after his victory over the republic of the aristocrats.

The annual rather prosaic assumption of office of a new cousul on the first of January is related (in the poem) to the onset of the "last age" and the "birth" of a "great order (sequence) of generations (epochs)" (*Ecl.* 4.4f.). The cosmic renewal ("Great Year") and the taking of office, in turn, are associated with Hesiod's myth of the races of humanity (4.8f.): the iron race will cease, the golden will rise. Thus the succession of races of humanity will be transformed from an open sequence (according to Hesiod) to a circle. Biological cycle (the birth of the child), politics (the taking of office of the consul), astronomical constellations ("Great Year," rule of the sun), mythic speculation (*Saturnia regna;* metal time periods), the timeless wonder-world of Arcadia and indeed even the life expectancy of the poet (4.53): this overlapping of events, actions, and processes produces a deep background in the philosophy of history, increases the poetic expression and the embarrassment of interpreters, who attempt to synchronize various courses and rhythms in one single bar. The wealth of the aspects under which the changing world is seen is overwhelming: the new return of the old (4.5f. 34 ff.), the necessarily unclear boundary between the old and new time at the moment of the transition (4.13.31), the cosmic joy "about the generation (epoch) that is coming." The cosmos too takes part in history. The infinity and the regularity of movement, hardly unified in the motif of the "return" (*Ecl.* 4.6, 34ff.), makes possible rational action, freedom, and history. Virgil refers to the Cumean sibyl. He sets his poem in a long literary and, in Rome, living religious tradition: the next *ludi saeculares* are imminent. The sibyl speaks darkly "with raving mouth"; she gives only hints: the human reader is required to determine what is right in the proposed setting.

The problem of poetic ambiguity (polyvalence, *ambiguitas*), be it frustrating or be it stimulating, should not obscure the reflective naiveté of the bucolic nature and its motifs, whether utopian or regressive. The lion will lie near the cattle;[33] poisonous snakes and plants will fail (4.22–25); there will be no more seafaring, no trade, no agriculture; even the cattle will be released from their yokes. The earth bears everything bountifully, by itself, everywhere, even lambs with colorful wool (37–45): thus commerce is really not necessary any longer. The child is Hope and Peace (4.17: *pacatus orbis*) and a scion of Jupiter (4.49). Hellenistic ruler cult is adumbrated here. The explanation of Virgil's "messianic" poem should, however, not be distorted either by Christian theology (*praeparatio evangelica*) or by the political propaganda of the later Augustan restoration or by the history of its reception in the West.

"The Dominion without End" (Aeneid 1.278f.)

In January of the year 27 B.C.E. through the formal restoration of the republic, Octavian assured his unique power as Emperor Caesar Augustus. The beginning of a new era was marked by counting the years of the Augusti, *anni Augustorum.* Soon thereafter Virgil set about writing his mythohistorical epic about the origin of the city of Rome, the Romans, the Julian family, which had already set itself up as a dynasty, and the Italian cities and peoples. In a typical revelatory situation, Jupiter teaches the mother of Aeneas about the "secrets of the fate" (*Aen.* 1.262: *fatorum arcana*), that is, about the history of Rome. Three years remain still for Aeneas, who will found his city Lavinium; after thirty years follows the *translatio imperii* of Lavinium to Alba Longa; after three hundred years, the founding of Rome. The point of this list is its conclusion:

For these (the Romans) I set neither bounds nor periods.
Dominion without end I gave to them. (*Aen.* 1.278f.)

The dominion is universal; the Orient too will serve; the Greeks will be punished for the destruction of Troy. War is abolished; the enemy brothers Remus and Romulus (Quirinus) are reconciled. There will be no more civil war; they dispense justice together.

This promise indeed reflects the end of history. The enemies of Rome, who had to endure the Augustan peace, had prophesied the end of the city. The Romans themselves had feared it often enough (see pp. 107–10 above). In this respect the promise of Virgil's Jupiter is simply triumphant counter-propaganda. But his view of history is not uneschatological, but posteschato-logical. Rome has its demise behind it: the ruins of Troy, which would not be rebuilt and may not live on in the name of the new city in Italy (*Aen.* 12.826ff.), and the last civil war. The epoch, which was supposed to come (*venturum saeculum*), is now arrived. This is how the fulfilled collective eschatology of a victor sounds. The realized apocalypticism serves, like myth, as a justification of empire, yet an empire that promises freedom and justice. The promise of Virgil's Jupiter is affirmative theology of history and praise of rulers but also a warning and *Fürstenspiegel.*

"The Journey through the Underworld" (Aeneid 6)

Virgil guaranteed his revelation about the underworld doubly—cultically and psychologically. Aeneas descends after an elaborate ritual, with a dangerous leap down into the darkness. Through the gates of dream he returns to earth (Cancik 1980). A further context is the cult of the dead: before the descent Misenus, the weapon bearer of Hector, is buried (6.156–235), then Gaieta, the nursemaid of Aeneas (7.1–6). Thus Aeneas loses family and companions the nearer he comes to his goal: his wife, his father Anchises, the old helmsman (5.833–871). His beloved he had sacrificed for the sake of duty (book 4). Thus arise the need and place for new friends, allies, women—the future. In the netherworld Aeneas meets his past: the enemies of Troy and many companions, who were lost in the long wandering. Freed from the past, at the end of his Katabasis he comes to the future Roman history.

Not the Cumean sibyl, who had led him up to this point, who had shown him the judgment of the individual dead, the places of punishment (6.548–627) and the Elysium (6.637–768), but his father Anchises "reveals" (*pandit*) to the son in a instructional speech (6.722–51) the history of the soul, which falls into the "blind prison" of the body. After death it will be cleansed, by wind, water, and fire, of stain incurred because of its body. Later, when they have "rolled the wheel" for a thousand years, souls at the behest of God will return to bodies again. The drink from the River Lethe takes from them all memory of the netherworld.

Old mythic traditions and rites from the mystery cults combine with motifs that the interpreter can classify as Stoic, Pythagorean, or Platonic (Norden 1957, 305ff.). With its wealth of eschatological traditions and in the art with which contradictions are forced together, the passage is similar to the *Fourth Eclogue*. No naive, triumphalist portrayal of Roman history can follow this complex anthropology. Even the praise of Augustus, who establishes the golden time period for Latium (*Aen.* 6.792f.), will be taken back in the grief for Marcellus (d. 23 B.C.E.), the nephew, son-in-law, and pillar of the dynastic plans of the emperor. Elegiac, with grief and cult of the dead, Anchises ends his speech (6.882–86): "Give lilies with full hands, / I wish to strew purple blossoms." The portrayal of Roman history on the shield of Aeneas is triumphalistic (*Aen.* 8.608–731): the future triumphs of the Romans "in the coming time" (8.626ff.), at the end the threefold triumph of Augustus (29 B.C.E.). Aeneas, however, does not understand (8.730f.): "He rejoices at the images, ignorant of the facts, and takes on his shoulder the fame and destiny of his descendants." Actually Aeneas, on the basis of the instruction of Anchises, should have been able to recognize a few of the portrayals, and especially Augustus. Virgil, however, having laid out a kind of Summa of ancient eschatology and apocalypticism, insists on the ignorance of people acting in history.

⤳ NOTES _____

1. Aristotle, *Physics* 5.4; cf. Plato, *Phaedo* 95. Theagenes A15 DK; Leucippus A1 DK = 563 KRS; Melissos B4 DK = 528 KRS: "Nothing that has both beginning and end (*telos*) is either eternal or unlimited"; Anaxagoras A46 DK = 496 KRS.

2. Varro, *Ant.*, book 16; the nature of the soul is discussed again here (frag. 226f.); cf. Cicero, *De legibus* 2.14.36. See pp. 96–97 above. Cf. Varro, *Ant.* frag. 209.

3. On the rebellion of the Titans, see Aristotle, frag. 18 (Ross); Lucretius 5.110–21 (the enlightened, as Giants, shatter the walls of the world with reason); Plutarch, *De facie,* chap. 12 (926 D–E).

4. The concept "philosophy of history" is attributed to Voltaire (*La philosophie de l'histoire* [Amsterdam, 1765]).

5. B. Kytzler, K. Rudolph, and J. Rüpke, eds., *Eduard Norden (1868–1941): Ein deutscher Gelehrter jüdischer Herkunft,* Palingenesia 49 (Stuttgart: Steiner, 1994); J. Rüpke, *Römische Religion bei Eduard Norden* (Marburg: Diagonal, 1993). Norden

began his great commentary on Virgil's account of the netherworld in 1898. From the history of scholarship the following names must suffice: H. Diels, *Sibyllinische Blätter* (Berlin: Reiner, 1890); F. Boll, *Aus der Offenbarung Johannis* (Leipzig/Berlin: Teubner, 1914). The concept of eschatology is taken up by K. Reinhardt, *Kosmos und Sympathie* (Munich: Beck, 1926) and P. Schubert, *Die Eschatologie des Posidonius* (Leipzig: Pfeiffer, 1927).

6. *Tübingen Theosophy* §37 (ed. H. Erbse, *Theosophorum Graecorum Fragmenta* [Stuttgart: Teubner, 1995]); cf. Lactantius, *Divine Institutions* 7.13. Compare the conversation in the oracular cave of Trophonius (Plutarch, *Gen. Socr.* 591A–592E).

7. In Plutarch, *De pyth. or.* 6.397A; see Parke 1988, 63f.

8. Goethe, *Venetianische Epigramme* (1790) 1 (J. W. v. Goethe, *Sämtliche Werke in 18 Bänden*, ed. E. Beutler [Zurich: Artemis 1960–66] 1:221).

9. Marmor Parium: FGH 239 A 14; cf. "Homer" *Hymn to Demeter;* Kern 1922, 115ff.

10. K. Tsantsanoglou and G. M. Parassoglou, "Two Gold Lamellae from Thessaly," *Hellenika* 38 (1987): 3–16; F. Graf, "Dionysian and Orphic Eschatology," in T. H. Carpenter and C. A. Faraone, *Masks of Dionysos* (Ithaca, N.Y./London: Cornell University Press, 1993), 239–58. For the history of religions, see Zuntz 1971.

11. Orpheus (Hieros Logos) in Olympiodorus, commentary on Plato's *Phaedo* (Kern, frag. 232); F. Graf, "Dionysian and Orphic Eschatology," 243f.; parallels in Kern.

12. V. Ehrenberg and A. H. M. Jones, *Documents Illustrating the Reigns of Augustus and Tiberius* (Oxford: Clarendon Press, 1955; reprint, 1976), no. 98, Greek and Latin; cf. the *lex arae* of Narbonne (Gaul, 12/13 C.E., Ehrenberg-Jones, no. 100): foundation of the cult on 23rd and 24th of September, because on this day "the happiness of the epoch" (*saeculi felicitas*) brought forth the "leader of the world" (Augustus).

13. With him a new era also begins in Rome: the "years of the Augusti" (*anni Augustorum*), in January, 27 B.C.E. According to official propaganda, this point marks the "renewal of the republic" (*restitutio rei publicae*); cf. Censorinus, *De die natali* 21.8.

14. Inscription on coins of Hadrian (BMC, Emp. III p. 334) and Antoninus Pius (BMC, Emp. IV pp. 205–6).

15. Servius, commentary on Virgil, *Aeneid* 8.398; Censorinus, *De die natali* 14.6; Macrobius *In somnium Scipionis* 1.7.1; 1.7.7.

16. Zosimus's source was probably Phlegon, "Concerning the celebrations of the Romans," which for its part (indirectly) goes back to Varro. A *saeculum* celebration under Maximian (304 C.E.) is uncertain.

17. Note, however, *Theogony* 713ff.: Tartarus; the children of the night; sleep and death; Hades and Persephone; Styx. These are all analogous to the Homeric Nekyia.

18. H. Otten, *Mythen vom Gotte Kumarbi: Neue Fragmente* (Berlin: Akademie, 1950); West 1966; H. A. Hoffner, Jr., *Hittite Myths* (Atlanta: Scholars Press, 1990); Burkert 1987b. On the epoch of nine years, see Hesiod, *Theog.* 795–805.

19. Cf. the numbering of the succession of the gods in the Orphic tradition (Kern 1922, no. 107).

20. Varro, *De gente populi Romani,* frags. 3 and 4 (ed. H. Peter) in Censorinus, *De die natali* 21; and Augustine, *City of God* 22.28. Cf. H. Peter, "Die Epochen in Varros Werk de gente populi Romani," *Rhein. Mus.* 58(57) (1902): 231–51.

21. Appian's source was Polybius 38.4.22, which is fragmentary at this passage. Cf. Jesus' prophecy about the destruction of Jerusalem: Matt. 23:37; Luke 13:34–35; cf. Luke 18:41–44.

22. The Greek composition (second–third century C.E.) is lost. A Latin translation comes from the third–fourth century; a coptic is preserved in NHC VI 7 and 8 (340/370 C.E.). See M. Krause, "Ägyptisches Gedankengut in der Apokalypse des Asclepius," *Zeitschrift der deutschen morgenländ. Gesellsch.* Suppl. 1 (1969): 48–57. All these texts are available in German translation with notes in C. Colpe and J. Holzhausen, *Das Corpus Hermeticum Deutsch* (Clavis Pansophiae 7.1–2; Stuttgart: Frommann-Holzboog, 1997).

23. *Sib. Or.* 3.350ff.; 652; Josephus, *Jewish War* 6.312–34; "Oracle of Hystaspes" (second or first century B.C.E.) in Lactantius, *Divine Institutions* 7.15.11; 1.17.11. See H. G. Kippenberg, "Dann wird der Orient herrschen und der Okzident dienen," in *Spiegel und Gleichnis: Festschrift für Jacob Taubes,* ed. N. Bolz and W. Hübener (Würzburg: Königshausen & Neumann, 1983), 40–48.

24. For Tacitus's own doubts, see *Hist.* 4.54, concerning the burning of the capitol; see also G. Baudy, *Die Brände Roms: Ein apokalyptisches Motiv in der antiken Historiographie* (Hildesheim: Olms, 1991).

25. Theophrastus (372/370–288/286 B.C.E.) in Simplicius (sixth century C.E.) on Aristotle, *Physics* 24.13 = Anaximander, A9 DK; text and commentary in KRS 101.

26. The basic studies are K. Gaiser, *Platon und die Geschichte* (Antrittsvorlesung, Tübingen, 1960; Stuttgart-Bad Canstatt: Frommann-Holzboog, 1961); idem, *Platons ungeschriebene Lehre: Studien zur systematischen und geschichtlichen Begründung der Wissenschaften in der Platonischen Schule,* 2nd ed. (Stuttgart: Klett, 1968) 205ff.

27. Rohde 1925, 2:263–95. Cf. H. Cancik, "Erwin Rohde—ein Philologe der Bismarckzeit," in *Semper Apertus: Sechshundert Jahre Ruprecht-Karls-Universität Heidelberg* (Berlin/Heidelberg: Springer, 1985), 2:436–505.

28. Technical terms that first appear among later authors are "rebirth" (*palingenesia*), renewal (*renovatio mundi*), restoration (*apokatastasis*). Cf. SVF II. frags 593, 620, 625. Cf. Acts 3:21; Eph. 1:10; Col. 1:20.

29. On the battle of the stars, see Seneca, *Hercules furens* 944ff.; *Thyestes* 844ff. Cf. *Sib. Or.* 5.512ff.

30. For the analogy between macrocosmic and microcosmic death, cf. Seneca *Epist.* 65.24. Cf. Schubert, *Die Eschatologie des Posidonius,* 86f.

31. Constantine, *Oratio ad coetum Sanctorum;* cf. Lactantius, *Divine Institutions*

7.24.11. P. Courcelle, "Les exégèses chrétiennes de la quatrième Eclogue," *Revue des Etudes Anciennes* 59 (1957): 294–319; idem, "Les pères de l'église devant les enfers Virgiliens," *Archives d'histoire doctrinale et littéraire du moyen âge* 22 (30/31) (1955): 5–74.

32. Norden 1958; H. Hommel, "Vergils 'messianisches' Gedicht," in *Wege zu Vergil*, ed. H. Oppermann (Darmstadt: Wissenschaftliche Buchgesellschaft, 1963), 368–425; H. D. Betz, "Eduard Norden und die frühchristliche Literatur," in *Eduard Norden*, ed. B. Kytzler et al., 107–27.

33. *Ecl.* 4.22; cf.. Isaiah 11. See J. Ebach, "Konversion oder Vertilgung: Utopie und Politik im Motiv des Tierfriedens bei Jesaja und Vergil," in *Spiegel und Gleichnis*, ed. Bolz and Hübener, 23–39. A critical comparison between bucolic Utopia and Greco-Roman eschatologie, on the one hand, and Jewish messianism on the other, is undertaken by R. Faber, *Politische Idyllik: Zur sozialen Mythologie Arkadiens* (Stuttgart: Klett, 1977).

BIBLIOGRAPHY

Abbreviations

CAH   *Cambridge Ancient History,* vol. 8. Cambridge: Cambridge University Press, 1965.

CIL   *Corpus Inscriptionum Latinarum*

DK   H. Diels, ed. *Die Fragmente der Vorsokratiker: Griechisch und Deutsch.* Berlin: Weidmann, 1903. Fifth edition, with notes edited by W. Kranz (Berlin, 1934). Sixth revised edition (Berlin, 1951/52). A = testimonia; B = fragments.

FGH   F. Jacoby, ed. *Die Fragmente der griechischen Historiker.* Leiden: Brill, 1957–.

KRS   G. S. Kirk, J. E. Raven, and M. Schofield, eds. *The Presocratic Philosophers: A Critical History with a Selection of Texts.* Cambridge: Cambridge University Press, 1957. Second edition, 1983.

LSAM   F. Sokolowski, ed. *Lois sacrées de l'Asie Mineure.* Paris: Boccard, 1955.

NHC   Nag Hammadi Codex

SVF   J. von Arnim, ed. *Stoicorum Veterum Fragmenta.* 4 vols. Stuttgart: Teubner, 1964.

Bibliography

Alföldi, A. 1965–66. "Die alexandrinischen Götter und die vota publica am Jahresbeginn." *Jahrbuch für Antike und Christentum* 8/9:53–87.

Andresen, C. 1952–53. "Justin und der mittlere Platonismus." *Zeitschrift für die neutestamentliche Wissenschaft* 44:157–95.

Betz, H. D. 1983. "The Problem of Apocalyptic Genre in Greek and Hellenistic Literature." In Hellholm 1983, 577–97.

Burkert, W. 1987a. *Ancient Mystery Cults*. Cambridge, Mass.: Harvard University Press.

———. 1988. "Oriental and Greek Mythology." In *Interpretations of Greek Mythology*, edited by J. Bremmer, 10–40. London: Routledge.

Cancik, H. 1980. "Der Eingang in die Unterwelt: Ein religionswissenschaftlicher Versuch zu Vergil, Aeneis 6.236-72." *Der Altsprachliche Unterricht* 23.2:55–69.

———. 1983a. "Libri fatales: Römische Offenbarungsliteratur und Geschichtstheologie," in Hellholm 1983, 549–76.

———. 1983b. "Die Rechtfertigung Gottes durch den 'Fortschritt der Zeiten': Zur Differenz jüdisch-christlicher und hellenisch-römischer Zeit- und Geschichtsvorstellungen," in *Die Zeit*, edited by A. Peisl and A. Mohler, 257–88. Munich: Oldenbourg.

———. 1990. "Geschichte." In *Handbuch religionswissenschaftlicher Grundbegriffe*, edited by H. Cancik, B. Gladigow, and K.-H. Kohl, 2:491–500. Stuttgart: Metzler.

———. 1995a. *Nietzsches Antike: Vorlesung*. Stuttgart: Metzler..

———. 1995b. "Militia perennis: Typologie und Theologie der Kriege Roms gegen Veji bei Titus Livius." In *Töten im Krieg*, edited by H. von Stietencron and J. Rüpke, 197–211. Historische Anthropologie 6. Freiburg/Munich: Alber.

Collins, J. J. 1974. *The Sibylline Oracles of Egyptian Judaism*. Missoula, Mont.: Scholars Press.

———. 1987. "The Development of the Sibylline Tradition." In *ANRW* 20.1: 421–59.

Demandt, A. 1978. *Metaphern für Geschichte, Sprachbilder und Gleichnisse im historisch-politischen Denken*. Munich: Beck.

De Martino, E. 1977. *La fine del mondo: Contributo all' analisi delle apocalissi culturali*. Turin: Einaudi.

Flusser, D. 1972. "The Four Empires in the Fourth Sibyl and the Book of Daniel." *Israel Oriental Studies* 2:48–75.

Fuchs, H. 1938. *Der geistige Widerstand gegen Rom in der antiken Welt*. Berlin: de Gruyter.

Gatz, B. 1967. *Weltalter, goldene Zeit und sinnverwandte Vorstellungen*. Spudasmata 16. Hildesheim: Olms.

Graf, F. 1974. *Eleusis und die orphische Dichtung Athens in vorhellenistischer Zeit*. Berlin/New York: de Gruyter, 1974.

Graf, M. 1950. *Roman Anniversary Issues*. Cambridge: Cambridge University Press.

Hellholm, D., ed. 1983. *Apocalypticism in the Mediterranean World and the Near East: Proceedings of the International Colloquium on Apocalypticism, Uppsala, August 12–17, 1979*. 2nd ed. Tübingen: Mohr, 1989.

Jaeschke, W. 1986. *Die Suche nach den eschatologischen Wurzeln der Geschichtsphilosophie: Eine historische Kritik der Saekularisierungsthese*. Munich: Kaiser.

Kern, O. 1922. *Orphicorum Fragmenta*. Berlin: Weidmann.

Kurtz, D. C., and J. Boardman. 1971. *Greek Burial Customs*. London: Thames & Hudson.

Momigliano, A. 1987. "Daniele e la teoria greca della successione degli imperi." In idem, *Pagine ebraiche*, 33–39. Turin: Einaudi.

Norden, E. 1957. P. Vergilius Maro, *Aeneis Buch VI*. 4th ed. Darmstadt: Wissenschaftliche Buchgesellschaft.

———. 1958. *Die Geburt des Kindes: Geschichte einer religiösen Idee*. Darmstadt: Wissenschaftliche Buchgesellschaft. First published 1924.

Overbeck, F. 1996. *Christentum und Kultur* (1919). In *Werke und Nachlass* 6.1, edited by B. von Reibnitz. Stuttgart: Metzler.

Parke, H. W. 1988. *Sibyls and Sibylline Prophecy in Classical Antiquity*. Edited by B. C. McGing. London: Routledge.

Riedweg, C. 1995. "Orphisches bei Empedocles." In *Antike und Abendland* 41:34–59.

Rohde, E. 1925. *Psyche: Seelencult und Unsterblichkeitsglaube der Griechen*. Tübingen: Mohr. First published 1890.

Rosenmeyer, T. G. 1957. "Hesiod and Historiography." *Hermes* 85:257–85.

Stierle, K., and R. Warning, eds. 1996. *Das Ende: Figuren einer Denkform*. Poetik und Hermeneutik 16. Munich: Fink.

Swain, J. W. 1940. "The Theory of the Four Monarchies: Opposition History under the Roman Empire." *Classical Philology* 35:1–21.

Taubes, J. 1991. *Abendländische Eschatologie*. Munich: Matthes & Seitz. First published 1947.

Teuffel, W. S. 1871. *Studien und Charakteristiken zur griechischen und römischen Litteraturgeschichte*, 1–44. Leipzig: Teubner.

Toynbee, J. M. C. 1971. *Death and Burial in the Roman World*. London/Southampton: Thames & Watson.

von Wilamowitz-Moellendorff, U. 1948. *Platon: Sein Leben und seine Werke*. 4th edition. Berlin: Weidmann. First published 1918.

West, M. L. 1966. *Hesiod, Theogony*. Oxford: Clarendon Press.

———. 1983. *Orphic Poems*. Oxford: Clarendon Press.

Wright, M. R., ed., 1981. *Empedocles: The Extant Fragments*. New Haven: Yale University Press.

Zuntz, G. 1971. *Persephone: Three Essays on Religion and Thought in Magna Graecia*. Oxford: Clarendon Press.

PART 2

Apocalypticism in Ancient Judaism

4

From Prophecy to Apocalypticism: The Expectation of the End

John J. Collins
University of Chicago

IN POPULAR CONSCIOUSNESS, NO IDEA IS MORE CHARACTERISTIC of apocalyptic eschatology than the expectation of the end of the world. Eschatology, after all, means "talk about the end," even though, as we shall see, it can never be reduced to just the end of anything. While some scholars have traced this idea to the teaching of Zoroaster in ancient Iran (Cohn 1993), a clearer line of transmission can be traced to the Hebrew prophets. The ultimate roots of the concept lie in the combat myths that can be found in various cultures of the ancient Near East. In Israel, this mythology was adapted to celebrate the triumph of God over the forces of chaos, in the Psalms (e.g., Psalms 96, 98). The prophets, however, projected the conflict into the future and used the mythology to evoke the judgment of God, both on the Gentile nations and on Israel itself.

It was the prophet Amos in the eighth century B.C.E. who first proclaimed that "the end" (Amos 8:2; Hebrew *haqqēṣ*) was at hand. By this Amos meant that the kingdom of northern Israel was doomed. There was no concept as yet of an end of this world. Amos also spoke of this event as "the day of the Lord," which would be darkness and not light (Amos 5:18–20). In the centuries that followed, other prophets used poetic hyperbole to expand this notion into a day of cosmic judgment. An oracle preserved in the book of

Isaiah predicts the fall of Babylon in cosmic terms: "the day of the Lord comes, cruel, with wrath and fierce anger, to make the earth a desolation and to destroy its sinners from it. For the stars of heaven and their constellations will not give their light; the sun will be dark at its rising and the moon will not shed its light. . . . Therefore I will make the heavens tremble and the earth will be shaken out of its place at the wrath of the Lord of hosts, in the day of his fierce anger" (Isa. 13:9–13). Here the prophet is still concerned with the destruction of a specific city, Babylon, but his language evokes a catastrophe of cosmic proportions. Thus, the notion of the end of this world has its origin in the cosmic imagery of Hebrew prophets in their oracles of destruction against specific places, including Jerusalem.

This imagery, however, underwent significant development in the period between the Babylonian Exile (586–539 B.C.E.) and the rise of Christianity. We will consider three phases in the development. The first is located in the latter part of the sixth and early fifth centuries B.C.E., at the time of the Jewish restoration in Jerusalem under the Persians, and is often called "proto-apocalyptic." The second occurs in the Hellenistic period and reached its climax in the time of persecution under Antiochus IV Epiphanes (168–164 B.C.E.) and the Maccabean revolt. The third is contemporaneous with the rise of Christianity and arises in the context of Jewish reflection on the second destruction of Jerusalem, by the Romans in 70 C.E.

POSTEXILIC PROPHECY

In the period that followed the Babylonian Exile we often find heightened cosmic imagery in oracles that are difficult to pin down as to their specific historical referents. Some of the most colorful examples are found in Isaiah 24–27, a passage of uncertain historical provenance that may be related to the sack of Babylon by Xerxes in 485 B.C.E.. (These chapters are sometimes called "the apocalypse of Isaiah," but in form they are simply prophetic oracles.) "Now the Lord is about to lay waste the earth and make it desolate, and he will twist its surface and scatter its inhabitants" (24:1); "for the windows of heaven are opened, and the foundations of the earth tremble. The earth is utterly broken, the earth is torn asunder, the earth is violently shaken" (24:19). These oracles also draw motifs from ancient Canaanite myths, by promising that God "will swallow Death (*Môt*) forever" (25:7) and that he will punish Leviathan and slay the dragon that is in the sea (27:1). Significantly, we also find here the language of resurrection: "Your dead shall live, their corpses shall rise. O dwellers in the dust, awake and sing for joy"

(26:19). Most probably, the reference here is to the restoration of the Israelite nation, in contrast to their erstwhile rulers, of whom it is said that their dead will not live (26:14). Resurrection of the dead was already used as a metaphor for the restoration of Israel in Ezekiel's vision of the valley full of dry bones in Ezekiel 37, which dates from the time of the exile. In any case, the resurrection language here reminds us that these oracles are not only predictions of destruction. They are also looking for a new beginning beyond the disaster.

We can only guess at the historical and social matrix that inspired the prophet of Isaiah 24–27. There is clearly resentment against "the fortified city, the palace of aliens" (25:2; Babylon is perhaps the most plausible candidate). There is also a great desire for the restoration of Israel, likened to a resurrection of the dead. In the prophet's vision, the physical world symbolizes the political order; the world as constituted must be broken apart to allow a new order to emerge. The prophet evidently identifies with the poor and disenfranchised, but the poor may be the Jewish people in relation to the Gentiles, or some smaller group within Israel. The lack of historical specificity is characteristic of many eschatological oracles from the postexilic period. Another example is found in Ezekiel 38–39, where the prophet conjures up the fantastic figure of Gog from the land of Magog. (The name may be suggested by Gyges of Lydia, but Gyges had no contact with Israel.) Gog becomes a generic representative of Gentile power, which is to be brought low by God on the mountains of Israel. Yet another example is found in Joel 3:9–16, where God judges the nations in the valley of Jehoshaphat. Again, we can only guess at the historical context of this oracle. (Joel 3:6 rebukes Tyre, Sidon, and Philistia for selling Jews as slaves to the Greeks, but the slave trade flourished throughout the Persian and Hellenistic periods.)

All of these passages were probably composed with specific crises in mind. Since we no longer know the historical circumstances, however, the oracles take on the character of general eschatological predictions that evoke an expectation of the end of history, which may or may not be imminent. Since these oracles were embedded in scripture, later generations could interpret them in various ways and could see their fulfillment in various historical circumstances.

Only in the period immediately after the exile can the emerging eschatological expectations of the later biblical period be set in historical and social context. In the year 518 B.C.E. the prophets Haggai and Zechariah were instrumental in motivating the returned exiles to complete the rebuilding of the Temple. Haggai told the people that their lack of material prosperity was due to the fact that they had given higher priority to their own houses. When the building of the Temple was finally undertaken, he told them to take courage:

> For thus says the Lord of hosts: Once again, in a little while, I will shake the heavens and the earth and the sea and the dry land; and I will shake all the nations, so that the treasure of all nations shall come, and I will fill this house with splendor, says the Lord of hosts. (Hag. 2:7)

In the brief text of Haggai's oracles, there are signs that the promised transformation was delayed. Haggai is insistent: "From this day on I will bless you" (2:19). It is apparent, however, that the Jewish community did not experience a transformation of fortune such as Haggai had promised.

Haggai expected the rebuilding of the Temple to be the catalyst for a new age. Not all his contemporaries shared his views. The final section of the book of Isaiah (chapters 56–66) preserves a skeptical view of the Temple project:

> Thus says the Lord: Heaven is my throne and the earth is my footstool; what is the house that you would build for me, and what is my resting-place? All these things my hand has made, and so all these things are mine, says the Lord. But this is the one to whom I will look, to the humble and contrite in spirit, who trembles at my word. (Isa. 66:1–2)

The tremblers (*ḥārēdîm*) have given their name to apocalyptically oriented ultraorthodox Jews in modern Israel. They probably constituted a distinct group also in the Persian period (Blenkinsopp 1990). They were no less eschatological in their outlook than the proponents of the rebuilding: "For I am about to create new heavens and a new earth" (Isa. 65:17) and "as the new heavens and the new earth, which I will make, shall remain before me, says the Lord; so shall your descendants and your name remain . . ." (65:22).

In a seminal study published in 1975 Paul Hanson argued that Isaiah 56–66 represented *The Dawn of Apocalyptic.* He posited a sharp division in the postexilic community between the hierocratic party, represented by Haggai, Zechariah 1–8, and Ezekiel 40–48, whose piety focused the preservation of the sacred, and a visionary party, represented by Isaiah 56–66, that gave a higher priority to social and humanitarian concerns. In the categories of the sociologist Karl Mannheim, the hierocrats were ideological, while the visionaries were utopian. While both sides used eschatological symbols, the use made of them was different: one side used them to underpin the existing power structures of the Temple and priesthood, while the other side used them to undermine these structures. Hanson used a complex system of prosodic typology (that is, the changing poetic style of the prophets), to reconstruct the history of the visionary party, from the initial enthusiasm shown in Isaiah 60–62 to eventual disillusionment with history and the desperate hope for a new creation.

This ingenious reconstruction has been criticized on several grounds. The twofold division of postexilic society is almost certainly too simple, and the unsympathetic portrayal of the hierocratic movement requires modification. The hierocrats must be credited with genuine religious motives and not merely the desire to maintain the current power structures. Moreover, the "hierocratic" books of Zechariah and Ezekiel 40–48 are no less visionary than Isaiah 56–66 and may equally well be considered forerunners of apocalypticism (Cook 1995; Tigchelaar 1996). The reliability of prosodic typology as an instrument for tracing historical development is also open to question. Nonetheless, Hanson must be credited with an imaginative reconstruction of a situation where the hope for a new heaven and earth made sense: it arises from profound alienation and a sense of hopelessness in the present world. While it is certainly possible to find "millennial groups in power" (Cook 1995, 55), we must remember that even those who wielded power in postexilic Judah experienced relative deprivation in the broader context of the Persian empire. Haggai and Zechariah may have been close to the center of power in Jerusalem, but they were very marginal figures in the broader Persian context. The significance of Hanson's work, however, lies in the light it shed on the role of inner-community conflict in the rise of apocalypticism. Eschatological hope in the early postexilic period was not only prompted by the powerlessness of the Jewish people in the international context. It also arose from division and alienation within the Jewish community. Both factors, the international situation and internal division, continue to play a part in generating eschatological expectations throughout Jewish history.

The hope for a new heaven and a new earth (Isa. 65:17) is certainly relevant to the history of apocalypticism, but it should not be labeled "apocalyptic" without serious qualification. Formally, the last chapters of Isaiah are prophetic oracles, just like the oracles of the preexilic prophets. The content of the oracles also has much in common with older prophecy. The conditions of the new creation that are spelled out in Isaiah 65 are closer to the expectations of the prophets of old than to those of the later apocalyptic visionaries:

> No more shall there be in it an infant that lives but a few days or an old person who does not live out a lifetime; for one who dies at a hundred years will be considered a youth, and one who falls short of a hundred will be considered accursed. They shall build houses and inhabit them; they shall plant vineyards and eat their fruit . . . for like the days of a tree shall the days of my people be. (Isa. 65:17–25)

The passage concludes by evoking Isaiah 11: "The wolf and the lamb shall feed together." What is envisaged here is an earthly life such as we know, but longer and free of pain and care. This is a utopian hope, which can properly be called eschatological. It is very different, however, from the hope that we will find in the apocalyptic literature of the Hellenistic age.

We may summarize the developments of the early postexilic period as follows. There is increased use of cosmic imagery to express the hope of a radical transformation of human affairs. In many cases, the expected judgment takes on a general character that cannot be tied specifically to any known historical events. The ancient myth of God's combat with the dragon is projected into the future as a paradigm for a new creation. We find eschatological hopes in various theological traditions, some oriented toward the Temple cult, some critical of it. Eschatological hopes arise both to compensate for the powerlessness of Israel among the nations and to console groups that were alienated from the power structures within Jewish society. The hopes that we find in these late prophetic texts, however, are still oriented toward a restored earthly society in a way that has more in common with earlier prophets than with later visionaries.

It must be conceded, however, that we know extremely little about the groups that transmitted eschatological expectations in Judaism in the Persian period. When apocalypticism emerges full-blown in the books of Enoch and Daniel in the Hellenistic period, it is a far more developed and complex phenomenon than is the case in any of the fragmentary prophetic texts hitherto discussed. It is not possible to show any social continuity between the visionaries of the Persian period and their Hellenistic successors. The prophetic oracles were taken up into the canon of scripture, and so became part of the source material of the apocalyptists, who picked up motifs like the creation of a new heaven and a new earth. The apocalypticism of the Hellenistic period, however, is a new phenomenon in many crucial respects.

THE HELLENISTIC PERIOD

The Books of Enoch

The oldest Jewish apocalypses are found in the *Book of Enoch,* a composite work that is fully preserved only in Ethiopic. Greek fragments of the work have long been known, and Aramaic fragments have been found among the Dead Sea Scrolls (Milik 1976). The book includes at least five distinct works: the Book of the Watchers (chapters 1–36), the Similitudes (chapters 37–71), the Astronomical Book (chapters 72–82), the Book of Dreams (chapters 83–90), and the Epistle (chapters 91–105). Within these books, the Animal Apocalypse (chapters 85–90) and the Apocalypse of Weeks (93:1–10 + 91:11–18) stand out as distinct compositions, while the concluding chapters of the book, 106–8, contain further material. (Chapters 106–7 deal with the birth of Noah; 108 is "another book Enoch wrote for his son Methuselah.) The Similitudes are not attested in the Dead Sea Scrolls and can be dated no earlier than the first century C.E. The other books, however, must be dated to the third or early second centuries B.C.E. on the basis of the paleography of the Dead Sea fragments and also on internal evidence. (The Apocalypse of Weeks and the Animal Apocalypse allude to historical events and also presuppose the story of the Book of the Watchers.)

While the prophets of old had spoken in their own names, and oracles such as Isaiah 24–27 probably circulated anonymously, the books of Enoch are pseudonymous, since they are ascribed to an antediluvian patriarch who cannot possibly have been their actual author. Pseudonymity henceforth is a trademark of Jewish apocalypses. Other pseudonymous authors include Daniel, Moses, Ezra, Baruch, and Abraham. There was a precedent for pseudonymity in Jewish tradition: the book of Deuteronomy was ascribed to Moses, although it was promulgated by King Josiah in 621 B.C.E. and probably took its present form during the Babylonian Exile. In the Hellenistic period the device was widespread. New oracles were uttered in the name of the sibyl in the Greek world, and in the names of Zoroaster and Hystaspes in the Persian world. But pseudonymity was not peculiar to oracles and apocalypses. In Hellenistic Judaism we find new psalms of David and Solomon and a new wisdom book also in the name of Solomon. New writings circulated in the Greek and Roman world in the names of Plato and Heraclitus. Pseudonymity, then, was something of a literary fashion and could serve different purposes in different contexts. In all cases, it presumably enhanced the authority of a work by giving it an aura of antiquity. While the authors of such works must have been aware of the fiction involved, their effectiveness depended on the credulity of the masses. This is not to say that the authors sought to deceive; they may have had a sophisticated understanding of their literary device. In general, the pseudonyms are appropriate to their material. Enoch is the authority on heavenly mysteries, since he had been taken up to heaven before the flood (Gen. 5:24). Solomon is the authority for wisdom teaching, and Moses for matters pertaining to the law.

In the context of apocalyptic writing, pseudonymity offered some other advantages. It permitted the author to create an extended "prophecy" of history, most of which could be verified, because it was written after the fact. The actual prophecy of future events was thereby rendered more credible. Such prophecies conveyed a sense that the course of history was predetermined, since events could be predicted so far in advance. They also allowed the readers to identify their own place in the unfolding drama and to see the events of their time in a cosmic perspective.

The oldest parts of the Enoch tradition are found in the Astronomical Book and the Book of the Watchers. The Astronomical Book is largely taken up with the movements of the stars. These were important for establishing the true calendar, which was a major cause of sectarian division in ancient Judaism. Much of this material is scientific, or pseudo-scientific, in character, and it suggests that the tradents of the Enoch literature were learned scribes, even if their learning was crude and outdated by Greek or Babylonian standards. Enoch views the stars as animated beings and speaks of their leaders, who are responsible for their movements. Moreover, he warns that at a future time "many heads of the stars in command will go astray, and these will change their courses and their activities, and will not appear at the times which have been prescribed for them" (*1 Enoch* 70:6). We are also told that the regulations in this book are valid "until the new creation shall be made which will last forever" (72:1). Apart from these hints, however, there is little eschatology in the Astronomical Book of Enoch. The book is primarily a treatise on the movements of the stars (VanderKam 1984, 76–109).

The Book of the Watchers also contains much material that might be regarded as speculative and that suggests that the authors were learned scribes rather than prophets. In this case, however, eschatology also has an important role. There are two major themes in the Book of the Watchers, the story of the Watchers, or fallen angels, in *1 Enoch* 6–11 and the story of Enoch's ascent to heaven and his journeys to the ends of the earth (chapters 12–36; the two themes overlap in chapters 12–16). The story of the Watchers has its point of departure in Genesis 6, where the "sons of God" become enamored of the daughters of men and come down and beget giants. In *1 Enoch,* this story is developed into an explanation of the spread of sin on earth. (Enoch also knows the story of Adam and Eve, but he does not use it to explain the prevalence of sin in later generations.) On this explanation, sin results from the influence of supernatural, demonic forces on human behavior. The fallen angels impart to humanity forbidden knowledge: "and they taught them charms and spells and showed to them the cutting of roots and trees" (7:2).

> And Azazel taught men to make swords and daggers and shields and breast-plates, and he showed them the things after these, and the art of making them: bracelets, and ornaments and the art of making up the eyes and of beautifying

the eyelids and the most precious and choice stones and all kinds of colored dyes. And the world was changed. And there was great impiety and much fornication, and they went astray, and all their ways became corrupt." (8:1–2)

Later we are told that evil spirits come out of the flesh of the giants, to cause evil and sorrow on earth (15:8–16:1). This myth is developed in the book of *Jubilees,* where Mastema, the chief of the spirits, gets permission from God for one-tenth of the spirits to remain on earth so that humanity can be corrupted and led astray (*Jub.* 10:7–11).

Paolo Sacchi has argued that the story of the Watchers is the kernel in which the essence of apocalypticism is contained and from which the whole tradition grows (Sacchi 1996). The underlying problem that all apocalyptic literature addresses is the problem of evil. The characteristic apocalyptic explanation lies in the appeal to supernatural, demonic forces. There is no doubt that Sacchi has highlighted a very fundamental element in the Enoch tradition, but its importance must be seen in perspective. Even the story of the Watchers is not concerned only with the origin of evil; it also entails judgment and punishment. Moreover, we find various explanations of the origin of evil in apocalyptic tradition. The Qumran *Community Rule* says that God created two spirits, one of light and one of darkness, an explanation that is patently indebted to Zoroastrian dualism. Later apocalypses (4 Ezra, *2 Baruch*) make extensive use of the story of Adam and Eve and ignore the Watchers. But nonetheless, Sacchi has performed an important service in highlighting the role that the origin of evil plays in several apocalyptic texts. It should also be noted that the story of the Watchers very probably has an allegorical quality. The passage cited above from *1 Enoch* 8 complains that "the world was changed." It is difficult not to read this passage as a loose allegory for the cultural crisis brought on by the advent of Hellenism, which entailed the spread of information and new ideas of morality that were often scandalous to traditional Jews. The story of the Watchers, then, is not only an etiology of the spread of wickedness before the flood. It is also paradigmatic of the way the world was changed in the author's own time in the Hellenistic age.

The author evidently perceived the way the world was changed as negative, but his composition does not end in despair. Rather, he offers two resolutions of the crisis. First, the story of the Watchers ends with their imprisonment by the archangels; second, Enoch's tour reveals that the apparatus of judgment and retribution is already in place.

In *1 Enoch* 11, the punishment of the Watchers is described. The angel Raphael is bidden: "Bind Azazel by his hands and his feet, and throw him into the darkness. And split open the desert which is in Dudael, and throw him there . . . and cover his face that he may not see light and that on the great day of judgment he may be hurled into the fire. And restore the earth, which the angels have ruined" (10:4–7). Again, the angel Michael is told to bind Shemi-ḥaza, the other leader of the rebel angels, "for seventy generations under the hills of the earth until the day of their judgment and of their consummation, until the judgment which is for all eternity is accomplished" (10:12). The passage goes on to describe how the earth will be transformed and cleansed from corruption. The prospect of a final judgment provides the ultimate solution to the crisis of the Watchers. We do not, however, get the impression that this judgment is imminent. In the narrative context of the book, it is deferred for seventy generations, until the end of history.

The eschatology of the Book of the Watchers is filled out in the account of Enoch's journeys. Enoch is introduced in chapter 12 as a "scribe of righteousness," whom the Watchers ask to intercede for them. There follows an intriguing scene in which Enoch sits down "by the waters of Dan" and reads out the petition of the Watchers until he falls asleep. Then in his vision clouds call him and the winds lift him up to heaven. We have no way of knowing whether the author was reporting his own visionary experience here, but the recitation and the proximity of water are often associated with visions in many cultures. Enoch then describes his entry into the heavenly palace and the presence of God enthroned (chapter 14). He is told to tell the Watchers that they should intercede for humans, not the reverse, and that they should have remained spiritual and holy, living an eternal life, and not have lain with women and begotten children. We see here that the fundamental antithesis in the Book of the Watchers is between heaven and earth, spirit and flesh (although the latter distinction should not be confused with the Greek distinction between body and soul). The ideal life is the holy, spiritual, eternal life in heaven, which the Watchers have forsaken. Enoch, in contrast, is a human being admitted to the heavenly court, whose elevation betokens a new possibility for human existence. The negative attitude toward sex and procreation should also be noted. A similar tendency toward asceticism is found in the Dead Sea Scrolls and in the Greek accounts of the Essene sect, some of whose members are said to have been celibate.

Enoch's actual tour begins in chapter 17 and takes him to the ends of the earth, accompanied by angelic guides. He sees the storehouses of the winds and the elements and the cornerstone of the earth and other such cosmological marvels. A major part of his revelations, however, concerns places of judgment. In chapters 18 and 19 he sees the prison of the stars and the host of heaven, where the Watchers also are kept until the great judgment day, and another form of this vision is repeated in chapter 21. In chapter 22 he sees chambers inside a mountain, where "the spirits of the souls of the dead" are kept to await judgment. While there is some confusion in the text as to whether there are three chambers or four, it is clear that distinctions are made between the righteous and the wicked, while they await the judgment day. *This is earliest attestation of the judgment of the dead in Jewish tradition.* The following chapters go on to describe the place where God's throne will be set when he comes down to visit the earth for good (chapter 25), the tree of life whose fruit will be given to the chosen after the judgment (chapter 26), and the valley of judgment (chapter 27). In a later chapter (32) Enoch sees the tree of knowledge, from which Adam and Eve ate.

The world that Enoch tours in chapters 17–36 is normally hidden from human sight and is accessible here only by supernatural revelation. It is antithetical to the world defiled by the Watchers. The message of the book is that all is not as it seems on earth. In the hidden regions, all is in order. The places of judgment are prepared to ensure the triumph of justice and provision has been made for retribution on an individual basis. Moreover, the holiness of the divine throne and its surroundings provide the greatest contrast to life on earth. The expectation of a future day of judgment is of basic importance in this book, but it is not the only, or even the primary, focus of the author's attention. Rather, the emphasis is on the present reality of everything that Enoch sees. While most human beings can only hope for access to the angelic world after death, the revelation of Enoch assures them that it is already there, waiting for them.

The hope for fellowship with the angels in the heavenly world is more explicitly stated in the Epistle of Enoch (chapters 91–105), which probably dates from the early second century B.C.E. Much of this document is taken up with woes against the rich, who trust in their wealth and do not remember the Most High, and exhortation to the righteous. The hope of the righteous is expressed in chapter 104: "you will shine like the lights of heaven and will be seen, and the gate of heaven will be opened to you . . . you will not have to hide on the day of the great judgment . . . for you shall be associates of the host of heaven." Even though the author of the Epistle cares deeply about injustice on earth, his ultimate hope is not just for a reversal of earthly fortune but for an angelic life in heaven.

While both the Book of the Watchers and the Epistle of Enoch anticipate a day of judgment, their focus is on the contrast between the heavenly and the earthly, the hidden and the visible. Concern for chronology appears more clearly in two Enochic apocalypses from the Maccabean era, the Apocalypse of Weeks and the Animal Apocalypse. The Apocalypse of Weeks divides history into ten "weeks" (presumably weeks of years), which will be followed after a new creation by "many weeks without number forever." The turning point of history comes in the seventh week, when there is an apostate generation, but at the end of the week "the chosen righteous from the eternal plant of righteousness will be chosen, to whom will be given sevenfold teaching concerning his whole creation" (93:10). The eighth week will be that of the righteous and "a sword will be given to it that the righteous judgment may be executed on those who do wrong" (93:12). If the apocalypse was written in the eighth generation, the sword would presumably be a reference to the Maccabean revolt. It is more likely, however, that it was written in the seventh week, at the time of the emergence of the chosen righteous. It is clear, however, that this apocalypse envisages a militant role for the righteous in the last generations. In the ninth generation, the world will be written down for destruction, and in the tenth there will be an eternal judgment on the Watchers. Then the first heaven will vanish and pass away, and a new heaven will appear. The Apocalypse of Weeks is probably the first Jewish document to envisage the end of the world in a literal sense.

This apocalypse is also noteworthy for literary reasons. The revelation takes the form of an extended prophecy, most of which is after the fact. The time of the author can be identified as the point of transition in the apocalypse, from the woeful present to the glorious future. The idea that history can be divided into a set number of periods is a very common idea in Jewish, and later Christian, apocalyptic literature. The division into ten periods most probably derives from Persian eschatology, which expected a great transition at the end of a millennium (e.g., in the *Bahman Yašt,* chapter 1). We find here a distinctively historically oriented apocalypse that is formally quite different from the otherworldly journeys of Enoch in the Book of the Watchers. It is closer to much of what we will find in the book of Daniel. It conveys a sense that history is predetermined and serves to legitimate the group called "the chosen righteous" (to which the author surely belonged) as playing a providential role in history.

The Animal Apocalypse is another extended prophecy after the fact, although the division into periods is less clearly defined. The apocalypse gets its name from its dominant literary device—the representation of human beings as animals. Adam is a white bull; the fallen angels are stars who have members like the members of horses and whose offspring are elephants and camels and asses, and so forth. In the postexilic period, Israel is subjected to the rule of seventy shepherds. The turning point of history comes when small lambs are born and horns grow upon them, and a big horn grows on one of them. The lamb with the big horn is clearly Judas Maccabee, and the context is the Maccabean revolt. The outcome of the revolt, however, is not described simply in historical terms. The Lord of the sheep comes down in anger, and a judgment scene unfolds. A big sword is given to the sheep (Israel) to kill the wild animals (Gentiles). The judgment extends not only to the seventy shepherds (the patron angels of the nations) but also to the Watchers of old. Here again the device of prophecy after the fact serves to locate the author and his group at the turning point of history. Like the Apocalypse of Weeks, this apocalypse is unabashed in its endorsement of violence as a means of executing justice. As in all of these Enochic writings, however, the final judgment is executed by God, and it affects all generations simultaneously. The sheep that had been destroyed are assembled at the judgment (90:33), which is a figurative way of giving expression to the resurrection of the dead.

In the writings attributed to Enoch, then, we can trace a progression, from those that are more speculative in content to those that are more concerned with history. The pseudonym of Enoch was chosen presumably because Enoch was preeminently qualified to disclose the mysteries of the heavenly world. Already in the Book of the Watchers, which shows no awareness of the Maccabean crisis, these mysteries include the judgment of the individual dead. There are indications in several of these apocalypses that the authors belonged to a group that considered itself to be chosen by God. In the heat of the Maccabean crisis, the interest shifts from the mysteries of the cosmos to those of history, and the sense of imminent expectation becomes greater. At least the Animal Apocalypse, and possibly the Apocalypse of Weeks, expresses outright support for the militant policies of the Maccabees.

The Book of Daniel

The book of Daniel is also a composite book. Chapters 1–6 contain a collection of traditional tales, often legendary in character, about Daniel and his companions in the Babylonian Exile. These tales were written down sometime in the third or early second century B.C.E. Chapters 7–12 report the visions of Daniel, interpreted by an angel. Already in antiquity the Neoplatonist Porphyry showed that these visions did not come from the time of the Babylonian Exile. They give an accurate report of history down to the time of Antiochus Epiphanes (to about 167 B.C.E.) but not beyond that point. Although Porphyry did not realize it, the account of the death of the king "between the sea and the holy mountain" (11:45) was inaccurate, and so we know that this prophecy was completed before the news of his death reached Jerusalem. (He died in Persia, late in 164 B.C.E.) The visions of Daniel are pseudonymous, just like those of Enoch. Even though Daniel is supposed to have lived during the Babylonian Exile, it is likely that his name was derived from ancient myth. Ezekiel, who certainly lived during the exile, associated Daniel with Noah and Job (Ezek. 14:14) and regarded the wisdom of Daniel as legendary (28:3). A hero named Daniel is found in the Ugaritic myths from the late second millennium, but it is uncertain whether the name of the biblical figure was suggested by the mythic tradition.

The stories in Daniel 1–6 represent the tradition lying behind the apocalyptic visions in chapters 7–12. In the stories, Daniel is preeminently an interpreter of dreams and mysterious signs. Most notable for our purpose is the interpretation of Nebuchadnezzar's dream in chapter 2. The king refuses to tell his dream, so Daniel can only know it by divine revelation. The dream concerns a large statue composed of different metals: the head of gold, the chest and arms of silver, the middle and thighs of bronze, and the feet of iron mixed with clay. Daniel interprets the statue in terms of four kingdoms, in declining succession, beginning with Nebuchadnezzar as the head of gold. The use of metals to symbolize a declining sequence has a famous parallel in Hesiod's *Works and Days,* where the ages of humankind are represented as gold, silver, bronze, and iron. A closer parallel to Nebuchadnezzar's vision is found in the Persian *Bahman Yašt,* where Zoroaster sees "the trunk of a tree, on which there were four branches: one of gold, one of silver, one of steel, and one of mixed iron." While the Persian text in its present form is several centuries later than Daniel, it is likely to derive from a common source. There is no reason to think that it was influenced by the biblical book. In the context of the book of Daniel, the four kingdoms must be identified as Babylon, Media, Persia, and Greece. (Daniel introduces the fictitious figure of Darius the Mede to represent the Median empire.) This sequence also points to Persian influence, since the Medes never ruled over Judea.

The sequence of four kingdoms followed by a fifth of a different character was well known throughout the Near East in the Hellenistic and Roman periods. Another Jewish example is found in the fourth *Sibylline Oracle.* Assyria, rather than Babylon, is usually the first kingdom. In Daniel 2, the end of the sequence is represented by a stone cut from a mountain that destroys the statue. The stone represents the kingdom of God, which will last forever. In Daniel 2, however, there is no sense of imminent expectation. The coming of the kingdom of God is in the distant future from the viewpoint of Daniel and Nebuchadnezzar. The point is rather that the God of Israel is in control of history and that this control will eventually be made manifest.

The theme of four kingdoms is picked up again in Daniel's vision in chapter 7, but this time the imagery is very different. Daniel sees four beasts coming up out of the sea, one more fearsome than the other, and the fourth, which has ten horns plus an additional upstart one, is the most fearsome of all. Then he sees thrones set, and the deity, in the form of an ancient one, takes his seat and passes judgment on the beasts. Then "one like a son of man" appears with an entourage of clouds and is presented before the ancient one. He is given "dominion and glory and kingship" that shall never be destroyed. An angel subsequently explains to Daniel that the four beasts are four kings, or kingdoms, and that "the holy ones of the Most High will receive the kingdom." Finally the angel explains further that the little horn will attempt to change the times (i.e., the cultic calendar) and the law, and that "the people of the Holy Ones of the Most High" will receive the kingdom.

Daniel 7 is arguably the most influential passage in Jewish apocalyptic literature, and it had a profound influence on the Synoptic Gospels, where Jesus is identified as the Son of Man. It is also a powerful vision in its own right. Like some of the passages we have cited from Isaiah 24–27, it draws on the imagery of the Canaanite combat myth, where Baal, rider of the clouds, triumphs over Yamm, the turbulent sea. It is clear that the little horn represents Antiochus Epiphanes, and that the vision predicts his overthrow. But as Daniel sees it, the struggle is not just between Greeks and Jews. It is a reenactment of the primordial struggle where the beasts of chaos rise from the sea in rebellion against the rightful God. The most striking aspect of the imagery is that there seem, prima facie, to be two divine figures. Elsewhere in the Hebrew Bible it is always YHWH, the God of Israel, who rides on the clouds; here he must be identified with the Ancient of Days. This anomaly reflects the Canaanite background of the imagery. In the ancient myth, El is the ancient one while Baal is the rider of the clouds. In the Jewish context, the "one like a son of man" has often been taken as a symbol for Israel. He does indeed represent Israel in some sense, but such an interpretation misses the significance of the imagery. Elsewhere in Daniel, human figures in visions often represent angels (e.g., 10:5, 18; 12:5–6). "Holy Ones" nearly always represent angels both in Daniel and in the contemporary Jewish literature. In the context of Daniel, the one like a son of man is most satisfactorily identified as the archangel Michael, who is introduced as the "prince" of Israel in 10:21 and 12:1. The Holy Ones of the Most High are the angelic host and Israel is the people of the Holy Ones. The vision predicts the exaltation of Israel, but the real conflict is between the angelic hosts and the infernal beasts. (See further Collins 1993, 274–324.)

This reading of Daniel 7 is confirmed by the dialogue between Daniel and the angel Gabriel in chapter 10. There the angel explains that he is engaged in conflict with "the prince of Persia," and that shortly "the prince of Greece" will come, but he is aided in his struggle by "Michael, your prince." Conflicts between peoples on earth are understood as reflections of struggles between their patron angels. Chapter 11 continues with an extended "prophecy" of the history of the Hellenistic age. At the end Michael arises in victory (12:1) and the resurrection and judgment follow.

Much of the "prophecy" of Hellenistic history is focused on the persecution of the Jews by Antiochus Epiphanes in the Maccabean era. Unlike the Enochic apocalypses, however, Daniel evinces no support for the Maccabees. Instead, the heroes of the drama are the "wise" (*maśkîlîm*), who instruct the common people and some of whom are killed. Their instruction presumably corresponds to the understanding of events found in the book of Daniel itself. They are not said to fight. At the resurrection, however, these wise teachers are said to shine like the brightness of the firmament and be like the stars forever and ever. Like the righteous in the Epistle of Enoch, they become companions to the host of heaven. They can afford to lose their lives in this world, because they are promised a greater glory in the next. They cooperate with the angelic hosts in defeating the enemy, not by fighting but by keeping themselves pure. A very similar viewpoint is found in the *Testament of Moses* 9–10, where a man called Taxo reacts to persecution by taking his sons into a cave and telling them to die rather than transgress the commandments of the Lord, "for if we do this and die, our blood will be avenged before the Lord and then shall his kingdom appear throughout all his creation . . . and God will exalt you and set you in heaven above the stars." The innocent righteous are, in effect, martyrs. By sacrificing their lives they ensure their eternal reward and also hasten the coming of the kingdom of God.

Two other motifs in the book of Daniel are especially important for the development of apocalypticism. In chapter 9, Daniel ponders Jeremiah's prophecy that Jerusalem would be desolate for seventy years (Jer. 25:11–12; 29:10). The angel Gabriel appears to him and explains that the seventy years are really seventy weeks of years, or 490 years. This passage is important for several reasons. First, it shows the importance of biblical prophecy in apocalyptic thought. But the prophecies are not understood in their historical context. Rather, they are reinterpreted in light of the circumstances of the apocalyptic author. The logic behind this move is expressed very clearly in the commentary on Habakkuk from the Dead Sea Scrolls (col. 7): "God told Habakkuk to write what was going to happen to the last generation, but he did not let him know the end of the age." Biblical prophecy is treated like the writing on the wall or Nebuchadnezzar's dream. It is a coded message, to be deciphered by the inspired interpreter. Second, Daniel 9 offers a calculation of the duration of the period from the end of the exile to the end of the persecution. The seventy weeks of years would be reinterpreted over and over again in early Christianity in an attempt to calculate the end of the world (see Collins 1993, 116–17).

The final motif in Daniel that influenced later apocalypticism is related to this. In chapter 12 we are told the exact number of days until the coming of "the end." This is in fact the only instance in an ancient Jewish apocalypse of an attempt to calculate the exact number of days. According to Dan. 8:14 the Temple cult would be disrupted for 2,300 evenings and mornings, or 1,150 days. At the end of the book, however, we are given two further calculations: "From the time that the regular burnt offering is taken away and the abomination that makes desolate is set up, there shall be 1,290 days. Happy are those who persevere and attain the 1,335 days" (Dan. 12:11–12). Two things about this latter passage are remarkable. First, we are given two different numbers side by side. Both may be regarded as approximations of three and a half years, but the fact that two different figures are given strongly suggests that the second calculation was added after the first number of days had passed. The phenomenon of re-calculation is well known in later apocalyptic movements such as the Millerite movement in nineteenth-century America (Festinger et al. 1956, 12–23). Second, Daniel is not specific as to what will happen when the number of days has passed. Since the days are calculated from the time that the Temple cult was disrupted, we might expect that the expected "end" is simply the restoration of that cult, and this would seem to be the implication in Dan. 8:14. But, according to 1 Macc. 1:54; 4:52–54, Judas purified the Temple three years to the day after it had been polluted, so both numbers in chapter 12 point to a date after that restoration. At least the last date must have been added after the purification had taken place. Presumably, the author of Daniel did not think that the restoration under Judas was satisfactory. But there is probably more at stake here. The numbers in Daniel 12 follow the prophecy of the victory of Michael and the resurrection of the dead. In Dan. 12:13 Daniel is told that he will rise from his rest at the end of the days. The end, then, is the time when the archangel Michael intervenes and the resurrection takes place, roughly what later tradition would call the end of the world.

A New Kind of Literature

One of the major modern debates about Jewish apocalypticism has concerned the origin of the phenomenon. The most influential schools of thought have seen it either as a child of prophecy (e.g., recently Hanson) or as a product of wisdom circles (von Rad). There is manifest influence of biblical prophecy in both Enoch and Daniel, especially in the crucial expectation of a day of judgment. It is also true that both Enoch and Daniel are depicted as wise men rather than as prophets (von Rad 1965). But this whole debate about the origins of apocalypticism is misplaced. In the books of Enoch and Daniel we are dealing with a new phenomenon in the history of Judaism, which was very much a product of the way in which "the world was changed" by the impact of Hellenism on the Near East. The apocalyptic visionaries drew on materials from many sources: ancient myths, biblical prophecies, Greek and Persian traditions. But what they produced was a new kind of literature that had its own coherence and should not be seen as a child or adaptation of something else. The vision form as we find it in Daniel has prophetic precedents (e.g., Zechariah) but is also indebted to Babylonian dream interpretation. Neither prophetic oracles nor wisdom instructions can be said to play a major role in these books.

There has also been debate as to whether these books, and the later Jewish and Christian apocalypses, can be said to constitute a literary genre. Von Rad argued that they were a "*corpus permixtum*," embracing various *Gattungen* (von Rad 1965, 330). In this he was thinking of the constituent forms that make up the apocalypses: visions, heavenly journeys, *ex eventu* (after-the-fact) prophecies, dialogues, etc. But on a higher level of abstraction, these books also have significant commonalities in form and content. The common elements of apocalypses are summed up in the following definition (Collins 1979, 9):

> [A]n apocalypse is a genre of revelatory literature with a narrative framework, in which a revelation is mediated by an otherworldly being to a human recipient, disclosing a transcendent reality which is both temporal, insofar as it envisages eschatological salvation, and spatial insofar as it involves another, supernatural world.

Every individual apocalypse has some distinctive features, but this common core identifies a new macro-genre in the history of Jewish religious literature.

The definition of an apocalypse given above should be qualified in a few respects. As Paolo Sacchi especially has argued, this literature has a history and evolved over time. In the early books of Enoch and Daniel, the genre is in an experimental stage. No subsequent otherworldly journey is quite like that of Enoch in the Book of the Watchers. Both the early Enoch books and Daniel incorporate material that would not be considered apocalyptic if taken on its own (e.g., the stories in Daniel 1–6). Further, it is important to recognize at least two distinct types of apocalypses—the otherworldly journey, typified by the Book of the Watchers, and the historically oriented apocalypses, such as the Apocalypse of Weeks or Daniel 7–12. The popular stereotypes of apocalypticism are dominated by the historical type, but the otherworldly journeys also have an illustrious history in mysticism and even in literature (culminating in Dante's *Inferno*). Finally, while the functions of apocalypses may vary from one situation to another, one may say, on a fairly high level of abstraction, that they serve to exhort and console their addressees. The books of Enoch and Daniel arise out of a cultural crisis precipitated by Hellenism and aggravated by the persecution of Antiochus Epiphanes. Regardless of their status within the Jewish community, the authors of these books surely felt relatively deprived, because of the impact of foreign culture and religious persecution. The nature of the crises may vary, however, in other apocalyptic situations.

The definition given above concerns a literary genre. Implicit in that genre, however, is a worldview that can also find expression in other ways (Collins in Collins and Charlesworth 1991, 11–32). The crucial elements of this worldview are (1) the prominence of supernatural beings, angels and demons, and their influence on human affairs and (2) the expectation of a final judgment not only of nations but of individual human beings. Both of these elements can be paralleled elsewhere in the Hellenistic world, but in Jewish tradition they constituted a new and distinctive worldview, as can be seen if we contrast the book of *Enoch* with the Deuteronomic tradition or with the roughly contemporary writings of Ben Sira or 1 Maccabees. Especially important was the belief in the judgment of the dead and the hope for a blessed immortality. Ancient Israel was exceptional in the ancient world in its reluctance to embrace such notions. In most of the Hebrew Bible, the hope of the individual was for long life, prosperity, and offspring, in the context of a prosperous nation. In the apocalyptic literature we still find hope for a glorious kingdom, but the hope of the individual is for eternal glory with the angels. Consequently, the Enoch literature could look on sexual relations with women as defiling activity, unworthy of spiritual beings, and the wise men of Daniel could let themselves be killed rather than compromise their convictions. The expectation of judgment after death brought with it a profound change of values and laid the foundation for one of the more significant shifts in spirituality in the Jewish tradition.

THE ROMAN ERA

The Spread of Apocalyptic Ideas

The first major cluster of Jewish apocalyptic writings originated in the period shortly before and during the Maccabean revolt. For another comparable cluster of writings we must wait until the next great crisis in Jewish history, the revolt against Rome in 66–70 C.E., which led to the destruction of the Jerusalem Temple. In the intervening period of more than two centuries we do not find many apocalypses, but we find considerable evidence of the spread of apocalyptic ideas in several areas of Jewish life. The following are some examples:

The Dead Sea Scrolls are the subject of a separate essay in this volume. While they do not yield many apocalypses in the literary sense (there are a few fragmentary works of uncertain genre), they provide plenty of evidence for apocalyptic eschatology, most strikingly in the *Scroll of the War of the Sons of Light against the Sons of Darkness*. The sect that produced the major scrolls evidently adapted the apocalyptic tradition for its purposes. We find very little resurrection language, but several texts speak of present fellowship with the angels. It would seem that the sectarians claimed to enjoy in the present the exalted life that was promised to the faithful after death in Daniel and Enoch. The Scrolls are remarkable also for their strongly exegetical character, and the foundational role given to the Torah of Moses. This exegetical focus, coupled with the charismatic authority of the Teacher of Righteousness, may explain why the sectarians did not compose apocalypses in the names of ancient heroes or base their revelations on visionary experience.

The Dead Sea sect is most probably to be identified with the Essenes, whom Josephus describes as one of the three main Jewish groups around the turn of the era. The Sadducees, according to Josephus, rejected belief in angels and in life after death, and so can have had little sympathy for apocalyptic ideas. The Pharisees are said to "attribute everything to Fate and to God; they hold that to act rightly or otherwise rests, indeed, for the most part with men, but that in each action Fate co-operates" (*Jewish War* 2.163). They are also said to believe in some form of resurrection ("the soul of the good passes into another body"). Whether Josephus's account of the Pharisees is accurate is open to question, but presumably it has some basis. By analogy with this account, the *Psalms of Solomon*, which were composed some time after the Roman general Pompey entered Jerusalem in 63 B.C.E., are sometimes ascribed to the Pharisees. These Psalms clearly affirm resurrection and also express the hope that God will raise up an heir to the Davidic line—in effect, a kingly Messiah. Whether the *Psalms* are Pharisaic or not, they show that other groups besides the Essenes were interested in messianism and eschatology.

The *Testament of Moses* is a further witness to eschatological ideas around the turn of the era. We have already referred to this text in our discussion of Daniel. There are indications that the text was originally composed in the Maccabean era and updated later, after the death of Herod the Great in

4 B.C.E. The *Testament* purports to be the parting speech of Moses and is heavily influenced by Deuteronomic theology, with its tendency to see historical crises as punishment for sin. Most important for the present context is the fact that Moses concludes his prediction with the coming of the kingdom of God and the exaltation of Israel to the stars. The *Testaments of the Twelve Patriarchs* are also permeated with an eschatologically oriented view of history, but the *Testaments* are Christian in their present form, and it is difficult to reconstruct a Jewish stratum with any confidence.

One apocalypse that should be dated before 70 C.E. and probably originated in the land of Israel is the Similitudes of Enoch (*1 Enoch* 37–71). The Similitudes are presented as heavenly visions of Enoch, but their content is most notably indebted to the book of Daniel. In *1 Enoch* 46:1, Enoch sees "one who had a head of days and his head was white like wool; and with him there was another, whose face had the appearance of a man, and his face was full of grace, like one of the holy angels." The latter figure is subsequently referred to as "that Son of Man." It is said that his name was named before creation, and later he is seated on a throne of glory, just like the Most High (chapter 62). The wicked are confounded when he is revealed, but the righteous share his life in heaven forever. In chapter 71, Enoch is told "you are the Son of Man who is born to righteousness." There are literary indications that this chapter is a secondary addition to the Similitudes, added perhaps to contradict the Christian claim that Jesus was the Son of Man. In later Jewish tradition, however, Enoch is identified with Metatron, a heavenly viceroy who has much in common with Enoch's Son of Man. The Similitudes are not found among the Dead Sea Scrolls and presumably were the work of a different sect. They are typically apocalyptic in their focus on the coming judgment and the hope for a heavenly afterlife for the righteous.

The *Sibylline Oracles* constitute a distinct genre that flourished in the Jewish Diaspora. Books 3 and 5 of the standard collection were composed in Egypt between the middle of the second century B.C.E. and the early second century C.E. These were in the form of oracles or inspired speech; they include no vision reports or interpretations. They were modeled to some degree on pagan sibylline oracles, but they also show significant similarities to apocalypses of the historical type, insofar as they claim to predict the course of history, which is often divided into periods, and culminate in eschatological change. Surprisingly, neither book 3 nor book 5 of the *Sibylline Oracles* envisages resurrection or the judgment of the dead. Book 5 is considerably more pessimistic and hostile to the Gentiles than book 3, and it probably reflects the atmosphere of the great Diaspora revolt of 115–117 C.E. The fourth book of *Sibylline Oracles* reflects a different tradition (possibly originating in Syria).

Here history is divided into four kingdoms and ten generations, and the oracle concludes with a prediction of cosmic conflagration and resurrection. In its present form, book 4 dates from the period after the destruction of the Temple in 70 C.E. There is evidence that an older, Hellenistic oracle has been updated. The fourth kingdom and tenth generation is that of Macedonia; Rome is introduced after the end of the numerical sequence. It is impossible to be sure, however, whether the older oracle included the predictions of conflagration and resurrection, or whether these were part of the update in the Roman era. A somewhat similar oracle is found in books 1 and 2 of the *Sibyllines*, which also divide history into ten generations and end with conflagration, resurrection, and judgment. In this case, however, a Jewish oracle has been updated by a Christian, and the provenance of the Jewish original is uncertain, although there are some grounds for locating it in Asia Minor, around the turn of the era.

One particular motif that appears in the fourth and fifth books enjoyed a prolonged afterlife in sibylline and apocalyptic prophecy. This is the motif of *Nero redivivus* (*Sib. Or.* 4.138; 5.28–34, 138–53, 215–24, 363–70). At the time of Nero's death there was a popular belief that he had escaped and fled to the Parthians. Several pretenders appeared subsequently claiming to be Nero. In the *Sibylline Oracles*, however, the expectation is no longer for the historical Nero but for a figure of mythic proportions: "A man who is a matricide will come from the ends of the earth. . . . He will destroy every land and conquer all. . . . he will destroy many men and great rulers, and he will set fire to all men as no one else ever did" (5.363–69). The figure of *Nero redivivus* also appears in the book of Revelation (Rev. 17:11) and was assimilated to the Antichrist in later tradition.

Finally, mention should be made of the proliferation of eschatological prophets and messianic pretenders in Judea in the first century C.E. John the Baptist and Jesus were most probably eschatological prophets, and several other figures are described by Josephus. When Fadus was governor of Judea (about 45 C.E.) a man named Theudas "persuaded most of the common people to take their possessions and follow him to the Jordan River. He said he was a prophet, and that at his command the river would be divided and allow them an easy crossing" (*Antiquities* 20.97–98). Theudas apparently presented himself as a new Joshua, but his actions might also bring to mind Moses and the exodus. A decade later, a similar movement was instigated by an Egyptian, who "made himself credible as a prophet and rallied about thirty thousand dupes and took them around through the wilderness to the Mount of Olives. From there he intended to force an entry into Jerusalem, overpower the Roman garrison and become ruler of the citizen body" (*Jewish War*

2.261–62). But in another account (*Antiquities* 20.169–71) Josephus says that "he said that from there he wanted to show them that at his command the walls of Jerusalem would fall down and they could then make an entry into the city," clearly evoking the capture of Jericho. Josephus distinguishes prophets of this kind from armed rebels:

> Besides these (the "dagger-men") there arose another body of villains, with purer hands but more impious intentions, who no less than the assassins ruined the peace of the city. Deceivers and impostors, under the pretense of divine inspiration fostering revolutionary changes, they persuaded the multitude to act like madmen, and led them out into the desert under the belief that God would there give them tokens of deliverance. (*Jewish War* 2.258–60)

Unfortunately, these prophets left no writings, but the authors of the books of *Enoch* and Daniel, in their day, could equally well have been said to be fostering revolutionary changes under the pretense of divine inspiration. We have no apocalyptic books that can be dated either to the period leading up to the revolt or to the revolt itself. Yet it seems likely that eschatological prophecies of the kind reported by Josephus played a part in fomenting the rebellion, just as the apocalypses of Daniel and Enoch had played a part in the turmoil of the Maccabean revolution. Josephus claims that "what more than all else incited them to the war was an ambiguous oracle, likewise found in their sacred scriptures, to the effect that at that time one from their country would become ruler of the world" (*Jewish War* 6.312). It is not clear what scriptural passage is in question. (Daniel 7 is often considered a possibility.) Evidently the passage in question was popularly understood as a messianic oracle, but Josephus argues that it actually predicted the rise of Vespasian, who was proclaimed emperor on Jewish soil.

Apocalypse as a Medium of Reflection:
4 Ezra, 2 Baruch, 3 Baruch

The second major cluster of Jewish apocalypses dates from the end of the first century C.E., in the aftermath of the Jewish revolt. 4 Ezra, *2 Baruch,* and *3 Baruch* are all reflections on the catastrophe that had come to pass. While they continue to console and exhort, they represent a rather different use of the genre from that of the early Enoch writings and Daniel. Unlike the "ambiguous oracle" of Josephus, they could scarcely have incited anyone to revolt. Instead they are attempts to understand and come to terms with failure and destruction.

4 Ezra, which is preserved in Latin and several other secondary transla-

tions, stands out among the Jewish apocalypses as the most acute formulation of a theological problem. Ezra, located anachronistically in Babylon thirty years after the destruction of Jerusalem, acknowledges the familiar Deutero-nomic theory that the destruction was punishment for sin, but then raises an all-too-obvious question: "Are the deeds of Babylon better than those of Zion? Or has another nation known thee besides Israel? Or what tribes have believed thy covenants as these tribes of Jacob?" (3:31–32). The angel with whom he speaks does not respond to this question directly but tells Ezra: "Your under-standing has utterly failed regarding this world, and do you think you can comprehend the way of the Most High?" (4:2). He assures him, however, that "the age is hastening swiftly to its end" (4:26) and proceeds to tell him the signs that will precede the eschaton. Ezra, however, is not easily deterred. He renews his questions about the justice of God, only to be again diverted with an eschatological prediction (6:17–28). Yet a third time Ezra probes more deeply: "O sovereign Lord, behold, thou has ordained in thy law that the righteous shall inherit these things, but that the ungodly shall perish" (7:17). But in that case most of humankind is doomed to perish: "For all who have been born are involved in iniquities, and are full of sins and burdened with transgressions" (7:68). The angel's reply is harsh: "You are not a better judge than God, or wiser than the Most High! Let many perish who are not living, rather than that the law of God which is set before them be disregarded!" (7:19–20). The angel urges Ezra to think about what is to come rather than about what now is (7:16) and discourses on the messianic age and the judg-ment after death. The Most High, we are told, made not one world but two (7:50), this world for the sake of the many but the world to come for the sake of the few (8:1). Ezra is not consoled:

> It would have been better if the earth had not produced Adam, or else, when it had produced him, had restrained him from sinning. For what good is it to all that they live in sorrow now and expect punishment after death? O Adam, what have you done? For though it was you who sinned, the fall was not yours alone, but ours also who are your descendants. (7:116–18)

Even though he gradually resigns himself to the will of God, he still com-ments ruefully on the paucity of those who will be saved (9:15).

After the third dialogue, Ezra is told to go into the field and eat the flow-ers (9:24, 26). After this he has a vision of a woman in mourning. At first Ezra scolds her, for being concerned with her personal grief while "Zion, the mother of us all" is in affliction. Then he tells her not to dwell on her grief but to "let yourself be persuaded because of the troubles of Zion, and be consoled because of the sorrow of Jerusalem" (10:20). While he is speaking, she is transformed into a city with massive foundations. Then the angel Uriel appears and explains to Ezra that the woman was Zion and that God had shown him the future glory of Jerusalem because of his wholehearted grief over her ruin. From this point on, Ezra raises no further complaints. In chapters 11–12 he sees a vision of an eagle rising from the sea that is confronted by a lion. The eagle stands for Rome, and the lion for the Davidic Messiah. In chapter 13 a man rises on clouds from the heart of the sea. He takes his stand on a mountain and repulses the Gentiles, and then gathers in the lost tribes of Israel. In the final chapter, Ezra is inspired to reproduce the Torah that has been burnt, but also seventy secret books that are to be given to "the wise among your people, for in them is the spring of understanding, the fountain of wisdom and the river of knowledge" (14:46–47).

4 Ezra is remarkable for the fact that the pseudonymous author, Ezra, adheres to a theology that is rejected by the angel. Some scholars have argued that Ezra is the voice of heresy, which the author meant to refute, but it is surely implausible that heresy would be given such an authoritative voice. Rather, the dialogue between Ezra and the angel must be taken to reflect the conflict of theologies in the author's heart and mind (Stone 1990, 21–36). In this respect, it is reminiscent of the book of Job, which also articulates a deeply felt problem before submitting to a divinely imposed solution. Ezra articulates the traditional Deuteronomic theology but finds it wanting. The angel does nothing to rehabilitate this theology, but tells Ezra in effect that God's ways are inscrutable in this world, and that he must be content to wait for the revelation of justice in the world to come. In the end, the eschatological visions carry the day. The high value placed on the seventy secret books in the final chapter is highly significant. While the Torah remains important, it does not contain "the spring of understanding and the fountain of wisdom." That wisdom requires higher revelation, such as Ezra receives in this apocalypse.

The actual eschatology of 4 Ezra, however, is based on the Hebrew Scriptures, although the themes are developed in original ways. There is no influence here from the Enoch tradition. The origin of sin is discussed with reference to Adam. There is no mention of the Watchers. The picture of the future combines various strands of traditional eschatology. In chapter 7 the Messiah (called "my son") is said to reign for four hundred years and then die. After this, there will be seven days of primeval silence, followed by the resurrection and judgment. In this way, the apocalypse accommodates both the expectation of national restoration under a messianic king and the more typically apocalyptic hope for a new creation. We find a similar two-stage eschatology in the roughly contemporary book of Revelation, where Christ reigns on earth for a thousand years before the resurrection and new creation (Revelation 20). In chapters 11–13, 4 Ezra draws heavily on the book of Daniel. The Roman eagle rises from the sea like the beasts in Daniel 7 and is identified as "the fourth kingdom which appeared in a vision to your brother Daniel. But it was not explained to him as I now explain or have explained it to you" (11:11–12). The lion, who has no place in Daniel's vision but is derived from Gen. 49:9, is "the messiah whom the Most High has kept until the end of days, who will arise from the posterity of David." In chapter 13, the man who rises from the sea on clouds is clearly a reinterpretation of the "one like a son of man" in Daniel. He is identified, however, as the Davidic Messiah ("my son"), and the description of his stand on the mountain (Zion) is reminiscent of Psalm 2. The messianic age serves to restore Israel and thereby partially answer one of Ezra's complaints. Ultimately, however, this apocalypse insists that the Most High made not one world but two, and full retribution can only be expected after the resurrection, in the world to come. It should be noted that 4 Ezra has virtually no interest in the heavenly world, despite the role of the revealing angel. There is no sense that the other world is already present, as it is in the Dead Sea Scrolls. Nonetheless, like all apocalypses, it requires the belief that this world is not all there is; hope is based on belief in an alternative universe.

2 Baruch is in many ways a companion piece to 4 Ezra. It is similar in structure and contains both dialogues and visions. Baruch also raises questions about the justice of God, but he does not probe them the way Ezra does. He is more easily satisfied that justice is served by a judgment based on the law (54:14: "justly do they perish who have not loved thy law"). Like Ezra, Baruch asks, "O Adam what have you done to all those who are born from you" (48:42), but a little later he answers his own question: "Adam is therefore not the cause, save only of his own soul, but each of us has been the Adam of his own soul" (54:19). In the end, Baruch warns the tribes that "we have nothing now save the Mighty One and His law" (85:4). The message of the book is that the Jewish people should keep the law and trust in the justice of God. The teaching accords well with that of mainstream rabbinic Judaism.

This message is framed, however, by an eschatological teaching very similar to that of 4 Ezra. "The youth of the world is past, and the strength of the creation already exhausted and the advent of the times is very short" (85:10). There is an elaborate division of history into twelve periods in a vision of a cloud that rains alternately black and white waters (chapters 53–74). The twelfth period, however, is not the last but the restoration after the exile. This in turn is followed by a dark period, which presumably includes the time of the real author. Finally comes the messianic age, symbolized by lightning. In chapters 27–32 the time of tribulation is divided into twelve woes. Then the

Messiah is revealed, but after a time "he will return in glory." This presumably corresponds to the death of the Messiah in 4 Ezra, although it is expressed in more positive terms. The resurrection and judgment follow. In chapters 35:1–47:2 there is an allegorical vision, in which a vine rebukes a cedar. The vine, representing the Messiah, rebukes the cedar, just as the lion rebuked the eagle in 4 Ezra. Although there is no allusion to Daniel in the vision, the interpretation identifies a sequence of four kingdoms (chapter 39). Like 4 Ezra, 2 Baruch shows no awareness of the Enoch tradition, but integrates the eschatology of Daniel and of traditional messianism into a Deuteronomic theology.

4 Ezra and 2 Baruch can be seen as two voices in the discussion of theodicy in the wake of the destruction of Jerusalem. Both have much in common with emerging rabbinic Judaism and place a high value on the law, although neither deals with specific halakic issues. The common eschatological presuppositions of these works show that such ideas were widely shared in Palestinian Judaism at the end of the first century. Whatever role apocalyptic ideas may have played in stirring up revolutionary fervor at the outbreak of the war, they are not used for that purpose in these books. Here eschatology becomes an element in theological reflection. Although both books assure us that the time is short, neither conveys a great sense of urgency. What is important is that there will be an eventual judgment that will establish that God is in control. Hope is sustained but deferred. There is a clear attempt here to integrate different strands of Jewish eschatology, providing both for national restoration on earth and for the resurrection of the dead in a new creation.

A quite different reaction to the destruction of Jerusalem can be found in the Greek apocalypse of 3 Baruch, which was most probably composed in the Egypt (Harlow 1996). This text opens with Baruch grieving over the destruction of Jerusalem. An angel appears to him and tells him: "Do not be so distressed about the condition of Jerusalem . . . argue with God no more, and I will show you other mysteries greater than these. . . . Come and I will show you the mysteries of God." The angel then escorts Baruch on an upward tour of five heavens. (There has been much speculation as to whether there were originally seven, the usual number in apocalypses of this period, but there is no good reason to believe that anything has been lost. Rather, Baruch's revelation is limited insofar as he is not taken up to the highest heaven.) In the course of this ascent he sees various cosmological mysteries and also the places where the dead are rewarded and punished. In the fifth heaven he sees the archangel Michael, who takes the merits of the righteous up to the presence of the Lord. It appears that people are judged strictly on their individual merits regardless of their membership in a covenant people. The final chapter of the apocalypse indicates that Israel has suffered the curses of the covenant:

Inasmuch as they angered me by what they did, go and make them jealous and angry and embittered against a people that is no people, against a people that has no understanding. And more—afflict them with caterpillar and maggot and rust and locust and hail with flashes of lightning and wrath and smite them with sword and with death, and their children with demons. For they did not heed my voice, neither did they observe my commandments nor do them. (16:2–3)

The reference to "a people that is no people" alludes to Deut. 32:21, while the remainder of the passage recalls the curses of the covenant (Lev. 26:16; Deut. 32:24). A Jew might take some comfort in the thought that the Romans are "a people that is no people," but there is little consolation for Israel here. Whereas 4 Ezra and 2 Baruch had held that individuals who broke the law deserved to perish, 3 Baruch seems to hold that Jerusalem deserved its fate on the same grounds. All that is left in this apocalypse is the merit of individuals and the consolation of pondering the heavenly mysteries.

3 Baruch does not express the only reaction to the destruction of Jerusalem in the Hellenistic Diaspora. The fifth Sibylline Oracle, written around the time of the Diaspora revolt of 115–117 C.E., rages against Rome for its insolence in destroying the Temple. In the tradition of the Third Sibyl, however, this oracle lacks the typically apocalyptic motifs of resurrection and judgment of the dead. While it contains some prophecies of hope for a restored Jerusalem, it ends on an extraordinarily pessimistic note by describing a battle of the stars, at the end of which all the stars are destroyed and heaven is left starless. While the anger against Rome that we find in these oracles may have been a factor in the events that led to revolt in the Diaspora, the sibyl ultimately ends on a note of bitter resignation.

The Decline of Historical Apocalypses

After the failure of a series of revolts against Rome in the late first and early second centuries C.E., the rabbis who undertook the codification of Jewish tradition seem to have turned away from apocalypticism. Mythological and eschatological motifs can still be traced in the Talmud and midrashim, but the primary emphasis in rabbinic Judaism was placed on the Torah and its interpretation. Claims of higher inspiration were viewed with skepticism and suspicion. With the exception of the book of Daniel, the apocalypses of the Hellenistic and Roman periods were not preserved by the rabbis. Those books have come down to us through Christian hands, in various translations— Greek, Latin, Syriac, Ethiopic, Old Church Slavonic. Only in the last half-century have we recovered fragments of apocalyptic literature in Aramaic and Hebrew in the Dead Sea Scrolls.

In general, the "historical" type of apocalypse fades from view in the second century C.E., both in Judaism and in Christianity, although it would reemerge in the Byzantine period and in the Middle Ages. The heavenly journey becomes the standard medium of apocalyptic revelation. The ascent through a numbered sequence of heavens had its origin in Judaism, as can be seen in *3 Baruch* and *2 (Slavonic) Enoch,* although the provenance of the latter work is far from clear. This strand of apocalypticism finds its continuation in Judaism in the mystical Hekalot literature, notably in the work known as *3 Enoch* or *Sefer Hekalot,* which represents the culmination of the Enoch tradition. Apocalypses of this type also proliferate in Christianity after the first century C.E. They reflect a world with little anticipation of revolutionary change but with a strong orientation toward another, heavenly world beyond this one.

CONCLUSION

The Apocalyptic Worldview

Our rapid sketch of developments over a period of six hundred years allows us to draw some conclusions about the origins of apocalypticism in ancient Judaism. Apocalypticism is a worldview that is indebted to ancient Near Eastern myths and to Hebrew prophecy, but which arose in response to the new challenges of the Hellenistic and Roman periods. The essential ingredients of this worldview were a reliance on supernatural revelation, over and above received tradition and human reasoning; a sense that human affairs are determined to a great degree by supernatural agents; and the belief that human life is subject to divine judgment, culminating in reward or punishment after death. In the context of Israelite and Jewish tradition, this worldview was novel in the Hellenistic period, especially in its expectation of a final judgment, which had far-reaching implications for ethical values and attitudes in this life. The dominant form of Jewish apocalypticism, which we have traced in this essay, also anticipated a denouement of history, culminating in divine intervention and a judgment of all nations on a cosmic scale. This judgment, however, would typically be followed by a resurrection of the dead, which allowed for retribution on an individual as well as a national scale. This worldview found its typical medium of expression in the rather loose macro-genre "apocalypse," which was a report of supernatural revelation, with an eschatological dimension. But the worldview could also come to expression in other genres, that were not directly reports of visions or otherworldly journeys.

The worldview that we have sketched here is fairly broad and could be embodied in different sociological formations and theological schools. The Enoch literature says little, at least explicitly, about the law of Moses. In contrast, the Torah is fundamental to the priestly apocalypticism of the Dead Sea Scrolls. The "proto-apocalyptic" prophecies of Isaiah 65–66 seem to question the importance of Temple and sacrifice. Even though the Dead Sea sect was evidently alienated from the Jerusalem Temple, it evidently still attached great importance to cultic worship. The origin of evil might be variously understood in terms of the myth of the Watchers, with an emphasis on the role of fallen angels, or in terms of the sin of Adam, underlining human responsibility. Finally, we should not think that apocalyptic ideas were confined to sectarians living apart from the rest of Judaism, on the model of the Qumran community. The book of Daniel was accepted as canonical scripture by all Jews and Christians. 4 Ezra and especially *2 Baruch* have much in common with rabbinic theology and give no indication that they were produced in sectarian communities. Apocalypticism, then, was not the exclusive property of any one sect or movement, although it was characteristic of various movements from time to time.

The Functions of Apocalyptic Literature and Ideas

Most scholars would probably agree with the view of David Hellholm that apocalypses are "intended for a group in crisis with the purpose of exhortation and/or consolation, by divine authority" (1986, 27). A few qualifications are in order, however. All the texts we have considered in this essay can be said to have been written for a group in crisis, if only because the entire Jewish people can be said to have been in crisis for most of the period in question. The crises were of various kinds. For the authors of the Book of the Watchers, it was a cultural crisis, when the world was changed by Hellenism; for the author of 4 Ezra it was a crisis of theodicy, the apparent failure of divine justice in light of the destruction of Jerusalem. Since the "group in crisis" can be either the whole Jewish people or a specific group with a specific problem, like the Qumran sect, the designation is only of limited help. The same may be said of the sociological theory of relative deprivation: almost everyone can feel deprived relative to someone or something. Nonetheless, it is true that all the apocalypses we have considered here are born out of a sense that the world is out of joint. The visionaries look to another world, either in the heavens or in the eschatological future, because this world is unsatisfactory. This sense of

dissatisfaction is not necessarily an invariable aspect of apocalyptic expectations. In principle, it is possible to conceive of an apocalypticism of the powerful. Divine revelation can be used to buttress established authority and one
might look for its ultimate confirmation in the eschatological judgment. (Virgil's *Aeneid* might arguably be taken to exemplify this kind of apocalypticism.)
But in practice none of the Jewish apocalyptic writings of the Second Temple
period reflects the viewpoint of established power. Typically, the appeal for
divine intervention is necessitated because the world is believed to be in the
grip of hostile powers.

Apocalypses surely were written to exhort and console. We should note,
however, that exhortation and consolation are not the same thing, and that
the nature of the exhortation is in no way implied in the apocalyptic form.
Some of the apocalypses we have reviewed here were militant: the Apocalypse
of Weeks and the Animal Apocalypse may be understood to exhort their readers to support the Maccabean revolt. The "ambiguous oracle" reported by
Josephus was also evidently understood as a call to arms. Other apocalypses
are quietistic. Daniel shows little enthusiasm for the Maccabees. 4 Ezra and
2 Baruch are primarily reflections on a catastrophe that has befallen. The
exhortation of *2 Baruch* is quite explicitly directed to Torah observance. In
some of these texts, the expectation of an "end" seems to neutralize any urge
toward militant action: God will act in the proper time; the pious person
should wait patiently.

The consolation of apocalyptic hope may have been considerable in the
short term, but it was highly prone to disillusionment. It is in the nature of
apocalyptic eschatology that it cannot be fully realized in this life. Even when
the hopes could be realized in principle, they most often failed to materialize.
The Jewish visionaries rarely ventured specific dates for their predictions, and
so avoided the pitfalls that beset such groups as the Millerites in modern times.
Nonetheless, the eventual rejection of the apocalypses by the rabbis bespeaks a
sense of disillusionment that is readily understandable. The pathos of apocalyptic hope is nicely captured in the alleged exchange between Rabbi Akiba
and R. Yoḥanan b. Torta at the time of the Bar Kokhba revolt. When Akiba
hailed Bar Kokhba as "the king, the Messiah," Yoḥanan allegedly replied:
"Akiba, grass will grow between your cheekbones and he [the Messiah] will not
have come." Apocalyptic hope is invariably hope deferred. Nonetheless, it has
persisted as a recurring feature of Western religion for over two thousand years.
While it can never deliver on its promises, it continues to speak eloquently to
the hearts of those who would otherwise have no hope at all.

⌒BIBLIOGRAPHY————————————————————————————

Blenkinsopp, J. 1990. "A Jewish Sect of the Persian Period." *Catholic Biblical Quarterly* 52:5–20.

Charlesworth, J. H., ed. 1983. *The Old Testament Pseudepigrapha,* Volume 1. New York: Doubleday. Translations and annotations of most of the relevant non-canonical literature.

Cohn, N. 1993. *Cosmos, Chaos, and the World to Come.* New Haven: Yale University Press. Review of mythological backgrounds, arguing for the primacy of Zoroastrianism.

Collins, J. J. 1984. *The Apocalyptic Imagination.* New York: Crossroad. Reprint, Grand Rapids: Eerdmans, 1998. Introduction to the Jewish apocalypses in historical context.

———. 1993. *Daniel.* Hermeneia. Minneapolis: Fortress Press. Comprehensive introduction to the book of Daniel.

Collins, J. J., ed. 1979. *Apocalypse: The Morphology of a Genre.* Semeia 14. Chico, Calif.: Scholars Press. Analytical outline of the genre in the ancient world.

Collins, J. J., and J. H. Charlesworth. 1991. *Mysteries and Revelations.* Apocalyptic Studies since the Uppsala Colloquium. Sheffield: Sheffield Academic Press. Eight studies on developments in the study of apocalypticism in the 1980s.

Cook, S. L. 1995. *Prophecy and Apocalypticism: The Postexilic Social Setting.* Minneapolis: Fortress Press. Study of late prophecy with extensive anthropological parallels.

Festinger, L., H. W. Riecken, and S. Schachter. 1956. *When Prophecy Fails: A Social and Psychological Study of a Modern Group That Predicted the Destruction of the World.* New York: Harper.

Hanson, P. D. 1975. *The Dawn of Apocalyptic.* Philadelphia: Fortress Press. Groundbreaking sociological study of postexilic prophecy.

Harlow, D. C. 1996. *The Greek Apocalypse of Baruch (3 Baruch) in Hellenistic Judaism and Early Christianity.* Leiden: E. J. Brill. Study of *3 Baruch* in both its Jewish and its Christian redactions.

Hellholm, D. 1986. "The Problem of Apocalyptic Genre." *Semeia* 36:13–64.

Hellholm, D., ed. 1983. *Apocalypticism in the Ancient Mediterranean World and the Near East.* Tübingen: Mohr. Proceedings of International Colloquium at Uppsala in 1979, with comprehensive coverage of ancient sources and rich diversity of viewpoints.

Himmelfarb, M. 1983. *Tours of Hell: An Apocalyptic Form in Jewish and Christian Literature.* Philadelphia: University of Pennsylvania Press.

———. 1993. *Ascent to Heaven in Jewish and Christian Apocalypses.* New York: Oxford University Press.

Milik, J. T. 1976. *The Books of Enoch.* Oxford: Clarendon Press. First publication of the Enoch fragments from Qumran.

Murphy, F. J. 1985. *The Structure and Meaning of Second Baruch*. Atlanta: Scholars Press. Excellent recent study of *2 Baruch*.

Nickelsburg, G. W. E. *1 Enoch*. Hermeneia. Minneapolis: Fortress Press, forthcoming. Comprehensive commentary on *1 Enoch*.

Rowland, C. 1982. *The Open Heaven*. New York: Crossroad. Synthetic treatment of apocalyptic literature emphasizing its mystical aspects.

Sacchi, P. 1996. *Jewish Apocalyptic and its History*. Sheffield: Sheffield Academic Press. Collected essays on Jewish apocalypticism, originally published in Italian.

Stone, M. E. 1984. "Apocalyptic Literature." In *Jewish Writings of the Second Temple Period*, edited by M. E. Stone, 383–441. Philadelphia: Fortress Press. Excellent short survey of apocalyptic literature.

———. 1990. *Fourth Ezra*. Hermeneia. Philadelphia: Fortress Press. Comprehensive commentary on 4 Ezra.

Tigchelaar, E. C. 1996. *The Prophets of Old and the Day of the Lord*. Leiden: E. J. Brill. Study of Zechariah and the Book of the Watchers.

Tiller, P. A. 1993. *A Commentary on the Animal Apocalypse of 1 Enoch*. Atlanta: Scholars Press. Detailed commentary on the Animal Apocalypse.

VanderKam, J. C. 1984. *Enoch and the Growth of an Apocalyptic Tradition*. Washington: Catholic Biblical Association. Study of the early Enoch tradition against its Mesopotamian background.

von Rad, G. 1965. *Theologie des Alten Testaments*. 4th ed. Munich: Kaiser. Argument that apocalyptic literature is rooted in ancient wisdom.

5

Apocalypticism in the Dead Sea Scrolls

Florentino García Martínez
University of Groningen

I F "APOCALYPTICISM" IS BROADLY DEFINED (AS IT IS IN this Encyclopedia) as "the belief that God has revealed the imminent conclusion of the ongoing struggle between good and evil throughout history," there can be no doubt that the Qumran community was an "apocalyptic" community. The writings that most probably can be considered a product of the Qumran community and which better represent its thought show clear indications that the authors believe that their own lives and the life of the community were part of the ongoing struggle between good and evil, that God had revealed to them the approaching end of the struggle, that they were preparing themselves for an active participation in the final climax, and even that they were already living somehow in the final phase.

Since some of the elements that show the apocalypticism of the Scrolls, such as the participation in the final struggle of several messianic figures have been dealt with in other articles in this volume (see especially chapter 6 below) I will present a summary of the other most relevant topics: the origin of evil; the periods of history and expectation of the end; the communion with the heavenly world; and the eschatological war.

At the outset, it seems necessary to offer a short *status quaestionis* with reference to the literature on the topic listed at the end of this article.

The hard questions posed by Klaus Koch (1972) definitively ended the optimism of the previous decade of research, which saw in the Dead Sea Scrolls the solution to all the problems that had vexed scholarship in the field of apocalypticism. The announcement that the most characteristic apocalypses, such as Enoch or Daniel, were abundantly represented in the new finds, the discovery that other compositions previously unknown had characteristics similar to these apocalypses and could therefore be legitimately considered new apocalypses, the awareness that the most typical sectarian writings had a remarkable eschatological dimension and showed a very radical dualistic thinking, and above all the fact that the group from which the manuscripts were supposed to have come was a secluded community, providing for the first time a model for the sociological background of the apocalypses all helped to create a *pan-Qumranism* in the investigation of apocalypticism. But after many years of intensive research, this optimism proved to be ill grounded, and the contribution of Hartmut Stegemann to the Uppsala Colloquium in 1979 concluded that the expected master key to unlock the secrets of apocalypticism had not been found in the Dead Sea Scrolls. The Qumran manuscripts had not provided the solutions hoped for; the apocalyptic elements to be found within the Scrolls were scanty, and they could be foreign bodies, to which it is impossible to assign any central position in the life or organization of the Qumran group (Stegemann 1983). At the same time, there was a growing awareness of the inadequacy of the traditional way of defining apocalypticism by a mélange of literary and thematic elements, or by a mixing of form and content. On the one hand, a large number of elements used to characterize apocalyptic were to be found in many compositions that no one would dream of defining as apocalypses, and, on the other hand, many compositions recognized as apocalypses were lacking elements that were thought to be characteristic of apocalypticism. The intensive efforts of the Society of Biblical Literature group on the genre apocalypse, which culminated with the publication of *Semeia* 14, brought the necessary refinement of the terminology used to chart the problem and provided a definition of apocalypse commonly accepted today (Collins 1979). The definition of *Semeia* 14 and its distinction of two basic types of apocalypses—the *historical* and the *heavenly ascent* types—proved very fruitful and paved the way for the developments of the next decade. In these years we saw the development of the *syntagmatic* or *text-linguistic* analysis of several apocalypses as well as the *sociological approach* to apocalypticism (in which the insights gained by the study of millenarian movements through history [medieval millenarianism, Puritan groups in England in the sixteenth century, etc.], or by means of anthropological study of contemporary sectarian apocalyptic movements or groups [fringe groups in the United States, for example] were applied to the study of apocalypticism, but also the detailed study of single apocalypses [such as VanderKam 1984; Stone 1990]) and a systematic mapping of the developments of apocalypticism in a historical perspective, both in a synchronic (Collins 1984) and in a diachronic way (Sacchi 1996 [English 1997]). As a result, we can observe a decline in the importance of the Dead Sea Scrolls for understanding the phenomenon of apocalypticism, and a more differentiated way of understanding the individual apocalypses and the phenomenon of apocalypticism. Nonetheless, the contribution of the Scrolls to this field of study remains considerable.

As I formulated the issue in the introduction to my book *Qumran and Apocalyptic*:

> The study of the Qumran manuscripts has completely transformed the way in which we nowadays understand the most ancient apocalypses, those composed within the Enochic tradition, has had a profound effect on the study of the origins and the development of the apocalypse of Daniel and has indicated a number of new factors demonstrating the variety and the ideological richness of the apocalypses written within, or transmitted by, the Qumran community itself. (García Martínez 1992, xi)

I think this is still a fair, and rather nonpolemical, representation of the situation. Everybody agrees now on the characteristics of the literary genre apocalypse and its basic division of "cosmic" and "historical" apocalypses. Everybody agrees also that in the definition of the literary genre apocalypse the function of the genre (absent in the definition of *Semeia* 14) should be included in one way or another. And most tend to agree that this function could be defined as was done in *Semeia* 36: an apocalypse is "intended to interpret present earthly circumstances in the light of the supernatural world and of the future, and to influence both the understanding and the behavior of the audience by means of divine authority." This has resulted in a better understanding of the best representatives of both basic types: the books of Enoch and the book of Daniel. This would also, in my opinion, allow some of the compositions from Qumran lately published to be categorized as apocalypses despite their fragmentary condition.

Everybody also agrees that apocalypticism cannot be reduced to the literary genre apocalypse. The number, certainly limited, of apocalypses found at Qumran (or the even smaller number of apocalypses that can be attributed to the activity of the group) (Dimant 1994) do not need to limit us in the study of the apocalypticism of the Scrolls. The major sectarian scrolls, which are certainly not apocalypses, provide us in spite of their generic differences with a worldview similar to the worldview we find in the apocalypses, a worldview that can be considered representative of the group's way of thinking. Since this worldview has been clearly influenced by ideas characteristic of well-known apocalypses, mainly Enoch and Daniel, it can be described as "apocalyptic." In the words of John J. Collins:

> A movement or community might also be apocalyptic if it were shaped to a significant degree by a specific apocalyptic tradition, or if its worldview could be shown to be similar to that of the apocalypses in a distinctive way. The Essene movement and Qumran Community would seem to qualify on both counts. (Collins 1997b, 37)

Everybody also agrees that the worldview we find in the Scrolls presents also obvious differences from the ideas of these apocalypses. But there are several ways to interpret these differences, and so scholars are divided.

The basic question seems to be: Are the different solutions given to the same problem in Qumran and in some apocalyptic writings disagreements within a common framework in the interpretation of the same original myth (as seems to be the case between the Book of Watchers and the Epistle of Enoch, for example, or between 4 Ezra and 2 Baruch), or are they due to the use of different premises, referring to different myths? Should we see the relationship as one of continuity within a certain tradition or rather of discontinuity and derivation from different traditions?

For Paolo Sacchi, the differences remain within the same basic framework and we can speak thus of a continuity within the tradition (Sacchi 1996). For Collins, they indicate derivation from a different tradition. In the words of Collins: "I agree with Sacchi, against Carmignac and Stegemann, that apocalypticism can not be reduced to a literary genre. . . . I do not agree, however, that apocalypticism can be reduced to a single stream of tradition, or to a single socially continuous movement" (Collins 1997b, 298).

It is usually assumed that the circles responsible for the different Enochic compositions formed a single movement or belonged to a single tradition in spite of the differences, implying something more than a common worldview. After all, we usually speak of a "prophetic tradition" and of "a wisdom tradition," and we imply by this something more than a common worldview, in spite of our ignorance of the concrete sociological basis for these "prophetic" and "sapiential" traditions. In this way it does indeed seem appropriate to speak of an "Enochic tradition" even if the sociological basis remains rather vague. And because the Enoch books are apocalypses, it seems also appropriate to speak of an "(Enochic) apocalyptic tradition" (VanderKam 1984). By the same token it would be equally legitimate to speak of a "(Qumranic) apocalyptic tradition," and it would be equally legitimate to investigate the relationships (genetic or other) between the several apocalyptic traditions.

In my opinion, the *status quaestionis* boils down to the following: Is apocalypticism simply a worldview (an umbrella term for different apocalyptic traditions), or it is something more? Can the cluster of ideas we find in the Qumran writings be attributed to an apocalyptic tradition? As we shall see in the following summaries, the cluster of ideas appearing in the sectarian scrolls is something more than an umbrella term; it represents a genuine apocalyptic tradition, connected with, but different from, other apocalyptic traditions.

THE ORIGIN OF EVIL AND THE DUALISTIC THOUGHT OF THE SECT

The core of the oldest part (the Book of the Watchers) of the oldest apocalypse (*1 Enoch*) is dedicated to giving an explanation of the origin of evil in the world. And the explanation given to this topic, using the old myth of the "rebellion in heaven," is that evil was not introduced into the world by men, but is the result of the sin of the Watchers, the fallen angels lead by Asael and Shemiḥaza, who consorted with women and taught them heavenly secrets. The fallen angels introduce a disruption in the harmonic order of nature: "The whole earth has been devastated by the works of the teaching of Asael; record against him all sins" (*1 Enoch* 10:7). Sin originates in heaven not in earth, and it is introduced on earth by the action of angelic beings. Within the Enoch tradition itself, we will find a direct refutation of the conclusion of the Book of the Watchers about the heavenly origin of evil. In the last composition incorporated into the Enochic collection, the Epistle of Enoch, we can read (in Ethiopic, the Greek version is somewhat different): "I swear to you, sinners, that as a mountain has not, and will not, become a slave, nor a hill a woman's maid, so sin was not sent to the earth, but man of himself created it" (98:4). It is impossible not to conclude that the author of the Epistle is completely turning around the conclusion of the Book of the Watchers in order to arrive at the opposite conclusion. In spite of this direct rebuttal, both compositions, the Book of the Watchers and the Epistle of Enoch, seem to have originated within the same ideological tradition (which some people call the Enoch school, much in the same way others talk about a Johannine school); they were in any case considered compatible enough not only to fraternize in the same shelves of a library but to be included as part of the same book, our *1 Enoch*.

I thus conclude that it was perfectly possible within one and the same tradition to hold divergent (and even opposite) views on some central theological problem; and that we cannot expect dependence to be expressed only as agreement.

We do not know precise antecedents for the idea put forth by the author of the Book of the Watchers. In the short form in which we find the myth in Genesis 6 it is not put to use to explain the origin of evil. Nor is it used in this way by the book of *Jubilees*, which is dependent on the Book of the Watchers in many respects, but does not accept the idea that evil comes into the earth through angelic mediation and gives a different explanation of the origin of evil. For *Jubilees*, sin begins in the earth with the fall of Adam, long before the fall of the angels. *Jubilees*, on the other hand, presents the fallen angels as an army, led by Mastema, who is described as a prince, and who obtains from God that a tenth of the fallen spirits will not be directly destroyed but will be left under his command in order to harass, mislead, and destroy humanity. The idea that evil originates in heaven is also dismissed in the wisdom tradition as represented by Sir. 15:11: "Do not say, 'It was the Lord's doing that I fell away.'" But Sirach does not attribute evil either to the sin of Adam, which he never mentions (some manuscripts even change the famous reference to the sin of Eve in Sir. 25:24, attributing it to the "enemy"). Sirach introduces the idea of the "inclination" (the *yēṣer*): "God created man in the beginning and placed him in the hand of his inclination" (15:14). But he also insists that everything is in the hands of God: "In the fullness of his knowledge the Lord distinguished them and appointed their different ways. Some he blessed and exalted, and some he made holy and brought near to himself; but some he cursed and brought low, and turned out of their places" (33:11–12). Most of the interpreters rightly insist that the *yēṣer* in Sirach is very different from the *yēṣer* as it will be understood in 4 Ezra (the *cor malignum*) and especially in the rabbinic tradition, where it is even identified with Satan. Sirach does not exploit the potentiality of the *yēṣer*, and at the end, he is unable to resolve the tension created by his adherence to the traditional biblical conception, which preserves free will and the equally biblical conception that underlines God's omnipotence. As Collins says: "Sirach's over-all position remains ambiguous" (Collins 1997b, 370), and he limited himself to observing the duality of evil and good: "As evil contrasts with good, and death with life, so are sinners in contrast with the just" (33:14).

It is my contention that all these strands of thought are interwoven in the thought on the origin of evil that we find in the Dead Sea Scrolls, and that all of them contribute in some way to shape the new solution they gave to the problem. It is clear that the Scrolls know the myth as it is presented in the Book of the Watchers. Not only have several copies of the composition appeared in Cave 4, but the story itself is used in some other Qumran compositions such as 4Q180, a *pesher* on the periods, in which Asael plays a leading roll. Even more significantly, the *Damascus Document* (CD) uses the story of the Watchers as the first example in a review of human unfaithfulness to the will of God (CD 2:15–16). Similarly, *Jubilees* has had a deep influence in the thought of the community, which sees the angelic forces as organized armies under an angelic leader, and which even knows Mastema as one of the names used for this leader. Copies of *Jubilees*, of course, are among the compositions best represented in their library, as are (to a lesser extent) copies of Ben Sira. No wonder then that the *yēṣer* of the wisdom tradition has also left its traces within the Dead Sea Scrolls. As expected, its presence is more notorious in the wisdom texts, such as *4QSapiential A*, where we find expressions such as: "Do not be deluded with the thought of an evil inclination" (4Q417 2 ii 12), but it is also used in more clearly sectarian compositions such as CD 2:15–16: "so that you can walk perfectly on all his paths and not follow after the thoughts of a guilty inclination."

However, the most characteristic explanation of the origin of evil, the one we find in the Treatise of the Two Spirits, does not limit itself to incorporating and blending together these influences but offers us an original solution to the problem. This treatise, embodied in the *Community Rule* (1QS 3:13–4:26; all translations from the Dead Sea Scrolls are taken from García Martínez 1996), is at the same time the most systematic exposition of the dualistic thinking of the community.

The treatise begins with a solemn introduction (3:13–15), followed by the basic principle: "From the God of knowledge stems all there is and all there shall be. Before they existed he made all their plans, and when they come into being they will execute all their works in compliance with his instructions, according to his glorious design without altering anything" (3:15–16).

From this deterministic formulation the author deduces the basic dualistic structure of humankind, expressed with the traditional symbols of light and darkness: "He created man to rule the world and placed within him two spirits so that he would walk with them until the moment of his visitation: they are the spirits of truth and of deceit" (3:17–19). The author develops in detail his dualistic conception, applying it not only to each individual but to all humanity, which he describes as divided into two camps (two dominions), led respectively by the Prince of Light and the Angel of Darkness: "And in the hand of the Prince of Light is dominion over all the sons of justice; they walk in the paths of light. And in the hand of the Angel of Darkness is total dominion over the sons of deceit; they walk in the path of darkness" (3:20–21). He even extends this dualistic division explicitly to the angelic world, which is divided, as are humanity and each individual, in two camps: "He created the spirits of light and of darkness and on them established all his deeds, and on their paths all his labors. God loved one of them for all eternal ages and in all his deeds he takes pleasure for ever; of the other one he detests his advice and hates all his paths forever" (3:25–4:1). The treatise goes further, describing the characteristic deeds that result from the dominion of each one of the two angelic hosts, the conflicting human conduct that results from the influence of the opposing spirits, and the contrasting retribution of each person according to their share of light and darkness.

Not only the origin of sin is explained by the treatise in this way. The sin of each individual also finds an explanation in this dualistic context. Human life is seen as a battle between the forces of light and darkness, a violent conflict in which there is little left to human initiative:

> Until now the spirits of truth and of injustice feud in the heart of man and they walk in wisdom or in folly. In agreement with man's birthright in justice and in truth, so he abhors injustice; and according to his share in the lot of injustice he acts irreverently in it and so abhors the truth. For God has sorted them into equal parts until the appointed end and the new creation. (4:24–25)

A person can, of course, sin; even the righteous do. But these sins are explained as caused by the influence of spirits of darkness:

> Due to the Angel of Darkness all the sons of justice stray, and all their sins, their iniquities, their failings and their mutinous deeds are under his dominion in compliance with the mysteries of God, until his moment, and all their punishments and their period of grief are caused by the dominion of his enmity; and all the spirits of their lot cause the sons of light to fall. (3:21–24)

At the end, at the time of God's visitation, however, sin will disappear and justice will triumph:

> God, in the mysteries of his knowledge and in the wisdom of his glory, has determined an end to the existence of deceit and on the occasion of his visitation he will obliterate it for ever. Then truth shall rise up forever in the world which has been defiled in paths of wickedness during the dominion of deceit until the time appointed for judgment. Then God will refine, with his truth, all man's deeds, and will purify for himself the configuration of man, ripping out all spirit of deceit from the innermost part of his flesh, and cleansing him with the spirit of holiness from every irreverent deed. He will sprinkle over him the spirit of truth like lustral water (in order to cleanse him) from all the abhorrences of deceit and from the defilement of the unclean spirit. In this way the upright will understand knowledge of the Most High, and the wisdom of the

sons of heaven will teach those of perfect behavior. For these are those selected by God for an everlasting covenant and to them shall belong the glory of Adam. (4:18–23)

This eschatological perspective is an essential part of the treatise and puts in perspective the solution to the problem of evil given by its author.

For him, as for the Book of the Watchers, evil clearly has its origins not on earth but in heaven. But the author the Treatise of the Two Spirits is apparently not satisfied with the solution given in the Book of the Watchers; after all, if the Watchers are the origin of evil on earth, their own capability of doing evil also needs to be explained. The solution given to the problem by the author of the Treatise is much more radical than the one given in the Book of the Watchers. For him there is no rebellion in heaven. The Watchers are part and stock of the evil spirits, the army of the Prince of Darkness; they are created as evil spirits directly by God. Evil comes thus from heaven, and directly from God. The author also has used the conception of the angelical army as represented in *Jubilees*, and has fully developed the deterministic and dualistic implications of the *yēṣer* of the wisdom tradition. But its thought has a radicality that cannot be explained only by these influences. It was recognized almost as soon as the scroll was published that the thought of the Treatise of the Two Spirits is most akin to the myth of Persian dualism with its twin spirits, the twin sons of the supreme God, one identified as good and the other as evil from the beginning, and one associated with light and the other with darkness. This myth is already present in the oldest part of the Avesta, the *Gāthās,* generally considered to be the work of Zoroaster. The dualism of the Treatise of the Two Spirits does not imply the initial option of humans for one or the other spirit in the manner of the Persian myth, and, even more importantly, the Treatise emphatically views the two spirits as created by God and completely subordinate to him. It is thus far removed from the later Persian thought that considers evil to be primordial. Yet it seems clear that the thought of the author of the Qumran text is deeply indebted to some form of Zoroastrian thought and has used it in order to radicalize the ideas he has received from the apocalyptic and sapiential traditions.

It is true that the Avesta is known to us in a collection from the Sassanian period, but the centrality of dualism in Zoroastrian thought is already attested by Plutarch (*On Isis and Osiris*), and, although we do not know the exact channels of transmission, the possibility of its influence in a Jewish context poses no special problem during the Hellenistic period.

Although the explanation of the origin of evil and the expression of dualistic thought in the Treatise of the Two Spirits is perhaps not the most widespread idea in the Dead Sea Scrolls, we find it attested in enough different writings that we may consider it one of the trademarks of the thought of the Qumran community. I have already quoted a sentence of the *Damascus Document* in which the human *yēṣer* is qualified as "guilty." One of the parenetic sections of the same document, CD 2:2–13, shows not only a very close verbal parallel to the Treatise of the Two Spirits, but the same emphatic deterministic outlook. Another section, CD 4:11–18, describes Israel under the dominion of Belial and the people falling in his three nets, and CD 5:18–19 offers a perfect example of dualistic thinking presenting Moses and Aaron raised up by the Prince of Light and Jannes and his brother Jambres by the hand of Belial. The end of the original composition (as shown by 4QD^b 18 v) contains a ceremony of expulsion from the assembly which exactly parallels the ceremony of entry into the covenant of 1QS 1–2 and has the same general dualistic overtone.

Another composition closely related to the worldview of the Treatise is 4QAmram, an Aramaic composition recovered in five copies, all very poorly preserved. In it, Amram tells his sons about a vision he has had in which two angelic figures who "control all the sons of Adam" quarrel over him. One of them "rules over darkness"; the other "rules over all what is bright." Each figure has apparently three names, although the only name preserved is Melchireša^c. The assumed counterpart, Melchizedek, is the central figure of another composition from Cave 11, where he is the agent of the eschatological judgment and saves "the men of his lot," freeing them from the hand of Belial and the spirits of his lot. Although visions and revelations are involved, the literary genre of the composition is more that of testament than apocalypse. The Qumranic origins of 4QAmram have been disputed because it is in Aramaic, but the fact that the same cluster of ideas and expressions is to be found in a series of liturgical texts (4Q280–4Q287) which explicitly mention the Council of the *yaḥad* and abound in curses against Melchireša^c, Belial, and other angelic figures seems to me to place the composition within the corpus of sectarian writings.

The deterministic view of the Treatise appears also in a good part of the *Hodayot*, especially in the so-called Hymns of the Teacher, to the point that some people have speculated that both compositions were penned by the same author, the Teacher of Righteousness. The dualistic understanding of the world is equally obvious in the *War Scroll*. There it is not related to a description of human nature but concerns the development of human history and its final denouement in the eschatological war.

Summarizing the evidence on this point, I think we can conclude that the Dead Sea sect inherited from the Enochic tradition a view of the origin of evil that it further developed using elements coming from other traditions (like the Sapiential tradition and Zoroastrianism) so as to arrive at a full dualistic and deterministic view of the world.

⊂THE PERIODS OF HISTORY AND THE EXPECTATION OF THE END

One of the most characteristic features of the "historical" apocalypses is the division of history into periods and the expectation that God will intervene in the last of these periods in order to bring an end to evil in the world. Introducing these periods into history allows the apocalypses the possibility to integrate the past and the present reality with the future that the author intends to "reveal" and with the expected intervention of God, which will bring the end of history. The systems used to divide history into periods, bringing in this way some order into the chaos, are based on the numbers 4, 7, 10, 49 (7 x 7), 70, and even 490 (70 x 7 or 10 x 49). We find different ways of indicating this division of history into periods in different apocalypses, or even within the same composition. Daniel, for example, uses the schema of four successive kingdoms but also, and most characteristically, the schema of seventy weeks (of years), transforming the seventy years of Jeremiah into 490 years, which equals ten jubilees and can be correlated with the use of the number 10 in other apocalyptic compositions.

Within the different components of *1 Enoch*, we find different ways to express the division of history into periods. In the Book of the Watchers there is an allusion to a division of seventy periods before the end: "Bind them (the Watchers) for seventy generations under the hills of the earth until the day of their judgment and of their consummation, until the judgment which is for all eternity is accomplished" (10:12). The so-called Animal Apocalypse, which presents the protagonists in the history of Israel as various animals, also introduces periods into history; seventy shepherds pasture the sheep, each at his own time (89:59), and these seventy shepherds are divided into four unequal groups which pasture the sheep during four periods of different length (corresponding to the four kingdoms of Daniel). At the end of these periods the judgment takes place, the Messiah comes, and all the sheep become white bulls. But the most interesting view of the division of history is the one found in the so-called Apocalypse of Weeks, embedded in the Epistle of Enoch and now restored to its original order (disturbed in the Ethiopic translation) with the help of the Aramaic fragments from Qumran. As in Daniel, history is here divided into "weeks," presumably weeks of years, but the schema is based on the number 10, or, better said, on a combination of 7 and 10. The author compresses history from the birth of Enoch to his own days in seven weeks, and places himself obviously at the end of the seventh week, a week in which an apostate generation has arisen and at the end of which "the chosen righteous from the eternal plant of righteousness will be chosen [or "rewarded" according to other Ethiopic manuscripts], to whom will be given sevenfold teaching concerning his whole creation" (93:10). He obviously belonged to the chosen group to which he addresses his composition. Similarly, the author of Daniel belonged to the *maśkîlîm*, and the author of the Animal Apocalypse to the *ḥāsîdîm*. The great originality of the Apocalypse of Weeks lies in the fact that history does not end with this week. The Apocalypse goes on to reveal what will happen in the following weeks, introducing the organizing principle also in the future, and unfolding the progressive development of meta-history: in the eighth week a sword will be given to the righteous, who execute judgment on the sinners, and at its end "a house will be built for the great king in glory forever" (91:12–13); in the ninth week "the judgment of the righteous will be revealed to the whole world, all the deeds from the impious will vanish from the whole earth, and the world will be written down for destruction" (91:14); in the tenth week (in its seventh part) there will be apparently the judgment of the Watchers (the Ethiopic text is rather confused) and "the first heaven will vanish and pass away, and a new heaven will appear" (91:15–16) Then: "And after this there will be many weeks without number forever in goodness and in righteousness, and from then on sin will never again be mentioned" (91:17). The author of the Apocalypse of Weeks periodizes not only history but meta-history; the "end" is for him not one event, but rather the unfolding of a process in which several moments can be discerned.

In the Dead Sea Scrolls we find attested almost all the models used in the apocalyptic writings to periodize history, and also a conception of the "end" of history as an unfolding process in which several moments can be discerned.

A composition in Aramaic, preserved in two copies, 4Q552 and 4Q553, contained apparently a division of history following the model of the four kingdoms of Daniel; but the text is so badly preserved that we can say almost nothing. There is at least one vision and there is question of an interpretation. There is a king and there are trees that are able to talk and answer questions; one of the trees gives his own name as Babel, and of him it is said that he rules over Persia. This is almost all that can be gathered from the surviving fragments, but because it is also said that these trees are four, we can assume the author was following the well-known model of the four kingdoms.

Another very fragmentary text contained a commentary expressly dedicated to the division of history into periods that comprise the diverse phases of human history, which have been preordained by God and engraved in the heavenly tablets (4Q180–181). It begins: "Interpretation concerning the ages which God has made." This composition, certainly authored within the Qumran community and marked by the strongly deterministic outlook of the Treatise of the Two Spirits, could have provided us with a complete view of the problem within the community, but unfortunately it has also been badly preserved. Even combining the material of the two manuscripts (which are not necessarily part of the same composition) only part of the assertions concerning the first period (the ten generations from Noah to Abraham) can be recovered: the first is characterized by the sin of the fallen angels; the last by the sin of Sodom and Gomorrah. It is not clear how many periods were reckoned, but one of the fragments used the expression "in the seventieth week," apparently implying that a system of subdivisions was worked out inside the main divisions.

Another composition (4Q390) uses a system of jubilees to offer a review of the history of Israel, similar to the historical reviews of the apocalypses and of the beginning of the *Damascus Document,* but put into the mouth of God: "And when this generation passes, in the seventh jubilee of the devastation of the land, they will forget the law, the festival, the sabbath and the covenant, and they will disobey everything and do what is evil in my eyes" (4Q390 1:6–9). The author also uses other units to mark the divisions: a week of years ("and there will come the dominion of Belial upon them to deliver them up to the sword for a week of years" (4Q390 2:3–4), and a period of seventy years: "and they will begin to argue with one another for seventy years, from the day on which they break this vow and the covenant. And I shall deliver them to the hands of the angels of destruction and they will rule over them" (4Q390 2:6–7). Curiously enough, all the periods preserved in this document are characterized by a negative connotation: infidelity to the covenant and all sorts of transgressions, and especially the dominion of Belial and the "angels of destruction," a clear allusion to the Mastema of the book of *Jubilees.*

More clear, although also fragmentary, is the system we find in 11QMelchizedek, a thematic *pesher* that interprets Leviticus 25 (the jubilee year), Deuteronomy 15 (the year of release), and Isaiah 52 and 61 (which proclaim the liberation of the prisoners), applying these (and other biblical texts) to the eschatological period, the "last days." In this text, which knows Daniel and refers explicitly to it, history is divided into ten jubilees. The preserved part of the composition concentrates on the last of these ten jubilees: "This will happen in the first week of the jubilee which follows the nine jubilees. And the day of atonement is the end of the tenth jubilee in which atonement will be made for all the sons of God and for the men of the lot of Melchizedek" (11Q13 2:6–8). The protagonist of the text is Melchizedek, who is presented as a heavenly figure. The remission of debts of the biblical text is interpreted as referring to the final liberation, which will occur during the Day of the Expiation. Melchizedek, the agent of this liberation, is presented as the eschatological judge mentioned in Ps. 7:8–9 and Ps. 82:1–2. He is also presented as the chief of the heavenly armies, the leader of the "sons of God," who will destroy the armies of Belial, identifying his figure in terms of practical functions with the "Prince of Light" (a figure we find in 1QS 3:20, CD 5:8, and 1QM 13:10) and with the angel Michael (a figure appearing in 1QM 17:6–7). The victory of Melchizedek against Belial and the spirits of his lot, will usher in an era of salvation, which is described in the words of Isaiah.

In this text we have encountered the most usual expression within the Dead Sea Scrolls to indicate the period of the end, the phrase ʾaḥărît hayyāmîm. The expression is well attested (in Hebrew and once in Aramaic) within the Hebrew Bible. The phrase occurs more than thirty times in the nonbiblical scrolls and is especially frequent in exegetical compositions. The phrase originally meant "in the course of time, in future days," and this (noneschatological) meaning seems to be best suited to many of the biblical occurrences of the expression, although its use in Isaiah 2, Micah 4, Ezekiel 38, and Daniel 2 and 10 may have a more specifically eschatological meaning.

In Qumran this is certainly the case, as the expression seems to be used to designate the final period of history. Nowhere are the precise limits of this period defined, but it is the last of the divinely preordained periods and the period in which the community exists. According to the latest study published on ʾaḥărît hayyāmîm in the Scrolls (Steudel 1993), the phrase may refer, depending on the context, to the past, to the present, or to the future from the point of view of the writer. The last days are thus a period already started but not yet completed, somehow coextensive with the present of the community. As CD 4:4 put it: "the sons of Zadok are the chosen of Israel, 'those called by name' who stood up at the end of days."

The text most often quoted as asserting that the last days have already begun is 4QMMT, where the complete expression occurs twice in the hortatory section. But in the first occurrence (C 13–15) the expression may have a meaning more akin to the biblical usage, and the second—"And this is the end of days" (C 21)—can be linked both to the preceding sentence in the past tense ("We know that some of the blessings and the curses as written in the book of Moses have come, and this is the end of days," and to the following sentence in the future tense: "And this is the end of days, when in Israel they will return to the Law." In neither case will the phrase have the fully developed eschatological connotation characteristic of other Qumran usages; it will rather represent a first stage in the development of Qumranic thought.

The most characteristic usage is the one we find in the exegetical compositions, where the meaning of the biblical text, "for the last days," is directly applied to the life of the community, which is seen as fulfillment of the prophetic text. The phrase has two different aspects in the Scrolls. The last days are a period of testing and refining, a period of trial, but the expression also designates the time beyond the trial, the period in which salvation will start.

The first element is explicit in 4Q174, which interprets Ps. 2:1 as referring to the elect of Israel in the last days and continues: "That is the time of refining which comes . . . ." The participle used can be translated with a past or with a future meaning, but there is no doubt that the time involved is a time of trial: Belial is mentioned, and also a remnant, and the text explicitly refers to Dan. 12:10, where the just "shall be whitened and refined." Other texts use the same expression, "time of refining," referring to the persecution of the Teacher of Righteousness or of the men of the community (4QpPs^a 2:17–19) or to locate during the last days the hostile actions of the "violators of the covenant," as well as the suffering and tribulations of its members and its leaders (1QpHab, 4QpNah, etc.).

The second element is equally explicit. The last days comprise the beginning of the messianic age. The same 4Q174 locates in the last days the rising up of the "shoot of David" and the construction of the new temple. A *pesher* on Isaiah (4Q161), commenting on Isa. 11:1–5, presents the same "shoot of David" (also called the Prince of the Congregation in the same document, and the Messiah of Israel in other writings) waging the eschatological war against the Kittim in the last days, destroying its enemies and judging and ruling over all the peoples. CD 6:11 extends the duration of age of wickedness "until there arises he who teaches justice at the end of days." 11QMelchizedek announces the ushering in of the age of salvation in the last days. The *Rule of the Congregation of Israel in the Last Days* (1QSa), which legislates for the eschatological community, assumes as a matter of fact that the Messiahs are present in these last days and take an active part in the life of the community. One of the most famous and disputed passages of the Scrolls announces God's begetting the Messiah "with them." For the rest, as L. Schiffman (1989) put it: the document describes the eschatological future as a mirror of the present. 1QSa reflects the everyday life of the community as we know it from the *Community Rule*—its purity concerns, its hierarchical structure, and its meals—but addresses at the same time particular concerns of the communities of the *Damascus Document*, as if indicating that in the last days the *yahad* community and the communities of the camps will be reunited in a single eschatological congregation.

The precise limits of the end of days are nowhere clearly stated, but it is said that this period of time will be closed by God's "visitation." In the Treatise of the Two Spirits we read: "God, in the mysteries of his knowledge and in the wisdom of his glory, has determined an end to the existence of deceit and on the occasion of his visitation he will obliterate it forever" (1QS 4:18–19). It is thus a period of time of limited duration, and it would be surprising if the members of the community had not attempted to calculate exactly the moment when the evil would be obliterated forever. Indeed, in some texts indirect traces of these calculations can be found. I do not think (as Steudel does) that the Day of Atonement of the tenth jubilee of 11QMelchizedek could gives us this date, nor that it can be provided by the 390 years of the beginning of the *Damascus Document* (the year 72 B.C.E.). But I do think that other texts, the *pesher* Habakkuk and the *Damascus Document* preserve traces of these calculations.

This last text tells us that the traitors to the covenant "shall not be counted in the assembly of the people and shall not be inscribed in their list, from the day of the gathering in of the unique Teacher until there arises the Messiah of Aaron and Israel" (19:35–20:1). A little further on it adds: "And from the day of the gathering in of the unique teacher, until the destruction of the men of war who turned back with the man of lies, there shall be about forty years" (20:13–15). If we identify the "men of war who turned back with the man of lies" with the traitors "who turned and betrayed and departed from the well of living waters," and if we understand both the coming of the Messiahs and the destruction of the men of war as an indication of the beginning of the divine visitation, we can see here a trace of these calculations: the end will come *about* forty years after the death of the Teacher. I do not think we can calculate an exact date on the basis of this "about forty years," but its presence in the *Damascus Document* is a sure indication that such calculations were made.

The other text, 1QpHab 7:1–14 does not offer any more precision, but it is a precious witness to the way the community coped when the calculations proved to be wrong and the expected end did not materialize. The text concerns Hab. 2:1–3, which is quoted, section by section, and interpreted:

> And God told Habakkuk to write what was going to happen to the last genera-
> tion, but he did not let him know the end of the age. And as for what he says:
> "So that the one who reads it may run": Its interpretation concerns the Teacher
> of Righteousness, to whom God has disclosed all the mysteries of the words of

his servants, the prophets. "For the vision has an appointed time, it will have an end and will not fail." Its interpretation: the final age will be extended and go beyond all that the prophets say, because the mysteries of God are wonderful. "Though it might delay, wait for it; it definitely has to come and will not delay." Its interpretation concerns the men of truth, those who observe the Law, whose hands will not desert the service of truth when the final age is extended beyond them, because all the ages of God will come at the right time, as he established for them in the mysteries of his prudence.

In its extreme conciseness, this text teaches us many things: that the true meaning of the word of the prophet concerns the last period of history, the last days in which the community lives, although this meaning is not known by the prophet; that this deep meaning is known to the community thanks to the revelation the Teacher of Righteousness has received; that the core of this revelation is that the community lives in the last days, but this revelation does not include the exact time of arrival of the final salvation; that this arrival is part of the divine mystery, which includes prolongation as part of the divine plan; that the moment of salvation will come anyway, at the precise moment God has decreed; and that what really matters for the members of the community is not to abandon the service of truth during this prolongation.

The text clearly implies that the community has calculated the arrival of the end but that their prediction has not been fulfilled at the moment of the writing of the *pesher:* "the final age has extended beyond them." The text also shows that the community has already found a way to explain this delay without losing either the certainty of living already in the last days or the hope of the approaching final salvation.

This calculation of the end is nothing new. Daniel had already attempted to make even more specific calculations of the same end, and the biblical text shows traces of new calculations when the end did not come (Daniel 12).

Summary

The historical apocalypses were characterized by the division of history into periods and the expectation that God would intervene in order to bring an end to the evil in the world. These ideas are abundantly represented in compositions we can attribute to the Qumran community that are of very different literary genres. They also seem to have profoundly shaped the worldview of the sect, which considered itself to be living in the last period of history.

⌒COMMUNION WITH THE HEAVENLY WORLD _____

One of the elements that distinguishes apocalyptic literature from the traditional biblical worldview is an increased interest in the heavenly world. This is shown by the number, and the concrete names, of the heavenly beings, be they angels or demons, that we encounter in this literature (Mach 1992). These heavenly beings appear named for the first time in such books as *1 Enoch* and Daniel, where their numbers "cannot be counted," but they are no fewer than "a thousand thousands and ten thousand times ten thousand." The angelology of *1 Enoch* is particularly developed, where a multitude of angelic beings exercise multiple functions. They are servants of the deity who stand before the throne of glory or outside the heavenly residence; they are intercessors before God, ministers of the heavenly liturgy but also executioners of the divine will. They are intimately related to the seer; they interpret dreams for him and disclose to him heavenly secrets. They guide the visionary in his heavenly tours and communicate to him divine decisions. They are also deeply involved in the affairs of this world. They rule over the stars, the winds, the rains, the seasons, and over all celestial elements which form part of their own names. They record the deeds of human beings and execute the punishment of the Watchers and of the sinners, but also they help the righteous and watch over Israel.

Already in the classical description of the Essenes it is said that they cherished "the knowledge of the names of the angels." So it comes as no surprise that the angelology of the scrolls is rather developed, more in line with the angelology of *1 Enoch* than with the sober angelology of the biblical texts. We have already mentioned the dualistic division of the angelic world with the Prince of Light and the Angel of Darkness at the head of two angelic hosts, and we have also alluded to Belial, the most common name for the demonic leader in the Scrolls, to the "angels of destruction" (a designation that echoes the proper name of Mastema, their angelic leader in the book of *Jubilees*), and to Michael, the opponent of Belial in the eschatological war. But in the Scrolls we find also explicitly stated that another of the names of this angelic prince is Melkirešaᶜ; (4Q544), in parallel to Melchizedek (11Q13), who in the Scrolls is apparently identified with Michael and with the Prince of Light.

In the Scrolls we find also a strongly hierarchical structure of the heavenly world, similar to the one that appears in the apocalypses, with different roles and different degrees of proximity to the deity. The Scrolls also attribute to angels many of the functions assigned to angelic beings in *1 Enoch* and other apocalyptic writings: angels interpret dreams and visions to the seer (such as to Amram); they guide the visionary on a tour to the future city and the future temple (as in the New Jerusalem), or read for him from a heavenly book or inscription in the temple (as in 11Q18, 19 5–6). A fragmentary Aramaic composition (4Q529) even records "The Words of the book which Michael spoke to the angels of God."

But the most characteristic view of the heavenly world we find in the sectarian scrolls is the idea, expressed several times, that the angels are present in middle of the community, and consequently that its members somehow share already the life of the angels. This communion with the heavenly world and fellowship with the angels is explicitly stated as the reason for the high degree of purity required of those who take part in the eschatological battle: "And every man who has not cleansed himself of his 'spring' on the day of battle will not go down with them, for the holy angels are together with their armies" (1QM 7:5–6). But it is also invoked as an absolute reason to refuse entry into the eschatological community to anyone with an imperfection:

> No man defiled by any of the impurities of a man shall enter the assembly of these; and everyone who is defiled by them should not be established in his office amongst the congregation. And everyone who is defiled in his flesh, paralyzed in his feet or in his hands, lame, blind, deaf, dumb or defiled in his flesh with a blemish visible to the eyes, or the tottering old man who cannot keep upright in the midst of the assembly, these shall not enter to take their place among the congregation of famous men, for the angels of holiness are among their congre[gation.] (1QSa 2:3–9)

That this fellowship with the angels is not something reserved for the eschatological time, for the "last days" to which these two documents are addressed, is proved by one of the copies of the *Damascus Document* from Cave 4, which legislates who can become members of the present community:

> And no-one stupid or deranged should enter; and anyone feeble-minded and insane, those with sightless eyes, and the lame or one who stumbles, or a deaf person, or an under-age boy, none of these shall enter the congregation, for the holy angels are in its midst. (4Q267 17 i 6–9)

It is also shown by the repeated use of this idea both in *Rule of the Community* and in the *Hymns*, perhaps the most characteristic documents of the Qumran community, as indicated by the following two samples:

> To those whom God has selected he has given them as everlasting possession; until they inherit them in the lot of the holy ones. He unites their assembly to the sons of the heavens in order (to form) the council of the Community and a

foundation of the building of holiness to be an everlasting plantation through-out all future ages. (1QS 11:7–9)

And I know that there is hope for someone you fashioned out of clay to be an everlasting community. The corrupt spirit you have purified from the great sin so that he can take his place with the host of the holy ones, and can enter into communion with the congregation of the sons of heaven. (1QH 11:20–22)

The idea of communion with the heavenly world gives us the key to understanding the document in which the angelology of the Qumran group is most explicitly stated: the *Songs for the Sabbath Sacrifice*. This composition, the title of which has been taken from the sentence that begins each one of its thirteen songs, has been found in ten fragmentary copies: eight from Cave 4, one from Cave 1, and another one found in the excavations of Masada. All of them were made between the second half of the first century B.C.E. and the first half of the first century C.E. (Newsom 1985, 19). The peculiarities of the language, dominated by nominal and participial sentences with elaborate construct chains, the omnipresence of constructions with the preposition *l-*, many lexical novelties, and peculiar syntax, indicate that the original composition should not be dated very much earlier than the oldest copy.

The composition comprises thirteen songs intended for consecutive sab-baths, apparently designed to be repeated in each quarter of the year. Each song starts with a fixed formula but has no fixed end, and each one consists of a call to different sorts of angelic beings to praise the deity. Although the angels are insistently exhorted to praise, nowhere in the composition is their praise recorded, except as "the serene sound of silence" (4Q405 19 7), or "the voice of a divine silence" (4Q405 20–22 7) of the blessing.

The first four songs deal with the establishment of the angelic priest-hood, its responsibilities and functions in the heavenly sanctuary ("[Because he has established] the holy of holies among the eternal holy ones, so that for him they can be priests [who approach the temple of his kingship,] the ser-vants of the Presence in the sanctuary of his glory" [4Q400 1 i 3–4]), as well as with the relationship of the angelic priesthood to the human priesthood: "And how will our priesthood (be regarded) in their residences? What is the offering of our tongue of dust (compared) with the knowledge of the divini-ties?" (4Q400 2 6–7). The fifth song deals with the eschatological battle: "the war of the gods in the per[iod . . .] for to the God of the divinities belong the weapons of war [. . .] the gods run to their positions, and a powerful noise [. . .] the gods in the war of the heavens" (4Q402 4 7–10), placing this escha-tological battle in the same deterministic perspective we have seen in the Treatise of the Two Spirits: "Because from the God of knowledge comes all that existed for ever. And through his knowledge and through his decision all that is predestined exists for ever. He does the first things in their ages and the final (things) in their appointed periods" (4Q402 4, completed with the copy from Masada). The sixth and eighth songs detail respectively the seven praises uttered by the seven sovereign angelic princes who are the seven high priests of the seven heavenly sanctuaries, and the praises by their seven deputies, "those second among the priests who approach him, the second council in the wonderful dwelling among the seven . . . among all those having knowledge of eternal things." The seventh song, the center of the whole cycle, contains a very elaborate exhortation to praise, followed by the praise uttered by the different elements of the heavenly temple: "the foundations of the holy of holies, the supporting columns of the highest vault, and all the corners of his building," but also "all its beams and walls, all its shape, the work of his construction." This praise is continued in more detail in songs 9–11, which proceed with the description of the praise of the elements of the heavenly temple, described as animate beings, from the outside in the ninth song ("the lobbies of their entrances, spirits who approach the holy of holies"), to the inside in the tenth song, as far as the veil of the sanctuary with all that is engraved there, to reach finally in the eleventh song the inside of the *děbîr,* which describes the praise uttered by all its elements "living gods are all their works and holy angels the images of their forms." The twelfth song describes the appearance of the chariot-throne, the movement of the heavenly beings which surround it and the praises they utter:

> They bless the image of the throne-chariot (which is) above the vault of the cherubim, and they sing the splendor of the shining vault (which is) beneath the seat of his glory. And when the *ofanim* move forward, the holy angels go back; they emerge among the glorious wheels with the likeness of fire, the spirits of the holy of holies. Around them, the likeness of a stream of fire like electrum, and a luminous substance with glorious colors, wonderfully intermingled, brightly combined. The spirits of the living gods move constantly with the glory of the wonderful chariots. And (there is) a silent voice of blessing in the uproar of their motion, and they praise the holy one on returning to their paths. (4Q405 20–22 8–13)

The climax of the whole composition is reached in the thirteenth song, in which the sacrifices that appear on the heading of each song are finally mentioned: "agreeable offerings," "the sacrifices of the holy ones," "the odor of their offerings," "the odor of their libations." The angels are described as officiating priests wearing the ephod and the breastplate, and the praise of the whole heavenly temple is summarized (11Q17 cols. 10–11).

Although the *Songs* do not preserve personal names of the angels (except perhaps the name of Melchizedek in two broken instances) and it is difficult, not to say impossible, from the generic names used (gods, holy ones, glorious ones, spirits, angels, princes, priests, deputies, angels of the face, angels who approach, angels who serve, and so on) to extract the assigned or intended functions of the different classes of angels, there is no doubt that the number of beings and the differentiation of the heavenly world in the *Songs* is as great and variegated as it is in other apocalypses. In the *Songs* even all the material elements of the heavenly abode—the structures of the heavenly temple and the components of the chariot-throne—are presented as animated heavenly beings of angelic nature who utter praise and participate in the heavenly liturgy. And, though the hierarchical structure of the angelic realm is somewhat blurred in the *Songs,* at least there is explicit mention of the seven princes and their seven deputies in the sixth and eighth songs. These are clearly two categories of angelic beings superior to the others, the first corresponding perhaps to the seven archangels of the Greek text of *1 Enoch* or to the four archangels of the Ethiopic text, who are also named in other Qumran scrolls.

In spite of the nonpolemical and neutral character of the *Songs* and of the absence of clearly sectarian terminology in the composition, the abundant parallels with other clearly sectarian scrolls, such as the 1QH or 1QS, suggest that the *Songs* are a product of the Qumran community. Other considerations supporting this view include the use of *lĕmaśkîl* in the headings (which is common to many sectarian compositions); the close parallels between the description of the angelic praise and the heavenly temple in the *Songs* and in compositions such as 4QBerakot (4Q286–290) and the *Songs of the Maskil* (4Q510–511), whose sectarian character cannot be doubted; the great number of copies found; the late date of all of them and the equally late date assumed for the original. The idea of communion with the angels, which we find to be characteristic of the Qumran community, provides the most illuminating setting for the composition.

The function of the *Songs* within the community has been diversely explained. For those who value most the detailed descriptions of the components of the heavenly temple, the text would function as revelation of the heavenly realities. For those who underline the numinous character of the language used and the importance of the description of the chariot-throne, the *Songs* would function as an instrument of mystical meditation or even mystical ascent to the divine throne, similar to the mystics of the *Merkavah.* For those who emphasize the priestly character of the *Songs,* its function would be to validate and justify the priestly character of a community that has no control over the earthly temple by its association with the heavenly cult. In my view the most likely function of the *Songs* within the Qumran community was to substitute for the participation in the sacrifices of the earthly Temple the association with the heavenly liturgy and the sabbath offerings. We know that the community, in the expectation of the new situation "at the end of the days" had developed an interim theology of the community as spiritual temple, in which praise substituted for the sacrifices (see 1QS 8:4–10; 9:3–6). We have also seen (in the texts from 1QSa and 1QM quoted above) that the community had developed the idea of fellowship with the angels, and other texts show that the priests of the community considered themselves to be associated with the angelic priesthood. The blessing over the priests, the sons of Zadok, says: "May the Lord bless you from his holy residence. May he set you as a glorious ornament in the midst of the holy ones. For you may he renew the covenant of eternal priesthood. May he grant you a place in the holy residence" (1QSb 3:25–26), and even more clearly in the next column: "You shall be around, serving in the temple of the kingdom, sharing the lot with the angels of the face and the council of the community . . . for eternal time and for all the perpetual periods" (1QSb 4:25–26). The recitation of the *Songs of the Sabbath Sacrifice* on the successive sabbaths of the four quarters of the year gave the members of the community the possibility of participating in the sabbath sacrifice of the heavenly temple, compensating for their absence from the sabbath sacrifice of the Jerusalem Temple and giving a concrete expression to the life shared with the angels already in the present.

Summary

The complexity and structured organization of the heavenly world that we find in the apocalypses are represented also in the Scrolls, which add a most notable element: the idea that the angels are already living among the members of the community. This fellowship with the angels is not restricted to the future but is a reality also of the present and allows participation in the liturgy of the heavenly temple.

THE ESCHATOLOGICAL WAR

One of the basic themes of the prophets is the announcement of the final triumph of God and of the people of Israel against the evil forces and against the enemies who oppress the people in the present. Very often this triumph takes the form of a future military victory in which the Israelites will destroy the hostile powers who actually oppress them. This expectation is rooted in the realities of the political history of the people of Israel with its repeated experience of invasions and defeats by foreign powers and in the confidence that the God of Israel, who has overpowered the forces of chaos, will deliver his people from oppression. Although in some cases this liberation takes the form of a victory against a very concrete enemy (such as in the various oracles of Jeremiah against different nations), very often it is generalized in the form of a victory against all the nations (Psalm 2) or against a mythical enemy, such as Gog, king of Magog, who represents all the hostile powers (Ezekiel 38–39); a famous oracle of the prophet Joel links this victory with the day of the Lord, when the nations will be judged (Joel 3:9–16)

The apocalypses develop further this idea of the victory over all the nations, placing it in a clear eschatological perspective (as in the Animal Apocalypse, which ends with the destruction of all the hostile nations [*1 Enoch* 90]), and introduce in this eschatological war, as participants or as protagonists, the angelic forces with a celestial leader (as in Daniel, where Michael is the leader who overpowers the angels of the nations).

In the Scrolls the biblical elements of the final victory against all the nations are clearly present, and they are placed in an eschatological perspective. *4QFlorilegium* (4Q174) interprets Psalm 2 in the context of the "end of days" and "the time of the trial"; 4QpIsa[a] (4Q161) refers to Magog and "the war of the Kittim" together with the Branch of David, the Davidic Messiah who participates in the eschatological victory; the same figure, called there "the Prince of the Congregation," appears in the *Damascus Document* as "the scepter" of the oracle of Balaam "who will smite the children of Sheth" (CD 7:20–21). The angelic participation in the final battle is also well attested in the Scrolls, which refer to "the war of the heavenly warriors" (1QH 11:35), and which (as we have already seen) anticipate the final victory of the forces of light against the forces of darkness "at the time of his visitation" in the Treatise of the Two Spirits (1QS 3–4).

But in the Scrolls the eschatological battle does not simply coincide with the biblical and apocalyptic vision of the final victory against the foreign nations, because it comprises the victory against all evil forces. The dividing line is not between Israel and the foreign nations but between the Sons of Light (which are the elected ones of Israel) and the Sons of Darkness (a term that covers not only pagans but also unfaithful Israelites). In the thought of the Qumran community, the eschatological battle will not be restricted to a battle against the foreign nations; it will also be a battle against all the evildoers, including the part of Israel that has not joined the community.

The document in which the thought of the group on the eschatological battle and final victory is best reflected is the *Rule of the War of the Sons of Light against the Sons of Darkness* (1QM), which has been best preserved in a copy from Cave 1, but which is also attested in several fragmentary copies from Cave 4 (4Q492, 4Q494–496). Other manuscripts, such as 4Q491 and 4Q493, have preserved materials related to this composition or even different recensions of the same composition, while two other manuscripts (4Q285 and 11Q11) that also deal with the eschatological war may represent part of the lost end of 1QM or may come from another composition dealing with the same topic (Duhaime 1995).

The contents of 1QM may be summarized as follows:

Column 1 and part of column 2 contain a summary of the development of the war, which ends with the victory of the Sons of Light and the restoration of the cult in Jerusalem.

Columns 2–9 record the organization and the military tactics that should be employed in this war: rules of the trumpets to conduct each one of the phases of the war (2:15–3:11); rules of the banners with their inscriptions (3:13–5:2); rules of the formation of the battle arrays, the weapons, and the tactical movements (5:3–7:7); and the rules to conduct the war with the different trumpets (7:9 until the end of column 9).

Columns 10–14 contain the prayers that are to be said during the different phases of the war: in the camps (cols. 10–12), during the battle (col. 13), and after the victory (col. 14).

Column 15 to the end of the manuscript preserves another version of the war against the Kittim, with the exhortation of the high priest before the battle, the first engagement, the use of the reserve troops when the Belial army seems to have the upper hand, the final battle and the celebration after the victory.

The unity and coherence of the document in its present form have led some scholars to defend the unity of composition of 1QM. But, because of certain repetitions, inconsistencies, and especially because there are two basically different conceptions of the eschatological war, most scholars recognize that 1QM is the result of the fusion of at least two documents.

One of them, inspired by Daniel 11–12 and Ezekiel 38–39, developed the idea of an eschatological conflagration on seven lots in which each one of the sides has the upper part during three lots and which ends with the victory of God. As stated in col. 1: "In the war, the sons of light will be the strongest during three lots, in order to strike down wickedness; and in three (others), the army of Belial will gird themselves in order to force the lot of [. . .] to retreat. . . . And in the seventh lot, God's great hand will subdue [Belial, and a]ll the angels of his dominion and all the men of [his lot]" (1QM 1:13–15).

The same idea is found in cols. 14–19, in which, in spite of the bad state of preservation, we can discern that these seven lots alternate, a victory following a defeat, until the final victory of the Sons of Light in the seventh lot, when "the Kittim shall be crushed without a [remnant . . .] when the hand of the God of Israel is raised against the whole horde of Belial" (1QM 18:2–3). This war is envisaged in two levels, the human and the angelic: "On this (day), the assembly of the gods and the congregation of men shall confront each other for great destruction" (1QM 1:10), but the angelic hosts appear to have no leader apart from God himself, who at the end decides the victory. These two ideas characterize cols. 1 and 14–19.

These two elements allow us to distinguish this original document from the second one, reflected in cols. 2–13, in which the war of seven lots is transformed in a progressive battle of forty years against each one of the nations enumerated in Genesis 10, and in which the angelic army is guided by an angelic leader, the Prince of Light: "From of old you appointed the Prince of Light to assist us, and in [. . .] and all the spirits of truth are under his dominion" (1QM 13:10). This progressive battle, which evidently is based on the forty-year schema of Exodus, does not know any interruption other than the obliged rest of the sabbatical years, five in a forty-year period. This leaves thirty-five years for the conduct of the war. For the author of this document (or for the redactor who has united it with the previous one), the war of seven lots of the first document seems to be understood as the first seven of the forty years, of which the seventh year is not the final victory but the first sabbatical year, and the other six either a general preparation for the war or a general battle of the whole congregation against the main enemies, according to the interpretation one gives to the problematic expression of 2:9. The remaining twenty-nine years are dedicated to eradicating all the enemies of Israel: nine years of war against the sons of Shem, ten years against the sons of Ham, and the last ten years against the sons of Japheth:

> During the remaining thirty-three years of the war, the famous men called to the assembly, and all the chiefs of the fathers of the congregation shall choose for themselves men of war for all the countries of the nations; from all the tribes of Israel they shall equip for them intrepid men, in order to go out on campaign according to the directives of war, year after year. However, during the years of release they shall not equip themselves in order to go out on campaign, for it is a sabbath of rest for Israel. During the thirty-five years of service, the war will be prepared (or waged) during six years; and all the congregation together will prepare it (or wage it). And the war of the divisions (will take place) during the remaining twenty-nine years. (1QM 2:6–10)

If the idea of the forty-year war is clearly based on the biblical tradition and reminds us of the wandering in the wilderness, it is difficult to find a biblical precedent for the idea of the war of seven alternate lots, although there is an obvious similarity between the seven lots and the sabbatical structures that inform so much of Jewish thought. The closest parallel to this idea is provided by a passage in Plutarch that attributes a similar idea to the Persians: "Theopompus says that, according to the Magians, for three thousand years alternately the one god will dominate the other and be dominated, and that for another three thousand years they will fight and make war, until one smashes up the domain of the other. In the end Hades shall perish and men shall be happy "(*On Isis and Osiris* 47; see chapter 2 above).

Although there are many uncertainties in this text, it provides some basic elements, like two supernatural forces that battle each other and alternately hold sway until the victory of the supreme God, which may have helped to give shape to the thought of the author of the *War Scroll*. This possible Persian influence comes at no surprise since we have already noted the most plausible Persian influence on the Treatise of the Two Spirits, and the first document of the *War Scroll* shares the characteristic dualistic framework of this tractate.

The redactor who has combined both documents to form the *War Scroll* that we have in 1QM has also used other elements. Most prominent is a collection of prayers for the time of the war, which could have had an autonomous existence. This is suggested by the text itself:

> The High Priest will take up position, and his brothers the priests and the levites and all the men of the rule shall be with him. And he will say in their hearing the prayer for the time of war, [as it is written in the "Bo]ok of the Rule for this time," with all the words of thanksgiving. (1QM 15:4–5)

This clearly echoes the biblical order: "before you engage in battle, the priest shall come forward and speak to the troops" (Deut. 20:2), but the specific reference to a "book" seems to indicate that these prayers were already at the disposal of the redactor of the composition, an assumption that is corroborated by the use of the same prayers in other closely related but different compositions on the same topic such as 4Q491. These prayers are mostly grouped in cols. 9–14, but we can find them also in other places of the scroll. The prayers are very closely based on biblical material; many of them recall incidents from biblical history that show examples of divine intervention in favor of Israel, and their language is mostly a mosaic of biblical expressions. They are put in the mouths of levites, of priests, or of the high priest (who are also the ones who exhort the people by means of speeches and enforce the purity regulations), and they help to accentuate the priestly preeminence in guiding the people and the ritualistic character of the whole war.

The redactor has also sought inspiration from Greco-Roman tactical military manuals to specify the regulations for warfare that he applies to the development of the war in cols. 2–9. These regulations for warfare show some general similarity to Maccabean battles, but they are more akin to the Roman military tactics (such as the use of the "gates of war," the Roman *intervalla* [see Yadin 1962]). The knowledge of these tactics and the descriptions of the weaponry (such as the square shield, the Roman *scutum*) indicate a certain familiarity with the Roman army but do not imply that the redaction of 1QM is posterior to the intervention of Pompey, because this knowledge could be obtained well before the Roman conquest of Palestine. The author has been influenced by the biblical tradition more than by Greco-Roman military manuals or Maccabean warfare. The organization of the army in thousands, hundreds, fifties, and tens is patterned after the Israelite army as described in Exodus 18; the overall use of the banners to distinguish each unit and their elaborate inscriptions are dependent on Numbers 2 and 17; and the use of the trumpets has its basis in Numbers 10, although in the *War Scroll* the use of trumpets is much more complex and elaborate than in the biblical tradition, and its function in conducting each phase of the war goes far beyond the biblical text. This use of trumpets and horns accentuates the ritualistic character of the whole composition and recalls the ritual character of the conquest of Jericho in Joshua 7.

Because we do not have the end of the 1QM manuscript, we do not know in detail what expectations its author had for the time after the eschatological war or how he imagined the life of the community after the final divine intervention. But if he accepted, as it seems, the summary of the first document of the war of seven lots, one of the first results of the final victory (col. 2) would be the reconstruction of the temple service according to the proper order and the right calendar of 364 days. This implies return to Jerusalem after the necessary purification of the earth from the corpses of those slain in battle, and the reorganization of the whole of life according to the regulations of the community, which would be no more in exile but would control the whole country. Because all the Sons of Darkness, the "army of Belial," would be completely destroyed, the Sons of Light would no longer be a remnant but would be the whole of Israel. Hence, the *War Scroll* shares the perspective of other sectarian documents, such as the *Rule of the Congregation* (1QSa), in which membership of the community seems to be coextensive with the Israel "of the last days." Characteristically, the same people who are excluded from the community "of the end days" are also excluded from participating in the final battle (compare 1QM 7:4–5 with the already quoted text of 1QSa 2:5–8).

The function of the *War Scroll* has been defined in very different terms by various scholars: as the apocalyptic revelation of the several phases, enemies, and general development of the eschatological war; as a composition designed to instruct the perfect soldier, a manual to be used on the battlefield to oppose the enemy; as a propaganda pamphlet to oppose the way rival Jewish leaders were conducting the war indicating the right way to proceed; as a composition written more for liturgical than for practical purposes, more to celebrate the future victory than to prepare for or to conduct the war. But in fact these readings of the function of the text do not need to be mutually exclusive, and perhaps the best way to understand this complex document is by combining these apparently contradictory functions. The *War Scroll*, by representing the dramatic final conflict of the forces of good and evil as a liturgy in which the trumpets are as effective as the weapons, the priestly prayers as necessary as the movements of the troops, and the purity regulations as essential as the presence of the heavenly warriors, stimulates the hope for the future intervention of God, helps to organize the present as a preparation for this intervention, justifies the present opposition to other forces, and conveys the certitude that the actual dreams and hopes will be fulfilled in the final victory.

Summary

The apocalypses developed the traditional idea of a final victory against the enemies of Israel and placed it in an eschatological context, with participation of angelic forces. In the Dead Sea Scrolls this idea is further developed and transformed into an eschatological war of seven lots or of forty years which will end with the final victory against all forces of evil.

CONCLUSION

In the four topics examined we have seen that characteristic ideas of the apocalyptic tradition have not only contributed to the thought of the Qumran community but have undergone there equally characteristic developments. The idea of the origin of evil has been developed to a fully dualistic and deterministic view of the world; the apocalyptic division of history into periods and the expectation that God will intervene to bring an end to the evil in the world have profoundly marked the worldview of the community, which considers itself living in the last of these periods; the Scrolls add to the complexity and structured organization of the heavenly world of the apocalypses the idea that the angels are already living among the community, allowing its members to participate in the liturgy of the heavenly temple; the Scrolls also develop the apocalyptic idea of an eschatological war in which the heavenly forces help Israel to defeat the nations in a final war in which all evil will be destroyed.

We can thus conclude that the apocalypticism indicated by this cluster of ideas in the sectarian scrolls is something more than an umbrella term. It represents genuine continuity with the worldview of Daniel and *1 Enoch* even while it adapted the tradition inherited from these earlier apocalypses in its own distinctive ways.

≈BIBLIOGRAPHY

Collins, J. J. 1984. *The Apocalyptic Imagination.* New York: Crossroad. Second edition, Grand Rapids: Eerdmans, 1998. Broad introduction to the Jewish apocalypses in their historical context.
———. 1997a. *Apocalypticism in the Dead Sea Scrolls.* London: Routledge. The most comprehensive and detailed analysis of apocalypticism in the Scrolls.
———. 1997b. *Seers, Sibyls and Sages in Hellenistic-Roman Judaism.* Leiden: E. J. Brill. Important essays on apocalypticism and the Scrolls.
———, ed. 1979. *Apocalypse: The Morphology of a Genre. Semeia* 14. Chico, Calif.: Scholars Press. Definition of the literary genre Apocalypse, description of the paradigm and classification of the two main subtypes.
Dimant, D. 1994. "Apocalyptic Texts at Qumran." In *The Community of the Renewed Covenant,* edited by E. Ulrich and J. C. VanderKam, 175–91. Notre Dame, Ind.: University of Notre Dame Press. Classification of the Qumran texts that can be labeled apocalyptic.
Duhaime, J. 1995. "War Scroll (1QM; 1Q33; 4Q491–496; 4Q497)." In *The Dead Sea Scrolls: Hebrew, Aramaic, and Greek Texts with English Translation,* edited by J. H. Charlesworth, 2:80–203. Tübingen: Mohr; Louisville: Westminster/John Knox Press. Critical edition of all the fragments of the *War Sroll* and some related documents.
García Martínez, F. 1992. *Qumran and Apocalyptic.* Leiden: E. J. Brill. Collection of articles on Aramaic texts relevant to apocalypticism from Qumran.
———. 1996. *The Dead Sea Scrolls Translated. Second Edition.* Leiden: E. J. Brill; Grand Rapids: Eerdmans. Translations of most of the nonbiblical Dead Sea Scrolls.
Hellholm, D., ed. 1983. *Apocalypticism in the Ancient Mediterranean World and in the Near East.* Tübingen: Mohr. Proceedings of the Uppsala Colloquium on Apoca-

lypticism and the most complete collection of articles on the phenomenon of apocalypticism, the literary genre of apocalypses, the sociology of apocalypticism, and the function of apocalypticism.

Koch, K. 1972. *The Rediscovery of Apocalyptic.* Naperville, Ill.: Allenson. German original, *Ratlos vor Apokalyptik.* Critical analysis of the problems posed by the indiscriminate use of the term "apocalyptic."

Mach, M. 1992. *Entwicklungsstadien des jüdischen Engelglaubens in vorrabbinischer Zeit.* Tübingen: Mohr. Comprehensive and detailed study of the developments of Jewish angelology.

Newsom, C. 1985. *Songs of the Sabbath Sacrifice: A Critical Edition.* Atlanta: Scholars Press. Critical edition of all the preserved copies of the composition and analysis of its contents.

Sacchi, P. 1996. *Jewish Apocalyptic and its History.* Sheffield: Sheffield Academic Press. Italian original, *L'Apocalittica Giudaica e la sua Storia* (Brescia: Paideia, 1990). Collection of articles on the development of apocalypticism, focusing mainly on *1 Enoch.*

Schiffman, L. H. 1989. *The Eschatological Community of the Dead Sea Scrolls.* Atlanta: Scholars Press. Comprehensive and detailed analysis of 1QSa

Stegemann, H. "Die Bedeutung der Qumranfunde für die Erforschung der Apokalyptik." In Hellholm 1983, 495–530. Critical view of the importance of the Scrolls for the study of apocalypticism.

Steudel, A. 1993. "ʾaḥărît hayyāmîm in the Texts from Qumran." *Revue de Qumrân* 16:225–46.

Stone, M. E. 1990. *Fourth Ezra.* Hermeneia. Minneapolis: Fortress Press.

VanderKam, J. C. 1984. *Enoch and the Growth of an Apocalyptic Tradition.* Washington: Catholic Biblical Association. Monograph on the early Enoch tradition and its Mesopotamian background.

Yadin, Y. 1962. *The Scroll of the War of the Sons of Light against the Sons of Darkness.* Oxford: Oxford University Press. Comprehensive and detailed commentary on 1QM.

6

Messianism and Apocalypticism

James C. VanderKam
University of Notre Dame

I N ONE FORM OR ANOTHER JEWISH BELIEFS ABOUT A MESSIAH
surface in a number of texts dating from the Greco-Roman period. The
presence of the term *messiah* in a series of Jewish texts and especially the large
role the title plays in the New Testament works have ensured the popularity of
the topic to the present day. The purpose of this essay is to explore and document the varied messianic ideas present in the Jewish texts and to study their
connections (or lack of them) with apocalypticism. The introductory section
will be devoted to clarifying terms and to the biblical roots of messianism and
apocalypticism. The next section will present the evidence for messianic
expectations in early Jewish texts, and the final part will summarize the results
for the variety of messianic expectations and their relations with apocalyptic
concerns.

INTRODUCTION

Messiah and Messianism

The first term to be defined is *messiah,* a word reflecting the Greek transcription of the Hebrew *māšîaḥ,* which refers to a person who has been anointed

with oil. The Hebrew term appears moderately often in the Bible in connection with several types of officials or characters. It is used for the following: (1) Kings of Israel who have oil applied to their head as a way of marking divine designation of them for the role (e.g., 1 Sam. 12:3, 5; 16:6; 24:7, 11). A distinction should be drawn between those historical passages that refer to Saul or David or the like as anointed monarchs and a passage such as Ps. 2:2, in which the king, in a more mythical or ideal context in which he is identified as the son of God, is mentioned together with the deity himself as the object of assault by the rulers of the earth (see also Ps. 18:51 = 2 Sam. 22:51; Ps. 89:39, 52; 132:10, 17). (2) High priests of Israel, whom the Priestly writer calls "the anointed priest" (Lev. 4:3, 5, 16; 6:15; Ps. 84:10). (3) Cyrus of Persia, who was set apart for the purpose of carrying out the Lord's will (Isa. 45:1). (4) A future prince (Dan. 9:25, 26). (5) The patriarchs (Ps. 105:15 = 1 Chr. 16:22). While the third usage (for Cyrus) is consistent with the general concept that an anointed one is a high-ranking person who has been set aside to a lofty position or chosen by God for a noble purpose, numbers (1) and (2) are the most important for the present purposes. In the Bible both the king and the high priest can be designated the anointed ones of the Lord, and at times the term is put to a specialized use for a leader of the future (as also in the fourth usage).

From the normally mundane biblical employment of the term, the belief that there would be a divinely marked ruler in the future developed over time. Dan. 9:25–26 predicts: "from the time that the word went out to restore and rebuild Jerusalem until the time of the anointed prince, there shall be seven weeks; and for sixty-two weeks it shall be built again with streets and moat, but in a troubled time. After the sixty-two weeks, an anointed one shall be cut off and shall have nothing. . . ." The "anointed prince" in v. 25 may be the first postexilic high priest, Joshua, and the "anointed one" in v. 26 is often understood to be the high priest Onias III, who was forcibly removed from office in 175 B.C.E. and eventually executed (Collins 1993, 355–56). Passages such as Ps. 2:1–2 document the belief that an anointed Davidic ruler would also be a world ruler: "Why do the nations conspire, and the peoples plot in vain? The kings of the earth set themselves, and the rulers take counsel together, against the Lord and his anointed. . . ." This anointed king is later identified in the psalm as God's king (v. 6) and as the divine son (v. 7) who will conquer the nations and possess the ends of the earth (v. 8).

If one were to confine the survey only to the term "anointed one," the results from the Hebrew Bible would not be overly impressive. There are some thirty-eight occurrences of the word, and in all cases it is used for a leader. However, there has been a debate about the proper use of the terms *messiah* and *messianism:* Should these words be restricted to those places in which an anointed one is mentioned and those eschatological contexts in which a person explicitly designated Messiah appears? Or is it permissible to use the words more broadly to refer to any leader of the end-time and the thought patterns that include such characters?

If we go by the usage of ancient texts, there can be little doubt that the broader understanding is an acceptable one. A variety of prophetic texts in the Hebrew Bible make reference to a royal leader of the future but do not call him Messiah. For example, Isaiah prophesies: "A shoot shall come out from the stump of Jesse, and a branch shall grow out of his roots" (11:1). He will be given extraordinary qualities; his reign will be ideal; and in his time the dispersed will be gathered and their enemies defeated (11:2–16). Or Jeremiah, in one of his pictures of the future, quotes the Lord as saying:

> The days are surely coming, says the Lord, when I will raise up for David a righteous Branch (*ṣemaḥ*), and he shall reign as king and deal wisely, and shall execute justice and righteousness in the land. In his days Judah will be saved and Israel will live in safety. And this is the name by which he will be called: "The Lord is our righteousness." (23:5–6)

Neither Isaiah nor Jeremiah resorted to the term *anointed* in these contexts, but they do make clear that the present earthly "anointed" ones, that is, the Davidic kings, will have successors in the future of God's reduced people (see also Isa. 7:14; 9:1–6; Jer. 33:14–16; Ezek. 17:22–24; 34:23–24; 37:24–25; Mic. 5:1–3; Hag. 2:20–23; Zechariah 4 and 6). That point also emerges from the promise to David:

> When your days are fulfilled and you lie down with your ancestors, I will raise up your offspring after you, who shall come forth from your body, and I will establish his kingdom. He shall build a house for my name, and I will establish the throne of his kingdom forever. I will be a father to him, and he shall be a son to me. . . . Your house and your kingdom shall be made sure forever before me; your throne shall be established forever. (2 Sam. 7:12–14a, 16)

In later texts, *anointed* and other titles for end-time leaders are used side by side or interchanged for the same individual (see, e.g., the Similitudes of Enoch). Hence, despite the absence of the title Messiah from such contexts, it is possible to speak of at least an incipient messianism in the Hebrew Bible in that the prophetic pictures of the future at times include a new leader from the line of David, whether he is called a king or a prince or given some other title. As John Collins writes, "a messiah is an eschatological figure who sometimes, but not necessarily always, is designated as a משיח in the ancient sources" (Collins 1995, 12). Messianism, then, would be a mode of thought centering about such a leader or in which he plays a significant role. Postbiblical Jewish literature evidences a richer flowering from these rather limited biblical roots.

Apocalypse and Apocalypticism

There has been an extensive discussion in modern times concerning the proper usage of *apocalypse, apocalypticism,* and related terms. Since the definitions of these words have been discussed in the introduction to this volume, it suffices simply to note that here *apocalypse* is being used in the sense of Collins's expanded definition (see Collins 1991, 19 for the added section about the function of apocalypses). The tendency among scholars has been to focus on the eschatological side of teachings in the apocalypses and less on the other kinds of material found in them, but the future was not the only concern of the seers. They contain revelations about cosmological or heavenly phenomena as well as about eschatological mysteries. Yet it is accurate to say that disclosures about noneschatological subjects (e.g., about the heavens) are often if not always connected in some way with eschatological matters and are intended to reassure the reader that God ultimately reigns over the universe and is thus able to rectify what is now wrong with the world. It should be noted, too, that apocalyptic ways of thinking are not confined to works formally defined as apocalypses; they are also to be found in other genres such as testaments and oracles.

Collins and the other authors in the *Semeia* volume distinguished two major types of apocalypses: some apocalypses have and others lack an otherworldly journey by the individual who receives the revelation. Both those with and without otherworldly journeys can be further subdivided:

> (a) the "historical" type which includes a review of history, eschatological crisis and cosmic and/or political eschatology; (b) apocalypses which have no historical review but envisage cosmic and/or political eschatology . . . ; and (c) apocalypses which have neither historical review nor cosmic transformation but only personal eschatology. (Collins 1979, 13)

As with Messiah/messianism, the Hebrew Bible supplies the foundations for later Jewish apocalyptic writing and thinking. The only unmistakable apocalypses in the Hebrew Bible are the several visions disclosed to Daniel in chaps. 7–12, but a number of scholars have regarded earlier, especially prophetic texts as being *proto-apocalypses*. If one adopts Collins's definition of *apocalypse,* none was written by a Jewish author before the Hellenistic period began. This implies that those who consider passages such as Isaiah 24–27 or Zechariah 1–8 to be apocalypses or at least proto-apocalypses are operating with different definitions. F. M. Cross, who argues that "the origins of apocalyptic must be searched for as early as the sixth century B.C." (1973, 343), has pointed to "reformulations of the prophetic tradition and of the royal ideology" in some later prophetic texts in the Hebrew Bible; these manifest "rudimentary traits and motives of apocalypticism." He lists three: "democratizing and eschatologizing of classical prophetic themes and forms"; the doctrine of two ages; and "the resurgent influence of myths of creation used to frame history and to lend history transcendent significance, significance not apparent in the ordinary events of biblical history" (1973, 346). O. Plöger and P. Hanson have also located the first literary examples of apocalyptic phenomena at the beginning of postexilic history and have tried to describe the nonhierocratic, eschatologically minded groups who were responsible for the birth of apocalyptic thinking (Plöger 1968; Hanson 1975). Although it is obvious that the authors of the apocalypses drew upon earlier scriptural material and to a certain extent imitated biblical forms, no Jewish writer composed an apocalypse in Collins's sense of the term until the third century B.C.E. The evidence now suggests strongly that the most ancient Jewish apocalypses were texts that centered on the antediluvian seer Enoch.

Important models and sources for the apocalypses were supplied by the biblical prophetic literature. One prophetic model was the throne vision report in which the prophet was given access to the divine presence and the discussion of earthly matters that transpired between God and his angelic advisors (1 Kings 22; Isaiah 6; see *1 Enoch* 14). Another model came from passages such as Ezekiel 40–48, in which an angel gives the prophet a tour of the renewed Jerusalem, Temple, and country. Mention should also be made of symbolic visions that are disclosed to a prophet and explained by God or an angel (e.g., Amos 7–9; Zechariah 1–8) or of other cryptic messages that were clarified for a prophet (Daniel 9). In general the sequence in prophetic eschatology of decisive judgment followed by extraordinary renewal for a purged remnant is reflected in even stronger form in the apocalypses. However, there is also evidence that divinatory procedures and assumptions (as in dream interpretations) have left their mark on apocalyptic works. For example, in the apocalypses cryptic, symbolic dreams are disclosed to the seer who also receives a celestial explanation of the encoded message. The explanations reveal information about the future which will arise out of the circumstances of the past and present (see Daniel 7 for an example; VanderKam 1984, 52–75).

MESSIANISM IN EARLY JUDAISM

The purpose of this section is to survey the references to messiahs in early Jewish texts and to gather information about who the Messiah(s) was (were) thought to be and what he (they) was (were) expected to do. The survey falls into two parts. First, those texts that belong to the genre *apocalypse* as defined above will be examined; second, texts that are not apocalypses but in which a Messiah appears will be studied. It should be remembered that it is not only instances of the title Messiah that will be under consideration; others that are applied to the future ruler(s) and the nature of the qualities and roles assigned to these leaders will also be studied.

Messianic Leaders in the Early Jewish Apocalypses

Collins has identified a series of early Jewish texts that qualify under his definition as apocalypses. These should be studied in chronological order (insofar as that is possible) to determine which apocalypses assign a role or roles to messianic leaders, understood in a broad sense, and which do not. The survey will show that it is not until the first century C.E. that messianic leaders begin to appear consistently in the texts; even then, however, not all apocalypses envision such a leader in their eschatological tableaux.

THE ASTRONOMICAL BOOK OF ENOCH (*1 ENOCH* 72–82). Ever since J. T. Milik published some of the Qumran Aramaic fragments of the Astronomical Book, it has become customary to date it to the third century B.C.E. (Milik 1976, 7–11). It is at times considered an apocalypse because it claims to be the record of Uriel's revelations to Enoch (who is on a tour of the universe) about astronomical and geographical matters; however, the work does not consist of such instructions alone. According to 72:1 the disclosures are "for each year of the world and for ever, until the new creation."[1] In this early, perhaps apocalyptic work there is no hint of a messianic leader at the end-times.

THE BOOK OF THE WATCHERS (*1 ENOCH* 1–36). A third-century date has also been advocated for this collection of what appear to have been a series of originally separate works (Milik 1976, 22–23). Parts of the booklet have apocalyptic traits (see chapters 1, 10–11, 14–15, and 17–36). While these chapters contain many eschatological topics, not a word is said about a Messiah or any human leader. That is, the earliest Enochic apocalypses (if they may be called apocalypses) do not include a Messiah in their vivid pictures of the end. God and his angels act without messianic assistance.

THE APOCALYPSE OF WEEKS (*1 ENOCH* 93:1–10; 91:11–17). This short historical apocalypse, which appears in the correct order in the Aramaic fragments from Qumran but has been split and the parts reversed in the Ethiopic, presents Enoch as speaking from extraordinarily authoritative sources (books, heavenly vision, words of holy angels, tablets of heaven [93:1–3]). From them he reveals to his children the course of history and the judgment divided into ten schematic segments called *weeks*. Weeks 8–10 detail the different stages of the judgment. In week 8 the righteous receive a sword to punish the sinners; in week 9 righteous judgment is revealed to the entire world and the deeds of the impious vanish, with the world recorded for destruction; and in week 10 there is an eternal judgment on the watchers and the creation of a new heaven. These stages will be followed by innumerable weeks forever in which sin has been entirely eliminated. The text of the Apocalypse of Weeks is exceptionally brief and allusive, but no character in it can be construed as a messianic leader.

THE ANIMAL APOCALYPSE (*1 ENOCH* 85–90). The Animal Apocalypse, which follows an apocalyptic-sounding vision in chapters 83–84, also surveys biblical history and moves beyond it, as the Apocalypse of Weeks does. The experience behind the text is termed a dream and dream vision (85:1–2). The apocalypse uses animals as symbols for people, while people represent angels or the like. The numerous details of the symbolic biblical history are not pertinent in this context, but as the overview reaches the author's time (in the 160s B.C.E.) it refers to defeat after defeat for the sheep (= Israel), "until a big horn grew *on* one of those sheep" (90:9). The enemies "wished to make away with its horn, but they did not prevail against it" (v. 12). This sheep or ram (both terms are used) becomes the object of a unified assault by Israel's enemies. However, "it fought with them and cried out that its help might come to it" (v. 13). A recording angel assures the ram that divine assistance for it was coming (v. 14). A final assault by the combined foes leads to decisive divine intervention and victory for the sheep (vv. 16–19). It is possible to understand the sheep/ram with the large horn as a Messiah, but the conclusion seems unlikely, and commentators often identify it as a representation of Judas Maccabeus (yet note the reference to "that ram" in v. 31 [Tiller 1993, 62–63, 355]). One argument against seeing the sheep/ram with the large horn as the Messiah is the fact that he appears before another figure who seems to be a Messiah.

A more likely candidate for a Messiah is the individual called "a white bull" in 90:37. One learns that it was born at the end, and "its horns (were) big, and all the wild animals and all the birds of heaven were afraid of it and entreated it continually. And I [= Enoch] looked until all their species were transformed, and they all became white bulls; and the first one among them was a wild-ox, and that wild-ox was a large animal and had big black horns on its head. And the Lord of the sheep rejoiced over them and over all the bulls" (vv. 37–38). The image of the white bull reverts to the symbol used for the patriarchs from Adam through Isaac (85:3–89:12). Yet the bull hardly stands out as unusual in the end-time, since "all their species" became white bulls. "The function of this end-time figure seems to be unique in the literature of the period. Like the 'one like a son of man' in Daniel 7, he comes at the end of world history and is granted universal dominion. Contrary to Daniel's figure, he is a human individual, as is shown by the fact that he is symbolized by an animal" (Tiller 1993, 384). The fact that the white bull is soon joined by others entails that his mission is "apparently only to be a sort of catalyst for the transformation of all humanity" (Tiller 1993, 385). Consequently, the Animal Apocalypse appears to be the earliest Jewish apocalypse that mentions a messianic leader of the end-time. He is a special individual who exercises power over the nations, although he is not a different kind of being from his contemporaries.

DANIEL. Several sections in the second half of Daniel, the only fully apocalyptic unit in the Hebrew Bible, qualify as apocalypses.

1. Daniel 7. Daniel's famous vision of the four beasts who emerge from the sea climaxes in a scene of judgment in which "an Ancient One" (that is, God) serves as the enthroned judge before whom the horned fourth beast was executed and the other beasts were deprived of their dominion. "As I [= Daniel] watched in the night visions, I saw one like a human being [traditionally and more literally: one like a son of man] coming with the clouds of heaven. And he came to the Ancient One and was presented before him. To him was given dominion and glory and kingship, that all peoples, nations, and languages should serve him. His dominion is an everlasting dominion that shall not pass away, and his kingship is one that shall never be destroyed" (7:13–14). This figure appears to have clear messianic qualities and has traditionally been so identified, but there is a good chance that the "one like a son of man" is a symbol either for the people of God (see v. 27, where the dominion is given to the "people of the holy ones of the Most High") or for the angel Michael (Collins

1993, 304–10). In either case, the "one like a son of man" would not be a messianic individual who belonged at least in part to the human realm.

2. Daniel 8. After his vision of the four beasts, Daniel sees another in which a ram with two horns (specifically explained as the kings of Media and Persia), a goat (interpreted as the king of Greece; see 8:20–21), and four kingdoms into which the great horn of the goat was split play the central parts. The vision pertains, as the text says, to "the appointed time of the end" (v. 19). The judgment that will be meted out to the last foe is that "he shall be broken, and not by human hands" (v. 25). No Messiah or other human representative of the good appears in this vision about the end of time.

3. Daniel 9. As Daniel ponders Jeremiah's prophecy that Jerusalem would lie desolate for seventy years (Jer. 25:11–12; 29:10), he prays for national forgiveness and for the Lord to remember his ravaged sanctuary and city. The scene is an example of how the mantic tradition has influenced apocalyptic writers, since Daniel is attempting to derive a message from an encoded text that requires expert handling. The message lies hidden beneath the surface appearance of the medium. The angel Gabriel then came to explain the meaning of the puzzling prophetic words to him. Gabriel points out that the seventy years actually mean seventy weeks of years and further notes that there is to be a seven-year period from the command to restore Jerusalem "until the time of an anointed prince" (9:25). "After the sixty-two weeks, an anointed one shall be cut off and shall have nothing, and the troops of the prince who is to come shall destroy the city and the sanctuary" (v. 26). As noted above, this anointed one is thought to be the high priest Onias III, who was ousted from his position in 175 B.C.E. and eventually murdered. There is no indication in the text that he functioned as a messianic leader in any other than the most literal sense that he, like the high priests of old, had been anointed with oil upon taking the position. He does nothing specifically "messianic"; his appearance and death serve only to mark the turning point from a troubled time to one of catastrophe.

4. Daniel 10–12. In the longest of the visions (see 10:1, 7, 8) Daniel encounters a "man clothed in linen" (10:5–6) who had a frightening appearance and who came "to help you [= Daniel] understand what is to happen to your people at the end of days. For there is a further vision for those days" (10:14). The man was sent "to tell you what is inscribed in the book of truth" (10:21). The apocalyptic vision contains a historical survey covering individuals who are identified as the kings of Persia (11:2) and of Greece and successor kingdoms (11:3–45), but it provides particularly detailed information about

the kings of the south (the Ptolemies) and of the north (the Seleucids). Antiochus IV (175–164), "a contemptible person on whom royal majesty had not been conferred" (11:21), receives the largest amount of attention (11:21–45). The only leaders of eschatological times who are portrayed in a positive way appear to be "the wise among the people" (11:33), who give understanding to others, suffer violence and execution, and receive "a little help" (v. 34) from others whom commentators regularly identify as the Maccabees. After Antiochus meets his lonely end (11:45), "Michael, the great prince, the protector of your people, shall arise" (12:1). A time of anguish will occur, but Daniel's people, "everyone who is found written in the book" (12:11), will be delivered and many of the dead will rise, some to everlasting life, others to everlasting contempt (12:2). Throughout the relatively detailed scenario sketched by the author, not a word is said about a Messiah or any other eschatological leader, apart from the angel Michael.

Thus, the viewpoint expressed in all the apocalyptic visions in the second half of the book of Daniel is that there is no messianic king or the like at the last times. The only leader of God's people in those tumultuous and fateful days is an angel through whom God himself works.

THE BOOK OF *JUBILEES.* Various sets of internal and external data point to approximately the mid-second century B.C.E. as the time when the book was written. Although the book itself, which is presented as a revelation to Moses, is not formally an apocalypse, it does contain two passages that could be classified as apocalypses. One is the first chapter, which is set on Mount Sinai, where God is speaking directly to Moses. Much of the Lord's address deals with Israel's future apostasy from the covenant despite remarkable divine faithfulness and patience. The pattern that the Lord predicts to Moses is that Israel will sin and God will send witnesses (= prophets) to warn them but their missions will fail to accomplish a return to the covenant. God will then hide his face from his people and hand them over to the nations. When they are separated from their land, they will continue sinning but will later repent in their places of dispersion. As a result the Lord will gather them and transform them into a righteous plant in their own land, build his temple among them, and reestablish proper covenantal relations with them. Nothing that is said in the first chapter, however, even affords a hint that the author anticipates the rise of a Messiah. One learns there only about God's relations with the entire people and the mediating role that Moses plays in those relations.

The same may be said about parts of chapter 23, which are more clearly apocalyptic in character. The Lord will eventually arouse the nations against an especially wicked generation, and only later will a new generation of people who study the law be born. They will obey by returning to the right path, and the ages of God's people will again become as lengthy as and even longer than they were before the flood. There are several participants in the eschatological drama—the Lord, the nations, and the new generation who are called "children"—but there is no Messiah.

Before leaving *Jubilees* a note should be added about a theme in the book that caused messianic repercussions in later literature. The author highlights Levi and Judah as the most important among Jacob's twelve sons; their grandfather, Isaac, predicts that Levi and his descendants will serve as the Lord's priests and that Judah's line will provide the kings of Jacob's offspring (31:11–17, 18–20; cf. 30:18). *Jubilees* depicts neither Levi nor Judah as a leader in eschatological days, nor does it anticipate that one or two will arise from their children; nevertheless, its emphasis on priestly and kingly leadership seems to be an earlier stage in the development of the dual messianism found at Qumran (see below).

SIBYLLINE ORACLES 3. Much of the third *Sibylline Oracle* was written around the mid-second century B.C.E. It has been claimed that *Sib. Or.* 3.652–795, although a king is mentioned only at the beginning of the section, is "almost exclusively messianic in content" (Schürer 1979, 501), but Collins thinks that the king who comes from the sun is a "benevolent Ptolemy," not a Jewish Messiah. "The Sibyl, then, resembles Deutero-Isaiah in endorsing a Gentile king as the agent of deliverance. The hopes of most Jews in the period 550–150 B.C.E. were for a benevolent overlord who would protect and promote the Jewish people, rather than for national independence" (Collins 1995, 39).

TESTAMENT OF LEVI 2–5. It is not at all certain that the *Testament of Levi* belongs at this point in the chronological survey. In its present form the testament is Christian (see the reference to Jesus Christ in 4:4), but there is reason to believe that an older Jewish work underlies the extant text. The Aramaic Levi text from Qumran appears to be one of the sources (whether direct or indirect) from which the author drew in composing the testament, and the Aramaic Levi may be a third-century B.C.E. work.

In the *Testament of Levi* 2–5 Levi recounts a dream vision that he experienced while feeding the family flocks in Abelmaul. His dream vision belongs to the tour-of-heaven class of apocalypses: an angel shows him three heavens, and he learns about four others. He is told that the Lord will save the whole human race through him and through Judah (2:11). The angel explains to Levi the nature of the seven heavens, speaks of the baffling character of human sin, and predicts that various natural disasters will occur when the Lord judges humanity (chapter 3). Levi prays that he may be separated from unrighteousness and serve in the divine presence; his request is accepted. In chapter 5, during a throne vision in which he sees God in his heavenly temple, Levi is appointed as God's priest (5:1–2). This appointment, however, is presented as an event of the past and as affecting an ancient character. The vision does not describe Levi's investiture as eschatological priest. Only Jesus Christ, whose arrival is predicted in the passage, is accorded a messianic title; he is called God's son.

The situation is different in chap. 18, where the writer predicts that, at the end of history, "the Lord will raise up a new priest" (v. 2), whose accomplishments will be extraordinary: among other feats, he will execute judgment, remove darkness through the light he will dispense, receive the spirit of understanding and sanctification, enlighten the Gentiles, and remove sin. There is ample reason for thinking, however, that this chapter belongs to the Christian redaction of the testament and relates to Jesus Christ, not to a priestly Messiah who will be descended from Levi (Hollander and de Jonge 1985, 179–82).

The *Testament of Levi* and the *Testament of Judah*, along with several other statements elsewhere in the *Testaments of the Twelve Patriarchs*, present a teaching about Levi and Judah parallel to what we find in *Jubilees*, but they usually do not present their descendants as Messiahs. *Testament of Reuben* 6:12, in which the patriarch is speaking about Judah's posterity, predicts that he (or his descendants) will die in visible and invisible wars and be an eternal king. Such sentiments are probably Christian (Hollander and de Jonge 1985, 108). *Testament of Dan* 5:4–15, a pericope dealing with the last days, predicts unsuccessful opposition to Levi and Judah (v. 4) and that the Lord's salvation will come from Judah and Levi (v. 10). Once again, however, the passage has Christian motifs. An especially clear case is found in *Testament of Joseph* 19:11, where one reads about the lamb of God who takes away the sin of the world and saves all the nations; this lamb is to arise from the seed of Levi and Judah (see also *T. Sim.* 7:1–2; *T. Naph.* 8:2–3; *T. Gad* 8:1; and also *T. Levi* 2:11; 8:14–15).

It is particularly two, somewhat parallel texts that have been understood messianically—*Testament of Levi* 18 and *Testament of Judah* 24. The former was considered above; it refers to Jesus as the new priest who will not be from

Levi's line. The latter (which like *Testament of Levi* 18 directly follows a sin–exile–return passage) forecasts:

> And after these things a star will arise to you from Jacob in peace and a man will arise from my seed like the sun of righteousness, walking with the sons of men in meekness and righteousness, and no sin whatever will be found in him. And the heavens will be opened to him to pour out the blessing of the spirit of the holy Father, and he will pour out the spirit of grace upon you; and you will be sons to him in truth and you will walk in his commandments from first to last. This (is) the branch of God Most High and this (is) the fountain unto life for all flesh. Then the sceptre of my kingdom will shine, and from your root a stem will arise; and in it a rod of righteousness will arise to the nations to judge and to save all who call upon the Lord.

Commentators such as Hollander and de Jonge have noted the author's heavy reliance on a variety of passages from the Hebrew Bible but have also determined that several parts of the chapter clearly betray a Christian hand (e.g., the reference to Jesus' baptism). Hence, it is safest to say that, at least in its present form, *T. Judah* 24 is Christian and not a witness to a type of specifically Jewish messianism. After surveying all the relevant passages in the *Testaments of the Twelve Patriarchs,* Hollander and de Jonge conclude: "In any case, there is no 'double messianism' in the *Testaments.* Whenever a saviour figure occurs in L.J. passages [i.e., passages dealing with Levi and Judah], there is only one, and clearly Jesus Christ is referred to" (1985, 61).

THE SIMILITUDES OR PARABLES OF ENOCH (*1 ENOCH* 37–71). The lengthy section of *1 Enoch* that contains three parables uttered by the antediluvian patriarch is the earliest Jewish apocalypse to provide an extended and complicated treatment of a messianic individual. There has been a long scholarly debate about when the booklet was written, and that debate has taken on a new character after it was learned that no fragments of this part of *1 Enoch,* unlike the case with the other four sections, had been identified in Qumran Cave 4. Milik, the editor of the Qumran Aramaic copies of *1 Enoch,* argued that the Similitudes is a Christian work, written in the late third century C.E.; it was only later incorporated into *1 Enoch* when the Book of Giants was removed from the collection (Milik 1976, 89–98). Other scholars have continued to debate whether it dates from the first century B.C.E. or the first–second century C.E. There appears to be no decisive evidence for dating it any later that the end of the first century B.C.E.

There are four titles given to a messianic leader who is identified in 71:14 as Enoch himself. Two of the four occur only rarely, while the other two are more frequent. The first of these, *the righteous one,* seems to be used collectively in 47:1, 4, but it is used for an eschatological individual in 53:6: "And after this the Righteous and Chosen One will cause the house of his congregation to appear." The term "righteous one" is a descriptive word applied here to the character designated often in the book as the chosen one (see below). In 53:6 he seems to have a congregation associated with him. This same individual is explicitly termed Messiah in two places in the Similitudes. The first is in *1 Enoch* 48:10: "And on the day of their [= the kings' and the mighty ones'] trouble there will be rest on the earth, and they will fall down before him and will not rise; and there will be no one who will take them with his hands and raise them, for they denied the Lord of Spirits and his Messiah." Here, echoing the words of Ps. 2:2 about the Lord and the Davidic king, the writer pictures evil groups as finding no help at the end because they have denied both God himself and his anointed one. In 52:4, the only other use of "Messiah" for this leader, an angel explains to Enoch that some natural phenomena which he sees will serve the dominion of his anointed one. Thus, the messianic individual is to exercise some sort of rule.

While "righteous one" and "anointed one" appear infrequently in the Similitudes, the titles *chosen one* and *son of man* figure much more often. "Chosen one" is used in fifteen or sixteen passages, and "son of man" in sixteen. The chosen one is associated with a group appropriately designated the "chosen ones" (e.g., 39:6; 40:5; 45:3–4; etc.); on the day of judgment he will sit on a glorious throne (45:3; 51:3; 55:4; 61:8) and judge the different classes of evildoers (55:4). He is a source of comfort and strength for the chosen; his glory is eternal (see 49:2); and "all the secrets of wisdom will flow out of the counsel of his mouth" (51:3). Mountains will melt like wax before him (52:6), and various metals will be destroyed when he appears (52:9). It should be recalled that in 53:6 this figure is also called the "righteous one."

The sixteen cases in which "son of man" is employed for an eschatological figure also disclose important information about the functions he is expected to perform. For reasons that are not evident in every case, the Ethiopic text uses three different formulations for "son of man." One (*walda sab'*) appears only in 46:2, 3, 4; 48:2, where the vision of Daniel 7, with its "one like a son of man," exercises a noticeable influence. A second (*walda be'si*) is employed in 62:5; 69:29 (two times), and 71:14, that is, at later points in the Similitudes. The son of man sits on his glorious throne, evil passes from his presence, and his word is strong. The most interesting use of *walda be'si* comes in 71:14, where Enoch himself is identified as the son of man who was born for righteousness. Despite efforts to emend the text, the reading is secure. The third way of formulating the title (*walda 'eg^wāla 'emma-ḥeyāw* = son of the offspring of the mother of the living) occurs eight times and is thus the most frequent one. It, like the second form, figures in the latter parts of the Similitudes. *1 Enoch* 62:7 says that the son of man is hidden but is revealed to the chosen. The kings and mighty ones fall before him (62:14; 63:11), while the righteous and chosen ones will live with him eternally. According to 69:25–27 the ones to whom the son of man was revealed will be happy but the sinners are destroyed by his judgment; and 70:1 and 71:17 say that Enoch, the son of man, after his removal from earth, is to enjoy a long life in the heavens.

Scholars have debated whether chapters 70–71 belong to the original form of the Similitudes and thus whether the teaching that Enoch was the son of man is the conclusion intended by the author of the three parables (that is, of chapters 37–69). It can be argued that all of chapters 37–69 are set within Enoch's 365-year life and that the three stages of exaltation pictured in chapters 70–71 are a natural conclusion to that life as they describe his final removal (the one mentioned in Gen. 5:24). It has also been claimed that the Similitudes speak of the son of man as preexistent—a condition incompatible with identifying him as Enoch the son of Jared and seventh from Adam. It is reasonable to infer, however, that in passages such as *1 Enoch* 62:7 the son of man is not preexistent but was elected before the world began. Or possibly the verse means only that from an early time Enoch was hidden (see *1 Enoch* 12:1), that is, removed from human society (see VanderKam 1992, 176–82).

All four terms for the eschatological leader refer to the same individual, as equivalences and interchanged titles in the text demonstrate (VanderKam 1992, 185–86). It appears that in much of the material that describes the eschatological leader, the author of the Similitudes is dependent on the servant passages in Deutero-Isaiah; these he interprets as referring to a messianic individual. His messianic individual does not, however, suffer as the servant does in Isaiah. Some passages (especially *1 Enoch* 46–48) show heavy indebtedness to Daniel 7, whose "one like a son of man" the author has also read in an individualistic sense. The complicated messianic leader in the Similitudes is an exalted individual who will judge the wicked at the end and vindicate the suffering chosen ones, thus bringing about the great reversal from the present miserable conditions of oppression.

2 BARUCH. One of the literary responses by a Jewish author to the defeat and destruction to which the Romans subjected the Jews in 70 C.E. is *2 Baruch,* which has been preserved only in Syriac. It may date from near the end of the first century C.E. The book contains a lengthy dialogue between Baruch and God about the disaster that has occurred and the reasons for it. Statements about God's long-term purpose in what he has done lend themselves naturally to predictions about the end-time. In those predictions the author has lodged several references to a Messiah.

An apocalypse begins in chapter 26 with Baruch's question: "That tribulation which will be, will it last a long time; and that distress, will it embrace many years?"[2] The divine reply indicates that the calamitous time in question will be divided into twelve parts, which will overlap with one another to some extent. Baruch learns that what is being said to him applies to the entire world, although God will protect only those found in the holy land. "And it will happen that when all that which should come to pass in these parts has been accomplished, the Anointed One will begin to be revealed" (29:3). The end of time (29:8) will be marked by the act of consuming the two monsters Behemoth and Leviathan, by extraordinarily abundant crops, and by the reopening of the treasury of manna. The reader soon learns that the epiphany of the Messiah does not go unnoticed: "And it will happen after these things when the time of the appearance of the Anointed One has been fulfilled and he returns with glory, that then all who sleep in hope of him will arise" (30:1). The souls of the righteous rejoice, while the souls of the wicked waste away, knowing that the time of their torment has arrived (30:5).

Later, during an apocalypse that uses the images of a forest, vine, fountain, and cedar (chapters 35–40), the Messiah reappears. In a night vision (36:1) Baruch sees the vine with a fountain running under it submerge and uproot the forest and overthrow the mountains that surround it. Eventually the fountain grows so powerful that just one cedar is left. The vine condemns the cedar for making evil endure and consigns it to present pain and future judgment. Eventually the cedar was burned, the vine grew, and the valley around it became full of unfading flowers. Baruch requests an explanation for the night vision (chapter 38) and receives it from God. The forest is a fourth power, as in Daniel's vision of the four beasts. "And it will happen when the time of its fulfillment is approaching in which it will fall, that at that time the dominion of my Anointed One which is like the fountain and the vine, will be revealed. And when it has revealed itself, it will uproot the multitude of its host" (39:7). It turns out that the cedar is the last ruler who, after his army is killed, is brought to Mount Zion:

> . . . my Anointed one will convict him of all his wicked deeds and will assemble and set before him all the works of his hosts. And after these things he will kill him and protect the rest of my people who will be found in the place that I have chosen. And his dominion will last forever until the world of corruption has ended and until the times which have been mentioned before have been fulfilled. (40:1–3)

2 Baruch includes the Messiah one more time in a picture of the future. In chapter 53 the reader encounters an apocalypse that centers on clouds. There is a long explanation of alternating periods of darkness and light, represented by clouds of the corresponding color. At the very end of the explanation the Messiah appears: ". . . all will be delivered into the hands of my Servant, the Anointed One. For the whole earth will devour its inhabitants" (70:9–10). Chapters 72–73 detail what will happen at the time of bright waters following black ones. "After the signs have come of which I have spoken to you before, when the nations are moved and the time of my Anointed One comes, he will call all nations, and some of them he will spare, and others he will kill" (72:2). Once all of this has been completed, "after he has brought down everything which is in the world, and has sat down in eternal peace on the throne of the kingdom, then joy will be revealed and rest will appear" (73:1). Idyllic conditions ensue.

2 Baruch's Messiah is a conquering king whose glorious appearance marks a change after the eschatological calamities have occurred. He defeats the last, hideous foe and rules until the world of corruption ends. He judges all peoples, and when he sits on his throne in everlasting peace there is great joy. Those who have hoped in him, even if they have died, share in the benefits of his splendid reign.

2 ESDRAS (= 4 EZRA). Another response to the Roman destruction of Jerusalem, the Temple, and the nation was written under the pseudonym of Ezra, a leader during reconstruction more than a century after the first Temple was burned to the ground. The book has survived only in Latin but has the traits of a Jewish work composed in Hebrew, perhaps around the same time that *2 Baruch* was written. Like *2 Baruch*, 4 Ezra consists of dialogues in which the Jewish seer questions how God could justify the calamity that his people had experienced. In this case the dialogue takes place between Ezra and the angel Uriel, whom God had dispatched to converse with Ezra (see 4:1). As it has survived, the Jewish portion of the work is found in chapters 3–14, while chaps. 1–2 (= *5 Ezra*) and 15–16 (= *6 Ezra*) are Christian booklets that testify to the fact that Christians preserved and transmitted the Jewish work. *5 Ezra* contains teachings about a savior who is pictured as a young man of great stature, but, as one expects in a Christian work, this savior is Jesus Christ.

The Jewish composition (chapters 3–14) offers its own distinctive picture of a Messiah. In the third vision (6:35–9:25) the angel makes the first disclosure to Ezra concerning the Anointed One:

For behold, the time will come, when the signs which I have foretold to you will come to pass . . . . And everyone who has been delivered from the evils that I have foretold shall see my wonders. For my son the Messiah shall be revealed with those who are with him, and those who remain shall rejoice four hundred years. And after these years my son the Messiah shall die, and all who draw human breath. And the world shall be turned back to primeval silence for seven days, as it was at the first beginnings; so that no one shall be left. And after seven days the world, which is not yet awake, shall be roused, and that which is corruptible shall perish. (7:26–31)[3]

After the resurrection the Most High exercises judgment for about one week of years (7:32–44).

The Messiah, then, is God's son, who will have a temporary messianic reign of four hundred years, after which he will die. Nothing is said about whether he will rise to take part in the judgment.

The next reference to a Messiah occurs in the fifth, or eagle, vision (chapters 11–12). The eagle, which "had twelve feathered wings and three heads" (11:1), came from the sea and exercised rule over the entire earth (v. 5). The sundry parts of this amazing creature and their functions are set forth in chapter 11. Eventually a lion emerges to excoriate the eagle for its misrule and to announce its annihilation (11:36–46). The eagle, which is identified as the fourth beast of Daniel's vision (11:39; 12:11), is finally destroyed (12:1–3). Ezra requested an explanation of the strange vision and received one from the angel. The wings and heads of the creature are clarified, and the eagle is again presented as the fourth beast in Daniel 7.

And as for the lion that you saw rousing up out of the forest and roaring and speaking to the eagle and reproving him for his unrighteousness, and as for all his words that you have heard, this is the Messiah whom the Most High has kept until the end of days, who will arise from the posterity of David, and will come and speak to them; he will denounce them for their ungodliness and for their wickedness, and will cast up before them their contemptuous dealings. For first he will set them living before his judgment seat, and when he has reproved them, then he will destroy them. But he will deliver in mercy the remnant of my people, those who have been saved throughout my borders, and he will make them joyful until the end comes, the day of judgment, of which I spoke to you at the beginning. (12:31–34)

Here, unlike in chapter 7, the Messiah carries out the function of judging, but the object of his sentence is the eagle, although it is addressed in the plural. Also, the final judgment is not under consideration here; it is mentioned at the end of v. 34 as coming after the blissful rule of the Messiah. In that sense, the picture in chapter 12 is consistent with the temporary messianic reign in chapter 7. The Davidic Messiah is also the agent through whom God's people are delivered or saved.

Ezra's sixth vision provides the final scene in which the Messiah is mentioned, although he is not called an "anointed one." In a dream Ezra sees a wind stirring the sea and making "something like the figure of a man come up out of the heart of the sea. And I looked, and behold, that man flew with the clouds of heaven; and wherever he turned his face to look, eveything under his gaze trembled, and whenever his voice issued from his mouth, all who heard his voice melted as wax melts when it feels the fire" (13:3–4). When an enormous multitude of people from all directions gathered to attack the one resembling a man, "he carved out for himself a great mountain, and flew upon it" (13:6). The attack took place nevertheless. The manlike being did not use normal weapons to fight but "sent forth from his mouth as it were a stream of fire, and from his lips a flaming breath, and from his tongue he shot forth a storm of sparks" (13:10). These combined long-range weapons consumed the attackers. "After this I saw the same man come down from the mountain and call to him another multitude which was peaceable. Then many people came to him, some of whom were joyful and some sorrowful; some of them were bound, and some were bringing others as offerings" (13:12–13).

As was his practice, Ezra requested an interpretation. He learns that the man coming from the sea "is he whom the Most High has been keeping for many ages, who will himself deliver his creation; and he will direct those who are left" (13:26). The attack that Ezra had observed meant that in a time of universal war and confusion

> when these things come to pass and the signs occur which I showed you before, then my son will be revealed, whom you saw as a man coming up from the sea. And when all the nations hear his voice, every man shall leave his own land and the warfare that they have against one another; and an innumerable multitude shall be gathered together . . . desiring to come and conquer him. But he will stand on top of Mount Zion. And Zion will come and be made manifest to all people, prepared and built, as you saw the mountain carved out without hands. And he, my Son, will reprove the assembled nations for their ungodliness . . . and he will destroy them without effort by the law. . . . And as for your seeing him gather to himself another multitude that was peaceable, these are the ten tribes. . . . (13:32–40)

Ezra is later told that the man's rising from the sea signified that "no one on earth can see my Son or those with him, except in the time of his day" (13:52).

In 2 Esdras (= 4 Ezra), then, the messianic leader, termed God's son, is hidden until the end, when he as conqueror destroys the wicked and reunites God's people on Mount Zion. He is from David's line, and his joyful, four-hundred-year reign ends with his death and the deaths of all others just before the last assize.

THE *APOCALYPSE OF ABRAHAM*. Another Jewish apocalypse written after the disastrous result of the war against Rome is the *Apocalypse of Abraham,* which is preserved now only in Old Slavonic, transmitted by Christians. It is likely, however, that it was written in Hebrew and that it dates from some point at the end of the first or beginning of the second century C.E.[4] The first part of the work (chapters 1–8) deals with the youthful Abraham's rejection of his father's idolatry, while the second (chapters 9–32) is an apocalypse that is introduced into the scene of Abra(ha)m's sacrifice in Genesis 15. God tells him on that occasion: "in this sacrifice I will place the ages. I will announce to you guarded things and you will see great things which you have not seen" (9:5–6; cf. vv. 9–10). God sends the angel Iaoel to make the revelations to him (10:3).

In the course of many disclosures, Abraham is told about the messianic leader at the end of time. Not all of the details are crystal clear, but in chapter 29 some twelve periods of impiety leading up to the end are under discussion. Abraham looks down at a picture that is being shown to him and says: "I looked and saw a man going out from the left, the heathen side. From the side of the heathen went out men and women and children, a great crowd, and they worshiped him. And while I was still looking, those on the right side came out, and some insulted this man, and some struck him and others worshiped him. And I saw that as they worshiped him Azazel ran and worshiped and, kissing his face, he turned and stood behind him" (29:4–6). Abraham asks who the man is and is told:

> [H]e is the liberation from the heathen for the people who will be (born) from you. In the last days, in this twelfth hour of impiety, in the twelfth period of the age of my fulfillment, I will set up this man from your tribe, the one whom you have seen from my people. All will imitate him, . . . (you) consider him as one called by me . . . (they) are changed in their counsels. And those you saw coming out from the left side of the picture and worshiping him, this (means that) many of the heathen will trust in him. And those of your seed you saw on the right side, some insulting him, some beating him, and others worshiping him, many of them shall be offended because of him. It is he who will test those of your seed who have worshiped him in the fulfillment of the twelfth hour, in the curtailing of the age of impiety. (29:8–12)

The text goes on to speak about ten plagues that will be sent on creation. Once they are past, "I will sound the trumpet out of the air, and I will send my chosen one, having in him one measure of all my power, and he will summon my people, humiliated by the heathen" (31:1). The judgment follows this scene.

Thus, in the *Apocalypse of Abraham* the messianic figure is called a man who is worshiped by some but insulted by others. He liberates Abraham's descendants from the control of the heathen, but some of the nations and some of Abraham's descendants will worship him. He will summon God's people after they have been humiliated by the nations. Textual problems in chap. 29 prevent one from understanding more fully what is said there, but it is difficult to avoid the impression that this passage is a Christian interpolation.

OTHER APOCALYPSES. A few other apocalypses that are of uncertain date and origin should be mentioned briefly here. The *Apocalypse of Zephaniah* may be attested as early as Clement of Alexandria's *Stromata,* and arguments have been offered that it is a first century B.C.E. to first century C.E. work.[5] Much of the fragmentarily preserved text tells of the prophet's experiences and encounters in the fifth heaven, of Hades and the abyss, the heavenly city, and so on. Though the last days seem to be envisioned, no messianic figure plays a role.

The same is the case for the lengthy *2 Enoch.* It is set in Enoch's final earthly days and involves revelations given to him before he bids farewell to his children. The topic that receives an extended treatment is the creation. Throughout the apocalypse, while the end is in view, there is no Messiah. Enoch himself also does not seem to play any such role. Instead, he receives spectacular revelations, conveys the key information to his children, and is finally removed.

The *Testament of Abraham* (first to second century C.E.) is, of course, placed near the time when Abraham is to die. He resists God's various messengers (Michael, Death) who are to take him and is shown what sorts of judgments the different kinds of souls undergo after leaving their bodies. While the judgment does play a major part in the story, nothing is said about an end-time leader.

Finally, *3 Baruch* may also belong here. It was written in the early centuries of the Christian era and contains a tour by Baruch through the five heavens. Among the mysteries disclosed to Baruch are the results of obedience and disobedience to God's commandments. The final judgment is not an important theme in the book, and it never mentions a Messiah.

Messianic Leaders outside the Apocalypses

Another way in which to approach the question of the relation between messianism and apocalypticism is to survey those texts that are not apocalypses in a formal sense but in which a messianic figure appears. The earliest such occurrences of "anointed one" for a leader of the last times are in the Dead Sea Scrolls and the *Psalms of Solomon*. The Scrolls present the unusual picture of two messianic figures, while *Psalms of Solomon* 17–18 speaks of a single Messiah from the line of David. The Qumran Scrolls are associated in some way with what may be termed an apocalyptic community, but a community that seems to have produced no apocalypses of its own. That is, it inherited apocalypses, such as the ones in the Enochic tradition, but there is no evidence that any author at Qumran wrote an apocalypse (see below for two possible exceptions).

MESSIAHS IN THE SCROLLS. A series of passages documents the fact that in the Qumran texts both a priestly and a Davidic/secular Messiah were expected to come. Each of the two Messiahs is designated by three different titles. The Davidic/secular Messiah is also called Branch of David and Prince of the Congregation. Besides Messiah, the priestly leader is named Interpreter of the Law and (High) Priest. In the following paragraphs those passages in which both are or may be referred to as Messiah in the same expression will be examined. Once those passages have been considered, other messianic ones will be studied to isolate the functions they attribute to these eschatological individuals and also to check whether the Scrolls preserve evidence of other messianic expectations.

1. The Two Messiahs Together. The Scrolls speak of a Messiah from Israel and a Messiah from Aaron, that is, of a Davidic and a priestly Messiah. What appears to be the earliest such reference is also the best known one. The *Rule of the Community* includes the following statement: "They should not depart from any counsel of the law in order to walk in complete stubbornness of their heart, but instead shall be ruled by the first directives which the men of the Community began to be taught until the prophet comes, and the Messiahs of Aaron and Israel" (1QS 9:9–11).[6] While the number of Messiahs is not specified here, the fact that the words "of Aaron and Israel" complete the construct phrase favors the conclusion that there are two. The plural Messiahs is an unmistakable reading in the manuscript, but the genuineness of the passage has been disputed because one of the Cave 4 copies of the *Rule of the Community*, which on paleographical grounds is considered by some scholars

to be the oldest copy, lacks these and surrounding lines. Although ten copies of the work have been identified among the myriad fragments from Cave 4, only the fourth and fifth are relevant because they alone preserve the general part of the text found in the vicinity of the ninth column in the Cave 1 copy (where the messianic reference occurs). The fourth copy (4Q258) is broken in the context (although it contains the equivalent of 9:10 at the end of frag. 2 col. ii and has the equivalent of 9:15 at the beginning of frag. 2 col. iii), but the text preserved in 4Q259 moves from the equivalent of 8:15 in the Cave 1 copy to the equivalent of 9:12 in the Cave 1 copy. That is, it (apparently uniquely) lacks all the material between 8:15 and 9:12, including the reference to the Messiahs. The correct explanation for this state of affairs is not clear. Absence of the material could be explained as omission of a full column (similar expressions precede and follow the missing text), in which case the material would be original and the shorter text defective; or the extra material in the Cave 1 copy could be an addition (see VanderKam 1994, 212–13). Since 4Q259 may be the oldest copy of the *Rule of the Community,* some scholars have concluded that the work did not refer to the Messiahs in its original form. While there is clear evidence of conceptual development in the different copies of the work (the role of the sons of Zadok is a case in point), it remains debatable whether 4Q259 retains a more ancient form of the text than the Cave 1 copy in this place. The important point is, nevertheless, that a text dating from ca. 100 B.C.E. (1QS) contains a reference to a priestly and to a secular Messiah. In the text the appearance of the prophet and Messiahs serves to mark the end of an era: the members of the community are to follow the original directives of the group until they arrive. That is, their advent ushers in the end of this evil age. Nothing more is said about the Messiahs' activities in the *Rule of the Community.*

The evidence from the *Damascus Document* should probably be understood in the same sense. This work, which stems from the larger movement of which the Qumran community was a small part, resorts to similar but not identical language in speaking about messianic matters. The key distinction between the formulation in the *Rule of the Community* and that in the *Damascus Document* is that while the former uses the plural "Messiahs" the latter has the singular "Messiah." There are four passages in the *Damascus Document* that remind one of the messianic statement in 1QS. In CD 12:23–13:1 we read: "Those who walk in them, in the time of wickedness until there arises the messiah of Aaron and Israel. . . ." CD 14:18–19 is similar: "And this is the exact interpretation of the regulations by which [they shall be ruled until there arises the messiah] of Aaron and Israel. He shall atone for their sins]." CD

19:10–11 speaks of a military situation, as it explains Zech. 13:7: "These shall escape in the age of the visitation; but those that remain shall be delivered up to the sword when there comes the messiah of Aaron and Israel." Finally, 19:33–20:1 uses the messianic arrival to define the end of the present era: "And thus, all the men who entered the new covenant in the land of Damascus and turned and betrayed and departed from the well of living waters, shall not be counted in the assembly of the people and shall not be inscribed in their [lis]ts, from the day of the session {of him who te<aches>/ of the teacher} of the unique Teacher until there arises the messiah of Aaron and Israel." Although in all four instances the term *messiah* is singular and in the only case where a finite verb is used with the title it, too, is singular, the Messiah has both Aaronic and Israelite qualities. In fact, each of the two terms *Aaron* and *Israel* in CD 20:1 is supplied with a preposition (literally: from Aaron and from Israel). The fragmentary Cave 4 copies offer little help since they usually do not preserve the relevant parts of the text, but in the only instance in which one of the messianic passages is extant—4QD^a 10 i 12–13 for 14:18–19 (cf. 4QD^d 11 i 2)—it verifies the reading of the Geniza copy quoted above.

2. Messiah and Priest. There are no other occurrences of the expressions "the Messiahs of Aaron and Israel" or "the Messiah of Aaron and Israel" in the Scrolls, but there are several passages in which the Davidic Messiah appears together with a priest. These may reflect the same dual messianism even though they do not give the title Messiah to the priest. 1QSa (the *Rule of the Congregation*), which was copied on the same scroll as 1QS (the *Rule of the Community*), describes an eschatological meal in which the Messiah and a priest play roles. The text opens by saying, "this is the rule of the congregation of Israel in the final days, when they gather" (col. 1, line 1). The section dealing specifically with the messianic meal contains several lines that are important for the present purposes. According to García Martínez's rendering, 2:11–12a reads: "This is the assembly of famous men, [those summoned to] the gathering of the community council, when [God] begets the Messiah with them." However, the term "God" has to be imported into the text, and "begets" is an emendation. E. Puech has now shown that the verb, owing to a supralinear correction, is to be read "reveals," not "begets" (1994, 351–65). In other words, the text is speaking about an assembly at which God reveals the Messiah together with the members of the community. At that time, the text continues:

> the chief [priest] of all the congregation of Israel shall enter, and all [his brothers, the sons] of Aaron, the priests [summoned] to the assembly, the famous men, and they shall sit befo[re him, each one] according to his dignity. After,

[the Me]ssiah of Israel shall ent[er] and before him shall sit the chiefs [of the clans of Israel, each] one according to his dignity, according to their [positions] in their camps and in their marches. (2:12–15)

Then, when the meal is ready,

[no-one should stretch out] his hand to the first-fruit of the bread and of the [new wine] before the priest, for [he is the one who bl]esses the first-fruit of bread and of the new wine [and stretches out] his hand towards the bread before them. Afterwards, the Messiah of Israel shall stretch out his hand towards the bread. [And after, he shall] bless all the congregation of the community, each [one according to] his dignity. And in accordance with this regulation they shall act at each me[al, when] at least ten m[en are gat]hered. (2:18–22)

The last line suggests that this messianic meal is a recurring event, while the beginning of the text declares that the rules found in it are for the last days. The nonpriestly leader alone is given the title Messiah in the extant portions of the text. The priest may also be considered a Messiah, but the title is never specifically attached to him.

This pattern found in the *Rule of the Congregation,* according to which the two eschatological leaders appear together though the title Messiah is not assigned to both, is repeated in a number of other texts from the Qumran caves. 4Q174 (*Florilegium*) is a prime example. In a section of the text that deals with the promise of an eternal dynasty to David, the writer says: "This (refers to the) 'branch of David,' who will arise with the Interpreter of the law who [will rise up] in Zi[on in] the last days" (1–3 i 11–12). There is no doubt that Branch of David is a title for the Davidic Messiah, and Interpreter of the Law is one of the epithets used for the priestly Messiah. The text is explicit about the expectation that the two will appear together in the last days. It seems that 4Q252 (*Commentary on Genesisᵃ*) fits in the same mold. In his interpretation of the blessing on Judah in Gen. 49:10 the expositor writes:

A sovereign shall [not] be removed from the tribe of Judah. While Israel has dominion there will [not] lack someone who sits on the throne of David. For "the staff" is the covenant of royalty, [the thou]sands of Israel are "the feet." Until the messiah of justice comes, the branch of David. For to him and to his descendants has been given the covenant of royalty over his people for all everlasting generations, which he has observed [. . .] the Law with the men of the Community. (5:1–5)

It is likely that in the gap in the last line quoted (the space indicated as [. . .] before "the Law") the term "Interpreter of " should be restored; if so, then the Interpreter of the Law is present with the leader, who is called both Messiah and Branch of David (thus showing that the two royal titles refer to the same individual).

The *Damascus Document* contains a similar passage, one that supports the idea that in the recurring expression "Messiah of Aaron and Israel" (see above) two Messiahs are envisaged. The passage in question is CD 7:14–21, where the writer is clarifying the meaning of Amos 5:26–27 by using the complementary information found in Amos 9:11 and in Num. 24:17. About the star in Amos 5:26 ("Kaiwan your star-God") he writes: "the star is the Interpreter of the Law, who will come to Damascus, as it is written: 'A star moves out of Jacob, and a sceptre arises out of Israel' [= Num. 24:17]. The sceptre is the prince of the whole congregation and when he arises he will destroy all the sons of Seth" (7:18–21). The expositor finds that Num. 24:17 refers to two future leaders, and these two are the two Messiahs of the *Rule of the Community* and the *Damascus Document.*

4Q161 (4QpIsaᵃ) seems to belong in this category as indicated by 7–10 iii 22–29, where the writer is commenting on Isaiah 11. The long citation of Isa. 11:1–5 occupies lines 15–20, and an empty line separates the biblical lemma from the commentary. The Isaian text furnishes an obvious peg on which to hang statements about a Davidic Messiah. The name *David* appears immediately after a gap in line 22; it is followed by a reference to the end of days in the same line and by "throne" and "crown" in line 24 and the verbs "rule" and "judge" in line 25. Line 27 then gives a recitation of Isa. 11:3. The interpretation of the verse is broken, but lines 28–29 say: "28. [. . .] as they teach him, so will he judge, and according to their command 29. [. . .] with him. One of the priests of repute will go out. . . ."[7] The reputable priest is not identified as a Messiah, but at least he seems to be with the Davidic Messiah described in the preceding lines, and a group of priests appear to be the ones who provide instruction for the Messiah in matters of justice.

4Q285 (the so-called *War Rule*) frags. 4–5 also associate a Davidic leader with a priest. Here again the biblical base is from Isaiah, specifically Isa. 10:34–11:1. Frag. 4 refers to the Prince of the Congregation twice (lines 2 and 6) and apparently describes a war that he conducts against the Kittim. Frag. 5 opens with a quotation from Isa. 10:34–11:1 and continues with: "3 [. . .] the bud [= branch] of David will go into battle with [. . .] 4 [. . .] and the Prince of the Congregation will kill him, the bu[d of David . . .] 5 [. . .] and with wounds. And a priest will command [. . .] 6 [. . .] the destruction of the Kittim [. . .]." The Davidic Messiah, under two of his Qumran titles, figures prominently, but a priest, not further identified, also plays a commanding part in the battle.

3. Other Messianic References in Qumran Texts. Another group of texts mentions a single Messiah, whether Davidic or priestly, but fails to employ the title Messiah. The *War Rule* includes one reference to the Prince of the Congregation (1QM 5:1), on whose shield names representative of all groups in Israel are inscribed. 1QM 15:4 introduces the high priest as offering a prayer before the final struggle with the Kittim; he strengthens the troops with his words during the battle (16:13); during the last assault he and his fellow priests bless God (18:5; see also 2:1). 1QSb (the *Rule of the Blessings*) 5:20–29 contains a benediction for the prince of the congregation. The blessings heaped upon him are based on those given to the davidic shoot in Isaiah 11. He is to defeat the nations, establish the covenant, and rule with justice. The same text should contain a blessing for the high priest, but no rubric marks where it might have occurred.

Two Qumran texts that have been labeled apocalypses also preserve passages that should be treated in this context. It is debatable whether, under the definition offered above, either of these works should be assigned to the genre *apocalypse*. Perhaps if more of the texts had survived the point would be clear, but in their present, fragmentary form they lack some of the ingredients of apocalypses. 4Q521 (*Messianic Apocalypse*), at the top of what is called col. 2 in frag. 2, reads: "1 [for the heav]ens and the earth will listen to his Messiah 2 [and all] that is in them will not turn away from the holy precepts." The text goes on to speak of mighty deeds and miracles that will take place, but they are apparently performed by the Lord. The second text under this rubric, 4Q246 (*Aramaic Apocalypse*), predicts the rise of a remarkable ruler:

> 1 7 [. . .] and he will be great over the earth 8 [. . .] they will do, and all will serve 9 [. . .] great will he be called and he will be designated by his name. 2 1 He will be called son of God, and they will call him son of the Most High. Like the sparks 2 of a vision, so will their kingdom be; they will rule several years over 3 the earth and crush everything; a people will crush another people, and a city another city. 4 *Blank* Until the people of God arises and makes everyone rest from the sword.

Some scholars maintain that a messianic figure is here being called "son of God" and "son of the Most High" (as Jesus is in Luke 1:32, 35); but the pattern of the text seems to be that of Daniel 7, in which the quintessentially evil fourth kingdom is replaced by the rule of the saints. If so, the sequence would entail that the titles are ascribed falsely to a ruler in this last, wicked kingdom and hence are not being attributed to a Messiah.

THE *PSALMS OF SOLOMON*. The set of poems that were transmitted under the name of Solomon was written in the latter part of the first century B.C.E.

Psalms 17 and 18, the last two in the collection, express a vivid, detailed hope for a Messiah from the line of David. The author takes pains to locate his beliefs about a Messiah within the context of a repeated confession that God is the eternal king (17:1, 26; cf. v. 34, where the Lord is the Messiah's king) who is the savior and whose kingdom is also forever (17:3). He refers to the promise of an eternal dynasty for David but also notes that national sin has led to the rise of evil, non-Davidic rulers (apparently the Hasmoneans, "[t]hose to whom you did not [make the] promise" [v. 5]) who established themselves as kings. The Lord judged and overthrew them through an alien, who seems to be Pompey (vv. 6–9). Terrible times ensued because of the arrogance and violence of the foreign conquerors. In this context of all that had gone wrong during the periods of rule by the Hasmoneans and Romans, the author enunciates his yearning for a new Anointed One from David's line (17:21–44). The passage is too lengthy to quote, but its teachings and those of the shorter section in chap. 18:5–9 can be summarized under four headings.

1. The Nature of the Messiah. He is a king (17:21, 32) who is a descendant of David (17:21); he is called Lord Messiah,[8] is said to be free from sin (17:36), and whatever he does is characterized by righteousness.

2. The Messiah's Relation with God. God, the eternal king, is always the superior one who acts and is in control. God will raise the Anointed One in his own time (17:21) and will support him with the ability to drive out the Gentiles (17:22). The people led by the Judge-Messiah are the ones whom God sanctified (17:26; cf. v. 27). The Messiah will glorify God in an exalted place (Jerusalem, v. 30) where the nations see the Lord's glory (v. 31). As a righteous king he will be taught by God (17:32). The Lord is the Messiah's king, the one on whom he relies (17:32–34, 37). "God made him powerful in the holy spirit and wise in the counsel of understanding, with strength and righteousness" (v. 37). God's blessing remains with him (17:38), and his hope lies in the Lord (17:39), as he is "strong in the fear of God" (17:40). He will shepherd the Lord's flock (17:40). God is the one who will cause Israel's good fortune at the time of the Messiah (17:44), and he is the one who will cleanse Israel in preparation for that blessed time (18:5). The fear of the Lord will be the mark of the Messiah's reign (18:7–9).

3. The Messiah's Relation with Israel. The Messiah is to reign over God's servant Israel (17:21, 35; 18:5). He will gather and lead them in righteousness (17:26), will judge them (17:26, 43), and will be their righteous king (17:32). He purges Jerusalem of Gentiles (17:30–31). He blesses the Lord's people with wisdom and happiness (17:35); he shepherds them and leads them in

holiness and discipline (17:40-42; see 18:7). He also directs them in righteous acts in the fear of the Lord (18:8-9).

4. The Messiah's Relation with the Nations. The Messiah is to purge Jerusalem of Gentiles (17:32), and he will destroy "the unlawful nations with the word of his mouth" (17:24). The nations will flee from him when he warns them (17:25). As one might expect, he judges "peoples and nations in the wisdom of his righteousness" (17:29). The nations will serve him (17:30) and will stream to Jerusalem to observe his and the Lord's glory (17:31). He will be compassionate to the peoples who revere him (17:34).

In the *Psalms of Solomon* the Messiah is an extraordinary individual to whom God will grant great gifts such as wisdom, righteousness, holiness, and the fear of the Lord, but he remains a human monarch who is subservient to God, the eternal king.

PHILO AND JOSEPHUS. Philo has left no clear indication about any messianic beliefs he may have entertained, although he may be hinting in this direction in *On Rewards and Punishments* 95. There, in his explanation of the Greek version of Num. 24:17 ("there shall come forth a man"), he writes that the man, aided by God, will subdue many nations. He does not stipulate whether the text intends an eschatological or a historical ruler. Josephus does resort to the term *messiah* in a few instances and uses other terms for future leaders. However, he does not tell the reader what his views about a Messiah might have been. One passage that has messianic overtones is the familiar "ambiguous oracle" that he reports in the *Jewish War* in a section in which he is reflecting on portents the Jews had received before the war against Rome.

> But what more than all else incited them to the war was an ambiguous oracle, likewise found in their sacred scriptures, to the effect that at that time one from their country would become ruler of the world. This they understood to mean someone of their own race, and many of their wise men went astray in their interpretation of it. The oracle, however, in reality signified the sovereignty of Vespasian, who was proclaimed emperor on Jewish soil. (6.312–13)[9]

Josephus does make two references to Jesus and includes the term *messiah* in both. In *Ant.* 18.63 the text has "[h]e was the Messiah," while in *Ant.* 20.200 he is said to be "Jesus who was called the Christ."[10] The first of these passages has, of course, been widely regarded as the product of at least some Christian editorial interference, while the second is simply a noncommittal report by Josephus.

Josephus also adduces several instances in which men whom he regarded as impostors tried to gather a crowd of followers by evoking historical themes such as the exodus, the trek in the wilderness, and the crossing of the Jordan. He alludes to a Samaritan who, during the procuratorship of Pontius Pilate (26–36 C.E.) assembled an armed crowd which he led to the sacred Mount Gerizim to show them the holy vessels still buried where, curiously, Moses was supposed to have placed them. Pilate's troops brought a premature halt to the movement (*Ant.* 18.85–87). At the time of Fadus (ca. 45 C.E.) a man named Theudas, claiming to be a prophet, attracted a fairly large number of followers who were to accompany him to the Jordan River. It was to part at his command, just as it had for Joshua. Roman troops again intervened and Theudas was beheaded (*Ant.* 20.97–99). Rabbi Gamaliel refers to the same incident in Acts 5:36, where he puts the number of Theudas's followers at "about four hundred." While Felix ruled in Judea (ca. 52–59 C.E.), another claimant to the prophetic mantle, a man called only "the Egyptian," lured some thirty thousand people to the wilderness and then to the Mount of Olives with the promise that the walls of Jerusalem would collapse at their approach. The predictable military response of the Roman regime ended this scheme as well (*Ant.* 20.169–72). In *War* 2.262–63 Josephus writes that the Egyptian intended to rule as a tyrant. The Egyptian appears to be the man for whom the apostle Paul was mistaken by the tribune in Acts 21:38. Josephus never refers to any of these individuals as Messiahs or even so-called Messiahs.

MESSIAHS AND REVOLTS. The Jewish revolts against Rome in 66–70 and 132–35 and the Diaspora uprising in 115–17 could be considered prime occasions for potential Messiahs to appear. There is really no evidence for any such claim during the first revolt. Menahem, the son of Judas the Galilean (see *War* 2.433–48), and Simon bar Giora (see *War* 7.26–36) had royal pretensions, but Josephus reports nothing regarding messianic assertions by or about them. The Diaspora revolt in the time of Trajan may have involved a messianic leader or leaders. Eusebius calls the chief in Cyrene *Lucuas* (*Ecclesiastical History* 4.2) and attributes to him the titles Leader and King; Dio Cassius gives his name as *Andreas* (*Roman History* 68.32). The latter also mentions a certain rebel leader on Cyprus named Artemion. While some scholars view the uprising as messianic in nature, the evidence for the character of the revolt is really very sparse.

The second Jewish revolt against Rome (132–35) was certainly messianic in the sense that the Jewish military leader, Simon bar Kosiba, was identified as King Messiah by Rabbi Akiba according to rabbinic sources (e.g., *y. Ta'an.* 4.8 [68d]). Akiba is supposed to have related to him the prediction of Num. 24:17 that a star (*kôkāb*) would come forth from Jacob. This brought about the wordplay on Simon bar Kosiba's name so that it became *bar Kokhba*, or son of the star (see also Eusebius, *Ecclesiastical History* 4.6, 2). The same talmudic passage (*y. Ta'an.* 4.8 [68d]) also indicates that Rabbi Akiba's opinion was not shared by all. The letters and coins associated with Simon's rule use neither the title King nor Messiah for him; rather, they designate him Prince of Israel. When the revolt failed, Simon's memory was condemned by dubbing him Simon ben Koziba, or son of the lie (Horsley and Hanson 1985, 127–29).

conc

CONCLUSIONS

The survey of the evidence for messianic teachings within Jewish apocalypses and outside them has yielded important if diverse results. These may be summarized briefly.

Chronology

No Jewish text written before the second century B.C.E. mentions a messianic leader. Some of the later works in the Hebrew Bible offer suggestive words and images that point in this direction (e.g., Isa. 9:1–6; Hag. 2:20–23), and others were later interpreted as referring to a Messiah (e.g., the suffering servant in Deutero-Isaiah, the one like a son of man in Daniel 7), but no pre-200 work describes a person who could be called a Messiah in the eschatological sense of the term. Texts failing to mention a Messiah in eschatological contexts continued to be composed throughout the period covered by the preceding survey. Nonmessianic portraits of the end-times were a frequent phenomenon in early Judaism.

Apocalypses and Messianism

None of the earliest Jewish apocalypses (the Astronomical Book, the Book of the Watchers, the Apocalypse of Weeks, parts of *Jubilees,* Daniel 7–12) contains references to messianic leaders. The earliest one to make such an allusion—the Animal Apocalypse—dates from the late 160s B.C.E. After that time a number of apocalypses include messianic teachings (the Similitudes of Enoch, *2 Baruch,* 4 Ezra, *Apocalypse of Abraham*), but others do not (the *Apocalypse of Zephaniah, 2 Enoch,* the *Testament of Abraham,* and *3 Baruch*). If one divides the apocalypses into the categories defined in *Semeia* 14, four types are represented in the early Jewish apocalypses. Type Ia ("Historical" Apocalypses with No Otherworldly Journey) includes some with a messianic figure (the Animal Apocalypse, *2 Baruch,* 4 Ezra) and some without (Daniel 7-12, the

Apocalypse of Weeks, *Jubilees* 1 and 23). The same is the case for IIb (Other-worldly Journeys with Cosmic and/or Political Eschatology) in which the Astronomical Book, the Book of the Watchers, *2 Enoch,* and *Testament of Levi* 2–5 lack a Messiah, while the Similitudes of Enoch has one. Type IIa ("Historical" Apocalypses with an Otherworldly Journey) includes only the *Apocalypse of Abraham* among the works considered here, and it has a messianic leader. Type IIc (Otherworldly Journeys with only Personal Eschatology) contains the *Apocalypse of Zephaniah,* the *Testament of Abraham,* and *3 Baruch,* none of which mentions a Messiah (Collins 1979, 14–15). No author explains why a Messiah is not mentioned, but those texts which lack such a figure are able to emphasize the actions of God, perhaps executed through angels, to a greater extent than are those which include a Messiah.

Messiahs and Writings That Are Not Apocalypses

Some works that are not formally apocalypses but offer apocalyptic or eschatological teachings contain references to or entire sections on messianic figures, but few of them do so. That is, the vast majority of Second Temple Jewish texts have no reference to a messianic leader of the end-time. A number of works, such as historical reports, would not be expected to include one, but it is still obvious that messianic thinking was not a dominant approach among Jewish writers whose works have survived from that period.

Images of the Messiah(s):

The texts that speak about messianic beliefs present not a unitary but a varied picture of who the Messiah(s) was (were) thought to be and what he (they) would do.

1. The texts show that some writers anticipated the arrival of one and others awaited two Messiahs. Expectation of one Messiah is much more frequently represented; a dual messianism is attested only in the Dead Sea Scrolls.

2. Early Jewish authors used several titles for the Messiah(s):

Messiah	Similitudes of Enoch, *2 Baruch,* 4 Ezra, the *Rule of the Community,* the *Damascus Document,* the *Rule of the Congregation,* the *Commentary on Genesis^a,* 4Q521 (*Messianic Apocalypse*), *Psalms of Solomon* (where he is called Lord Messiah), Josephus, *Antiquities,* Talmud Yerushalmi
Righteous One	Similitudes of Enoch

Chosen One	Similitudes of Enoch, *Apocalypse of Abraham*
Son of Man	Similitudes of Enoch; 4 Ezra refers to one having the figure of a man, and the *Apocalypse of Abraham* calls him a man.
Son (of God)	4 Ezra
(God's) Servant	*2 Baruch*
Prince of the Congregation	*Damascus Document*, 4Q285 (*War Rule*), *War Scroll*, the *Rule of the Blessings*
Branch of David	4Q174 (*Florilegium*), *Commentary on Genesis*[a], 4Q285 (*War Rule*), 4Q161?
Interpreter of the Law	*Damascus Document*, 4Q174 (*Florilegium*), 4Q252 (*Commentary on Genesis*[a])
(High) Priest	*Rule of the Congregation*, 4Q161?, 4Q285 (*War Rule*), *War Scroll*

Other symbolic references are attested: a white bull (the Animal Apocalypse), a vine/fountain (*2 Baruch*), and a lion (4 Ezra).

3. The most common belief was that the Messiah would be from the lineage of David, that he would engage in warfare to defeat the nations, and that he would judge the wicked. In these senses he would be involved in delivering God's people and would appear at the turning point of history. His rule would be marked by justice. 4 Ezra alone expresses the belief that the messianic reign would be temporary and that the Messiah would die.

4. Only texts in the tradition prepared for by *Jubilees* (and perhaps Aramaic Levi; cf. the *Testaments of the Twelve Patriarchs*) and embodied in the Dead Sea Scrolls articulate the belief that there would be two Messiahs, one Davidic and one priestly. Their appearance with a prophet will mark the end of this evil age and usher in a new era. The Davidic Messiah is associated with ruling and judging, while the priest instructs and blesses. In one place it is said that the Messiah(s) will atone for the sins of the chosen.

5. Other than in the *Jubilees*-Qumran tradition, there is no clear evidence in early Jewish texts about the messianic beliefs or lack of them among the Jewish parties such as the Pharisees or Sadducees.

Concluding Speculations

The evidence does not permit sure conclusions about the reason(s) why messianism arose when it did and appeared where it is attested, but some tentative

tentative

suggestions may be offered. The lack of messianic expectation in the Second Temple and the fact that the most ancient apocalypses do not envisage a Messiah may in part be related to Jewish attitudes toward non-Jewish rule over them. The Jewish nation had centuries of experience with such a governmental arrangement, and there is evidence that Gentile rule was at times viewed neutrally or even somewhat positively, as long as the regime permitted exercise of Judaism. The first authors to include Messiahs in the scenarios for the future were hostile to the reigning power. The Animal Apocalypse includes the periods of rule by all the foreign powers in exilic and postexilic history within the time of despotic rule by the seventy shepherds; it does, however, show a positive attitude toward native rule (Judas Maccabeus). Parts of Daniel show, nevertheless, that attitudes to Gentile rule were not the sole cause for the rise of messianism, since in its apocalyptic sections, unlike some of the court narratives, the foreign powers are pictured most negatively and the Maccabees are presented somewhat positively.

In the Qumran texts, the *Psalms of Solomon,* and the Similitudes of Enoch both foreign and native rulers are castigated and hopes are placed on a Messiah (or Messiahs) who will end the present evil age of injustice. Much later, in the aftermath of the first Jewish revolt against Rome (66–70 C.E.) the gross failure of both Gentile and Jewish leadership led to the despair found in works such as *2 Baruch* and 4 Ezra and the yearning for the arrival of a Davidic Messiah. If attitudes toward the Gentile power were a strong factor in arousing messianic hopes, it is quite understandable that neither Philo nor Josephus would have a place for a Messiah in their writings.

The factors that determined the status assigned by the different authors to their Messiahs are not clear. It may be that the choice of which biblical passages to use in developing the picture of the Messiahs played a role, but that would leave unexplained why those passages were selected in the first place. Of all the texts surveyed, the Similitudes of Enoch presents the most exalted portrait of a Messiah; other apocalypses such as *2 Baruch* and *4 Ezra* also view him as a highly impressive individual but not one of the same heavenly status as the Messiah of the Similitudes. It is difficult to define the status of the Messiahs in the Qumran texts, but they appear to be human leaders; the same is true for the great and righteous descendant of David in the *Psalms of Solomon.* Moreover, there is no reason for thinking that Simon bar Kosiba was envisaged as superhuman. Consequently, while it may be the case that the apocalypses anticipate a somewhat more exalted messiah than the leaders one finds in the nonapocalyptic texts, the contrast is not a strong one in most cases.

NOTES

1. Quotations from *1 Enoch* are taken from M. Knibb, *The Ethiopic Book of Enoch*, 2 vols. (Oxford: Clarendon Press, 1978), vol. 2.

2. The translations of *2 Baruch* are from A. F. J. Klijn in *Old Testament Pseudepigrapha*, ed. J. H. Charlesworth, 2 vols. (= *OTP*) (Garden City, N.Y.: Doubleday, 1983, 1985), vol. 1.

3. The translation used for *2 Esdras/4 Ezra* is that of B. M. Metzger in *OTP*, vol. 1.

4. See R. Rubinkiewicz in *OTP*, 1:682–83. The translations of the *Apocalypse of Abraham* are those of Rubinkiewicz.

5. See O. Wintermute in *OTP*, 1:499–501.

6. Translations of the Dead Sea Scrolls come from F. García Martínez, *The Dead Sea Scrolls Translated* (Leiden: E. J. Brill, 1994).

7. The translation of this passage is from M. Horgan, *Pesharim* (CBQMS 8; Washington: Catholic Biblical Association, 1979), 76.

8. For the textual situation here, see R. B. Wright in *OTP*, 2:669–70, n. z. Quotations are from Wright's translation.

9. The translation is that of H. St. J. Thackeray, *Josephus* III: *The Jewish War, Books IV–VII*, Loeb Classical Library (Cambridge, Mass.: Harvard University Press; London: Heinemann, 1979).

10. These renderings are from L. H. Feldman, *Josephus* IX: *Jewish Antiquities, Books XVIII–XIX*, Loeb Classical Library (Cambridge, Mass.: Harvard University Press; London: Heinemann, 1981); and idem, *Josephus* X: *Jewish Antiquities, Book XX*, Loeb Classical Library (Cambridge, Mass.: Harvard University Press; London: Heinemann, 1981).

BIBLIOGRAPHY

Charlesworth, J. H., ed. 1992. *The Messiah: Developments in Earliest Judaism and Christianity.* Minneapolis: Fortress Press.

Collins, John J. 1991. "Genre, Ideology and Social Movements." In *Mysteries and Revelations: Apocalyptic Studies since the Uppsala Colloquium*, edited by J. J. Collins and J. H. Charlesworth, 11–32. Journal for the Study of the Pseudepigrapha Supplements 9. Sheffield: Sheffield Academic Press.

———. 1993. *Daniel.* Hermeneia. Minneapolis: Fortress Press.

———. 1995. *The Scepter and the Star.* Anchor Bible Reference Library. New York: Doubleday.

Collins, John J., ed. 1979. *Apocalypse: The Morphology of a Genre. Semeia* 14. Chico, Calif.: Scholars Press.

Cross, F. M. 1973. *Canaanite Myth and Hebrew Epic.* Cambridge, Mass.: Harvard University Press.

García Martínez, F. 1994. *The Dead Sea Scrolls Translated.* Leiden: E. J. Brill.

Hanson, Paul. 1975. *The Dawn of Apocalyptic.* Philadelphia: Fortress Press.

Hollander, H. W., and M. de Jonge. 1985. *The Testaments of the Twelve Patriarchs.* Studia in Veteris Testamenti Pseudepigrapha 8. Leiden: E. J. Brill.

Horsley, R. A., and J. S. Hanson. 1985. *Bandits, Prophets, and Messiahs: Popular Religious Movements at the Time of Jesus.* Minneapolis: Winston.

Milik, J. T. 1976. *The Books of Enoch.* Oxford: Clarendon Press.

Neusner, J., W. S. Green, and E. Frerichs, eds. 1987. *Judaisms and Their Messiahs.* Cambridge: Cambridge University Press.

Oegema, G. 1994. *Der Gesalbte und sein Volk.* Göttingen: Vandenhoeck & Ruprecht.

Plöger, O. 1968. *Theocracy and Eschatology.* Richmond: John Knox. An English translation of the second German edition, which appeared in 1962.

Puech, E. 1994. "Préséance sacerdotale et messie-roi dans la Règle de la Congrégation (*1QSa* ii 11–22)." *Revue de Qumran* 16/63:351–65.

Rowland, C. 1982. *The Open Heaven.* New York: Crossroad.

Schürer, E. 1979. "Messianism." In *The History of the Jewish People in the Age of Jesus Christ,* Volume 2, revised and edited by G. Vermes, F. Millar, and M. Black, 2:488–554. Edinburgh: T. & T. Clark.

Stone, M. 1968. "The Concept of the Messiah in IV Ezra." In *Religions in Antiquity: Essays in Memory of E. R. Goodenough,* edited by J. Neusner, 295–312. Leiden: E. J. Brill.

Tiller, P. 1993. *A Commentary on the Animal Apocalypse of I Enoch.* Society of Biblical Literature Early Judaism and Its Literature 4. Atlanta: Scholars Press.

VanderKam, J. 1977. *Textual and Historical Studies in the Book of Jubilees.* Harvard Semitic Monographs 14. Missoula, Mont.: Scholars Press.

———. 1984. *Enoch and the Growth of an Apocalyptic Tradition.* CBQMS 16. Washington: Catholic Biblical Association.

———. 1989. *The Book of Jubilees.* 2 vols. Corpus Scriptorum Christianorum Orientalium 510–11, Scriptores Aethiopici 87–88. Louvain: Peeters. Translations of *Jubilees* are taken from this volume.

———. 1992. "Righteous One, Messiah, Chosen One, and Son of Man in 1 Enoch 37-71." In *The Messiah,* edited by J. H. Charlesworth, 169–91. Minneapolis: Fortress Press.

———. 1994. "Messianism in the Scrolls." In *The Community of the Renewed Covenant,* edited by E. Ulrich and J. VanderKam, 211–34. Christianity and Judaism in Antiquity 10. Notre Dame, Ind.: University of Notre Dame Press.

7

From Apocalypticism
to Early Jewish Mysticism?

Michael Mach
University of Tel Aviv

T HE TOPIC OF THIS PAPER IS HIGHLY SPECULATIVE IN NATURE.
The following survey seeks to single out some elements that may be seen
as pointing to an inner-religious development from ancient apocalyptic texts
toward later mystical ones. The attempt as such has to struggle with considerable difficulties of method and evidence. It seems advisable, therefore, to
address some of these problems at the outset and to discuss the relevant apocalyptic texts only thereafter.

APOCALYPTICISM AND RABBINIC LITERATURE

Ancient Jewish apocalypticism has produced a considerable amount of literature. Within the Jewish community, however, the writing of apocalypses
seems to have ceased some few decades after the destruction of the Second
Jewish Temple in 70 C.E. The first known document released by the rabbis
thereafter, the Mishnah, mentions the "days of the Messiah" no more than
once (*Mishnah Berakot* 1:5; the term "Messiah" is mentioned once again in an
eschatological meaning in a later gloss in *Mishnah Soṭa* 9:15). The works of
Jewish apocalypticism have been copied and transmitted by different Christian churches.

One gets the impression that for a short period of time the apocalyptic heritage and all that goes with it have been suspended from rabbinic definitions of Jewish religion. Only a short while after the Mishnah, official rabbinic documents will mention the Messiah again and will come back to some notions of apocalyptic literature. The change is not as radical and one-sided as might be expected. Yet most characteristic features of the apocalyptic literature and its eschatology are either not really represented or appear only as possible background for rabbinic polemics or other theological discourses. Could it indeed be that such an enormous theological (not necessarily social) movement was erased from the intellectual landscape? In the later talmudic period and shortly thereafter apocalyptic ideas will reenter the rabbinic discussion, and outside the *Talmudim* some minor apocalypses will be written (Even Shmu'el 1968). The ongoing stream of that literature, marginal as it might have been, testifies at least that apocalypticism was not totally abandoned. It was kept in the background of the more official works such as the Mishnah that were given to serve the community as a new basis for religious self-definition. However suppressed, it will continue to influence some thinkers.

Nevertheless, one cannot fail to see a major change that occurred in Jewish piety once the works of apocalypticism were abandoned (being, indeed, no longer transmitted by the synagogue but by the Christian church alone). But eschatology and every other form of hope for the future had to undergo substantial reinterpretation. One might go so far as to define the rabbinic reformulation of Judaism as sanctification of the nation within this world, attaching no real importance to any otherworldly salvation (see Neusner 1984). The question to be asked is, therefore, quite naturally whether other strands of Jewish piety—be they at the fringes of rabbinical teaching, as a suppressed part of it or totally outside—reflect the former apocalyptic traditions and to what degree. Formulated in a different direction: What other forms of religious thought might have been created out of former apocalyptic ideas, and in what religio-social context are these to be expected? An outstanding candidate for a remodeled piety, based on the earlier apocalypses is found in the literature of what is commonly called "early Jewish mysticism," that is, the so-called Hekhalot literature. The following lines will, therefore, deal with the possible connections between apocalypticism and the early mystic traditions in Judaism treating especially the possible (proto-)mystical elements occurring in the former.

JEWISH MYSTICISM

The renewed interest in ancient Jewish apocalypticism has gone side by side with a relatively new academic field of Jewish studies, namely, Jewish mysticism. If the former was *inter alia* due to the new finds of, for example, the Dead Sea Scrolls, the latter owes its existence mainly to the life work of Gerhard Gershom Scholem. He elevated mystic texts to a level of academic discussion and investigation that could and indeed still does take its place at the side of more traditional fields of academic Jewish learning (see mainly Scholem 1946; 1960).

Yet it was only later that, following Scholem's more general remarks, both groups of texts, apocalypses and Jewish mystic lore, were brought into closer relation. The first work in this regard is Ithamar Gruenwald's Ph.D. thesis, conducted under Scholem's supervision and consequently published in a totally reworked form (Gruenwald 1980; later followed by other scholars). The direction of scholarly interest articulated in this later work is to a certain degree indebted to Scholem's definition of the different stages of inner development detectable within Jewish mysticism. What is under discussion here is especially the literature known as *Hekhalot* ([heavenly] palaces through which the mystic passes) or *Merkavah* ([God's] chariot, the aim of the mystic's vision). The main purpose of this literature was defined by Scholem and his followers as the mystic's passing through the (seven) heavenly palaces in order to gain a vision of God enthroned on his chariot. Thus, the apocalyptic ascent stories, have been considered the direct soil that nurtured the later mystic ascents. Following this line of argumentation scholars working on Jewish apocalyptic texts have taken some interest in Hekhalot literature and its motifs, using them partly as proof of the ongoing existence of apocalyptic traditions. Only recently the so-called *3 Enoch,* a part of the Hekhalot texts, has been included in J. H. Charlesworth's collection of apocalyptic texts (see also Himmelfarb 1993). To be sure, the name given to this specific text is a misnomer introduced by its modern editor (H. Odeberg). In the manuscripts it is called *Sēper Hēkālôt, Book of the Palaces*). On the other side, scholars have tried to deal with the mystic qualities of apocalyptic literature (e.g., Rowland 1982).

The outlined development alone would have sufficed to justify a discussion of early Jewish mystic texts and their dependence on the older apocalypses within the frame of a broader study on apocalypticism. However, before entering into such a comparison it should be made clear that this whole line of relating one group of texts to another is open for discussion because of various considerations. These concern the nature of the Hekhalot texts regarding the manuscripts, the fluctuation of the textual tradition, and the date and character of this whole literature. Only thereafter may the broader issue of possible transformations from apocalypticism as a basically prophetic, politically critical type of religion into a quite different, more individual (not necessarily uncritical), yet more quiet form of religion be approached.

It is, however, still another question whether or not mystic elements may already have been part of the underlying traditions behind the apocalypses. In such a case the transformation of these eschatological texts into mystic experiences would take on another dimension and would affect our understanding of these topics within the Hekhalot literature. We will have to come back to this issue too.

In short, despite the considerable amount of scholarly activity to clarify the precise relations between both corpora of texts there remains a lot to be done. Here some of the main questions should be pointed out, without attempting to solve them.

HEKHALOT WRITINGS

Before we enter into the real subject, some features of the Hekhalot writings should be outlined that will considerably restrict any comparison between the two streams of literature. The first and most important objection against the assumption of a direct historic link between ancient apocalypses and the Hekhalot literature has come up relatively recently. The manuscripts of these mystic texts differ notably from those of other texts. Ancient texts are normally copied by scribes—sometimes together with others—as whole units. The Hekhalot manuscripts, on the other hand, combine the material quite often in different orders, sometimes overlapping, and so on (Schäfer 1981, vi–viii). It has, therefore, been asked whether one is indeed permitted to see in the different writings "books," "treatises," or defined works of religious literature, or whether one should think of a stream of ongoing tradition reworked more or less by every scribe (Schäfer 1988). This specific characteristic of the manuscript tradition has led the editor of the texts to a synoptic printing of the evidence instead of establishing a "critical text" as we are accustomed to do for other "books." P. Schäfer describes the situation as a "fluctuation" of traditions. Yet even in this open fluctuation certain macro-structures recur (Gruenwald 1988, 175–89). The so-called *3 Enoch* and some parts of the *Sar Torah,* for example, are not only scattered paragraphs put together by modern editors. Great portions of text recur in various manuscripts. Accordingly, some of the older "treatises" have been edited and studied despite Schäfer's assumptions (M. S. Cohen, R. Elior 1982, M. D. Swartz 1992). Nevertheless, the fact that later copyists redacted the material time and again allows for certain doubts concerning even the actual wording of the texts (though at this point most of the later scribes are more bound to their traditions). Indeed, in a more recent publication Schäfer himself comes back to the study of the older "treatises" as macro-forms of the Hekhalot traditions (Schäfer 1992).

Given the fact that the manuscripts themselves are products of the medieval period, such a fluctuation has significant consequences for the dating of the whole tradition. The difficulties created by the nature of the manuscript tradition have not always been known to modern scholars. Yet throughout the history of modern scholarship in Judaism the Hekhalot texts received quite opposing dates.

The different opinions are very often constructed on just the same grounds: If apocalypticism was prominent in the period before the destruction of the Second Temple and seems to be almost totally absent from the early rabbinic documents, one may theorize that the Hekhalot must be relatively late, since eschatological ideas would have been of broader concern again only in late talmudic and posttalmudic times. The older consensus, therefore, was a date from the eighth century on (recently reaffirmed in part by some, for example, Halperin 1988). On the other hand, however, such a late date would not necessarily coincide with the development of other mystic texts and would not allow for a more intense link between apocalypticism and the Hekhalot (Scholem, followed by Gruenwald and others).

In such a case the Hekhalot texts would belong to a kind of Judaism alongside the official mishnaic and talmudic academies. This does not necessarily imply that the rabbis were not aware of or might even have been removed from such activities. The distinction of Merkavah speculations from other rabbinic teaching may not necessarily lie in the social group engaged in these but much more in the character of the documents that have been deemed worthy to be transmitted throughout the centuries in a more or less defined form, as the Mishnah, the Tosefta, and the two Talmuds. Here mystical activity as expressed in the Hekhalot writings is sometimes restricted (*Mishnah Ḥagiga* 2:1) or mentioned in passing only. There are, however, some texts that evince some kind of mystical conduct even by such well known rabbis as R. Yoḥanan ben Zakkai and his disciples. On the basis of these texts Scholem stated that Merkavah mysticism had a place in orthodox rabbinic circles. He was criticized for this thesis (E. Urbach), yet other scholars have been more positive toward the assumption that even within "orthodox" rabbinical academies the issues of the Merkavah and the Hekhalot were not neglected (e.g., I. Chernus, M. Fishbane, D. J. Halperin 1980). Read closely, even Urbach would allow for an amoraic date of the Hekhalot, yet he would like to distinguish this literature from such stories as the ones related to R. Yoḥanan ben Zakkai and his circle. The discussion of this point is still going on. Some kind of Merkavah activity seems to have been known already quite early in the rabbinic period. Just the precise nature of that activity remains shrouded in mystery. It seems, therefore, advisable not to deal with the dates of the Hekhalot manuscripts alone but with the age of the mystical experience as such.

If the connection of R. Yoḥanan ben Zakkai, R. Akiba, and R. Yishma'el to this activity is to be taken seriously (and at least partly it should), then one has to acknowledge that the Hekhalot kind of mysticism started in the Land of Israel and was carried over from there to the Babylonian Diaspora. Those who distinguish between Babylonian and Palestinian Hebrew have mostly characterized the style of a good amount of Hekhalot texts as Palestinian (e.g., Cohen 1985, 7). One has to bear in mind the words of L. Blau, who observed that though magical practices have been performed in both Jewish communities, Babylonian and the Palestinian, normally only the Babylonian texts preserved these traditions (Blau 1898, 23, 26–27). In other words, the attestation in the Babylonian Talmud has only limited significance for the question of geographical origins. Most of the persons named in the Hekhalot texts are to be identified as Palestinian rabbis. This might be no more than a pseudepigraphic attribution to the early generations of generally accepted rabbinic authorities; however, it might bear some witness to the real sources of the early mystic traditions. Are we allowed to deny these attributions any credibility whatsoever?

One other issue of central importance, however, must be discussed briefly before the actual comparison between the two kinds of literature may be undertaken: I. Chernus, among others, lamented the lack of a precise definition of what Merkavah mysticism is. He assumed that "a broad range of experiences, all related to ecstaticism and the realm of the divine 'upper world'" is denoted by that term. Yet it was mainly Scholem who stressed time and again that the main purpose of the Hekhalot writings lies in the ascent of the mystic to see God in his glory. That ascent is quite often called "descent." Schäfer, on the other hand, has minimized this aspect and stated contrarily that the reader of these documents will find only random notions of the ascent/descent story and will confront instead a sheer amount of magical adjurations, prayers, and the like not only in order to descend safely and to ascend again, but much more so for the sake of revelations of the hidden truth of Torah. Magical formulas and endless descriptions of the heavenly liturgies and hierarchies fill much of the manuscripts, which are mostly quite unsystematic. Schäfer modified this sharp statement later on; yet there remains a basic controversy about the main purpose of this literature and the means and instruments to reach it (cf. Deutsch 1995, 21–28). This, besides, is the main reason why we have referred to the Hekhalot literature as "what is commonly called early Jewish mysticism."

The dichotomy between mysticism and magic includes two terms that are only vaguely defined. It seems that at least the definition of "magic" depends on the religio-cultural framework for which and within which it is defined. A similar limitation might be true for "mysticism." Not every communication between the divine and human beings can be classified as "mystical." Revelation, including revelation of the details of the heavenly world, is a basic ingredient of religious thought (*pace* any *theologia negativa*). It even seems to be an understatement if the core of mysticism is defined only as visions "in which the soul of the mystic sees itself as being transported to heavenly realms, receives information there, and thereafter returns to the body" (Gruenwald 1988, 134, though this author has stressed the human initiative in other places). What might be labeled "mystical," however, has its starting point in human initiative. The mystic's arrival before the throne of glory or the gaining of heavenly secrets becomes a mystical experience not so much in itself but by the qualification of the initiator. Yet it is mainly the Jewish-Christian tradition that has rejected any human attempt to force the deity to any kinds of deeds as "magic" (Swartz 1996). The same mystic that transcends the borders set by the divinity imposes on God the will of the human. The more or less conscious knowledge of this transgression might explain the repeated affirmations in the Hekhalot literature that God really longs for the mystic to arrive before his throne. The "descent" to the divine chariot is full of dangers, caused especially by the angelic beings who guard, as it were, the divine realm against possible human conquest. In other words, the descending mystic is well aware of the fact that he transgresses natural borders and by doing so imposes his own wish on God. Accordingly, the mystic will feel some need for protective devices such as, for example, seals, names, and so on. Within the Jewish and Christian tradition magic and mystic are, therefore, firmly tied together. Another associated item in this discussion is the real aim of the ascent/descent, which as such might be related to some of the topics singled out by Schäfer. We will have to come back to this issue later.

Yet once the step toward imposing one's will on the deity is taken, there are no real reasons not to use otherwise known magical formulas. What is of utmost importance here is the fact that the descenders to the Merkavah are consciously undertaking that journey—or else are dreaming that such a journey is possible, has been undertaken in the past, and might well be within the realm of today's possibilities, granted only that the right devices will be at hand.

One possible misunderstanding of the following discussion should be prevented at the outset: there is scarcely any direct historical link between the two literatures involved. The problems of dating the Hekhalot traditions have been addressed in the previous paragraphs. The apocalyptic literature relevant for the following comparison is surely much older. It dates from the end of the third century B.C.E. to the middle of the second century C.E. The later Hekhalot traditions use some traditional elements that originated in apocalypticism. One might therefore look for some ongoing traditions. Yet it must be stressed that a direct development from one part of the literature involved to the other is not apparent directly from the texts. We have the apocalyptic beginning and the "mystical" end; we lack the evidence for the transitional stages. To stress a religious continuity in this case does not imply, therefore, a direct historical link (though such a possibility cannot be ruled out either). As with some of the mythological rewritings of biblical material in the apocalypses themselves, one often faces the problem that much earlier strata of religious literature reappear much later. In part this fact is to be explained by the nature of our sources: as much as the biblical writings have been edited by later theological schools, allowing only certain myths of old to be transmitted, the rabbinic writings too have been censured first from within and reflect, therefore, only what certain groups wanted to transmit. The apocalypses as well as the mystical literature or magical recipes and spells have not been part of that "official" literature. As indicated above, however, the stream of apocalyptic thought had not really stopped. It is hard to imagine that later authors of apocalypses during the early medieval period should have reinvented the genre as well as the worldview of people who lived centuries earlier. Yet every such comparison is in a sense highly speculative and cannot really be "proved." The older apocalyptic literature will, therefore, be surveyed for what roads it could have opened up for later generations.

ASCENT STORIES

The ascent stories of the apocalypses are the most outstanding phenomenon that has to be discussed in search of the emerging Hekhalot mysticism. These stories, however, are themselves a new phenomenon in the Jewish religious tradition. It has been argued that they are not so much a unique Jewish development but rather reflect a more widespread interest of the Hellenistic period. This claim is indeed easily verified. Yet at the same time the Jewish ascent stories have some distinctive features mostly because of their relation to scripture.

During the period of the Second Temple there is still no generally acknowledged canon of binding scriptures (Collins 1997, 3–21). For this reason new writings are plausible; they may, *inter alia,* narrate new revelations. Yet many authors have a still undefined sense of the growth of such an assembly of authoritative writings. Therefore, later authors will not simply relate new revelations. They are in part restricted by older traditions, which might be rewritten or otherwise reused. However, there is still something new to be told. The ambivalence lies precisely in the fact that the new revelations are at least partly interpretations and yet aim to be original and authentic. In some extreme cases the new knowledge lies in the revealed meaning of the older prophecies (Dan. 9:2, 21; *2 Baruch* 4:3–4; *Jubilees* 1:26; cf. 6:22 and passim; 1QpHab 7:5). The attitude toward prophecy and other comparable ways of knowing about the divine has changed: during the transitional stage of the Second Temple period, writing is still conceived of as addition to or even replacement of older traditions with just the same authority. This is done, however, by exploring already existing traditions.

The biblical prophet may have seen God enthroned in heaven like Micaiah ben Imlah (1 Kgs. 22:19) and may have thus listened to the heavenly council (e.g., Jer. 23:18; but see Job 15:8). Yet he never really left the earth in order to take part in that council. This is surely so in Ezekiel 1 and most probably also in Isaiah 6. Even the famous revelation of God on Mount Sinai has Moses climbing the rock and entering "the cloud where God was" (Exod. 20:21; 24:18). During the Sinai revelation the cloud is a most prominent device to circumscribe God's presence. This motif will recur in the texts to be discussed below.

These three texts, Exodus 20–24, Isaiah 6, and Ezekiel 1, will provide most of the motifs for apocalyptic ascent stories—at least in the beginning of that tradition. However, there is more to the fact, that precisely these biblical references will serve as basic texts of reference. Moses enters the cloud in order to gain Torah (and the later tradition will identify the revelation on Mount Sinai as the law giving *par excellence*). Isaiah actually does see God in the Temple and the "Seraphim" attend him, singing their thrice-holy. It is important to note already here that Isaiah feels himself to be at a place where a normal human being should not stand. One of the Seraphim, therefore, has to purify the prophet's lips. Ezekiel describes a theophany and adds the divine chariot and the "living creatures," who are later identified with the cherubim (1:5; 10:22–23). They will sing their song to glorify God in turn. The two visions just mentioned combine the river (Ezekiel 1), and the Temple (Isaiah 6) as scenarios. However, none of these texts needs to transfer the prophet into heaven. They all represent the basic distinction made in Ps. 115:16: "Heaven is the heaven of the Lord, but the earth he has given to the children of men." This limitation is transcended with the apocalyptic ascent stories.

1 Enoch 14–36 seems to be the oldest example for the new approach. The text is part of the Book of the Watchers (*1 Enoch* 1–36). Fragments of this part have been identified among the Qumran writings. The earliest of these fragments has been dated in the first half of the second century B.C.E., which means that the work as such seems to be at least some decades older (see Collins 1984, 36–46). A comparison of this early text with one of the latest additions to *1 Enoch,* the Similitudes (*1 Enoch* 37–71), is quite telling and will allow us to link the other ascent stories into a frame established by these two texts.

Astonishingly enough, *1 Enoch* 14–16 already includes some protomystical qualities—"mysticism in a nutshell," so to speak. Yet before the actual ascension "Enoch" is compelled to state:

> I saw in my sleep what I now speak with my tongue of flesh and the breath of the mouth which the Great One has given to man (so that) he may speak with it—and (so that) he may have understanding with his heart as he (the Great One) has created and given it to man. Accordingly he has created me and given me the word of understanding so that I may reprimand the Watchers, the children of heaven. (*1 Enoch* 14:2–3)

In clear contrast to the biblical prophets, this author is struggling with a central problem of mystic-ecstatic experience—namely, language. The normal vehicle of human conversation is unable to express the real experience adequately. He might speak with a "tongue of flesh and the breath of mouth"; however, this seems to be inadequate to communicate the vision and his feelings during the ascent.

The dilemma of the adequacy of language to describe the contents of a mystical encounter will be one of the most powerful impulses for centuries thereafter. Not only the elaborate style of the Hekhalot literature but also *Sefer Yezira* (*The Book of Creation*) and *Sefer HaBahir* (*The Book of the Light*) will put this issue into the center of their discourse. To be more precise, the problem of adequate language is not to be seen as a mere motif of revelatory literature. On the contrary, it lies at the core of the human meeting with the divine. The description of that confrontation with the source of holiness needs a language different from that of daily parlance. *1 Enoch* does not elaborate this subject, but the author feels the difference in quality. What one reads here is an account of a very personal experience.

The author of the introductory passage just quoted aims nevertheless at disclosing his encounter with the divine. His solution is as simple as it is revolutionary: God has given to humanity not only the breath of the mouth but he has created a heart for human understanding: "Accordingly he has created me and given me the word of understanding." It is not entirely clear how far *1 Enoch* is really willing to go with this statement. In other words, one feels a certain consciousness regarding the actual difficulty. The uneasiness felt by the author still does not force him to elaborate on it in a broader discourse.

After this opening statement by the apocalyptic visionary, it should be clear that the text aims at more than a repetition of prophetic call narratives. Yet these are in the background and serve as the basic model for the ascent, that is, the meeting of the prophet (Enoch) with God. The text uses these older models. In contrast to the prophetic call narratives, however, Enoch ascends primarily in order to hear the divine decision about the watchers, that is, the "fallen angels," and their offspring (see chapter 4 above). The revelatory meeting between God and the prophet does not so much serve to legitimate the human partner (although that aspect is included) as to announce judgment.

Yet this judgment is not really comparable to the announcements of the ancient prophets. Here the punishment of angels is proclaimed. The event has cosmic dimensions and transcends the human sphere. Not only the "wicked" and "evildoers" will stand in court, but the heavenly council is divided and some of its members will be called to God's forum. It belongs to the specific features of some apocalypses that this-worldly evil is understood to be caused by heavenly powers and not only by human agents. One might argue that this development necessitated the transfer of the judgment scene to heaven.

Be that as it may be, the situation described in *1 Enoch* connects Enoch's ascent with the three biblical revelations mentioned above: Enoch sits at the riverside (as did Ezekiel), at the foot of Mount Hermon (which recalls Mount Sinai), and he will ascend into a heavenly building that must be understood as a temple (hinting at Isaiah 6). The use of these specific biblical background texts is evidenced also by other elements. Enoch is invited to enter by the clouds and the fog (the double terminology reflects the two Hebrew terms used for Moses' ascent in Exodus). The whole terminology of lightning and so on employed by the author reflects the Sinai revelation as well as that of Isaiah 6.

Of even greater importance is the description of the heavenly house—more precisely, the two houses that Enoch approaches. The first one is built of hailstones and surrounded by tongues of fire. These two elements will be repeated throughout the description of this heavenly building. Their combination indicates either that the dividing part between heaven and earth was conceived of as a mixture of ice, snow, and the like with the heat of fire (cf. the midrashic material discussed by Fishbane) or else that in heaven elements might exist in proximity that in earthly experience would destroy one another. It is clearly at this point that the author comes back to his struggle with language for the appropriate description. The second house cannot be described (14:16). Even the repeated expressions of the visionary's fear, horror, and trembling point to more than a rewritten prophetic call narrative or a literary repetition of the well-known motif of fear caused by an epiphany. Combined with the other elements just discussed, this is language of emotion.

Actually, Enoch does not even enter this second house: he is called and brought to the gate (14:25). A most striking parallel to later Hekhalot traditions (mainly of *Hekhalot Rabbati*) is the statement that "no angel was able to enter this house, or to look at his face, by reason of its splendor and glory; and no flesh was able to look on him" (14:21; see Schäfer 1992). This statement notwithstanding, the second house is filled with ten million angels.

Yet the house in heaven still needs further explanation. Interpreters of *1 Enoch* are quite unanimous in assuming that this house is a heavenly temple constructed literally according to the basic structure of the earthly one in Jerusalem. Therefore, God's throne is located there in the inner house, and the Cherubim mentioned in both houses are a relic of that Jerusalem Temple (where they have been depicted). Of particular interest is the fact that the author of *1 Enoch* singles out the wheels for special mention. (These will become a kind of angelic group in later traditions.) The concept of a heavenly temple would not be too astonishing in the ancient world; however, this revelation is intentionally affiliated with Isaiah 6 and Ezekiel 1. God is seen as seated upon his throne within his temple and the heavenly creatures surround him.

The intercultural references between the apocalyptic author and his prophetic predecessors might go a decisive step further. Isaiah already included severe strictures against the people's approach to the cult. Ezekiel was even more dramatic by relating a series of visions concerning Israel's idol worship (mainly chapter 8). It is not the Temple as such that is attacked here but the priests and parts of the nation.

It has been argued convincingly that the story of the "fallen angels" implies a critique of the Jerusalem priesthood in a remythologized cryptography. Together with the priestly interests behind some of the apocalyptic descriptions, one cannot rule out the impression that the heavenly temple of *1 Enoch* 14–16 serves in itself as a counterpoint to the traditional one in Jerusalem (Suter 1979; Gruenwald 1988, 125–44). Indeed, M. Himmelfarb has argued recently that the conception of heaven as a temple is fundamental for the understanding of the ascent stories. One may be justified, then, in inferring that the real meeting point with God is no longer in that earthly house but in heaven. Yet the alternative to the Temple of Jerusalem is still another house where God is enthroned as he was depicted formerly in the traditional Temple. In other words, there are good reasons to suspect that the text just discussed includes a serious amount of social and cultic critique—maintaining, however, the basic concept of God enthroned in a house with at least two chambers, surrounded mostly by the cherubim and other multitudes of angels. This so-called conservative attitude is nearly self-explanatory. The form of Jewish religion at this point of time is still temple-oriented. Even in the case of harsh critique, the basic structure of the religion as such is still unchanged. The alternative to the Temple of Jerusalem is still a temple (for a different view, see Isaiah 66).

When compared to the later Hekhalot texts, the first ascension of Enoch contains some striking parallels. Yet there are some important differences too. The most outstanding one is Enoch's relative passivity: he saw in his sleep what he will later recount. Clouds and fog are calling him, and the course of the stars and other things hastened him and drove him up into heaven (14:8). The seer is not actually contriving the vision to follow; it is bestowed upon him. Later apocalyptic texts will know about fasting and other means of preparation for an angelic revelation. These techniques are still not used for the aim of a heavenly ascent. Even so the vision or angelic revelation is understood as something granted or even imposed upon the seer. It does not yet appear as the natural outcome of some devices that automatically cause a heavenly ascent or an angelic revelation. On the other hand, visions like that of Enoch are not really raptures (however, see Himmelfarb): the clouds call Enoch—invite him, so to speak—and he follows that option.

Another difference is the inner structure of the angelic world. In the Book of the Watchers, the cherubim and the Watchers are mentioned alongside ten thousand times ten thousand angels. We are told only once about a special group of seven archangels. The motif of that distinguished group of seven is already known from other, nonapocalyptic works (Tobit). The distance of the angels from God is quite similar to that mentioned in some Hekhalot texts (Schäfer 1992) and distinct from the Moses narratives as contained in the rabbinic literature. Yet there is still no real attempt to systematize the heavenly hierarchy. These angels, who cannot come close to God, are indeed a silent "chorus": No heavenly song is reported here. Both elements, the inner order of the celestial world and the angelic liturgy, will become central to the Hekhalot texts.

Assuming some kind of development from texts such as *1 Enoch* 14 to the

Hekhalot tradition, three religio-historical problems pose themselves before the modern reader:

1. After the destruction of the earthly Temple, the later descriptions of the ascent to heaven will no longer be bound to the architectural—and theological—structure of that model. Hence, the two-chamber system might give room to other symbolic structures such as a sevenfold construction. Still, the later literature will keep the term *hekhalot*, which in Biblical Hebrew was used for either a royal palace or God's temple. Insofar as the older Temple symbolism will be given up, this terminology is meaningful only if God is understood to reign as a king as in *Hekhalot Rabbati* and elsewhere in that literature (Schäfer 1992).

2. It is open to discussion to what degree social and religious critique characterizes the later Hekhalot writings (Halperin argued in that direction [1988]). One cannot rule out the possibility that other elements will replace this critical stratum. One point must be made, however: The apocalyptic ascent stories owe quite a lot of their elements to priestly interests.

3. Inasmuch as Temple sacrifices no longer define Jewish religion, the rabbinic tradition offers two alternatives: the liturgy and the study of God's law, the Torah. Both are to be expected as substitutes for sacrifice, or even as reward for the visit to the heavenly temple. They are, therefore, the two sides of the same basic development that has turned Jewish religion from a temple cult into a different form of spirituality (see Elior 1997).

At this stage, however, we should come back to the story of *1 Enoch*. In total contradistinction to the biblical revelation stories alluded to previously, Enoch's ascent does not end with the reception of the divine message. From chapter 17 on, he is on a heavenly journey. The text says quite laconically "and they lifted me up (and brought me)." It is not clear who has lifted Enoch; one might suggest angels (as compared with *2 Enoch*) or winds (as later on in *1 Enoch*). Enoch arrives at a high mountain and oversees the whole of creation—including heavenly places of light, fire, and so forth. In his journey he is granted a sight of the future place of punishment for the "fallen angels," who are now identified with the stars (chapters 18 and 21), the rooms for the souls of the dead, the tree of life, sand so on.

The single elements that Enoch is granted to see fall into different categories. They reflect in part what the modern mind takes as natural phenomena, including the stars and other astrological items: the place of the great fire in the east, the darkness in the west, the chambers of the winds, lightning, and thunder. These "revelations" not only answer questions of cosmological interest. In doing so they revolutionize the biblical worldview according to which such heavenly wisdom is out of human reach (Job 38). Yet the comparison of these revelations with God's famous answer from the whirlwind has more to tell about the nature of some apocalypses and the goals of their authors. The righteous Job suffered unjustly—according to his understanding. He accused God and demanded his response. God, however, denied any obligation to justify himself before human beings. The series of God's questions, "Where were you when I created X?" is, of course, rhetorical and stresses Job's inability to understand God's thought and his way in history. Whosoever claims to know the answer to God's questions either has the right to raise Job's demand anew or even understands the ways of God's justice (Gruenwald 1980). In other words, the author of the Book of the Watchers is not interested simply in nature as such; he *knows* what Job could not have claimed to understand. This knowledge has, therefore, a new quality as compared to the biblical worldview.

The other elements are directly connected to these phenomena of nature; mythical and eschatological items are seen as heavenly places. The two elements are blended into one on several occasions. The place of future punishment for the fallen angels is a mythological place that awaits a certain event in the last days.

Of special interest in this heavenly journey is the fact that the names of the seven most important angels and the scope of their responsibility are revealed. The list appears in several versions (six or seven angels—the names are not always identical). However, the fact that the heavenly world includes the respective fields of angelic authorities as parts of the cosmological description is of utmost importance for the later Hekhalot traditions. Here sometimes endless lists of angelic names are provided in order to describe the heavenly hierarchy.

Enoch's journey is a "guided tour." The angels Uriel, Raguel, and Michael are mentioned, each at various times, as the one "who was with me." They answer Enoch's questions and thereby explain the different places and items for the readers. The phenomenon of an interpreting angel is known from scripture (mainly Zechariah). Yet these angels are friendly companions. Such an idyllic picture contradicts the hostile angels of both the rabbinic midrash concerning the ascent of Moses and the Hekhalot traditions regarding the numerous dangers that await the mystic during his ascent—although in both traditions the hostile angels become friendly once they recognize the adept as worthy.

The journey, then, serves to answer urgent problems of theodicy (as does the first part of the ascent story). The cosmological secrets revealed to Enoch have granted him an understanding of God's justice and a hope for the future of the righteous. The actual ascent was still modeled on the prophetic call narratives (including for our purpose the ascent of Moses on Mount Sinai). The journey is without a biblical antecedent. Here, more than in the previous ascent, the attitude toward the world has basically changed. Already in the first ascent (chapters 14–16) heaven had become an additional option for escape, so to speak, from this-worldly reality. This part of the story already offered more than a reformulation of older meetings between the seer and the divine, though such an encounter must have undergone a most serious change, once God could no longer be supposed to dwell in an earthly temple (cf. Isaiah 66), at least not in the actually existing one.

The following journey adds the seer's hope for a happier and more just future that lies in heaven as a place. The heavenly secrets as such—differing as they do from any biblical conception of human knowledge—are only part of the answer. It is not only the end of days but also heaven as the place where God's justice will again govern the events. Heaven understood in this way is not only a storehouse of secret knowledge but much more the intact alternative to a wicked reality. It can hardly be underestimated that from now on ascent to heaven with all its mystic and proto-mystic qualities is at the same time the occasion of a most exciting personal encounter with the divine *and* an escape from reality. Such a worldview points to the historical conditions of its authors. Yet, in order to understand their religious heritage within a given world, they inaugurated a new dimension in Jewish religion. After the destruction of the last Jewish Temple in 70 C.E., this hope penetrated into Jewish piety at quite distinct points. A discussion of the later Hekhalot literature must keep in mind this manifold function of the ascent in its connection to the heavenly journey.

Summary

The ascent includes a very emotional religious experience, legitimates the adept through direct contact with God (or his angels), reveals heavenly secrets that carry a soteriological hope and allows for an alternative to the reality of this world. Since Scholem has chosen to link Hekhalot traditions about ascent and heavenly wisdom (and their apocalyptic forerunners as he saw them) to the term "Gnostic" it should be stressed here that the knowledge offered by the Gnostics is of a different nature (see Gruenwald 1988, 65–123). Without going into the details of the latter one may generally say that Gnostic knowledge is itself part of the act of salvation. This aspect is not really characteristic of the heavenly secrets seen by and explained to the ascending visionary.

⌒THE SIMILITUDES OF ENOCH _____

Another unit of *1 Enoch* commonly treated as of much later date (see Collins 1984, 142–54) alludes to the first sections just discussed. In the Similitudes, *1 Enoch* 37–71, Enoch's ascent is already taken as a known fact (Himmelfarb). *1 Enoch* 39:3 may, therefore, summarize the whole ascent by the single statement: "In those days whirlwinds carried me off from the earth and set me down into the ultimate ends of the heaven." The heavenly places shown to Enoch this time are mostly comparable to those of the older portions of *1 Enoch;* however, the heavenly temple plays only a minor role. Again, four special angels are singled out by name out of "a hundred thousand times a hundred thousand, ten million times ten million, an innumerable and uncountable (multitude)" (40:1).

On the basis of the earlier journey, the Similitudes add at least three points that are important for the later mystical traditions: the place of wisdom, the angelic song, and the transformation of the righteous.

The actual need for an ascent in order to receive divine knowledge presupposes that the relevant knowledge is to be found in heaven. In line with this idea, the author of the Similitudes adds an enigmatic chapter about wisdom and iniquity (chapter 42). The text is not directly connected with the surrounding chapters, which list several revealed items. Neither does it fit into the lists of things described there. The relevant passage reads:

> Wisdom could not find a place in which she could dwell;
> but a place was found (for her) in the heavens.
> Then Wisdom went out to dwell with the children of men,
> but she found no dwelling place.
> (So) Wisdom returned to her place and settled permanently among
>   the angels. (42:1–2)

The next verse tells how iniquity was well accepted and dwelt with humanity.

The text takes wisdom as a hypostasis, as it was understood elsewhere in biblical and noncanonical literature (see Prov. 8:22–31). For an apocalyptic author there is nothing unexpected in the fact that such wisdom cannot be found on earth. On the contrary, this is just the basic attitude presupposed by those who long for heavenly wisdom and accordingly ascend to heaven.

Yet, for the later development and especially for the problematic combination of ascent, revelation of Torah, and the angels, it is necessary to consider Sirach 24 also. The latter—by no means an apocalyptic visionary—embedded in his moral teachings a song of praise sung by wisdom herself. Generally he follows certain conventions. His text includes, however, innovations as compared to older material. Since Sirach's lifetime is quite close to the Book of the Watchers, these changes are all the more illuminating. For Sirach too wisdom is part of the heavenly council: "In the assembly of the Most High she opens her mouth, in the presence of his host she declares her worth" (24:2). The language involved points much more strongly to the descriptions of the heavenly council as known from several biblical passages. Again, as in *1 Enoch* 42, she looks for a dwelling place:

> Then the Fashioner of all gave me his command,
> and he who had made me chose the spot for my tent,
> Saying, "In Jacob make your dwelling, in Israel your inheritance." (24:8)

It is a well-known fact that this wisdom according to the same song in Sirach 24 is identified with Israel's Torah:

> All this is true of the book of the Most High's covenant,
> the law which Moses enjoined on us
> as a heritage for the community of Jacob. (24:23)

The first line is an allusion to Exod. 24:7, whereas the two following ones quote Deut. 33:4.

The two texts dealing with God's wisdom as a hypostasis of the creator, looking for a dwelling place have two strictly opposed answers to that request. One will hardly find another couple of texts that might emphasize the contrasting worldviews in a more transparent way. The author of the *Similitudes* is unable to find divine wisdom in this world. The teacher Sirach identifies wisdom with the traditional law. We have no idea of whether and how these texts are interrelated, or whether one reacts to the other or not. Yet it seems likely that both were nourished from a more widespread myth: both understand Wisdom as heavenly hypostasis, part of the divine council. Both describe Wisdom's search for a dwelling place on earth. The final answer is different. The contradiction reflects the general attitudes of the respective authors to life in this world. If so, we might be justified in assuming that the last part of Sirach's text, that is, the identification of Wisdom with Torah, was also widespread. It is attested in Philo as well as in the rabbinic writings. This common aggadic core has allowed for different developments. One is the rabbinic attitude scattered throughout this literature telling the story of how God offered his Torah to different nations; yet only Israel was willing to accept it (and will, therefore, be rewarded). This midrash exists side by side with the other one, which claims the preexistence of Torah based on the identification with wisdom as in Proverbs 8. This Torah could, therefore, be used as the basic plan for creation.

On the other side one might look for divine wisdom in heaven. If that (basically apocalyptic) wisdom is again identified with Torah, the later mystical expectation of learning Torah in order not to forget is fully understood as a reward for the ascent. One of the fundamental dichotomies, rightly pointed out by Schäfer, might be explained this way: Wisdom dwells in heaven; she is Torah. That is what the apocalyptic visionary already longed for. Not in vain is the biblical ascent of Moses already interwoven into the first ascent story in *1 Enoch* 14.

The second development attested to in the Similitudes as compared to the Book of the Watchers regards the hymnic element, which is by now much stronger. Enoch, the angels, and exalted righteous humans are repeatedly reported to bless and praise God—mostly by formulas that are quite close to Jewish liturgical ones that are still used (see Gruenwald 1988, 145–73). Whereas in Daniel 7 and *1 Enoch* 14–16 the multitudes of angels are reported as surrounding God's throne, merely filling the stage, in the Similitudes they fulfill specific tasks. The most outstanding one is praise and song.

Angelic song has a long prehistory already in scripture; however, as a rule one may say that most of the biblical references call the heavenly beings to join the human praise (e.g., Ps. 103:20–22; Tob. 8:15; 11:14). The actual wording of such angelic song is mentioned only in Isa. 6:3 and Ezek. 3:12. Both texts recapitulate theophanies and are not reacting to an extraordinary event in normal human life that caused the praise (e.g., rescue from danger, etc.). The song of the Seraphim in Isaiah 6 appears as celestial routine, and the short praise in Ezekiel 3 comes closer to that than to the psalmist's call to join him in his thanksgiving.

Yet in the Similitudes the praise offered to God is built into the overall structure of that work. This fact alludes to more than the poetic artistry of the author. It fulfills a theological task. The first one to praise God is Enoch (chapter 39). He reacts to the sight of the future place for the righteous and the promise that his place will be among them. This is still personal thanksgiving as in the Psalms. Yet at that point he hears the liturgical praise of the angels. It seems that both are parallel but distinct songs, though for a part they use the same formulas. Next Enoch hears the four angels (Michael, Raphael, Gabriel, and Phanuel) uttering their songs, a song of praise to God, a praise to the Elect One and the elected, a song of supplication for the humans and a song for expelling the demons that accuse the humans before God. This combination will be discussed shortly, but first mention should be made of the other occurrences of song in the Similitudes. All those who dwell on the earth will glorify and bless God when the Elect One will be installed (chapter 48), and angels and humans alike shall bless at the day of judgment (chapter 61). In other words, the first praise is the individual's reverence for future salvation, followed by a routine liturgy of the angels. The second occasion is a totally angelic praise, merging the standard ritual with the praise for the Elect, a messianic figure (Collins 1993, 304–10, 313–17), and the human elect who are saved. The first praise will be that of all the humans at the time of the Elect's installation, whereas angels and humans join in one voice at the day of judgment.

This outline makes the heavenly praise a reaction to the act of salvation alongside the celestial routine. For the author of the Similitudes that event lies mostly in the future. Those who are to be saved and accordingly ascend to heaven will join there the celestial liturgy in unison with the angels. The eschatological expectation of uttering one's praise to the saving God seems still to be implied in the common Jewish liturgy. The *sanctus* follows the benediction for God "who revives the dead." Moreover, it opens according to all the different rites, by calling the human community to join the heavenly praise.

The four angels referred to in *1 Enoch* 40–41 are of special interest for the later mystical developments. Besides the standard liturgy and the eschatological hope, the last two of these angels have to do with practices that otherwise are seen as closely connected with magic. According to this text the supplication for the living humans and the expelling of demons are accomplished by "voices," apparently songs. The next parallel for such an attitude is the magical spell. Once the eschatological middle part is taken out we are left with normal heavenly ritual, supplication, and antidemonic rituals. All these will return in the Hekhalot writings (with scarcely any eschatological outlook). Yet it must be stressed time and again that all these songs (and spells) are to be heard only by those who have ascended to heaven.

The eschatological climax is surely typical for the apocalypses, but what is to be expected once Jewish religion lost its messianic orientation? Indeed, as has already been pointed out, the later rabbis of the Mishnah did their best not to mention the Messiah. At least for a certain period of time, the study of Torah (including not only the biblical text but at least as much so the religious law based on that text) in the main replaced imminent eschatological hopes. Should one wonder, then, that at the side of magical or quasi-magical practices the request for a better learning of that Torah governs a considerable part of the Hekhalot traditions? These contain long hymnic compositions that are supposed to be either an angelic liturgy to be recited by the mystic during the different stages of his ascent, or else an adjuration of those angels that might help to gain a better knowledge of Torah.

The last point at which the Similitudes differ remarkably from the earlier Book of the Watchers is the transformation of the ascending visionary into an angelic being. Only here the heavenly temple is mentioned quite briefly. The mutation of a human into a heavenly being has been discussed quite often in recent years. Yet in relation to the heavenly ascent it has not always been stressed markedly enough that this transformation is not restricted to the ascending person alone.

According to *1 Enoch* 39:4–5; 41:2; 70:3–4, the future dwelling place of the righteous ones is together with the angels. This implies at least a common future if not an identical status. Yet the concluding chapters of the Similitudes have a more radical point to make. Standing before the heavenly house and holding sight of multitudes of angels and of God himself Enoch says: "I fell on my face, my whole body mollified and my spirit transformed. Then I cried with a great voice by the spirit of power, blessing, glorifying and extolling."

This seems to be the first description of a human's transformation into an angelic being in the Jewish tradition (see, however, Zechariah 3). The Ethiopic text is not free of difficulties at this point in the text. Yet the chapter will be understood in the way just indicated, namely, as transformation, by those authors who elaborate this tradition.

Enoch is transformed into a heavenly being so that he may dwell together with the angels. Yet that communion is by no means restricted to the few ancient figures mentioned; it is the common hope for all those righteous ones who will somehow follow in the footsteps of the transformed person. The ascent becomes thereby a model for other righteous ones.

Again, even in the quite extraordinary transfiguration of *1 Enoch* 71 the seer is brought before a heavenly temple. This building is described so much in the same terms as those of chapter 14 as to make us assume that the later author knew the former passage and used it consciously.

The transformation of a human person is, so to speak, the opposite of a mystical ascent. The angel-like righteous one is not supposed to return to earth and to tell his experience there. At this point apocalypticism and mysticism go in divergent directions (yet see Borgen 1993).

THE HEAVENLY ASCENT IN OTHER WRITINGS

The two text units discussed so far have allowed us to observe significant developments. They are by no means the only texts containing these peculiar elements. Other writings contribute even further motifs, though not all of these works are apocalypses in the strict sense of the literary definition. During the process of transmission these ancient Jewish texts underwent some redactional reworking. Nevertheless, the Jewish kernel of the works under consideration is mostly evident. Yet for some of the additional motifs it must be asked to what stage of tradition they really belong. It will appear that some motifs have found their way into the Jewish tradition even if they cannot be attested before the destruction of the Second Temple. A clear indication for the later works will be found in those instances where other Jewish literature attests the same motifs. Yet it is still an open question at what point in history these elements entered into Judaism.

The following writings contain further accounts of heavenly ascents: *Testament of Abraham, Apocalypse of Abraham, Testament of Levi, 3 Baruch, 2 Enoch,* and *Ascension of Isaiah.* At least two of these writings are "testaments"; that is, they belong to a more specific category of last words, which may include a prophetic vision of the future. In *Testament of Abraham* this is coupled with the patriarch's ascent to heaven.

However, this later work does not really fit into the model of heavenly journeys discussed here. Suffice it, therefore, to indicate in passing that according to this document the patriarch ascends while still in his body as he demanded. We meet here an exceptional case, that a human consciously asks for the grace to be brought up to the heavenly realm before his death. This request is granted. Yet the objects seen by Abraham belong to quite distinct categories and deal mostly with the judgment and future life of the individual. There is no angelic song, no heavenly temple, and nothing else that links this journey to the apocalyptic ones.

The basic structure of *2 Enoch* resembles that of a testament: Enoch is taken shortly before his death, and the heavenly ascent serves to provide him with the necessary instructions for his sons. The work is generally dated to the first century C.E. and located in the Diaspora; however, it contains several redactional additions. To complicate the situation even more, the book exists in two versions. Yet what is of interest here is mostly found in both versions. Undoubtedly, the author knew *1 Enoch* and the ascent stories told there.

Yet the whole situation has changed. In his sleep Enoch sees two remarkably huge men with wings. As he wakes up they tell him to prepare his house, since they will take him into heaven. Indeed, these two angels lead Enoch through the seven heavens showing him the different angels in these heavens, calendrical information, and so on. On some occasions the angels of the different heavens are praising and serving God with their songs, but these songs are no longer bound to eschatological events like the day of judgment, the appearance of the Elect, and the like. Enoch's surprise that there is no praise in the fifth heaven makes it obvious that the song belongs to an ongoing, quite static liturgy. In the seventh heaven the two angels leave Enoch, and Gabriel takes the seer before the throne of God. Enoch is transformed into one of the archangels: "And the Lord said to Michael: 'Go and extract Enoch from his earthly clothing. And anoint him with my delightful oil, and put him into the clothes of my glory.' And so Michael did. . . . And I looked at myself and I had become like one of his glorious ones, and there was no observable difference" (*2 Enoch* 22:8–10). He is then appointed heavenly scribe. God reveals to him the secrets of creation that even the angels do not know. He is returned to the earth and given some time to tell his sons what has happened to him. In doing so he enlarges upon the "secrets" revealed to him earlier.

In comparison with the various units included in *1 Enoch, 2 Enoch* demonstrates a series of significant changes in regard to our understanding of early mysticism and its possible apocalyptic backgrounds. The whole journey is clearly structured according to the system of seven heavens. What in *1 Enoch* was recorded as traveling in different directions during the same heavenly journey is now systematized into a model of seven heavens. There is a continuing discussion about the ultimate sources of this concept (Yarbro Collins 1996). However, it seems more than only accidental that the first Jewish text to structure the heavenly journey within such a framework is late and seems to be of Diaspora provenance. In other words, the concept of heaven as temple is not as important here as it used to be for those who longed for an alternative to the existing cult.

There are some hints at the importance of ongoing sacrifices. Yet if heaven should be understood in this work as a kind of temple, that concept has been modified considerably. There is not the slightest hint of any critique of an existing temple. The transformation of Enoch is told in clear combination with the older experience of Joshua the high priest (Zechariah 3) and the anointing of priests, thereby indicating some priestly connection. But this holds true only for the person of Enoch, not for heaven as a temple, since the structure of seven does not match any forms of architecture of the earthly building. The exaltation of the hero has no exemplary meaning for other righteous ones in the future.

Enoch feels the impossibility of describing God's face, yet he does see him and stands before his throne. The repeated short rhetorical question, Who am I to describe? (chap. 22), seems to be a literary device. In contrast to *1 Enoch* 14, the author of *2 Enoch* has no real problem of language. Later on "Enoch" will even be seated at the side of God. The exaltation to a rank higher than that of the angels as well as the seating at God's side have their parallels and considerable development in Enoch's/Metatron's transformation and enthronement as depicted in *3 Enoch* (*Sēper Hēkālôt*).

Another obscure text reporting a journey through seven heavens is *Testament of Levi* 2–6, but this text is very inconsistent in itself. To complicate the situation, the contents of several heavens are described differently in the manuscript tradition. The commentators mostly agree that the text as it now stands is the product of a later redactor who has combined several traditions in order to arrive at a system of seven heavens. In the form known to us the text is Christian and belongs to the second century. Scholars disagree about whether this is the original work or a Christian rewriting of an earlier Jewish text. It is difficult to tell to what level of textual growth the seven heavens belong.

The author associates the vision with the patriarch's dream during which an angel called Levi to enter the suddenly opened heaven. From there he proceeds to another one. Levi is said to arrive at a third heaven, where God sits upon his throne. Yet, given the inconsistencies of the text, the patriarch actually never arrives there. The next chapter already interprets the seven heavens that Levi has allegedly seen, but even that exposition is not consistent.

The actual goal of Levi's ascent is open for discussion; however, there is good reason to suppose that the ascent wishes to tie Levi's investment as high priest to a heavenly scene (as described 4:2–6 as well as 5:1–2). It is interesting to note that according to some Hekhalot traditions the real hero of the revelation is R. Yishmaʾel, the high priest.

The *Testament,* then, shows different levels of redaction, and we cannot define ultimately which of the distinct elements belongs to what stratum. It seems very likely that an original three-heaven conception was enlarged into a seven-heaven one. We have no idea of the date of that development. It should be noted, however, that in the second investment account Levi does see God in a holy temple sitting on the throne of glory (5:1).

The difficulties of the redactional growth of this text mirror somehow the situation that has to be emphasized. It is the transitional stage from a temple-oriented religion to another stage that involves at the same time a vision of the heavenly temple and a sevenfold structure for the heavenly journey. It should be stressed here that besides *2 Enoch* no other text that can be dated in the period of the Second Jewish Temple has such a seven-heaven model.

As the tradition about heavenly journeys and especially the seven heavens goes on, it loses the immediate urgency and the emotional impact. A notable example for this later approach is *3 Baruch.* This apocalypse has been transmitted in Greek and in two Slavonic versions. In its present form it has undergone at least a thorough Christian redaction, the traces of which, however, are not as strong in the Slavonic versions. Since the admittedly Christian parts are more prominent in the later chapters, one might justifiably suspect that the concluding part has replaced a more original text. This possibility recommends itself especially in light of the fact that Baruch is said to see God in his glory (7:2; 11:2; also 4:25 and 16:45 Slavonic). Yet he arrives only at the fifth heaven and sees the archangel Michael there but not God himself. (See, however, Harlow, who argues that the extant text is original.)

Already the opening sentences disclose the gap between the earlier emotional language and *3 Baruch's* exclusively literary usage of motifs that have already become conventional within this genre. The seer is lamenting the destruction of the Temple, yet his lament ceases immediately once the angel promises to show the visionary greater secrets. The relatively short passage has to be compared, for example, with the ongoing mournings of Ezra in 4 Ezra. There the hero is disputing with the angel for at least three long discussions about the severe divine judgment. Only slowly does he accept a future reward in return for what appeared to him as divine injustice. In *3 Baruch* all that is dealt with within some few sentences.

The seer sits at the side of the (Kidron) river and ascends from there to the gates of the Holy of Holies. The geography of the opening verse in the Greek is not really consistent. Yet it seems that we are dealing again with a theological map and not necessarily with real places. The angel calls Baruch by an expression otherwise known in its precise form from the angelic revelation in Dan. 10:11. The biblical seer was sitting at the side of the Tigris. Yet Daniel 9 relates another vision, and here the address of the angel Gabriel is quite similar to the later one (Dan. 9:23). This revelation takes place while Daniel is praying on the Temple mount (Dan. 9:20); however, Daniel's prayer of lament is a most emotional piece of religious literature. *3 Baruch* is using all these elements quite technically: Ezekiel, Daniel, and Enoch gained their visions by the side of a river; Isaiah, Daniel, and Enoch had a clear relation to the Temple. All of this is taken up, but briefly and without emphasis. In other words, the heavenly journey has become a topic of religious literature that serves to narrate some kind of revelation. Indeed, the first heavens as described by Baruch are repeating related items. At some point one gets the impression that *3 Baruch* might have known *2 Enoch* (the phoenix, for example, is again mentioned together with the sun, etc.).

The angel promises Baruch a vision of God's glory (see above). However, be it because of later redactional changes or because of the author's inconsistency, Baruch arrives only in the fifth heaven. Here again the author's attitude differs markedly from the older descriptions. A gate marks the border to the sixth heaven, yet that gate is closed. It will be opened only when the archangel Michael appears to collect the prayers of the righteous ones. During the time he delivers these prayers to God and gets some oil as reward for the people, the gate will again be closed. Baruch does not see God.

An important variation regards the liturgy: only the Greek version knows at one place (10:7) about some miraculous birds "who continuously praise the Lord." The author's indifference toward the heavenly liturgy conforms paradoxically with his emphasizing the earthly one. All in all, this text seems to be already far removed from the other ones discussed here.

In many particular aspects the *Ascension of Isaiah* is much closer to the older Enoch traditions. In the known (Ethiopic) version, the work is combined with the *Martyrdom of Isaiah*. Both works are Christian in character, but certain Jewish elements point toward originally Jewish compositions. The combination of the two texts was later interpolated by another Christian redactor.

Chapters 6–11 report the prophet's vision, which takes the form of a journey through the seven heavens, guided by an angel. Already the description of the opening circumstances reminds the reader of a similar situation in the later Hekhalot writings: The prophet sits in the middle of a group of people. He relates his words while all the attendants listen. All of a sudden he becomes silent, since he sees a vision. The other members of the group are helplessly left aside. In the *Ascension of Isaiah* they wait until the prophet is again capable of describing his vision. The most striking parallel to this story is R. Nehunja ben HaKana's sudden silence before the entrance to the sixth heaven (*Synopse*, §§ 225–27). What is of importance here is not the detailed practice of how to call the seer back (this is, indeed, specific for the Hekhalot tradition) but much more the setting of the vision: Isaiah and R. Nehunja are not alone; they sit in the middle of a select group of people.

Like the Jewish mystic, the now christianized Jewish prophet experiences the danger of the ascent just before entering the seventh heaven. A voice comes forth and asks, "How far will he who dwells with strangers ascend?" Yet another voice answers: "May it be allowed for the holy Isaiah to ascend since his garment is here."

Isaiah recounts his vision later. He was taken by an indescribably glorious angel. For the time of the ascent the prophet is granted the ability to speak the angel's language. As the text stands, this means that all the time a human being is in the body he or she will be unable to speak or understand the angelic tongue. The history of this motif is not of real relevance here. The author of the *Ascension* wants to make clear that Isaiah has left his body but will return to it.

Prophet and angel ascend through the firmament and the seven heavens listening to the songs of praise offered in most of the heavens. In the sixth heaven the prophet joins the heavenly chorus, primarily giving thanks for his future lot among the angels. Without real specification, the song is declared to be more glorious in each successive heaven, as is the light that shines brighter from one heaven to the next. What has indeed changed from one heaven to the other is not really signified. As in the Similitudes, angels and righteous ones offer their song of praise before the Messiah. This will be the reaction of those who listen to the prophet's account of his vision.

Isaiah describes a kind of transformation as he and the angel ascend. The closer they come to the seventh heaven the more the prophet becomes like one of the angels. This process starts already in the third heaven and comes to its climax in the seventh. Interestingly, the book knows about the reverse change of the heavenly figure of Jesus, who changes from heaven to heaven until he becomes like a human. The most important device for the change of the prophet lies in the garments, in part also in the crowns awaiting the righteous, who will ascend in the future (after having left their bodies). This detail recalls Zechariah 3 as well as *2 Enoch* 22, mentioned above.

Yet there is another element connected to Isaiah's transformation: after all, his vision is now combined with the story about his martyrdom. Starting with the first Christian martyr, Stephen (*Acts* 6–8), the gradual transformation of the martyr has become a topic in these Christian works. As noted above, transformations are by no means a Christian motif, yet the connection to the martyr's death is more widespread in that literature.

Reviewing the texts discussed in the last paragraphs, one encounters a double trend: the language of emotion and the exegetical link to the Hebrew Scriptures diminishes over time. Naturally, this holds true in varying degrees for each of the documents. However, it seems that this general trend is to be understood in light of the fact that the documents move from Palestinian Judaism through Diaspora settings to texts with increasing Christian reworking. This, of course, does not imply that considerable Christian influence is in itself opposed to explication of scripture, nor do we intend to deny the later redactors any emotion. We would rather like to point to very specific ways of midrashic use of scriptural references and a personal urgency when dealing with the center of one's religious life.

An explanation of what is meant by the foregoing observation might be given through consideration of the last text belonging to this group. The *Apocalypse of Abraham*, generally dated at the second century C.E., is a mostly Jewish text with only minor redactional additions. It combines the story of Abraham's astral observation that ultimately brings him to the recognition of monotheism with a heavenly journey that includes an apocalyptic overview of Jewish history. The first part of the account is already well known from earlier noncanonical sources (e.g., the book of *Jubilees*). The second part draws intensively upon a midrashic interpretation of Genesis 15. The concluding chapters foretell, so to speak, the latest events of Jewish history, mostly the destruction of the Second Temple, allowing for a more optimistic expectation in the future. The middle part is of primary interest here.

Following Abraham's prayer in search of the one true God and creator of all, a heavenly voice warns the patriarch to leave his father's house. Immediately a great thunder burns the house. Then a voice is heard instructing Abraham to prepare certain sacrifices (a quotation of Gen. 15:9) and promising him a revelation of the ages. Since nobody is seen, Abraham trembles and ultimately falls down. The description of his fear is quite dramatic. However, the voice continues, now calling Jaoel "of the same name through the mediation of my ineffable name" (10:4). Jaoel is an angel who will help Abraham rise again and finally ascend. The explanation of his name resembles Exod. 23:21. The same verse is used mostly to explain Metatron's exalted rank in *3 Enoch* and elsewhere in the Hekhalot writings. He is the angel who has to "restrain the threats of the living creatures of the Cherubim against one another." Jaoel's appearance is similar to that of God in Dan. 7:9. Abraham and the angel leave for the mountain of God—that is, Horeb—for forty days without eating and drinking. This is another allusion to scriptures, this time to the forty days Moses spent on the mountain and to the escape of Elijah (1 Kgs. 19:7–8). The midrashic use of scripture goes on: according to Gen. 22:7, Abraham and Isaac reach the mountain of God without an animal for the sacrifice and the son inquires of his father. In the *Apocalypse of Abraham* the patriarch asks the angel.

In short, this text is an ongoing midrash connecting one verse of scripture with another, sometimes by allusion, at other times by partial quotation. This is the aspect of midrashic exploration that had diminished in the other works surveyed before.

The ongoing story of the actual sacrifice, the attending angels, the attacks of Azazel (depicted like the "bird of prey" in Gen. 15:11) and finally the journey to heaven on the wings of the pigeon is filled with other references to Genesis 15. The meeting with God will fit that general framework, since God will appear as a fire in a great sound of sanctification (some manuscripts emended, "saying, holy, holy, holy"). The fire is taken over from Gen. 15:17; however, the text of the apocalypse adds an important detail: "like a voice of many waters, like a voice of the sea in its uproar." This may be an allusion to Ezek. 1:24. What counts more, however, in our discussion is the fact that precisely the image of water is connected with the entrance to the seventh heaven in the Hekhalot writings. The direct link to the later mystical texts is obvious in the ensuing prayer. The angel had instructed Abraham to recite it now, invoking God with formulas that in part have their nearest parallels in magical papyri or in the Hekhalot texts as, for example, "Eli, eternal, mighty one, holy, Sabaoth, most glorious El, El, El, El, Jaoel" (17:10). Many-eyed creatures recite a song, and the four living creatures are singing. The author describes some of the beings more closely; however, without going too much into detail it should be apparent by now that the *Apocalypse of Abraham* offers the reader a blend of midrashic exploration, emotional language, and first traditions about what finally will become Hekhalot mysticism.

The text continues with God's revelation of history referring briefly to the concept of the seven heavens. Yet the author speaks only about the three highest ones (the others are not mentioned and, as it seems, are dispensable). The general account did not aim only at a heavenly journey; neither was it intended to reveal an apocalyptic history. It seems fair to summarize this extraordinary work as a comfort for a shaken nation just after the downfall of the Temple, which was the main means of its religious self-definition. The author attempts to strengthen his fellow Jews by pointing to the real characteristic of Jewish religion as he understood it—that is, Jewish monotheism—the divine election of Israel and a happier (messianic) future. The catastrophe of 70 C.E. is part of the divine plan and comes as a reaction to Israel's sins. By looking for the ideal hero from the past to convey that message, the author has chosen Abraham, who had served as an ideal type of Jewish religion for some centuries. The main text for this midrash, Genesis 15, includes the announcement of Israel's slavery in Egypt and thus fits the general atmosphere in the time of the later author. It is hardly coincidental that the text used besides Genesis 15 was Ezekiel 1, the theophany after the destruction of the first Jewish Temple.

In order to console his fellow Jews, the author has tied Abraham's election to one of those biblical stories that includes a sacrifice and a theophany, yet without a proper temple. Several elements in the text allow for the assumption that the author of the *Apocalypse of Abraham* was aware of the earlier writings like those of the Enoch cycle. The critique against an existing temple was out-of-date now: the Temple no longer existed. Accordingly, Abraham does not ascend to a heavenly building for his meeting with God. Yet the biblical narrative describing a theophany on earth was no longer appropriate either. The author was not interested in a detailed list of the heavens and their contents. He knew about the seven heavens. Yet the actual encounter of the patriarch with God was the main aim to be reported. For that purpose the later author again employed emotional language and interpreted scripture. He incidentally introduced some elements that would become more prominent in the mystical literature.

EARLY JEWISH MYSTICISM

It was stated at the beginning of this chapter that the question of the precise relationship between apocalyptic literature and early Jewish mysticism is in itself highly speculative. As pointed out above, we do have some ancient apocalypses and quite later manuscripts containing instructions of a mystical character; however, we know from later sources that the writing of apocalypses was not totally abandoned during the interval, though neither can it claim a central role. Given the single items we possess, one must decide whether to describe each of these separately or to search for their possible correlation. In our case the texts hint at some vague combining links. Yet how far may we connect the later mystical manuals with the earlier apocalypses?

As we have seen, the writers of apocalyptic works did link their own thoughts to those of their predecessors. Motifs, scriptural references, and the like may, therefore, be found equally in both corpora. Yet they are only a partial proof, since the same biblical sources may have given rise to similar associations at different times. It seems self-evident that the assembly of motifs and so on is not in itself sufficient to establish a clearcut connection.

Moreover, the apocalyptic tendency to criticize reality reaches dangerous levels at times. The fact is well known, and so a short reminder may suffice at this point. Apocalypticism quite often conceives this world as spoiled; in other words, this world is at least under conditions that necessitate an urgent improvement, but humans cannot perform this on their own. Naturally, the literary genre conveying such messages might itself well be reused for less revolutionary ideas. Yet it is worthwhile to pay due attention to the many attacks against the kings and reigning persons, for example, in the Similitudes. The plea of the oppressed may well find a literary expression transcending the limits of the social order. Again, the danger is inherent within the apocalyptic worldview. It depends on each specific author whether or not such language will dominate the work. Yet it must be evident that every religious establishment seeking to keep a community in stable conditions will at least frown upon if not openly reject the possible apocalyptic threat. The whole aspect just touched on needs to be dealt with at some length, but this is not the place to do so. However, the affinity of apocalypticism to social critique at least accounts for a basic difference when compared with rabbinic literature. The latter is part of a religious establishment. Whatever the actual social position of the single rabbi was, he was engaged in keeping that religion and its community in order. In short, there is nothing unexpected in the fact that the rabbis did not transmit the earlier apocalypses. On the contrary! We would have to redefine both apocalypticism and rabbinic literature, if the latter would have allowed for significant apocalyptic topics. Again, apocalypses may deliberately relate to less subversive subjects. Some ideas promoted first by the apocalypses may find their way into the world of the religious establishment. One must resist the simplifying "either-or" description for the reality of historical texts. Nonetheless, the basic distinction has to be made. It offers a partial answer for the lack of evidence for any apocalyptic writings during the classical rabbinic period.

Yet the dichotomy just pointed out must not disqualify any later utilization of apocalypses. The *Apocalypse of Abraham* offers a useful example in this direction. Here the structure of an apocalypse is maintained together with some prominent features of that literature. However, in the new setting the principal aim of that work lies in comfort. In other words, once the apocalypses did exist, they could have been reused for a variety of purposes. They need not react to a social crisis and are not restricted to exercising inner critique. Positively put, apocalypses may be taken as a way of introducing new religious ideas based, as it were, on revelations. At stake are the content, function, and determination of these new ideas.

When it comes to the question of possible connections between the apocalypses and the Hekhalot literature there is more to be accounted for. Historically, the two bodies of literature are separated from one another by an event that can hardly be overestimated: the destruction of the Temple. The historical date marks not only the end of national or even nationalistic desires. It signals, first of all, the end of a religious and, therefore, sociological self-definition. A whole nation lost its center of worship, of contact with the divine and thereby itself. Judaism was in urgent need of a new definition of its religion now without a temple. It seems to be significant that the temple image indeed weakens in the ongoing ascent stories that have been discussed above.

Different ways offered themselves to close the gap. One could try to establish a new self-definition by denying or minimizing the importance of the former center. Another way could have been to proclaim that whatever one is doing now is just a continuation of the former way. There are rabbinic statements that may evince both options in turn, but it was also possible to carry on as if nothing had really changed. This way is the one the mystics seem to have preferred. For reaching this goal they might have been assisted by earlier models. Yet the evidence for such a thesis is not beyond question.

One of the more prominent Qumran texts may illustrate this last part of the discussion. In the famous *Songs of the Sabbath Sacrifice* (Newsom 1985) the fragments of thirteen songs are preserved. The songs, to be recited at the time of the sabbath sacrifice, describe the angelic world and the heavenly temple and liturgy. Historians still discuss whether or not the Qumranites could have attended the Jerusalem Temple service. The songs are understood more easily by assuming that they could not. In that case the Qumranites would have recited the description of the heavenly liturgy instead of joining the earthly one. Indeed, the relation of both liturgies has been discussed in both the rabbinical and the Hekhalot writings. Interestingly enough, the two traditions have some features in common. The point to be made here is mainly the idea that the angels share Israel's worship of praise. Yet the mystical manuals will go much further in their detailed reports of the heavenly songs as well as in their use of liturgical formulas for the purpose of the ascent.

The literary affinities of the known Hekhalot texts to earlier Jewish apocalypses vary considerably in degree. The so-called *3 Enoch* mentions the actual ascent of its hero, R. Yishma'el, only briefly in the opening paragraphs and proceeds to an elaborate description of Enoch's transformation into the angel Metatron, a secondary deity, presiding over the angels. The section is followed by lists of angels and their respective tasks and responsibilities, including details about the heavenly liturgy, cosmological revelations, and so on. In the last part some items of earlier apocalypses are repeated, such as a description of the dwelling places of the dead righteous, a general overview of Israel's history (but without any precise information, in contrast to some of the historical apocalypses), and the spirits of the punished angels. This short outline shows the attempt to keep the framework of an apocalypse. Yet there can be no doubt that the revealed things have been reshaped notably. Moreover, *3 Enoch* is a compilation of older units. At some places the gaps are still felt. Yet it is an open question whether further investigation of these redactional units will promote our understanding. The compiler of the work deemed it meaningful as it stands now.

Of still more composite character is the work generally known under the name *Hekhalot Rabbati*. It contains an elaborate description of the actual ascent as well as a short apocalypse concerning the ten martyrs. In the printed editions, this work ends with the *Sar Torah* section. Other parts of the text deal with heavenly liturgies, the advantages of the ascent, and so on. Other texts will more fully emphasize the adjurations of angels, especially as aids for the study of Torah. We do not propose to discuss these singular items any further in this context, nor do we intend to provide additional surveys of the mystical texts. What must be pointed out here is the conglomerate makeup of these texts.

Because of the conglomerate character of the Hekhalot texts, every attempt at an overall definition of the aims and goals of the later mystics is disqualified as a simplification. Yet one may suggest that attending the heavenly liturgy and keeping sight of God in his beauty are substitutes for the older Temple cult (especially Gruenwald 1988; Elior 1997). The possibility of reaching a high level of learning fast and easily by means of adjurations was also a factor, and this encountered a certain resistance from the rabbinic establishment (see Halperin 1988). Moreover, what we regard as distinct phenomena worked together in the minds of ancient authors.

The apocalypses and the Hekhalot texts are linked by the belief that human visionaries have access to a transcendent reality. This reality was out of reach for the people of biblical times. The door to heaven was opened by the apocalypses. Whether they were directly known to the later mystics or not, the apocalyptic writings are, therefore, the necessary precondition for the Hekhalot type of mysticism.

BIBLIOGRAPHY

Black, M. 1985. *The Book of Enoch or I Enoch.* Studia in Veteris Testamenti Pseudepigrapha 7. Leiden: E. J. Brill. A new English edition with commentary and textual notes. Translation and notes use the Greek, Ethiopic, and Aramaic texts and fragments; in this paper this translation was sometimes preferred.

Blau, L. 1898. *Das altjüdische Zauberwesen.* Budapest: Landes-Rabbinerschule. Jahresbericht für 1897–98. Reprinted several times, this remains a standard work for the field of ancient Jewish magic within the "orthodox" writings.

Borgen, P. 1993. "Heavenly Ascent in Philo: An Examination of Selected Passages." In *The Pseudepigrapha and Early Biblical Interpretation,* edited by J. H. Charlesworth and C. A. Evans, 246–68. Sheffield: Sheffield Academic Press.

Charlesworth, J. H., ed. 1983. *The Old Testament Pseudepigrapha.* Volume 1, *Apocalyptic Literature and Testaments.* Garden City, N.Y.: Doubleday. Basic collection of translations for the apocalyptic texts, as well as for *3 Enoch.*

Chernus, I. 1982. *Mysticism in Rabbinic Judaism: Studies in the History of Midrash.* Studia Judaica 11. Berlin/New York: de Gruyter. Important collection of studies concerning mystical elements in the rabbinic literature.

Cohen, M. S. 1983. *The Shiʿur Qomah: Liturgy and Theurgy in Pre-Kabbalistic Jewish Mysticism.* Washington, D.C.: University Press of America. Includes a translation of this specific text as well as a rich discussion of some basic issues.

———. 1985. *The Shi'ur Qomah: Texts and Recensions.* Texte und Studien zum antiken Judentum. Tübingen: Mohr. Text edition with translation.

Collins, J. J. 1984. *The Apocalyptic Imagination: An Introduction to the Jewish Matrix of Christianity.* New York: Crossroad. Introduction to the Jewish apocalypses.

———. 1993. *Daniel.* A Commentary on the book of Daniel with an essay, "The influence of Daniel on the New Testament," by A. Yarbro Collins. Hermeneia. Minneapolis: Fortress Press.

———. 1997. *Seers, Sybils and Sages in Hellenistic-Roman Judaism.* Leiden/New York/Cologne: E. J. Brill. Collection of essays on apocalypticism and related subjects.

Dean-Otting, M. 1984. *Heavenly Journeys: A Study of the Motif in Hellenistic Jewish Literature.* Judentum und Umwelt 8. Frankfurt am Main/Bern/New York: Lang.

Deutsch, N. 1995. *The Gnostic Imagination: Gnosticism, Mandaeism, and Merkabah Mysticism.* Leiden/New York/Cologne: E. J. Brill. Discusses Scholem's work in light of his later critics.

Elior, R. 1982. *Hekhalot Zutarti.* Jerusalem Studies in Jewish Thought, Suppl. 1. Jerusalem: Magnes. The Hebrew title indicates that this edition is mainly based upon MS New York 8128 (828); it includes a list of different readings as compared to Schäfer's *Synopse,* an introduction, rich notes, etc., which will be available, however, only to readers of Hebrew.

———. 1993–94. "Mysticism, Magic, and Angelology: The Perceptions of Angels in Hekhalot Literature." *Jewish Studies Quarterly* 1:3–53. Beginning of a study completed in the following Hebrew article. Elior argues for an understanding of the mystical traditions as replacing the temple spirituality.

———. 1997. "From Earthly Temple to Heavenly Shrines: Prayer and Sacred Song in the Hekhalot Literature and its Relation to Temple Traditions." *Jewish Studies Quarterly* 4:217–67. Important study for the actual place of the Hekhalot traditions in the spiritual life of the community.

Even Shmu'el, Y. 1954. *Midrashej Ge'ula: Pirkej Ha-apocalypsa ha-yehudit.* Jerusalem/Tel Aviv: Bialik. [= 1968, "Salvation-Midrashim: Jewish Apocalyptic Pieces" (in Hebrew)]. Edition of apocalyptic texts of the amoraic period and later.

Fishbane, M. 1992. "The 'Measures' of God's Glory in the Ancient Midrash." In *Messiah and Christos: Studies in the Jewish Origins of Christianity presented to D. Flusser,* edited by I. Gruenwald, S. Shaked, and G. G. Stroumsa, 53–74. Texte und Studien zum antiken Judentum. Tübingen: Mohr.

Gruenwald, I. 1980. *Apocalyptic and Merkavah Mysticism.* Arbeiten zur Geschichte des antiken Judentums und Urchristentums 14. Leiden/Cologne: E. J. Brill. The basic study for the inner relations of both religious traditions as indicated by the title; includes the appendices by S. Liebermann, "Metatron, the meaning of his name and his function," and "The Knowledge of *Halakha* by the Author (or Authors) of the Heikhaloth."

———. 1988. *From Apocalypticism to Gnosticism: Studies in Apocalypticism, Merkavah Mysticism and Gnosticism.* Beiträge zur Erforschung des Alten Testaments und des Antiken Judentums 14. Frankfurt am Main: Lang. Complementary volume of studies following the aforementioned book, important for the author's answers to his critics; chapter 4 is a shortened version of a study otherwise only available in Hebrew.

Halperin, D. J. 1980. *The Merkabah in Rabbinic Literature.* New Haven: American Oriental Society.

———. 1988. *The Faces of the Chariot: Early Jewish Responses to Ezekiel's Vision.* Texte und Studien zum antiken Judentum 16. Tübingen: Mohr. Overall attempt to connect the Hekhalot texts and the interpretation history of Ezekiel with social questions, etc. Sometimes controversial important work.

Harlow, D. C. 1996. *The Greek Apocalypse of Baruch (3 Baruch) in Hellenistic Judaism and Early Christianity.* Studia in Veteris Testamenti Pseudepigrapha 12. Leiden/New York/Cologne: E. J. Brill. Most recent discussion of this pseudepigraphon.

Himmelfarb, M. 1988. "Heavenly Ascent and the Relationship of the Apocalypses and the *Hekhalot* Literature." *Hebrew Union College Annual* 59:91–96.

———. 1991. "Revelation and Rapture: The Transformation of the Visionary in the Ascent Apocalypses." In *Mysteries and Revelations: Apocalyptic Studies since the Uppsala Colloquium,* edited by J. J. Collins and J. H. Charlesworth, 79–90. Sheffield: Sheffield Academic Press.

———. 1993. *Ascent to Heaven in Jewish and Christian Apocalypses.* New York/Oxford: Oxford University Press. Most important recent study of the ascent stories, partly prepared for by the preceding articles.

Kuyt, A. 1995. *The 'Descent' to the Chariot: Towards a Description of the Terminology, Place, Function and Nature of the Yeridah in Hekhalot Literature.* Texte und Studien zum antiken Judentum 45. Tübingen: Mohr. Highly technical discussion of the "descent" terminology.

Lieberman, S. 1960. "Mishnat Shir Hashirim. In Scholem 1960.

———. 1980a. "Metatron, the meaning of his name and his function." In Gruenwald 1980.

———. 1980b. "The Knowledge of *Halakha* by the Author (or Authors) of the Heikhaloth." In Gruenwald 1980.

Mach, M. 1992. *Entwicklungsstadien des jüdischen Engelglaubens in vorrabbinischer Zeit.* Texte und Studien zum antiken Judentum 34. Tübingen: Mohr. Aims at describing the development of Jewish angelogy from the Hebrew Scriptures through the early second century C.E.; of special interest here, pp. 159–240—the union with angels, be it as transformation, in liturgy, or otherwise.

Neusner, J. 1984. *Messiah in Context: Israel's History and Destiny in Formative Judaism.* Philadelphia: Fortress Press.

Newsom, C. 1985. *Songs of the Sabbath Sacrifice: A Critical Edition.* Harvard Semitic Studies 27. Atlanta: Scholars Press. The edition offers a critical reading of the text, an introduction, translation, and critical notes.

Odeberg, H. 1928. *3 Enoch or the Hebrew Book of Enoch.* Cambridge: Cambridge

University Press. Reprint, New York: Ktav, 1973. Prolegomenon by J. C. Green-field. First edition of this text that comes closest to earlier apocalypses.

Rowland, C. 1982. *The Open Heaven: A Study of Apocalyptic in Judaism and Early Christianity.* London: SPCK. Treatment of apocalypticism with special attention to mystical elements in the apocalypses and in early rabbinic literature.

Schäfer, P. 1988. *Hekhalot-Studien.* Texte und Studien zum antiken Judentum 19. Tübingen: Mohr. Includes mostly German studies and also two very important articles in English: "Tradition and Redaction in Hekhalot Literature" and "The Aim and Purpose of Early Jewish Mysticism."

———. 1992. *The Hidden and Manifest God: Some Major Themes in Early Jewish Mysticism.* Albany: State University of New York Press.

Schäfer, P., ed. 1981. *Synopse zur Hekhalot-Literatur in Zusammenarbeit mit M. Schlüter u. H.G. v. Mutius.* Texte und Studien zum antiken Judentum 2. Tübingen: Mohr. Basic text edition for the Hekhaloth, presenting the seven most important manuscripts in parallel printing; references to Hekhalot mater-ial not otherwise translated are to the section numbers of this edition.

———, ed. 1984. *Geniza-Fragmente zur Hekhalot-Literatur.* Texte und Studien zum antiken Judentum 6. Tübingen: Mohr. Complementary volume to the *Synopse,* including important fragments.

———, ed. 1986–88. *Konkordanz zur Hekhalot-Literatur in Zusammenarbeit mit G. Reeg u.a.* Texte und Studien zum antiken Judentum 12–13. 2 volumes. Tübingen: Mohr.

Scholem, G. G. 1946. *Major Trends in Jewish Mysticism.* New York: Schocken. Reprinted several times, this is the classic discussion of the subject. Chapter 2 deals directly with the topic of this paper.

———. 1960. *Jewish Gnosticism, Merkabah Mysticism, and Talmudic Tradition.* New York: Jewish Theological Seminary. 2nd ed., 1965. Radicalizes the author's assumptions as discussed in *Major Trends* and argues for a much earlier dating of the Hekhalot as well as for a stronger connection with the apocalypses; includes the important appendix by S. Lieberman, "Mishnat Shir Hashirim Rabbah" (in Hebrew).

Suter, D. 1979. "Fallen Angels, Fallen Priests: The Problem of Family Purity in I Enoch 6-16." *Hebrew Union College Annual* 50:115–35.

Swartz, M. D. 1992. *Mystical Prayer in Ancient Judaism: An Analysis of Maʿaseh Merkavah.* Texte und Studien zum antiken Judentum 28.Tübingen: Mohr.

———. 1996. *Scholastic Magic: Ritual and Revelation in Early Jewish Mysticism.* Princeton, N.J.: Princeton University Press. Especially important for *Sar Torah.*

Wolfson, E. 1993. "Yerida la Merkavah: Typology of Ecstasy and Enthronement in Ancient Mysticism." In *Mystics of the Book: Themes, Topics and Typologies,* edited by R. Herrera, 13–44. New York: P. Lang.

Yarbro-Collins, A. 1996. *Cosmology and Eschatology in Jewish and Christian Apocalyp-ticism.* Leiden: E. J. Brill. Of special interest here is the article "The Seven Heav-ens in Jewish and Christian Apocalypses," pp. 21–54.

PART 3

*Apocalypticism in
Early Christianity*

8

The Eschatology of Jesus

See esp. 281-85

don't miss biblio, p. 301-be

Dale C. Allison, Jr.
Pittsburgh Theological Seminary

good sym of 3 legs of conventional reduction

WHAT JESUS BELIEVED ABOUT THE LAST THINGS IS A CON-
troversial topic. Throughout most of church history Christian readers
of the New Testament have related Jesus' prophecies primarily to three
things—to Pentecost and the life of the church, to the destruction of
Jerusalem in 70 C.E. and God's supposed abandonment of the Jewish people,
and to the resurrection of the dead and final judgment at the distant end of
the world. Many modern scholars, however, now believe that Jesus had little if
anything to say about the church, that he anticipated not God's abandonment
of Israel but Israel's eschatological restoration, and that he spoke of the end
not as distant but as near to hand. Indeed, many are convinced that much of
Jesus' message can be fairly characterized as apocalyptic eschatology. This
chapter will clarify just why this is the case and why other interpretations of
the evidence are unlikely to be correct.

THE OLD CONSENSUS

The modern discussion of Jesus and eschatology began with the first edition
of Johannes Weiss's *Die Predigt Jesu vom Reiche Gottes,* which appeared in
1892. In this Weiss argued that Jesus' proclamation of the kingdom, rightly

apoc eschat

was WISE

understood, was consistent with neither traditional Christian piety nor the nineteenth century's liberal lives of Jesus. When Jesus spoke of the kingdom, he was not referring to the church, that is, the body of dead and living saints, nor was he speaking of God's rule in the human heart. He was, rather, announcing the imminent advent of an eschatological reality that would transform the physical world. That reality would be ushered in by the final judgment, which would mean punishment or annihilation for the condemned and reward in paradise for the righteous. According to Weiss, although Jesus originally thought the end to be very near, later, after his call for repentance went widely unheeded, he came to believe that the kingdom would not come before he had died as a ransom for the people.

In 1906 Albert Schweitzer, when surveying the nineteenth century's quest for Jesus, wrote that Weiss's little book "seems to break a spell. It closes one epoch and begins another" (1961, 239). Schweitzer had independently come to the same conclusion as Weiss: Jesus was an apocalyptic preacher. Schweitzer, however, believed that Weiss "showed a certain timidity" (1961, 351 n. 1), for he failed to see that Jesus' conduct in its entirety was ruled by an eschatological scenario. This was the significance of Schweitzer's famous term "thoroughgoing eschatology" (*konsequente Eschatologie*). More so than Weiss, Schweitzer explained every aspect of what Jesus said and did by reference to eschatology. Schweitzer indeed went on to contend that we must choose between two alternatives, between thoroughgoing eschatology and thoroughgoing skepticism. By this he meant that either Jesus lived in the same imaginative world as those responsible for the old Jewish apocalypses, or the Gospels are so unreliable that we know next to nothing about him.

Since Schweitzer, many have accepted his dichotomy and embraced the eschatological option. Even when disagreeing with Schweitzer about this or that, they have believed that Jesus expected God to put an end to the normal course of things by raising the dead, judging the world, undoing evil, and transforming the earth into a perfect reflection of the will of God. They have also thought that for Jesus this eschatological metamorphosis was near to hand. The generalization includes Rudolf Bultmann, who affirmed that "Jesus' message is connected with the hope . . . primarily documented by the *apocalyptic* literature, a hope which awaits salvation not from a miraculous change in historical (i.e. political and social) conditions, but from a cosmic catastrophe which will do away with all conditions of the present world as it is" (1951, 4). The generalization also includes the more conservative Joachim Jeremias, who attributed a whole series of very concrete eschatological expec-

So this goes with my Jewish interests.

wow

tations to Jesus—that eschatological suffering would soon fall upon the saints, that Satan would soon be defeated, that angels would soon separate the living righteous from the wicked, that the dead would soon be raised, that Gentiles would soon stream in from east and west to the mountain of God (1971, 122–41, 241–49). More recently, E. P. Sanders has argued that Jesus was an eschatological prophet who prophesied the eschatological destruction and rebuilding of the temple and looked forward to the restoration of the twelve tribes of Israel.

REJECTION OF THE CONSENSUS

Schweitzer's interpretation of Jesus as an apocalyptic preacher has always had its opponents. One suspects that in this matter theological sentiment has unduly interfered with intellectual history. However that may be, perhaps the foremost among Schweitzer's opponents in the first half of the twentieth century was the British scholar C. H. Dodd. In *The Parables of Jesus,* first published in 1935, he sought to counter the seemingly humiliating discovery that Jesus was, in effect, a false prophet. (In the 1960 Preface he states candidly that "my work began by being orientated to the problem as Schweitzer had stated it.") Dodd urged that "Jesus conceived His ministry as moving rapidly to a crisis, which would bring about His own death, the acute persecution of His disciples, and a general upheaval in which the power of Rome would make an end of the Jewish nation, its city and temple" (1935, 50–51). But all this trouble was not to be followed by a supernatural age of bliss. For the sayings that can be so understood (e.g., Matt. 19:28; Mark 14:58) point rather to "the transcendent order beyond history" (1935, 53). Dodd believed that on the historical or mundane plane the kingdom had already arrived, or was already, so to speak, accessible. Jesus proclaimed the kingdom as "a present fact" (1935, 29). As Matt. 12:28 has it, "the kingdom of God has come upon you."[1] What the prophets foretold was for Jesus a matter of present experience.

Although most have judged Dodd to be unpersuasive in much of his exegesis and appraised his work a failed attempt to find the eschatology of John's Gospel in the sayings of the historical Jesus, his rejection of a Jesus who expected the natural course of things to be interrupted by God's supernatural intervention is shared by many. Perhaps the most prominent exponent of a noneschatological Jesus today is John Dominic Crossan. As early as 1973 he wrote that the scholarly consensus that Jesus' message was "apocalyptic eschatology" had become "extremely problematic." For Jesus "was not announcing that God was about to end the world (i.e., for us, the planet), but he was proclaiming God as the One who shatters the world repeatedly and always. If, for instance, he forbade calculations of the signs of the end, it was not calculations nor signs he was opposed to, but end" (Crossan 1973, 109).

Crossan has continued to forward this view in recent books. While Jesus, as a follower of John the Baptist, began as an apocalyptic believer, he did not, for Crossan, so continue. Jesus broke with the Baptist and developed his own program.

Crossan's method of developing a Jesus dissimilar from Schweitzer's is different from that of Dodd. Although Dodd believed the eschatological discourse in Mark 13 to be "a secondary composition," so that it cannot stand as evidence of Jesus' "own forecast of the future" (1935, 36–37), Dodd took the Synoptics to be very reliable. So his dismissal of Schweitzer was based primarily on a reinterpretation of pertinent passages. Crossan, unlike Dodd, freely confesses that a great many sayings in the Jesus tradition state and presuppose eschatological expectations that contradict his reconstruction; he simply regards these as not authentic. In this Crossan carries forward the project of Norman Perrin, who, although he did not go as far as Crossan in eliminating eschatological elements from the tradition, ousted so-called apocalyptic items as secondary, that is, argued that they were not from Jesus himself.

It has recently been claimed that the position staked out by Crossan has become the new consensus. While this is debatable, many do now reject Schweitzer's old dichotomy. Although denying that Jesus thought something like a millennial kingdom or the rabbinic world-to-come to be just around the corner, they do this without giving up the quest for the historical Jesus. They contend rather that earlier scholars made at least two big mistakes. First, they attributed to Jesus eschatological texts that should instead be attributed to the early church. Second, they misinterpreted other texts that Jesus did compose.

As illustration of the first error, many now doubt that Jesus uttered any of the sayings that feature "the Son of Man" and the last judgment. Mark 8:38 ("Those who are ashamed of me and of my words in this adulterous and sinful generation, of them the Son of man will also be ashamed when he comes in the glory of his Father with the holy angels") and related texts are thought to have been created by Christians. There is said to be no convincing evidence that "the Son of Man" was a recognizable title for a messianic figure among Jesus' Jewish contemporaries, so Jesus could not have used it. The appellation was rather created by Jesus' followers and applied to him on the basis of a Christian interpretation of Dan 7:13–14. On this view of things, if Jesus ever used "son of man" (as most think he did on at least a few occasions) he was only using a common Aramaic idiom for speaking about oneself in a round-about fashion.[2] The expression had nothing to do with the last things (see Vermes 1973).

As illustration of the second supposed error, some now say that Jesus' sayings about the kingdom or rule of God have been roundly misunderstood, because it has been assumed that the kingdom—the central theme of Jesus' proclamation—was imminent and eschatological. The common conviction may seem an obvious inference from Mark 14:25 ("I shall not drink again of the fruit of the vine until that day when I drink it new in the kingdom of God"). But the authenticity of these words is now disputed, and there are other texts that clearly indicate that Jesus spoke of the kingdom as present. Matt 12:28 = Luke 11:20, for instance, declares that "the kingdom has [already] come to you," and Luke 17:20–21 says that "the kingdom of God is not coming with things that can be observed; nor will they say, 'Look, here it is!' or 'There it is!' For, in fact, the kingdom of God is among you." Crossan and others have urged that Jesus proclaimed a "sapiential" kingdom, one having to do with living under God's power and rule in the here and now.

Two catalysts in particular have disturbed the old consensus regarding Jesus and eschatology and have encouraged the new position. The first was the discovery of the *Gospel of Thomas,* part of the Nag Hammadi library, a corpus of Gnostic texts discovered in 1945 in Egypt. This extracanonical collection of sayings of Jesus, which seems in part independent of the canonical Gospels, was, according to many, composed sometime between the middle of the first century C.E. and the middle of the second century C.E. So it is relatively early. It moreover contains not a word about the eschatological Son of Man. Nor is there any sense that the world is about to undergo an eschatological transformation. Several scholars have proposed that *Thomas* reflects a very early stage of the Jesus tradition, one that had not yet been touched by the apocalyptic expectation of the Son of Man. For them, *Thomas* is reason to suppose that the sayings in the Jesus tradition which promote an apocalyptic eschatology are secondary.

A second catalyst toward the new picture of Jesus has been discussion of the compositional history of Q, the hypothetical document supposedly used by both Matthew and Luke. Several recent scholars have decided that the earliest, or at least an early, version of Q contained no future Son of Man sayings, and that the eschatological pathos present in Q as it was known to Matthew and Luke was a secondary development (so Kloppenborg 1987). If accepted, this result would be consistent with the theory that the Christian tradition, without help from Jesus, was responsible for the eschatological character of so much in the Gospels.

DEFENSE OF THE OLD CONSENSUS

But there are problems. Some would hesitate to put much confidence in the hypothetical compositional history of the hypothetical document Q. Others would offer alternative histories of Q that do not eliminate a strong eschatological element from the earliest stratum.

For the sake of argument, however, what follows if one grants that the first level of Q was indeed empty of eschatological feeling? Probably very little. One can readily imagine that the initial compiler of Q had interests different from the compiler of some later, expanded edition. But why those first interests, as opposed to later interests, would alone favor the preservation of authentic sayings is unclear to many of us. If we were envisaging a documentary history that spanned generations, then an earlier contributor would certainly be in a privileged position. Q, however, was opened and closed within, at most, a thirty- or forty-year period. One might accordingly even suppose that the enlarged Q, by virtue of additional, authentic material, resulted in a fuller and less distorted impression of the historical Jesus. Is arguing that the first stratum of Q alone gives us an accurate picture of what Jesus did or did not say about eschatological matters really any more persuasive than urging that the first biography written about, let us say, John F. Kennedy, must be more reliable than all of those that have come later? Should we, because we learn of Jesus' crucifixion not from Q but from other sources, perhaps entertain the notion that Jesus was not crucified? Obviously Q leaves much out of account, even much of importance, which it must have known.

As for the *Gospel of Thomas*, whatever its compositional history may be, there is every reason to believe that its final redactor had no fondness for sayings promoting an apocalyptic eschatology. The truth is that *Thomas* both knows and disparages an eschatological understanding of Jesus. This being so, *Thomas* shows only that competing interpretations existed at an early period. It does not tell us which of those interpretations was congruent with Jesus himself.

There is, however, yet another reason for questioning the old consensus. Contemporary work on the Jesus tradition has plausibly urged that Jesus was a teacher of subversive wisdom, an aphorist, a creator of sapiential sayings. This matters for us because wisdom is about coping with the present whereas apocalypticism seemingly rejects the present in the hope of a better future. We appear to have here two different ways of looking at the world. If so, and if Jesus saw things through the wisdom tradition, is it not natural to intuit that he did not also see them through the apocalyptic tradition? Many have discerned a tension between sayings that assume the continuing flow of the natural order and others that prophesy the end of that order.

Although one sees the point, surely Jesus the eschatological prophet could have uttered provocative one-liners and lived partly out of the wisdom tradition. As historians of Second Temple Judaism are well aware, significant connections run between wisdom literature and the apocalypses. Further, an imminent expectation or strong eschatological interest is combined with wisdom materials in Daniel, the *Testaments of the Twelve Patriarchs,* the Synoptics, and Paul. So why not also with Jesus? One needs only a little knowledge of contemporary American fundamentalism to realize that fervent attention to practical social questions can go hand in hand with authentic belief in a near end. In any case both the subversive and often unconventional wisdom of the Jesus tradition and its expectation of a quick end to things as they now are function similarly, namely, to undo the status quo.

Those who reconstruct a noneschatological Jesus sometimes defend their position with the claim that Jesus' message was misunderstood or misinterpreted within a generation. As Robert Funk has affirmed,

> We can understand the intrusion of the standard apocalyptic hope back into his [Jesus'] gospel at the hands of his disciples, some of whom had formerly been followers of the Baptist: they had not understood the subtleties of Jesus' position, they had not captured the intensity of his vision, and so reverted to the standard, orthodox scenario once Jesus had departed from the scene. (Funk 1996, 164)

This strategy is not new. C. H. Dodd, in trying to save Jesus from Schweitzer's brand of eschatology, wrote that Jesus' reporters, "understandably anxious to find his words relevant to their own urgent preoccupations, have given them a twist away from their original intention" (1970, 123).

This sort of apology against eschatological error indeed has a very long and ancient pedigree. For it already appears in the New Testament itself. Luke tells us that as Jesus went up to Jerusalem he told his disciples a parable, "because they supposed that the kingdom of God was to appear immediately" (Luke 19:11). Luke, like Dodd, is telling us that while the disciples got it wrong, Jesus got it right. He made no mistake. He was just misunderstood.

Now, of course, great figures who stand above their times can be misunderstood. But this is too easy a way out. Rabbinic texts tendentiously explain sectarianism by positing that the disciples of Antigonus of Socho and Shammai and Hillel inadequately understood their masters' teaching. Is not Luke 19:11 equally tendentious? If the early Christians really failed to comprehend Jesus' pronouncements about the kingdom, then is it realistic to think that we, who have access to him only through their erroneous memory, can ever understand him aright? Would it not be more realistic just to give up the quest for Jesus?

More worthy of our attention is the proposition that the presence of the kingdom in certain sayings is incompatible with a Jesus who believed in a yet-to-come eschatological kingdom. One way around this—more plausible than is often imagined—is simply to assert that the sayings so often taken to mean that the kingdom was in some sense present mean no such thing. But even if one thinks this a desperate strategy, one still would not have sufficient reason for attributing one idea to Jesus, another to his followers. Rudolf Otto, observing that although Muhammad announced the day of Allah to be near, the prophet nonetheless gave himself to long-term political and military projects, stressed what he called the "essential irrationality" of eschatological thinking (63). He had a point; and when we remember how often people have found tensions and outright contradictions within the authentic letters of Paul, we should perhaps hesitate to apply with any confidence criteria that demand consistency from Jesus.

In this particular, however, there seems to be a natural resolution. First, Jesus' Bible itself exhibits a similar tension. Dan. 2:44 announces that "in the days of those kings the God of heaven will set up a kingdom that shall never be destroyed." Here the kingdom is eschatological and yet to come. But in 4:34 we read that God's "kingdom endures from generation to generation." Here the kingdom is somehow already present.

Second, Judaism was familiar with the notion that the eschatological transition would be a protracted process, a series of events taking place over a period of time; and this notion appears in texts for which the process has already begun, for which eschatological blessings have entered the present.

The author of *Jubilees*, for example, writing around the middle of the second century B.C.E., believed that the eschatological era had already begun. This is evident above all in chapter 23, which first describes the Maccabean revolt and then apparently moves on to allude to the author's present as a time when "people will begin to study the law and the commandments anew and to return to righteousness" (v. 26; trans. Wintermute, in Charlesworth 1983). The text, then, draws no sharp line between the happy present and the days of eschatological redemption when people will live to be a thousand years old and "there will be no Satan or evil creature" (v. 29). The one time will gradually become the other: "And the days will begin to increase and grow longer" (v. 27). Evidently the eschatological tribulation is past. The kingdom of God has begun to arrive.

The so-called Apocalypse of Weeks (= *1 Enoch* 93 + 91:12–17) offers a similar eschatology. Here history is divided into ten weeks. The first six weeks run from Adam to the destruction of the Temple. The seventh week then introduces eschatological time. There is first a period of great wickedness, after which the elect become manifest and receive knowledge. There follow three weeks of eschatological judgment. The author clearly belongs to the end of the seventh week, when eschatological tribulation ceases and eschatological knowledge enters the world. So although God's kingdom has not yet come in its fullness, God is already bestowing the blessings of the new age.

One can take Jesus' statements about the presence of the kingdom to imply that he thought himself to be in the middle of the unfolding of the eschatological scenario. The term "inaugurated eschatology" has often been used to refer to this sort of idea.

A point regularly missed by those who give us a noneschatological Jesus is that, among sayings thought to declare the kingdom present, we find the language of advent, not reference to a changeless reality. Luke 10:9 says that the kingdom has come or has come near. Similar is Luke 11:20: "upon you has come the kingdom of God." Whatever else these statements mean, they give a temporal character to the kingdom. Presumably there was a time when the kingdom of God had not come upon people. Does this make sense if Jesus had in view an "always available divine dominion"? (Crossan 1991, 292). Does not the use of temporal verbs with the kingdom reflect Jesus' belief that something new and unprecedented had happened? Are we not impelled to think in terms of an eschatological scenario?

Given the inconclusive nature of the arguments so far considered, it is no surprise that the old consensus still has its vigorous supporters. Declarations of its demise or of its replacement by a new consensus are premature. In addition to Sanders, John P. Meier has recently written a major work in which Jesus looks much more like Schweitzer's Jesus than the nonapocalyptic, Cynic-like sage of Crossan. Many in fact remain confident that the eschatological Jesus must be the historical Jesus. Among their reasons are the following.

1. The apocalyptic writings put us in touch with a type of eschatology that was well known in the Judaism that nurtured Jesus. Not only did the sacred collection itself contain apocalyptic materials—Isaiah 24–27, Daniel,

Zechariah 9–14—but portions of *1 Enoch,* some of the Jewish *Sibylline Oracles,* and the *Testament of Moses* were in circulation in Jesus' day; and the decades after Jesus saw the appearance of 4 Ezra, *2 Baruch,* and the *Apocalypse of Abraham.* His time was also when the Dead Sea Scrolls, so many of which are charged with eschatological expectation, were presumably being composed or copied and studied. The point, reinforced by Josephus's remarks on the general popularity of Daniel (*Antiquities* 10.268), is simply that the sort of eschatology Schweitzer attributed to Jesus was indeed flourishing in Jesus' day. The sense of an imminent transformation appears to have been shared by many. So to propose that Jesus thought likewise is just to say that he believed what many others in his time and place believed.

2. The apocalyptic view of things was not just held by many Jews in general; it was also held by many of the first Christians in particular. Passages from a wide variety of sources leave little doubt that many early followers of Jesus thought that the eschatological climax was approaching. Examples include Acts 3:19–20; Rom. 13:11; 1 Cor. 16:22; 1 Thess. 5:1–11; Heb. 10:37; Jas. 5:8; 1 Pet. 4:17; 1 John 2:8; Rev. 22:20; and *Didache* 16.

If in the post-Easter period there were Jesus people who believed that "the ends of the ages have come" (1 Cor. 10:11), in the pre-Easter period Jesus was associated with John the Baptist, whose public speech, if the Synoptics are any guide at all, featured frequent allusion to the eschatological judgment, conceived of as imminent.[3] According to Q (as preserved in Matthew 3 and Luke 3), John warned people "to flee from the wrath to come," asserted that "even now the axe is laid to the root of the trees," prophesied a baptism "with fire," affirmed that the winnowing fan of judgment was about to clear the threshing floor, and spoke of him "who is coming after me."

The direction of all this is unambiguous. For Jesus himself was baptized by John. Further, we should not doubt that Jesus had positive things to say about his baptizer (see, e.g., Mark 11:30; Luke 7:24–28 [Q], 31–35 [Q]). Obviously then there must have been significant ideological continuity between the two men. So, as many have observed over and over again, to reconstruct a Jesus who did not have a strong eschatological orientation entails unexpected discontinuity not only between him and people who took themselves to be furthering his cause but also between him and the Baptist, that is, discontinuity with the movement out of which he came as well as with the movement that came out of him. Presumption is against this. Certainly the Synoptic evangelists seem to have been unaware of major discrepancy between John and Jesus, for they tended to assimilate the two figures.

Crossan resists the inference from Jesus' relationship to John by citing *Gos. Thom.* 46 ("whoever among you becomes a child will know the kingdom and shall become higher than John"; trans. Guillaumont et al.) and its parallel in Luke 7:28 (Q) ("the least in the kingdom of God is greater than he"). This tradition supposedly shows that if—as Crossan admits—Jesus once shared and "even defended" John's "apocalyptic" vision, he must later have "changed his mind" (1991, 237). But Crossan's interpretation of *Gos. Thom.* 46 and Luke 7:28, which sets Jesus at odds with John, is far from obvious. So one can hardly be chided for preferring the plain and unqualified endorsement of John's message ascribed to Jesus in Luke 7:26 (Q): "What did you go out to see? A prophet? Yes, I tell you, and more than a prophet." One also wants to ask Crossan why, if Jesus abandoned John's apocalyptic vision, the contributors to Q thought it fit to preface their collection of Jesus' sayings with John's sayings about eschatology. Did they not understood that Jesus had "changed his mind" and gone far beyond John? Did they fail to see what Crossan sees?

Marcus Borg for his part resists the natural implication of the expectation of the early churches by crediting that expectation "to a deduction based upon the Easter event itself. . . . To some within the church, the fact that a resurrection had occurred was an indicator that the general resurrection must be near; Christ was the 'first fruits' of those to be raised from the dead" (1986, 95–96). This seemingly sensible suggestion, however, leaves the big question unanswered: Why did anyone proclaim a resurrection in the first place? "The fact that a resurrection had occurred" is an infelicitous formulation. How can one here speak of a "fact"? The declaration of Jesus' resurrection was not the recording of a clear observation but an act of interpretation. So what made that particular interpretation the favored one among certain people?

Borg himself observes that "'resurrection' (as distinct from resuscitation) in Judaism was an event expected at the end of time" (1986, 96). Given this and the observations already made, does not the post-Easter, eschatological interpretation of Jesus' vindication—God has already raised Jesus from the dead—imply a closely related pre-Easter eschatological expectation?

3. The Synoptics contain statements that almost certainly regard the eschatological kingdom of God as temporally near:

> Truly, I tell you, there are some standing here who will not taste death until they see the kingdom of God has come with power. (Mark 9:1)

> Truly, I tell you, this generation will not pass away until all these things have taken place. (Mark 13:30)

When they persecute you in one town, flee to the next; for truly, I tell you, you will not have gone through all the towns of Israel before the Son of Man comes. (Matt. 10:23)

The Synoptics also contain parables admonishing people to watch for the coming of the Lord or of the Son of Man (e.g., Luke 12:39–40 [Q]; Luke 12:35–38 [Q?]; Matt. 25:1–13), pronouncements of eschatological woes on contemporaries (e.g., Mark 13:17; Luke 6:24–26; 10:12–15 [Q]), and miscellaneous traditions that either announce or presuppose that the final fulfillment of God's saving work is nigh (e.g., Mark 1:15; 13:28–29, 33, 37; Luke 18:1–8; 21:34–36).

If Jesus uttered just one of these sayings, then Schweitzer was probably close to the truth. But even in the unlikely event that they were all created by the early church, that is still no sound reason to deny an apocalyptic outlook to Jesus. That some Christians believed one thing is no strong reason to hold that Jesus believed something else. It is theoretically possible that the Jesus tradition was so amorphous or devoid of character that it could not resist the wholesale importation of foreign ideas into it. But it is more likely that people felt free to compose eschatological sayings and add them to the tradition because they thought them in accord with Jesus' message.

4. In ancient Jewish literature "kingdom (of God)" is associated with both imminence and eschatology proper. Consider the following texts:

Then his [God's] kingdom will appear throughout his whole creation. Then the devil will have an end. Yea, sorrow will be led away with him. (*Testament of Moses* 10:1; Priest, in Charlesworth 1983)[4]

But when Rome will also rule over Egypt . . . then indeed the most great kingdom of the immortal king will become manifest. (*Sibylline Oracles* 3.46–48; Collins, in Charlesworth)

And then, indeed, he will raise up a kingdom for all ages. (*Sib. Or.* 3.767–68; Collins in Charlesworth)

Their kingdom will be an everlasting kingdom and all their path will be truth. They will jud[ge] the earth in truth and all will make peace. The sword will cease from the earth, and all provinces will pay homage to them. (4Q246)[5]

He will glorify the pious on the throne of the eternal kingdom. . . . (4Q521 frag. 2, col. 2)

May you attend upon the service in the Temple of the kingdom and decree destiny in company with the Angels of the Presence. . . . (1QSb 4:25–26)

May he establish his kingdom in your lifetime and in your days, and in the lifetime of the whole house of Israel, speedily and at a near time. (Kaddish prayer)

No one would dispute that many first-century Jews were indeed "looking forward to the consolation of Israel" (Luke 2:25), nor that this consolation was often conceived of as an eschatological transformation of the world, nor that this transformation was sometimes spoken of as "the kingdom (of God)." So when we find that the Jesus tradition links "the kingdom (of God)" with eschatological imagery in sayings that are not obvious creations of the community, it is natural to suppose that for Jesus himself the kingdom had strong eschatological associations. One thinks, for example, of the following sayings, which make the kingdom something to be experienced in the future:

How hard it will be for those who have wealth to enter the kingdom of God. (Mark 10:23)

I will never again drink of the fruit of the vine until that day when I drink it new in the kingdom of God. (Mark 14:25)

Then people will come from east and west, and north and south and will eat in the kingdom of God. (Luke 13:29 [Q])

Your kingdom come. (Luke 11:2 [Q])

5. A common Jewish conviction about the latter days was that God would finally defeat Satan and the forces of evil. As it says in *Jub.* 23:29, then, "there will be no Satan and no evil (one) who will destroy" (Wintermute, in Charlesworth 1983; compare *1 Enoch* 10:4–6; 54:4–6; *Testament of Zebulon* 9:8; Rev. 20:1–15). This matters because the Jesus tradition contains sayings which refer to Satan's downfall:

I watched Satan fall from heaven like a flash of lightning. (Luke 10:18)

But if it is by the finger of God that I cast out the demons, then the kingdom of God has come to you. (Luke 11:20 [Q])

No one can enter a strong man's house and plunder his property without first tying up the strong man; then indeed the house can be plundered. (Mark 3:27)

Three things may be said about these sayings. First, at least the last two are widely thought to come from Jesus himself. Second, the tradition associates these same two sayings with Jesus' ministry of exorcism. Third, the three sayings naturally reflect the conviction that Satan has already begun to be defeated. The devil has fallen from heaven. He has been cast out. He has been tied up and plundered. These are very strong statements. It is not just that the devil is meeting opposition but rather that he is being routed—as people expected him to be in the latter days. So are we not invited to believe that Jesus was a successful exorcist who, given his eschatological convictions, associated the defeat of Satan in his ministry with Satan's expected defeat before the eschatological coming of the kingdom?

6. Despite its moral focus, the Jesus tradition fails to supply guidance for changing political or social realities. This very strongly implies that if Jesus hoped for better circumstances he must have assumed that they would be brought about by God himself. In other words, Jesus' imperatives are not akin to the *Analects* of Confucius: they do not offer human solutions to concrete problems but rather look forward to God himself, through a miracle, setting all things right.

7. Many early Christian texts associate the death and resurrection of Jesus with what appear to be eschatological events. According to Matt. 27:51–53, when Jesus died there was strange darkness (cf. Amos 8:9–10), a strong earthquake (cf. Zech. 14:5), and a resurrection of the dead (cf. Ezekiel 37; Zech. 14:4–5). According to John's Gospel, Jesus' death was "the judgment of the world" (12:31) and brought down the reign of Satan (16:11). And according to Paul, Jesus is "the first fruits of those who have died" (1 Cor. 15:20)—a metaphor which assumes that the eschatological harvest (see below) is under way, that the resurrection of Jesus is only the beginning of the general resurrection of the dead.

Given its attestation in Paul, the Synoptics, and John, the habit of associating the end of Jesus with eschatological motifs must go back to very early times. What explains it? The most natural answer is that, while Jesus was yet with them, his followers—as Luke 19:11 plainly tells us—"supposed that the kingdom of God was to appear immediately." That is to say, they foresaw eschatological suffering followed by eschatological vindication, tribulation followed by resurrection. So when Jesus was, in the event, crucified and seen alive again, his followers, instead of abandoning their eschatological hopes, did what one would expect them to do: they sought to correlate expectations with circumstances. This is why they believed that in Jesus' end the eschaton had begun to unfold.

JESUS' EXPECTATIONS

It seems more likely than not, despite recent arguments to the contrary, that Jesus and those around him held strong eschatological hopes, which they thought would soon be realized. But beyond that, what details can we offer?

The Eschatological Judgment

To begin with what we can know with assurance: the theme of eschatological reversal runs throughout the sayings of Jesus, and this theme presupposes that the eschatological judgment is just around the corner. Consider the following:

> Blessed are you who are hungry now,
>   for you will be filled. (Luke 6:21 [Q])

> For all who exalt themselves
>   will be humbled,
> and those who humble themselves
>   will be exalted. (Luke 14:11 [Q])

> Those who try to make their life secure
>   will lose it,
> but those who lose their life
>   will keep it. (Luke 17:33 [Q])

> Many who are first
>   will be last
> and the last
>   will be first. (Mark 10:31)

Regarding authenticity, perhaps no words in the tradition are more often reckoned authentic than the beatitudes in Luke 6:20–21; and Rudolf Bultmann spoke for many when he included Luke 14:11; 17:33 (cf. Mark 8:35); and Mark 10:31 among those sayings of which he said, "here if anywhere we can find what is characteristic of the preaching of Jesus" (1963, 105).

As for interpretation, these pithy sayings are neither secular proverbs begotten of experience, akin to "pride goes before destruction" (Prov. 16:18), nor expressions of hope for a world reformed by better people. The first half of each declaration picks out a circumstance in the mundane present, while the second half declares its reversal in the surprising future. What conviction underlies the certainty with which it is announced that unhappy present circumstances will be undone? One supposes that it was only his firm belief in God's near judgment that allowed Jesus to prophesy the reversal of present circumstances. One recalls the story in the Talmud, in which Rabbi Joseph ben Joshua ben Levi catches a glimpse of the next world, which is "topsy–turvy," because "those who are on top here are at the bottom there, and those who are at the bottom here are on the top there" (Babylonian Talmud Pesaḥ 50a). This is not secular wisdom but an affirmation, based upon revelation, about what God will do. One may compare Isa. 60:22:

The least of them
  shall become a clan,
and the smallest one
  a mighty nation;
I am the Lord;
  in its time I will accomplish it quickly.

Also closely related are the promises of reversal in *Testament of Judah* 25:4:

And those who died in sorrow
  will be raised in joy;
and those who died in poverty for the Lord's sake
  shall be made rich;
those who died on account of the Lord
  shall be awakened to life.

If the Synoptic sayings quoted above presuppose, as do Isa. 60:22 and *T. Jud.* 25:4, a coming judgment that will overthrow the current state of things, other sayings often ascribed to Jesus plainly refer to God's judgment. Consider the following three sayings, all from Q:

Do not judge, and you will not be judged. (Luke 6:37)

I tell you, on that day it will be more tolerable for Sodom than for that town. (Luke 10:12)

The queen of the South will rise at the last judgment with the people of this generation and condemn them. . . . The people of Nineveh will rise at the judgment with this generation and condemn it. (Luke 11:31–32)

Sayings about the judgment appear throughout the Synoptic tradition. While this in itself does not guarantee that Jesus himself spoke of the judgment, surely the sayings offer some reason for supposing that he did.

The interesting question is not whether Jesus believed in or spoke of eschatological judgment but whether he gave that belief definite shape, whether he offered a picture of it. Was Norman Perrin right to affirm that Jesus expressed confidence in divine vindication but said "nothing about its form" and that, when this result is compared with the ancient sources, Jewish and Christian, the difference is "spectacular" (1967, 203)?

The Synoptics contain only one detailed picture of the last judgment. In Matt. 25:31–46 the Son of Man, accompanied by angels, comes in glory, sits on a throne, and, like a shepherd who separates sheep from goats, divides humanity into two groups, one for the kingdom, one for exclusion from the kingdom. This scene, however, appears only in Matthew, and it seems to owe as much to the evangelist and to the Similitudes of *1 Enoch,* where the Son of Man also sits on his glorious throne in judgment, as it owes to Jesus.

We have no good evidence then that Jesus ever painted a picture of the last judgment, but the implications of this are not large. We have here only a difference in emphasis or style from the apocalypses, not a difference in conviction. If Jesus did not depict the last judgment in detail, the explanation is not that he thought such depiction inappropriate but that he could take such detail for granted. That is, his tradition already supplied his audience with pictures of the last judgment, so Jesus could simply assume them. Certainly there is no evidence that he rejected traditional images or sought to correct them. To go by the extant evidence, Jesus' focus was not on depicting the judgment but on drawing out its ramifications for behavior in the present. When he warned that one would be taken, another left (Luke 17:34–35 [Q]), he did not elaborate on how that would happen. The point was instead to get people to change their behavior. Christianity began as a sectarian movement precisely because Jesus, following John the Baptist, denied that membership in Israel—that is, physical descent from Abraham—would place one well in the afterlife. Jesus, like his first followers, believed that the verdicts of heaven and hell corresponded to acceptance and rejection of Jesus and his cause.

The Resurrection of the Dead

Soon after his crucifixion, several of Jesus' pre-Easter followers declared, "God raised Jesus from the dead." Upon this fact the canonical Gospels, traditions in Acts, and the letters of Paul all concur.

To proclaim a man's vindication by "the resurrection of the dead" (Acts 4:2) was to proclaim the occurrence of an eschatological event. There is no evidence that Christians ever understood Jesus' resurrection to be (like Lazarus's experience) a return to earthly life. It was, rather, always conceived of as an entrance into heavenly glory. But to say this, to say that God had raised somebody from the dead, was to claim that God had already begun to do what he had formerly been expected to do only at history's culmination.

Why do we have texts that associate Jesus' postmortem vindication with the language of resurrection? Why not texts announcing the heavenly vindication of Jesus' spirit, or declaring his *future* resurrection from the dead, or interpreting Jesus as an angel who only appeared to die before he returned to heaven, or using terms linked with the assumptions to heaven of earlier Jewish heroes such as Enoch and Elijah?

The best answer is that several influential individuals came to their Easter experiences—whatever they were—with certain categories and expectations already fixed, that they already envisaged the general resurrection to be imminent. This would explain why Jesus' vindication was <u>interpreted not as an isolated event but as the onset of the consummation</u>. As anyone familiar with the sociology of messianic movements knows, every effort is usually made to clothe the unfolding of events with material already to hand. In the year 1666, the so-called Old Believers in Russia declared that the end would come shortly. When it did not, they did not throw away their expectation but rather decided that the Antichrist ruled in the Russian Orthodox Church.

That Jesus expected the general resurrection is not just an inference. Mark 12:18–27 has Jesus, in debate with Sadducees, arguing that God can raise the dead. The unit has often been reckoned to rest on a pre-Easter encounter. The early church, as far as we know, did not engage Sadducees in debate,[6] and to judge from the New Testament, the early church argued for the resurrection and speculated on its nature by reference to Jesus' resurrection, not scripture. But Jesus' resurrection is not part of Mark 12:18–27. We seemingly have here an inner-Jewish debate, which makes sense on the level of the historical Jesus.

There is also a pertinent Q saying, Luke 11:31–32 par. According to this, "the queen of the south will be raised at the judgment with this generation and will condemn it," and "the people of Nineveh will be raised at the judgment with this generation and will condemn it." Although these words do not offer details, the universal judgment is presupposed, and it is natural, in view of the future tenses, to give "will be raised" its literal sense.[7]

The general resurrection is further presupposed in Mark 9:43–47, where Jesus says it is better to enter life maimed or lame or with one eye than to be thrown into hell whole. The language, like that of some rabbinic texts, implies that the body is raised exactly as it was buried. If a limb has been cut off, then it is missing at the resurrection. The language may, to be sure, be hyperbolic and so intended to startle. Still, Mark 9:43–47 presupposes that speaker and audience expect the dead to come forth from their graves.

Belief in the resurrection of dead appears not only in Mark 9:43–47; 12:18–27; and Luke 11:31–32 but also in the explicit passion predictions (Mark 8:31; 9:31; 10:33–34). These are often dismissed, perhaps rightly, as obviously composed after the event. But Jesus probably did anticipate an untimely death, and it would hardly be surprising to learn that he hoped that God would, notwithstanding all opposition, vindicate his cause. So it is at least possible that, in accord with his eschatological outlook, Jesus foretold tribulation and death for the saints, including himself, and their and his subsequent vindication at the general resurrection. The passion predictions as they now stand would then supply an example of what is so common in the history of broken eschatological expectations, namely, the reinterpretation of a prediction in order to align it with its fulfillment.

Whatever one makes of the passion predictions, there is reason enough to believe that Jesus looked forward to a general resurrection. The implications of this are considerable. Jesus' eschatological future was not mundane but was rather some sort of new, supernaturally wrought state. Whether he thought of something like a millennial kingdom, or a transformed world in which the boundaries between heaven and earth would begin to disappear, or something like the supramundane rabbinic "world to come," he expected its inauguration to be marked by extraordinary events, including the resurrection of the dead. We are not here in the world of preexilic prophecy but in that of Daniel and the apocalypses.

The Restoration of Israel

Turning now to things that are less certain but still probable, it seems likely enough that Jesus, despite his focus on individuals, expected the eschatological restoration of Israel. The hope was common. It appears in the First Testament as well as intertestamental literature.[8]

The widespread expectation is found in the earliest Jesus tradition. In Luke 22:28–30 (Q) Jesus promises his disciples that they will sit on thrones "judging the twelve tribes of Israel." "Judging" here almost certainly means not "condemning" but "ruling," and the saying presupposes the belief that the gathering of the lost and scattered twelve tribes belongs to the eschatological events.

But can we attribute this conviction to Jesus himself? Whether Luke 22:28–30 goes back to Jesus is unfortunately an open question that cannot be definitively answered. But surely it is suggestive that Jesus associated himself with a special group of twelve disciples. Did he not thereby indicate his belief in the eschatological restoration of the twelve tribes?

There is another Q saying, one whose authenticity is usually accepted, in which Jesus speaks of many coming from east and west and reclining with Abraham, Isaac, and Jacob in the kingdom of God (Luke 13:28–29; cf. Matt. 8:11–12). Most exegetes have assumed that the "many" should be identified with Gentiles. But a minority of interpreters have entertained the possibility that Jesus had in mind the eschatological ingathering of Israel (e.g., Sanders 1985, 119–20). The minority is probably right. For the Q context (see Luke 13:24–30) says nothing about Gentiles, and the phrase "east and west" occurs in Jewish texts in connection with the return of Jews to the land promised to Abraham.[9] On the other hand, there does not appear to be a single text in which "east and west" refers to an eschatological ingathering of Gentiles. Further, there is otherwise little or no evidence that Jesus spoke of the eschatological coming of the Gentiles. So Luke 13:28–29 appears to tell us that Jesus drew a stark contrast not between unbelieving Jews and believing Gentiles but between saved and unsaved Jews. In this case he made a prophetic threat that while Jews scattered abroad who had not had the benefit of encountering him or his message would find eschatological salvation, those in the land who had heard him would not. The meaning would then be close to Jer. 24:1–10, where the good figs are identified with the exiles from Judah, whom God will return to the land and make his own, while the bad figs are identified with Zedekiah, his princes, the remnant of Jerusalem in the land and those in Egypt, who will be condemned. One may also compare Ezekiel 11, which promises return to Palestine for those in exile but foretells terrible punishment for those who have remained in the land.

One final point about Luke 13:28–29 is that it assumes that the land of Israel will be the geographical center of the eschatological scenario. This accords with traditional expectations. At the same time, the saying seemingly negates any advantages that might accrue from dwelling in Palestine. We have here the rejection of the sort of thinking found in *2 Bar.* 29:2; 71:1; 4 Ezra 9:7–8; and Babylonian Talmud *Ketub.* 111a. In these and other texts it is prophesied that the land will protect its own from the dangers of the latter days. In Jesus' proclamation, however, inhabitants of the land will be cast out. Their living in Palestine will not bring them merit. Quite the contrary. It is precisely those inside the borders of Israel, those who have been blessed with the presence of God's eschatological herald, who will face the more dire consequences. Of those to whom much is given, will much be required.

Eschatological Tribulation

Jewish apocalypticism is by nature catastrophic; that is, it stresses the difficulties that lie between the painful present and the ideal future; and ancient Jewish sources regularly depict the birth of a better world as accompanied by terrible labor pains (Allison 1985, 5–25). The rabbis spoke of the "birth throes of the Messiah," and the sorts of disasters catalogued in Mark 13 can be found in many documents, Jewish and Christian. As Dan. 12:1 says, "there shall be a time of anguish, such as has never occurred since the nations first came into existence."

Some have, with good reason, supposed that when Jesus looked into the future he saw what so many others did—not just a new world coming but its attendant birth pangs—and further, that he, like other ancient Jews (Allison 1985, 6–22), interpreted his own work in terms of those pangs. Schweitzer suggested that Jesus originally anticipated, in a generalized fashion, suffering for himself and his followers before the coming of the kingdom; but later, as this expectation went unfulfilled, he conceived the notion that he would die in Jerusalem and take unto himself alone the tribulation of the latter days. According to Joachim Jeremias, Jesus believed instead that his death would be "the prelude to the time of the sword," that the eschatological time of distress would commence with his passion and cover the period of his subsequent absence (1971, 241–44).

What is the evidence that Jesus took up and used to his own ends the traditional motif of the messianic woes? Jesus saw difficulties all around him. He used the image of lambs in the midst of wolves (Luke 10:3 [Q]). He said he had no place to lay his head (Luke 9:58 [Q]). He spoke to people who were poor and hungry and in mourning (Luke 6:20–21 [Q]). He said that those who were not against him and his cause were for him (Mark 9:40)—implying that some were against him (Luke 11:23 [Q]). He told a story in which the invitations to a banquet were roundly rejected—a fictional circumstance surely mirroring his own experience (Luke 14:15–24 [Q]). He spoke of disciples hating their parents (Luke 14:26 [Q]). He may also have enjoined people to take up a cross (Mark 8:34), and he may have composed a parable in which the workers of a vineyard shamefully treat the owner's messengers, a parable that perhaps climaxed with a murder (Mark 12:1–9).

To all this one may add that Jesus' self-conception and experience together pointed to difficulties ahead. For (a) Jesus considered himself a prophet (see below), and Jewish tradition had many tales about the persecution of prophets;[10] (b) Jesus came out of the Baptist movement, and the Baptist was arrested and killed; and (c) Jesus was a controversial figure, and his activities put him into conflict with some Jewish authorities. Certainly someone put him to death, and we may doubt that he was blind to the fact that his provocations might lead to trouble. Now because the Jewish prophetic and apocalyptic traditions foresaw a time of tribulation for the saints before God's final victory, and because Jesus spoke of that victory as near, one wonders whether he might not have spoken of his own present and expected suffering as belonging to that time.

It is possible that the Lord's Prayer alludes to the eschatological woes. In

Luke 11:4 (Q) the disciples are to pray that they not be brought to the time of trial. Whether or not the rest of the Our Father is given an eschatological interpretation, its concluding line probably envisions not the trials or temptations of everyday life but the final time of trouble which precedes the renewal. Here, as in Rev 3:10, the Greek word *peirasmos* can stand for the messianic woes, from which one prays to be delivered (Jeremias 1971, 202).

Whatever one makes of the Lord's Prayer, that Jesus interpreted his own difficult time as the eschatological trouble appears from the Q text behind Luke 12:51–53 and Matt. 10:34–36. It included something close to the following: "Do you think that I came to give peace on the earth? I did not come to give peace but a sword. For I came to divide a man against father and daughter against mother and a daughter-in-law against mother-in-law." This passage depends on Mic. 7:6: "For the son treats the father with contempt, the daughter rises up against her mother, the daughter-in-law against her mother-in-law; your enemies are members of your own household." In *Mishnah Soṭa* 9:15 this biblical text is drawn upon to characterize the discord of the time right before the Messiah's coming: "Children shall shame the elders, and the elders shall rise up before the children, for the son dishonors the father, the daughter rises up against her mother, the daughter-in-law against her mother-in-law; a man's enemies are the men of his own house." Similar statements appear in other texts.[11] The conviction that the eschatological trial would turn those of the same household against each other was common. That Q's adaptation of Mic. 7:6 should be given an eschatological sense is confirmed by the statement about the sword. For talk of the sword within prophecies of eschatological affliction and judgment was also widespread.[12] For Jesus, then, the eschatological time of affliction had come or was near.

Possible confirmation appears in Luke 16:16, which is usually assigned to the historical Jesus and which in Q was close to the following: "The Law and the prophets were until John; from then the kingdom of God has suffered violence and violent men take it by force." Norman Perrin strongly argued that here "the use of the kingdom of Heaven . . . evokes the myth of the eschatological war between God and the powers of evil and interprets the fate of John the Baptist, and the potential fate of Jesus and his disciples, as a manifestation of that conflict" (1976, 46). In other words, Jesus linked opposition to the Baptist's cause with opposition to his own cause and saw both as part and parcel of the eschatological tribulation. This may very well be the correct interpretation.

Luke 12:49–50, which may have stood in Q even though it has no Matthean parallel, makes Perrin's reading all the more plausible. Here Jesus declares, "I came to cast fire upon the earth; and would that it were already kindled! I have a baptism to be baptized with; and how I am constrained until it is accomplished!" Throughout the Jesus tradition fire is associated with eschatological judgment. Moreover, Jewish tradition commonly uses water and flood as symbols of calamity (e.g., Ps. 18:16; Isa. 43:2; Amos 5:8). Jewish tradition also links fire and water together as symbols of judgment, as in Isa. 43:2: "When you pass through the waters I will be with you; and through the rivers, they shall not overwhelm you; when you walk through fire you shall not be burned, and the flame shall not consume you" (compare Ps. 66:10–12; Isa. 30:27–28; *Sib. Or.* 3.689–91). Jewish tradition, presumably under the influence of Iranian eschatology, where a flood of molten metal burns up sinners but refines saints at the end of time, also combines fire and water into one eschatological symbol. In Dan. 7:10 there is a stream of fire; in Rev. 19:20 a lake of fire (compare *1 Enoch* 14:19; *Sib. Or.* 3:54; 4 Ezra 13:10–11). In view of all this, one can make a very good case that in Luke 12:49–50 Jesus is relating his own fate to the end of the eschatological trial, when flood and fire will come upon all. As Mark 9:49 says, "every one will be salted with fire." In Luke 12:49–50, however, Jesus shrinks from this prospect; he is torn between conflicting attitudes toward the fearful expectation. One is reminded of the words attributed to both Ulla and Rab in Babylonian Talmud *Sanhedrin* 98b concerning the terror of the latter days: "Let him [the Messiah] come, but let me not see him!"

One final point should be made about the messianic woes. Schweitzer observed that certain traditions seem to join Jesus' fate with the fate of his disciples, yet others focus entirely on Jesus and his solitary passion. Schweitzer eliminated the tension between these two traditions by positing a change within Jesus' thought. At an early time Jesus expected the tribulation to encompass all; later he anticipated taking it up in himself alone. If, however, one takes account of the post-Easter reinterpretation of the Jesus tradition, there is no need to postulate development in Jesus' thinking here. Jesus expected to suffer in the final drama. This accounts for the traditions that link his fate with the fate of his followers (see, e.g., Mark 10:35–45). The church then interpreted and modified his words in the light of what actually happened. This accounts for the texts that focus on Jesus' fate alone. On this view it becomes possible that even the so-called passion predictions are, as already suggested, reinterpretations and specifications of more general prophecies. Any prediction of death and resurrection would originally have meant this: suffering lies ahead for the saints, but afterwards God will vindicate us. Such a pre-Easter forecast, if Jesus gave one, would naturally have been revised, after the fact, to correspond to his isolated suffering and belief in his isolated resurrection.

JESUS' SELF-CONCEPTION

Anointed Prophet

According to Mark 6:15 and 8:27–28, some of Jesus' contemporaries thought him a prophet (see also Matt. 21:11, 46; Luke 7:39; 24:19). There is no reason to reject this testimony, and every reason to suppose that Jesus himself shared this evaluation. In Mark 6:4 he says that a prophet is without honor except in his own hometown. The implication is that Jesus understood his own ministry in prophetic terms. Again, in Luke 13:33 (whose authenticity is less assured) Jesus says that he must be on his way today and tomorrow and the day following, for it cannot be that a prophet should perish away from Jerusalem.

Given that Jesus apparently considered himself a prophet, and given that he thought himself to belong to the latter days, did he associate his ministry with any particular eschatological prophecies? Q's beatitudes, now found in Luke 6:20–23, suggest that he did. The beatitudes draw upon Isaiah 61, which opens thus:

> The spirit of the Lord God is upon me,
> because the Lord has anointed me;
> he has sent me to bring good news to the poor,
> to bind up the broken-hearted,
> to proclaim liberty to the captives,
> and release to the prisoners;
> to proclaim the year of the Lord's favor,
> and the day of vengeance of our God;
> to comfort all who mourn.

Q's "Blessed are those who mourn, for you will be comforted" borrows from Isa. 61:2.[13] "Blessed are the poor, for yours is the kingdom of God" alludes to Isa. 61:1. One may also observe that "Rejoice and be glad" recalls Isa. 61:10. What follows?

The Dead Sea Scrolls (11QMelchezedek and the fragmentary 4Q521) use Isa. 61:1–3 to portray the eschatological liberation of Israel's captives, and an eschatological interpretation of these verses also appears in the targum on Isaiah. Moreover, another Q text, Luke 7:22, takes up Isaiah 61 to demonstrate that Jesus is to be identified with the eschatological figure of John's proclamation. When John the Baptist asks whether Jesus is the Coming One, Jesus says, among other things, that the poor have good news preached to them—a clear reference to Isa. 61:1.

Unfortunately, the authenticity of Luke 7:22 is controverted; there is no consensus that it goes back to Jesus. But the beatitudes by themselves tell us that Jesus linked his work with Isaiah 61. And, given that we have other reasons for believing that he took himself to be a prophet, the inference that Jesus identified himself with the eschatological prophet of Isaiah commends itself.

Jesus' interpretation of his own ministry in terms of Isaiah 61 may also help explain why early Christians came to confess him as Messiah. The indications that Jesus associated himself with Davidic hopes are, as scholars have long recognized, few and far between. The two scenes that must bear the burden of proof—Peter's confession at Caesarea Philippi (Mark 8:27–30) and Jesus' confession before the Sanhedrin (Mark 14:61–62)—are often dismissed, rightly or not, as post-Easter products. At the same time, no persuasive explanation for the post-Easter confession of Jesus as the Messiah has been forthcoming. But if Jesus was already, in his own lifetime, thought to be an eschatological figure "anointed" by God (Isa. 61:1), then the step to confession of him as "the Messiah," that is, "the Anointed One," would perhaps not have been such a large one. Particularly suggestive in this connection is 4Q521 (4QMessianic Apocalypse). This says that "[the hea]vens and the earth will listen to His Messiah," then goes on to list miraculous healings reminiscent of Luke 7:22 (see below), and finally cites Isa. 61:1 ("He will heal the wounded, and revive the dead, and bring good news to the poor"). The case has been made that "His Messiah" not only preaches good news to the poor but performs the miracles listed (Collins 1994). We seem to have here an example in Judaism of how one who was thought to fulfill the oracle in Isaiah 61 could be identified as "Messiah."

Son of Man

Several Synoptic sayings refer to the eschatological coming of "the Son of Man" (e.g., Matt. 10:23; Mark 13:26; 14:62; Luke 12:40; 18:8). But many now suppose that the church created all these sayings. Jesus may have used the Aramaic idiom "the son of man" to speak about himself in a roundabout fashion, but he could not, it is said, have used this circumlocution to prophesy his own coming on the clouds of heaven. The church, with its belief in the *parousia,* or second coming of Jesus Christ, used Daniel 7, where one like a son of man comes on the clouds of heaven, to depict Jesus as the judge of the last day.

This solution to the puzzle of the Son of Man sayings has become popular of late (Vermes 1973), and it could be correct. But some remain troubled by the fact that outside the Gospels "the Son of Man" rarely appears. The point has all the more force because we know that although Lord and Christ were all-important titles in the early church, they have left scarcely a trace in the sayings of Jesus. One may doubt that the church freely introduced christological titles into the Jesus tradition.

Another approach to the Son of Man sayings holds that Jesus did in fact refer to the coming of the Son of Man, but he was not speaking about himself. This position was held by Bultmann and was once very popular; its adherents are fewer today. The parables of *1 Enoch* as well as 4 Ezra show us that even if "the Son of Man" was not a recognizable title in Jesus' day, there was at least an exegetical tradition that identified Daniel's humanlike figure with a preexistent Messiah. This makes it reasonable, for those who recognize Jesus' kinship with Jewish apocalypticism, to suppose that he looked forward to the heavenly appearance of the Son of Man. On this view of things, the formal distinction between Jesus and the Son of Man in Luke 12:8–9 makes sense: those who confess Jesus will be confessed by the Son of Man; those who deny Jesus will be denied by the Son of Man.

One objection to this viewpoint is that outside the Son of Man sayings there is no evidence that Jesus looked for or spoke of eschatological figures other than the Baptist and himself. It has been replied, however, that the church would hardly have been anxious to preserve references to such a figure, and also that, after the resurrection, Jesus' followers would have identified him with the figure of Dan 7:13. Still, why could they not have been content to proclaim Jesus' resurrection and simultaneously look forward to the coming of another figure, the Son of Man?

Another objection to the proposal that Jesus did not think of himself as the Son of Man is that he may well have believed himself to be Israel's messianic king. That he was crucified as a messianic pretender, that his first followers confessed him to be the Messiah, and that he associated his own work with that of the anointed herald of Isaiah 61 may tell us, when taken together, that he took himself to be not just an important prophet but Israel's eschatological king. This conclusion is consistent with the fact that he apparently placed himself outside of the symbolic group of twelve that he assembled: he stood above them as their leader and so, perhaps, implicitly made himself out to be the leader of regathered Israel.

All this matters because those who believe that Jesus took himself to be Israel's king might also believe that he spoke of himself as the Son of Man coming on the clouds. Both the Similitudes of Enoch and 4 Ezra, which are literarily independent, identify Daniel's "one like a son of man" as the Messiah; so if Jesus took himself to be the latter, he could have made himself out to be the former. It can be retorted that the identification of Jesus with Daniel's "one like a son of man" would not have made sense before the crucifixion, when Jesus was on earth. But this protest is not decisive if Jesus interpreted his own time in terms of the eschatological tribulation, for he then could have thought of vindication on the far side of suffering and death. Certainly Judaism was familiar with the notion that God's chief agent in the final judgment might be a character from the past who was now waiting in heaven.[14]

Given the current lack of scholarly consensus about the Son of Man problem, this is not the place to put forward my own conclusions on this matter. But two final observations may be offered. First, even if Jesus took himself to be the messianic king in Jerusalem, he might still have expected the coming Son of Man to be someone else. Jewish messianism was quite variegated, and if some of the Dead Sea Scrolls speak of two Messiahs, or two Anointed Ones, Jesus could have done something similar. If he believed in two eschatological prophets—the Baptist and himself—he could, at least in theory, have also believed in two Messiahs or messianic deliverers.

Second, it has occasionally been asserted that without the authenticity of the coming Son of Man sayings, there is little reason to suppose that Jesus' teaching about the kingdom had anything to do with an imminent end. This is untrue. Neither Johannes Weiss's nor Albert Schweitzer's account of things rested solely or even mainly on the Son of Man sayings; nor did Rudolf Bultmann's, nor E. P. Sanders's. The truth is that even if Jesus never said anything about "the Son of Man," one could still construct a solid case for an apocalyptic Jesus. The popularity of apocalyptic eschatology in Jesus' day, Jesus' close relationship to John the Baptist (attested in Q, Mark, and John's tradition), the selection of a symbolic body of twelve men, the eschatological expectations of so many in the early church, the primitive proclamation of Jesus' resurrection, and Jesus' execution as "king of the Jews," a would-be deliverer, all cohere with the view that Jesus' words were from the beginning linked with a strong eschatological expectation.

THEMES AND MOTIFS RELATED TO ESCHATOLOGY

When Schweitzer spoke of "thoroughgoing eschatology" he was urging not just that Jesus promoted a certain sort of eschatology but that Jesus' entire ministry, including just about everything he said, could be directly related to it. In what follows it will be argued that, in accord with Schweitzer's contention, many different themes in the authentic Jesus tradition, over and above those already introduced, can and indeed should be closely linked with Jesus' imminent apocalyptic eschatology.

Revelation

Consider the following sayings:

> I thank you, Father, Lord of heaven and earth, because you have hidden these things from the wise and the intelligent and have revealed them to infants; yes, Father, for such was your gracious will. (Luke 10:21 [Q])

> Blessed are the eyes that see what you see. For I tell you that many prophets and kings desired to see what you see but did not see it, and to hear what you hear, but did not hear it. (Luke 10:23 [Q])

> To you has been given the secret of the kingdom of God, but for those outside, everything is in parables. (Mark 4:11)

These three sayings, which depict the present as a time of unprecedented divine disclosure, are easily associated with the conviction that the eschatological consummation will bring special knowledge to the elect. Already Jer. 31:34 says, "No longer shall they teach one another, or say to each other, 'Know the Lord,' for they shall all know me, from the least of them to the greatest, says the Lord." Hab. 2:14 puts it this way: "The earth will be filled with the knowledge of the glory of the Lord, as the waters cover the sea." The commentary on Habakkuk from the Dead Sea Scrolls, when commenting on this line, similarly declares that "afterwards knowledge will be revealed" in "abundance" (1QpHab 11:1). The author of this commentary probably connected his own ability to fathom Habakkuk's prophecies with this sort of eschatological expectation. Certainly this conviction lies behind the composition of the apocalypses, in which eschatological revelations are made known. In Daniel the seer explicitly announces that his book will be sealed until "the time of the end," when "the wise will understand" (compare *1 Enoch* 104:12–13; *Testament of Judah* 18:3, 5).

Particularly interesting in this regard is the Apocalypse of Weeks (= *1 Enoch* 93 + 91:12–17). As already observed, in this work the present is already eschatological time, and it is characterized by the entrance of eschatological knowledge into the world: in the latter days the righteous will be given "sevenfold instruction." Do we not have something similar in the Jesus tradition? And do we not have it precisely because Jesus himself interpreted his own teaching not just as revelation but precisely as eschatological revelation? Is this not how we should account for Luke 10:21, 24 and Mark 4:11? One remembers that, in the Dead Sea Scrolls, God has "made known all the mysteries of the words of his servants the prophets" to the so-called Teacher of Righteousness, who belongs to "the last generation" (1QpHab 7:1–5). One also recalls that *1 Enoch* 51:3 prophesies that God's Elect One will sit on the divine throne and pour forth all the secrets of wisdom, and that in the Animal Apocalypse in *1 Enoch* the final events commence with snow-white sheep beginning to open their eyes and see (90:6)—an allegorical way of saying that near the end special revelation will be given to the righteous (compare also CD 3:13–14).

Harvest

The tradition assigns three parables of harvest to Jesus: the parable of the sower (Mark 4:2–9), the parable of the scattered seed (Mark 4:26–29), and the parable of the tares (Matt. 13:24–30). It also has Jesus say that "the harvest is plentiful" (Luke 10:2 [Q]; compare John 4:35–38). Crossan (1991) accepts the authenticity of this saying and the three parables, but he does not seem to recognize that they speak against his nonapocalyptic Jesus. For the Jewish Bible uses the images of threshing, winnowing, and harvesting in prophecies of judgment,[15] and in apocalyptic literature the same images are associated with the eschatological consummation. In Rev. 14:14–16 the judgment comes when a man seated on a cloud puts forth his sickle and reaps the fruit of the eschatological harvest. In 4 Ezra the end can be called without explanation "the time of threshing" (4:30, 39). In *2 Bar.* 70:2 we read that the last days will come when "the time of the world has ripened and the harvest of the seed of the evil ones and the good ones has come." We evidently have here a common way of speaking into which Jesus' talk of harvesting, if given an eschatological sense, fits nicely. One may cite as a parallel a saying that Q assigns to the Baptist: "His winnowing fork is in his hand, to clear his threshing floor and to gather the wheat into his granary; but the chaff he will burn with unquenchable fire" (Luke 3:17). This, whether or not it goes back to John, shows us how those steeped in Jewish tradition naturally construed language about harvesting.

That Jesus' use of such language should turn our thoughts to eschatology is strongly suggested by the yields in the parable of the sower: the good soil offers yields of thirty- and sixty- and a hundredfold. Recent study has seemingly demonstrated that these yields would be truly miraculous in Jesus' time and place. This matters so much because the theme of supernatural fertility or yield was strongly associated with God's eschatological restoration of the land.[16] Once again, then, the Jesus tradition moves one to think of eschatology.

Periodization of History

The Jesus tradition reflects the conviction that the present is a time of unprecedented significance:

> When you see a cloud rising in the west, you immediately say, "It is going to rain"; and so it happens. And when you see the south wind blowing, you say, "There will be scorching heat"; and it happens. You hypocrites! You know how to interpret the appearance of earth and sky, but why do you not know how to interpret the present time? (Luke 12:54–56 [Q])

These words are readily given eschatological sense: even though the consummation is near, people fail to recognize the fact and to take it into account. That this is the correct interpretation appears from another Q saying, that behind Matt. 11:12 (compare Luke 16:16):

> The law and the prophets were until John. From then the kingdom of God has suffered violence and the violent take it by force.

We have already looked at these enigmatic words in connection with the subject of eschatological tribulation. Here it may be remarked that John the Baptist marks a division within history. After him, or with his appearance, the kingdom of God suffers violence. Now it is a characteristic of several Jewish apocalypses that they divide history into segments. Daniel 7 offers a vision of four beasts, which are four consecutive kingdoms. Daniel 9 tells us about the seventy weeks of years. The *Testament of Moses* divides the time between Moses and God's eschatological advent into 250 units. The Apocalypse of Weeks teaches that seven weeks of world history are past and three weeks are yet ahead. Compared to these detailed schemes Matt. 11:12 is relatively rudimentary. Nonetheless, the division of times it offers reminds one of nothing so much as the systematization of history one finds in apocalypses.

Dualism

Jesus was undoubtedly known as an exorcist, and it is perhaps this above all else which, in his lifetime, made him so popular with so many. It has already been observed that Jesus probably associated the defeat of Satan in his exorcisms with Satan's defeat before the eschatological coming of the kingdom.

That is, Jesus seems to have interpreted his own work within the context of the great battle between good and evil.

This cosmic dualism has its natural correlate in the tendency of the Jesus tradition to see things in black and white, to divide people into two groups or types. There are those who build their houses on the sand and those who build their houses on the rock (Luke 6:47–49 [Q]). There is Lazarus and there is the rich man (Luke 16:19–31). There are the two sons, one who speaks well but does wrong, one who speaks wrongly but does rightly (Matt. 21:28–32). There are those who use the money entrusted to them to gain wealth for their master, and there is one who fails to do so (Luke 19:11–27 [Q]). There are the wise and intelligent from whom things are hidden, and there are the infants who possess revelation (Luke 10:21 [Q]). There are those who are for Jesus and those who are against him, and seemingly no one in between (Luke 11:23 [Q]; but note Mark 9:40).

These traditions, some of which surely go back to Jesus, reflect more than the excessive clarity of the moral visionary. For in some of these units those who do the wrong thing are punished. Floods sweep away the house without a foundation. The rich man who does not feed Lazarus is tormented in Hades. The man who buries the talent has everything taken away from him. Throughout church history these images have most often been taken to stand for the final judgment of God, for the sentence of judgment that is to be passed upon the wicked. Here, it seems, the church has got it right. Jesus' division of his hearers into two groups carries forward the old biblical prophecies of salvation for the righteous and disaster for the wicked, and it presupposes that at the eschatological judgment only two sentences will be passed.

Ethics

Jesus' ethical teaching—his demand to love enemies, to hate father and mother, to lose one's life, to forgive seventy times seven—has often been thought to be at odds with a fervent eschatological orientation. C. H. Dodd urged that the ethical teaching of Jesus "appears to contemplate the indefinite continuance of life under historical conditions" (1935, 79). But the objection is misguided. For one thing, Jesus' prohibition of divorce, according to which the monogamy of creation overrides Moses' permission (Mark 10:2–9), may well presuppose that the end will match the beginning (a common belief): the coming of the kingdom will bring the restoration of paradise, when Adam and Eve were united as man and wife (Sanders 1985, 256–60). For another thing, the Dead Sea Scrolls show us that people expecting a near end could also draw up detailed institutional rules, while *2 Baruch* combines the conviction that "the youth of the world has passed away" (85:10, trans. Klijn, in Charlesworth 1983) with conventional exhortations to keep the Torah (32:1; 46:3; etc.). The situation is similar in the *Testaments of the Twelve Patriarchs*: the ethics and the eschatology are not logically linked, but they nonetheless appear side by side. So it would be unwise to set eschatology over against imperatives that seem to us to envisage "the indefinite continuance of life under historical conditions." When Mark summarizes Jesus' proclamation by combining the nearness of the end with a call to repent (1:15), the evangelist probably catches the spirit of Jesus' exhortations. It is just common sense, confirmed by the experience of those who are told that they have little time to live, that the present takes on added seriousness if the end is near. Even if most of Jesus' imperatives have parallels in noneschatological texts, that is no reason to deny that, on his lips, imminence lent them an added earnestness.

Healing

The tradition has Jesus healing the blind, curing the lame, and raising the dead. It also has him interpreting these remarkable events as eschatological signs: "Go and tell John what you have seen and heard: the blind receive their sight, the lame walk, the lepers are cleansed, the deaf hear, the dead are raised, the poor have good news brought to them" (Luke 7:22 [Q]). This list is offered as evidence that Jesus is an eschatological figure, John's "coming one." Whether or not Bultmann was right to suppose that the words just cited go back to Jesus, they do plainly connect healing miracles with eschatology. This connection is now illuminated by a fragmentary Dead Sea Scroll, 4Q521, which includes the following:

> [the hea]vens and the earth will listen to his Messiah, and none therein will stray from the commandments of the holy ones. . . . The Lord will consider the pious and call the righteous by name. Over the poor his Spirit will hover and will renew the faithful with his power. And he will glorify the pious on the throne of the eternal kingdom, he who liberates the captives, restores sight to the blind, straightens the b[ent]. . . . He will heal the wounded, and revive the dead and bring good news to the poor. . . .

Whether or not the miracles which the Lord performs in this text are done through his Messiah, we have here evidence that at least some pre-Christian Jews expected miracles of the sort Jesus worked to belong to the eschatological scenario. The point is that even Jesus' healing ministry can, if one is so inclined, be associated with eschatological expectation.

To conclude this section: if the nonapocalyptic Jesus were the historical Jesus, it is peculiar that so much in the tradition, even so much that is regarded as authentic by those who offer us such a Jesus, can be so easily related to apocalyptic eschatology.

FINAL REMARKS

In most respects the eschatology of Jesus must be regarded as conventional. The nearness of the consummation, the coming of judgment, and belief in the general resurrection were all things handed to him by his tradition. What was new was the connection he made with his own time and place. He probably interpreted John the Baptist as an eschatological prophet who suffered during the messianic woes. He interpreted his own ministry as a fulfillment of the prophecies of Isaiah 61. He foresaw judgment upon those who rejected his proclamation, and he associated his own teaching with the special revelation expected to be made known to the righteous in the latter days. In other words, Jesus, like the sectarians of Qumran, construed what he saw around him in terms of certain eschatological expectations.

Focus on matters eschatological and hope for a near end often arise out of suffering or dissatisfaction with the present. It was almost surely the same with Jesus. Not only was Judea under the Roman thumb, but his words, as observed above, have much to say about difficult times. Moreover, the many polemical barbs against scribes and Pharisees and the stories of conflict with them tell us that Jesus was disillusioned with and alienated from many religious authorities. Beyond this, however, it may be impossible to go. There may have been some particular political or social crisis that fostered his eschatological enthusiasm and gave him a receptive audience, but, if so, the details sadly appear to be lost to history.

NOTES

1. Biblical quotations are from the NRSV, although the author has occasionally made minor revisions.

2. E.g., Mark 2:28 ("the Son of man is lord even of the sabbath") has been taken to mean that human beings in general (including therefore Jesus in particular) stand above the sabbath.

3. It might be argued that one should follow not the Gospels but Josephus, whose John is not an apocalyptic prophet but a social reformer (*Ant.* 18:116–19). Josephus, however, sought to underplay the eschatological fervor of Judaism. It is telling that his portrait of the Essenes includes nothing about the restoration of Israel, cosmic dualism, or messianic hope. Only from the Dead Sea Scrolls—presumably written by Essenes—do we learn these things.

4. The context encourages the reader to hope that this kingdom will come soon.

5. All translations of the Dead Sea Scrolls are from Vermes 1995.

6. There is no evidence of real Christian debate with Sadducees in Q or any of the four Gospels (with the possible but unlikely exception of Matthew), and Sadducees are missing entirely from the New Testament epistles. They are only marginal in Acts (4:1–2; 5:17–18; 23:6–10).

7. Jewish sources vary as to who will be raised. Most refer only to the righteous being resurrected; see, e.g., *Psalms of Solomon* 3; *1 Enoch* 83–90; and Josephus, *Jewish War* 2.163 (compare Ps. 1:5 LXX?). Luke 11:32–33 par. seems to indicate that Jesus on the contrary believed that all the dead would be raised. His belief in this matter may explain why a universal resurrection appears in some early Christian sources (e.g., John 5:28–29). But a universal resurrection also appears in *Sib. Or.* 4.179–90; *Testament of Benjamin* 10:8; and perhaps Dan. 12:1–3, which says that "many" (= "all"?) will be raised, some to life, some to shame.

8. E.g., Isa. 27:12–13; 43:5–6; Hos. 11:11; 2 Macc. 1:27; 2:18; Bar. 4:37; 5:5; *Psalms of Solomon* 8:28; 11:2–3; *1 Enoch* 57:1; 11QTemple 57:5–6; 4 Ezra 13:32–50; *2 Bar.* 78:1–7; *Sib. Or.* 2.170–73; *Testament of Joseph* 19:3–8 (Armenian); *Mishnah Sanhedrin* 10:3.

9. E.g., Deut. 30:4 LXX; Zech. 8:7–8; Bar. 4:4; 5:5; *Pss. Sol.* 11:2; *1 Enoch* 57:1. While Matt. 8:11–12 uses "east and west," Luke 13:28–29 uses the longer expression "from east and west and north and south." This phrase too was traditionally associated with Israel's return: Ps. 107:2–3; Isa. 43:5–6; Zech. 2:6 LXX; *Pss. Sol.* 11:2–3.

10. See, e.g., 1 Kgs. 18:4, 13; 19:10; Neh. 9:26; Jer. 2:30; 26:20–24; *Jub.* 1:12; Josephus, *Ant.* 10.38; *Ascension of Isaiah* 5:1–16; Letter of Jeremiah 9:21–32.

11. E.g., *Jub.* 23:16, 19; *1 Enoch* 56:7; 99:5; 100:1–2; 4 Ezra 5:9; 6:24; *2 Bar.* 70:3.

12. E.g., Isa. 66:16; *Jub.* 9:15; *1 Enoch* 63:11; 90:19; 91:11–12; *Pss. Sol.* 15:7; *Sib. Or.* 3.796–99; 4.174; Rev. 6:4; *2 Bar.* 27:6.

13. Matthew's form is here original.

14. See, e.g., 11QMelchizedek; *1 Enoch* 71 (if v. 14 identifies Enoch with the earlier "one like a son of man"); and *Testament of Abraham* A 12–13. Also relevant are 1 Cor. 6:2 and Rev. 20:4. One might protest that Daniel's "one like a son of man" is an angel, maybe Michael, but in any case not a man (a plausible interpretation). But Jewish eschatology (including the teaching of Jesus) could erase the line between

humans and angels. The Dead Sea Scrolls turn Melchizedek into an angelic figure (11QMelchizedek) and perhaps even identify him with the archangel Michael (see 4Q401 frag. 11).

15. E.g., Isa. 41:14–16; Jer. 15:7; 51:33; Hos. 6:11; Joel 3:13; Mic. 4:12–13.

16. Cf. Isa. 51:3; Ezek. 36:35; 47:7–12; Rev. 22:2; *1 Enoch* 10:19; *2 Bar.* 29:4–8; Papias in Irenaeus *Against Heresies* 5.33.3–4; Babylonian Talmud *Ketubot* 111b–112a; *Šabbat* 30b.

⁀BIBLIOGRAPHY

Allison, Dale C., Jr. 1985. *The End of the Ages Has Come: An Early Interpretation of the Passion and Resurrection of Jesus.* Philadelphia: Fortress Press. This study argues that many early Christian passion traditions are best explained as attempts to reconcile Jesus' fate with his eschatological prophecies.

Beasley-Murray, G. R. 1986. *Jesus and the Kingdom of God.* Grand Rapids: Eerdmans. A detailed exegesis of every Synoptic saying about the kingdom of God. It consistently reviews the history of the discussion.

Borg, Marcus. 1986. "A Temperate Case for a Non-Eschatological Jesus." *Forum* 2 (September):81–102. A clear presentation of what the title indicates.

Bultmann, Rudolf. 1951. *Theology of the New Testament.* Vol. 1. New York: Charles Scribner's Sons. Contains a very influential portrait of Jesus as an eschatological prophet.

———. 1963. *History of the Synoptic Tradition.* Oxford: Basil Blackwell.

Charlesworth, James H., ed. 1983. *The Old Testament Pseudepigrapha.* 2 vols. Garden City, N.Y.: Doubleday.

Collins, John J. 1994. "The Works of the Messiah." *Dead Sea Discoveries* 1:1–15.

Crossan, John Dominic. 1973. "The Servant Parables of Jesus." In *Society of Biblical Literature 1973 Seminar Papers,* edited by G. W. MacRae, 2:94–118. Cambridge, Mass.: Society of Biblical Literature.

———. 1991. *The Historical Jesus: The Life of a Mediterranean Jewish Peasant.* San Francisco: Harper. According to Crossan, Jesus was a Cynic-like sage who began as a follower of the apocalyptic Baptist but later adopted another view of things. The work is characterized by the use of extracanonical sources.

Dodd, C. H. 1935. *The Parables of Jesus.* London: James Nisbet. The classic presentation of "realized eschatology," according to which Jesus proclaimed not an apocalyptic message but the presence of the kingdom.

———. 1970. *The Founder of Christianity.* New York: Macmillan.

Funk, Robert W. 1996. *Honest to Jesus: Jesus for a New Millennium.* New York: Macmillan.

Guillaumont, A., et al., eds. 1959. *The Gospel according to Thomas.* Leiden: E. J. Brill.

Jeremias, Joachim. 1971. *New Testament Theology.* New York: Charles Scribner's

Sons. This summation of Jeremias's conclusions after a lifetime of study interprets the entire message of Jesus in terms of the expectation of a near end.

Kloppenborg, John S. 1987. *The Formation of Q*. Philadelphia: Fortress Press.

Meier, John P. 1994. *A Marginal Jew: Rethinking the Historical Jesus*. Vol. 2, *Mentor,
Message, and Miracles*. New York: Doubleday. This contains a long and thorough
discussion of the meaning of Jesus' proclamation of the kingdom. Meier concludes that Jesus believed both in the presence of the kingdom and in a near end.

Otto, Rudolf. 1943. *The Kingdom of God and the Son of Man: A Study in the History of
Religion*. London: Lutterworth.

Perrin, Norman. 1976. *Jesus and the Language of the Kingdom*. Philadelphia: Fortress
Press. Here Perrin argues that Jesus used "kingdom" as a "tensive symbol," that
is, as something whose meaning cannot be exhausted or adequately expressed by
any one referent.

———. 1967. *Rediscovering the Teaching of Jesus*. New York: Harper & Row. This
influential book argues that Jesus expressed confidence in God's future but did
not give his expectation any definite form. He did not, for example, refer to
Daniel's "one like a son of man."

Sanders, E. P. 1985. *Jesus and Judaism*. Philadelphia: Fortress Press. According to
Sanders, Jesus was an eschatological prophet who looked forward to the restoration of Israel.

Schlosser, Jacques. 1980. *Le Règne de Dieu dans les dits de Jésus*. Etudes bibliques. 2
vols. Paris: J. Gabalda. A systematic examination of Synoptic sayings about the
kingdom which Schlosser judges to be from Jesus.

Schweitzer, Albert. 1961. *The Quest of the Historical Jesus*. New York: Macmillan.
This is the standard review of nineteenth-century research on Jesus. It concludes
with Schweitzer's memorable portrait of a Jesus consumed by eschatological
expectation.

Vermes, Geza. 1973. *Jesus the Jew*. London: Collins, 1973.

———. 1995. *The Dead Sea Scrolls in English*. Revised 4th ed. London: Penguin.

Weiss, Johannes. 1971. *Jesus' Proclamation of the Kingdom of God*. Philadelphia:
Fortress Press. This book opened the modern discussion of Jesus and eschatology and remains interesting reading.

9

The Kingdom of God and the Renewal of Israel: Synoptic Gospels, Jesus Movements, and Apocalypticism

Richard A. Horsley
University of Massachusetts, Boston

SINCE THE BEGINNING OF THE TWENTIETH CENTURY, JESUS and the Gospels have been interpreted as "apocalyptic," even as direct expressions of Jewish apocalypticism. In reaction to the "apocalyptic" or "eschatological" Jesus emphasized by Albert Schweitzer and others has arisen a more recent movement to rescue a Jesus more compatible with modern rational sensibilities from the "enthusiasm" of Jewish apocalypticism. The apocalyptic elements in the Gospel traditions of Jesus are therefore ascribed to the Gospels themselves or the traditions they used as a way of isolating a non-apocalyptic Jesus. Debates rage regarding the degree to which and ways in which a given Gospel or gospel tradition is "apocalyptic" (e.g., Beasley-Murray 1993; Mack 1988).

Ironically, many of those debates may have more to do with modern theology than with ancient Jewish and Christian literature and movements. The concept of apocalyptic(ism) that dominates many of these discussions was developed over a century ago, when many of the documents of Jewish apocalyptic literature were (re-)discovered. It is a synthetic construct of typical elements or features abstracted from a variety of Jewish "revelatory" literature ranging over several centuries from the third century B.C.E. to late antiquity. This concept was developed, moreover, during a time when scholars read the language of revelatory texts somewhat literally, without taking into account the way in which given imagery may have been used. For example, ancient Jewish apocalypticism supposedly involved the expectation of the imminent end of historical, earthly conditions in a "cosmic catastrophe"; historical life, meanwhile, was determined by superhuman forces, and apocalyptically minded people were "alienated from history" and oriented to an otherworldly existence. This highly synthetic concept, constructed out of motifs from a variety of different texts from different historical situations, was then determined to be present in a given document such as the Gospel of Mark. Even an individual Gospel saying was categorized as "apocalyptic" on the basis of the occurrence of one of the typical motifs, such as judgment or imminence.

During the last three decades, however, more critical analysis has resulted in a far more subtle and sophisticated understanding of Jewish apocalyptic literature and the scribal circles that produced it (Collins 1984; and see especially chapter 4 above). There seems to be little point, therefore, in rehearsing the debates about Jesus and the Gospels carried on in terms of the standard old synthetic concept of apocalypticism. What was discerned as being present or absent—for example, in the Gospel of Mark or in a given set of Jesus' sayings—was the modern construct "apocalypticism" (e.g., Perrin 1974; Mack 1988). We now have a clearer sense of the general historical situation of the people who produced Judean apocalyptic literature and of those who produced the Gospels. We can therefore now understand particular pieces of literature much more precisely in the historical contexts in which they originated and which they addressed (Collins 1984; Nickelsburg 1981). This enables us to use Judean apocalyptic literature to illuminate the Gospels in two ways. We can note some key common features of Judean apocalyptic literature in the period prior to the Gospels, replacing the old concept with a clearer understanding of how apocalyptic literature was related to historical circumstances. And we can make particular comparisons between a given Gospel or Gospel passage and particular Jewish apocalyptic texts or passages that seem historically appropriate, a far more defensible procedure than the old method of categorizing a text according to a broad synthetic concept (Horsley 1987, 129–45; 1993).

THE PRINCIPAL CONCERNS OF JEWISH APOCALYPTIC LITERATURE

Generally speaking, Judean apocalyptic literature was the product of and was addressed to certain crises that emerged from the imperial situation that prevailed in Judea under the Hellenistic and Roman empires. Following the Babylonian destruction of Jerusalem and deportation of the Judean ruling class in 587 B.C.E., Judea was under the control of one empire after another. Whereas the Persian imperial regime had sponsored the return of the Judean ruling class to Jerusalem to rebuild the Temple and consolidate Judea's (Israelite) cultural and legal traditions, the "Western" empires, beginning with Alexander the Great, fostered a cultural as well as political-economic imperialism. The Hellenistic and Roman empires encouraged the ruling classes of the ancient Near East in particular to assimilate to the dominant Greek cultural as well as political forms.

That policy placed Judean scribes, who aided the high priestly families in governing the Judean Temple-state, in a difficult situation. Scribes were the professional guardians and interpreters of the traditional Judean way of life, including the Torah (literally "teaching") of Moses. When the Judean high priestly rulers in Jerusalem collaborated too closely with the Hellenistic and Roman imperial rulers and even adopted some of the dominant cultural and political forms, some scribes felt their own position as well as the traditional way of life threatened. In the escalating crisis that led up to the Maccabean Revolt, for example, the high priestly families appeared to "sell out" completely to the empire in an attempt to transform Jerusalem into a Greek type of government along with its attendant culture. The scribal circle known as "the wise" (*maśkîlîm*) steadfastly resisted the hellenizing "reform." When the resisters were arrested and persecuted, they began to receive "revelations" in the form of dreams and interpretations that now appear in the book of Daniel (chapters 7–12), the prototypical apocalyptic literature. The visionary revelations in Daniel not only explained how history had come to such an extreme crisis but also reassured the faithful that God was still in control and would eventually take action to deliver them from the intolerable situation.

In addressing specific historical crises, Judean apocalypses such as Daniel 7–12 and sections of *1 Enoch* articulated three main concerns. Most important is a twofold resolution of the historical crisis: God will intervene (1) to defeat or judge the oppressive imperial or indigenous rulers and (2) to restore the people. Apocalyptic literature addressed to circumstances of persecution also articulated a third principal concern closely related to the judgment of the oppressive rulers and the restoration of the people: (3) those martyred in the struggle to maintain the traditional way of life will be vindicated. All three of the principal concerns of Judean apocalyptic literature appear together at the climax of the long review of the people's suffering under the increasingly repressive Seleucid imperial rule in Daniel 10–12. (1) The emperor Antiochus

Epiphanes will be defeated; (2) the Judean people will be delivered after action by their protective angel Michael in a restoration that includes the resurrection of the dead (to either everlasting life or contempt); and (3) "the wise" martyred in the struggle against the imperial violence will "shine . . . like the stars forever" (Dan. 11:45–12:3). Although here in Dan. 12:2 and earlier in Isa. 26:19 bodily "resurrection" symbolizes the restoration of the people, it could also be used for the vindication of martyrs.

Judean apocalyptic literature displays both continuities and innovations in comparison with late prophetic literature in the Hebrew Bible. As in late prophecies, such as the "new heaven and new earth" in Isa. 65:17, apocalyptic literature often expresses the restoration of the people in fantastic imagery. Among those fantastic images is that of bodily resurrection. The resurrection in Dan. 12:2 stands in continuity with the same image in late prophetic literature, such as Isa. 26:19, yet is utterly unprecedented in earlier prophetic literature. God's intervention to defeat the oppressive rulers is often accompanied by disturbances in the cosmic order in apocalyptic literature. This stands in continuity with prophetic representations of "the day of the Lord" and even with early biblical portrayals of the divine warrior's action against oppressors of Israel (e.g., Judg. 5:4–5; Isa. 13:10). A focus on divine judgment also continues from late prophecy into apocalyptic literature. In a significant shift from even late prophetic literature, however, superhuman forces that decisively influence human affairs, such as angels and demons, appear in apocalyptic literature. It was difficult to understand how God could have been responsible for the prolonged or intense experiences of suffering, evil, and oppression. It was also impossible for those who were striving mightily to maintain the traditional way of life under circumstances of oppression or persecution to believe that their suffering was due only to their own sins. Superhuman evil forces must be causing the difficulties, and superhuman forces of good were needed to help the faithful. Similarly dualistic worldviews and focus on demonic spirits are found also in modern colonial situations where an imperial culture and indigenous culture stand in uncompromising opposition.

Nearly all of these principal features of apocalyptic literature appear at the conclusion of the *Testament of Moses* (which is technically not an "apocalypse"): the three dominant interrelated themes of defeat of the oppressive empire, restoration of the people, and vindication of the martyrs, along with the defeat of the evil force(s) and the cosmic disturbances that accompany God's deliverance. An elaborate assurance that God will avenge them (*T. Moses* 10) follows an exhortation to potential martyrs. "Then [God's] kingdom will appear throughout his whole creation. Then the devil will have an end." When God arises against the enemies of his people, the earth will tremble, the sun and moon will be darkened, and the stars will be thrown into disarray.

> Then you will be happy, O Israel!
> And you will arise upon the neck and wings of the eagle
>   and they will be brought to an end.
> And God will raise you to the heights.
> Yea, he will fix you firmly in the heaven of the stars.
> And you will behold from on high.
> Yea, you will see your enemies on the earth.

Before proceeding to the Gospels, however, we should raise an important issue seldom addressed in study of Jesus and the Gospels (Horsley 1987, 129–31). It is generally simply assumed that Judean literature from around the time of Jesus provides evidence for a common Jewish culture or "Judaism" shared by everyone in the society except the high priests and Herodian rulers. That assumption, however, does not take into account clear differences in social location. Apocalyptic literature was written by the literate, cultural (although not political-economic) elite. Jesus and his followers, among whom the Synoptic Gospel traditions originated, were illiterate peasants who cultivated their own Israelite traditions in village communities.

A distinction used by anthropologists may help us understand the possible interaction and relationship between the literary products of the scribal elite and the traditions and ideas of the peasantry. In many societies like that in ancient Judea and Galilee, two parallel traditions operate at different social levels. The elite cultivate a "great" tradition, usually oral but often in written form. Meanwhile, the peasants cultivate a "little" or popular tradition, completely in oral form, according to which life in local communities is conducted. Particularly if the scribal elite attempt to get the peasantry to follow their legal rulings and versions of the people's sacred history, there can be considerable interaction between the great and little traditions. Because of their different social locations and social interests, however, there is often considerable difference, even conflict, between "great" and the "little" traditions. A good example of such a conflict appears in Mark 7:1–13. There Jesus defends the Galilean peasants' concern for retaining their economic produce in order to feed their families, according to the basic "commandment of God" ("Honor your father and mother") against the scribal "traditions of the elders" that, in this instance, encouraged the peasants to "devote" those economic resources to the Temple.

While Judean apocalyptic literature was produced by scribal circles, however, they were often making common cause with the peasantry. In the crises of the imperial situation that evoked apocalyptic literature, the scribes were undergoing some of the same conflicts with, even oppression by their rulers that the peasantry experienced on a regular basis. Particularly in times of crisis, as they engaged in common struggles, there would have been much more interaction between the Judean scribes and the peasantry than is usual in traditional agrarian societies. Thus, we may presume a considerable degree of common culture across the social divide between scribal circles and peasant villages around the time of Jesus. For example, both apparently believed in resurrection as a mode of vindication for martyrs and in superhuman forces such as demons. Nevertheless, we would not expect distinctively scribal lore and systematic reflection on deterministic schemes to appear in peasant movements. Insofar as the Gospel traditions stem originally from peasant circles and only secondarily were overwritten by "scribes" such as Matthew and cultivated writers such as Luke, we would not expect to find much scribal lore and schematic reflection in earlier stages of the Gospel tradition.

In this connection it may be of considerable significance that we have windows onto several popular prophetic movements among the Judean peasantry in the decades immediately following Jesus' ministry. Theudas, for example, persuaded his followers to go out to the Jordan River, which he prophesied would be divided to allow the people to cross over. Such prophets and their followers were obviously acting out a certain "script" in the "little tradition." We can recognize Theudas as a new Moses or Joshua enacting a new exodus or entry into the promised land. Obviously the expectations on which they acted were fantastic, given the realities of the imperial situation. Yet without more information on these popular prophetic movements it would be unwarranted to classify them as "apocalyptic."

One of the more significant differences among pieces of apocalyptic literature (and the communities who produced them) is the degree to which the anticipated judgment, renewal, and vindication are imminent or even already under way. The author of the *Testament of Moses* was eagerly hoping that God's kingdom would appear soon. The "wise" who authored Daniel 10–12 see themselves as living midway through the last "week" of years before God's anticipated intervention in judgment and restoration. The Qumran community that authored the Dead Sea Scrolls was so convinced by revelations received by their "righteous teacher" that God's decisive "visitation" was imminent that they went out into the wilderness of Judea to "prepare the way of the Lord." Their successors, moreover, sustained the keen anticipation in their celebration of meals as if the Messiahs of Aaron and Israel were already present. Yet the decisive action of God to defeat both the Prince of Darkness and his historical agents, the Romans, was still clearly in the future. The popular prophets and their followers apparently believed that the time for God's decisive intervention had arrived, but the repressive military action by the Roman governors gave them little time to celebrate the new deliverance. More than any other Jewish literature, the earliest Gospel literature claims that fulfillment is already under way. In the Gospel of Mark Jesus declares that "the kingdom of God is at hand." It is already being manifested in Jesus' preaching and healing. The Jesus movements that produced the Gospel literature lived in a keen sense of excitement that the long-awaited renewal of Israel had already begun in the ministry of Jesus. The keen sense that renewal was already under way—and the emphasis on building the movement that Jesus had started—focused attention on the present more than on the future.

Finally, before proceeding to the Gospels, we should take note of the important functions or effects of Judean apocalyptic literature and the comparable quasi-apocalyptic perspective manifested in popular prophetic and other movements (Horsley 1987, 143–45). As can be seen especially in these three dominant concerns (judgment of oppressive rulers, restoration of the people, and vindication of martyrs), Judean apocalyptic literature served generally to bolster people's resolve to remain faithful to the traditional covenantal way of life and to resist foreign or domestic oppression, even if it meant martyrdom. More particularly, apocalyptic literature reinforced the people's *memory* of God's promises of blessings to the people and of God's great acts of deliverance from foreign rule or domestic oppression in the past. That memory then informed the apocalyptic *imagination* or creative vision of a life of justice and plenty, a society again free of oppression, a life that, given the present circumstances, must have seemed a virtual "new heaven and new earth." The apocalyptic perspective also involved a *critical demystifying* of the pretenses and practices of the dominant order. High priests were not sacrosanct. They could be "wicked" (as in certain Dead Sea Scrolls). Emperors were not divine. They were beastly (as in Daniel 7). Judean apocalyptic literature and "apocalyptic" movements were manifestations of indigenous resistance to the threats posed by internal oppression and imperial encroachment to the independent and just society that God had willed and previously established in the sacred traditions of Israel.

THE DISCOURSE GOSPEL Q:
THE PROPHETIC RENEWAL OF ISRAEL

The standard understanding of the relationship among the Synoptic Gospels —Matthew, Mark, and Luke—is that Mark wrote first and that Matthew and Luke then, while basically following Mark's narrative, each inserted a great deal of additional material. The large amount of non-Markan material in both Matthew and Luke, much of it identical in wording, must have come (it is believed) from a common source known as "Q" (from the German word *Quelle,* "source"). This is hypothesized to be the earliest written source among Christian Gospels.

This earliest of the "gospels," however, is different from Matthew, Mark, Luke, and John in highly significant respects. It consists largely of Jesus' sayings, with very little narrative. It makes no mention of Jesus' crucifixion and resurrection and has no concern for Jesus' identity as the Messiah/Christ. Those omissions were not found to be particularly significant so long as Q was understood to be basically "catechetical" (teaching) material supplementary to the fundamental "gospel" proclaimed in Mark and followed by Matthew and Luke. Once Q was viewed as an independent gospel document, however, it also appeared to be the product of and to provide evidence for a Jesus movement different from the one for which Mark was written.

Until recently the Synoptic Sayings Source "Q" was understood simply as a collection of sayings. The discovery of the *Gospel of Thomas* earlier this century seemed to provide another example of the same literary genre. Among those who have studied Q closely, opinions are sharply divided over the degree to which it displays "apocalyptic" features. In reaction against the tendency to read Q, like other Synoptic Gospel materials, as an expression of "apocalyptic Christianity" (Perrin 1974), some have claimed that "apocalyptic" material in Q belongs to a secondary "apocalyptic" layer, as opposed to the supposedly original document, which consisted exclusively of wisdom sayings. One motive in this effort has been the desire to free Jesus as a wisdom teacher acceptable to late-twentieth-century liberal sensibilities from the eschatological visionary who predicted a "cosmic catastrophe," as envisioned earlier in the twentieth century by Albert Schweitzer and Rudolf Bultmann.

One particular division of Q into an earlier "sapiential" or wisdom layer and a secondary "apocalyptic" layer has become highly influential among members of the "Q Seminar" of the Society of Biblical Literature (Kloppenborg 1987a). Five clusters of Q sayings (3:7–9, 16–17; 7:1–10, 18–35; 11:14–26, 29–32, 37–52; 12:39–59; and 17:23–35) are assigned to a later "apocalyptic" layer on the basis of three common features. The *projected audi-*

ence supposedly consists of the impenitent opponents of the Q people, all of Israel. The literary form of "prophetic judgment" and "apocalyptic" sayings, it is claimed, dominate these clusters. And supposedly preponderant in these five clusters are *motifs* related to the theme of judgment, such as imminence and the *parousia*, with Israel obstinately rejecting Jesus and the Q preachers while the Gentiles respond positively. When one examines these five clusters of sayings, however, it is difficult to find these hypothesized "common features." The vast majority of material in these clusters is directed to the "in-group" of Jesus' followers themselves (3:16–17; 7:18–35; 11:14–26; 12:39–59; 17:23–35). Part of one cluster is ostensibly directed against the "scribes and Pharisees" (11:37–52). Yet there is no reason to think that "this generation" accused in 11:29–32 refers to "Israel" as opposed to "Gentiles." Moreover, in *form* virtually none of the sayings in these clusters can be classified as "apocalyptic." Rather, many would more legitimately be classified as "prophetic," raising questions about why the label "apocalyptic" should be used for this supposed layer in Q in the first place. The *motifs* that dominate these clusters of sayings, finally, are not particularly "apocalyptic." For example, judgment is not particularly "imminent," and the expectation of the "*parousia*" is not found in Q itself but is introduced in Matthew's resetting of certain sayings. We shall find that Q expresses the same basic concerns as apocalyptic literature. Yet since it lacks many of the key forms and motifs typical of apocalyptic literature, attempts to distinguish an apocalyptic literary stratum are not persuasive.

What has come out of the sharp debate about the hypothetical "apocalyptic" and "wisdom" layers in Q has been the growing recognition that Q is not merely a collection of sayings like the *Gospel of Thomas*. Whereas the sayings in the *Gospel of Thomas* appear separately or in pairs, most of the sayings in Q appear in larger clusters focused on some topic. It is now increasingly being recognized that Q is a series of discourses, each focused on some particular issue such as instructions for mission or exhortation to fearless confession when on trial. Q is more like the *Didache* (*Teaching of the Twelve Apostles*), a sort of handbook providing instruction on basic issues for early Christian churches in Syria. To a degree the issues dealt with in Q come in the same sequence as the same issues in the *Didache*. Q can thus be read as a coherent set of discourses addressing key concerns of an early Jesus movement (Horsley 1991).

The series of discourses in Q even has a dominant connecting theme. Sayings about the "kingdom of God" occur prominently at crucial points in most of the discourses. In Jesus' first words to his followers he offers the kingdom to the poor (6:20); the envoys Jesus sends out are to announce that in the healing of the sick "the kingdom of God has come near" (10:9). Indeed, in his exorcisms it has "come upon you" (11:20). If those anxious about food and clothing will earnestly "seek the kingdom of God, then these things will be added" to them (12:31). The reality, nearness, or presence of the kingdom is accompanied by a sense of experiencing something utterly new, unprecedented in the history of Israel, a fulfillment of age-old longings and expectations. Now that the kingdom is coming, the hungry will be filled, those who weep will laugh (6:21). In the practice and preaching of Jesus the blind now see, the lame walk, the deaf hear, and the poor receive good news, in fulfillment of well-known prophecies of the prophet Isaiah (7:22). While the greatest figure in history is John the Baptist, "the least in the kingdom is greater than he" (7:28). Those who experienced Jesus' ministry are seeing what many prophets and kings desired to see (10:24). This is something greater than the famous wisdom of Solomon or the preaching of Jonah (11:31–32). An intense sense of a new historical time, a fulfillment of age-old longings, of renewal of personal and community life, dominates Q.

The unprecedented situation created by Jesus' preaching and practice is in fact a historical crisis with a tone of finality. John the Baptist announced that he would baptize with both "Holy Spirit and fire," that he would "burn the chaff with unquenchable fire" as well as "gather the wheat into his granary." That is exactly what the Q discourses portray as under way. As indicated in the instructions for the "workers in the harvest," the kingdom of God comes near in the healings of the sick, but it also comes near in the judgmental mode for those who reject the movement, its message, and its workers (10:8–11, 12–16). Those who think they can rely on their aristocratic genealogy or those who presume upon their wealth and privilege will find themselves cast out when all Israel gathers for the glorious feast of fulfillment. Those who do not respond now will be accused and condemned in "the judgment" (11:31–32). Holy Spirit *and* fire, grain gathered into the granary *and* chaff burned with fire.

Given the prominence of both fulfillment and judgment running through its discourses, it may not be surprising that earlier interpreters found "apocalyptic Christianity" in Q. Like the scribal dream-vision in Daniel 7 that fantasized God's imminent return of sovereignty (the kingdom) to the oppressed "people of the saints of the Most High," the prophetic discourses in Q proclaim the benefits of God's kingdom already under way for the desperate villagers of Israel. Just as the scribes of the Epistle of Enoch anticipated judgment against their wealthy and powerful rulers in Jerusalem, so the prophets John and Jesus in Q pronounced judgment against those of power and privilege. Now that we have a far more precise historical sense both of ancient Jewish "apocalypticism" and of the contours of Q discourses, however, we can explore more closely many particular expressions in Q and compare them with features found in the Jewish apocalyptic literature of near contemporary Jewish scribal groups (Horsley 1991).

John the Baptist's preaching of repentance and prophecy of a stronger one coming after him who would "baptize in Holy Spirit and fire" (Luke 3:7–9, 16–17 // Matt. 3:7–12) would appear to have opened this discourse gospel. The images of "the wrath to come" as a harvest-time winnowing of wheat from chaff and a burning of unfruitful trees drew on both familiar experiences in an agrarian society and a long Israelite prophetic tradition of impending divine judgment. John sets his call for repentance and renewal of the Mosaic covenant directly over against the upper-class Jerusalemite trust in the unconditional Abrahamic promise and their cultivation of proper genealogies. In the context of Q, the "stronger one" coming with "Spirit and fire" is Jesus, who is about to proclaim and manifest the kingdom of God. In subsequent discourses Jesus performs in his ministry what John prophesies (see especially Luke/Q 7:18–28). In that respect (despite the obvious differences in social location) Q seems very similar to key texts from the Qumran community, where the new exodus and new (Mosaic) covenant community are already under way (see especially the opening "covenant renewal" sections of the *Community Rule* and the *Damascus Document*). The long-awaited renewal of Israel is already happening in the communities' very foundation, and the communities live in intense anticipation of fuller realization of their now-intensified hopes and expectations. None of the imagery used by the Baptist, however, suggests an imminent "last judgment," let alone "cosmic catastrophe."

Next comes the only extended narrative in Q, the story of Jesus' temptation by the devil. This section of Q does not seem to fit well with the rest of the series of discourses. Especially interesting is the opposition of the devil and the Spirit, which leads Jesus into the Moses-like (or early Israel-like) "forty days in the wilderness." The same opposition between the devil/Satan and Jesus in the power of the Spirit (or "finger") of God appears later in the Beelzebul discourse (Luke/Q 11:14–26). This resembles the dualism between divine and demonic spirits that occurs in some Jewish apocalyptic literature, particularly that between the Spirit of Light and the Spirit of Darkness (= Belial) in the *Community Rule* from Qumran. But the opposition in Q is nowhere near as all-encompassing and determinative of human affairs in general, nor is it as systematically developed as in the scribal reflection evident in the Dead Sea literature.

The Q "sermon" (Luke/Q 6:20–49) presents a renewed (Mosaic) covenant, with many similarities to the renewed covenant in the opening columns of the *Community Rule* from Qumran. As interpreters of the Mosaic covenant in Exodus 20 and the covenant renewal in Joshua 24 have explained, the covenant that served as Israel's basic form of governance under the direct rule of God had three interrelated parts. God's great acts of deliverance (from Egyptian slavery, etc.) were recited first; then the principles of (exclusive loyalty to God and the principles of) social relations (the Decalogue) were presented; and finally sanctions such as "blessings and curses" were declared to motivate the people's compliance. The identical pattern is evident in the Q sermon, although the blessings and curses seem displaced. The set of sayings about "love your enemy, do good and lend" and "turn the other cheek" in Luke/Q 6:27–38(–42), which closely resemble traditional covenantal exhortations (e.g., Leviticus 19), constitute the principles of social relations, in this case renewed reciprocity and mutual care in the (village) communities. The sayings about good and bad trees and the double parable about building one's house on rock versus sand in Luke/Q 6:43–49 serve as sanctions on maintaining the renewed covenantal relations.

Consideration of the historical social context addressed may help clarify the seeming displacement of the blessings and curses to the beginning of the renewed covenant in Q (Horsley 1987, 246–73). As in most agrarian societies, the Galilean and Judean peasantry were economically marginal at best. Compounding the people's burdens of tribute to Rome and Temple and priestly dues, Herod the Great and Herod Antipas intensified economic exploitation of their subjects to fund their massive building projects. The struggling people, however, would presumably have understood their worsening conditions of poverty and hunger as God's curses for their having violated the covenantal principles (the Decalogue). In the opening of the Q sermon Jesus offers the "poor" and "hungry" people the kingdom of God as an imminent blessing, and announces that God's curses are falling on the rich and well-fed, not on the poor. That is, God's imminent bringing of the kingdom to the poor is the new act of deliverance on the basis of which the people can now renew the covenantal care and cooperation of their community life. To those who have "ears to hear," that is, who are attuned to Israelite covenantal traditions and the historical social context, the "beatitudes" of the renewed covenant in Q indicate an intense sense of renewal of Israel, already under way as well as in anticipation of further fulfillment of expectations.

The next major discourse, Luke/Q 7:18–35 (following the fragmentary story in 7:1b, 6b–9) confirms this intense sense of fulfillment as already under way. The age-old longings of the people are now being satisfied in the good news Jesus is preaching and the healing and liberation he is practicing, in fulfillment of cherished prophecies (7:22; cf. Isa. 35:5–6; 61:1). Not only is John the Baptist's work set over against the Herodian rulers (against whom he prophesied, according to Mark 6 and Josephus), but he is held up as the greatest figure of history, in comparison with whom even the least in the kingdom of God is greater! This discourse intensifies the sense of unprecedented renewal now happening, a sense of fulfillment that goes far beyond that expressed in Qumran literature. It also indicates that the prophetic pronouncements and the work of John and Jesus have provoked sharp criticism and accusations (7:31–35).

The "mission" discourse in Luke/Q 9:57–10:16 makes unavoidably clear that Q is the document of a movement, not a mere collection of Jesus' pithy teachings addressed to individuals. The introduction to the mission instructions alludes to the famous stories of the prophet Elijah's calling of his successor Elisha, who carried on his prophetic project of renewing an Israel suffering under alien and exploitative rule. The harvest imagery is now completely positive, in contrast with the double-edged imagery of John's preaching: the huge harvest requires sending out workers. The village-by-village preaching and healing by the workers, however, vividly illustrate the dual impact and effect of the kingdom now at hand: healing for the receptive, but proleptic judgment for those who reject the offer. Jesus' woes consigning the unreceptive villages to judgment cite "Sodom," the standard "historical" example of God's destructive punishment in Israelite prophetic tradition, as well as Tyre and Sidon, standard foils in earlier prophetic oracles, as well as nearby alien and wealthy cities. The kingdom of God is already effective in anticipation of its nearness and the rhetoric of rejection intense, but judgment does not seem particularly imminent.

The most "apocalyptic" language in Q comes in the next sayings, Luke/Q 10:21–24, the contours of whose discourse cannot be fully discerned from Matthew's and Luke's editing. Jesus gives thanks to the Father that he has "revealed" ("apocalypsed") all these things to "babes," that is, the ordinary people, and in fact hidden them from sapiential elite, the professional scribes and sages who cultivated and on occasion received "revelations." This indicates explicitly that the Q discourses were products of a popular movement opposed to and by the political and cultural elite of rulers and their scribal representatives. Apocalyptic literature such as the sections of *1 Enoch* was produced by dissident scribal circles also opposed to and by the high priestly rulers of Judea. Q, however, was "revelation" specifically for a popular movement of renewal, self-consciously set over against scribes as well as rulers. We should thus not expect in these discourses the kind of scribal lore, reflection, and speculation that we find in apocalyptic literature.

The content of the following section in Q, which contains the Lord's Prayer, was transformed into a more distinctively religious mode by Luke, then variously spiritualized through generations of Christian recitation. While Luke has surely retained the shorter form more original to the Q prayer for the kingdom, Luke 11:2–4, Matthew has probably preserved more of the original wording of particular phrases. The third petition in particular, Matt 6:12 // Lk 11:4, enables us to discern just how concrete and down-to-earth the "kingdom of God" was understood to be among the Q people. The more serious problems for Galilean as for any peasants would have been chronic hunger and the spiral of indebtedness necessary to meet obligations for taxes as well as to feed hungry families. In the prayer for the kingdom, Jesus taught the people to petition the Father in heaven for subsistence bread and for cancellation of debts! The concrete economic meaning of the "kingdom of God" in Q is reminiscent of the concrete economic meaning of the "new heaven and new earth" in Isa. 65:17–22. In severe circumstances prophetic fantasy resorts to extreme hyperbole in its symbolization of longings for a simple decent life free of war, oppression, and exploitation. The prayer in Luke/Q 11:2–4 is also consistent with the covenantal exhortations in the Q sermon, which admonish the people to reciprocal cooperation and sharing (Luke/Q 6:27–36). Those who petition for cancellation of their debts are reciprocally therewith forgiving the debts of their neighbors.

The words ("seek and you will find," etc.) that follow the prayer for the kingdom in Luke/Q 11:9–13 and the similar discourse addressing anxiety about food and clothing in Luke/Q 12:22–31 offer sensitive reassurance that God will take care of the people's basic needs. The key is the people's single-minded pursuit of the kingdom. And if the latter is understood in the terms already indicated in the renewed covenant and the prayer for the kingdom, then the pursuit of the kingdom involves that key to community life, reciprocity of sharing and cooperation.

The matter-of-fact language about demons in the Beelzebul discourse in Luke/Q 11:14–26 suggests that Q and the Q people lived in a world in which demons and demon possession were familiar. It would appear that in Judean and Galilean society in the Second Temple period, particularly under the highly intrusive Seleucid and Roman imperial rule, the traditional covenantal explanation of suffering as punishment for sin was no longer adequate. Surely God could not be responsible for the extreme evil and suffering of his people.

Surely superhuman forces were at work. Like colonized peoples in modern times who dare not focus directly on imperial violence as the cause of their malaise, the ancient Judeans and Galileans understood various forms of their personal and social disorder in terms of possession by alien spirits or hostile demons. Indeed, such colonial situations seem to be caught in a struggle between two superhuman/divine forces, of good and of evil.

The Qumran community developed a systematic and comprehensive scheme whereby all history was understood as caught in a struggle between the Spirit of Light and the Spirit of Darkness, created at the beginning by God. By contrast with the *Community Rule* and the *War Scroll* from Qumran, the dualism of Holy Spirit and Satan in Q is relatively undeveloped. It is nowhere nearly as pervasive and comprehensive in Q as among that scribal-priestly community. It may also be noteworthy that this opposition is introduced into the discussion ostensibly by Jesus' opponents who accuse him of witchcraft (working in cahoots with Satan). Comparative materials such as the sixteenth- to seventeenth-century western European witch-hunts suggest that the intellectual and/or political elite of a society can press a comprehensive dualistic ideology on a population precisely in order to eliminate "deviants." The Beelzebul discourse appears to be cleverly formulated. Opponents (evidently scribal) representing a systematically dualistic ideology ascribe Jesus' remarkable influence over demons to the Satanic side of the dualism. This provides Jesus with the occasion to demonstrate (logically) that even on the establishment's own terms Satan's rule is collapsing, as manifested in his own exorcisms, hence the kingdom of God has come upon the people. Thus also Q's Beelzebul discourse represents God's final victory over Satan as already under way (Luke 11:17–22), whereas the Qumran community was still awaiting "the time of his visitation."

The group of sayings in Luke/Q 11:29–32 juxtaposes a blunt rejection of "this generation seeking a sign" with a vivid portrayal of "this generation's" condemnation at "the judgment." Luke/Q 11:32 indicates that "the preaching of Jonah" was the "sign of Jonah" for the Ninevites (who repented!). Thus, in the analogy drawn with "the sign of Jonah" in 11:30, the "Son of Man" must be a self-reference by Jesus, somewhat like "Son of Man" in the fourth Q beatitude (Luke 6:22; cf. Matt. 5:11) and the introduction to the mission discourse (Luke 9:58), and not a reference to the judgment, which is mentioned explicitly in 11:31–32. The "Son of Man" in 11:30, moreover, stands parallel to "something greater than Solomon . . . [and] Jonah" that "is here" in 11:31–32. Thus, besides excoriating "this generation" for its lack of response, these sayings parallel the point made in earlier Q discourses (especially Luke/Q 7:18–28; 10:23–24), that in Jesus preaching and healing something long-awaited but historically unprecedented is happening. "The judgment," however, does not seem particularly imminent. Also noteworthy is the matter-of-fact way that the sayings assume the resurrection of earlier generations to appear as accusers at the judgment. These are not simply literary motifs. Resurrection and judgment have become integral parts of the prevailing cultural "symbol system" or "symbolic universe" that Q and the Q community presuppose.

The series of woes against the Pharisees and scribes, Luke/Q 11:37–52, mocks their concerns for purity and indicts them for the debilitating effect of their role as retainers of the Temple-state on the people, for example, when they urge the people to pay the full levy of tithes and other (economic) "burdens." The pronouncement of "sentence" on these "indictments" in 11:49–51 indicates that the Q people understand the hero-founder of their movement to stand in a long line of Israelite prophets killed by the elite, (by implication) the rulers as well as their scribal retainers. The Q discourses portray Jesus, like John the Baptist, in a prophetic role in both his preaching and healing, with reminiscences of Moses (6:20–49) and Elijah (9:57–62). Jesus himself is evidently the greatest and perhaps final prophet in that line, since the kingdom of God is clearly under way in his ministry.

That "hidden" things are "revealed," at least to the elect, is a prominent theme in Jewish and Christian apocalyptic literature and movements. Perhaps such language lends a certain additional overtone of reassurance in the discourse of assurance to members of a movement under attack in Luke/Q 12:2–12. The "hidden revealed" in this Q discourse refers not to what the apocalyptic visionary has received from an interpreter-angel, but to the eventual public triumph of the mission of the Q people that is currently pursued surreptitiously, because of the threat of repression by the authorities (12:3, 11). In the further words of assurance given in 12:4–5, Gehenna, the ravine south of Jerusalem that had become a symbol for the fiery punishment upon condemnation in "the judgment," seems to be another component in the basic "symbolic universe" presupposed in Q. Similarly standard in the symbol system that Q presupposes is the picture in 12:8–9 of the judgment as carried out before "the angels of heaven," a traditional picture of the divine court. It seems most likely that the Son of Man in 12:8 is another self-reference by Jesus (as in 6:22; 9:57; and 11:30). Jesus/the Son of Man will appear before the divine court of judgment as a witness, somewhat in the same way that the Ninevites or the Queen of the South will. But he is not portrayed here as the agent of judgment and salvation, as in Mark 8:38 and 14:26–27.

Another saying referring to the Son of Man in Luke/Q 12:(39–)40 appears to go together with—indeed to be interpreted by—Luke/Q 12:41–46. This discourse would appear to be an admonition to the members (or leadership?) of the movement to maintain rigorous discipline, for they simply do not know when the judgment will occur. The Son of Man seems to be a standing symbol for the judgment (as in Luke/Q 17:24, 26, 30 below). Any possible reference to Jesus would have to be transferred from previous discourses.

The discourse in Luke/Q 12:49–56 refers to the crisis in families and local communities provoked by Jesus' mission and movement. Jesus uses the ominous hyperboles of fire, flood, and war, and cites the traditional prophetic (not distinctively "apocalyptic") scenario of generational division in households (12:49–51, 52–53; cf. Micah 7:6). He then draws the analogy from interpreting the appearance of earth and sky to interpreting historical events of the present, meaning apparently the significance of the movement under way, in which the kingdom of God is finally present. It is unclear if the parables of the kingdom in Luke/Q 13:18–21 belonged to a larger discourse. In any case, the comparisons they make parallel the discourses in Luke/Q 12:2–12; 12:22–31; and 12:49–56. They suggest that Jesus' mission and movement (in which the kingdom is now coming or is about to come), while seemingly insignificant at the outset, will grow dramatically, having a transforming effect on society.

The two prophetic sayings in Luke/Q 13:28–29 and 13:34–35 have often been interpreted according to a certain Christian paradigm of salvation history that has seriously skewed the reading of Q generally. It is assumed that in the Gospels as well as in Paul, the new, universal religion Christianity was replacing the old, particularist religion Judaism. According to this scheme, "the sons of the kingdom" in Matt. 8:12 and "Jerusalem" in Luke 13:34 // Matt. 23:37 are taken as symbols of a monolithic "Judaism," and these sayings appear to be prophetic condemnations of "all Israel" or "Judaism." It is difficult to discern the possible contours of the one-time Q discourse of which they were components. Yet read against the background of a more precise understanding of the Judean Temple-state, these prophetic sayings can now be seen as condemnations of the ruling house in Jerusalem, not "all Israel." The parallel references from earlier prophetic literature to the "pilgrimage" from east and west into the banquet of fulfillment in 13:29, moreover, refer not to "Gentiles" but to Israelites. These sayings thus express the same basic opposition between rulers and ruled within "Israel" that prevailed at the time in the political-economic-religious structure of the Judean Temple-state, including ideological conflict over the form that "Israel" should take. Luke/Q 13:28–29 is thus a prophetic vision of the finally restored Israel banqueting with its founding ancestors, but significantly without the rulers who presumed on their ancestry (cf. John's words in 3:7–9). Luke/Q 13:34–35—which is paralleled strikingly thirty years later by the woes on Jerusalem by another rustic prophet, Jesus son of Hananiah—is a prophetic lament over the Jerusalem ruling house, which has repeatedly blocked God's attempts at restoration of Israel through the ministry of the prophets.

Matthew and Luke present widely differing versions of the "great supper" parable. The version in Luke 14:16–24 and the parallel in *Gospel of Thomas* 64 portray the invited guests who are too busy to come as the wealthy. That suggests that this parable in Q should be read together with the immediately preceding Q materials in 13:28–29, 34–35 as another way of declaring that the Jerusalem rulers and other wealthy and powerful people will be shut out of the kingdom-banquet, while the poor will be invited in, as in the blessings and woes of 6:20–26.

What is perhaps the next to the last discourse in Q, Luke/Q 17:23–24, 26–30, 33–34, 37, focusing on the suddenness of "the day of the Son of Man," is probably a sanction on all of the exhortation in the preceding Q discourses. This discourse is the locus of most of the "future Son of Man" sayings, which have been claimed as proof texts for the "apocalyptic" character of Q in general and/or for the secondary "apocalyptic" layer in Q (Jacobson 1992; Yarbro Collins 1989). "Logia apocalypse" is an inappropriate designation, since it lacks any narrative presentation of final events ("and then . . . ," etc.). The concept of the "coming" (Greek *parousia*) is Matthew's contribution (24:27, 37, 39). Within the discourse there is nothing even to suggest that "the Son of Man" is Jesus, although that meaning may carry over from earlier discourses in Q. The series of parallel sayings in Luke/Q 17 simply emphasize the suddenness of judgment symbolized in "the day of the Son of Man." Jewish prophetic tradition had long used "Sodom (and Gomorrah)" and the escape of Lot as a prime symbol of God's judgment against wickedness. Jewish apocalyptic literature also used Noah or Noah's generation as an analogy to the time preceding the final judgment. But nothing in this Q discourse comes close to the portrayal of the present generation as so wicked that it, like that of Noah, needed to be utterly destroyed. Noah's time in Luke/Q 17:26–27 serves simply as an analogy for the future judgment and how sudden and unexpected it will be. The Q discourse does not appear to be directed against apocalyptic-style calculation or prediction of "signs," but against the Q people becoming distracted by any *other* movements or leaders. This discourse could even be comforting to the Q people, on whose behavior it is a sanction, insofar as the correlatives indicate how the suddenness took the others unawares, while the heroes Noah and Lot were saved.

It seems likely that Luke 22:30 // Matt. 19:28 was (part of) Jesus' final words in Q. This saying, read, like Luke/Q 13:28–29 and 34–35, through a Christian paradigm of salvation history, has been taken to mean that the Twelve are to be (negatively) "judging" Israel. This reading involves a misleading translation of the Greek verb *krinein,* which clearly carries the positive meaning of "doing justice for" or even "delivering" in the Greek translation of the Hebrew Bible (the Septuagint)—as when God "defends" the widow, the orphan, and the poor in the Psalms and elsewhere (Horsley 1987, 201–8). Matthew's interjection of "the Son of Man sitting on his glorious throne" may have contributed to the skewed Christian reading of the saying. But the term "renewal" in Matt. 19:28, used by the Jewish historian Josephus for the restoration of Israel on its land, suggests what "kingdom" in Luke/Q 22:30 means. Indeed, the whole series of discourses known as Q, consistently focused on the theme of the kingdom of God, constitutes a sustained presentation of various aspects of the renewal of Israel.

The symbol of "twelve tribes of Israel" makes this meaning unavoidable. The Q people (or the leadership, symbolically also "twelve," as in Matthew's version) are to be *establishing justice for* or *delivering* the twelve tribes of Israel. This concept is closely paralleled in Jewish literature of that time such as the *Psalms of Solomon* (17:28–32) and the *Community Rule* from Qumran (1QS 8:1–4). In the latter, "the council of the community," consisting of twelve men and three priests, is to effect "righteousness, justice, loving-kindness, and humility, . . . preserve faith in the land, . . . and atone for sin by the practice of justice." Thus, Q does not end with Jesus' setting up the Twelve to condemn Israel at the last judgment. Like the scribal-priestly community at Qumran, the peasant movement that produced the Q discourses was engaged in a renewal of Israel. The Q movement aimed at renewal of Israel, however, did not withdraw from the rest of society either as a monastic community in the wilderness or as a bunch of "wandering charismatics," but focused on revitalization of the village communities, the fundamental social form in which Israel was constituted.

There appears to be little basis for classifying the discourse "gospel" Q as "apocalyptic" in the older sense that has dominated the field of New Testament studies. No imminent cosmic catastrophe looms. The imagery of harvest or fire upon the earth or allusion to historical destructions (in Luke/Q 3:9, 17; 12:49; 17:27) does not point to any sort of "catastrophic destruction of the world" (Kloppenborg 1987b, 296). There is no feeling of "historical determinism." References to "the judgment" abound, but it is not particularly imminent. Contrary to much recent scholarly discussion, Jesus does not appear to be identified with a heavenly judge or redeemer with the title "the Son of Man." When "the Son of Man" refers to Jesus, he is not playing the role of an eschatological judge or redeemer, and when "the day of the Son of Man" refers to the judgment, it does not appear to be identified with Jesus. The most prominent image of the future fulfillment of the people's longings is that of a banquet in the kingdom of God, central to the Israelite prophetic tradition since Jeremiah. References to heaven and the divine court; to hell, Hades, and Gehenna; to resurrection; and even to the Holy Spirit and Satan/demons appear to be components of the standard "symbolic universe" of late Second Temple society under foreign imperial rule. Certainly Q does not fit the synthetic modern concept of "apocalyptic" constructed by biblical scholarship about a century ago.

On the other hand, the discourse gospel Q (along with the movement that produced it) displays a number of significant similarities to, as well as distinct differences from, Judean apocalyptic literature of the immediately preceding centuries.

Even more striking are the similarities and differences with the scribal-priestly Qumran movement and its literature. The three principal concerns of apocalyptic literature (judgment of oppressive rulers, restoration of the people, and vindication of martyrs) are all central in Q. The images in which they are portrayed, however, are less elaborate, derived from the basic covenantal and prophetic traditions of Israel, and the anticipated fulfillment is much further advanced than in the scribal apocalyptic literature. Daniel 7 looks forward to God's restoration of the people to sovereignty; Q presents the kingdom as already under way in Jesus' ministry and movement. The hopes and expectations of the common people are being wondrously fulfilled in the message and actions of Jesus and continue in the mission of the movement, if the people remain single-mindedly focused on "seeking first the kingdom of God." Similar to the Qumran community (and certain late-medieval movements in Europe), the program of the renewal of society now under way in the Q community is derived from the sacred traditions of Israel, in this case the Mosaic covenantal tradition and previous prophetic movements among the people. Also similar to the Qumran community as well as to *1 Enoch* (and many late-medieval European movements), the Q people sharply condemn their own rulers. In Q as in *1 Enoch,* the prophetic condemnation of rulers focuses only on oppressive domestic rulers. By contrast, the Qumran community included its own opposition to the Romans ("the Kittim") in its vivid portrayal of the final battle against "the hosts of Satan" entitled *The War of the Sons of Light against the Sons of Darkness.* Q also promises vindication for those who are persecuted or killed for the kingdom's/Jesus' sake (Luke/Q 6:23; 7:35; 11:49–51; 12:2–12), although the Q people anticipate nothing as fantastic as "shining like the stars."

Perhaps because of its emphasis on the renewal of Israel already under way in the preaching and manifestation of the kingdom of God, Q has no portrayal of a future intervention by God accompanied by disturbances in the cosmic order similar to that in *T. Moses* 10. Even the future judgment in Q functions more as a sanction on the discipline of the Q community itself than it does as a condemnation of its opponents. The most striking differences between Q and scribal apocalyptic literature are Q's lack of scribal apocalyptic lore and the kind of schemes that resulted from more systematic scribal reflection. The very cultural symbol system or symbolic universe presupposed by Q included an expectation of a resurrection in connection with God's future judgment and a belief in demons and Satan—perhaps partly as a result of the dissemination of ideas that originated in scribal apocalyptic circles (although the Qumranites do not share the belief in resurrection). Q, however, includes nothing like the elaborate portrayal of resurrection in Daniel 12 or the systematic reflection on the dualism of divine and demonic Spirits at Qumran or the reflection on angels, heavenly bodies, and heavenly journeys found in *1 Enoch.*

THE GOSPEL OF MARK

Mark's Gospel portrays Jesus engaged in a programmatic renewal of Israel, over against the Jerusalem rulers and Temple, according to a basically prophetic "script" that is overlaid with a radically transformed understanding of the role of a Messiah. More programmatically but less prominently than in the discourse gospel Q, "the kingdom of God" forms the theme running throughout the Gospel. At the outset of his mission in Galilee, Jesus summarizes the "good news" he proclaims as the imminence of the kingdom of God in the time of fulfillment: "The time is fulfilled, and the kingdom of God has come near; turn your lives around, and trust in the good news" (Mark 1:15). The kingdom, the plan of which has been communicated in private to the disciples and other followers, like seeds that grow secretly and eventually produce an abundant harvest or large bushes, is already "planted" and "growing" (4:11, 26–32). In the near future it will "come with power" (8:34–9:1). Meanwhile, Jesus warns that "whoever does not receive the kingdom of God as a little child will never enter it" (10:14–15). Indeed, for wealthy people (who have gained their wealth only by defrauding others) it will be virtually impossible. "It is easier for a camel to go through the eye of a needle than for someone who is rich to enter the kingdom of God" (10:17–25). At his last meal with his disciples, at which he institutes the Lord's Supper with his followers, he declares that in the future he will once again "drink the fruit of the vine . . . new in the kingdom of God" (14:25). The distinguished member of "the council" who receives his body for burial, finally, is "waiting expectantly for the kingdom of God" (15:43). *Testament of Moses* 10 and Daniel 7 looked for God to implement his/the people's kingdom imminently. Like Q, Mark portrays the kingdom of God as, in effect, already under way in Jesus' ministry, although the kingdom is to "come with power" only in the imminent future (9:1), as in *T. Moses* 10.

The "kingdom of God" theme is just one among many ways in which Mark indicates that fulfillment of long-standing expectations and prophecies of the renewal of Israel was set in motion first by John the Baptist's preaching and then especially by Jesus' preaching and practice. John was God's messenger "preparing the way of the Lord" (1:2–3; cf. Mal. 3:1; Isa. 40:3). Jesus himself was a Moses- and Elijah-like figure engaged in the restoration of Israel, in sea crossings, exorcisms, healings, wilderness feedings, and appointing the Twelve as representatives of and envoys to the people now undergoing renewal (Mark 9:2–8; 4:35–8:26; 3:13–19; 6:7–13). In his instruction on marriage Jesus even restored the conditions of God's original creation and in his economic exhortation renewed the original egalitarian reciprocity of the Mosaic covenant (10:2–9, 17–31).

In the course of his programmatic preaching and practice of the renewal of Israel, Jesus comes into conflict with the scribes and Pharisees, authorities who have "come down from Jerusalem," and (like John) with Herod Antipas and his representatives, "the Herodians." In contrast to the former, Jesus teaches "with authority/power" (1:22–27). The Pharisees keep him under surveillance (2:1–3:5; 7:1–5) and, with the Herodians, conspire to destroy him (3:6). In a story that prefigures Jesus' martyrdom, Herod Antipas imprisons and beheads the prophet John (6:17–29). More ominous than the Pharisaic-Herodian conspiracy, moreover, Jesus engages the demonic forces in battle. Right from the outset of his manifestation of the kingdom of God, Jesus casts out "unclean spirits" from demon-possessed people and restores them to productive lives among the people (1:21–28, 32–34, 39; 3:11–12, 15). Indeed, it is the "unclean spirits" who know who he really is, "the holy one of God" (1:24; 3:11–12; 5:7). It is clear at points that these "unclean spirits" represent the political as well as cultural-spiritual dimension of the imperial forces under which the people live: "My name is Legion (Roman troops); for we are many." Although they beg Jesus not to "send them out of the country," the demonic forces named "Legion," pointedly self-destruct by drowning in the "Sea" (5:10–13).

As in the discourse gospel Q, Jesus takes the occasion of the scribes' (Pharisees') accusation that he is working in cahoots with "Beelzebul, the ruler of the demons," to point to the deliverance already accomplished precisely in his exorcisms (3:22–27). The Gospel of Mark is not permeated throughout with a sense that all actions are determined by the struggle between "the Prince of Light" and "Belial," as in the priestly-scribal Qumran literature. Perhaps one reason for this can be seen precisely in Jesus' argument in the "Beelzebul controversy." Jesus ostensibly accepts the assumption of the scribal accusation (all actions are determined either by "Satan" or God), as well as their observation that he is casting out demons. If indeed Satan's house is divided, it will fall. But surely Satan is not so foolish as to be divided against himself. Thus, since "the strong man's" house is clearly being "plundered" in the exorcisms, then Satan must have been "tied up" (by Jesus or God). Again, as in the Legion story, the political implications are evident precisely on the assumption of the scribal demonology, such as that articulated in Qumran literature. According to this demonology, which Mark as well as Q shared with the Qumran scribal literature, oppressive rulers such as the Romans ("Kittim") or the Jerusalem high priests (the "Wicked Priest") are under the control of superhuman forces headed by Belial, the "Prince of Darkness/Lies." But if Satan has been "tied up," the oppressive rulers' days must be numbered (Horsley 1987, 184–90).

Indeed, as the demonological language disappears in the second half of the Gospel of Mark, the conflict becomes much more explicitly and ominously political. Jesus informs the disciples three times that "it is necessary" (in God's plan) for "the Son of Man" to be condemned by the high priestly and scribal rulers, to be killed, and after three days to rise (8:31; 9:31; 10:33). That is Mark's way of transforming the role of the Messiah into martyrdom and vindication, as opposed to leading troups of peasants in more active opposition to Jerusalem and/or Roman rule. Then he enters the capital city in a noisy messianic demonstration and even carries out a dramatic prophetic demonstration against the Temple, the sacred center of religious-political-economic power (11:1–10, 15–19). In a sequence of further stories, Jesus embarrasses the high priestly rulers, indeed tells a prophetic parable declaring their condemnation by God as rebellious "tenants" of God's vineyard (Israel), and prophesies the destruction of the Temple (11:27–13:2). Accordingly, Jesus is apprehended by an armed posse, tried and condemned for his prophecy against the Temple, and handed over to the Roman governor for crucifixion as an insurrectionary against the imperial order.

The Gospel of Mark thus has the same dominant concerns as scribal apocalyptic literature: judgment of oppressive rulers and restoration of Israel. As in sections of *1 Enoch,* as opposed to Daniel and the *Testament of Moses,* judgment is directed primarily against the Jerusalem rulers of Israel, not against the alien imperial rulers. Renewal of Israel and judgment against Jerusalem rulers in Mark, however, follow distinctive prophetic traditions and patterns, with Jesus portrayed primarily as a new Moses and new Elijah in chaps. 1–10, to which reminiscences of Isaiah and Jeremiah are added in the Jerusalem climax. Mark superimposes messianic motifs and titles only at Jesus' baptism at the beginning, in Peter's confession at the middle, and in the high priestly trial and the crucifixion toward the end. In contrast with scribal apocalyptic literature, Mark has no fantastic imagery of restoration of the "end," no "new heaven and new earth." Mark makes almost no mention of a transcendent world inhabited by angels. It is difficult to discern any "last judgment" in Mark. No temporal dualism dominates the discourse. "This age" and "the age to come" appear in passing in 10:30, but emphasis there falls explicitly on manifold social-economic restoration "now in this age." Even Jesus' battle with "unclean spirits" fades as the action escalates into direct political confrontation in Jerusalem. Compared with scribal apocalyptic literature, Mark pursues a basically prophetic "script" rooted in popular Israelite prophetic traditions of Moses and Elijah.

While the prophetic script dominates the narrative in Mark, there are nevertheless valid reasons why Mark has been described as "apocalyptic" in tone and character. We may focus on three of these for purposes of analysis. First, since the renewal of Israel is already under way in Jesus' mission of preaching and healing and the kingdom of God "at hand," a tone of urgency and excitement permeates the Gospel. The vindication of the martyred Messiah evident from the empty tomb serves to further intensify this sense of fulfillment in Mark. Second, the lengthy discourse of Jesus in Mark 13 includes several motifs paralleled in Jewish apocalyptic literature, some even derived from Daniel. The heavy concentration of motifs categorized as apocalyptic in Mark 13 has led many to posit a "Synoptic" or "Little Apocalypse" of Jewish or Jewish-Christian origin that Mark adapted at this point in his Gospel. Third, what have been labeled the "apocalyptic (or future) Son of Man" sayings appear to give the Gospel an orientation toward an imminent "end-time" or last judgment.

First, the announced resurrection of Jesus, confirmed by the empty tomb story, which forms the open ending of the Gospel, adds appreciably to the sense of fulfillment already under way and excitement over imminent completion. Jesus was martyred, but has also been vindicated. The rising again implied in the empty tomb intensifies the sense of fulfillment and renewal that continues in the Jesus movement which Mark expresses and addresses. Significantly, however, Mark makes no reference to the vindicated Jesus "shining like the stars of heaven" (in contrast to Dan. 12:3 and *T. Moses* 10:9) or to Jesus' enthronement in glory (cf. Phil. 2:9–11; 3:20–21). Mark rather directs Jesus' followers back to Galilee (whence Jesus has gone before them), presumably to resume the work of community renewal. The excitement and urgency about fulfillment are thus more intense in Mark than in Jewish apocalyptic literature. Whereas Jewish scribal literature looks for eventual vindication in the future, Mark's Gospel assumes and articulates vindication accomplished in the case of the martyred prophet-Messiah Jesus. And that confirms and reinforces both the conviction that God's judgment on the rulers is certain and the sense that renewal of Israel is already under way—as well as the motivation to expand and solidify the movement Jesus started.

Second, the concentration of "apocalyptic" motifs in Mark 13 is the most important basis on which Mark as a whole has been viewed as "apocalyptic." It also provides the material for numerous reconstructions of a "Little Apocalypse" supposedly adapted here in Mark. Such theories of a Jewish or Jewish-Christian apocalypse behind Mark 13 are questionable on a number of grounds (Beasley-Murray 1993; Yarbro Collins 1992, 73–91). They began in the nineteenth century as defensive attempts to explain that Jews or Jesus' followers, and not Jesus himself, were responsible for the mistaken prediction that the end was imminent (cf. 13:30). Attempts to distinguish apocalyptic narrative units from parenetic (exhortative) units falter because prophecy and parenesis are combined at key points, such as 13:7 and 14–20.

We must also be careful not to read Mark 13 in terms of later Christian theories of salvation history, according to which Jerusalem was destroyed by the Romans as a direct result of the crucifixion of Jesus. As noted above, Mark portrays Jesus engaged in a renewal of Israel centered in Galilee and in opposition to the rulers in Jerusalem. Nothing in the Gospel of Mark itself suggests a "Christian" community separated from "Judaism" or "Israel." Matthew and Luke, written after the Roman destruction of Jerusalem, assume that the discourse in Mark 13 refers to those events. But Jesus' prophecy in Mark 13:2 of the destruction of the Temple/Jerusalem, which provides the occasion of the discourse in Mark 13, is not sufficiently specific to be read as a prophecy "after the fact." While the "abomination that desolates" in Daniel (9:27; 11:31; 12:11) referred to the profanation of the Temple by the Seleucid emperor Antiochus Epiphanes, nothing in the immediate literary context in Mark 13 indicates that "the desolating sacrilege" in Mark 13:14 refers to the Romans' destruction of the Temple in 70 (contrast Matt 24:15 and Luke 21:20–21). Although Jesus' prophecy about Jerusalem and the Temple provide the occasion for the discourse, it is written from a perspective apparently outside Jerusalem and Judea (13:14) and evidently prior to the Roman destruction of Jerusalem.

The historical context of Mark 13, as of the rest of the Gospel, was the intense social conflict that was escalating throughout the middle of the first century (Yarbro Collins 1992; Horsley and Hanson 1985; 1987, 26–58, 90–120). That conflict had erupted in widespread revolt at the time of Herod's death (and Jesus' birth) in 4 B.C.E. and erupted again in the great revolt of 66–70. The Synoptic Gospel traditions included in Mark developed during decades of extensive social unrest, periodic protests, resistance movements, and violent repression by Roman military actions. It may be impossible to reach any degree of precision regarding particular events to which sayings in Mark 13 refer. Yet the numerous movements and conflicts of these decades provide plenty of possibilities.

The many "prophecies" and warnings in Mark 13:5–27 appear to refer to future events, although they are similar to experiences that must have been common among Judeans and Galileans throughout this period. It is thus difficult to discern in Mark 13 the break between past (and present) and future events typical of the rehearsal of events in Jewish apocalyptic literature (Daniel 7; 10–12; *Testament of Moses*). It might be argued on the basis of the end of 13:7 and 13:8 as well as 13:20 and 23 that Mark 13 was written in the middle of the great revolt, and that all of the events mentioned in 13:5–23 are in the immediate past. Yet all of those statements could also refer to the future, with 13:20 being an affirmation that God remains in ultimate control throughout, despite appearances. It seems most likely that the transition from past to future occurs at 13:24 and that Mark is thus written in the midst of the war against Rome.

Several of the references in 13:5–23 illustrate the difficulty of fixing the particular point before or during the great revolt at which Mark 13 was written. For example, the "wars and rumors of wars" in 13:7 could refer to the crisis caused by the emperor Caligula's order to install his image in the Temple (in 40?), presumably in the past. "Nation will rise against nation" could refer to the great revolt, already begun, and the extreme distress described in

13:14–20 could refer to the people's suffering under the "scorched earth"/ "search and destroy" tactics of the Roman reconquest of northwest Judea in 67–68. Yet these could be prophecies delivered at any time in the decades leading up to the great revolt. The "scorched earth" practices of the Roman military were still fresh in people's memories from the reconquest led by Varus in 4 B.C.E. And at several points during the escalating conflicts of the 50s and 60s the Roman governors reacted to actual or perceived popular unrest with severely repressive military violence. Especially after the crisis touched off by Caligula's madness, no clairvoyance was necessary to prophesy an imminent major crisis and to describe how the Romans would treat people such as pregnant or nursing women who remained in their villages (Horsley 1987, 28–49, 116–20). A prophet or an evangelist would not need to have experienced the Roman reconquest of Galilee or northwestern Judea in 67–68 to have articulated Mark 13:14b–18.

Similarly, after the disastrous effects of the severe drought of the late 40s, the possibility of further famines in the near future would have been on everyone's mind. The "false Messiahs" and "false prophets" of 13:6 and 21–22 could be the ones who appeared in the middle of the great revolt. Yet, as the Jewish historian Josephus informs us, popular prophets had been active since shortly after Jesus' death, and memories were alive of the popular messiahs who arose at the death of Herod. Given the continuing conflicts of this period, more could reasonably be expected. Like the warnings and exhortations about trials before councils, governors, and kings in 13:9–13, the warnings, prophecies, and exhortations of 13:5–9 and 14–23 refer to what appears as future escalation of the severe conflicts that the Judean and Galilean people were already undergoing during the mid-first century.

More than elsewhere in the Gospel, Mark 13 features some of the terms and motifs typical of Jewish apocalyptic literature (Beasley-Murray 1993). The whole discourse is touched off by the disciples' questions about "when will this be?" and "what will be the sign?" It is organized in terms of "birth pangs" (13:5–8), "sufferings" (13:14–23), and finally the eventual restoration of the people (13:24–27). In the list of wars, nation against nation, earthquakes, and famines (13:7–8), Mark uses traditional prophetic rhetoric (Isa 8:21; 13:13; 14:30; 19:2; Ezek. 5:12) that became elaborated and stereotyped in later apocalyptic literature (4 Ezra 9:3; 13:31; 2 Bar. 27; 70:8). In addition to possible allusions elsewhere, Mark makes explicit reference in 13:14 to Daniel in the "desolating sacrilege" (Dan. 9:27; 11:31; 12:11) and in 13:19 the suffering unprecedented since creation (Dan. 12:1). The "desolating sacrilege" in Mark 13:14, however, may well not have the same reference to an abominable corruption of the Temple as in Daniel. With its sharp condemnation of the Temple (as in *1 Enoch* and the Qumran literature) and its focus on Galilee, the Gospel of Mark would likely have a very different orientation from that of the Judean "wise" who wrote Daniel.

The most apocalyptic-sounding part of Mark 13 is the climactic restoration of the people prophesied in 13:24–27. The reference to cosmic disturbances derived from prophetic tradition (Isa. 13:10; 34:4), which apocalyptic literature continued. This standard prophetic representation of disruptions accompanying "the day of the Lord" usually referred to God's "military" action against foreign rulers (see also Ezek. 32:7–8; Joel 2:10), as he acted in deliverance of his people. Mark 13:24–27 focuses solely on the divine restoration of the people, with the barest if any allusion to judgment of Rome. Moreover, not God but, in seeming allusion to Dan. 7:13, "the Son of Man coming in clouds with great power and glory" performs the deliverance. He sends out the angels to gather his elect from the four winds. We may also wonder just how explicitly or directly Mark had Dan. 7:13 in mind. In Daniel the "humanlike one" symbolized the people who were about to be delivered, whereas Mark has "the Son of Man" preside over the deliverance.

All of the apocalyptic predictions in Mark 13, however, are framed, balanced, and interpreted by the exhortations in 13:5–6, 9–13, and 18–37, particularly by the carefully positioned and repeated "watch" (13:5, 9, 23, 33) and "keep awake" (13:35, 37). The important function of exhortation in this context resembles that in the Epistle of Enoch. The main point of the exhortations in Mark 13, and thus of the prophecies and warnings framed by them, seems to be "Do not be diverted from the struggle by the difficulties attendant upon the struggle." The first main section of exhortation (13:9–13) focuses on the movement's persecutions by rulers. Far from being distracted by wars and famines, members of the movement are to "Watch! Expect repression, but do not worry." The climactic prophecy of deliverance reassures the readers that God is ultimately in control. The second main section of exhortation (13:28–37) follows up this prophecy of divine deliverance in two steps. First comes assurance of both the imminence of deliverance and the veracity of Jesus' words (13:28–31). It is worth noting that the only comparable saying in Mark, that the kingdom of God will come with power soon, also functions as a reassurance to Jesus' followers to remain focused on their cause in similar circumstances of persecution and repression ("take up the cross . . . ," 8:34–9:1). Second, and the concluding point in the discourse, is the insistence that, since no one knows precisely when deliverance will come, the people are to "keep awake" and focused on the work of building the movement—to which they are directed by the open-ended conclusion of the Gospel in 16:8. In sum, the discourse in Mark 13 uses several apocalyptic motifs and allusions to reassure Jesus' followers that the renewal of Israel already inaugurated in Jesus' preaching and practice will finally be completed despite the crisis they are living through in the period just before or during the great revolt.

The third reason Mark appears apocalyptic is because of the "apocalyptic Son of Man" saying in 13:26–27 as well as those in 8:38 and 14:62. Most of the Son of Man sayings in Mark, which refer to Jesus, have nothing to do with gathering the elect or judgment or the influence of visionary imagery from Daniel 7. They are rather the three announcements of Jesus' suffering, condemnation, death, and rising (8:31; 9:31; 10:33–34) and four or five related Markan references to Jesus' death or rising (9:9, 12; 14:21, 41; 10:45). The sayings about the authority of the Son of Man to forgive sins and the Son of Man as lord of the sabbath (2:10, 28) similarly pertain to the ministry of Jesus and perhaps also still have the general sense of humankind/people having authority to forgive/over the sabbath. It is the three "future Son of Man" sayings that have provided one of the principal bases for an apocalyptic reading of Mark in general.

In 8:38, a variation on the saying also found in Luke/Q 12:8–9, the Son of Man seems more of an accuser than a judge, although the scenario is clearly the divine judgment, with the attending company of the angels. Both Mark 13:26–27 and 14:62 allude to the "humanlike one" of Dan. 7:13 in the phrase "coming in/with the clouds." In these two Markan passages, the Son of Man is not a symbol of the people but an eschatological judge or deliverer, as in the contemporary Similitudes of Enoch (*1 Enoch* 62). The Son of Man in Mark 13:26–27 presides over the gathering of the elect from the four winds. The Son of Man in 14:62 appears to be a heavenly judge "coming with the clouds of heaven" to condemn the high priests and/or vindicate Jesus, on whom they are sitting in judgment. In none of these sayings is Jesus explicitly identified with the Son of Man. Indeed, in 14:62 the Son of Man appears as a figure who is coming to vindicate Jesus. By using the same phrase "Son of Man" both for Jesus as the martyred Messiah and for a future accuser/deliverer/judge, Mark may have been the first in the Synoptic Gospel tradition to suggest that the two were the same person. Mark has thus taken an important step toward the more elaborate Christian apocalyptic scenario of the *parousia* (second coming) of Jesus as heavenly Lord, as we find in Matthew and later Christian doctrine. As can be seen in the open ending of the empty tomb with

Jesus "gone before them into Galilee," Mark's emphasis was not as much on the resurrected and exalted Lord who was coming again as on the continuation of Jesus mission of the renewal of Israel.

THE GOSPEL OF MATTHEW

Matthew's Gospel presents simultaneously a less intense feeling of the fulfillment of longings for the renewal of Israel and an eschatological expectation elaborated in more apocalyptic terms. As in both Mark and Q, which Matthew has appropriated, the kingdom is the central theme of Jesus' teaching. Also as in Mark and Q, Jesus' and his disciples' preaching and activities focus on the renewal of Israel. Matthew's preference for "kingdom of heaven" is simply a circumlocution to avoid uttering the divine name, not an indication of an otherworldly orientation. Reading Matthew, however, one does not have the same feeling as in reading Mark of being caught up in the struggle of the kingdom's manifestation in Jesus' and his envoys' preaching and practice. Matthew organizes the gospel traditions received from Mark, Q, and elsewhere more systematically into five major sections, each consisting of both narrative and discourse. For example, in constructing the famous Sermon on the Mount, he dramatically expands the renewed covenant discourse from Q into an unavoidably explicit new covenant charter for the movement. The communities of the movement seem more settled. Peter is named as the rock on which Jesus founds the "assembly" (Greek *ekklēsia,* 16:17–19). And Matthew establishes procedures for community discipline (18:15–20). In many ways Matthew's Gospel resembles the *Community Rule* from Qumran, another apocalyptic renewal movement in Israel that had seemingly settled into an indefinite period of waiting for the final divine intervention into history that would complete the provisional fulfillment that they already embodied. And since the intensity of fulfillment in the present has subsided somewhat, more is pushed off into the future, to the more distant "end of the age."

One major reason that Matthew displays both a less intense tone and a more elaborate scenario of future judgment than Mark is surely the sequence of events that intervened between their respective writing. Mark appears to address the situation in Palestine either just before or during the great revolt. Matthew addresses communities fifteen or twenty years after the Roman destruction of Jerusalem. He alludes to it in the parable of the wedding feast (22:1–14, especially 22:7). When the Romans destroyed Jerusalem, they also destroyed the Judean priestly regime centered in the Temple, leaving no centralized Jewish political-religious institution with authority over the Jewish communities of Palestine and Syria. The rabbinic movement located initially at Yavneh on the Judean coast and later in the cities of Galilee did not come into prominence until several generations later. A currently prominent interpretation views Matthew's Gospel as addressed to communities that understood themselves as a renewal movement of Israel that had expanded its mission to include other peoples as well (Saldarini 1994). Matthew makes explicit again and again throughout the Gospel in "formula quotations" that Jesus' ministry is the fulfillment of what Israel's prophets had prophesied, but the fulfillment of the hopes of Israel is now offered to all peoples, not just Israel.

The decline of intensity compared with Mark may not be evident in the first sections of Matthew's Gospel. Indeed Matthew's combination and elaboration of the Markan and Q mission discourses make the movement's struggle against opposing forces all the more ominous. Efforts of Jesus' disciples to expand his program of renewal in Israel will only further exacerbate the social conflict already rife in society: "I have come not to bring peace, but a sword!" (10:34–36). Their continuation of his mission can only be expected to bring divisions between the younger and older generations, in fulfillment of a standard prophetic tradition of "a man against his father, and a daughter against her mother, and so on" (e.g., Micah 7:6). Jesus demands unwavering commitment to the cause (10:37–39). The missionaries themselves could only expect to be abused, beaten, and dragged before governors and kings. But, like the faithful scribal sages who were martyred by Antiochus Epiphanes two centuries earlier (see Dan. 11:33–12:3), they would be vindicated at the judgment (Matt. 10:16–33).

Into this expanded mission discourse Matthew inserts a saying that loomed central in Schweitzer's insistence that Jesus thought the end of the world was imminent: "For truly I tell you, you will not have gone through all the towns of Israel before the Son of Man comes"(10:23). Given Matthew's indications elsewhere in the Gospel of the prolonged period of time during which the renewal movement begun by Jesus will continue before "the end of the age," it is unlikely that this was meant to be taken at face value. Yet it indicates the urgency of the original mission, some degree of which carried over into Matthew's own time partly by the repeated readings or performances of just such a discourse in the Gospel. The lower level of intensity of the mission in Matthew's own time may be indicated in the last set of sayings in the discourse: "Whoever welcomes a prophet in the name of a prophet will receive a prophet's reward" (10:40–42).

In his third major discourse Matthew indicates an elongated perspective of continuing history from which he views Jesus' ministry. Among the several "parables of the kingdom" that he adds to those in Mark 4 is the parable of the weeds (13:24–30). The interpretation of this parable given privately to the disciples (13:36–43) lays out a grand scenario of the fulfillment begun with Jesus. There is no hint of any "cosmic catastrophe." But the "explanation" of the parable draws significantly upon traditions and motifs familiar from Jewish prophetic and apocalyptic literature, such as the harvest image for the "end of the age" and the dualism of good and evil, God and Satan. The Son of Man sows good seed, "the children of the kingdom," in the "field" of the world, but the devil simultaneously sows "children of the evil one." At the close-of-the-age "harvest," however, the angels as "reapers" will gather out of his kingdom "all causes of sin and all evildoers . . . and throw them into the furnace of fire, where there will be weeping and gnashing of teeth. Then the righteous will shine like the sun in the kingdom of their Father."

Mark used the imminent but uncertain hour of the angels' gathering of the elect to alleviate the community's anxiety about the troubles whirling around them so that they could concentrate on furthering the work of the now risen Jesus in Galilee (Mark 13:3–37). Matthew's explanation delays the end of the age indefinitely, before the angels will gather the evil ones for fiery punishment. Whereas Mark has Satan disappear from the scene after Jesus' Galilean ministry, in Matt. 13:36–43 the devil is still very active during an indefinite growth of the intermixed seeds of kingdom and of evil. Moreover, while Mark has no portrayal even of Jesus in glorious vindication, Matthew has all of the righteous "shine like the sun" in their glorious exaltation "at the end of the age." Matthew's apocalyptic elaboration on the fulfillment of history corresponds to a decline in the intensity with which the fulfillment was experienced. Matthew's communities must wait patiently until the indefinite end of the age. During that patient period of waiting, what is required is community discipline (including mediation of conflict and mutual forgiveness), to which Matthew devotes the fourth major discourse (chap. 18).

Matthew concentrates his full elaboration of the "end of the age" scenario in the fifth and final discourse (chapters 24–25). He sets the stage in the changes he makes in the Markan and Q traditions he uses at 16:27–28 and 19:28. Matthew focuses both of these references to the final establishment of the kingdom on the Son of Man. Like the saying inserted at 10:23 mentioned above, these alterations to his sources are part of Matthew's program of focusing on the future coming of the Son of Man as eschatological judge and/or vindicator, who will "repay everyone for what has been done." In these three cases, the coming Son of Man functions as the future vindicator for Jesus' disciples who are undergoing persecution or making extreme sacrifices for the sake of the kingdom. In 19:28 it is clear that Matthew still views the "renewal" as the final establishment of just social-economic relations, not some sort of life in heaven, and a restoration of Israel. That is, the disciples will be "establishing justice for," versus the standard mistranslation of "judging," the twelve tribes of Israel. Yet Matthew has significantly dropped the phrase in Mark about the restoration coming "in this age," so that the "renewal" focuses primarily on "inherit eternal life," which, in turn, is relegated to the indefinite future.

The *parousia*—popularly thought of as the "second coming"—of Christ is really Matthew's construction, at least in Gospel literature. Given Mark's identification of Jesus with the Son of Man, the idea of the eschatological "coming" was implicit in "the Son of Man coming in the clouds" in Mark 13:26. The term *parousia*, however, occurs only in Matthew 24, where it is the focus of the whole discourse about the coming of the Son of Man in final judgment at the end of the age in Matthew 24–25. This discourse is the source of the standard picture of the last judgment in subsequent Christian art, architecture, and literature. Such representations of the last judgment and the second coming of Christ, however, miss the thrust of this last, "apocalyptic" discourse in the Gospel of Matthew.

This final discourse of Jesus in Matthew 24–25 is ostensibly addressed to the disciples just before his arrest, trial, and crucifixion. Yet it was actually written in and addressed to a situation some sixty years (two generations) later, ten to twenty years after the Roman destruction of Jerusalem. Far more than Jesus' final discourse in Mark, Jesus' "apocalyptic testament" to his disciples in Matthew is a review of history up to the situation of the readers, similar to that in Daniel 7, 10–12. Matthew's final discourse is nearly three times as long as Mark's, incorporating several long parables in addition to material from Q. As indicated in the introductory questions of the disciples, Matthew's concerns run well beyond the events covered in Mark 13:5–23 (–27), the rather vague "these things." In contrast to Mark, Matthew really does focus (ostensibly) on "the end," on "last things": "what will be the sign of *your coming* and of *the close of the age*." Like the *parousia*, "the close of the age" is distinctive to Matthew among the Gospels, figuring prominently in the explanations of the parables of the weeds and the dragnet, as well as here and at the very end of the Gospel (13:39, 40, 49; 24:3; 28:20).

In fact, while the Roman destruction of Jerusalem figures prominently in the Gospel, Matthew's concerns focus on the situation of the movement in the new circumstances created by that destruction. Matthew had already implied the destruction of Jerusalem and its high priestly rulers in the parable of the wedding feast: when those invited to the feast killed his servant messengers, the enraged king "sent his troops, destroyed those murderers, and burned their city" (22:1–7; cf. taking away the vineyard from the tenants in 21:43). By concluding the woes on the scribes and Pharisees with Jesus' prophetic lament on the Jerusalem ruling house in 23:37–38, Matthew ties the destruction of Jerusalem closely with the apocalyptic testament that follows in chapters 24–25. The destruction of Jerusalem and the Temple, however, is by no means the crucial point reviewed in the narrative of events. Matthew (24:15) does indicate, in a way that Mark (13:14) does not, that the "desolating sacrilege" would be "standing in the holy place," surely an indication of the Temple. The ensuing travails of war taken from Mark, however, do not constitute "all things" that Jesus has "told [them] beforehand" (which Matthew, in 24:25, significantly deletes from Mark 13:23).

Although Matthew does not focus on the destruction of Jerusalem, that event and the vacuum of central institutionalized authority for Jewish Palestine and Jewish communities in Syria created a completely new situation for a renewal movement in Israel such as the one Matthew addressed (Saldarini 1994). Suddenly the authorities that had exercised some check on the movement (if we place any trust in key sections of the book of Acts) had disappeared from the historical stage and no centralized leadership of Israel had emerged or been appointed by the Romans. The fact that the capital and symbolic center of Israel was now in ruins, moreover, might well have led the renewal movement behind Matthew to turn outward. The destruction of Jerusalem would almost certainly have provided a major impetus in expanding the movement's mission to include all peoples in a more programmatic way than the earlier outreach to "Gentiles" in Antioch and elsewhere. This is exactly the program delineated at the very end of Matthew's Gospel: "Go therefore and make disciples of all nations (peoples), baptizing them . . . and teaching them to obey everything that I have commanded you" (28:19–20a). In the revelatory narrative of Jesus' "apocalyptic testament" the point at which the mission to the peoples is announced (for the first time in the Gospel) is as the destruction of Jerusalem is pending: "And this gospel of the kingdom [which Jesus had preached before in Galilee] will be preached throughout the whole world, as a testimony to all nations (peoples)" (24:14a). The period of this new mission, moreover, is the present to which the "apocalyptic testament" is addressed. Only after that program of evangelizing all the peoples, only "then," would the end come (24:14b). Meanwhile, the exalted Jesus to whom "all authority in heaven and on earth had been given" would be with them "every day" (literally "all the days"), "to the end of the age" (28:18, 20b).

The importance of the time during which the wider mission of Jesus' kingdom-movement takes place for Matthew helps us understand why the apparent *climax* of the revelatory narrative in 24:30–31 is only the *apparent* climax. The apocalyptic testament is a response to the disciples' question, "What will be the sign of your *parousia* and the end of the age" (24:3b). The answer is given apparently in 24:29–31: "immediately after the tribulation of those days" (the violence and chaos of the Roman reconquest of Judea [24:16–28]), accompanied by the cosmic disturbances traditional in prophetic and apocalyptic descriptions of divine deliverance, "then the sign of the Son of Man will appear in heaven." Matthew even enhances the Danielic coming of the Son of Man on the clouds of heaven and sending out of the angels to gather in the elect with "a loud trumpet call" (24:30–31; cf. 1 Cor. 15:52). There ensues a lengthy delay in the narrative of the *parousia* to explain the implications of "the delay of the *parousia*" (delay mentioned explicitly in 24:48; 25:5, 19). Matthew devotes more than half of the discourse, including repeated exhortations and three long didactic parables (24:37—25:30), to the importance of behavior and relationships in the communities of the movement during the "delay."

After reproducing the Markan point about the imminence of "all these things" (24:32–35), Matthew then uses the next point from Mark, that the day and hour are unknown (24:36), to launch his lengthy exhortation on watchfulness and responsibility. As in the rehearsals of past history by seers in apocalyptic literature such as Daniel 7 and 10–12, the preceding predictions in Matt. 24:5–28 lend credibility to the prophecy of the *parousia* of the Son of Man in judgment and deliverance. Matthew then uses the certainty of judgment looming in the future to insist upon discipline and responsible relations within the communities of the movement. A principal function of apocalyptic literature was to reinforce the solidarity of community in an uncertain or threatening situation by assuring them that God would act soon and/or that judgment was sure. Matthew does not appear to be in the urgent situation of Mark or Daniel, although the Roman reconquest of Judea and the destruction of Jerusalem must have sent shock waves through any and all Jewish groups and movements. Matthew rather addresses communities settling in for prolonged periods of further building and solidification of the movement. Thus, the point of the exhortative analogies as well as all these parables in 24:37–25:30 is not simply passive watching but active service. As he goes Matthew embellishes the parables with "Christian" apocalyptic motifs such as the "cry" and the summons "to meet" the bridegroom in the parable of the maidens (25:6; cf. 1 Thess. 4:16–17).

In the climactic scene of the apocalyptic discourse, Matthew portrays the peoples gathered before the Son of Man on his glorious throne for judgment. If it had not become clear from the preceding exhortations and didactic parables, then it becomes clear in this judgment scene that the real "crisis" (Greek *krisis* means "judgment") lies in people's behavior in the present, not in the *parousia* of the Son of Man at the end of the age. The assumption within the discourse is that since the end would not come before the gospel of the kingdom was preached to the peoples, the peoples gathered for judgment have been evangelized. The judgment scene is therefore directed basically to the communities of the movement itself. The "similitude" in Matthew's judgment scene is similar in certain ways to the Similitudes of Enoch (*1 Enoch* 39–71, first century C.E.). The criteria for judgment, however, which are repeated four times, direct attention back into the present of the readers. Only insofar as they have fed the hungry, clothed the naked, visited the imprisoned, and so on among the least of the Son of Man's brothers and sisters have they done it to him and thus become eligible to inherit the kingdom prepared from the foundation of the world. The Son of Man, who will appear on his glorious throne, is hidden in, or rather is identical with, the least among the communities of the movement. The obvious clue earlier in the Gospel, of course, was the suffering and crucified Son of Man, who both had authority to forgive sins and over the sabbath and had nowhere to lay his head. The final "judgment" scene in Matthew's last discourse thus comes back around to a main principle in the first section of the first discourse. The "kingdom" movement inaugurated by Jesus focuses on active love (loving-kindness or mercy as action, not attitude) toward others, particularly the needy. This renewal of mutual care and reciprocity in community life is in Matthew motivated by the fulfillment manifested in Jesus' ministry but also by the final judgment. But far more than in Mark or Q it is motivated also by the promise/threat that one's fate in the judgment at the end of the age is determined by present actions.

We should not imagine from the remarkable twist given to the judgment scene, however, that Matthew has dissolved the apocalyptic perspective and its embellishment into a sanction on community discipline and cooperation. He continues his embellishment of Markan narratives with apocalyptic motifs at key points in the passion narrative. In the arrest scene, Matthew's Jesus insists that at his appeal the Father would send the heavenly armies to the rescue—a motif derived ultimately from the "holy wars" of early Israelite traditions, but revived in Jewish apocalyptic literature. Then both at the moment of Jesus' death on the cross and at the resurrection Matthew makes ominous additions to the Markan narrative he is following. When Jesus breathed his last, a great earthquake opened tombs and many bodies of saints were raised! Again at the tomb came another earthquake and the appearance of an angel "whose appearance was like lightning and clothing white as snow." The Gospel then ends with a grand embellishment of one of the key themes or events of Jewish apocalyptic literature. (The risen) Jesus is not only vindicated by exaltation to heaven but receives "all authority in heaven and on earth." Matthew directs the kingdom movement Jesus inaugurated to continue under precisely that sign.

⌒THE GOSPEL OF LUKE

Like Matthew, Luke also follows Mark's narrative and assimilates the prophetic discourses of Q. Far more noticeably than Matthew, however, Luke tones down many of the apocalyptic overtones he finds in his sources (Tannehill 1986). With a few deft deletions of words from Mark's narrative, he effectively tones down the sense of imminence. As Jesus begins his ministry in Galilee in 4:15, Luke deletes completely Mark's summary of Jesus' preaching as "the kingdom of God is at hand." In 9:23–27 Luke follows Mark in retaining the reference to the future judgment of the Son of Man coming in glory. But in 9:27 he tones down the sense of imminence in Mark 9:1, "some standing here will not taste death before they see the kingdom of God," by deleting "come with power." In rewriting the Markan "apocalyptic" discourse, Luke minimizes the sense of imminence in Mark 13:30 somewhat, by deleting "these things" in 21:32. He also suppresses some of the apocalyptic motifs, by deleting "to the end" in connection with "enduring" in 21:19 (cf. Mark 13:13b) and the allusion to Dan. 12:1 (in Mark 13:19) in 21:23b and the reference to the angels gathering the elect (in Mark 13:27) in 21:27 (but what does 21:28 mean?). Any sense of an imminent coming of the kingdom or an imminent appearance of "the Son of Man" in judgment is merely a carryover from the Markan materials Luke has assimilated.

The Gospel of Luke reconfigures in matter-of-fact historical terms what Mark and Matthew expressed in more prophetic and apocalyptic terms. The longings and prophecies of Israel have indeed been fulfilled, in part, in the ministry of Jesus. "Luke," however, narrates the history not only of Jesus but of the movement that he founded that has spread from Galilee and Jerusalem to the imperial metropolis, Rome. The Roman destruction of Jerusalem, moreover, is not simply a past event but a major turning point in the history of fulfillment. That history has taken a different course from what was expected (in Jewish prophetic and apocalyptic circles) because of Jerusalem's resistance to Jesus as the Messiah who was to have restored Israel. The most telling example of Luke's matter-of-fact historical treatment of events is his substitution for Mark's allusive "desolating sacrilege" (in Mark 13:14) of "when you see Jerusalem surrounded by armies, then know that its desolation has come near" in 21:20.

The disciples' ostensible misunderstanding plays an important role in Luke's presentation of the unexpected turn of history on account of Jerusalem's rejection of Jesus. They are not completely mistaken in their supposition "that the kingdom of God was to appear immediately" when Jesus went to the city (19:11) or in their hope that this "prophet mighty in deed and word before God and all the people" was "the one to redeem Israel" (24:19, 21). Indeed, the disciples' acclamation of Jesus as "the king who comes in the name of the Lord!" indicated precisely what was happening in the "triumphal entry" into the city. The Jerusalem rulers and their Pharisaic retainers, however, did not recognize "the time of their visitation from God." Luke has Jesus articulate the historical result of Jerusalem's rejection: "Your enemies will surround you . . . and crush you to the ground . . ." (19:41–44; cf. 13:34–35).

Even more than Mark 13 and the Q discourse concerning "the day of the Son of Man," Luke warns against a sort of jumping to apocalyptic conclusions with regard to current events and the struggles in which the movement is engaged. In 17:20–21 (which may be derived from Q) Jesus warns that "the kingdom of God is not coming with things that can be observed . . . for the kingdom of God is among you." To the Q sayings about the unpredictable timing and suddenness of "the day of the Son of Man" Luke adds a warning against yearning for it, for first he (= Jesus, in Luke) must suffer and be rejected (17:22, 25). Luke's revision of the Markan "apocalyptic" discourse is similar. The disciples should not heed false teachers who claim that "the time is near" because they themselves must first endure rejection and persecution (21:8, 9–19).

For all his deletion and downplaying of apocalyptic language and excitement, however, Luke is not devoid of prophetic motifs that evoke a sense of fulfillment and crisis, motifs also found in Jewish apocalyptic literature of the time. That Jesus has come "to cast fire upon the earth," has "a baptism with which to be baptized," and has come to bring not peace but division (12:49–53, probably from Q) lends Luke's narrative a sense of crisis and of straining forward to completion. Besides integrating the Q saying about the eschatological banquet as a future judgmental sanction on discipline necessary for the kingdom in 13:18–29, Luke frames the "great supper" parable from Q with the traditional prophetic motif of the eschatological banquet in

14:15. In those and many other discourses used by Luke, "the day of the Son of Man" as a symbol of future judgment and/or the future return in judgment by the Lord plays an important role in exhortation, as in 12:35–48; 17:20–37; 21:34–36. That day may appear suddenly, so Jesus' followers must both keep awake and maintain ethical discipline in the movement.

NB - comparison to today

CONCLUSION

The rise of apocalyptic literature was the Judean scribes' creative response to the pressures against the traditional Israelite way of life presented by Western imperialism. How could their God, who had promised them blessings and delivered them from distress in the past, allow continued foreign domination and even apostasy and oppression by their own high priestly rulers? God, who had previously spoken through prophets like Moses, Elijah, and Isaiah, seemed remote and silent. Through dreams, visions, and heavenly journeys, certain scribes or sages received revelations from angels and ancient wise men, reassuring them that God was still in control of history and the universe. Indeed, the principal concerns of such revelations were that God would soon judge the oppressive rulers, foreign and/or domestic, restore the "kingdom" to the people themselves, and vindicate those who had died in defense of the traditional way of life. In the course of their struggles to comprehend the imperial situation in which they were caught, they also developed explanations of the domination, evil, and suffering to which they were subjected that were unprecedented in biblical traditions. History was caught in the grip of a struggle between divine and demonic forces. A decisive divine intervention was necessary if Satan was to be defeated. Moreover, it was intolerable to imagine that the wise who were leading the resistance to unjust rulers or outright persecution were not to participate in the restored society: the martyrs would be vindicated through resurrection or glorification.

Movements of resistance to imperial domination and/or oppressive domestic rulers also arose among the ordinary Judean and Galilean peasantry. Those we know about through our limited sources follow either a prophetic script or a messianic script. That is, they are informed by and patterned after either the great acts of deliverance led by Moses and Joshua or those led by Saul and David. Since our sources for these movements are so minimal, we cannot tell the degree to which they may have shared the key images and views of the scribal apocalyptic literature. Yet because the circles of dissident scribes at times made common cause with popular resistance, there must have been some interaction and mutual influence. It is clear from the Synoptic Gospel tradition generally, for example, that both belief in demons and expectation of a resurrection of the dead had become standard features in the symbolic universe of Judean society (except for the high priestly elite) by the time of Jesus.

Because the Gospels function primarily as scripture for the Christian religion, it is easy to lose sight of the fact that the communities for which they were written were originally movements of renewal of Israel and resistance to imperial rule. The Gospel literature produced by and for these movements both parallels and resembles Judean apocalyptic literature. The principal concerns are the same: renewal of the people, condemnation of oppressive rulers, and vindication of the martyrs. While the Gospels, particularly the earliest, Mark and the discourse gospel Q, follow primarily a prophetic script, they share many images and motifs with Judean apocalyptic literature. Because Q and the pre-Markan gospel traditions and Mark itself are not scribal literature, they lack most of the distinctively scribal features present, for example, in Daniel or *1 Enoch* (e.g., dream-interpretation, angel interpreters, heavenly journeys, cosmological lore). The relationship of similarity and difference can be seen particularly in the demonology, which is simple, ad hoc, and relatively undeveloped and unreflective in Q and Mark, but reflectively systematic in Qumran literature.

In addition to their differences in social location, the Gospels, particularly Mark and Q, proclaim that God's saving action, the fulfillment of the people's longings, is already happening in Jesus' preaching and practice of the kingdom of God. This emphasis on the fulfillment that is already under way in Jesus shifts the focus to the present, to the renewal of Israel embodied in the Jesus movement itself. In Mark, followed by Matthew and Luke, the sense of fulfillment already accomplished is confirmed by the resurrection of Jesus himself, which constitutes the vindication of his cause, the validation of his preaching and practice, including his prophetic oracles and demonstrations against the rulers and ruling institutions. Correspondingly, the future judgment in the Gospels has a function somewhat different from that in Judean apocalyptic literature. In the latter, God's judgment will focus primarily on the rulers. In the Gospels, the judgment functions more as a sanction on the movement's own discipline than as vengeance on the rulers, who have already been decisively condemned by Jesus' prophetic pronouncements.

In the move from Q and Mark to Matthew and Luke, the Gospel tradition moves much further along the spectrum from the originally oral expressions of a popular movement to scribally authored literature. Luke merely eliminates some of the apocalyptic motifs and softens the anti-imperial impact of some of the material he incorporates from Mark and Q. Matthew, however, is still more of an apocalyptic scribe. Matthew is the one who gives what became the classic form to Christian apocalyptic ideology, particularly the *parousia* of the Son of Man and the appearance of Christ/the Son of Man at the last judgment. As noted above, however, the function of this now classic form of Christian apocalypticism is to direct the faithful followers of Jesus to acts of justice and mercy in the care of "the least of these," his brothers and sisters. Like Judean apocalypticism, the apocalypticism of the Gospels is directed to the renewal of the people in their faithful struggles to maintain an independent and righteous community amid an oppressive imperial situation.

BIBLIOGRAPHY

Beasley-Murray, G. R. 1993. *Jesus and the Last Days: The Interpretation of the Olivet Discourse.* Peabody, Mass.: Hendrickson. Review of investigations into the eschatological discourse in Mark 13.

Charlesworth, J. H., ed. 1983. *The Old Testament Pseudepigrapha.* Vol. 1. New York: Doubleday. Translations, with notes, of Jewish apocalyptic literature.

Collins, J. J. 1984, 1998. *The Apocalyptic Imagination.* New York: Crossroad. 2nd ed., Grand Rapids: Eerdmans, 1998. Introduction to Jewish apocalypses in historical context.

———. 1993. "Wisdom, Apocalypticism, and Generic Compatibility." In *In Search of Wisdom: Essays in Memory of John G. Gammie,* edited by L. G. Perdue et al., 165–85. Louisville: Westminster/John Knox. A critical historical argument for qualifying the dichotomy between "wisdom" and "apocalyptic" often operative in biblical studies.

Harrington, D. J. 1991. *The Gospel of Matthew.* Collegeville, Minn.: Michael Glazier/Liturgical Press. Recent commentary on the Gospel of Matthew.

Horsley, R. A. 1987, 1993. *Jesus and the Spiral of Violence: Popular Jewish Resistance in Roman Palestine.* San Francisco: Harper & Row. Reprint, Minneapolis: Fortress, 1993. Analysis of basic concerns of Judean apocalyptic literature and of its relationship to popular movements.

———. 1991. "Q and Jesus: Assumptions, Approaches, and Analyses." *Semeia* 55:175–209. Examination of Q as series of discourses.

———. 1993. "Wisdom and Apocalypticism in Mark." In *In Search of Wisdom: Essays in Memory of John G. Gammie,* edited by L. G. Perdue et al., 223–44. Louisville: Westminster/John Knox. An attempt at precise comparisons between Mark and Jewish apocalyptic literature.

Horsley, R. A., and J. S. Hanson. 1985, 1987. *Bandits, Prophets, and Messiahs: Popular Movements in the Time of Jesus.* Minneapolis: Winston. Reprint, San Francisco: Harper & Row, 1987. Analysis of popular Jewish leaders and movements in historical context.

Jacobson, A. D. "Apocalyptic and the Synoptic Sayings source Q." In *The Four Gospels 1992: Festschrift Frans Neirynck,* edited by F. van Segbroeck et al., 403–19. Leuven: Leuven University Press. Review of interpretation of Q as "apocalyptic."

Kee, H. C. 1984. *Community of the New Age.* 2nd ed. Macon, Ga.: Mercer University Press. Interpretation of Mark as an apocalyptic Gospel for an apocalyptic community.

Kloppenborg, J. S. 1987a. *The Formation of Q.* Philadelphia: Fortress Press. Argument for sapiential and apocalyptic layers in Q.

———. 1987b. "Symbolic Eschatology and the Apocalypticism of Q." *Harvard Theological Review* 80:287–306. Questions previous characterization of Q as apocalyptic.

Mack, B. L. 1988. *A Myth of Innocence: Mark and Christian Origins.* Philadelphia: Fortress Press. Argument that Mark apocalypticizes Jesus traditions in composing his Gospel.

Nickelsburg, G. W. E. 1981. *Jewish Literature Between the Bible and the Mishnah.* Philadelphia: Fortress Press. Survey of Jewish apocalyptic and wisdom literature.

Perrin, N. 1974. *The New Testament: An Introduction.* New York: Harcourt Brace. Interpretation of Q and Mark as "apocalyptic Christianity/drama."

Saldarini, A. J. 1994. *Matthew's Christian-Jewish Community.* Chicago: University of Chicago Press.

Stanton, G. A. 1992. *A Gospel for a New People: Studies in Matthew.* Edinburgh: T & T Clark. Critical studies on key issues in Matthew.

Tannehill, R. C. 1986. *The Narrative Unity of Luke–Acts: A Literary Interpretation.* Vol. 1, *The Gospel According to Luke.* Philadelphia: Fortress Press. Thematic survey of Luke including prophecy, revelation, and eschatology.

Tuckett, C. M. 1996. *Q and the History of Early Christianity.* Peabody, Mass.: Hendrickson. Critical studies of topics in Q, including eschatology and the Son of Man.

Yarbro Collins, A. 1989. "The Son of Man Sayings in the Sayings Source." In *To Touch the Text: Biblical and Related Studies in Honor of Joseph A. Fitzmyer, S.J.,* edited by M. P. Horgan and P. J. Kobelski, 369–89. New York: Crossroad. Critical analysis of the Son of Man sayings in Q.

———. 1992. *The Beginning of the Gospel: Probings of Mark in Context.* Minneapolis: Fortress Press. Critical analysis of Mark's genre "apocalyptic discourse" and other issues.

Wilder, A. N. 1958–59. "Eschatological Imagery and Earthly Circumstance." *New Testament Studies* 5:229–45.

10

Paul and Apocalyptic Eschatology

M. C. de Boer
Vrije Universiteit, Amsterdam

THIS CHAPTER DISCUSSES ESCHATOLOGY OR, MORE PRECISELY, *apocalyptic* eschatology, in the writings of Paul the Apostle (d. ca. 65 C.E.). The New Testament contains thirteen letters under Paul's name. According to many scholars, Paul may actually be the author of only seven of these (Romans, 1 and 2 Corinthians, Galatians, Philippians, 1 Thessalonians, Philemon). The authorship of the other six (Ephesians, Colossians, 2 Thessalonians, 1 and 2 Timothy, and Titus) remains disputed. In this article, therefore, references to Paul are in the first instance references to the Paul of the seven undisputed letters.

To the minds of many readers, Paul's apocalyptic eschatology is most readily, or even exclusively, discernible in those passages which present a scenario of events anticipated to occur at Christ's *parousia* ("presence," "coming," "advent"), an event that Paul can refer to as "the revelation [Greek *apocalypsis*, 'apocalypse'] of our Lord Jesus Christ" (1 Cor. 1:7; cf. 2 Thess. 1:7). 1 Thess. 4:13–18 and 1 Cor. 15:20–28, 50–56 are the classic examples from the undisputed letters. Both concern the resurrection of the dead. In the first, Paul claims:

> We [believers] who are alive, who are left until the coming [*parousia*] of the Lord, will by no means precede those who have died. For the Lord himself, with

a cry of command, with the archangel's call and the sound of God's trumpet, will descend from heaven and the dead in Christ will rise first. Then we who are alive, who are left, will be caught up in the clouds together with them to meet the Lord in the air; and so we will be with the Lord forever.[1]

In the second, Paul writes:

All will be made alive in Christ. But each in his own order: Christ the first fruits, then at his coming [*parousia*] those who belong to Christ. Then is[2] the end, when he hands over the kingdom[3] to God the Father, after he has destroyed every ruler and every authority and power. . . . The last enemy to be destroyed is Death. . . . We will not all die, but we will all be changed, in a moment, in the twinkling of an eye, at the last trumpet. For the trumpet will sound, and the dead will be raised imperishable, and we will be changed. . . . (15:23–24, 26, 51–52)

A notable (and challenging) example from the disputed Pauline letters occurs in 2 Thess. 2:1–12, which reads in part:

As to the coming [*parousia*] of our Lord Jesus Christ and our being gathered together to him, . . . Let no one deceive you in any way; for that day will not come unless the rebellion comes first and the man of lawlessness is revealed, the son of destruction . . . whom the Lord Jesus will destroy with the breath of his mouth, annihilating him by the manifestation of his coming [*parousia*]. . . .

This study will indicate, however, that apocalyptic eschatology in the letters and thought of Paul cannot, and therefore must not, be confined to these scenarios of the *parousia,* nor then to the expectation of such a *parousia.*[4] Jesus' *parousia,* along with the events that will accompany it, is the culmination of a series of apocalyptic-eschatological events. This series began at least as early as God's raising Jesus from the dead, an event that has already taken place. As Paul writes in 1 Thessalonians, Christians eagerly await God's "Son from heaven, *whom he raised from the dead*—Jesus, who rescues us from the wrath to come" (1 Thess. 1:10). Here two references to the *parousia* (awaiting the Son from heaven, rescue from the wrath to come) sandwich a reference to Jesus' own resurrection. In 1 Corinthians 15, Paul claims that "Christ has been raised from the dead"; it is for this reason that he is "the first fruits of those who have died" (1 Cor. 15:20), the first installment of the full harvest of resurrection to come. God's raising of Christ here constitutes the first act in the apocalyptic-eschatological drama of which the *parousia* is but one element:

each in his own order: [1] Christ the first fruits, [2] then at his coming [*parousia*] those who belong to Christ. [3] Then is the end . . . . (1 Cor 15:23–24)

Paul's understanding of Christ and his saving work is permeated from begin-

ning to end (from Christ's resurrection to his *parousia*) by the categories and
the perspectives of apocalyptic eschatology. Indeed, Paul goes further, since he
also applies these categories and perspectives not only to Jesus' resurrection
but also to his death by crucifixion, and even, in some contexts, to God's
sending of Jesus into the world (see, e.g., Gal. 4:4).

PAUL AND JEWISH APOCALYPTIC ESCHATOLOGY

The understanding of Paul as an apocalyptic thinker owes most to Albert
Schweitzer, who wrote two studies on Paul and his eschatology early in the
twentieth century: *Paul and His Interpreters: A Critical History* (1912; German
1911) and *The Mysticism of Paul the Apostle* (1931; German 1930). The latter
was actually drafted in 1906 and was intended as a sequel to the former.
Schweitzer momentously claimed that Paul lived "in the conceptions of the
dramatic world-view" of Jewish apocalyptic eschatology, which Schweitzer
referred to, somewhat unfortunately, as "the late Jewish Eschatology" (1931,
11). Schweitzer thus interpreted Paul's eschatology with primary reference not
to the eschatology of Jesus nor to that of other early Christians but to the
eschatology to be found among Jews of Paul's time. The writings attesting the
Jewish eschatological view were for Schweitzer "mainly the Book of Enoch
[*1 Enoch*], the Psalms of Solomon, and the Apocalypses of Baruch [*2 Baruch*]
and Ezra [*4 Ezra*]." As additional sources, Schweitzer listed the book of
Jubilees, the *Testaments of the Twelve Patriarchs,* and the "Ascension" (*Assumption*) of Moses, with a passing nod also to "the earlier and later Prophets"
(1931, 54–55). (Schweitzer did not of course know the Dead Sea Scrolls.)

Ever since Schweitzer, students of Paul who have tended to label Paul's
eschatology (and even his whole theology) as "apocalyptic" have done so
largely because, following Schweitzer's lead, they have discerned conceptual
affinities between Paul's eschatological ideas and first-century Jewish eschatological expectations, which are also understood to be "apocalyptic" in some
sense (e.g., the resurrection of the dead). It is thus difficult, nay impossible, to
discuss Paul's apocalyptic eschatology apart from Jewish apocalyptic eschatology and what scholars have said about the latter since the time of Schweitzer.

In recent years, many scholars of Jewish apocalyptic, though not all, have
found it appropriate and useful (see especially Hanson 1976; 1979; 1992) to
distinguish between apocalypses (a literary type or genre), apocalyptic eschatology (a religious perspective not confined to apocalypses), and apocalypticism (a socioreligious movement or community that has recourse to

apocalyptic eschatology as a way of dealing with social or political alienation). Only the second of these (apocalyptic eschatology) can apply to Paul. He wrote no apocalypses and his apocalyptic-eschatological understanding of Christ did not emerge from social or political or any other kind of alienation. Indeed, according to his own testimony, exactly the *reverse* is true in his case, as in that of the communities he founded: social and political alienation (often leading to persecution) was a *consequence* of faith in Christ (the Christ whose *parousia* was eagerly awaited), *not* its cause (see, e.g., Phil. 3:5–9; 1 Thess 2:14). Hence, this chapter will discuss Paul's particular apocalyptic eschatology as it comes to expression in his letters.

According to Paul Hanson, "Apocalyptic eschatology is neither a genre, nor a socioreligious movement, nor a system of thought, but rather a religious perspective, a way of viewing divine plans in relation to mundane reality . . . it is a perspective which individuals or groups can embrace in varying degrees at different times" (1976, 29), and give a home in different genres of litera-ture. In an important and influential article first published in 1964, Philipp Vielhauer maintained that "the essential characteristic" of the apocalyptic-eschatological perspective is what he called "the eschatological dualism" of two world ages, "this age" and "the age to come" (1992, 549; see *1 Enoch* 71:15; 4 Ezra 7:50, 112, 119; *2 Baruch* 44:8–15; 83:4–9; *Mishnah ʾAbot* 4:1; *Mishnah Sanhedrin* 10:1; *Mishnah Berakot* 9:5; cf. Mark 10:30; Matt. 12:32; Luke 18:30; Eph. 1:21; 2:7; Heb. 6:5). This claim was echoed by Hanson: as "a religious perspective," the "essential characteristics" of Jewish apocalyptic eschatology are two ages separated by "a great judgment" (1979, 432, 440). Similarly, D. S. Russell wrote that the "dualistic view of the world, which is characteristic of apocalyptic eschatology, finds expression in a doctrine of two ages" (1964, 269).

The dualism of the two ages is "eschatological" (and thus also temporal) because it entails the final, definitive replacement of "this age," which is com-pletely evil or bad, by "the age to come." The latter puts an end to the former. There is and can be "no continuity" between the two ages (Vielhauer 1992, 550), since "this age" is the epoch and the realm (or sphere) of sin, evil, and death, whereas "the age to come" is the epoch and the realm (or sphere) of God and thus of righteousness, well-being, and life. As realms (or spheres) of activity, the categories "this age" and "the age to come" have spatial as well as temporal aspects. The locus of "this age" is the earth, whereas the locus of "the age to come" is heaven, from which the benefits of the new age will descend at the end of time or history. The dualism of the two ages characteristic of apoc-alyptic eschatology is thus *at once temporal and spatial.*

Furthermore, although Jewish apocalyptic eschatology naturally finds its focus in God's covenantal relationship to Israel, the scope of the two ages is cosmic: they both involve all people and all times. As Schweitzer pointed out, redemption in apocalyptic eschatology is "not a mere transaction" between an individual and God, but "a world-event in which he [or she] has a share" (1931, 54).

That Paul was familiar with some form of this eschatological dualism is minimally suggested by his use of the expression "this age" (*ho aiōn houtos,* Rom. 12:2; 1 Cor. 1:20; 2:6, 8; 3:18; 2 Cor. 4:4; cf. Eph. 1:21). In Gal. 1:4, he refers to "the present evil age." The phrase "this world" (*ho kosmos houtos*) is a synonym (1 Cor. 3:19; 5:10; 7:31; cf. Eph. 2:2; 4 Ezra 4:2; 8:1), as is shown by the parallelism in 1 Cor. 3:18–19:

> If you think that you are wise in *this age,* you should become fools so that you may become wise. For the wisdom of *this world* is foolishness with God.

The corresponding expression "the age (or world) to come" occurs only in Ephesians among the Pauline letters (1:21; cf. 2:7), though there may be an allusion to it in the reference to "the ends of the ages" (i.e., the end of the old age and the beginning of the new) in 1 Cor. 10:11. But the idea of a coming age is implied when the present world-age is characterized as *this* world-age (Keck 1984, 234). Moreover, such expressions as "the kingdom [kingly rule] of God" (Rom. 14:17; 1 Cor. 4:20; 6:9, 10; 15:24, 50; Gal. 5:21; 1 Thess. 2:12; see also Eph. 5:5; Col. 4:11; 2 Thess. 1:5; cf. *Testament of Moses* 10:1), "eternal life" (Rom. 2:7; 5:21; 6:22, 23; Gal. 6:8; see also 1 Tim. 1:16; 6:12; Titus 1:2; 3:7; cf. Dan. 12:2), and "new creation" (2 Cor. 5:17; Gal. 6:15; cf. *1 Enoch* 72:1; 4 Ezra 7:75; *2 Bar.* 32:6) are surely other ways of speaking about the age or world to come. These are eschatological realities, that is, the realities of the new age of God.

APOCALYPTIC ESCHATOLOGY AND REVELATION

While a two-ages dualism characteristic of Jewish apocalyptic eschatology underlies Paul's thought, the apostle does not, of course, write about "apocalyptic eschatology." He does not use this technical phrase, nor do other ancient writers of his time. The phrase is an invention, and also a convention, of biblical scholars (see Sturm 1989). It provides a convenient, shorthand way of labeling and discussing a distinctive form of eschatology (teaching concerning "last things") that scholars have discerned not only in Paul's letters but also in other ancient Jewish and Christian literature. Christian versions of apocalyptic eschatology, including that of Paul, are deeply indebted to, or are modifications of, Jewish apocalyptic eschatology, which already existed in the time of Jesus and the early church. Jewish apocalyptic eschatology, in short, was the matrix within which Christian apocalyptic eschatology, including that of Paul, arose and developed (see Collins 1984).

Eschatology has traditionally (within the history of Christian thought) referred to the theological doctrines of heaven, hell, judgment, and life after death (see the *Oxford English Dictionary* [1897]), often treated separately and with an eye on the destiny of the individual believer. *Apocalyptic* eschatology, however, concerns visible, objective, and public events that are cosmic in scope and implication, for example, the general resurrection of the dead and the last judgment.[5] Apocalyptic eschatology is fundamentally concerned with God's active and visible rectification (putting right) of the created world (the "cosmos"), which has somehow gone astray and become alienated from God.

This form of eschatology is in turn often differentiated from the eschatology of the Hebrew prophets (e.g., Amos, Isaiah, Jeremiah), which has a more limited frame of reference. This "prophetic" eschatology is often seen as the precursor of the apocalyptic variety (see Rowley 1963, 13–53; Russell 1964, 73–103), though this is a much-debated question (Collins 1984, 19–28). Prophetic eschatology—the eschatology of the Hebrew prophets—has in view a future divine intervention in the ongoing history of Israel. This divine intervention is a corrective measure in the continuing story of God's people. Furthermore, God's intervention is not publicly visible but is hidden in the historical process of national disaster or restoration. Postexilic or "late" prophecy (e.g., Ezekiel, Zechariah, Trito-Isaiah) tends to portray God's intervention in the affairs and history of Israel against a backdrop of cosmic upheaval and discontinuity, which gives this "late" prophecy a proto-apocalyptic flavor (see Hanson 1979). According to Collins (1992, 283), a "novelty" of apocalyptic eschatology (relative to prophetic eschatology) is a judgment of the dead as well as of the living (see already Isa. 25:8; 26:19, part of the so-called Isaiah Apocalypse; Dan. 12:1–3). A distinctive element of apocalyptic eschatology, at least in such works as *1 Enoch, 2 Baruch,* and *4 Ezra,* is its cosmic scope and interest: all times and places and thus all human beings are involved and at stake in the eschatological drama about to unfold, so that God's eschatological action of rectifying the creation reaches back to the beginning of human history even as it brings it to an end.

But why call this form of eschatology "apocalyptic"? The adjective is derived from the noun "apocalypse," a near transliteration of the Greek *apokalypsis,* literally meaning "unveiling" (which is also the meaning of the Latin *revelatio,* from which the English term "revelation" comes). The use of this term to characterize "apocalyptic" eschatology was inspired primarily by the New Testament book of Revelation (the Apocalypse of John). The opening verse, from which the traditional title derives, reads: "The revelation [*apokalypsis,* apocalypse] of Jesus Christ, which God gave him to show his servants what must soon take place" (Rev. 1:1). Apocalyptic eschatology refers, then, to the kind of eschatology found in the book of Revelation, and this eschatology is a matter of divine revelation: apocalyptic eschatology is *revealed* eschatology. It needs also to be recognized, however, that the book of Revelation is in many ways distinctive and cannot be taken as the measure of all expressions of an apocalyptic-eschatological worldview. The sheer quantity and richness of Revelation's symbolism and imagery are really without parallel in contemporary sources, whether Jewish or Christian (see Bauckham 1994, 9–12). Apocalyptic eschatology can be given expression in much less vivid, certainly less lurid, imagery and language, and Jewish apocalyptic eschatology, of course, would not have the Christian elements found in Revelation. Nevertheless, what is called "apocalyptic eschatology," whether in Jewish or Christian sources, is normally assumed to bear at least a "family resemblance" to the eschatology found in the book of Revelation; the family resemblance is discernible in the dualism of the two world ages, which is a matter of divine revelation.

For understandable reasons, apocalyptic eschatology has been closely associated with books that are seemingly of the same genre as the New Testament book of Revelation and thus sharing its distinctive generic features at least to some extent. The Jewish apocalypses Daniel, *1 Enoch,* 4 Ezra, and *2 Baruch* are the commonly cited examples (though unlike these works Revelation is not pseudonymous). In recent years, in fact, some scholars have begun to insist that the term "apocalyptic" should be used exclusively in connection with works of this genre or with the themes attested in them. These scholars also maintain that the term "apocalyptic" cannot then be limited to eschatology (understood narrowly as expectations about future events) since eschatology is not always the sole or even the major concern or topic of an apocalypse. Christopher Rowland, the major champion of this approach, has argued that the term "apocalyptic" ought to be used only in connection with what, in his view, is distinctive about apocalypses, namely, their interest in the revelation of "divine mysteries" (1982, 1–3, 29–37, 70–72). "Apocalyptic," he claims, "seems essentially to be the revelation of the divine mysteries through visions or some other form of immediate disclosure of heavenly truths" (1982, 70). According to Rowland, such divine mysteries can include not only the future but also "the movement of the stars, the heavenly dwelling of God, angelology, the course of human history, and the mystery of the human plight." All of these "fall within the category of the mysteries which can only be solved by higher wisdom through revelation" (1990, 34). He concludes: "To speak of apocalyptic, therefore, is to concentrate on the theme of direct communication of the heavenly mysteries in all their diversity" (1982, 14). B. Matlock, in his extensive survey and critique of scholarship on Paul as an apocalyptic thinker, has followed Rowland's lead (Matlock 1996, 258–62, 282–87).

Rowland does make a significant contribution in his insistence that apocalyptic is not only concerned with future events:

> Apocalyptic is as much involved in the attempt to understand things as they are now as to predict future events. The mysteries of heaven and earth and the real significance of contemporary persons and events in history are also the dominant interests of the apocalypticists. There is thus a concern with the world above and its mysteries as a means of explaining human existence in the present. (1982, 2)

Thus, if the essential characteristic of apocalyptic eschatology is the dualism of two ages, cosmically conceived, the notion of revelation in "apocalyptic" eschatology encompasses *both* ages, not just the one to come, since it is only through the disclosure of the coming age that the present can be perceived as "*this* (evil) age," as one destined to be brought to an end by God. Along similar lines, J. L. Martyn has written that apocalyptic involves "the conviction that God has now given to the elect true perception both of present developments (the real world) and of a wondrous transformation in the near future." A central concern of apocalyptic is "the birth of a new way of knowing both present and future" (Martyn 1985, 424 n. 28; cf. 1967). The knowledge granted of the future, of the last judgment, and of the new age beyond the judgment thus bears a close and reciprocal relationship to the knowledge granted of "this age"—which is to say that the solution (the age to come) must address the problem (this age). In apocalyptic eschatology, then, the notion of revelation applies not only to the last judgment and the coming age but also to "this age," its true nature, and its destiny.

In other respects, however, Rowland's proposal contains considerable difficulties. First, in his account apocalyptic is reduced to something mystical and individualistic. The consequences for studying Paul as an apocalyptic thinker are considerable. As Matlock points out, Rowland's view that apocalypses are more concerned "with secret knowledge and with revelatory experi-

* yes: only in light of salvin do we cog. the prob

ence" than with eschatology means that when "applied to Paul, attention shifts from the 'apocalyptic eschatology' of 1 Corinthians 15 to the rapture to paradise in 2 Corinthians 12" (Matlock 1996, 286–87, pointing to Rowland 1982, 374–86; similarly Segal 1990, 34–71). This peculiar restriction of apocalyptic in Paul's thought and experience to his personal journey to the heavenly realm in 2 Cor. 12:1–10 (an ecstatic experience Paul recounts only in order to devalue its importance) is in stark contrast to what is normally understood by apocalyptic, in Paul or elsewhere, and cannot even be substantiated by Paul's own use of the language of revelation in a number of other passages (see below). For Rowland, apocalyptic becomes curiously focused on the human experience of the divine world, rather than on God's own revelatory action of rectifying a world gone awry.[6]

Second, John J. Collins has pointed out against Rowland that "the essential role" eschatology plays in the Jewish apocalypses must not be underestimated (1984, 8). In Rowland's account, the mysteries disclosed about contemporary persons or events, about the human plight, about angels, and much else are implicitly divorced from the expected future events, from eschatology, when such mysteries should probably be understood only (or at least primarily) in relation to this eschatology. The divine mysteries disclosed are arguably of no interest apart from the expectation of God's cosmic act of rectification.

Third, as I pointed out above, the definition of apocalyptic eschatology is partly a matter of scholarly tradition and convenience even though it is based, as it ought to be, upon the data of the available sources, namely, such books as Revelation, Daniel, *1 Enoch, 2 Baruch,* and 4 Ezra. It really makes no difference to this definition that there are apocalypses that may contain no eschatology or an entirely different one. Nor does the fact that the language of revelation is used outside of the framework of apocalyptic eschatology affect the soundness of the basic definition.

Fourth, as also pointed out previously, apocalyptic eschatology (the revealed dualism of the two world ages) is not confined to apocalypses (see Collins 1984, 2; Hanson 1976, 29) even if it finds its most vivid and memorable expression in some works that seem to fit that genre. An apocalypse itself "is not constituted by one or more distinctive themes but by a distinctive combination of elements, all of which are found elsewhere" (Collins 1984, 8–9). There are some notable works, such as *Jubilees,* the *Testaments of the Twelve Patriarchs,* and the *Community Rule* (1QS) and the *War Rule* (1QM) from Qumran, which assume a clearly apocalyptic-eschatological perspective (the dualism of the two world ages) but are not apocalypses at all.[7]

Fifth, the book of Revelation itself, which is often regarded as the paradigmatic example of the genre apocalypse, has the formal framework of a letter reminiscent of Paul's own letters. Compare:

> John to the seven churches that are in Asia: Grace to you and peace from him who is and who was and who is to come. . . . (Rev. 1:4)

> Paul an apostle . . . to the churches of Galatia: Grace to you and peace from God our Father and the Lord Jesus Christ. (Gal. 1:1–3)

> The grace of the Lord Jesus be with all the saints. Amen. (Rev. 22:21)

> The grace of the Lord Jesus be with you. Amen. (1 Thess. 5:28)

The opening line of the book, "The revelation of Jesus Christ," may in fact describe not the genre of the book at all but its contents,[8] or the one to whom the contents point (Jesus Christ himself). It is even possible, given the Pauline flavor of its epistolary framework, that the opening line was derived from Paul (see Gal. 1:12 and below).

Sixth, the revelation that is an integral element of apocalyptic eschatology does not refer, as in Rowland's proposal, to the mere disclosure of information about the past, present, and/or the future to a seer who is to pass it on (in an apocalyptic writing, for example), but primarily to *God's expected eschatological activity itself.* That is, the final events themselves, when they occur, will constitute God's eschatological revelation (*apokalypsis*) of himself, of his justice or righteousness, and of his sovereign claim on the whole created world. The word "apocalyptic" properly evokes this idea of God's own eschatological and sovereign *action* of putting an end to this world-age and replacing it with the new world-age (the kingdom of God). To speak of apocalyptic, therefore, is to concentrate not on the theme of direct communication of heavenly mysteries to a human being (even if such can be involved) but on the theme of God's own visible eschatological *activity,* activity that will constitute the actual revelation, what we may call the apocalypse of God.

THE REVELATION (APOCALYPSE) OF JESUS CHRIST

The opening line of Revelation, with its claim that the revelation is "of Jesus Christ," points to a crucial modification of Jewish apocalyptic eschatology, one shared by Paul. In Revelation, the eschatological events of the imminent future take their point of departure from an eschatological event of the recent past, the resurrection (and thus ascension) of Jesus Christ to God's heavenly throne (cf. 1:9–20; 5:1–14). This event, in Paul as in Revelation, constitutes a crucial Christian modification of Jewish apocalyptic eschatology. For Paul (as for John of Revelation), the hour of the eschaton was not, as in Jewish apocalyptic eschatology, about to strike; it had already struck in God's raising of Jesus from the dead, an apocalyptic-eschatological event, as Schweitzer clearly perceived:

> While other believers held that the finger of the world-clock was touching on the beginning of the coming hour and were waiting for the stroke that would announce this, Paul told them that it had already passed beyond the point, and that they had failed to hear the striking of the hour, which in fact struck at the Resurrection of Jesus. (Schweitzer 1931, 99)

Paul's apocalyptic eschatology, like that of Revelation, is thus as much a matter of a *past* eschatological event (the resurrection of Jesus, the Messiah) as of an event still to occur (the *parousia*). Christians such as Paul and John of Revelation were convinced that God's Messiah had already made an appearance on the human scene and, just as important, that this appearance of the Messiah provided the essential and inescapable clue to a "right" understanding of this world and its events, of the human condition or plight, as well as of what was expected to happen in the near future. "For the man [person] of insight who dares to see things as they really are," Schweitzer wrote, "faith ceases to be simply a faith of expectation. It takes up present certainties into itself"; someone "who has true knowledge [a Christian] can be conscious of himself [or herself] as at one and the same time" living in both ages, in what Schweitzer here refers to as "the transient world and the eternal world" (1931, 99).

Paul also uses the term "revelation" (*apokalypsis*) in several passages. Indeed, as already noted, he can, like John in Rev. 1:1, speak of "the revelation of Jesus Christ" (Gal. 1:12; cf. 1 Cor. 1:7; 2 Thess. 1:7). Needless to say, the term is not a genre designation for Paul. However, it also cannot be assumed that the term as used by Paul is a technical one for his apocalyptic-eschatological understanding of Christ, as it is for modern scholars. Paul's use of the term and that of scholars may well diverge. It is clear that there are numerous instances where Paul uses this noun and its cognate verb (*apokalyptein*, "to reveal") in connection with the communication of heavenly or divine mysteries, particularly as mediated or induced by the Spirit. For example, he writes: "When you come together, each one has a hymn, a lesson, a *revelation*, a tongue, or an interpretation" (1 Cor. 14:26; cf. 1 Cor. 2:10; 14:6, 30; 2 Cor. 12:1, 7; Phil. 3:15; Gal. 2:2; Eph. 1:17). In 2 Cor. 12:1, he writes about "visions and revelations of the Lord." Paul's usage here approximates Rowland's linking of the term with the visionary disclosure of heavenly secrets or information to an individual (who mediates what he or she has seen and heard to others).

However, Paul also uses the term in connection with Jesus' *parousia:* the Corinthians, he writes, "are waiting for the *revelation (apokalypsis)* of our Lord Jesus Christ" (1 Cor. 1:7; cf. Rom. 2:5; 8:18–19; 1 Cor. 3:13). Paul continues: God "will strengthen" the Corinthians "to the End" (cf. 1 Cor. 15:24) so that they "may be blameless on the day [= *parousia*] of our Lord Jesus Christ" (1 Cor. 1:8). In this passage, then, the term *apokalypsis* does approach the technical usage of modern scholars when they talk about apocalyptic or apocalyptic eschatology: the "revelation" of Jesus concerns his visible eschatological appearance at his *parousia,* and this is clearly an apocalyptic *event,* as commonly understood. The Corinthians are "waiting" not for the direct communication of heavenly mysteries, of divine information, in a dream, mystical trance, or a moment of spiritual ecstasy, but for the visible reappearance on the world scene of Jesus himself. 2 Thess. 1:7 speaks similarly and more clearly of "the *revelation (apokalypsis)* of the Lord Jesus from heaven with his angels of power" (in 2 Thess. 2:3, 6, 8, it is Jesus' adversary who will "be revealed" at his *parousia*). The "revelation" here referred to is no mere disclosure of previously hidden heavenly secrets, is not simply information about future events, but is actual eschatological activity and movement, an invasion of the world below from heaven above, which is also in a sense an invasion of the present by the future.

Moreover, Paul does not confine this use of the language of revelation, of apocalypse, to the *parousia.* In Rom. 1:16–18, "the gospel" itself is decribed as "the power of God for salvation," and in this gospel "the righteousness (= rectifying act) of God is [now being powerfully] revealed through faith for faith." Indeed, "the [eschatological] wrath of God is [now also being] revealed from heaven upon all ungodliness and wickedness of those who by their wickedness suppress the truth." In Gal. 1:12, Paul claims that "the gospel that was proclaimed by me is not of human origin; for I did not receive it from a human source, nor was I taught it, but [it came or happened][9] through a *revelation (apokalypsis)* of Jesus Christ," an unmistakable allusion to the cataclysmic appearance of the risen Christ to Paul near Damascus (cf. 1 Cor. 9:1; 15:8–10; Phil. 3:7–9). A few verses later, he writes that "God . . . was pleased to *reveal* his Son to me (*en emoi,* in me, that is, in my life), so that I might proclaim him among the Gentiles" (Gal. 1:15–16). Paul did not travel up to heaven in a dream or a trance; rather, God came down (as it were) into Paul's Pharisaic life and shattered it: "I have been crucified with Christ; . . . it is no longer I who live, but it is Christ who lives in me" (Gal. 2:19–20); "the world has been crucified to me and I to the world" (Gal. 6:14). According to Paul's own understanding, God disclosed to him his Son, the Christ who faithfully died for sins "so as to deliver us from the present evil age" (Gal. 1:3–4). This Son, his saving death and resurrection, is the content of the gospel Paul proclaims (cf. 1 Cor. 15:1–5), a gospel that is not his gospel but God's (Rom. 1:1). Paul can even talk of faith itself as something "revealed" (Gal. 3:23), and this means that faith "came [on the scene]" as Christ himself did (3:24). Christ entered a world in subjection to inimical enslaving powers, here the law (Gal. 3:25).

> Now before faith came [on the scene], we were imprisoned and guarded under the law until faith should be revealed [apokalyphthēnai]. Therefore the law was our confining custodian until Christ came [on the scene], so that we might be justified by faith. But now that faith has come [on the scene], we are no longer subject to a confining custodian. (Cf. Martyn 1997)

Paul uses the language of revelation to characterize the whole of God's eschatological saving *activity* in Christ, from beginning to end. This activity includes the revelatory work of the Spirit in the churches (cf. 1 Cor. 14:26, etc. above), since the Spirit is the apocalyptic-eschatological presence of God and Christ on earth, in human history. And Paul's proclamation is itself part of the apocalyptic-eschatological drama inaugurated by the death-resurrection of Christ (cf. Rom. 16:25; Eph. 3:5), a drama that is to culminate in his *parousia*. The proclamation of the gospel elicits faith and creates eschatological communities that are the visible manifestations of God on the human scene, at least for those whose eyes have been opened by faith. The church is the community that lives at the juncture of the ages (cf. 1 Cor. 10:11), the point at which the forces of "this age" are being crushed (cf. 1 Cor. 1:18), to be replaced by a new world, the world of God disclosed in the person and the work of Jesus Christ.

PAUL AND THE TWO PATTERNS OF JEWISH APOCALYPTIC ESCHATOLOGY

According to Schweitzer, the Jewish eschatology that provides the interpretive background for Paul's own entails a dualistic contrast between the "natural" world or age and the "supernatural" world or age. The "natural" world-age is "characterized not only by its transience, but also by the fact that demons and angels exercise power in it . . . ," while the "supernatural" world-age "will put an end to this condition" (Schweitzer 1931, 55). Salvation is "thus cosmologically conceived" (Schweitzer 1931, 54), as the expurgation of evil demonic or angelic powers from the cosmos. The presence of angels and demons in such

Jewish apocalyptic literature as *Jubilees, 1 Enoch,* or the *War Rule* (1QM) goes considerably beyond what is found in the canonical Old Testament, apart from Daniel. As Russell writes: "Details of their numbers, their names, their functions, their natures are given which, though in many cases having their beginnings in the canonical scriptures, far outstrip anything to be found there" (Russell 1964, 240). Furthermore, in contrast to the Hebrew Old Testament (apart from Daniel), the world of the angels "is divided into two. On the one side are the angels who remain true to God . . . on the other side are the fallen angels and demons who obey the chief of the demons and commit all kinds of wickedness upon the earth" (1964, 238; cf. *1 Enoch* 6–16; 54–56; 69; *Jubilees* 10, 15; 1QS 3–4; 1QM; Daniel 10).

It is noteworthy, however, that of the four Jewish works named by Schweitzer as his main witnesses to Jewish apocalyptic eschatology—*1 Enoch, Psalms of Solomon,* and the apocalypses of Baruch and Ezra—the latter three do not mention evil angelic or demonic forces, nor then a conflict between angelic forces at the eschaton. Schweitzer himself acknowledged this fact: "In the Psalms of Solomon the Angels have no role assigned to them at all. The Apocalypses of Ezra and Baruch mention angels only as obedient servants of God and never as adversaries and oppressors of men [people]." The *Apocalypse of Baruch* mentions an angel of death (21:23), but "he too is thought of as standing in the service of God," not as a cosmic opponent. But this then means that the angelology of such works as *1 Enoch, Jubilees, Testaments of the Twelve Patriarchs,* the *Community Rule* (1QS) or the *War Rule* (1QM) is not an essential component of the dualism of the two ages which fundamentally characterizes apocalyptic eschatology.

The dualism of the two ages, in fact, exhibits two distinct patterns (or "tracks") in the available Jewish literature, one cosmological, the other "forensic" (legal, juridical) in which cosmic, angelic forces play no part (see de Boer 1989).

1. According to one pattern, the created world has come under the dominion of evil, angelic powers in some primeval time, namely, in the time of Noah (for the idea of an angelic "fall," cf. Gen. 6:1–6; *1 Enoch* 6–19; 64:1–2; 69:4–5; 86:1–6; 106:13–17; *Jub.* 4:15, 22; 5:1–8; 10:4–5; *Testament of Reuben* 5:6–7; *Testament of Naphtali* 3:5; CD 2:17–3:1; *2 Bar.* 56:12–15; *Liber Antiquitatum Biblicarum* 34:1–5; Wis. 2:23–24; Jude 6; 2 Pet. 2:4). God's sovereign rights have been usurped and the world, including God's own people, has been led astray into forms of idolatry. But there is a righteous remnant, chosen by God, who by acknowledgment of and submission to the Creator, the God of Israel, bears witness to the fact that these evil cosmological

powers are doomed to pass away. This remnant, the elect of God, await God's deliverance. God will invade the world under the dominion of the evil powers and defeat them in a cosmic war. Only God has the power to defeat and to overthrow the demonic and diabolical powers that have subjugated and perverted the earth. God will establish his sovereignty very soon, delivering the righteous and bringing about a new age in which he will reign unopposed.

This "cosmological" apocalyptic eschatology is to be found in perhaps its purest form in *1 Enoch* 1–36 but can best be illustrated here by *Testament of Moses* 10:

> And then his [God's] kingdom shall appear throughout all his creation,
> And then Satan shall be no more,
> And sorrow shall depart with him.
>
> . . .
>
> For the Heavenly One will arise from his royal throne,
> And he will go forth from his holy habitation
> With indignation and wrath on account of his sons.
> And the earth shall tremble. . . .

This form of Jewish apocalyptic eschatology, in short, appears to involve "a cosmic drama in which divine and cosmic forces are at work" (Russell 1964, 269). This drama in turn suggests that the two ages are not only temporal epochs but also two spheres or zones in which certain powers hold sway or in which certain kinds of activity take place. The final judgment entails God's defeat and destruction of evil cosmic forces.

2. The other pattern is a modified form of the first. In this pattern, the notion of evil, cosmological forces is absent, recedes into the background, or is even explicitly rejected (cf. *1 Enoch* 98:4–5; *Psalms of Solomon* 9:4–5). Instead, the emphasis falls on free will and individual human decision. Sin is the willful rejection of the Creator God (the breaking of the first commandment), and death is punishment for this fundamental sin. God, however, has provided the law as a remedy for this situation, and a person's posture toward this law determines his or her ultimate destiny. At the last judgment, conceptualized not as a cosmic war but as a courtroom in which all humanity appears before the bar of the judge, God will reward with eternal life those who have acknowledged his claim and chosen the law and observed its commandments (the righteous), while he will punish with eternal death those who have not (the wicked).

This "forensic" form of apocalyptic eschatology is to be found in both 4 Ezra and *2 Baruch,* both of which emphasize the fall and the responsibility of Adam, the first and paradigmatic human transgressor (4 Ezra 3:5–7,

20–21; 4:30–31; 7:118–19; *2 Bar.* 17:2–3; 23:4; 48:42–43; 54:14, 19; 56:6; cf. *1 Enoch* 69:6; *Jub.* 3:17–25; 4:29–30; *LAB* 13:8–9; Sir. 25:24; Wis. 10:1). Evil angelic powers are absent from both works, as noted above. According to *2 Baruch,* for example, "Adam sinned first and . . . brought death upon all . . . each of us has become his [or her] own Adam" (54:14, 19; trans. Klijn, in Charlesworth 1983). The destiny of each person is in his or her own hands: "each of them who has been born from him [Adam] has prepared for himself [or herself] the coming torment . . . each of them has chosen for himself [or herself] the coming glory" (54:15; cf. 51:16; 85:7). To choose the law is thus to choose the coming glory (cf. 17:4; 38:1–2; 48:22; 54:5). The present age is the time of *decision.* This form of apocalyptic eschatology, whose marks can still be traced in rabbinic literature, is characterized by a legal piety in which personal responsibility and accountability are dominant.

Some works exhibit a blend of the two patterns, notably the Dead Sea Scrolls, where one finds both subjection to evil cosmological forces and human control of personal destiny, both predestination and exhortation to observe the law, both God's eschatological war against Belial and his cohorts and God's judgment of human beings on the basis of their deeds or works (see 1QS 1–4; 1QM; CD). According to the Scrolls, the community as a whole as well as the individual members are under constant threat from evil cosmological powers (Belial, the Angel of Darkness, the Spirit of Falsehood or Deceit). To choose the law is thus to choose to stand in the protected sphere of God's own power (as represented by Michael, the Angel of Light, the Spirit of Truth). The law is God's powerful weapon whereby he enables the righteous believer to withstand the superhuman power of the demonic forces (cf. CD 16:1–3). Present existence is thus marked by a struggle between two contending groups of cosmological powers or spirits that seek to lay their claim on human beings. This struggle manifests itself not only in the sociological separation of the righteous (the covenantal community) from the wicked (the world outside) but also in the choice that the individual, especially the member of the community must make each day for God and his law. The struggle penetrates the heart of the individual (see especially 1QS 3–4). (See Sanders 1977, 237–321, especially 295.) Much the same could be said for the book of *Jubilees* and the *Testaments of the Twelve Patriarchs* (see Collins 1984, 111).

Paul's letters also exhibit the characteristic concerns and ideas, or at least the language, of these two different patterns or "tracks" of Jewish apocalyptic eschatology. His use of the story of Adam in 1 Cor. 15:21–22, 45–49 and Rom. 5:12–21 (cf. 2 Cor. 11:3; 1 Tim. 2:13–14) betrays the influence of the tradition of interpretation of Adam and his disobedience found in 4 Ezra and

2 Baruch, while his not infrequent references to Satan, always as the power hostile to God and the gospel of Christ (Rom. 16:20; 1 Cor. 5:5; 7:5; 2 Cor. 2:11; 11:14; 12:7; 1 Thess. 2:18; cf. 2 Cor. 6:14; 1 Thess. 3:5), suggest his deep indebtedness to the worldview of "cosmological" Jewish apocalyptic eschatology (cf. "the god of this age" in 2 Cor. 4:4; "Beliar" in 2 Cor. 6:15). The angelology of "cosmological" Jewish apocalyptic eschatology probably also lies behind the references to "the rulers of this age" in 1 Cor. 2:6–8, the principalities and powers mentioned in Rom. 8:38 and 1 Cor. 15:24, and Paul's personification of Sin and Death as oppressive cosmic powers that rule over human beings (cf. Rom. 5:12, 21; 1 Cor. 15:26, 56).

The two patterns of Jewish apocalyptic eschatology as just outlined have been reflected in the study of Paul, and particularly in the debate between Rudolf Bultmann and Ernst Käsemann. Bultmann acknowledged the importance of Schweitzer's insights but also argued that Paul had begun a process of existentially reinterpreting ("demythologizing") received apocalyptic tradition with its talk of cosmological powers and future cosmic transformation, a process that Bultmann sought to bring to fruition in his own existentialist interpretation of Paul (see Bultmann 1984; 1951, 185–352). Käsemann sought to refute Bultmann's approach in a series of essays published in the early 1960s (see especially 1969b). Bultmann's so-called anthropological approach maintained that Paul's primary concern was with the *individual* human being as he or she is addressed by the gospel message in the *present* and confronted with the *decision* of faith. Käsemann's "cosmological" interpretation maintained that Paul's primary concern was with God's destruction in the *future* of the inimical *cosmic powers* that now enslave the creation, a condition from which the individual human being cannot be abstracted. As Käsemann wrote:

> Man [the human being] for Paul is never just on his [or her] own. He [she] is always a specific piece of world and therefore becomes what in the last resort he [she] is by determination from outside, i.e., by the power which takes possession of him [her] and the lordship to which he [she] surrenders him[her]self. His [her] life is from the beginning a stake in the confrontation between God and the principalities of this world. In other words, it mirrors the cosmic contention for the lordship of the world and is its concretion. As such man's [a human being's] life can only be understood apocalyptically. (1969b, 136)

Both Bultmann and Käsemann sought in their respective interpretations of Paul to come to grips with the tension of "already" and "not yet" in Paul's thought. Nevertheless, Käsemann's interpretation was regarded as properly apocalyptic, whereas Bultmann's was regarded as a nonapocalyptic reading of Paul.

Both interpretations of Paul, however, assume the basic dualism characteristic of apocalyptic eschatology and for this reason both acknowledge in their own way the influence of Jewish apocalyptic traditions within Paul's thought, christologically adapted and modified of course. This can be seen most illuminatingly in their respective interpretations of Paul's theology of justification by faith, regarded by both as lying at the center of Paul's thought.

Bultmann argued that there was "complete agreement" between Paul and first-century Jews "as to the formal meaning of *dikaiosynē* ['justification,' 'righteousness,' 'rectification']: It is a forensic-eschatological term" (Bultmann 1951, 273; Bultmann appeals to Rom. 2:13; 4:3, 5, 6; Gal. 3:6). For Bultmann "righteousness" as a forensic term implies the imagery of the lawcourt and thus means the "favorable standing" one has in such a court; it does not mean "the ethical quality of a person," but "his [or her] relation to God" (1951, 272, 279). The event of Christ's death and resurrection, however, caused Paul to make two key modifications in the Jewish view:

1. *Present not future.* "What for the Jews," Bultmann wrote, appealing to Rom. 5:1, "is a *matter of hope* is for Paul a *present reality*—or, better, is also a present reality" (1951, 279 [emphasis original]). Thus, through the Christ-event, "God already pronounces His eschatological verdict (over the man [person] of faith) in the present; the eschatological event is a present reality, or, rather, is beginning in the present" (p. 276). Christ's death and resurrection was "the eschatological event by which God ended the old course of the world and introduced a new aeon" (p. 278). Through that event "God's acquitting decision" (p. 279) has been declared, a verdict that becomes a reality for the individual "hearer of the gospel" (p. 275).

2. *Faith not works.* Whereas "the pious Jew endeavors . . . to fulfill the conditions which are the presupposition" of God's eschatological justifying (acquitting) verdict (to be given at the last judgment), namely, "keeping the commandments of the Law and doing good works" (p. 273), the Christian does not seek justification by works of the law but receives it by faith: "Righteousness, then," Bultmann wrote, "cannot be won by human effort, nor does any human accomplishment establish a claim to it; it is sheer gift" (pp. 280–81). The "righteousness of God" (*dikaiosynē theou*) is thus "God-given, God adjudicated righteousness" (p. 285).

It is evident from this brief summary of Bultmann's views that Paul's "anthropological" understanding of justification or of God's righteousness was, apart from the two modifications mentioned, the same as that found in the forensic Jewish apocalyptic eschatology outlined previously. According to Bultmann himself, "In the apocalyptic view the individual is responsible for himself [herself] only . . . and the individual's future will be decided according to his [her] works. And this is a judgment over the whole world" (1975, 31). In another work (1956, 80–86), Bultmann relies primarily on 4 Ezra for his account of Jewish apocalyptic eschatology, while in his famous *Theology of the New Testament* (1951, 230), he attributes talk of cosmological powers in Paul to the influence of "the cosmological mythology of Gnosticism," rather than to Jewish apocalyptic traditions.

In reaction to Bultmann, Käsemann (1969a) argued that the expression "the righteousness of God" (*dikaiosynē theou,* Rom. 1:17; 3:5, 21; 10:3; 2 Cor. 5:21) referred in the first instance to God's own righteous eschatological saving action and power. This unified expression was not coined by Paul; it occurs as a technical term in Deut. 33:21, in *Testament of Dan* 6:10, and in 1QS 11:12: "If I stagger because of the sin of flesh, my justification shall be by the righteousness of God which endures for ever" (trans. Vermes). Paul, Käsemann argued, retained this meaning in his appropriation of the term. For Käsemann, then, the undoubted character of righteousness as a forensic-eschatological gift (acquittal to eternal life) cannot be separated from its character as God's saving presence and power: "God's saving activity . . . is present in his gift; the righteousness of God "partakes of the character of power, insofar as God himself enters the arena with it" (1969a, 174). God's righteousness is a gift only insofar as it also signifies submissive obedience to God's saving power (p. 182), without which all claims to righteousness are merely illusion. In the process of establishing this thesis, Käsemann also attacked the two modifications Bultmann attributed to Paul:

1. *Present but also still future.* According to Käsemann, what made Paul's use of the expression "the righteousness of God" unique over against the Jewish apocalyptic use of it was not, as Bultmann claimed, the present reality of righteousness. The *Thanksgiving Hymns* from Qumran show that its present reality was also stressed in one stream of apocalyptic Judaism (p. 178). But Käsemann's basic point was not that Bultmann had misunderstood apocalyptic Judaism but that he had misunderstood *Paul.* Though Käsemann conceded that "Paul lays the strongest stress on the present nature of salvation" (p. 178), he emphasized that Paul's "present eschatology cannot be taken out of its context of future eschatology. . . . Paul remained an apocalyptist" (p. 181). Käsemann here unfortunately, probably because he was reacting to Bultmann, equates apocalyptic eschatology in Paul with a future hope, with the "not yet"; elsewhere he can be more nuanced.

2. *God's cosmic act of salvation.* Similarly, in attacking Bultmann's second modification, Käsemann asserted that "the righteousness of God does not, *in Paul's understanding,* refer primarily to the individual and is not to be understood exclusively in the context of a doctrine of man [the human being]" (1969, 180 [emphasis added]). The Bultmann anthropological/individual constriction occurs when exclusive emphasis is laid on the gift character of righteousness and when the latter is interpreted in terms of the contrast between faith and works (pp. 172–73, 176). *Paul's* theology of God's righteousness is not "essentially concerned with anthropology" (p. 181), that is, with human activity and decision, but with God's own redemptive action in and for the world. It is here that the uniqueness of Paul's appropriation of the term "the righteousness of God" lies, according to Käsemann. Over against apocalyptic Judaism as well as pre-Pauline Jewish Christianity, the disclosure of God's righteousness in Christ can no longer signify only his covenant faithfulness but also, and primarily, his faithfulness toward the whole creation. It is "God's sovereignty over the world revealing itself eschatologically in Jesus" (p. 180), through whom, contrary to the Jewish view, God justifies not the godly but the ungodly (p. 178). The ungodly (Rom 4:5; 5:6) are not those who do bad things, nor those who willfully transgress the law, but those who *cannot* do the right thing, because they have become subjected to the enslaving powers of Sin and Death. God's righteousness is saving gift because it delivers human beings from these two cosmic powers, powers against which the law is weak and ineffectual.

It is evident from this summary that Käsemann's interpretation of God's righteousness in Paul's thought reflects the categories and perspectives of the "cosmological" Jewish apocalyptic eschatology previously outlined. The debate between Bultmann and Käsemann (and their respective followers) is a sufficient indication that the traditions of both patterns or "tracks" of Jewish apocalyptic eschatology, the forensic and the cosmological, are present in Paul's thought.

Schweitzer, however, had concluded that Paul, like Jesus, "stood *closer* to the world of thought represented by the Book of Enoch" than to that of "the Apocalypses of Baruch and Ezra" (1931, 57 [emphasis added]). This was of course also the view of Käsemann, in polemical opposition to Bultmann. That this is a correct interpretation of Paul would seem to be supported by Paul's argument in Romans 1–8. In the first five and a half chapters (Rom. 1:1–5:11), the language and perspectives of forensic apocalyptic eschatology are clearly prominent (not surprisingly, Bultmann found these chapters crucial to his own interpretation). In Romans 6–8, however, the language and perspectives of cosmological apocalyptic eschatology predominate (e.g., sin and death, righteousness, flesh, and the Spirit are conceptualized as cosmic powers in conflict). In Rom. 5:12–21, however, where Paul utilizes the figure of Adam, whose primeval disobedience and its result (death) play crucial roles in forensic Jewish apocalyptic eschatology (4 Ezra, *2 Baruch*), forensic and cosmological ideas completely interpenetrate, and the passage marks the shift from predominantly forensic to predominantly cosmological categories in Paul's argument in Romans. That shift finds its anticipation in 1:16–17 and 3:9, two texts that occur at crucial junctures in Paul's argument in the first three chapters. Thus, while such passages as 8:1 and 8:33–34 indicate that forensic categories have hardly been given up or left behind, the structure and progression of Paul's argument in Romans 1–8 suggest that motifs proper to cosmological apocalyptic eschatology circumscribe and, to a large extent, overtake forensic motifs.

If this assessment of Romans 1–8 is correct, the question is: Why are forensic motifs present at all? Or why are they so prominent in the opening chapters? The answer may have something to do with Paul's assumed or imagined conversation partners, perhaps especially those in Rome. If one of these partners was Judaism (as interpreters of Romans have often claimed), then it was also probably a Judaism embracing the categories and the perspectives of forensic Jewish apocalyptic eschatology. In Rom. 2:5–8 (cf. 2:13), Paul reproduces a nearly pure specimen of Jewish forensic apocalyptic eschatology, with its adaptation of the Two Ways: "by your hard and impenitent heart you are storing up wrath for yourself on the day of wrath and the revelation of the righteous judgment of God, who will repay to each person according to his [or her] works. . . ." Since Paul is writing to Christians in Rome, it is also quite possible, perhaps probable, that these imagined conversation partners, whether of Jewish or of Gentile birth, had appropriated the categories and the perspectives of forensic Jewish apocalyptic eschatology. For such Christians, presumably, Christ's death would have been understood as a sacrifice atoning for past sins (Rom. 3:25–26; 4:25; cf. 1 Cor. 15:3; Gal. 1:4). This sacrificial death did not put an end to law observance but quite to the contrary obligated those so forgiven to obey it all the more (cf. Matt. 5:17–20).

Throughout Rom. 1:18–3:19, Paul embraces the presuppositions of forensic Jewish apocalyptic eschatology (and/or its Jewish-Christian adaptation), most notably its understanding of the role and function of the law, only to claim that by the standard of the law, through which "the whole world may be held accountable to God" (3:19; cf. 2:12–16), the human situation is in fact hopeless (cf. 3:10–20; 4:15; 8:1). It is hopeless because, for Paul, every one is "under the power of Sin" (3:9), a claim that presumes what is made abundantly clear later in Romans, namely, the inability of the law to provide deliverance from Sin's lethal clutches (cf. 7:7–8:8). Reliance on "works (observance) of the law" (3:20, 28) is quite literally a dead end (4:15a) and, in any event, is ruled out by the justifying death of Christ (3:21–30; cf. 5:1–11), good news indeed. Faith is the appropriate human posture to this event, replacing (as Bultmann rightly claimed) "works of the law." But Paul's cosmological understanding of God's righteousness (1:16–17) and of Sin (3:9) indicate that faith is not, as Bultmann seemed at times to think, analogous to what it replaces; that is, it is precisely not a matter of human choice or "decision" (cf. 10:17). It is in fact a matter of being grateful beneficiaries of God's gracious, liberating power revealed (made effectively present in the world) in the death and resurrection of Christ (cf. 5:11). Thus, while Paul speaks of faith (or of rectification by faith) primarily when he is combatting the claim (among both Jews and Christians of his time) that "works (observance) of the law" provide the righteousness that will lead to eschatological justification (acquittal) and thus to life in the new age, the meaning of faith is actually determined by the cosmological-apocalyptic disclosure of God's righteousness and of sin in the crucifixion of Christ. Christ's death cannot be understood in exclusively forensic terms, since it marks God's triumphant invasion of the world "under sin" (Rom. 3:9) to liberate human beings (the ungodly) from sin's deadly power.

SOME SPECIAL PROBLEMS

What was the source of Paul's apocalyptic ideas?

In Phil 3:5, Paul declares himself a Pharisee (cf. Acts 26:5), and according to some interpreters Pharisaism was an essentially *non*apocalyptic form of first-century Judaism (see the overview of the debate in Russell 1964, 20–28, 73–103). Pharisaism was the immediate precursor of the rabbinic Judaism that developed after 70 C.E. (the year the Roman armies destroyed the Temple in Jerusalem), and the rabbis explicitly repudiated Jewish apocalyptic works such as *1 Enoch* (Daniel was the only apocalyptic work accepted into their canon of scripture.). It must be noted, however, that the rabbis shared and retained the two-ages dualism characteristic of apocalyptic eschatology, as indeed did the Pharisees before them (cf. Acts 23:6–8). But the apocalyptic eschatology of the rabbis was largely of the *forensic* variety attested in such works as the *Psalms of Solomon*, 4 Ezra, and *2 Baruch*. The Pharisaic rabbis thus repudiated only the "*cosmological*" manifestations of Jewish apocalyptic eschatology. As a former Pharisee, Paul's deep familiarity with the perspectives and assumptions of forensic Jewish apocalyptic eschatology is thus readily explicable.

But what then about his familiarity with, and even his preference for, the perspectives and categories of *cosmological* Jewish apocalyptic eschatology? Here it must be said that the precise character of Pharisaism *prior* to 70 C.E. is not easily ascertainable, since all the relevant sources (primarily Josephus, the Gospels, and Acts) date from after 70 C.E. There is one exception: Paul's own letters. In fact, Paul is the only known Pharisee who has left any writings behind at all. It cannot be excluded, therefore, that Pharisaism prior to 70 was characterized by, or could accommodate, the perspectives and categories of cosmological Jewish apocalyptic eschatology (cf. Acts 23:8, which mentions the Pharisaic beliefs in angels and spirits; Hengel 1991, 40–55, especially 51). By the same token, then, it cannot be excluded that Paul the Christian derived some of his cosmological-apocalyptic concepts from his earlier life as a devout Pharisee (cf. Gal. 1:13–14; Phil. 3:5–9).[10]

Does Paul simply fit his understanding of Christ into an apocalyptic-eschatological framework taken over from his pre-Christian past?

It could be argued in light of the foregoing discussion that while Paul the Christian repudiated the Pharisaic understanding of a righteousness predicated on observance of the law (Phil. 3:5–9; cf. Gal. 2:19–20; 6:14), he did not repudiate the apocalyptic-eschatological two-ages dualism of his previous Pharisaism. With respect to this dualistic understanding of time and history, there was no discontinuity between Paul's Pharisaic past and his career as an apostle of Christ. The conclusion is then at hand that Paul effectively fit his understanding of the gospel of Christ into the perspectives and assumptions of Jewish apocalyptic eschatology (whether that be forensic or cosmological). As Dodd wrote, "When Paul became a Christian, his new beliefs were fitted into this framework" (Dodd 1953, 109). According to J. C. Beker, despite the christological modifications, the coherent core of Paul's gospel remained "the imminent cosmic triumph of God" (Beker 1980, 19), which was the central hope of Jewish apocalyptic eschatology. Paul imposes and insists on "a particularist Jewish apocalyptic ideology to communicate the truth of the gospel" (ibid., 170).

It is clear from the discussion of Bultmann and Käsemann above, however, that the reverse must be true: the crucified Christ whom God raised from the dead is Paul's criterion for the appropriation of Jewish apocalyptic-eschatological categories; the latter serve the former, not vice versa. Jewish apocalyptic ideas or categories have no validity whatsoever apart from the validation they receive from God's action in raising from the dead the crucified Christ. (The same is true of Paul's use of, for example, Stoic or Epicurean ideas). Paul does not preach apocalyptic eschatology, not even Christian apocalyptic eschatology; he preaches the crucified Christ whom God raised from the dead, nothing else (cf. 1 Cor. 1:23; 2:2).

Is there apocalyptic eschatology in Paul's letter to the Galatians?

This question arises from the fact that there are no explicit or even certain references to the *parousia* or a future consummation in Galatians. Gal. 5:5 is the clearest possibility: "we eagerly wait for the hope of rectification" (cf. 2:16). As a result, Beker claimed that in Galatians Paul's dominant apocalyptic-eschatological perspective was effectively suppressed for reasons having to do with the specific problems he was seeking to address in the churches of Galatia (Beker 1980, 37–58). Once Paul's apocalyptic eschatology is not limited to his expectation of the *parousia,* however, this appraisal of Galatians falls away (see Martyn 1985, 1997). The two-ages dualism of apocalyptic eschatology permeates this letter (see especially the conflict between flesh and spirit in 5:16–26), though it has of course been brought into the service of proclaiming the gospel: Christ's self-sacrificial atoning death "for our sins" delivers human beings from "the present evil age" (1:4).

Did Paul's views concerning the parousia and concerning the resurrection of the dead change or develop?

In 1 Thess. 4:13–18, Paul assumes that Christians (including himself) can expect to live to the *parousia;* the death of Christians in Thessalonica (4:13) before that event was an unexpected development, causing considerable consternation. In 1 Cor. 15:50–58, however, the death of Christians before the *parousia* is no longer regarded as unusual or unexpected: "We will not *all* die," Paul declares. Those who remain alive until the *parousia* now seem to be in the minority.

Furthermore, the way Paul conceives of the resurrection seems to change as well. The issue in 1 Thess. 4:13–18 is whether those who have died before the *parousia* are lost or at a disadvantage. Paul solemnly declares to the Thessalonians that such is not the case, that "we who are alive, who are left until the coming of the Lord, will by no means precede those who have died." In fact, at the final trumpet, "the dead in Christ will rise first." Then "we who are alive, who are left, will be caught up in the clouds together with them to meet the Lord in the air." Thus, the dead in Christ as well as the living shall "be with the Lord for ever." In 1 Cor. 15:50–58, Paul's conception of what will happen at the *parousia* is much more elaborate: "we will all be changed. . . . For the trumpet will sound, and the dead will be raised imperishable, and we [the living along with the dead] will be changed"; the perishable body shall "put on imperishability," and the mortal body shall "put on immortality." Death will then have been "swallowed up in victory." There is nothing here about being caught up in the clouds to meet the Lord in the air. The emphasis falls on transformation into a new bodily form of existence and God's triumph over the power of death (cf. 15:26).

2 Cor. 5:1–10 seems to go further. Paul here echoes the language used in 1 Cor. 15:50–58 ("we wish not to be unclothed but to be further clothed, so that what is mortal may be swallowed up by life") but the *parousia* is not mentioned, nor is a last trumpet signaling a final resurrection. Rather, Paul now seems to be concerned with what happens immediately after physical, bodily demise: "we know that if the earthly tent [the physical body] is destroyed [dies], we have a building from God, a house not made with hands, eternal in the heavens." Paul seems not only to contemplate his own death but even to prefer it: "we know that while we are at home in the body we are away from the Lord . . . we would rather be away from the body and at home with the Lord." Paul's focus seems thus to have shifted from the *parousia* and the (future) resurrection of the dead to the prospect of life with Christ immediately after death; he no longer talks about a corporate meeting of Christ in the air at the *parousia* (as in 1 Thess. 4:13–18), nor about eschatological bodily "change" for all who are raised at the last trumpet (as in 1 Cor. 15:50–58), but about personal release from the earthly body at death. Has Paul given up the apocalyptic-eschatological expectation of a *parousia?* Has the *parousia* receded in imminence and thus in importance? Some scholars have argued as much, especially Dodd (1953, 108–28).

Dodd saw "the turning point" in Paul's developing thought "to lie somewhat about the time of II Corinthians." The letter to the Ephesians was for Dodd "the climax of that development" (1953, 117–18). In Ephesians, as in Colossians, Christians are said to "have been raised with Christ" and to "have been made alive together" with him (Eph. 2:4–6; Col. 2:12–14); the future expectation, though not given up (Eph. 6:13; Col. 3:4), has receded in vitality and in importance (a conclusion that could also apply to the Pastoral Epistles; cf. 1 Tim. 6:14; 2 Tim. 4:1; Titus 2:3). Paul, Dodd argued, "outgrew" the dualistic mentality of Jewish apocalypticism and he also "revised" his eschatological timetable (1953, 126–27). Dodd's views are easier to maintain if

Colossians and Ephesians (and the Pastoral Epistles) are deemed to be authentic letters of Paul, which most scholars today doubt with respect to Ephesians and the Pastorals (they are evenly divided over Colossians). But if we disregard these disputed letters, the claim that Paul's eschatology changed is doubtful.

In Galatians, as we saw above, there is no mention of the *parousia* and a future expectation plays a minor role in Paul's argument. If, as some scholars believe, Galatians (instead of 1 Thessalonians) was Paul's earliest letter, the thesis of a development in Paul's eschatological expectation (from vibrant to moribund) clearly falls to the ground. Galatians has much in common with Romans, a letter undoubtedly written toward the end of Paul's active missionary career. In Romans, the emphasis certainly falls, as in Galatians, upon the present benefits of Christ's death and resurrection (cf. Romans 5–6), but the expectation of a future cosmic transformation is neither absent nor peripheral to the theology (see especially Rom. 8:18–25; 13:11). In any event, Romans was written after Galatians and the future expectation is more vibrant in Romans than in Galatians. In Romans, furthermore, Paul still holds out hope for a bodily redemption (cf. 8:11). In Philippians, also probably written toward the end of Paul's active missionary career, the apostle combines the hope of being with Christ immediately after death with the expectation of a future consummation. His personal "desire is to depart [die] and be with Christ for that is far better [than remaining alive]"; indeed "dying is gain" (1:21–23). But Christians also await from heaven "a Savior, the Lord Jesus Christ" who "will transform" the lowly earthly body into a glorious one (3:20–21). The language here echoes 1 Thess. 1:9–10; 4:13–18; 1 Cor. 15:20–28, 50–58.

It is important to remember that Paul's undisputed letters are occasional works, addressing specific problems in specific places; they are not dogmatic nor systematic treatises on specified topics such as the *parousia,* the resurrection of the dead, or life after death. The differences from one letter to the next may not reflect changes in Paul's fundamental theological convictions (that Jesus will come again and that there will be a resurrection of the dead), but changes in the issues being addressed. Furthermore, the actual language Paul uses to describe the *parousia* and the resurrection of the dead is not only figurative and plastic (the last "trumpet," "put on" immortality as clothing, "change," "transform," etc.), but also contextually determined, that is, determined by the needs of the audiences being addressed (see Lindemann 1994). Paul's eschatology, then, may not have changed or developed but may have found constantly new forms of verbal and conceptual expression. His fundamental conviction, one that arguably unifies his thought, is expressed in Rom. 8:38–39:

For I am convinced that neither death, nor life, nor angels, nor rulers, nor things present, nor things to come, nor powers, nor height, nor depth, nor anything else in all creation, will be able to separate us [both now and in the future] from the love of God in Christ Jesus our Lord.

Does Paul believe all human beings will be saved at the end?

The question arises from seemingly irreconcilable statements (see Boring 1986), even in the same work. For example, in 1 Cor. 1:18, Paul writes that "the message about the cross is foolishness to those who are perishing, but to us [i.e., us Christians] who are being saved it is the power of God." This statement seems to imply a limited salvation, as do others (cf., e.g., 1 Thess. 1:10; 4:13–18). In 1 Cor. 15:22, however, Paul claims that "as all die in Adam, so all will be made alive [saved] in Christ." Here salvation appears to be universal, as it is elsewhere (see especially Rom. 5:12–21). Scholars have sought to come to grips with these seemingly contradictory claims in various ways, for example, by arguing that Paul's thought developed from limited salvation to universal salvation (Dodd), that while Paul may have regarded salvation as universal in intent (salvation is "offered" to all) it would be only limited in actual result (Bultmann and many others), or that Paul's statements cannot finally be reconciled: he maintains both points of view (Boring). The issue comes down to two sets of passages: (1) those that envisage Christians appearing before the judgment seat of God or Christ (see 1 Cor. 3:17; 2 Cor. 5:10; Rom. 14:10; cf. Rom. 2:1–16; 1 Cor. 9:24–10:13), and (2) those that envisage ultimate salvation for nonbelievers as well as believers (especially 1 Cor. 15:21–22; Rom. 5:12–21; cf. Rom. 11:25–36; 2 Cor. 5:14–15, 19). The issue is thus whether Christians can lose or be denied salvation at the *parousia,* on the one side, and whether nonbelievers can or will ultimately be saved on the other.

The first group of texts bears the hallmarks of "forensic" apocalyptic eschatology because of their emphasis on individual responsibility and accountability for one's actions: for example, "For all of us [Christians] must appear before the judgment seat of Christ, so that each may receive recompense for what has been done in the body, whether good or evil" (2 Cor. 5:10); "we [Christians] will all stand before the judgment seat of God. . . . So, then, each of us will be accountable to God" (Rom. 14:10, 12). Does Paul, therefore, believe that the sinful actions of Christians can and will put their ultimate salvation at risk? Will some of them be damned instead of saved? It is certainly true that Paul regards salvation in the *present* as under constant threat, and he cautions against the presumption of claiming to be already living beyond the *parousia,* especially in 1 Corinthians (see 1 Cor. 4:8; 9:24–10:13): "So if you think you are standing, watch out that you do not fall!" (1 Cor. 10:12; cf. Rom. 11:18–22). Christians are in danger and their faith is in jeopardy, but he goes on to assure his Corinthian readers that God is faithful and will enable those who put their trust in him to withstand such testing (1 Cor. 10:12–13; cf. 1:8). Thus, while Paul regards salvation as under constant threat in the short term (prior to the *parousia*), it is doubtful that he so regards it in the long term (Phil. 1.6). Christians will be held accountable for what they do, but their works have no effect on their salvation in the long term (for Paul, salvation is not a human achievement, or "work," in any sense of the word). When, in 1 Cor. 5:1–10, Paul counsels the Corinthian church to "drive out" an errant member (for gross sexual immorality) and no longer to associate with him, it is "so that his spirit may be saved in the day of the Lord," that is, at the *parousia.* The loss of even this person, whom Paul regards as a lapsed Christian, to the realm of Satan (where his behavior shows he belongs) is entirely temporary and provisional.

In 1 Cor. 15:21–22 and Rom. 5:12–21, both of which contrast the work of Christ with that of Adam, salvation seems to be universal. Scholars attempt to get around the difficulty of Paul's statement in 1 Cor. 15:22 ("all will be made alive in Christ") in three ways. First, they claim that Paul's *true* view is to be found in the following verse, which mentions only "those who belong to Christ" as being raised at his *parousia* (as in 1 Thess. 4:13–18). But this interpretation does not solve the problem presented by the wording of 15:22, while the reference to the raising of Christians in 15:23 may not in any case be meant exclusively. Indeed, some scholars argue that the phrase "Then is the end [*telos*]" could also mean "Then come the rest," that is, the remainder of the dead (see NRSV note). This would mean three groups: Christ, Christians, and the rest of humanity. Others would reject this interpretation of *telos,* probably rightly (cf. 1:8), but still discern a general resurrection, to occur at the end, given the parallelism of 15:21–22:

> through a human being, death,
> through a human being, *resurrection of the dead.*

> in Adam, all die,
> in Christ, *all* shall be made alive.

The parallelism demands that the "resurrection of the dead" encompass "all" people.

Second, some scholars attempt to get around this parallelism by claiming that the general resurrection in view is not a resurrection of all to salvation but of all to final judgment whereby those raised will be consigned *either* to salvation *or* to damnation (so Schweitzer 1931, 68, 93; cf. Luke 14:14; John 5:29). That this interpretation is improbable is once again shown by the parallelism in 15:21–22, where "resurrection of the dead" is parallel with "all shall be *made alive.*" Elsewhere Paul uses the verb "to make alive" (one word in the Greek) as a synonym for "to save" (Gal. 3:21; Rom. 4:17; 1 Cor. 15:45; cf. 15:36) and it seems likely that he does so here as well.

Third, some scholars claim that what Paul really means in 15:22 is that "all who are in Christ," that is, only believers, shall be saved. But this interpretation is not supported by the grammar or syntax, nor by the parallelism with "in Adam, all die." It also raises another problem: How can Christ's work be less effective, *less cosmic,* than Adam's transgression? The whole point of the comparison between Adam and Christ is that the effects of Christ's saving work (*all* shall be made alive) match the cosmic effects of Adam's primal transgression (*all* die). How could it be otherwise if God is to be "all in all" (1 Cor. 15:28)? Furthermore, Paul repeats the point in Rom. 5:12–21, where he reuses the Adam–Christ typology: "just as one man's trespass led to condemnation *for all,* so one man's act of righteousness leads to justification and life *for all*" (Rom. 5:18). The two italicized phrases are in parallel and must have the same reference and thus the same scope. There can be no doubt here that Paul's words signify universal salvation, even if here too there have been repeated attempts to suggest that that is not what Paul *really* means: Paul has merely been forced into this understanding of Christ's saving work, so the argument runs, only by the force of the analogy with Adam; he does not *really* mean to say this. However, the universality given expression in these passages is arguably consistent with Paul's fundamental theology. The universality of salvation corresponds to, and addresses, the universal hegemony of sin and death (1 Cor. 15:26, 54–56; Rom. 3:9; 5:12, 21). Unless salvation is universal, sin and death will not have been completely defeated, and God's saving action and thus his sovereignty will remain an extremely limited affair.

Furthermore, the claim of universal salvation has a significant rhetorical function in both 1 Corinthians 15 and Romans 5 (see de Boer 1988): it effectively destroys any notion that salvation is either a natural right (1 Corinthians) or a merited achievement (Romans). Salvation is thus no longer a matter of competition or triumphalist claims ("I am saved; are you?"). Paul's claim of a universal salvation is an expression of his "theology of the cross" (see 1 Cor. 1:18–2:4; cf. 2 Cor. 5:14–15). The upshot of this theology is that God justifies and thus saves not the righteous but the ungodly. In Paul's view, God saves only the ungodly, those who cannot save themselves, a category that includes all human beings from Adam onward ("for there is no distinction, since all have sinned and fall short of the glory of God" [Rom 3:23]). Adamic human beings cannot save themselves from the inimical cosmic powers of sin and death, and for this reason the gospel is not the "offer" of salvation (as is the law in forensic Jewish apocalyptic eschatology) whose saving effects depend on human acceptance or "decision" (Bultmann). Salvation is a gift granted by God and takes effect solely at God's initiative. The salvation God will bestow on all is thus no different in kind from the salvation to be bestowed on believers and in which they have already been graciously allowed to participate, having received the Spirit as "a first installment" (2 Cor. 1:22; cf. Rom. 8:23). The dualism between those perishing and those now being saved (1 Cor. 1:18), between unbelievers and believers, is thus entirely temporary and provisional.

Some would argue, as Boring does, that "Paul has statements in which salvation is . . . conditional on faith in Christ" (Boring 1986, 290; cf. Rom. 10:9) and thus limited, but faith for Paul involves the trustful acknowledgment that salvation is (has and will be) *un*conditionally given by God to the ungodly; that is, it is God who effects and thus freely grants salvation (cf. Rom. 5:9–11, 15–17). Faith for Paul is not a work that can lay claim to salvation as a just reward. Faith is the gracious result of God's prior saving act (the death and resurrection of Jesus), not the condition for it.

It is perhaps no surprise that Paul's assertion of a universal salvation just as much as his theology of the cross has proven to be a great stumbling block for Christians and non-Christians alike.

What is the destiny of unbelieving Israel in Paul's eschatology?

This question is closely related to the preceding, for in Rom. 11:25–32, Paul places the thorny issue of Israel's unbelief (more precisely, the unbelief of a *part* of Israel, probably the majority in Paul's time) within the context of the universality of salvation: "For God has imprisoned *all* in disobedience so that he may be merciful to *all*" (Rom. 11:32; cf. Gal. 3:22). God's universal mercy, extended to the ungodly Gentiles, is now paradigmatic for God's dealing with unbelieving, that is, ungodly, Israel (see Martyn 1988, 8–11). God's mercy is greater and more powerful than human disobedience, including the disobedience of his own people (cf. 11:1). Thus, this disobedience is temporary and provisional; it is also part of the divine purpose:

> I want you to understand this mystery: a hardening has come upon part of Israel
> [see 9:18], *until* the full number of Gentiles has come in. And so all Israel will
> be saved [by God]; as it is written, "Out of Zion will come the Deliverer; he will
> banish ungodliness from Jacob. And this is my covenant with them, when I take
> away their sins" . . . they have now been disobedient in order that, by the mercy
> shown to you [Gentile Christians], they may now receive mercy.

The unbelief of a part of Israel, whereby they have become God's enemies
(11:28), does not nullify God's call and God's promises (9:4–5; 11:18, 28–29).
Exactly how God will accomplish the salvation of all Israel is left rather vague,
perhaps intentionally so. Does this salvation necessarily involve conversion, the
recognition of Jesus as Messiah and Lord? Is "the Deliverer" in 11:26 Christ or
God? Does "out of Zion" mean "out of heaven"? Does Paul have the *parousia* in
view or some other event? What does "the full number of Gentiles" mean?
What is the meaning of the verb "to come in"? It may be idle to speculate about
such matters given Paul's words about God's inscrutable ways in 11:33–34
(though cf. 10:9–13; 11:14–15, 23). What is interesting here is that Paul's
ambiguous scenario of events presupposes that the salvation of Gentiles precedes rather than follows the salvation of God's own people (the unbelieving
part thereof), which is in effect a modification (tantamount to a reversal) of the
Jewish tradition of an eschatological conversion and pilgrimage of the Gentile
nations to Zion following upon God's deliverance of Israel (cf., e.g., Isa. 2:2–3;
25:6–9; 56:6–8). The key point, however, is that the salvation of all Israel
(which is brought about *by God* in his own way and time, and not by human
beings, not even by Christians) is part of the gospel itself and of its eschatological vision of cosmic redemption (see further Davies 1978).[11]

What about 2 Thessalonians?

2 Thessalonians is one of the disputed letters of Paul, one reason being its distinctive eschatology (see Menken 1994). This letter is very similar in structure
and wording to 1 Thessalonians, and a comparison of the eschatology of the
two letters is therefore instructive. The key passages are 1 Thess. 4:13–18
(with 1:9–10; 5:1–5) and 2 Thess. 2:1–12. Both passage speak explicitly
about the *parousia,* as we saw at the beginning of this article. But in other
respects the scenarios are strikingly different.

   1. In 1 Thessalonians, the *parousia* is understood to be *imminent,* but in
2 Thessalonians it is understood to be *delayed.* The readers are instructed not
to believe that "the day of the Lord is already here [i.e., imminent, around the

corner]" through some word or letter supposedly from Paul (a possible allusion to 1 Thessalonians, where that is precisely the assumption!).

2. In 1 Thessalonians, the *parousia* will come *suddenly,* without any warning, "like a thief in the night" (5:2); in 2 Thessalonians, however, the *parousia* will *not* come suddenly but will be preceded by a series of public events: "that day will not come unless the rebellion [Greek *apostasia,* 'apostasy'] comes first and the man of lawlessness is revealed, the son of destruction." The man of lawlessness "takes his seat in the Temple, declaring himself to be God." The passage continues: "And you know what is now restraining him, so that he may be revealed when his time comes. For the mystery of lawlessness is already at work, but only until the one who now restrains it is removed." It is extremely difficult to determine exactly what the author is here referring to (What is the rebellion? Who is the "man of lawlessness"? What and who does the "restraining"?), but that a series of discernible events is involved seems clear enough. The conception of the *parousia* here is really not compatible with that found in 1 Thessalonians (and indeed elsewhere in the undisputed letters of Paul).

3. In 1 Thessalonians, the tone is *warm* and the emphasis falls upon the *salvation* of (both dead and living) Christians and their eternal fellowship with the Lord. In 2 Thessalonians, however, the tone is *cold* and the emphasis falls upon the *eternal* destruction of unbelievers:

> For it is indeed just of God to repay with affliction those who afflict you . . . when the Lord Jesus is revealed from heaven with his mighty angels in flaming fire, inflicting vengeance on those who do not know God and on those who do not obey the gospel of our Lord Jesus. These will suffer the punishment of eternal destruction, separated from the presence of the Lord and from the glory of his might. (1:6–9; cf. 2:10)

These three features, taken together, set the eschatology of 2 Thessalonians apart from that of 1 Thessalonians, causing doubt about its genuineness as a letter of Paul (cf. 2:2, 15; 3:14, 17). Though the genuineness of 2 Thessalonians still has strong supporters, the theology of 2 Thessalonians is difficult, probably impossible, to reconcile with the theology of the undisputed letters in which God's love, mercy, and grace finally outweigh his justified wrath against human sinfulness (cf. Rom. 5:9; 1 Thess. 1:10; 5:9). Indeed, God's eschatological destructive action, his wrath, is finally directed not toward human beings at all, but toward the inimical spiritual forces (sin, death, flesh, Satan) that subjugate human beings and alienate them from God and life (1 Cor. 15:20–28; Rom. 5:12–21).

Does Paul contemplate a messianic interregnum
between the parousia *and the end?*

The question arises from 1 Cor. 15:20–28, which refers to Christ's reign or
rule:

> Christ has been raised from the dead, the first fruits of those who have died. . . .
> But each in his own order: [1] Christ the first fruits, [2] then at his *parousia*
> those who belong to Christ; [3] then is the End, when he hands over the king-
> dom to God the Father, after he has destroyed every ruler and every authority
> and power. For he must reign [rule as king] until he has put all his enemies
> under his feet. The last enemy to be destroyed is Death . . . so that God may be
> all in all.

Does this passage, then, envisage an extended period of time between the
parousia (2) and the end (3)? And is this the time of Christ's reign, a reign that
shall conclude with the destruction of the inimical powers, the last of these
being Death? Some interpreters, most notably Schweitzer (1931), have drawn
this conclusion, finding support in the thousand-year reign of Christ after his
parousia in Rev. 20:4–6 (which has as its background the idea of a messianic
interregnum in Jewish expectations, e.g., 4 Ezra 7:26–31 [four hundred
years]; *2 Bar.* 29:1–30:5: 40:3 [no specified duration]). This interpretation
then assumes the following scenario:

1. The resurrection of Christ
2. Then the *parousia* and the resurrection of Christians ("those who
   belong to Christ")

   Christ's reign (the messianic kingdom)

3. Then the end, when he hands over the kingdom to God the Father,
   after he has destroyed every ruler and every authority and power,
   Death being the last. The general resurrection of the dead occurs and
   God becomes "all in all" (15:28).

This interpretation of 1 Cor. 15:20–28 actually has little to commend it
(see Davies 1967, 285–98). There is no real indication that there is a significant lapse of time between the *parousia* and the end, or that this interval was
of any importance to Paul here. The "end" more probably immediately follows the *parousia* itself,[12] and signifies what the *parousia* will bring about.
Christ's reign, during which he takes on and destroys the powers, thus takes
place between his own resurrection and the *parousia* (cf. Col. 1:12–13). The
following scenario results:

1. Christ's resurrection from the dead
       Christ's reign (the messianic kingdom)
2. Then the *parousia:* the resurrection of Christians;
3. Then the end, when he hands over the kingdom to God the Father, after he has destroyed every ruler and every authority and power, Death being the last. The general resurrection of the dead occurs and God becomes "all in all."

Christ's reign actually extends from his resurrection to the end, and the end is signaled by the *parousia.* Christians now live in the midst of Christ's reign, where he carries on spiritual warfare with the powers of this evil age, as we have seen previously.

Paul's scenario of a messianic interregnum finds its most important background in the *War Scroll* (1QM), where the Messiah (here called "the Prince of all the Congregation," 5:1) is a warrior king who destroys the enemies of Israel ("the Kittim," Romans) in an eschatological war lasting forty years (2:5f.). The earthly war reflects and corresponds to a cosmological battle between the spiritual forces of Belial and the angels of God. In short, the messianic era of forty years is a time of war (not peace, as in 4 Ezra or Revelation) and marks the transition (as in *2 Baruch*) from the old age to the new, when God will reign supreme and unopposed. For Paul, however, the enemies of the Messiah (Jesus) and of Christians are not other human beings but solely the malevolent spiritual powers who enslave them (see de Boer 1988, 132–36). In 1 Corinthians 15, death itself is the supreme and "last" enemy (cf. Isa. 25:8), the partner and outcome of sin (1 Cor. 15:56; Rom. 5:12–21); when Christ has destroyed death, his mission will have been accomplished and all human beings will have been saved from death's hegemony.

CONCLUSION

It was a key insight of Schweitzer that Paul's eschatology was not, as so often thought, "a kind of annexe to the main edifice of Pauline doctrine" (Schweitzer 1911, 53). As Davies has summarized the point:

> Schweitzer has criticized . . . those writers who in their treatment of Pauline theology have assigned their discussion of Paul's eschatology to the last section of their work, as if eschatology were an aspect of the Apostle's thought which could be neatly isolated and treated as a kind of addendum, whereas in fact it is his eschatology that conditions Paul's theology throughout. (Davies 1967, 285)

Schweitzer's insight has force to the extent that Paul's apocalyptic eschatology is not reduced to his understanding of the *parousia* and the end but also encompasses his understanding of Christ's advent, death, and resurrection. A full account of Paul's apocalyptic eschatology would thus have to be a full account of Paul's theology, an exercise clearly beyond the scope of this chapter.

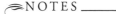NOTES _____

1. Translations follow NRSV, with occasional changes.

2. There is no verb in the Greek.

3. The sense here is kingly rule, not realm.

4. Scholars such as A. Schweitzer, E. Käsemann, and J. C. Beker, who have made significant contributions to an understanding of Paul as an apocalyptic-eschatological thinker, have also tended to identify the expectation of an imminent *parousia* as the central or defining element of Paul's apocalyptic eschatology (Schweitzer 1931, 52; Käsemann 1969b, 109 n. 1; Beker 1980, 18).

5. These events signal and effect the end of the world as previously known and experienced by human beings (i.e., the world characterized by sin, evil, death, and forces of lawlessness and rebellion, as in the scenarios of the *parousia* quoted above), as well as the transition to a new world marked by righteousness, peace, and life.

6. Schweitzer ran the same risk when he introduced the term "mysticism" in connection with Paul's eschatology and highlighted it in the title his seminal book *The Mysticism of Paul the Apostle* (1931). According to Schweitzer, however, Paul's mysticism was an "eschatological mysticism" whereby the individual believer participates in and benefits from God's *cosmic* act of eschatological salvation as effected in and through Christ (1931, 3). This distinctive eschatological mysticism was thus also a "Christ mysticism" (not a God mysticism), since the believer is "in Christ" or "in the Spirit," while Christ or the Spirit "lives" or "dwells" in the believer (Gal. 2:19–20; Rom. 8:9–11; cf. Gal. 3:26–28; 4:6; 5:24–25; 6:14; 2 Cor. 5:17; Rom. 6:10–11; 7:4; 8:1–2; 12:4–5; Phil. 3:1–11). Paul's "mysticism" does not, then, blur the boundaries between earth and heaven, or between the human and the divine, but between the present (existence in the flesh) and the future (the kingdom of God, now already effective in the activity of the Spirit). Furthermore, this mysticism encompasses all aspects of Christian existence (especially love, the primary fruit of the Spirit), not just (or even primarily) "out-of-body" experiences of the sort recounted in 2 Corinthians 12.

7. Collins also points out that in fact an apocalypse is "a generic framework" (1984, 3) within which passages of different literary genres can find a home.

8. The term "apocalypse" only clearly becomes a self-conscious genre designation in the course of the second century C.E. (Collins 1984, 3).

9. There is no verb in the Greek.

10. Various details of Paul's apocalyptic eschatology could well have been com-

monplace, even in the non-Jewish world. For example, Paul's claim that the creation is "in decay" (Rom. 8:21) may reflect the "widespread common acceptance of the idea of the world's senescence" (Downing 1995, 206), which also found a place in Jewish apocalyptic texts (4 Ezra 5:51; *2 Bar.* 85:10). This idea, "Epicurean in origin," was "in Paul's day widespread" (ibid.).

11. 1 Thess. 2:14–16, a disputed passage that some scholars do not believe to have been written by Paul, cannot speak against this view. Here certain Jews are charged with killing Jesus and the prophets, persecuting Paul, displeasing God, and hindering Paul from speaking to the Gentiles. "Thus," he concludes, "they have constantly been filling up the measure of their sins; but God's wrath has overtaken them at last" (NRSV). An alternate translation of the last phrase (*eis telos*) is "completely" or "forever" (so NRSV footnote), but this would be incompatible with Romans 11. If the passage stems from Paul he has moderated his views by the end of his apostolic career.

12. Again, there is no verb in the Greek. NRSV supplies "comes," which implies an event subsequent to the *parousia*.

BIBLIOGRAPHY

Bauckham, R. 1994. *The Theology of the Book of Revelation.* Cambridge: Cambridge University Press.

Beker, J. C. 1980 [1984]. *Paul the Apostle: The Triumph of God in Life and Thought.* Philadelphia: Fortress Press. A major study of Paul's theology which argues that apocalyptic, defined as the imminent cosmic triumph of God, is the unifying center of Paul's thought as a whole.

Boring, M. E. 1986. "The Language of Universal Salvation in Paul." *Journal of Biblical Literature* 105:269–92.

Bultmann, Rudolf. 1951. *Theology of the New Testament.* Volume 1. New York: Charles Scribner's Sons.

———. 1956 [1949]. *Primitive Christianity in its Contemporary Setting.* New York: Meridian.

———. 1975. *The Presence of Eternity: History and Eschatology.* Westport, Conn.: Greenwood.

———. 1984 [1941]. "New Testament and Mythology." In *New Testament & Mythology and Other Basic Writings,* edited by S. Ogden, 1–43. Philadelphia: Fortress Press. Bultmann's classic essay explores the problem of making sense of Paul's apocalyptic ideas in the modern world from an existentialist perspective.

Charlesworth, J. H. 1983. *The Old Testament Pseudepigrapha.* Vol. 1, *Apocalyptic Literature and Testaments.* Garden City, N.Y.: Doubleday.

Collins, John J. 1984. *The Apocalyptic Imagination: An Introduction to the Jewish Matrix of Christianity.* New York: Crossroad.

————. 1992. "Apocalypses and Apocalypticism (Early Jewish Apocalypticism)." In *Anchor Bible Dictionary*, edited by David Noel Freedman, 1:282–88. New York: Doubleday.

Davies, W. D. 1967 [1948]. *Paul and Rabbinic Judaism: Some Rabbinic Elements in Pauline Theology.* New York: Harper Torchbooks.

————. 1978. "Paul and Israel." *New Testament Studies* 24:4–39.

de Boer, M. C. 1988. *The Defeat of Death: Apocalyptic Eschatology in 1 Corinthians 15 and Romans 5.* Journal for the Study of the New Testament Supplement 22. Sheffield: JSOT Press. A detailed examination of two key passages in Paul's letters and an exploration of how Paul has adapted the two-ages dualism of Jewish apocalyptic eschatology especially in connection with his understanding of death.

————. 1989. "Paul and Jewish Apocalyptic Eschatology." In *Apocalyptic and the New Testament: Essays in Honor of J. Louis Martyn,* edited by Joel Marcus and Marion L. Soards, 169–90. Journal for the Study of the New Testament Supplement 24. Sheffield: JSOT Press. Argues that ancient Jewish apocalyptic eschatology exhibits two distinct patterns or "tracks" and that both provide important background for understanding Paul's own views.

Dodd, C. H. 1953 [1935]. "The Mind of Paul: II." In *New Testament Studies,* 108–28. Manchester: Manchester University Press. A classic exposition of the view that Paul's thought about the *parousia* and the resurrection of the dead developed and changed over time.

Downing, F. Gerald. 1995. "Common Strands in Pagan, Jewish and Christian Eschatologies in the First Century." *Theologische Zeitschrift* 51:196–211.

Hanson, Paul D. 1976. "Apocalypse, Genre" and "Apocalypticism." In *Interpreter's Dictionary of the Bible: Supplementary Volume,* 27–34. Nashville: Abingdon.

————. 1979. *Dawn of Apocalyptic: The Historical and Sociological Roots of Jewish Apocalyptic Eschatology.* 2nd ed. Philadelphia: Fortress Press.

————. 1992. "Apocalypses and Apocalypticism (Genre, Introductory Overview)." In *Anchor Bible Dictionary,* edited by David Noel Freedman, 1:279–82. New York: Doubleday.

Hengel, M. 1991. *The Pre-Christian Paul.* London: SCM; Philadelphia: Trinity Press International.

Käsemann, Ernst. 1969a [1961]. "'The Righteousness of God' in Paul." In *New Testament Questions of Today,* 168–82. Philadelphia: Fortress Press. A classic essay which argues that God's righteousness in Paul refers to God's eschatological saving action in Christ against the evil spiritual powers of this present evil age.

————. 1969b [1962]. "On the Subject of Primitive Christian Apocalyptic." In *New Testament Questions of Today,* 108–37. Philadelphia: Fortress Press. An important essay on early Christian apocalyptic, especially that of Paul.

Keck, Leander E. 1984. "Paul and Apocalyptic Theology." *Interpretation* 38:229–41. A plea for the idea that Paul's apocalyptic is not merely a matter of eschatology but of theology.

Lindemann, Andreas. 1994. "Paulus und die korinthische Eschatologie: Zur These von einer 'Entwicklung' im paulinischen Denken." *New Testament Studies* 37:373–99.

Martyn, J. Louis. 1967. "Epistemology at the Turn of the Ages: 2 Corinthians 5.16." In *Christian History and Interpretation: Studies Presented to John Knox,* edited by W. R. Farmer, C. F. D. Moule, R. R. Niebuhr, 269–87. Cambridge: Cambridge University Press. Also in *Theological Issues in the Letters of Paul,* 89–110. Edinburgh: T & T Clark, 1997. Introduced epistemological considerations into the discussion about Paul's apocalypticism.

———. 1985. "Apocalyptic Antinomies in the Letter to the Galatians." *New Testament Studies* 31:307–24. Also in *Theological Issues in the Letters of Paul,* 111–23. Edinburgh: T & T Clark, 1997. An argument for apocalypticism in Galatians.

———. 1988. "Paul and His Jewish-Christian Interpreters." *Union Seminary Quarterly Review* 42:1–15. Also in *Theological Issues in the Letters of Paul,* 37–45. Edinburgh: T & T Clark, 1997.

———. 1997. *Galatians: A New Translation with Introduction and Commentary.* Anchor Bible 33A. New York: Doubleday.

Matlock, R. Barry. 1996. *Unveiling the Apocalyptic Paul: Paul's Interpreters and the Rhetoric of Criticism.* Journal for the Study of the New Testament Supplement 127. Sheffield: Sheffield Academic Press. A searching appraisal of scholarship and the problems of talking about apocalyptic in Paul.

Menken, M. J. J. 1994. *2 Thessalonians.* New Testament Readings. London/New York: Routledge. An interpretation of 2 Thessalonians which pays particular attention to its eschatology.

Rowland, Christopher. 1982. *The Open Heaven: A Study of Apocalyptic in Judaism and Early Christianity.* New York: Crossroad.

———. 1990. "Apocalyptic." In *A Dictionary of Biblical Interpretation,* edited by R. J. Coggins and J. L. Houlden. London: SCM.

Rowley, H. H. 1963 [1944]. *The Relevance of Apocalyptic.* London: Athlone.

Russell, D. S. 1964. *The Method and the Message of Jewish Apocalyptic: 200 BC–AD 100.* Old Testament Library. Philadelphia: Westminster.

Sanders, E. P. 1977. *Paul and Palestinian Judaism.* Philadelphia: Fortress Press.

Schweitzer, Albert. 1912 [1911]. *Paul and His Interpreters: A Critical History.* London: Adam and Charles Black. A survey of scholarship on Paul, originally intended as the introductory chapter of the following work. Schweitzer faults his predecessors for not seeing the importance of eschatology for understanding Paul's thought as a whole.

———. 1931 [1930]. *The Mysticism of Paul the Apostle.* London: Adam & Charles Black. A classic exposition of Paul's thought as thoroughgoing eschatology.

Segal, Alan F. 1990. *Paul the Convert: The Apostolate and Apostasy of Saul the Pharisee.* New Haven, Conn.: Yale University Press.

Shires, H. M. 1966. *The Eschatology of Paul in Light of Modern Scholarship.* Philadelphia: Westminster. A readable discussion of various aspects of Paul's eschatology.

Sturm, R. E. 1989. "Defining the Word 'Apocalyptic': A Problem of Biblical Criticism." In *Apocalyptic and the New Testament: Essays in Honor of J. Louis Martyn*, edited by Joel Marcus and Marion L. Soards, 17–48. Journal for the Study of the New Testament Supplement 24. Sheffield: JSOT Press. A helpful survey of scholarship and of the problems of definition.

Vielhauer, Philipp. 1992 [German 1989]. "Introduction" to "Apocalypses and Related Subjects." In *New Testament Apocrypha: Vol. 2, Writings Related to the Apostles; Apocalypses and Related Subjects.* Cambridge: James Clarke; Louisville: Westminster/John Knox. First published 1964.

Whiteley, D. E. H. 1964. "Eschatology." In *The Theology of St. Paul,* 232–73. Oxford: Blackwell. A brief, technical discussion of numerous special problems in Paul's eschatology.

11

The Book of Revelation

Adela Yarbro Collins
University of Chicago

N**O OTHER SINGLE WORK HAS HAD AS GREAT AN INFLUENCE** on the apocalyptic tradition as the book of Revelation. Its opening word, "apocalypse" or "revelation," which serves as a kind of self-designation, has become the name of a kind of writing and the ideas and themes associated with it. Although its key images have precedents in Jewish literature and parallels in other early Christian writings, it is from the book of Revelation that the popular images of "Armageddon," the "tribulation," the "millennium," and the "New Jerusalem" come. The purpose of this essay is to place the book in its social-historical context and to consider its relationships with Jewish apocalypticism and the Jesus tradition.

⌒THE AUTHOR───────────────────────

The author of the book of Revelation refers to himself as "John" (Rev. 1:1, 4, 9; 22:8). Since the name was not uncommon among Jews and followers of Jesus at the time, we may not simply assume that this John is John the son of Zebedee, one of the Twelve, to whom the Gospel of John has also been attributed by Christian tradition. The author of Revelation never refers to himself as an apostle or a disciple of the Lord. Justin, surnamed Martyr, writing around 135 C.E., refers to the book and says that its author was John, one of the apostles of Christ (*Dialogue with Trypho* 81). Irenaeus refers to the author of Revelation as "John, the Lord's disciple" (*Against Heresies* 4.20.11; 5.35.2). The reliability of this tradition is called into question by a combination of two other factors. One is the likelihood that the book of Revelation was written in the mid-nineties C.E. (see below). The other is the tradition that John, the son of Zebedee, was killed for his allegiance to Christ, apparently before 70 C.E. (see Charles 1920, 1:xlv–xlix). The attribution of the book of Revelation to John, the son of Zebedee, therefore, occurred either by mistake or as a way of increasing the authority of the book.

Since ancient times, some have argued that the book of Revelation is pseudonymous, that is, that it was written by someone who wanted those who received the work to think that it had been written by John, the son of Zebedee. The Alogi, a group active in the second century who strongly opposed the New Prophecy (Montanists), argued that neither the Gospel of John nor the book of Revelation was composed by John. Rather, they were written by Cerinthus, a teacher criticized for various reasons, including his ideas about a future kingdom of God on earth. The reason for this strange accusation seems to be that the Gospel of John and the book of Revelation supported certain ideas of the New Prophecy (see Swete 1917, cxi–cxiv). In modern times, some scholars have argued that the book of Revelation was written pseudonymously, because pseudonymity is a typical feature of ancient Jewish apocalypses. This argument is not compelling because there was a revival of prophecy among the followers of Jesus, which led, for a short time at least, to the willingness to prophesy and to write books of prophecy in one's own name. The apocalyptic work from the second century called *The Shepherd of Hermas,* for example, was written by a Christian in Rome, Hermas, in his own name. Another reason that this argument is unpersuasive is that the author would probably have taken care to specify more clearly that he was an apostle or a disciple of the Lord, if he had intended to be so recognized.

The most reasonable conclusion about the authorship of Revelation is that it was written by a man named John who is otherwise unknown to us (see Yarbro Collins 1984, 25–53). Although John never claims to be a prophet, he describes his work as a "prophecy" (1:3; 22:7, 10, 18, 19). Further, he comes very close to designating himself as a prophet when he attributes the following words to the revealing angel in 22:9, "I am a fellow servant with you and your brethren the prophets" (RSV). Thus, the author presented himself indirectly as a prophet, that is, as one whose task it was to mediate an intelligible message to his fellow Christians, a message that he claimed derived ultimately from God (1:1). His intimate knowledge of Jewish scriptures and evidence that he knew Hebrew and Aramaic indicate that he was probably a Jew by birth and a native of Judea. The fact that he addressed several different communities suggests that he was an itinerant prophet. His presence in Asia Minor and his attitude toward Rome may be explained with the hypothesis that he was a refugee from the first Jewish war with Rome, which erupted in 66 and climaxed with the destruction of the Temple in Jerusalem in 70 C.E.

☞THE DATE

The earliest statement about the date of the book of Revelation is the remark of Irenaeus that the revelation was seen at the end of the reign of the Roman emperor Domitian (*Against Heresies* 5.30.3). There is no good reason to doubt this dating. Domitian ruled from 81 to 96 C.E. (see Yarbro Collins 1984, 54–83).

The most important internal evidence for the date consists of references to a city called "Babylon" and prophecies of its destruction (14:8; 16:19; 17:5; 18:2, 10, 21). It is unlikely that the author was referring to the city in Mesopotamia or the one in the delta of the Nile in Egypt, both of which bore that name. The name is not literal but symbolic, as the statement in Rev. 17:5 shows, "and on her forehead was written a name of mystery: 'Babylon the great, mother of harlots and of earth's abominations.'" The explanation of the "mystery" in 17:7–9 makes clear that the woman represents the city of Rome. She sits on a beast with seven heads; the heads represent seven hills on which the woman is seated. Writers of antiquity frequently referred to Rome as the city of seven hills. Furthermore, the woman is interpreted as "the great city which has dominion over the kings of the earth" (17:18). In the first century such a city could only be Rome.

It is likely that John took over this symbolic name from Jewish tradition current in his time. In ancient Jewish sources, "Egypt," "Kittim," "Edom," and "Babylon" are all used as symbolic or code names for Rome. "Kittim" is the most common name for Rome in the Dead Sea Scrolls, and "Edom" is the most common in rabbinic literature. Most of the occurrences of "Babylon" occur in apocalyptic works. In each occurrence, the reason for this choice of symbolic name is made clear in the context. It is the fact that Rome's forces, like those of Babylon at an earlier time, destroyed the city of Jerusalem and the Temple (4 Ezra = 2 Esdras 3:1–2, 28–31; *2 Baruch* 10:1–3; 11:1; 67:7; *Sibylline Oracles* 5.143, 159). The use of the name in Jewish tradition suggests that John used it not only to allude to the great power, wealth, arrogance and decadence of Rome but also and most especially to call to mind the events of

70 C.E. This interpretation implies that the book of Revelation was written after 70 C.E., but not necessarily immediately afterward. The two great Jewish apocalypses that react to those events, 4 Ezra and *2 Baruch,* were not written immediately after the destruction of Jerusalem, but around 100 C.E.

SUMMARY OF THE CONTENTS

The book of Revelation opens with a preface in the third person; that is, in it John does not speak but is spoken about (1:1–3). It is difficult to determine whether the preface was added later by someone else or whether John used the third person here as a literary device. In any case, the style and content of the preface are very similar to those of the rest of the work.

The preface refers to the work as an "apocalypse" or "revelation" that was given by God to Jesus Christ to show his servants what must soon take place (1:1). This emphasis on the imminence of significant events is repeated at the end of the preface, "for the time is near" (1:3). The revelation was mediated in a series of steps: from God to Jesus Christ to an angel to John to the servants of God (1:1–2). The work is also called "words of prophecy" and a blessing is pronounced on the one who reads it aloud (in a communal setting) and on those who keep or observe the things written in it (1:3).

Apart from the preface, the book has the framework of an ancient letter (1:4–22:21). In this part of the work, John speaks in the first person and also quotes other speakers. This part of the work begins with the typical opening elements of an ancient letter: the salutation, that is, the naming of the sender and the addressees (1:4a); the greeting, in this case the wish that God and Christ grant grace and peace to the addressees (1:4b–5); and a doxology (1:5b–6). The latter corresponds to the thanksgiving that typically occurs near the beginning of the letters of Paul. The work closes with a concluding blessing, typical of early Christian letters (22:21).

Attached to the epistolary prescript are two prophetic sayings (1:7, 8), which hint that this work is not a typical letter. Similarly, a series of prophetic sayings precedes the epistolary conclusion (22:6–20). These sayings enclose what may be called the body of the work, 1:9–22:5. This main part is a description of the revelation received by John and an account of how and from whom he received it. This report falls into two main parts: an account of an appearance of the risen Christ to John (1:9–3:22) and a description of visions and auditions of heavenly origin (4:1–22:5). The second part begins with a vision of the heavenly court (4:1–5:14), which introduces a series of symbolic visions (6:1–22:5).

THE STRUCTURE OF THE BOOK

It is clear that an organizing principle in the book of Revelation is the number seven: seven messages, seven seals, seven trumpets, and seven bowls are presented. The symbolic significance of this number is cosmic. According to late Pythagorean tradition and to the Jewish exegete and philosopher Philo, all reality is ordered and that order expresses itself in patterns of seven (see Yarbro Collins 1996, 90–99, 122–27). Jewish writers argued that the observance of the sabbath is thus in accordance with the cosmic order, but John does not make this point, at least not explicitly.

It is not so clear, however, how each of the series of seven relates to the others. They manifest parallels among themselves and some repetition. The similarities between the trumpets and the bowls are so close that the latter seem in large part to repeat the former. Some scholars think that the repetition results from the use of written sources. Others think that it is part of the author's literary design. Within the latter group, some think that the literary design involves a linear sequence of events, whereas others argue that the same events are described repeatedly from different points of view.

The theory that the book of Revelation describes the same events from different points of view was adopted by the author of the oldest surviving commentary on the work, written ca. 300 C.E. by Victorinus of Pettau. He stated that both the trumpets and the bowls predict the eschatological punishment of unbelievers (Haussleiter 1916, 84, line 14–p. 86, line 7). Victorinus's principle of recapitulation was taken up by Tyconius as an independent rule in his exegetical work *Three Books of Rules,* written around 382 C.E. (Steinhauser 1987, 32, 250). Tyconius then applied this rule in his influential commentary on the book of Revelation, written about 385 C.E. This commentary has unfortunately been lost, but it survives in fragments and something of its nature can be known by its influence on others. The approach to Revelation pioneered by Victorinus has been called the recapitulation theory.

The source-critical approach was first applied to the book of Revelation by Daniel Völter in 1882. An extreme source-critical analysis was proposed by Friedrich Spitta in 1889, who argued that the seals, trumpets, and bowls each reflect a source based on a sevenfold series (see Bousset 1906, 109, 113–14). In the twentieth century, the source-critical approach has been adopted by M. E. Boismard, J. Massyngberde Ford, and Ulrich B. Müller. Boismard used the repetitions in the book to distinguish two sources, one written under Nero and the other somewhat later (Boismard 1949). Müller used differences in messianic ideas to distinguish sources in Revelation from the minimal editorial work of the author (Müller 1972). Ford suggested that chaps. 4–11 constitute a source containing the prophecies of John the Baptist and that chaps. 12–22 represent another, later source, originating from among the disciples of John the Baptist (Ford 1975). It is now generally accepted that the author of the book of Revelation used sources, but not as many or as extensive ones as some source critics have argued. The argument for an extensive use of sources has been undercut by the demonstration of the unity of style in the work as a whole (Bousset 1906, 159–77; Charles 1920, 1:lxxxviii–lxxxix).

Charles argued that the literary design of Revelation describes a linear sequence of events. Most of the events are given in strict chronological order, but there are significant exceptions. Chapter 12 is a flashback intended to provide the background for chapter 13. Three "proleptic" or anticipatory visions interrupt the orderly unfolding of events in order to encourage the audience by flashing forward to some more distant point of the future; these are 7:9–17; 10:1–11:13; and chapter 14. The adequacy of this theory was called into question both by these significant exceptions and by the hypothesis that the text had been thrown into disarray by an incompetent disciple of the author after his death (Charles 1920, 1:xxii–xxiii, l–lv, lix).

The failure of the attempt to interpret the plan of the book as a linear sequence of events led to the revival of the recapitulation theory. Scholars had been reluctant to admit the validity of this approach, because it had been used by those who argued that Revelation prophesied history from the time of its composition to the time of the interpreter (see below). But Günther Bornkamm was able to show that this theory was compatible with a historical-critical approach to the book, that is, with an interpretation that understands the prophecies to refer to the past and present of the author and otherwise to the eschatological future. Bornkamm pointed out the close parallel structure between 8:2–14:20 and 15:1–19:21. He suggested that the former passage describes the same series of events as the latter, but in a mysterious, fragmentary, and proleptic manner (Bornkamm 1937). Another way of retrieving the recapitulation theory is the argument that the book of Revelation is composed of two great cycles of visions, 1:9–11:19 and 12:1–22:5. Each of these cycles is made up of three series of seven: (1) seven messages, seven seals, and seven trumpets; (2) seven unnumbered visions, seven bowls, and another series of seven unnumbered visions. Beginning with the seven seals, each series expresses the message of the whole book in its own particular way. The constant elements of the message are (a) persecution, (b) punishment of the persecutors, and (c) salvation of the persecuted. These themes are introduced in the first cycle in a way that seems deliberately veiled and fragmentary. The second cycle maintains the symbolic and mythic language of the first, but presents the message of the book in a fuller and more coherent manner. In particular, the second cycle is more explicit about the historical contexts of the visions. The first cycle makes clear that persecution is of major importance, but it is only in the second cycle that the identity of the persecutors is made explicit, namely, the Roman authorities (see Yarbro Collins 1976, 32–44).

Structural, thematic, and text-linguistic approaches have also been offered. Elisabeth Schüssler Fiorenza discerned a pattern of inclusion or symmetry in the book of Revelation. The first (1:1–8) and the last (22:10–21) units are related to one another as promise and fulfillment. The second (1:9–3:22) and sixth (19:11–22:9) units correspond because they each have an "inaugural" vision of Christ (1:12–20 and 19:11–16). The third (4:1–9:21) and fifth (15:1, 5–19:10) units are related to each other because both evolve out of the scroll with the seven seals. The fourth unit is then the center and climax of the book (Schüssler Fiorenza 1985, 170–75). Charles Homer Giblin, building on the work of Ugo Vanni, argued that the themes of divine judgment and divine disclosure are articulated and correlated in chaps. 16–22. The narrative of the seventh bowl, wrath against "Babylon" (16:17–21), describes the negative aspect of divine judgment. The narrative of the elimination of all eschatological adversaries (19:11–21:8) is the fulfilled aspect of divine judgment that entails a new creation. The disclosure of the significance of "Babylon" (17:1–19:10) is correlated with the disclosure of the New Jerusalem (21:9–22:6) (Giblin 1974). In his text-linguistic study of Revelation, David Hellholm concluded that the level of communication most profoundly embedded in the work is the speech of God in 21:5–8. This speech also occurs on the highest grade of the hierarchy of text sequences. This hierarchic embedment of divine speech enhances the authority of the message (Hellholm 1986, 45).

SOCIAL SETTING AND PURPOSE

The messages to the seven congregations in the seven cities reveal conflict among the followers of Jesus in this region and rivalry among their leaders. Each message is addressed to "the angel" of the congregation in that particular city. Since angels were equivalent to stars in Jewish tradition and the angels of the congregations are identified with stars in 1:20, it is clear that John refers to angelic beings in 2:1 and in the other messages, not to human messengers. This motif is a democratization of the Israelite and Jewish idea that each people or nation has an angel ruling over it, as representative and patron. At the same time, however, the address to the angel is a literary device through which the author can address each community as a whole, speaking in the name of Christ. It may be that the author employed this device in order to circumvent the institutional leaders of these communities (bishops, elders etc.) and to relativize their authority. The charismatic authority of the prophet may bypass the institutional authority of the local leaders.

The Christians in Ephesus are commended because they "cannot bear evil men but have tested those who call themselves apostles but are not, and found them to be false" (2:2). They are also praised for hating the works of the Nicolaitans, which Christ also hates (2:6). In the message to the followers of Jesus in Pergamum, the teaching of the Nicolaitans is equated with that of Balaam (2:14–15). According to Numbers 22–24, Balaam was a foreign priest and a diviner or seer, whom Balak, the king of Moab, paid to curse Israel. Moved by the power of the Lord, however, Balaam blessed Israel instead. But the book of Revelation seems to allude not to these mostly positive accounts but to Num. 31:16, which says that Balaam counseled the women of Midian to cause the people of Israel to act treacherously against the Lord in the matter of Peor. This text in turn alludes to the story in Num. 25:1–18, according to which some of the men of Israel married women of Moab and Midian, who then persuaded them to worship their god, Baal of Peor. The teaching attributed to Balaam which some in Pergamum are accused of holding involves eating food sacrificed to idols and practicing immorality (Rev. 2:14). It is not entirely clear whether either or both of these activities are meant literally or metaphorically. The eating of food, probably meat, sacrificed to idols is an issue addressed by Paul in 1 Corinthians 8–10. It could very well be meant literally here. Practicing (sexual) immorality could also be meant literally, but in some restricted sense regarding distinctions between permitted and forbidden types of marriage. If the terms are taken literally, the controversy here may be related to the so-called apostolic decree reported in Acts 15:29. Another possibility is that both terms are meant to symbolize laxness in monotheistic devotion to the one true god. "Harlotry" is a term used frequently in the prophetic books of the Jewish scriptures for honor paid to other gods. In either case, the point at issue seems to be how to live as a servant of God and a follower of Jesus in a pluralistic society. In antiquity there was no concept of a secular state; religious, social, economic, and political aspects of life were closely intertwined. John evidently disagreed with some traveling and local teachers in Ephesus and Pergamum on this question.

The issue is even more explosive in the message to Thyatira. The Christians in that place are criticized for tolerating the woman "Jezebel" (2:20). As "Babylon" is a symbolic name for the city of Rome, so "Jezebel" is a code name for a female prophet active in Thyatira. According to 1 Kgs. 16:31–33,

Jezebel was the daughter of the king of Sidon and a worshiper of Baal. Ahab, the king of Israel, married her, presumably to form an alliance with Sidon. Ahab then built a temple for Baal in Samaria. A struggle then followed between the devotees of Baal and those of Yahweh. In the end, Jezebel was thrown from a window and her body was eaten by dogs (2 Kgs. 9:30–37). John's endowment of the otherwise anonymous prophet with the name "Jezebel" is already in itself a harsh condemnation of her teaching. Her teaching is described in the same way as that of Balaam: practicing immorality and eating food sacrificed to idols (2:20). The words attributed to Christ hint that her teaching also involved "the deep things of Satan" (2:24). This phrase could be understood to mean that her teaching was similar to Gnostic speculation or that she was involved in the practice of magic. It could, however, simply mean that she taught "mysteries," that is, apocalyptic or heavenly secrets, perhaps through the interpretation of texts, about Satan and the evil angels associated with him. Such teaching is intelligible entirely within the context of Jewish and Christian apocalypticism. But we do not have sufficient information to be sure about what this teaching was.

The messages also reflect a social setting in which followers of Jesus are in conflict with their Jewish neighbors. Although the movement that originated with the historical Jesus could still be defined as a type of Judaism in the nineties C.E., it is likely that considerable social differentiation had taken place. The use of the term *ekklēsia* ("congregation" or "church") in the book of Revelation (1:4, 20; 2:1 etc.) indicates that the followers of Jesus in each city had their own association, separate from the *synagōgē* ("synagogue"), the assembly of the local Jewish community. In the message to Smyrna, the speaker refers to "the slander of those who say that they are Jews and are not, but are a synagogue of Satan" (2:9). "Those who say that they are Jews and are not" could be Jewish or judaizing Christians condemned for some reason by John. For example, they could be Gentiles by birth who argue that those who would be saved in Christ must be circumcised and observe all or some commandments of the Torah. This line of interpretation seems unlikely, however, since John shows no interest in the theological principles dear to Paul, such as salvation by faith rather than works of the law. Furthermore, the rhetorical force of the saying implies that "Jews" is a positive designation. The implication is that the *ekklēsia,* the Christian congregation, is the synagogue of God, and that the local Jewish community, which does not recognize Jesus as the Messiah, is a synagogue of Satan. The polemic is analogous to that of the community of the Dead Sea Scrolls against other Jews who have not joined in their new covenant with the Lord. For example, the *Community Rule* states: "They shall separate from the congregation of the men of falsehood and shall unite, with respect to the Law and possessions, under the authority of the sons of Zadok, the Priests who keep the covenant, and of the multitude of the men of the Community who hold fast to the Covenant" (1QS 5:1–3; trans. Vermes). The men of falsehood are equivalent to the men of the lot of Satan (Belial) (cf. 1QS 4:9–14 and especially 1:4–10). In the *Thanksgiving Hymns,* the (probably Jewish) opponents of the Qumran community are designated "a council of deceit and a congregation of Belial" (1QH 2:22 Vermes = 10:22 García Martínez; my translation).

Immediately following the reference to "the synagogue of Satan" is encouragement in the face of expected persecution. John uses the word "tribulation" to speak of the sporadic persecutions that have already happened and continue to occur (1:9; 2:9) and for the persecutions that he expects to happen in the future (2:10; 7:14). He uses the term once for the punishment that may fall upon a false prophet (2:22). In the message to Smyrna, the speaker says, "Do not fear what you are about to suffer. Behold, the devil is about to throw some of you into prison, that you may be tested, and for ten days you will have tribulation. Be faithful unto death and I will give you the crown of life" (2:10). These words imply expectation of official arrest and imprisonment, presumably to await trial. Now at this time, the Roman officials did not seek out Christians to arrest and interrogate them. They took action only when a citizen or resident with civil rights brought an official accusation or charge against Christians, in accordance with the normal legal process. The juxtaposition of the two remarks suggests that in Smyrna, conflict between Christians and Jews had led, or was about to lead, to the formal accusation of Christians by Jews before the Roman authorities. The charge could have been disturbing the peace or introducing a new (unlawful or subversive) cult. The message to the congregation in Philadelphia also mentions a "synagogue of Satan" and "those who say that they are Jews and are not, but lie" (3:9). The promise that those who claim to be Jews will come and bow down before the feet of the congregation and know that Christ has loved them expresses the hope for a reversal of the present situation in which the Christian congregation has little or no status and power.

The need to endure and the need to avoid denying the name of Christ are prominent themes in the messages. These themes reflect a social situation in which it is difficult to maintain the identity of the group in light of the dominant symbolic system and lifestyle and in which there is active opposition to the Christian communities. The messages reveal tensions between Christians and non-Christian Jews. It is likely that there were tensions between Christians and non-Christian Gentiles as well. As already noted in the discussion of the date of the work, the book of Revelation manifests great antipathy to

Rome because of the destruction of Jerusalem and the Temple. Another point of potential conflict was the imperial cult. This issue begins to emerge in chap. 12.

The revelatory report in chap. 12 consists of a vision with three scenes (vv. 1–6, 7–9, and 13–17) and an audition (vv. 10–12) that interprets the second scene of the vision. The first and third scenes constitute a birth narrative in which a suprahuman female figure gives birth to a son with a heroic or divine destiny. Mother and son are threatened by a great monster, but the mother receives divine aid and the child is saved. This narrative has similarities with several ancient texts, but it is most like stories about Leto giving birth to Apollo, in spite of the pursuit of Python, a monster who rightly fears that Apollo will take his place as ruler of Delphi and its oracle. During the period of the Roman Empire, Roman rule was likened to the golden age of Apollo, and various emperors were identified as Apollo manifest or incarnate. John co-opts this imperial propaganda to claim that the true golden age will come with the messianic reign of Christ (see Yarbro Collins 1976, 57–155).

The vision of the beast rising out of the sea (13:1–10) is a rewriting and adaptation of the vision of the four beasts rising out of the sea in Daniel 7. At the end of the previous vision, the dragon or serpent that threatened the woman is shown standing on the sand of the sea (12:17). The dragon thus watches as the beast arises from the sea in 13:1. The implication is that the beast is the agent of the dragon. This impression is confirmed by the statement in 13:2b, "And to it the dragon gave his power and his throne and great authority," and by 13:4, "Men worshiped the dragon, for he had given his authority to the beast, and they worshiped the beast, saying 'Who is like the beast, and who can fight against it?'" Since the dragon is identified with Satan (12:9), the beast is presented as an ally or agent of Satan. In the original context of Daniel, the four beasts represented the Babylonian empire, the Medes, the Persians, and the Greeks. Josephus provides evidence that the fourth beast was understood to be Rome in the first century C.E. That the beast of Rev. 13:1–10 represents Rome is clear from the statement in 13:7b, "And authority was given it over every tribe and people and tongue and nation." Rather than describe four beasts, each more terrible than the last, John has combined the attributes of all four to create one overwhelmingly monstrous creature. The result is a reduction of attention to history and a focus on the terrors of the recent past and the present.

The vision of the beast from the sea makes clear what the dominant concerns of John are. Like the beasts of Daniel 7, this beast, that is, Rome, is portrayed as rebelling against God, as an adversary of God. This theme is evoked by the very images of the sea and the sea monster (cf. Ps. 74:12–17; 89:10; Job

26:12–13; Isa. 27:1; 51:9). It is made explicit by the motif of the blasphemous name upon its heads and the mouth uttering haughty and blasphemous words (Rev. 13:1, 5). This theme reaches its climax in the statement that "it opened its mouth to utter blasphemies against God, blaspheming his name and his dwelling, that is, those who dwell in heaven" (13:6). So far, the language of conflict is symbolic or mythic. In 13:7a it becomes clear that this mythic conflict has a historical dimension: "Also it was allowed to make war on the saints and to conquer them." This statement may be understood in two ways. It reflects the incidents of persecution that have already occurred (cf. 2:13) and those that John expects to occur in the future (13:9–10; cf. 1:10). It also probably reflects the first Jewish war with Rome, which began during the reign of Nero. The Roman forces were at first under the command of the military leader Vespasian, until he was proclaimed emperor. His son, Titus, then took over the command. It was he who led the siege of the Temple mount and under whose command the Temple was burned and the city leveled. Later, he succeeded his father as emperor. Thus, the Romans made war on the saints (that is, the people of God; in Daniel, the "saints" or "holy ones" are angels and the people are "the people of the saints of the Most High"; cf. Dan. 7:27) and conquered them.

The blasphemous name and haughty and blasphemous words evoke not only rebellion and war but also the imperial cult. Worship of the living emperor was not a typically Roman phenomenon, but it was popular in the East. In the cultures of Mesopotamia and Egypt, it was traditional to view the king or pharaoh as a deity manifest or incarnate. The Greeks had a tradition of honoring the special dead with hero cults and of honoring living benefactors with religious rituals. When Alexander the Great conquered the Near East, he accepted and apparently even encouraged the peoples he ruled to give him divine honors. His successors did the same. Various ruler cults appeared among the Greeks during the Hellenistic period. When Roman hegemony was established in the eastern Mediterranean area, various cities established cults in which divine honors were given to Roma and Augustus and then to various other emperors, often while they were still alive. It is clear that these cults had important social and political functions. They expressed gratitude to Rome for creating social and political stability, and were part of a system of benefaction and patronage. The philosophical and religious dimensions of the phenomenon are debated. S. R. F. Price has argued that the imperial cult in the Hellenistic cities resulted from the attempt by Greek subjects of the Roman Empire to relate their ruler to their own dominant symbolic system (1984, 241).

The imperial cult was a ubiquitous and impressive phenomenon in the regions in which the seven cities of the book of Revelation were located. No resident could overlook it. There were eighty imperial temples in sixty cities in Asia Minor (Price 1984, 134). The cult was celebrated not only in temples but also in the major civic centers, the meeting place of the council, the theater, the stadium, and the gymnasium (ibid., 109). The emperor was regularly associated with the gods and sometimes presented as a god himself. For example, gold was normally used only in statues of the gods, but it was also often used in those of the emperors. Images of the emperor were often carried in processions (ibid., 186–89). Finally, many of the coins in use carried the portrait of the emperor, often depicted as Zeus, Apollo, or Hercules.

John's awareness of the imperial cult is evident in the remark, "and they worshiped the beast, saying, 'Who is like the beast, and who can fight against it?'" (13:4b). His disapproval of it is displayed in the statement that "all who dwell on earth will worship it, every one whose name has not been written before the foundation of the world in the book of life of the Lamb that was slain" (13:8). In the account of the last judgment, it is said, "and if anyone's name was not found written in the book of life, he was thrown into the lake of fire" (20:15). This lake of fire is the second death (20:14b). The remark in 13:8, then, is a heavy condemnation of those who worship the beast and a strong threat addressed to those who may be contemplating doing so. The threat in 14:9–11 is even more direct and terrifying.

By associating the emperor with the beast and the beast with Satan, John argued that honoring the emperor was betrayal of God. This position was not taken by all Christians. Paul instructed the Christians in Rome to be subject to the ruling authorities. He implied that the emperor is God's servant and minister and that he was worthy of respect and honor (Rom. 13:1–7). The author of 1 Peter similarly advised his audience to be subject to the emperor and to honor him (1 Pet. 2:13–17). Until the outbreak of the war with Rome, the Jewish people offered a daily sacrifice in the Temple in Jerusalem in behalf of the emperor. So early Christians may have debated with one another whether to honor the emperor and, if so, how to do so. Some, like John, chose to condemn, rather than honor the emperor. Others may have advocated praying for the emperor, as a kind of spiritual sacrifice. Yet others may have seen nothing wrong in pouring a libation to the emperor or in burning incense before his image. For John, however, doing so was idolatry, the worst offense imaginable.

Following the vision of the beast from the sea is a vision of a beast that arises out of the earth. On the mythic level, these two beasts recall Leviathan and Behemoth, primordial creatures that must be conquered by divine power (cf. Job 40:15–41:34). On the historical level, the beast from the sea represents the Roman Empire and its heads Roman emperors. The beast from the land is described as follows: "It exercises all the authority of the first beast in its presence and makes the earth and its inhabitants worship the first beast, whose mortal wound was healed" (13:12). Earlier it was said that one of the heads of the beast "seemed to have a mortal wound, but its mortal wound was healed, and the whole world followed the beast with wonder" (13:3). By adapting legends about Nero, John has created a picture of an Antichrist figure, even though he does not use the term (see Yarbro Collins 1976, 176–90). Both Jesus and the beast as Nero are kings who die and rise again. The vision of the beast from the land may refer to the future from John's point of view, but it reflects his present, a situation in which the local elite, wealthy, powerful families in Asia Minor, occupy positions of power with the blessing of Rome for mutual advantage. In order to maintain good relations with Rome and enhance their own prestige, local leaders in various cities of Asia Minor tried to outdo one another in building temples, statues, and other monuments honoring the emperor.

John says that the second beast had the power to cause those who refused to worship the first beast to be slain (13:15). This should not be taken to mean that the Roman governor or local leaders attempted systematically to force people to participate in the imperial cult. The pressure was cultural rather than legal. Since the imperial cult was a significant part of civic life in Asia Minor, it would have been difficult to resist joining in. The pressure to celebrate Christmas in American society today is formally analogous. The authorities did apply force, however, in one set of circumstances. They would not seek out Christians, but if anyone was accused of being a Christian, the governor would ask him or her to offer wine and incense before images of the gods and the emperor. If this act was refused, the individual would be executed (see Pliny *Letters* 10.96; Yarbro Collins 1984, 72–73).

John also says that "no one can buy or sell unless he has the mark, that is, the name of the beast or the number of its name" (13:17). As noted earlier, many of the coins in circulation in Asia Minor bore the image of the emperor with divine attributes and his name. This aspect of the vision expresses the offense caused by the virtual necessity of using such coins for strict monotheists and strict interpreters of the commandment against images (see Yarbro Collins 1996, 212–14). In the following verse, the allusion to "the number of its name" is explained as follows, "Here is wisdom: let him who has understanding calculate the number of the beast, for it is the number of a human being, and his number is six hundred sixty-six" (13:18). These remarks are based on the fact that Hebrew and Greek letters served sequentially as numerals. For example, the first letter of the alphabet is used as the numeral "one," the tenth as "ten," the eleventh as "twenty," and so forth. Thus, the letters of any name may be added up, and the sum may be used cryptically to refer to the name or the person bearing the name. The "wisdom" involved is not only the knowledge of what numerals the letters represent. To calculate the sum related to a name is easy; there is only one correct sum. But to determine what name is represented by a particular sum is difficult, since the same sum may represent the total of many different series of numerals. Two types of evidence support the theory that "Nero Caesar" is the name alluded to in Rev. 13:18. One is the fact that the references to the beast from the sea allude to the legend about Nero's death and return. The other is the fact that a number of manuscripts read "six hundred sixteen" rather than "six hundred sixty-six." Nero's name was sometimes spelled "Neron" and sometimes without the final *n*. If one uses Hebrew letters (another aspect of the "wisdom" needed to solve the riddle), the name "Neron Caesar" adds up to 666; without the final *n,* it adds up to 616.

John's thinking was dualistic in the sense that he perceived the situation in which he lived as characterized by a cosmic struggle between two diametrically opposed powers and their allies. God and Satan, along with their agents and spokespeople, were engaged in a struggle for the allegiance of the inhabitants of the earth. Jesus Christ, the primary agent of God, had been slain but would return to establish the rule of God on earth. At his return, he would be opposed by the primary agent of Satan. As the historical Jesus was transformed by his resurrection into a powerful, transhistorical figure, so Nero is presented as transformed by his descent into the underworld into an opposing, transhistorical figure. This symbolic or mythic construct expresses the insight, or makes the argument, that the primary conflict in John's time was the cultural tension between the views and lifestyles of a strictly monotheistic and exclusive type of Christianity, on the one hand, and the Roman imperial ideology on the other. A major purpose of the book of Revelation is to discourage its audience from accepting the ideology of the provincial elite, which involved a pyramid of power and patronage with the emperor at the pinnacle, and from participating in any form of the imperial cult, which was the religious aspect of that system. This purpose was accomplished by the imagery of the beast, which provided a highly negative redefinition of the imperial symbolic system, by threats, for example, the angelic proclamation of 14:9–11, and by promises, for example, the reward predicted for those who do not worship the beast (20:4).

The work's critical attitude toward Rome is also clearly expressed in the vision of the prostitute in chapter 17. As noted above, the depiction of the woman as sitting on a beast with seven heads and the explanation of the heads as seven hills show clearly that the woman is a symbolic representation of the city of Rome. The Hebrew prophets often personified cities. Isaiah exclaimed that the faithful city, Jerusalem, had become a prostitute, thereby condemning the corruption and injustice that occurred there (1:21). Ezekiel personified Jerusalem as a prostitute and associated this image with the worship of gods other than Yahweh (chapter 16). He also personified both Jerusalem and Samaria as prostitutes and defined their tributary alliances with other nations as prostitution (chapter 23). Given the lack of differentiation of politics and religion, such alliances would almost inevitably involve some recognition of the foreign religious symbolic system and thus of their deities. The prophet Nahum depicted Nineveh as a prostitute because of its deceitful and treacherous dealings with other cities (3:4). Isaiah described the commercial dealings of Tyre as prostitution (18:15–18). Analogously, and perhaps inspired by these texts, the author of the book of Revelation depicted the alliances and commercial activities of the city of Rome as prostitution (cf. 17:2 with 18:3 and 18:9–10 with 18:11, 15, 19, and 23). The association of prostitution with the worship of other gods is implied by the motifs of the blasphemous names and the abominations and impurities (17:3–4). The motif of injustice appears in the allusions to the persecution of the followers of Jesus in 17:6 and 18:24. Violence against non-Christians is also condemned in 18:24 and a critical attitude toward the slave trade is implied in 18:13.

Besides biblical precedent, the portrayal of the city of Rome as a prostitute may have another set of associations. Beginning with the second century B.C.E., cults of the goddess Roma appeared in cities of Asia Minor, the region to which the book of Revelation is addressed (Price 1984, 24, 40–43, 187–88, 250, 252, 254). Such a cult is attested for the city of Erythrae, which was situated on the mainland opposite the island of Chios, not far from Smyrna, one of the seven cities of the Apocalypse. Around the same time, the city of Chios voted to hold a procession, sacrifice, and games for Roma. When Octavian became emperor and the cities of Asia Minor wished to give him divine honors, he allowed himself to be worshiped only in conjunction with the goddess Roma. Temples dedicated to them are attested for the island of Samos and for the cities of Pergamum and Ephesus. If, as suggested above, the author of the Apocalypse was a native of Palestine, he may have seen the temple that Herod built in Caesarea Maritima in which stood a colossal cult statue of Augustus, modeled on the statute of Zeus at Olympia, and another of Roma, of the same size as that of Hera at Argos. The cult of Roma is a good example of the inseparability of the religious and the political in antiquity. She was a goddess and also a personification of the power of Rome. The cults of Roma probably arose in western areas under Greek cultural influence during the Roman republic, but soon spread to Greece and Asia Minor and continued into the imperial period, so that John was probably familiar with them. From this perspective, the portrayal of the city of Rome as a prostitute in Revelation 17 has a polemical edge. Instead of depicting her as a goddess like Hera (as she was presented in the temple at Caesarea mentioned above) or Athena (as she appeared on coins [Price 1984, 44]), John portrays her as an ostentatious, luxury-loving woman of loose morals, displaying her wealth in the finest clothing and jewelry and drinking to excess, even drinking blood. By painting such a picture, John expressed the outrage already felt by many Jews and Christians because of the destruction of Jerusalem; the portrait also had the effect of challenging any members of the audience who accepted the dominance of Rome and the symbolic and social system connected with it to reconsider their perceptions and their loyalties.

As we have seen, the book of Revelation reflects conflict among Christians, conflict between Christians and Jews, and conflict between Christians and the representatives of Rome. The work attempts to interpret these conflicts and to resolve them in accordance with its own perspective. These interpretations and proposed resolutions are intended to win or reinforce the commitment of members of the audience to that perspective, and they are reinforced by admonitions and threats. They are also reinforced by promises of future rewards and glory. Each of the seven messages in chapters 2–3 contains a promise to "the one who conquers." The Greek phrase could also be translated "the one who overcomes" or "the one who is victorious." The notion of Christian victory in the book of Revelation is complex and paradoxical. It is a metaphor that has its deepest root in the experience and language of victory in battle. According to Hesiod, the goddess of Victory was honored by Zeus for assisting the gods against the Titans (*Theog.* 383–403). The poets depicted her as ruling over athletic and all other competitions, as well as military contests. She appeared in Roman allegorical art as a symbol of victory over death. The paradox of the image is expressed most vividly in Revelation 5. The statement that "the lion of the tribe of Judah, the root of David, has conquered, so that he can open the scroll and its seven seals" (5:5) evokes for the audience with its messianic language the idea of a military victory. The vision that follows the statement, however, focuses on the slain Lamb. According to the announcement of the heavenly voice in chapter 12, "the brothers" have conquered the Accuser (Satan) by the blood of the Lamb and by the word of their own testimony, and they are acclaimed as those who "did not love their lives unto death" (12:10–11). These two passages imply that it is by dying that Christ and his followers become victorious over Satan and all their enemies. But later in the book, military imagery is used; for example, according to the vision of Rome as prostitute in chapter 17, "[the beast and the ten kings] will do battle with the Lamb, and the Lamb will conquer them, because he is Lord of Lords and King of Kings, and those with him are called and chosen and trustworthy" (17:14). The battle alluded to here is announced already in chapter 16. After the sixth bowl is poured out, the beast will assemble the kings of the earth for battle on the great day of God the Almighty. The scene of this great battle is to be a place called "Armageddon" in Hebrew (16:12–16). "Armageddon" is a reference to Megiddo, an ancient city on a plain in northern Israel that was the scene of several decisive battles in the history of Israel (Judg. 5:19; 2 Kgs. 9:27; 2 Chr. 35:22). Christ is also pictured as a victorious warrior in 19:11–21. The vivid depiction of the past metaphorical victory of Jesus and the future military victory of the risen Christ encourages the audience to stand firm in their loyalty to him. The main way in which they conquer the beast is to refuse to participate in the activities that involved giving the emperor divine honors, even if such resistance resulted in death (cf. 15:2 with 20:4 and 7:14).

In the message to Ephesus, those who are willing to make such a commitment, those "who conquer," are promised that they will eat of the tree of life that is in paradise or the garden of God (2:7). This is a clear example of the way in which visions of definitive salvation in the final age are similar to myths of origin. The one who conquers will be allowed to enter the garden from which Adam and Eve were driven and to eat from the tree of life, to which they were denied access (Gen. 3:22–24). The implication is clear: in the new age, death will be no more. The promise to Smyrna is similar: "The one who conquers will not be harmed by the second death" (2:11). Some in Smyrna may be killed (2:10), but this first death, the death of the earthly body, is of little consequence. A death faced in commitment and loyalty is like a triumph in a contest, and it will be rewarded by "the crown of life" (2:10). The victor in athletic and other contests received a crown of laurels, but those who suffer this noble death will be spared the second death, the death of the soul or eternal torment (cf. 20:14–15 with 14:10–11), and will enjoy eternal life. Such beliefs provided powerful motivation for resistance.

The promise to Pergamum involves the gift of manna and a new name (2:17). Like the promise of the tree of life, the promise of manna compares the future, definitive salvation to a former time. In this case it is the time of the wandering in the wilderness, when God nourished the people in an extraordinary, if not miraculous, way. The intimacy between God and the people enjoyed in the time of the exodus will be restored in the new age. The motif of the new name implies a new beginning; the former name, the lack of status, the suffering—all will be removed and a new, secret name of power will be granted.

The promise to Thyatira, that the one who conquers will rule the nations with a rod of iron, evokes the military aspect of victory once again (2:26–27). The victors will share in Christ's messianic rule and power (cf. 5:10; 22:5). Christ also promises to give the victor the morning star (2:28). In ancient Near Eastern and Greek myths, the morning star was a deity. According to the book of Revelation, Christ is the morning star (22:16). This promise seems to be a figurative way of promising that the victor will share in Christ's glory and divinity. The promise to Sardis, that the victor will be clothed in white garments (3:5), is similar. The white garments signify a glorious, exalted state like that of the angels and other immortals.

The promise to Philadelphia, that Christ will make the victor a pillar in the temple of God, is odd, because John explicitly states in the description of the New Jerusalem that he saw no temple there (21:22). Yet he also says that the temple of the city is the Lord God Almighty and the Lamb. This implies that, in effect, the whole city takes the place of the temple in which God or his name traditionally dwelled. The promise to Philadelphia, therefore, may be read as a figurative way of saying that the victor will participate in an important way in the life of the city, the focal point of the new age. This interpretation is supported by the association of the gates of the cities with the twelve tribes of Israel and the foundations with the apostles of the Lamb (21:12, 14).

The promise to Laodicea, like the one to Thyatira, indicates that the one who conquers will share in the victory of Christ. Not only will the victor have power over the nations (2:26–27); he will even share the throne of Christ, which is also the throne of God (3:21). Such language suggests the identification of the follower of Christ with Christ himself, a kind of mystical union that involves the deification of the one who conquers. At the very least, the image signifies that the victorious follower of Jesus enjoys a fulsome delegation of authority and will act as an agent of God and Christ in the new age. The image is similar to the dream of Moses narrated by Ezekiel the tragedian in the Greek drama *The Exodus* (Holladay 1989, 362–63). A figure, probably representing God, rises from a throne on Mount Sinai and commands Moses to sit on it.

A very important reward for those who resist the beast, especially those who lose their lives because of such resistance, is a share in the first resurrection. Those who have been beheaded for their testimony to Jesus and the word of God and who did not worship the beast are to come to life and to reign with Christ for a thousand years while Satan is bound. The rest of the dead are not to rise until after the thousand years are ended (20:4–6). This is the vision from which the apocalyptic theme of "the millennium" derives, "millennium" coming from the Latin word for a thousand.

The theme of the rewards of the victor is concluded with the words attributed to God in Rev. 21:7, "the one who conquers will inherit these things." "These things" include the new heaven and new earth (21:5) and the enjoyment of the intimate presence of God with God's peoples (21:6–7), symbolized by the water of life (cf. 22:1–2).

WOMEN AND FEMININE SYMBOLISM

Actual, historical women are invisible in the book of Revelation with two exceptions. The first is the message to Thyatira with its attack on "the woman Jezebel" (2:20). Some readers take the criticism of this early Christian female prophet at face value, perhaps because they accept the claim that these words were spoken by the risen Christ or acknowledge the authority of the author, whom they assume to be John the son of Zebedee, one of the twelve apostles, or simply because of the canonical authority of the book of Revelation itself. A more critical reading starts from the assumption that here the author is claiming the authority of the risen Christ for his own point of view in a struggle within the early Christian movement (see above). "Jezebel" is criticized for encouraging followers of Jesus to eat "food sacrificed to idols." Like some of the Christians in Corinth (see 1 Corinthians 8–10), this female prophet may have argued that it was permissible to eat such food because the gods worshiped by the Greek, Roman, and other residents of Asia did not exist. She may have called upon the criticism of idols in the book of Isaiah for support. She may have argued that, since there is one God, the Creator, all food is clean and may be eaten after giving thanks. In 1 Cor. 8:6, Paul agreed with this point of view in principle. If she communicated revelations concerning Satan and the spirits associated with him (Rev. 2:24), she may have argued that this revelation endowed her followers with power over these intermediary beings, who were identified with the Greek and Roman gods. Such power would allow her followers the freedom to eat dedicated food unharmed and without sin.

For "the strong" in Corinth and the followers of "Jezebel," the issue of dedicated food was not an abstract theological debate, but a practical matter. A tolerant position on this matter would allow Christians to mingle socially with non-Christian Gentiles. Such social contact would have been important for Christians who wanted to maintain contact with non-Christian relatives or who wished to join or maintain membership in one of the numerous local associations. Meals taken in common virtually always had a religious dimension. The associations normally had a patron god or goddess who was honored at meetings. The club's common meals often took place on the grounds of a temple. Christians may have wished to join local burial associations or associations of artisans who shared the same craft. Inscriptions provide evidence that there were many such trade associations in Thyatira (Hemer 1986, 108, 246 n. 10). John's teaching advocated a form of Christianity that would remove Christians from the social fabric of their surrounding communities.

Besides allowing the consumption of dedicated food, "Jezebel" is accused of advocating the practice of prostitution (2:20). In the text to which allusion is made (Num. 25:1–2), the "prostitution" of the Israelites was twofold: intermarriage with non-Israelites and idolatry. It is not clear whether the "prostitution" mentioned in Rev. 2:20 is purely metaphorical and thus refers to idolatry only, or whether some actual sexual practice was involved. In vv. 22–23, the sexual metaphor is extended. Those who accept "Jezebel's" teaching (or her partners in leadership) are described as those who commit adultery with her. The reference to her "children" is probably a way of describing her followers. This figurative language suggests that "prostitution" means idolatry only, although tolerance of mixed marriages may also have been a factor. In ancient Jewish tradition, such marriages were often associated with idolatry, because of the assumption that the non-Jewish spouse would lead the Jewish spouse away from Jewish tradition and into polytheistic practices.

It is unlikely that an early Christian leader advocated polytheism in a theological sense. What was at stake was the question whether the Christian faith and way of life were compatible with Greek and Roman cultures. This was a difficult issue, since no ancient culture even attempted to be religiously neutral. John implies that they are not compatible and that Christians must avoid Greek and Roman cultural institutions and practices. The position of "Jezebel" was, therefore, not as extreme as it appears when the text is taken at face value. Persons who took a position similar to hers were accepted as members of the Christian congregation in Corinth. Paul attempted to modify their views and especially their practices, but he did not vilify them as John does his rivals. John says that the female prophet "calls herself a prophet" (2:20), implying that she was not a genuine prophet. But evidently, she not only claimed to be a prophet but was recognized as such by a considerable number of Christians in the vicinity. If she had not been well received, at least in Thyatira, John would not have been so concerned about her influence. Prophecy was a gift often received by early Christian women. Paul acknowledged the activity of female prophets in 1 Cor. 11:2–16. According to the book of Acts, the female daughters of Philip prophesied in Caesarea Maritima, a city in the land of Israel and the Roman capital of the province of Judea. John's mention of "Jezebel" is evidence that a woman, whose actual name has not been preserved, exercised the gift of prophecy in Asia Minor toward the end of the first century. It is unlikely that she was the only woman to prophesy in her time and region. John's name-calling has obscured the fact that we have here an important indication of the leadership of women in the early church of this region.

The other text that bears on the lives of actual Christian women of this period is 14:1–5. This vision belongs to the second great cycle of visions that extends from 12:1 to 22:5. The 144,000 who are seen with the Lamb are making in this passage their second appearance in the book. They were introduced first in 7:1–8, where they are portrayed as an assembly consisting of 12,000 persons from each of the twelve tribes of Israel. Since John can dispute the Jewishness of members of the local synagogues, it is likely that he included Gentile Christians among the 144,000. The number clearly has symbolic significance as a multiple of twelve, but the use of a specific number (as opposed to the innumerable multitude of 7:9–17) suggests that a particular group within the whole body of the faithful is intended. In 14:4 it is said that they "follow the Lamb wherever he goes." According to chapter 5, the most distinctive characteristic of the Lamb is the fact that he was slain. The 144,000, therefore, seem to be those who are called to suffer death for the sake of their faith in Jesus. This hypothesis is supported by the citation of this passage in the *Letter of the Churches of Lyons and Vienne.* One of the martyrs, Vettius Epagathus is called "a true disciple of Christ, 'following the Lamb wherever he goes,'" because he laid down his life in defense of his fellow Christians (1.10). The description of the 144,000 is best understood as a rhetorical presentation of ideal discipleship. The description of the group includes the following statement, "These are the ones who have not defiled themselves with women, for they are virgins" (14:4). The language implies that any kind of heterosexual relation is defiling. The root idea, found both in Israelite and Jewish religion, on the one hand, and Greek and Roman religion, on the other, is that sexual relations make the parties unfit to enter the holy space of a sanctuary dedicated to a deity. But this was a temporary defilement, the removal of which was governed by certain regulations (see Lev. 15:18). But Rev. 14:4 goes beyond the idea of a temporary, removable defilement by speaking of the 144,000 as virgins. The passage thus expresses a point of view in which the defiling potential of sexual relations with women is to be avoided absolutely by avoiding such relations altogether. The question arises as to the occasion and rationale for this intensification of the quest for ritual purity and for the androcentric way in which the achievement of purity is expressed.

One possibility is that the occasion for the intensification of the value of purity was the adaptation of holy war tradition in the book of Revelation. The ancient Israelite notion of holy war involved the understanding that Yahweh and his angels fought alongside the men of Israel and were present in the military camp. Because of this heavenly presence, the camp had to be kept holy. Various regulations were developed to that end, among which were restrictions on sexual relations, which were forbidden for a time preceding the gathering of the military force and within the camp. The ancient holy war traditions had not been forgotten in John's time. The Maccabees had revived them in the second century B.C.E. (Yarbro Collins 1996, 199–200). The community of the Dead Sea Scrolls adapted the notion of holy war to articulate their understanding of the last days. Revelation also makes use of this tradition, especially in the account of the last battle in 19:11–21 (ibid., 205–7). The expectation that the faithful were to have an active role in the eschatological battle (Rev. 17:14) could be the occasion for the high value placed on sexual continence and for the androcentric point of view (warriors were normally men).

The ascetic tendencies in the Dead Sea Scrolls can also be understood as an intensification of the priestly purity regulations and their extension to the whole community. The notion of the priesthood of the whole Christian community is an important theme in the book of Revelation (1:6; 5:10; 20:6). As in the Dead Sea Scrolls, the notion that purity was necessary for holy war and the idea and practice of priestly purity may have reinforced one another in the milieu of the book of Revelation. The androcentric point of view would thus in part reflect the traditional Israelite-Jewish state of affairs in which only men were priests.

The priest had to be holy because of his special closeness to God. Similarly, around the turn of the era, in some contexts the prophet was seen as one especially close to God. Philo treated the priestly and the prophetic roles of Moses as virtually identical. Near the beginning of his treatment of the third aspect of the life of Moses, his priesthood, Philo states that Moses had to be clean in order to exercise his priesthood, which is the service of God. He had to purify himself from all the calls of mortal nature, food and drink and intercourse with women. Philo says that he disdained the latter almost from the time when, possessed by the spirit, he entered on his work as a prophet, since he had held it fitting to hold himself always in readiness to receive the oracular messages (*On the Life of Moses* 2.68–69). Philo's rationale for the sexual continence of Moses is clearly a metaphysical dualism in which material, earthly things are devalued in comparison with the heavenly. Nevertheless, one may ask whether the book of Revelation, as an apocalyptic work, did not link the prophet in a similar way to the heavenly world and thus to sexual continence.

Besides understanding themselves as priests and as potential holy warriors, the community of the Dead Sea Scrolls understood themselves to be living with and like the angels. This notion appears to be a characteristically apocalyptic one. The aim of apocalyptic revelation and piety is to share in the life of the heavenly world and to overcome the evils, dislocations, and limitations of finite, earthly life. This aim is often expressed by the expectation of human transformation into a heavenly or angelic existence (e.g., Dan. 12:3). In the present, special individuals may attain that angelic existence, at least temporarily (see the Book of the Watchers, i.e., *1 Enoch* 1–36, and the *Ascension of Isaiah*). The Book of the Watchers is especially interesting in relation to Rev. 14:1–5. This early apocalypse contains a narrative about the fallen angels that is similar to but much more elaborate than Gen. 6:1–4. It is said that some angels came down from heaven and took human wives for themselves. These angels taught the women heavenly secrets, including charms and spells, the arts of war, and so on. This illegitimate revelation (and the illegitimate children that they produced, the giants) was the cause of all the evils upon the earth (*1 Enoch* 6–9). The good angels comment that the fallen angels "lay with those women and became unclean" (9:8). Later in the text, the Lord, while decreeing the punishment of the wayward angels, remarks that they "have associated with the women to corrupt themselves with them in all their uncleanness" (10:11). Enoch, who had been "hidden" (cf. Gen. 5:24) and was dwelling with the angels, or Watchers, was sent to the fallen Watchers to inform them of the divine decree. They ask Enoch to intercede with the Lord in their behalf, so that they might be forgiven. Instead of forgiving the Watchers, the Lord instructs Enoch to go and say to them that they ought to petition in behalf of men and not men in behalf of them; they have left the high, holy, and eternal heaven and lain with the women and become unclean with the daughters of men; they were spiritual, holy, living an eternal life, but became unclean upon the women or through the blood of the women, begat children through the blood of the flesh, lusted after the blood of men, and produced flesh and blood as they do who die and are destroyed (15:2–4).

A clue for interpretation is the remark "You ought to petition in behalf of men, not men in behalf of you" (15:2). Enoch and some of the angels have exchanged places. The heavenly and spiritual existence of some angels has been transformed into an earthly existence, involving flesh and blood, procreation and death. Enoch's earthly and fleshly existence has been transformed into a heavenly and spiritual one. Sexual intercourse with women stands for earthly existence, as a part for the whole. The exchange by the angels of a spiritual existence for an earthly one is symbolized by their having sexual relations with women. Although it is not explicit in the narrative, the corollary is that a man's exchange of an earthly existence for a spiritual, heavenly one may be symbolized by abstaining from sexual relations with women. The underlying logic of Rev. 14:1–5 seems to be the same. The 144,000 exemplify the ideal of a Christian apocalyptic piety, in which the goal is a transformed human existence. Through a faithful death, Christians may participate in eternal, heavenly life (14:13; 12:10–11; 7:14–17). In the present, that existence may be anticipated by a life of sexual continence (14:4; cf. Luke 20:34–36).

Feminine symbols are prominent in the second half of the book of Revelation, which extends from 12:1 to 22:5. The three major feminine symbols are the woman clothed with the sun in chapter 12, the prostitute of chapter 17, and the bride of the Lamb in chapters 19 and 21. The roots and purpose of the image of the prostitute in chapter 17 were discussed above. A traditional interpretation of the woman clothed with the sun is that she is Mary, the mother of Jesus, since the child she brings forth is described as the Messiah. Other innerbiblical interpretations are that she is personified Israel, Jerusalem, or the people of God. Such personifications are common in the prophetic traditions of Israel. An approach based on the history of religions leads to the conclusion that the woman is presented as a high goddess with astral attributes: the sun is her garment, the moon her footstool, stars her crown. These attributes suggest that she is the queen of the universe who has power over the movements of the heavenly bodies and thus over human destiny. Only a few goddesses in Hellenistic and early Roman times were so depicted: the mother-goddess worshiped at Ephesus, who was identified with the Greek Artemis and the Roman Diana; the Syrian goddess Atargatis; and Isis, the Egyptian goddess who was worshiped in new forms all over the Mediterranean world in the Hellenistic and Roman periods. The plot of Revelation 12 involves an attack of a monster on a pregnant woman in order to destroy her and her child. As noted above, this narrative has similarities with several ancient texts, especially the pursuit of Isis by Seth-Typhon and of Leto by Python (Yarbro Collins 1993, 21–24). The author of Revelation has adopted motifs and stories about goddesses in order to create a glorious picture of the heavenly Israel. Her story serves as a model for the audience of the book. Like her, they have a heavenly identity: they are God's kingdom in the world, God's priests (1:6). But they are also vulnerable: some have been arrested, some killed; their legal status in the Roman Empire is precarious. The rescue of the woman and her being nourished in the wilderness suggest to the audience that God will deliver them as God delivered the people of Israel from Egypt.

The motif of the bride of the Lamb in chapters 19 and 21 is analogous to the sacred marriage of Zeus and Leto. Traditional interpretations have identified the bride with the church or with the soul of the individual Christian that is united with Christ after death. An approach based on the history of religions sees the influence of the mythic notion of a sacred marriage in the formation of this symbol. Such a marriage celebrates the establishment of cosmic, political, and social order, both on the narrative level and in the social world of the text. The vision of the bride has also been influenced by Isaiah 54, in which Jerusalem is portrayed as God's wife. The construction of the New Jerusalem out of precious stones may have been suggested by Isa. 54:11–12, "I will set your stones in antimony, and lay your foundations with sapphires. I will make your pinnacles agate, your gates of carbuncles, and all your wall of precious stones." In the Dead Sea Scrolls this text was interpreted as an allegorical description of the "Congregation of His Elect," the sectarian community that used the scrolls. The bride, the New Jerusalem, in Revelation symbolizes the community of the faithful at the time of their uniting with God and the Lamb in the new age. In this work, the fulfillment of God's creation and God's ultimate intimacy with humanity are not described in abstract terms or in metaphors that are only masculine. Both the masculine and the feminine are drawn upon to express the richness, complexity, and vitality of the created world and its fulfillment. This vision of the new creation as a wedding is a counterbalance to Rev. 14:1–5. Because of the present crisis, which John implied was about to intensify, the ideal was to renounce sexual relations and to prepare for the end. At the same time, as one of the fundamental characteristics of God's good creation, sexual union is a symbol of the new creation, of wholeness, of the time of salvation.

THE HISTORY OF INTERPRETATION

At least since the time of the early Christian scholar and theologian Origen, the crucial issue in the interpretation of the book of Revelation has been whether to take it literally or spiritually. One focus of the controversy in the early church was the prophecy expressed in Rev. 20:1–6. Some early Christian writers, for example, Papias, Justin Martyr, Irenaeus, and Tertullian, believed that this passage predicted an earthly kingdom of Christ that would follow his second coming and last for a thousand years. This interpretation, especially in the case of Irenaeus, may have arisen in opposition to the purely spiritual notion of salvation held by the Gnostics. Origen, however, taught that hope for an earthly kingdom was an indulgence of unworthy desires. He rejected literal interpretations of prophecies of the new age and argued that they ought to be interpreted figuratively (*De Principiis* 2.11.2–5). This approach flowered in the work of the late-fourth-century Donatist Tyconius (see above and McGinn 1987, 531). He interpreted the book of Revelation exclusively in terms of the struggle between good and evil throughout the history of the church and excluded any hope for a coming earthly kingdom.

The tension between those who looked forward to an earthly reign of Christ for a thousand years (the chiliasts or millenarians, from the Greek and Latin words for a thousand respectively) and those who did not (the allegorists) was mediated by Augustine's synthesis of teaching about the last things (eschatology). He interpreted Rev. 20:1–6 figuratively as a reference to the ministry of Jesus, because during that time Satan was bound (with reference to Luke 10:18). Thus, the reign of a thousand years was understood as the age of the church, which was to be followed by the second coming of Christ. Augustine's interpretation of the beasts of chapter 13, as this wicked world and hypocrisy respectively, undercut the tendency to identify these beasts with the Roman Empire and its agents or with other specific political or social institutions. Even though Augustine understood the thousand years and the events of the end literally, his spiritual interpretation of the present and his location of the end in the distant future significantly reduced speculations about the end and expectation of its imminent advent.

Augustine's view of eschatology became dominant. Eventually, the thousand years of the age of the church came to be understood symbolically rather than literally. From about 400 to about 1100 C.E., the book of Revelation was interpreted primarily in terms of the moral struggle between vice and virtue. The notion of an earthly reign of Christ or new age remained dormant until it was revived by Joachim of Fiore. Although he maintained the moral perspective of the Augustinian approach and affirmed the literary structure of recapitulation in his *Exposition on Revelation,* Joachim provided a historical reading that correlated the symbols of the book of Revelation with the major events of the history of the church. This interpretation also divided all of history into three great epochs related to the three persons of the Trinity. According to Joachim, the third age of history, which is to begin after the defeat of the Antichrist, is one in which the Holy Spirit will bring about a reformed and purified monastic church. He did not teach that this new age would last a literal thousand years, but he did reintroduce millenarianism by predicting a coming perfect age of indefinite duration.

The book of Revelation was frequently read and intensely debated in England during the period of the Reformation. Truly millenarian readings revived in radical Puritan circles in the seventeenth century and often included the idea of England as an elect nation. In the nineteenth century, American and British heirs of the apocalyptic Puritan tradition continued to produce treatises and commentaries giving apocalyptic interpretations of the American and French Revolutions and the activities of Napoleon I and Napoleon III.

In modern times, the issues have been analogous to those debated in the early church. In the twentieth century the old debate between the chiliasts and the allegorists has gone on in controversies between fundamentalists and modernists or between premillennialists and amillennialists. Those who expect a literal reign of Christ on earth for a thousand years believe that they hold the historic faith of the church. As a movement, they have more proximate roots in the teaching of John Nelson Darby, who founded the Plymouth Brethren in England, and in various movements in nineteenth-century America, such as the Millerites. Today such believers call themselves "premillennialists" because they believe that Christ will return before the thousand year reign on earth. They oppose the official eschatological teaching of the major denominations, which is rooted in Augustine, and describe it as "amillennial" because it does not include an earthly reign of Christ between the second coming and the final state.

In the United States in the twentieth century, several points of view on the question of the end may be distinguished. The position that has attracted the most attention and caused the most concern is that which combines premillennial faith with imminent expectation. This point of view sometimes includes calculations of various periods in history and a more or less specific prediction of the date of the second coming. One of its fundamental principles is the literal interpretation of scripture. Its adherents accuse "amillennialists" of being inconsistent, because they interpret other parts of scripture literally, but have a special hermeneutic for prophecy. The books of Daniel and Revelation are important resources for this point of view.

The modern premillennial position may be seen as a contemporary analogue to ancient chiliasm. A contemporary version of the spiritual or allegorical point of view is characterized by commitment to the scientific method and thus by considerable skepticism and agnosticism with regard to the actual events of the beginning and end of our universe. From this point of view, Daniel and Revelation suggest the inner meaning of our universe or of the human experience of its processes. The biblical apocalypses are viewed not as forecasts of what is to be but as interpretations of how things were, are, and ought to be. Their purposes are to inform and influence human life by means of the values and insights expressed in symbolic and narrative form.

⌒CONCLUSION

For the historically minded critical reader, the book of Revelation is not a cryptic summary of the history of the church or the world. It is not primarily a prediction of the timing of the end of the world. Rather, it is a work of religious poetry, inspired by the prophets of Israel and by the cosmic and political myths of the author's time. The author, an early Christian prophet by the name of John, believed himself authorized by God and his Messiah to interpret the times for his contemporaries. His message was harsh and demanding, both for insiders and outsiders. Insiders were to avoid compromise with the corrupt and idolatrous culture of the hellenized and romanized cities of Asia Minor, no matter what the cost. Some chance for the repentance and conversion of outsiders was envisaged (Rev. 11:13). But, for the most part, outsiders were expected to continue doing evil and to be condemned to eternal torment in the lake of fire (20:15; 22:11). The book of Revelation is also a work of religious rhetoric, intended to shape the beliefs and lifestyle of its audience. Its impact is far different from that of the teaching of Jesus as expressed in the Sermon on the Mount (Matthew 5–7), which calls for love of enemies and turning the other cheek. Historically speaking, however, the book of Revelation may have contributed to the survival of a Christian perspective that could not simply take its place as one ancient cult among many. Theologically and ethically speaking, it is a work that expresses the anguish of those who live on the margins. It expresses a vision of hope for the marginalized themselves and makes vivid and intelligible for the comfortable how the world of power relations looks from a perspective on the margins.

⌒BIBLIOGRAPHY

Aune, David E. 1981. "The Social Matrix of the Apocalypse of John." *Biblical Research* 26:16–32. An illuminating study of the social context of Revelation.
——. 1987. "The Apocalypse of John and Graeco-Roman Revelatory Magic." *New Testament Studies* 33:481–501. A suggestive study regarding the similarities between Revelation and the magical papyri.
——. 1997. *Revelation 1–5.* World Biblical Commentary 52A. Dallas: Word. Major commentary that appeared after this article was written.
Barr, David. 1984. "The Apocalypse as a Symbolic Transformation of the World." *Interpretation* 38:39–50. A study of the way in which the book of Revelation affects its audience.
Boismard, M. E. 1949. "'L'Apocalypse' ou 'les apocalypses' de S. Jean." *Revue biblique* 56:507–27. A classic example of a source-critical study of the book of Revelation.

Boring, M. Eugene. 1989. *Revelation*. Interpretation: A Bible Commentary for Teaching and Preaching. Louisville: John Knox. An interpretation that argues that the message of the book of Revelation is compatible with the teaching of nonviolence attributed to Jesus.

Bornkamm, Günther. 1937. "Die Komposition der apokalyptischen Visionen in der Offenbarung Johannis." *Zeitschrift für die neutestamentliche Wissenschaft* 36:132–49. Also in *Studien zu Antike und Christentum: Gesammelte Aufsätze, Band II*, 204–22. Beiträge zur evangelischen Theologie 28. Munich: C. Kaiser, 1959. The article that revived the recapitulation theory in modern scholarship on Revelation.

Bousset, Wilhelm. 1906. *Die Offenbarung Johannis*. Rev. ed. Göttingen: Vandenhoeck & Ruprecht. Reprinted, 1966. A classic commentary from the point of view of the history of religions.

Charles, R. H. 1920. *A Critical and Exegetical Commentary on the Revelation of St. John*. 2 vols. International Critical Commentary. New York: Charles Scribner's Sons. A classic commentary, still valuable for its comparisons with Jewish apocryphal and pseudepigraphical texts.

Ford, J. Massyngberde. 1975. *Revelation: Introduction, Translation and Commentary*. Anchor Bible 38. Garden City, N.Y.: Doubleday. The source-critical theories of this commentary have not been accepted, but it is valuable for comparisons with the Dead Sea Scrolls.

García Martínez, Florentino. 1994. *The Dead Sea Scrolls Translated: The Qumran Texts in English*. Leiden/New York/Cologne: E. J. Brill. A comprehensive translation of all the significant fragments.

Giblin, Charles Homer. 1974. "Structure and Thematic Correlations in the Theology of Revelation 16–22." *Biblica* 55:487–504. An important literary study.

Haussleiter, I., ed. 1916. *Victorini Episcopi Petavionensis Opera*. Corpus scriptorum ecclesiasticorum latinorum 49. Leipzig: Freytag. The oldest surviving commentary on the book of Revelation.

Hellholm, David. 1986. "The Problem of Apocalyptic Genre and the Apocalypse of John." *Semeia* 36:13–64. A sophisticated study of the language of the book of Revelation and the implications for its structure and genre.

Hemer, Colin J. 1986. *The Letters to the Seven Churches of Asia in Their Local Setting*. Journal for the Study of the New Testament Supplement. Sheffield, JSOT Press. A comprehensive collection and discussion of geographical and social data related to the seven cities of Revelation.

Holladay, Carl R., ed. 1989. *Fragments from Hellenistic Jewish Authors*: Vol. 2, *Poets: The Epic Poets Theodotus and Philo and Ezekiel the Tragedian*. Society of Biblical Literature Texts and Translations 30, Pseudepigrapha Series 12. Atlanta: Scholars Press. Text, translation, and notes on the fragments of Ezekiel the Tragedian, a Jewish work that casts light on some aspects of Revelation.

McGinn, Bernard. 1987. "Revelation." In *The Literary Guide to the Bible*, edited by Robert Alter and Frank Kermode. Cambridge, Mass.: The Belknap Press of Harvard University Press. A magisterial history of the interpretation of Revelation.

Müller, Ulrich B. 1972. *Messias und Menschensohn in jüdischen Apokalypsen und in der Offenbarung des Johannes.* Studien zum Neuen Testament 6. Gütersloh: Mohn. An important study of the presentation of Jesus Christ in Revelation and other works from the same period.

Pippin, Tina. 1992. *Death and Desire: The Rhetoric of Gender in the Apocalypse of John.* Louisville: Westminster/John Knox. A reading of Revelation from a twentieth-century feminist perspective.

Price, S. R. F. 1984. *Rituals and Power: The Roman Imperial Cult in Asia Minor.* Cambridge: Cambridge University Press. A very insightful history and analysis of the practice of the worship of the Roman emperor in Asia Minor.

Schüssler Fiorenza, Elisabeth. 1985. *The Book of Revelation: Justice and Judgment.* Philadelphia: Fortress Press. A brief but important commentary from the perspective of liberation theology.

Steinhauser, Kenneth B. 1987. *The Apocalypse Commentary of Tyconius: A History of its Reception and Influence.* European University Studies, Series 23, vol. 301. Frankfurt am Main/Bern/New York: Peter Lang. An important study of the surviving evidence for the lost commentary of Tyconius.

Swete, Henry Barclay. 1917. *The Apocalypse of St. John: The Greek Text with Introduction Notes and Indices.* 3rd ed. London: Macmillan. A classic commentary on the Greek text.

Thompson, Leonard L. 1990. *The Book of Revelation: Apocalypse and Empire.* New York/Oxford: Oxford University Press. A learned, but ultimately unconvincing reading of Revelation as a nondualistic response to a nonthreatening social situation.

Vanni, Ugo. 1971. *La struttura letteraria dell' Apocalisse.* Aloisiana 8. Rome: Herder. An important analysis of the literary structure of Revelation.

Vermes, Geza. 1995. *The Dead Sea Scrolls in English.* Revised 4th ed. London/New York: Penguin. A highly readable translation of most of the significant texts.

Yarbro Collins, Adela. 1976. *The Combat Myth in the Book of Revelation.* Harvard Dissertations in Religion 9. Missoula, Mont.: Scholars Press. A study of the literary structure of Revelation, the major symbols of chapters 12, 13, and 17, and the mythic character of the whole work.

———. 1984. *Crisis and Catharsis: The Power of the Apocalypse.* Philadelphia: Westminster. An analysis of the book of Revelation in its social context.

———. 1993. "Feminine Symbolism in the Book of Revelation." *Biblical Interpretation* 1:20–33. A study of the feminine symbols in which two approaches are explored: the history of religions and Jungian interpretation.

———. 1996. *Cosmology and Eschatology in Jewish and Christian Apocalypticism.* Supplements to the Journal for the Study of Judaism 50. Leiden: E. J. Brill. Essays on the book of Revelation and related texts.

12

Early Christian Apocalypticism: Literature and Social World

David Frankfurter
University of New Hampshire

THROUGH THE GRECO-ROMAN PERIOD AND ESPECIALLY IN THE later first century C.E. with the book of Revelation, we see a widespread and pronounced interest in apocalyptic texts, otherworldly revelation in general, and the whole notion of a book as medium of otherworldly gnosis. At the same time, we see widespread evidence of apocalyptic movements—groups organized around an expectation of the end of the world and a conviction in their own sainthood. Many of these texts and many of these movements seem also to have embraced one or another form of Christian ideology.

When we contemplate apocalypticism over the last two thousand years we think above all of beliefs or states of anticipation emphasizing the destruction of the world—or, more precisely, the world as culturally conceived—a culmination of some cosmic battle between good and evil taking place in that world, and a decisive purification of the old and polluting world to make way for a new and ideal cosmos. Thus we find versions not only in western religious traditions but also in ancient Mesoamerican and Indo-European mythologies as well. But when we go back to the beginning of Christian apocalypticism—to the time of Jesus, to the author of the book of Revelation, and to the spate of end-time tracts that emerge with the dawn of the Christian movement—we find ourselves dealing not with an eschatological literary tradition but rather a broad, intercultural, and multimedia fascination with otherworldly gnosis, secret teachings, and the sacred book of revealed wisdom. It was in this way, in fact, that people of the ancient Mediterranean world understood the notion of *apokalypsis* (literally, "unveiling," "revealing") (see Adler, in VanderKam and Adler 1996, 8–13). At the same time, the first, formative centuries of Christianity show a distinctive focus on eschatological anticipation. From the apostle Paul's anxious admonitions to Mediterranean congregations (1 Thess. 4:13–5:11; Rom. 8:18–25), to one congregation's stepped-up certainty of imminent arrival (2 Thess. 2:1–2), to the preservation of words from the risen Christ—still being channeled through prophets—revealing that the eschaton was nigh (Rev. 22:6–20), the first century of Christianity consisted for the most part of groups confident that the skies would open at any moment with trumpets and heavenly beings.

We might be led to expect people in such anticipation of the end of history to seek literary grounding in Jewish apocalypses, which quite often revealed a cosmic eschatology that would resolve all the present misfortunes of the righteous, sometimes even with timetables and precise details of heavenly intervention (Daniel 12; 4 Ezra 5:1–13; 7:26–44; see Collins, in Collins 1979, 21–59). But in fact we find the earliest Christian interest in apocalypticism characterized not by the search for eschatological details but rather by an attraction to heavenly revelation, and especially the heavenly book, as a mode of authority.

So even while the period and religious trends covered here produce a wild profusion of eschatological convictions (seemingly beyond any other period in ancient history), we must nevertheless try to understand the eschatology of earliest Christianity in the context of the religion's early emphasis on revelatory texts and wisdom. The texts to be examined as principal data in this chapter consist, therefore, of those books of an ultimately Christian orientation that self-consciously unveil otherworldly secrets and are datable with some certainty to the second and third centuries C.E.

A REGIONAL ASSESSMENT OF EARLY CHRISTIAN APOCALYPTIC LITERATURE

As is often the case in reconstructing ancient history, our entry into the religious world of an early Christian apocalypticism depends almost entirely on the historical evidence of the ancient texts: the apocalypses themselves, enigmatic and often esoteric books that convey little more than their authors' attitudes toward some "greater truth" at work in the world than historical reality itself, material of little use for documenting actual religious groups and figures. More objective witnesses in the form of church histories, letters, and heresiographies seldom complement the apocalypses directly. We are left with a great variety of data for what was apparently a great diversity of religious groups, which we collect together under the rubric "apocalypticism" by virtue of their pronounced interests in otherworldly gnosis preserved in books.

The first step in allowing the apocalyptic texts some significance in the history of early Christian religion must be to group them by *regional* affiliation, for this way apocalypses, along with other kinds of data from a region and a particular period, can together constitute parts of a manageable cultural puzzle. The region, as anthropologists have shown, provides the fundamental context for religious phenomena.

To be sure, numerous apocalyptic texts are subjects of ongoing debate as to provenance and date, and this essay will leave very few texts "unprovenanced," offering as it proceeds the rationales for placing texts in particular places or periods. Such assignments admittedly involve some circularity, and yet we must proceed with just this kind of experimentation if we are to understand these texts as products of particular cultures.

Egypt

We know quite a bit about apocalypticism in Egypt, not just through the manuscripts preserved there but also through the extensive documentation of Alexandrian Judaism and its neighbors. Through the end of the first century C.E. figures like Philo and the authors of the Wisdom of Solomon and the *Book of the Secrets of Enoch* (*2 Enoch*) demonstrate various kinds of interest in esoteric heavenly knowledge and the spiritual states involved in achieving this knowledge. The shadows of a "Sethian Gnosticism" are also apparent in this culture: Jewish groups maintaining what they allege to be secret antediluvian teachings about the cosmos (such as the *Apocalypse of Adam* [Nag Hammadi Codex (NHC)] V, 5).[1] Coincidentally, many priestly conventicles of the native Egyptian temple tradition were moving in a similar direction. Papyri, inscriptions, and "magical" spells show that members of this milieu were actively cultivating revelatory dream states and developing ideas of transcendent knowledge (see Podemann Sørensen 1992).

There are also hints in the Jewish *Sibylline Oracles* and in scattered papyri of a more eschatologically oriented, even millennialist, religious sentiment—both in Egyptian Judaism and in Egyptian native religion—which effectively explodes in the early second century. In 115 C.E. a messianic Jewish revolt swept from Cyrene in North Africa throughout Egypt and inspired Egyptians themselves to launch a counterattack with a fervor that could be compared to holy war. Virtually no more evidence of Jewish life exists in Egypt until the fourth century (see Frankfurter, in VanderKam and Adler 1996, 145–46).

Meanwhile, a highly diverse selection of Christian manuscript fragments, especially of texts of Syrian provenance such as the Gospels of John and Thomas, reflects the second-century growth of diverse Christianities, many if not most devoted to cultivating an otherworldly gnosis and realizing a concomitant spiritual nature (see Pearson 1990, 194–213).

The third century sees a progressive economic and social decline throughout the Roman world, which was felt especially catastrophically in Egypt; and papyri document the emperor Decius's attempt to reverse chaos by requiring uniform religious observance (249 C.E.). Perhaps most important for the genesis of apocalyptic texts at this period is the evidence, preserved in Eusebius's *Church History* (7.24), for a popular millennialist movement in the Fayyum of the mid-third century, linked to the book of Revelation and involving some learned apologists (see Frankfurter 1993, chaps. 9–10).

Apocalyptic literature from Egypt fits into these historical circumstances quite well, and also into the broader cultural sensibilities of Egyptian Judaism and Egyptian native religion. *3 Baruch*, which probably belongs to Egypt on the basis of its afterlife details (4:5; 13) and Origen's acquaintance with it (*De Principiis* 2.3.6), assumes in its rather formulaic description of heavenly ascent the kind of deep scribal respect for an apocalyptic genre that motivated many Gnostic texts. Assuming that the Christian appropriation of *3 Baruch*'s Jewish core took place in the same region (and probably in the fourth century), we can perceive, on the one hand, a Christian community devoted to the authority of the apocalyptic ascent text and to the biblical hero as exemplary seer and saint, and, on the other hand, the beginnings of an endeavor, well represented in later Coptic literature, to support regional cultic traditions (here the archangel Michael's services) and moral exhortations (against drunkenness) by appeal to heavenly revelation and paradigm (*3 Baruch* 11–14; see Harlow 1996, 186–87). *3 Baruch* seems to reflect a trajectory from the apocalyptic Judaism of *2 Enoch* and Wisdom of Solomon to the distinctive uses of apocalypse in early Egyptian Christianity.[2]

The Christian Gnosticism evidently based in Alexandria and other cities has roots both in first-century Judaism and in native priestly trends such as Hermetism; and this environment of religious synthesis provides the milieu for a number of texts that stressed the achievement of otherworldly knowledge according to early Jewish literary models of ascent and angelic mediation. They are essentially "Christian" to the extent that they work from Christian lore of the second and third centuries. The *Apocryphon of John*

(NHC II, 1; III, 1; IV, 1), *Allogenes* (NHC XI, 3), and a Coptic *Apocalypse of Paul* (V, 2), *Pistis Sophia,* and the *Books of Jeu* are all part of this Gnostic corpus of Egyptian Christian apocalypses. Cosmic eschatology is of little importance; but revelation itself, the notion of the revelatory book, and the nuances of ascent in a rather frightening cosmos are all of paramount interest. The *Apocryphon of John,* for example, opens with the "author's" crisis after the crucifixion and its resolution through the appearance of a polymorphic Christ (much as "Ezra's" crisis in 4 Ezra 3 is resolved through the appearance and teachings of the Lord-angel); but this narrative serves only to frame an extended discourse on the nature and imprisonment of the Gnostic soul, concluding with an admonition to write everything down and transmit secretly "the mystery of the immovable race." The extensive *Books of Jeu* offer instructions on passing through the gates of the heavens, using passwords and symbols to pacify the demonic toll collectors, while the *Apocalypse of Paul* describes the apostle's ascent through the same kinds of tolls, soaring even beyond the seventh heaven, where sits the god of older apocalyptic cosmologies, to the tenth, the home of the Gnostic, where Paul recognizes his fellow spirits (see Fallon, in Collins 1979, 123–58; and Frankfurter, in VanderKam and Adler 1996, 150–62).

At the same time we find texts of a more eschatological bent. The *Apocalypse of Peter,* although occasionally placed in Palestine, seems more at home in Egypt for many of its details (especially a brief discussion of animal worship in chap. 10 [Eth.]).[3] Cited with respect by Clement of Alexandria (*apud* Eusebius, *Hist. eccl.* 6.14.1), the book must have germinated at some point in the second century. It consists essentially of a protracted eschatological discourse revealed to Peter by Jesus, covering the final woes of the earth, the judgment, and then the lurid punishments that special angels will bring upon those who persecute the "elect." The very vengefulness that the *Apocalypse of Peter* expresses toward a shadowy outside world—complete with a special "punishment angelology"—develops a notion of vindictive judgment already present in the Wisdom of Solomon, a document of early Roman Alexandrian Judaism (*Apoc. Pet.* 3.1–5.16); but the *Apocalypse of Peter* carries it to an imaginative extreme reminiscent of the fiery Christ that one early Christian author imagined would come and smite his own historical adversaries (2 Thess. 1:6–10). These are the fantasies that maintain sectarian boundaries under stress.

The same combination of eschatological discourse, persecution imagery, and a focus on an elect occupies a text of the later third century, the *Apocalypse of Elijah.* Other Christian apocalypses that may have appeared in the intervening century or so cannot be identified, but the *Apocalypse of Elijah* is by no means an anomalous document for Egyptian Christianity of the period.

Indeed, its combination of traditions seems very much to epitomize a type of Christianity taking root outside the urban milieu of Clement and Origen and the conventicles responsible for the Gnostic texts.

The *Apocalypse of Elijah* is, properly speaking, not an "apocalypse"—a literary unveiling of heavenly secrets—but a prophetic discourse such as one might imagine delivered by a charismatic leader or a religious ecstatic. "The word of the Lord came to me thus," the speaker imitates Jeremiah and Ezekiel, "Say to this people, 'why do you sin and add sin to your sins, angering the Lord God who created you? Do not love the world, nor what is in the world, for the pride of the world and its destruction are of the devil,'" he loosely quotes 1 John. "Remember that he has prepared for you thrones and crowns in heaven . . ." (*Apoc. Elijah* 1.1–2, 8). "If you should hear that there is security and safety in Jerusalem, tear your garments, O priests of the land, because the Destructive One will not be long in coming!" (2.40). This mode of first-person address continues for most of the text. And partly on the basis of this literary form I have proposed an actual prophetic leader behind this text, much like the prophetic leaders in the testimony of Eusebius and the lives of desert saints.

The original audience of the *Apocalypse of Elijah* must have been sufficiently Egyptian in cultural sensibility to recognize as authoritative the author's extensive use of Egyptian traditions. Where the *Apocalypse of Peter* frames its entire revelation as a past event within the gospel legend of Jesus on the Mount of Olives, the *Apocalypse of Elijah* moves the anticipation of the eschaton—indeed, an actual millennium—into a distinctively Egyptian idiom, drawing on Egyptian concepts of beneficent rulership, staging the end-time events in the land of Egypt, and addressing distinctively Egyptian Christian concerns.

Most of the text consists of a protracted eschatological timetable, and the signs of woe here are drawn from a religious world now awash with apocalyptic motifs and fragments. Some of these motifs were already in circulation in the *Sibylline Oracles* or as unattributed prophecies, but most of the eschatological imagery in the *Apocalypse of Elijah* is inherited from classical Egyptian tradition: benevolent and malicious rulers, a king from the sun, the Nile running with blood, people seeking death out of despair, drought, economic collapse, the influx of dangerous animals.

In fact, the *Apocalypse of Elijah* exploits the same Egyptian symbolism and the same Egyptian *kingship ideology* as two roughly contemporaneous Egyptian texts: the Hermetic *Perfect Discourse* and fragments of the *Potter's Oracle,* a priestly tract first composed during the Ptolemaic era. All these texts cast in prophetic form a traditional Egyptian symbolism of the alternation of chaos and order: social harmony and the generations are maintained, fields flourish, foreign nations and desert animals stay away when the Pharaoh rules, while chaos reigns when proper kingship is not maintained (or, in later times, when the standing king is inimical to Egyptian order; see Frankfurter 1993, chapter 7). Taken together, the *Apocalypse of Elijah,* the *Perfect Discourse,* and the *Potter's Oracle* fragments seem to reflect either one of two cultural facts: either the existence of related scribal movements in third-century Egypt, or a literary-ideological idiom so entrenched in scribal tradition that any author of the culture, whether of Hermetic, Christian, Manichean, or temple affiliation, would naturally use it to describe the end-times.

The attitude of the *Apocalypse of Elijah* toward persecution and martyrdom also seems to reflect religious currents distinctive of Egypt. Its millennialist eschatology, distinctly influenced by the book of Revelation, seems to reflect the same worldview as the millennialist movement in the third-century Egyptian Fayyum region (Eusebius, *Hist. eccl.* 7.24). Its concern for martyrs anticipates many of the same concerns as the so-called Melitians, whom Bishop Athanasius opposed a century later in rural Egypt: Who is a true martyr—the fugitive or the executed? What happens to martyrs? Whom do martyrs resemble among the saints? The text's promotion of fasting anticipates later Coptic ascetic ideologies. Indeed, in promoting the practice of fasting against some shadowy opponents, the *Apocalypse of Elijah* appears to reflect a community caught in the crossfire between the Manichean movement, growing rapidly in the countryside, and the Alexandrian church, crusading against the ascetic virtuosities that, in its view, distinguished Manicheans (see Frankfurter 1993, chapter 11).

The problem of opponents occupies the author/speaker of the *Apocalypse of Elijah* quite early:

> Hear now, you wise men of the land, concerning the deceivers who will multiply in the end time, because they will adopt teachings that are not of God. They will put aside God's law—these people whose god is their belly—who say, "The fast does not exist, nor did God create it." . . . Do not let those people deceive you! Remember that the Lord made fasting from (the time of) his creation of the heavens. . . . (*Apoc. Elijah* 1.13–15)

The author thus warns against rival leaders who oppose ascetic fasting. What is most interesting—and telling—about the social setting of the *Apocalypse of Elijah* is that the speaker/author then turns immediately to the signs of the end, as if the occurrence of this conflict over fasting signaled for some group the beginning of the last days. Alerting the audience to the sign of end-time deceivers turns the present time of confusion, of rival teachings, into the first stage of a protracted eschaton—suddenly this and all coming woes are comprehensible and preordained (see Frankfurter 1993, 296–98).

Martyrdom, asceticism, millennialism are all issues that would preoccupy Egyptian Christianity in the fourth century; here they occupy—nay, *motivate* —the propaganda of a small sectarian movement in later-third-century Egypt. It was a movement that combined ideologically a deeply Egyptian worldview, the traditional scribal articulation of that worldview, and a fanatical Christian millennialism. It is even more remarkable how the impact of the *Apocalypse of Elijah* surpassed its parochial origins: Didymus the Blind knew it well, the Syrian author of the *Tiburtine Sibyl*, a fourth-century apocalyptic text, used it for eschatological details, and an apocalyptic text from Ireland seems to have known it as well (*The Two Sorrows of the Kingdom of Heaven* [tenth or eleventh century]; see Frankfurter 1993, 24–26, 51–54).

It is useful to mention three additional Egyptian Christian apocalyptic texts despite the fact that they do not necessarily fit into the period under discussion: the *Apocalypse of Paul,* the *Epistula Apostolorum,* and the *Testament of Abraham.* The *Apocalypse of Paul,* a late-fourth-century Greek compilation, is actually dependent on the *Apocalypse of Peter* for details of punishment and on some common introductory fragment with the *Apocalypse of Elijah* (*Apoc. Paul* 3a = *Apoc. Elijah* 1.1).[4] But the genius of the *Apocalypse of Paul* is in moving the eschatological punishments of the *Apocalypse of Peter* into an "ongoing status": where and how the sinners of this world perpetually and indefinitely end up. The text also portrays the delights of the blessed in and around the heavenly Jerusalem. In this world of judgment appear some of the religious constituencies that came under scrutiny during the fourth century: monks, anchorites, docetic heretics, heathens, and—in stark contrast to the *Apocalypse of Elijah*'s ascetic imperative (1:2, 13–22)—overachievers in the fasting domain (chapter 24). In its repeated translations and literary spin-offs throughout the medieval world, the *Apocalypse of Paul* provided a principal prototype for Dante's *Inferno.*

The *Epistula Apostolorum,* so named after its epistolary introduction, is an extended dialogue between Jesus' disciples and the risen Christ, thus utilizing a literary genre of special popularity among Christians of a Gnostic bent for recording otherworldly wisdom.[5] The text has often been dated to the second century by virtue of the number of years it seems to put between crucifixion and *parousia* (chapter 17); but it clearly has little interest in a precise date, and the general interests it conveys may be more at home in the fourth century, closer to the time of its first manuscripts. Commencing with a creedal declaration, the *Epistula Apostolorum* stands apart from the other Egyptian Christian apocalypses of the second and third century in moving deliberately and confidently away from such pressing topics as eschatology and the imminence of woes (chapters 16, 34–38), martyrdom (chapters 15, 36, 50), the details and satisfaction of a last judgment (chapters 39, 44), and the definition of radical sectarian boundaries (chapters 36, 43–45), and toward the consolidation of *doctrine:* a set of ideas that themselves might define an "elect" and a charge, not to remain in ascetic preparation for the coming end, but to spread those ideas far and wide. As a historical document, the *Epistula Apostolorum* seems to occupy a place between the Gnostic apocalypses, with which it is in closest conversation (by virtue of the shared dialogue genre and various matters of doctrine), and the eschatological apocalypses (*Apocalypses of Peter* and *Elijah*), with whose "this-worldly" sphere of action the author implies some basic affiliation.

The third apocalyptic text with possible relevance for the pre-Constantinian period is the *Testament of Abraham* and its additions, the *Testaments of Isaac and Jacob.*[6] The *Testament of Abraham* describes the patriarch's vision of an ongoing, and quite intricate, judgment process as administered by Michael and other angels, including one called "Death." Whether or not this kind of legend originated as a Jewish composition in Egypt or elsewhere, the *Testament of Abraham* such as we have it seems to have undergone a lively transmission in several versions during the fourth century, particularly in Egypt: the influence of native Egyptian mortuary myth in at least one of its versions is quite apparent.[7] Subsequently, the *Testament of Abraham* was extended with *Testaments of Isaac and Jacob,* distinctively Coptic works in their dual emphasis on asceticism and the cult of the saints.[8] But it was not just the popularity of the *Testament of Abraham* that inspired this multiplication of testaments. It was also the special meaning of these patriarchs and other biblical heroes for upper Egyptian Christianity, a cultural phenomenon to which we shall return.

Three trends, overlapping in some cases, seem to characterize the Egyptian apocalypses: first, in some circles, a purely "Gnostic" orientation toward gaining otherworldly wisdom, linked closely to a book culture, and exploiting the notion of heavenly ascent to develop extravagant cosmologies; second, a strongly sectarian millennialist expectation served by esoteric angelologies and timetables (*Apocalypse of Peter, Apocalypse of Elijah*); and third, linked to the second but obviously outlasting it, a thematic focus on judgment, its intricacies, drama, and implications for this world. Already in the early Roman period the Wisdom of Solomon developed the image of judgment as eschatological vindication for the persecuted righteous (3:1–5:16), an idea certainly developed to radical extreme in the *Apocalypse of Peter*. An *Apocalypse of Zephaniah* of Egyptian provenance but unclear (Jewish or Christian) leanings focuses on a perpetual judgment and punishment in heaven. (On the *Apocalypse of Zephaniah,* see Wintermute, in Charlesworth 1983–85, 1:497–515). But the judgment scene is also developed in as unearthly and noneschatological a text as the *Pistis Sophia* (4.144–48; cf. *Apoc. Paul* [NHC V, 2], 20–22). Spread out among such a diversity of Egyptian texts, the theme of judgment clearly brings together both Egyptian and Jewish scribal interests (see Frankfurter, in Vanderkam and Adler 1996, 195–200).

Syro-Palestine

What should distinguish apocalypses of Syro-Palestine? More likely than a direct reflection of the violent politics of the first and second centuries C.E., such texts should represent the very diversity of esoteric priestly, pseudo- (or would-be) priestly, and anti-priestly Judaisms that we know from Josephus, Qumran, and even rabbinic texts, carrying over into the Christianities of the Roman period. So, for example, the *Testaments of the Twelve Patriarchs,* a series of twelve brief discourses by each of the sons of Jacob concerning proper ethics, predictions of future salvation, and, for Levi and Naphtali, visions of the other world, reflect a Christian scribal milieu in continuity with some kind of Jewish milieu. Indeed, this continuous milieu maintained a very specific orientation toward the eschatological triumph of the tribes of Levi and Judah in the person of Christ;[9] that is, the Christianity that oriented this group's essentially Jewish religious world stemmed directly from their Levi-Judah interests—it was not a perfunctory addition. And a repeated reference to the patriarchs' burials at Hebron might also suggest, as do the Christian *Lives of the Prophets,* a provenance in which such shrines were actually accessible.[10] On the whole, the *Testaments* fit best in Palestine for these continuations of Palestinian *Jewish* apocalyptic themes, especially those of a rather esoteric priestly bent.

The *Testaments of the Twelve Patriarchs* resolutely participate in the Jewish apocalyptic tradition: not only in working over what appears to be a quite ancient legend of Levi's heavenly ascent but also in situating eschatological prediction in alleged books of Enoch. The references to Enoch's writings need not connect to known texts in order to reveal a culture in which eschatology was considered a subject based in antediluvian revelation and Enoch an established authority over such revelations.[11]

The *Testament of Adam,* either composed in or quickly translated into Syriac from Greek, is a compilation of (at present) three revelation discourses, one predicting the advent of Christ and two listing the activities of the heavenly world.[12] "The Hours of the Night" and "of the Day" describe the liturgical drama carried out by the elements of the cosmos in praise of God (an ancient theme in Jewish apocalyptic visions and one with distinctly mystical ramifications). "The Heavenly Powers" describes the nature of the seven "orders" of angels up to the enthroned "Lord Jesus the Messiah," an apocalyptic form used elsewhere in liturgy and as the structure of the Jewish ritual handbook *Sefer HaRazim*.[13] Although difficult to date, the *Testament of Adam* shows the concerted interest in collecting apocalyptic lore, especially lists of angels, signs, or prayers, which characterized Christian as well as Jewish scribal conventicles. While the scribe here included a prediction of Christ's advent framed as Adam's "testament," his overall interest was clearly in collecting all manner of otherworldly information.

Considering the widespread competition among proponents of Jesus, John the Baptist, Simon Magus, Paul, and no doubt other first-century charismatic leaders, all of whom were credited with revelatory powers, it is hardly surprising that two apocalyptic texts from Syro-Palestine offer quite personal claims to visionary authority. The *Book of Elchasai* and the autobiography of the third-century religious founder Mani might be called "quasi-Christian" in their departure from a strict Christocentrism, or (better) they might be viewed as testimony to the variety of apocalyptic Christianities possible in the Middle East.

Elchasai was the early-second-century founder of a Jewish-Christian sect that originated in Transjordan and eventually migrated to Mesopotamia. According to those sparse remains of his book that appear in early church fathers' writings, Elchasai claimed a vision of two giant figures, identified with Christ and the Holy Spirit, and on this authority offered a new religious system based on Jewish law and focused on repeated baptisms. The *Book of Elchasai* apparently wove together the ethical rules, the heavenly visions, and details of eschatological war and martyrdom.[14]

In the mid-third century, one Mani, an "Elchasaite" himself who was subsequently taken with Pauline and Marcionite teachings (deemed heretical by the Elchasaite sect), claimed a visionary experience of his own. His heavenly "twin" appeared to him and revealed otherworldly secrets, carried him to heaven and other lands, and convinced him he should be, more than Jesus, Buddha, or Zarathustra, an apostle to the world.[15] Mani himself was well acquainted with Jewish apocalyptic texts and traditions and claimed that his authority would lie not simply in the revelations he had received but also in his preservation of these revelations in books (*Cologne Mani Codex,* pp. 48–60).[16] He was to be the culmination of all apocalyptic wisdom, as he repeated several times, and he self-consciously wove together both revelatory imagery and eschatological motifs of chaos, war, and conflagration from numerous Mediterranean traditions (see Koenen 1986). While certainly steeped in the Jewish apocalyptic tradition, Mani used such a variety of literary forms, from discourses and hymns to the autobiographical "On the Origin of His Body," preserved in a three-inch-high codex, that he almost seems to have transcended the bounds of the apocalypse genre. Rather than retrojecting lore anonymously into books of distant antiquity, Mani took such books as foils to his own self-conscious mission: he made it clear that heavenly secrets all came straight to him from his own "twin" and were to be disseminated to the world under his own name, Mani.

It is hard to generalize about Christian apocalypticism in Syro-Palestine on the basis of these four texts, but perhaps we can make a few tentative inferences based on their continuities with Jewish traditions and their dissimilarities with other regional apocalypticisms. There is, for example, a tremendous diversity of forms and contents among these texts; and yet all reflect a self-conscious scribality in collecting and systematizing lore and revelation: the Levi propaganda in the *Testaments of the Twelve Patriarchs,* the scrapbook of apocalyptic lists in *Testament of Adam,* the compilation of autobiographical materials in Mani's "Origin of His Body," even—it seems—the ethical exhortations and visions attributed to Elchasai.

There also seem to be rather similar uses of heavenly ascent as a claimed *personal* experience in these texts. In the *Book of Elchasai,* in Mani, as in some other texts of the early Christian period (*Odes of Solomon* 11, 36; 2 Cor. 12:1–5), the heavenly ascent is not restricted to heroes of old like Enoch or Abraham, nor attached formulaically to one's pretensions as a biblical-style prophet, but emerges as the singular claim to authority of a contemporary charismatic leader or seer. Of course, the *Testament of Levi* is the interesting exception here, a legendary ascent apparently preserved for generations in some Jewish form before being rewritten in the Christian *Testaments of the Twelve Patriarchs* (see Hollander and de Jonge 1985, 17–25, 129–30); and materials from Asia Minor, to which we will turn next, show similar claims. Perhaps this pattern points to the particular concentration of independent seers in our Syro-Palestine sample.

Asia Minor

From the later-first-century composition of the book of Revelation, Asia Minor is distinctive for its prophetism—that is, the central religious function within early Christianity of figures reputed to speak as mediators of the super-natural and travelers to the heavenly world, who often predicted to their audi-ences imminent woes, cataclysm, and new worlds dawning. (Here the word "prophet" is used in its social-scientific sense, implying no historical relation-ship with "prophets"—*nĕbî'îm*—in the Bible).

The historian of antiquity is most familiar with this prophetism through the second-century movement that swept the Mediterranean called "New Prophecy," often referred to as "Montanism" after one of its major exponents. But there were numerous leaders (including women such as Maximilla and Priscilla) claiming ecstatic revelations and even heavenly ascents, and their various utterances were recorded and transmitted so widely as to galvanize a Christian millennialism as far as North Africa, remaining active well into the third century.[17] We cannot attribute this phenomenon to the cult of Cybele or its ecstatic priests, nor can we derive it easily from the Judaism of the area, whose archaeology tends to show a quite nonsectarian and economically established people (see Schürer 1973–87, 3.1:17–36). If anything, the Jewish communities of Asia Minor show a progressive endeavor to localize their tra-ditions within their physical and cultural environment. Numerous sources witness the development of the legend of Noah's Ark in Roman Phrygia, for example (Schürer 1973–87, 3.1:28–30); and the first *Sibylline Oracle,* whose initial composition seems to have taken place in that area and period, makes clear that the localization of the Ark legend served the self-determination of Phrygian Jews (lines 196–98, 261–82). One might imagine that this ten-dency could have prepared the way for biblical-style prophets to appear in the same area: syncretism often provides the opportunity for revitalizing religious paradigms in new surroundings. The first and second *Sibylline Oracles* might then represent a midpoint in this development from localization to prophetism and, neatly Christianized as they stand, the continuity of the same ideas into Christian-identified milieux.

Any more secure links between Christian prophetism in Asia Minor and distinctive Asia Minor religious traditions remain elusive. However, this prophetism as we see it in Revelation and, I will argue, three other texts of generally disputed provenance, presented itself as the explicit revitalization of Israelite prophecy: the authoritative self-definition of the Christian prophets derived from the traditions of biblical *nĕbî'îm,* and the numerous visions and predictions that they offered were a function of their status as imitation Isaiahs and Jeremiahs.

The *Martyrdom and Ascension of Isaiah* is a Christian ascent apocalypse with an accompanying narrative of Isaiah's martyrdom at the hands of one Belchira and his false prophets. This narrative may derive from earlier Jewish legends or compositions of debated magnitude, but the text is decidedly Christian as it stands; and what it reflects is an acrimonious intra-Christian dispute over prophetic authority and claims to heavenly vision.[18]

The narrative revolves around the opposition of Belchira and his false prophets to claims by Isaiah "and many of the faithful who believed in the ascension to heaven" (*Asc. Is.* 2.7) that Isaiah had actually beheld Christ in heaven. The substance of this claim in fact makes up the second half of the text, in which Isaiah describes the strange process of his ascent through the seven heavens to the throne of Christ, followed by the descent of Christ into the world. And despite rather haphazard editing of the narrative, the whole *Ascension of Isaiah*—from visions to martyrdom to a couple of eschatological discourses (3.13–4.18)—concerns the authority of "Isaiah"'s revelation.

It is not difficult to see the *Ascension of Isaiah* in the same cultural world as the book of Revelation: religion and—perhaps more important for the genesis of texts—religious *disputes* that revolve around the authority of prophets and their extravagant claims of heavenly visitation.[19] The typical dates assigned to the *Ascension of Isaiah* range across the second century, a period when such internecine disputes were preoccupying the diverse Christianities of Asia Minor. Both the Pastoral Epistles (e.g., 2 Tim. 3:1–13) and Ignatius of Antioch (*Letter to the Trallians* 5, *Letter to the Smyrnaeans* 6.1), for example, bear witness to intra-Christian movements in Asia Minor at this time, opposed to the hierarchical organization these authors were promoting, movements apparently based in claims of otherworldly revelations.[20]

This same cultural world offers a coherent context for the two rather breathless prophetic discourses included in the apocryphal corpus known as 2 Esdras (where they frame the important first-century Jewish apocalypse 4 Ezra). *5* and *6 Ezra*, as they are known, clearly imitate the prophetic voice and formulae of biblical prophets like Jeremiah and Isaiah, speaking floridly in the name of the Lord, invoking the same kinds of themes, threatening woes from (and against) neighboring nations, but also contain elements that are clearly Christian: *5 Ezra*, for example, is obviously dependent on the book of Revelation (*5 Ezra* 2:42). The putative author, Ezra the scribe, is cast in *5 Ezra* as a prophet who receives his commission, like Elijah, on Mount Horeb and sows his discourse with references to the divine status and the martyrdoms of the biblical prophets (*5 Ezra* 1:32, 39–40; 2:1, 18). Whereas it would be too much to assume that *5 Ezra* is an unedited transcript of someone's ecstatic utterance, it clearly depends on a milieu in which such traditional prophetic voices had an abiding authority (see Bergren 1990, 26–29, 269–70; Trevett 1996, 24–25).

6 Ezra is hardly different in this respect: another prophetic discourse whose most distinctive aspect is a reference to a coming "tribulation" in which the "elect" will be "forced to eat meat sacrificed to idols" (*6 Ezra* 16:68–74). This detail would certainly correspond to a public method of testing a citizenry's commitment to the imperial Fortune that was common in Asia Minor and Egypt, especially in the third century, and often served to root out those local Christians who would refuse to partake. Yet we should be less inclined to assume a reference to historical edicts or religious purges than to interpret the verse along the lines that scholars view "tribulation" imagery in the book of Revelation: that is, a symbol of the outer world's evil that a prophet projects in order to shore up sectarian boundaries (see Thompson, in Yarbro Collins, 1986, 147–74). The influence of the book of Revelation also explains *6 Ezra*'s brief nod to textuality: "Cause [the words of the prophecy] to be written on paper; they are trustworthy and true," the speaker quotes God as instructing (15:2). Prophetic charisma and prophetic revelation are, to be sure, phenomena that depend on dramatic oral performance. But as in the book of Revelation (22:10, 18–19), the abiding authority of the revelation depends on its broader circulation as some kind of apocalypse. On the whole, texts like *5* and *6 Ezra* and *Ascension of Isaiah,* like Revelation, display a kind of tension between the charisma of oral performance as it might be crudely maintained in the "prophetic transcript" genre, and the charisma of the apocalyptic text under a hero's name, with its pretense of antiquity and its nostalgic retrojection of claims to heavenly wisdom.

The same tension probably affected New Prophecy as well, since its prophets' oracles were collected and transmitted well beyond Asia Minor, and Montanus at least felt constrained to undergird the authority of these oracles with a tract on the ecstatic utterances of the biblical patriarchs and prophets.[21] Asia Minor, then, was an area where people held prophetic performance in high esteem yet sought earnestly—under the loom of Jewish scripture—to maintain prophetic authority in texts.

The last apocalyptic text we will attribute to pre-Constantinian Asia Minor is the *Vision of Dorotheus,* and it stands apart from the others in being self-consciously an apocalypse—actually a dream vision—rather than a prophecy, and in being a work of poetic artistry as well, replete with Homeric allusions.[22] Details in the text offer good reason to identify this Dorotheus as the son of a renowned Smyrnean poet who became a church official in Antioch in the late third century (Hurst et al. 1984, 46, with Eusebius, *Hist. eccl.* 7.32.2–4).

In his vision Dorotheus finds himself in the palace of heaven and is directed by the archangel Gabriel to guard the inner courtroom. But his curiosity about the activities of heavenly "elders" leads him to abandon his post, to be reassigned to the palace gates, and finally to be viciously whipped as punishment at the behest of Christ and Gabriel. Chastened, Dorotheus returns to the gate and, under the tutelage of Gabriel, he becomes a "giant hero," taking the name of the apostle Andrew. At the end he stands again at the inner gate, singing praises to God.

The text seems to reflect a distinctive period and milieu in Asia Minor Christianity: on the one hand, a debt to the tradition of the book of Revelation in its fascination with heavenly "elders" and its final image of a heavenly liturgy;[23] on the other hand, an author able to write in metrical Greek with Homer as a model, clearly enmeshed in imperial palace protocol, who is sufficiently accustomed to real Roman punishment (whether or not for proclaiming Christ) that he can describe flagellation with gory detail. It has been suggested, indeed, that at the time of composition Dorotheus was an upper-class crypto-Christian. In this regard *Dorotheus* seems to represent a literary departure from the other Asia Minor apocalypses, which base themselves in Jewish prophetic literature and on the ideal model of the prophet as mediator between heaven and community.

Carthage and Rome

Dorotheus's self-conscious authorial voice, together with the detailed psychic transformation through which he proceeds in the *Vision* put this text in a literary field with the *Martyrdom of Perpetua* and the *Shepherd of Hermas,* two important apocalyptic works of the western Mediterranean to which we now turn. The very self-consciousness of these texts seems to be distinctive of the early Christian dream account and perhaps may point to a particular social milieu. The dreamers in all three texts came from a fairly elevated class of citizenry and seem to have found their own psychic transformations to be the central experience of otherworldly revelation, unlike other apocalypses we have reviewed whose authors are veiled or even anonymous in order to highlight the power of the revelation itself or of the prophetic role (see Cox Miller, 1995).

The first text, a document of New Prophecy from early-third-century Carthage, contains a series of visions beheld by one Perpetua, an educated young matron, and two of her cell-mates in the days preceding her execution, visions that are all framed according to chronology and emotional context.[24] As an apocalyptic composition—a book proffering heavenly revelations as some saintly figure received them (see Aune, in Yarbro Collins 1986, 74)—

the *Martyrdom of Perpetua* actually rationalizes the authenticity and authority of its contents by arguing, in an introduction, that the same visionary and prophetic powers described in the Bible have been revitalized in figures like Perpetua (*Mart. Perp.* 1.1–5). But the series of visions that Perpetua undergoes while awaiting the arena has its own function independent of the introduction: it serves to clarify the "true," supernatural character of the punishments she would undergo in the arena. The visions also define her martyr's status as a virtual axis for the community between earthly and heavenly worlds. Subsequent visions recorded by her companion Saturus provide the same clarification of the role of martyr, revealing the heavenly community of martyrs so tangible to those awaiting execution.

The *Shepherd of Hermas,* from second-century Rome, also articulates a spiritual process through its progression of dreams and revelations delivered by a female figure distantly based on the ancient Roman Sibyl. In this case, the spiritual process involves the author Hermas's achievement of a saintly moral stance, in harmony with the heavenly world, while still remaining very much in the world.[25] The text takes a precise view on morality, criticizing especially the "double-mindedness" of the bourgeois Christian. Yet it also stands in some opposition to the various apocalyptic currents of the period. Rather than exalting the boundless visionary potential of prophets, Hermas's revealers support hierarchy (*Herm. Vis.* 3.5.1), excoriate false prophets (*Herm. Mand.* 11), and make clear that heavenly wisdom comes from, and should circulate in the medium of, books (*Herm. Vis.* 2.1.4–2.1; 2.3.4; 5.5). Despite Hermas's exemplary commitment to preparatory fasting and praying, all he can get from his revealers are lectures on the evils of double-mindedness (*Herm. Vis.* 3.10.7): eschatology, for example, is simply not to be discussed (*Herm. Vis.* 3.8.9).[26] On the other hand, the revealers refer consistently, if vaguely, to a coming "tribulation" and the privileged status of martyrs (*Herm. Vis.* 3.1.9–2.1) much as will the *Apocalypse of Elijah* a century later. Such tribulation language seems to have become a stock symbol of group boundaries quite early in Christianity, and it was eminently useful for convincing the comfortable to be "single-minded."

The immense popularity of the *Shepherd of Hermas,* as demonstrated by its early and broad circulation (see Tertullian, *De Pudicitia* 10), testifies to the interest among early Christian communities in cultivating some kind of otherworldly connection, some sense of sainthood. The text allows the Christian audience to appreciate the authority and the immediacy of apocalypticism while still not engaging with those prophets and millennialist sects who in many regions defined Christianity through the third century.

MOTIVATIONS FOR THE USE OF APOCALYPSES IN EARLY CHRISTIANITY

The thematic analysis of these texts has been kept rather cursory in order to emphasize their affiliation with regional literary and religious currents. But numerous broader currents have emerged among these texts, not the least of which are the implications of the term "apocalypticism" in selecting particular texts and inferring their religious value. Given that this essay understands the apocalypse in its broad, ancient Mediterranean sense of a "revelatory book" and the pursuit of such otherwordly gnosis as might be contained in such books, what motivated the use of apocalypses and apocalyptic materials in early Christianity?

First of all, apocalyptic literature as we have seen it served *to maintain the literary and legendary authority of traditional heroes* within the new ideological circumstances created with regional Christianities. The texts we have reviewed elevated the names and legends of numerous biblical characters— Adam, Abraham, Levi, Ezra, Isaiah, Elijah—either to demonstrate particular reverence for these figures or to collect unattributed materials under authoritative pseudonyms (as in the case of the *Testament of Adam*). Nonbiblical (including early Christian) figures are also maintained, or even *developed* as authoritative revealers: the apostles Peter, Paul, and John, as well as figures of broader Mediterranean appeal like Allogenes.

Here also the expanding authority of the Roman Sibyl as an apocalyptic seer provides an important illustration of the cultivation of legendary heroes. Notwithstanding the Syrian or Egyptian affiliation of individual books or sections, the *Sibylline Oracle* collection in its final, late antique redaction, has little identifiable provenance and so resists the regional interconnections we found for other texts. And yet, as a continuous literary project of over five hundred years that became thoroughly christianized, the twelve books[27] of the *Sibylline Oracles* testify to the abiding authority of the Sibyl as a revealer of divinely ordained events. Not only did the actual editors of the Christian *Sibyllines* hold her in eminent esteem, but so also did many prominent church fathers, and Jews before them.[28] Even in the second century C.E. the Sibyl provides the principal model for the female revealer in the *Shepherd of Hermas*—a "paganism" so blatant as to have required denial in the text (*Herm. Vis.* 2.4.1). In other texts the Sibyl's revelatory authority is bolstered—legitimized— through assertions of her kinship with Enoch or Noah.[29]

Second, apocalypses and apocalyptic forms allowed early Christians a basis for the *invention of new, personalized compositions* during the second and third centuries. The *Book of Elchasai,* Mani's autobiography, the *Shepherd of Hermas,* the *Martyrdom of Perpetua,* and the *Vision of Dorotheus* all represent, as texts, explicit hybrids of the apocalypse. We may well attribute this hybridizing to the reification of the apocalypse as a literary genre in the second and subsequent centuries, for now people of an esoteric religious bent knew the genre as a major vehicle of otherworldly wisdom (see Adler, in VanderKam and Adler 1996, 8–13).

Finally, and perhaps most importantly for the history of religions, apocalyptic literature in early Christianity served to *relate religious situations in this world to paradigms in the other world.*[30] The *Apocalypse of Peter* galvanizes sectarian boundaries against the outside world by fantasizing various punishments to be wreaked upon outsiders by an esoteric set of vengeance angels. The *Apocalypse of Elijah* casts an internecine dispute about fasting as a divinely ordained sign of the end, and it outlines criteria of true martyrdom according to the ideal, heavenly models of Elijah, Enoch, and Tabitha, returning martyr heroes of the end-times.[31] In the *Martyrdom of Perpetua,* Perpetua and Saturus find themselves shuttling actively between the supernatural and the Roman world as their martyrdom nears, and their visions "prove" their intermediary powers. The *Ascension of Isaiah* articulates current tensions among prophetic groups through a retelling of the Isaiah legend, suggesting that the stories of such heroes represented for some communities the ideal and, indeed, *only* relevant arena for articulating the situations in this world. Christian apocalypses of the fourth and later centuries (e.g., *Apocalypse of Paul, Testament of Isaac*) show the use of the apocalypse and the vision to warrant current practice and desirable institutions according to heavenly paradigms.[32]

In these cases the community situation clearly motivates the appeal to otherworldly paradigms and apocalypse in general. However, this is not to say that history itself governs apocalyptic composition but rather social dynamics. The difference is important to note, since it is often assumed that apocalyptic writers typically located their own period by writing recent history as prediction, then tacking on, in the same mode, what they expected would happen next. This compositional style of *vaticinia ex eventu,* so popular in Daniel, the *Sibylline Oracles,* and some Byzantine apocalypses, is often assumed to operate throughout apocalyptic literature. But for the early Christian apocalypses nothing could be further from the truth. The tableaux of woes and eschatological scenarios that appear in the *Apocalypses of Peter* and *of Elijah* and in 5 and 6 *Ezra* were assembled to give a general sense of global insecurity and breakdown, not to refer systematically to historical events. Early Christian apocalypticism is characterized by what Bernard McGinn has called "a priori" apocalyptic symbolism, an amassing of motifs, numerological schemes, oracular formulae, and sign lists that might be applied to current events (as, for example, in the book of Revelation) but is not generated by them. It is an enclosed symbolic world, and to some extent it implies a sectarian context seeking to maintain conviction in its own authority against the confusion of real historical events (see McGinn 1979, 33–36; Frankfurter 1993, chapter 8).

EARLY CHRISTIAN APOCALYPTICISM AS A RELIGIOUS PHENOMENON

Having assessed the earliest Christian apocalyptic texts in terms of their regional affiliations, stressing their links with other texts, with native traditions, and with regional religious tendencies, we can now move to a broad, pan-Mediterranean vantage, asking whether any general tendencies appear across the regional variations. What are the distinctive religious or ideological elements in early Christian apocalypticism?

Millennialism

First, there is a tendency among several of these texts to reflect actual millennialist sectarianism as social scientists have described the phenomenon: the group endeavor of preparing for an imminent eschaton and new world that would appear miraculously on earth, wiping away everything that stood before. Scholars of early Judaism and, indeed, of medieval Christianity have grown appropriately accustomed to distinguishing apocalyptic composition, which was often the endeavor of one or a few scribes with no broad popular charisma, from apocalyptic sectarianism as a social movement anticipating an imminent eschaton, a phenomenon with broad cross-cultural parallels (see McGinn 1979, 29–32).

But many texts of the early Christian period reflect just this kind of social movement. One can see it in the prophet-centered Christianity of Asia Minor and in the overwhelming group boundaries and eschatological imminence promoted in Egypt's *Apocalypse of Peter* and *Apocalypse of Elijah,* with the convenient evidence for a real millennialist movement in mid-third-century Egypt.[33] But one cannot find this millennialist background behind all Christian apocalypses: *Hermas,* the *Testaments of the Twelve Patriarchs,* and the Syrian texts show little eschatological anticipation even while including some eschatology and promoting a distinct "insiderness."

Prophetic Authority

A religious phenomenon much more broadly represented among these texts is prophetic authority and crises over its legitimacy. In a number of texts reviewed here an urgent orality dominates the composition to the exclusion (or diminishment) of any frame narrative (which might situate that voice for literary audiences): the *Apocalypse of Elijah,* 5 and 6 *Ezra,* and the book of Revelation. It is an orality, moreover, dedicated to parenesis, polemic, and eschatological prediction; and it quite likely reflects a social context of prophets, their audiences, and the secretaries that put their speech into broader circulation. Most important, one finds this "prophetic mode" inevitably coupled with references to ideal or rival prophets in the text (see Frankfurter 1993, 75–96; and, more generally on the prophetic mode of Christian apocalypses, Aune, in Yarbro Collins 1986, 65–96).

From Revelation onwards, almost all of the Asia Minor apocalyptic texts thus reflect the importance of prophetic leadership, almost to the exclusion of the kind of hierarchy promoted in the Pastoral Epistles and Ignatius's letters. Even beyond Asia Minor, Origen's opponent Celsus lampoons Christian prophets in Palestine and Phoenicia (Origen, *Contra Celsum* 7.9); and the *Apocalypse of Elijah* manifestly stems from a prophet figure probably much like the ecstatic Egyptian Christians whom Eusebius describes on trial in the late third century (*Martyrs of Palestine* 11.8; 13.7–8).

But true to sociological principles, many of these texts display the social chaos and internecine antagonism that inevitably arise in situations of charismatic leadership and minimal social organization—when inspired utterances conflict, authority and legitimacy are in doubt, and charges of "false prophecy" begin to fly about (see Tertullian, *De Pud.* 21, for an example of this situation). Indeed, the prominence of the figure Belchira in the *Ascension of Isaiah* (chapter 5) is good evidence that the whole notion of an eschatological adversary—an Antichrist figure, such as emerges so prominently in 2 Thessalonians (2:3–12), Revelation (chapter 13), and the *Apocalypse of Peter* (chapter 2) and the *Apocalypse of Elijah* (chapters 3–5)—received its most vivid definition and development among sects in which charismatic leadership prevailed and the identification of true *and false* authority was an abiding concern (Frankfurter 1993, chapter 5).

Of course, prophets and the mysteries of their authority were also a problem for people in more hierarchical Christian associations: both the *Shepherd of Hermas* (*Herm. Mand.* 11) and the second-century church manual the *Didache* (chapter 11) try to formulate systems for testing prophets' legitimacy—a perpetually fruitless task, since prophets will rarely conform to rules as subjective as these texts propose.[34]

Prophetic charisma gave early Christian groups both the ability to maintain strong sectarian boundaries and an inherent instability, a leadership crisis that was understood symbolically through the terror of deception and apostasy—an "inner evil." But this sense of "inner evil" tends in many sects to be projected onto the outside world: deception, harm, and woes derive from the outside world, requiring ever higher walls to protect the inside. Such boundaries are all the sect has to secure its being in situations of uncertainty. Thus, the leadership instability in prophet-led movements must also explain the common focus in Christian apocalypticism on "tribulation"—persecution, martyrdom. Indeed, this explanation of tribulation imagery should work even when Christians actually experienced forms of persecution through coming into conflict with Roman ritual edicts.

Tribulation and Martyrdom as Focal Concerns

We can no longer attribute the consistent references to martyrdom in early Christian apocalyptic literature to historical religious persecution. First of all, historians today admit the sporadic, unsystematic, and incomplete nature of edict enforcement in the Roman world (see Lane Fox 1987, chapter 9, especially 434–59). Second, extending from the time of the Gospels (Mark 13; Matthew 27) and the book of Revelation, there is abundant evidence that the fascination with martyrdom and the need to imagine persecution were characteristics of many Christian movements. Ignatius, Cyprian, and Tertullian in the first person and Eusebius in the third reveal both a veritable thirst for public death and a popular Christian view that would-be martyrs already had one foot in the heavenly world—and in that status might intercede for others. And apocalyptic literature, as Donald Riddle once observed, provided a principal instrument of martyrological propaganda.[35]

In the *Martyrdom of Perpetua* apocalyptic clairvoyance is one of the chief powers and social roles of would-be martyrs in their liminal status. (Tertullian himself asserts as much in *De anima* 55.4–5.) In the *Apocalypse of Peter* (2.2) and the *Apocalypse of Elijah* (chaps. 3–4) the martyrdom of the righteous is a necessary, almost glorious sign of the imminent end, and the "saints" of the present are compared to paradigmatic martyrs from the supernatural world: Enoch, Elijah, Tabitha. The *Apocalypse of Elijah* goes even further, distinguishing real martyrs from refugee hermits and describing the magical powers of martyrs' bodies (Frankfurter 1993, chapter 6).

The idea that martyrs are the most blessed of Christians and that apocalyptic clairvoyance is their reward continues, at least in Egypt, into the exaltation and lore of certain monks: their ascetic virtue is rewarded with visions of and even ascents to the other world, and occasionally revelations of the endtimes (see Frankfurter, in VanderKam and Adler 1996, 174–85). Some apocalypses—and the New Prophecy movement itself—paved the way for this continuity by prescribing ascetic practices like fasting and celibacy as means of purification toward heavenly status or visionary states. Thus, already by the fourth century an athletic self-denial might gain one the reputation of clairvoyance and heavenly congress as well.[36]

The Cult of the Biblical Saint

The promotion of Enoch and Elijah as eschatological paradigms in the *Apocalypse of Peter* and the *Apocalypse of Elijah* points to a theme of particular significance for the Christianities that spawned these apocalypses. As noted earlier, biblical heroes constitute the focal religious models in most of these texts. In the *Testaments of the Twelve Patriarchs,* Levi and Judah provide the keys for understanding Christ: Christ is simply the fulfillment of their lines. In the *Apocalypse of Peter,* the *Apocalypse of Elijah, 5 Ezra,* and the *Ascension of Isaiah,* the biblical prophets, along with Enoch and Moses, are in various ways types or ideals for the blessedness and fate of the community: standing in heaven, returning to destroy or die at the hands of the eschatological adversary, or, in the *Apocalypse of Paul* (and Coptic monastic literature more broadly), epitomizing pious self-abnegation and asceticism (*Apoc. Paul* 25). Even beyond the explicit invocations of biblical heroes we can detect various kinds of interest in Melchizedek the priest and Enoch the scribe as apocalyptic culture heroes, models of heavenly status and gnosis (see Frankfurter, in VanderKam and Adler 1996, 181–85, 187–89). Indeed, for a literary environment that raised the heroics of the biblical saint far above the nuances of Christology, we must be extraordinarily careful about speaking of "Christian" in any monolithic, clearly distinct sense. The "cult" of the biblical saint as it continued in Christian apocalyptic texts suggests that we should speak less of "Jewish materials taken over by Christians" than of continuously "evolving literature," the work of what we might call "continuous apocalyptic communities."[37]

Such communities, it is apparent, came to appropriate various Christian notions as plausible extensions of what they had already been thinking and writing about within Judaism—or native scribal tradition. Their reverence for biblical heroes could obviously work in several directions: for promoting martyrdom and asceticism, as we have seen, but also as a subject of ongoing scribal work. In the progressive compiling of the *Testaments of the Twelve Patriarchs,* the invention of a *Testament of Adam,* the notion of an Egyptian Christian prophecy of Elijah, the assembling of *Lives of the Prophets,* we find scribes actively filling in the legends, fleshing out the wisdom, reimagining the characters of these biblical heroes through the composition of new discourses, new revelations, new images of their perpetual mediation. (On the *Lives of the Prophets,* see Satran 1995.)

Christian Apocalypticism as a Scribal Project

There appears alongside of, and often overlapping with, the millennialist sectarianism and prophetism of some early Christian apocalypses a subculture of scribal conventicles. For these groups the very process of apocalyptic composition was an act of pious involvement with the other world. Textuality itself gave substance and verification to apocalyptic authority—of a legendary seer, of his prophecy or teachings, of subsequent revelations under his or her name.

This scribal apocalypticism appears increasingly during the third and fourth centuries. Porphyry refers to "apocalypses of Zoroaster and Zostrianos . . . and other people of that kind" produced by "sectarians" (*Life of Plotinus* 16); the Nag Hammadi Library uses "apocalypse" as a genre label; the millennialist movement in third-century Egypt is supported by an apologetic tract written by the local bishop (Dionysius of Alexandria *apud* Eusebius, *Hist. eccl.* 7.24, on which see Frankfurter 1993, 274–78); and fourth-century Melitian Christians in Egypt held up as authoritative various Enoch, Moses, and Isaiah pseudepigrapha (Athanasius, *Festal Letters* 39 [367], with Frankfurter, in VanderKam and Adler 1996, 170–74). We see elements of this extensive scribal culture in the obvious intertextuality among early Christian books: the *Apocalypse of Peter* adhered closely to the eschatological discourse of the Gospel of Matthew (chapter 27, with Bauckham 1994, 20–24); the *Pistis Sophia* (3.34) cites the *Books of Jeu,* and the *Apocryphon of John* cites a "Book of Zoroaster" (*Ap. John,* NHC II, 1, p. 19). Such book citations might be invented too, reflecting a romantic lore of "ultimate" apocalypses: Mani cites alleged apocalypses of Seth and Enoch to support his own textual authority (*Cologne Mani Codex* 48–60, with Frankfurter 1997), and the *Testaments of the Twelve Patriarchs* appeal to books of Enoch as a supreme heavenly authority in book form. Even in its most "prophetic" incarnations apocalypticism had always been a book culture of sorts: Montanus wrote tracts to ground New Prophecy in scripture (Trevett 1996, 80–86, 129–35);

the author of the *Ascension of Isaiah* describes books "not like the books of this world" up in the seventh heaven (*Asc. Is.* 9.22).

Many apocalyptic texts of Egypt and Syro-Palestine, like the *Testament of Adam* and the *Apocalypse of Elijah,* bear witness to a great circulation of fragments—oracles, lists, timetables, physiognomies—out of which scribes compiled ever-new apocalyptic texts. Sometimes they merely labeled a fragment with a pseudonymous attribution or frame, or they might collect a series of oracles and apocalypses of different ages under a single attribution, as in the corpus known as 2 Esdras. These trends bespeak established and dynamic—and probably quite diverse—scribal cultures, begun well before the consolidation of monasteries. Where once this scribal culture might have supported prophets and their authority (one thinks of Baruch, the secretary to Jeremiah, in Jeremiah 36), ultimately it provided the means for enshrining that authority—or redefining it for new times or circumstances, or even reining it in as of a bygone age.

The *Sibylline Oracles* certainly represent the ongoing endeavor of scribes, or even solitary intellectuals, committed to updating and exploiting the authority of the ancient seer, an endeavor that continued at least through the *Oracles'* codification in the fifth century as Christian propaganda. In this endeavor they followed a much more ancient tradition of promoting the authority of a local or regional Sibyl. As the Sibyl became Jewish in the *Third Sibylline Oracle* (thus demonstrating that local character could extend to ethnic or ideological character), so she became Christian and eschatologically oriented in the first, second, and sixth through eighth *Sibylline Oracles* in the third or fourth century. (On the historical and social world of the later Sibylline compilers, see Potter 1990, 95–140.)

Continuation of Native Scribal Traditions

The literary affiliation between texts like the *Apocalypse of Elijah,* the *Testament of Abraham,* and some of the *Sibylline Oracles,* and Egyptian temple materials has often been noticed. Many of the details and themes in these texts have immediate prototypes in Egyptian priestly literature. Viewed historically and alongside native Egyptian texts of the same period, these details show that Christian apocalyptic texts, even sectarian or pseudo-biblical texts, provided the vehicles for the perpetuation of native idioms and ideology. Whatever the affiliation of the immediate editors of these apocalyptic texts, this legacy of Egyptian priestly literature signals that the literary media of apocalypticism—whether Christian prophecy, Gnostic ascent, or Sibylline authority—served the rearticulation, even the reassertion, of native Egyptian religious materials. It is precisely this kind of apocalyptic scribalism continuous with the culture of native temple scribes that would have been responsible for those oft-recognized syncretisms in Egyptian Christian apocalypses—judgment themes, ascent imagery, demonology, signs of woe, some of which have almost verbatim parallels in Egyptian texts.[38]

Indeed, it is the scribal culture of apocalypticism, more than any other aspect, that implies a relationship between christianized and "prior" religious communities—Jewish, native priestly, or something else. Many of the regional Christian apocalypticisms we have examined show clear, or at least compelling, evidence of prior communities, working on the same materials, promoting the same biblical figures, seeking the same otherworldly gnosis, perhaps even organized in similar fashion, and yet not including Christ in their speculations.

The novelty of christianization in the history of these continuous communities was therefore twofold. Obviously it involved the assimilation of Christian ideas like the return of Christ into already established apocalyptic literary traditions. But Christianity's most vivid development in apocalyptic materials had less to do with changing the genre than with requiring those literary traditions to be *the means of* negotiating those particular problems endemic to the early stages of the movement: religious authority, especially that of prophets, and the definition of group boundaries. Functionally, this use of the apocalypse is not unique across religions, but what has been preserved in Christian apocalyptic writings is the various particular situations of early Christianity.

The Nature of Eschatology in Early Christian Apocalypses

A distinctive aspect of early Jewish apocalypses—Daniel, the Book of the Watchers (*1 Enoch* 1–36), 4 Ezra, among others—was their promotion of eschatology as the very culmination of a secret divine plan for the world. Integral to that "ulterior" order to which apocalyptic literature (as an heir to the wisdom tradition) always beckoned its reader was, in these texts, the certainty of catastrophes, of fiery cleansing, and of a new cosmos. Thus, in John Collins's programmatic definition of an apocalyptic "genre," apocalypses had both a "spatial axis"—details of a supernatural world to which an elect (or the elect) might travel and gain heavenly wisdom—and a "temporal axis": a teleological scheme of history whose violent and then glorious end would resolve all the traumas of the present (Collins, in Collins 1979, 9–12; cf. Vielhauer, in Schneemelcher 1991–92, 2:547–55).

To be sure, this conceptualization of history as having an "inner teleology"—a time divinely ordained for misfortunes and evils to occur before a pre-set time of purification—depended on Zoroastrian traditions, in which present times represented a "mixture" of Ahura Mazda and the demonic Angra Mainyu before Mazda and his hosts purged Angra Mainyu utterly from the universe. But by the Roman period the Zoroastrian scheme (and other Mediterranean eschatological ideas) had become thoroughly domesticated into the cosmology of Jewish apocalypticism. By the beginning of the Roman period the most influential Jewish apocalypses (Daniel, the Enoch corpus, 4 Ezra) were pointing readers toward similar schemes of present confusion and eschatological purge, hidden inside scripture and behind the signs of the present time, as the principal topic of otherworldly knowledge.

But the early Christian apocalypses surveyed here arose out of many more contemporaneous cultural influences than this synthetic Jewish apocalypticism with its eschatological focus; and consequently we must approach their genre according to looser categories and much more diverse cultural milieux. Christian texts patch together, often with little concern for a precise determinism, the motifs and traditions of regional scribal cultures, on the one hand, and a veritable marketplace of oracles, portentous images, and lores of books and prophets circulating around the Roman world, on the other. Thus, while some texts adhere closely to Jewish apocalyptic formulae and models (Revelation, *Ascension of Isaiah, Apocalypse of Paul, Apocryphon of John*), others consist largely of eschatological tableaux woven from this Mediterranean oracular culture (*5 and 6 Ezra, Apocalypse of Elijah,* the *Sibylline Oracles*), and still others combine a strong generic dependence on Jewish apocalyptic tradition with a lively eclecticism in what they reveal (*Testament of Adam, Vision of Dorotheus, Martyrdom of Perpetua,* revelations of Mani).

Of those texts that depend quite vividly on the Jewish apocalyptic literary tradition and its implications for a determined historical plan, the Asia Minor materials, the *Shepherd of Hermas,* the *Martyrdom of Perpetua,* and the revelations of Mani all exploit that tradition quite explicitly for the immediacies of prophetic charisma, sectarian self-definition, martyrology, and the definition of religious morality for particular communities. Thus, eschatology and its imminent expectation, when they appear as concerns, are *subordinated to* immediate social realities; they are not the texts' organizing problem. The "spatial axis"—the exploration of a supernatural world—remains distinctive of the genre as these authors exploited it, the "temporal axis" subsidiary.

There are a number of early Christian apocalypses, to be sure, that focus quite anxiously on eschatological scenarios (of quite diverse character), and we will examine the nature of these scenarios below. However, for the greater portion of the texts under discussion eschatological interests of the sort thought typical of "apocalypticism" are rather incidental to the authors' or editors' broader commitments to unveiling heavenly secrets: the *Ascension of Isaiah,* Mani's autobiography, the *Vision of Dorotheus,* the *Testament of Adam,* the *Shepherd of Hermas,* the utterances of the New Prophets, the *Martyrdom of Perpetua,* the Gnostic apocalypses, the *Epistula Apostolorum,* the *Apocalypse of Paul,* and the *Testament of Abraham.* It is quite evident that any broad "apocalypticism" that we might care to posit was, in its early Christian form, consistently assimilated to the kinds of immediate circumstances that only rarely required *eschatological* resolution or a historical self-definition that transcended the immediate orbit of the charismatic martyr or prophet. It was more important to define oneself as the "Elect" of this world than to project oneself desperately into the end-times. Eschatology in these latter apocalypses simply paled in relevance compared to the miracle of present gifts (see Himmelfarb, in Yarbro Collins 1986, 97–111; and Trevett 1996, 95–105 on New Prophecy).

For those authors who did underline the imminence of the end as a central otherworldly revelation (Revelation, *Apocalypse of Peter, Apocalypse of Elijah, 6 Ezra,* and perhaps the *Book of Elchasai* [frags. 7, 9]) the immediate concerns were not "present gifts" but rather internecine crises, projected into cosmic scope and vindicated through the eschatological scenario. In these eschatologically oriented texts, as we have already seen, the chief evidence that *present* traumas have led the authors to emphasize the end-times consists in the details of false leadership and persecution: the eschatological adversary, whether as Beliar, Antichrist, or Lawless One, becomes almost immediately a staple of the Christian eschatological scenario (see Frankfurter 1993, chapter 5). The *Apocalypse of Elijah* illustrates how fast-approaching schedules for cosmic destruction might be spun directly out of some immediate social trauma: apostasy, criticism or rejection from without, a blowup over meal purity, a leader's authority, or the definition of a "saint." On the other hand, the *Ascension of Isaiah* has no such schedules or scenarios despite its origin in a conflict situation. Eschatology thus functions as *one* means of social expression, related to but independent of that other symbol of the "insider," the apocalypse itself: the recorded wisdom of the other world, preserved in text for self-proclaimed *cognoscenti.*

What was the method in assembling eschatological tableaux? In most cases it conformed to older literary traditions. Tracts of the "timetable" format, best exemplified in the *Apocalypse of Thomas* (an early Christian text of indeterminable date that became popular in Ireland) and some sections of the book of Revelation, are spun out of the enumeration itself (e.g., *Apocalypse of*

Thomas's seven "days" of world decline). Now linked numerologically to creation, cardinal points, the structure of heaven, or any number of inner equivalences, the timetable conveys a profound sense of design behind the world's chaotic stage.

The *Sibylline Oracles* provide perhaps the most concentrated source of those catastrophic oracles of eschaton and judgment (and their ultimate resolution under Christ) normally associated with "apocalypticism":

> But whenever this sign appears throughout the world, / children born with gray temples from birth, / afflictions of men, famines, pestilence, and wars, / change of times, lamentations, many tears; / alas, how many people's children in the countries will feed / on their parents, with piteous lamentations. . . . / The gathering together is near when some deceivers, / instead of prophets, approach, speaking on earth. / Beliar also will come and will do many signs /. . . / And then a great river of blazing fire / will flow from heaven, and will consume every place, / . . . But the heavenly luminaries / will crash together, also into an utterly desolate form. / For all the stars will fall together from heaven on the sea. / All the souls of men will gnash their teeth, / burning in a river and brimstone and a rush of fire / in a fiery plain, and ashes will cover all. / And then all the elements of the world will be bereft— / air, land, sea, light, vault of heaven, days, nights. / . . . / When Sabaoth Adonai, who thunders on high, dissolves fate / and raises the dead, and takes his seat / on a heavenly throne, and establishes a great pillar, / Christ, imperishable himself, will come in glory on a cloud / toward the imperishable one with the blameless angels. / He will sit on the right of the Great One, judging at the tribunal / the life of pious men and the way of impious men. (*Sib. Or.* 2.154–59, 165–67, 196–97, 200–207, 238–44; trans. Collins, in Charlesworth, 1983–85, 1:349–51)

Is it urgency, mystery, or a sense of revealed conviction that impels such a concatenation of omens? In fact, this kind of tableau of signs and cataclysm is really quite generic to the Sibylline tradition, not a timetable or a call to action, and certainly not in any way distinctive of Christian apocalyptic concerns. The *Sibylline Oracles* had always, by the genre's very nature, stressed cosmic portents and woes and alerted readers to some greater religious way, by adherence to which the world might forestall misfortune (see Potter 1990, 109–14). Christian editors added little to the genre in orienting these signs toward the second coming or in including angels, Beliar, and a more distinct notion of those to perish, or in promoting Christ as the greatest Mediterranean god.

Individually, the omens and the layout of history's end in the *Sibylline Oracles*—what we might call the "eschatological components"—belong (along with those in the *Apocalypse of Elijah, 5* and *6 Ezra,* and Manichean apocalyptic materials) to that common Mediterranean store of oracular motifs and schemes mentioned above. By the third century of the Common Era the catalogue of possible eschatological scenes combined not only Jewish but also Egyptian, Babylonian, Zoroastrian, and Greek imagery (see, e.g., Koenen 1986, regarding Manichean ideology). Themes of cosmic portent—astronomical irregularities, geological disasters like famine or flood, conflagration—and of social reversal—the inversion of ethical norms, infertility and violence, disrespect toward religion, the disorder or malevolence of kings—provided stock (if frightening to our eyes) images of increasing chaos that had been preserved for centuries in various cultural traditions. In Egypt, for example, an archaic priestly literature that defined the ordering power of the kingship against the contrast of a land in disorder came to be applied generally to the present state of things—including present kings—in anticipation of an ideal king to come. The *Apocalypse of Elijah* draws explicitly on this royal scheme of disorder and order to define in Egyptian terms the powers of an imminently returning Christ (see Frankfurter 1993, chapters 7–8). The stock images of political and social chaos therefore contribute to a drawn-out *antithesis* to Christ's imminent cosmic order, rendered the more vivid for the third-century Egyptian through references to persecution, deceptive rumors, and a suffering Elect.

Long dedicated to the articulation of Roman policy, the *Sibylline Oracles* highlighted the chaotic shifts of political powers much like the *Apocalypse of Elijah*. And in a world of insecure political boundaries and shifting military fronts it is not surprising to find the movements of armies and rulers across borders as dominant motifs in Christian eschatological tableaux (*6 Ezra* 15:28–45; *Apoc. Elijah* 2.39–48; *Sib. Or.* 5; 7–8; 13). The intensity of a portent or sign had always grown in cosmic scope according to the size of the experienced world; and by Roman times the notion of disaster and eschatological chaos had to transcend all borders, be visible or audible across seas, crush vast populations. Even "when the Christ comes," assures the *Apocalypse of Elijah*, "the *whole world* will see him like the sun that shines from the east to the west" (*Apoc. Elijah* 3.2–3).

What subsequently happened to eschatology within Christian apocalyptic literature reflects very much the kinds of steadying, even anti-millennialist ideas that informed the canonical Gospels Luke and Matthew and patristic writers. Eschatological scenarios perhaps once composed in anticipation of imminent action became pro forma dressing for apocalyptic texts that espoused quite this-worldly doctrines: the *Epistula Apostolorum*'s litany of signs (chapters 34–38) stands far off from the text's present life and agenda, and the incorporation of the *Apocalypse of Elijah* into subsequent eschatological discourses in the Byzantine age suggests that once-imminent woes had become but well-turned vignettes of distant catastrophe (see Frankfurter 1993, 24–26, 224–26). Bishop Dionysius of Alexandria rescued the book of Revelation for the Christian canon in the same way in the 260s, recasting John's anxious visions as only abstruse symbols (*apud* Eusebius *Hist. eccl.* 7.24.4–5).

One important facet of this transformation of eschatology would have been the recasting of last *cosmic* things, especially, the judgment, into last *individual* things: the notion of a perpetual judgment of souls. Egypt provides a microcosm of this transformation, most vividly in the fourth-century *Apocalypse of Paul*'s use of the *Apocalypse of Peter*: the latter's visions of a last judgment reemerge altered and expanded in the *Apocalypse of Paul* as an ongoing judgment (see pp. 422–24 above). Yet what might appear a deliberate decision by anti–millennialist Christians (Tertullian, for example, himself stresses such a personalized judgment in *De resurrectione mortuorum* 35 and *De anima* 55–58) may have depended in Egypt, at least, on the continuing influence of native traditions. The somewhat earlier (and possibly *Jewish* Egyptian) texts *Testament of Abraham* and the *Apocalypse of Zephaniah* both demonstrate a profound interest in an ongoing judgment of souls and yet no interest in a last judgment. Gnostic ascent texts, attentive to the Gnostic soul's ability to penetrate the demonic guardians of the lower heavens, also reveal ongoing punishments (for those sinful and "unsealed" who seek to pass the guardians) to the neglect of a final judgment (*Apoc. Paul* [NHC 5, 2] 20–22; cf. *2 Jeu* 49 and Athanasius *Life of Anthony* 65). These visions owe at least as much to Egyptian mortuary traditions (some of which described the unpleasant fate of people not privileged to accompany the sun god on his underworld circuit) as they do to Jewish tradition (in which "ongoing" judgment also had greater antiquity than final judgment: see *1 Enoch* 21–23).

If Egypt is an indication of, or even an influence on, a broader Christian transformation of eschatology, we should conclude that an older tradition of ongoing judgment simply superseded another, more recent tradition of final judgment, assimilating some lurid "final" punishments in the process. In the *Apocalypse of Elijah*, for example, we find both traditions simultaneously and separately (*Apoc. Elijah* 1.8–12; 5.24–31). But all these kinds of eschatological details in Christian apocalypses depended on the availability to their authors of lists and prior oracles as much as on the authors' expectations of catastrophe, and on a sectarian feeling of unease and anxiety in *this world* as much as on a confidence in imminent vindication from the next.

Christian apocalypses were, fundamentally, literature with religious environments, dependent on notions of book, the lineage of a book, and what might be conveyed through a book. So ultimately we are left with the books themselves and with the question why certain people sought to write in such a manner, to articulate the present condition in terms of heavenly secrets disclosed, to endow a book or tract with such otherworldly authority. Christian apocalypticism, which continued regardless of eschatology's vicissitudes, consisted then in a more fundamental search for heavenly gnosis—whether in a scribal book culture and its lore or in the charismatic clairvoyance of living prophets, martyrs, and eventually desert hermits (see Frankfurter, in VanderKam and Adler 1996, 174–200).

NOTES

1. Wisdom of Solomon: especially 4:20–5:1 (afterlife speculation); 7:17–21 (list of esoteric lore); 9 (reception of divine Wisdom); *Epistle of Barnabas* 2.3–4; 5.4; 18.1; 19.1. On *2 Enoch,* see Andersen, in Charlesworth 1983–85, 1:91–221. On Jewish apocalypticism and Gnosticism in Egypt, see Pearson 1990, 10–28; and Frankfurter, in VanderKam and Adler 1996, 143–62.

2. See Gaylord, in Charlesworth 1983–85, 1:653–79, with Harlow 1996. Note also cautions in Schürer 1973–87, 3.2:791 on establishing *3 Baruch*'s provenance.

3. The *Apocalypse of Peter* has often been taken as propaganda against Bar Kokhba (Bauckham 1994), but chapter 11 is one convincing reason to take it as Egyptian (see Müller, in Schneemelcher 1991–92, 2:622; and Yarbro Collins, in Collins 1979, 72). In the fifth century, Sozomen reports that the text was being read aloud in some churches of Palestine (*Hist. Eccl.* 7.19).

4. Trans. in Duensing and de Santos Otero, in Schneemelcher 1991–92, 2:712–48. The date has often been retrojected to the mid-third century (see Yarbro Collins, in Collins 1979, 85–86), but the text's frame story and internal correspondences to fourth-century monasticism point to the fourth century (Piovanelli 1993).

5. Trans. Müller, in Schneemelcher 1991–92, 1:249–84, with important analysis in Hills 1990.

6. Trans. Kuhn, in Sparks 1984, 393–463, with important analyses in Nickelsburg 1972.

7. See Nickelsburg, in Nickelsburg 1972, 29–40. Francis Schmidt argues that only Recension A bears the imprint of Egyptian mythology (in Nickelsburg 1972, 78–79), and here it is indeed quite vivid: see chapters 12–13, 19–20. But the tradition of Enoch the scribe in Recension B, chapter 11, suggests distinctive Coptic influence (or at least "fit") (see Pearson, in Nickelsburg 1972, 243–48; and Frankfurter, in VanderKam and Adler 1996, 186–88, 194–95).

8. See Stinespring, in Charlesworth 1983–85, 1:903–18, with MacRae, in Nickelsburg 1972, 327–40; and Frankfurter, in VanderKam and Adler 1996, 187.

9. See especially *T. Levi* 8.14; 17; *T. Judah* 21–22; *T. Iss.* 5.7; *T. Dan.* 5.4–13; *T. Gad* 8.1, with analysis by Hollander and de Jonge 1985, 154, 174, and more generally 59–61, 76–79. De Jonge has elsewhere discussed the kinds of Christians probably involved in the compiling of the *Testaments of the Twelve Patriarchs* (1991, 255–62).

10. On the *Lives of the Prophets,* see Hare, in Charlesworth 1983–85, 2:379–99, especially 381, *pace* Satran (1995, 110–17), who rejects the references to tombs in this Byzantine text as reflecting an actual cultic geography.

11. *T. Sim.* 5.4; *T. Levi* 10.5; 14.1; 16.1; *T. Jud.* 18.1; *T. Zeb.* 3.4; *T. Dan* 5.6; *T. Napht.* 4.1; *T. Ben.* 9.1; see Hollander and de Jonge 1985, 39–40.

12. Trans. Robinson, in Charlesworth 1983–85, 1:989–95.

13. Compare, for example, the use of such liturgical descriptions in the Qumran *Shirot ha-shabbat* (11QShirShabb) (*Songs of the Sabbath Sacrifice*). A similar use of heavenly lists for explicitly liturgical imitation appears in the *Gospel of the Egyptians* (NHC IV, 2).

14. See Irmscher, in Schneemelcher 1991–92, 2:685–90; Yarbro Collins, in Collins 1979, 75–76; Luttikhuizen 1985.

15. As recorded in the *Cologne Mani Codex,* "On the Origin of His Body" (ed. Koenen and Römer 1988). *Cologne Mani Codex* pp. 2–99 can be found in English translation by Cameron and Dewey 1979.

16. See Adler, in VanderKam and Adler 1996, 11–12; Frankfurter 1997.

17. Sources conveniently collected in Heine 1989, with important analyses by Lane Fox (1987, 404–18); and Trevett 1996. On heavenly ascents in New Prophecy, see the anonymous historian quoted in Eusebius, *Hist. eccl.* 5.16.14; Tertullian, *De anima* 9.4.

18. On Jewish sources, see Knibb, in Charlesworth 1983–85, 2:143–55, especially 146–48 on Jewish characteristics of the martyrdom story (*Asc. Is.* 1–5). On the historical and social background, see Hall 1990; and Norelli 1993. Norelli argues convincingly that there were two different texts used in the composition of the final *Ascension of Isaiah,* but that both would have been Christian in inception (1993, 43–48, 73–78).

19. Revelation 1–3 and 22:6–19 generally defend the authority of the speaker's revelations. On *Ascension of Isaiah*'s prophetic milieu, see Hall 1990; Norelli 1993, 66–78, 87–99.

Note that Hall (1990, 306) and Norelli (1993, 95–99), while admitting parallels with situations behind Revelation and Ignatius, both place the book in Syria. Ignatius of Antioch's letters to Asia Minor cities are only one of several reasons not to separate the religious cultures of Asia Minor and Syria too strictly: Christological terms and symbols obviously flow between the Syrian Johannine community and the milieu of John of Patmos (e.g., the Lamb) and between that of the Syrian *Odes of*

Solomon and the *Ascension of Isaiah* ("Beloved"). But attempts to bring *Ascension of Isaiah* into the same milieu as the *Odes of Solomon* (Charlesworth, in Charlesworth 1983–85, 2:733; Hall 1990, 303–4) do not reckon with the considerable differences in prophetic self-definition and the relative importance given to visionary detail and angelology. *Ascension of Isaiah,* like Revelation but unlike *Odes of Solomon,* shows a thorough commitment to a self-definition modeled on the biblical *nābî².*

20. Norelli argues convincingly that Ignatius positions himself close enough to the ideology of *Ascension of Isaiah* in citing his own esoteric wisdom in the ranks of heavenly beings that he might be at least one of the author's chief opponents (1993, 95–99).

21. Montanus *apud* Jerome *Commentary on Ephesians* 2.3 = Heine 1989, §108. See Trevett 1996, 80–89.

22. Trans. and analysis in Hurst et al. 1984; Kessels and Van Der Horst 1987.

23. On the use of "elders" (using *gerontes* and *presbeis,* not *presbyteroi* as in Rev. 4:4; etc.), see Hurst et al. 1984, 26–28.

24. Ed. and trans. in Musurillo 1972, 106–31, with important analysis in Cox Miller 1995, chapter 6.

25. See Vielhauer and Strecker, in Schneemelcher 1991–92, 2:592–602; Osiek, in Yarbro Collins 1986, 113–21; Lane Fox 1987, 381–90; Cox Miller 1995, chapter 5.

26. Cf. *Herm. Mand.* 11.2 on false prophets. *Pace* Lane Fox (1987, 388–90), who views Hermas as distinctive of early Christian prophecy. A better discussion of Hermas's uniqueness in the prophetic tradition is Aune 1983, 299–310.

27. The standard collection of *Sibylline Oracles* is numbered books 1–8 and 11–14. The material in the manuscripts that was designated as books 9 and 10 duplicates material found in other books.

28. See Justin, *1 Apology* 20; Clement, *Stromateis* 6.5.43.1; Lactantius, *Divine Institutes* 1.6.6; etc.; Augustine, *City of God* 18.23. On the Jewish use of the Sibylline medium, see Collins, in Charlesworth 1983–85, 1:356–57, 381–83, 390–92.

29. On Sibyl-Enoch, see Pearson, in Nickelsburg 1972, 239–40. The Sibyl is Noah's daughter-in-law in *Sib. Or.* 3.823–27.

30. See Yarbro Collins's revised definition of the genre "apocalypse" as it pertains to early Christian apocalypses, in Yarbro Collins 1986, 7.

31. *Apocalypse of Elijah* 1.13–22 (fasting); 4.1–32, especially 24–29 (martyrdom). See Frankfurter 1993, chaps. 6 (martyrdom), 11 (fasting).

32. *Apoc. Paul* 9 (ascetics), 24 (prideful ascetics), 25 (prophetlike ascetics), 29 (simple monks), 31–39 (irresponsible ecclesiastics), 41 (heretics); *T. Isaac* 4:1–8 (superhuman fasting and charisma); 6:10–23 (memorial institutions in honor of Isaac; cf. *T. Jacob* 8).

33. On millennialism in Asia Minor, see Trevett 1996, 24–25, 95–105 (admitting the standard data for eschatological expectation but protesting too much against the label "millennialist"). On the millennialist background of the *Apocalypse of Elijah,* see Frankfurter 1993, 265–98.

34. See also Ignatius, *Letter to the Smyrnaeans* 8.1 and *Letter to the Trallians* 2–3,

with discussion by Norelli (1993, 95–99), who also proposes that the historical opponents of *Ascension of Isaiah*'s prophets were the increasingly hierarchical presbyters (ibid., 76). Further on the insecurity of identifying legitimate prophecy, see Aune 1983, 87–88, 222–29; and Lane Fox 1987, 409–10.

35. See especially Riddle 1931, 28–38, 133–46, and in general on the lust for martyrdom, 60–69, 72–76. For patristic voices, see Ignatius, *Letter to the Romans* 5–8; Cyprian, *Epistles* 10, 31, 37, 57, 67; Tertullian, *De anima* 55.4–5; *De fuga et persecutione* 9.4; Eusebius, *Martyrs of Palestine*. On the function of martyrological symbolism, see Thompson, in Yarbro Collins 1986,   147–74; and Frankfurter 1993, chapter 6.

36. Among many voices to this effect in early Christianity, see especially Rev. 14:1–5; *Apoc. Elijah* 1.13–22 (on which see Frankfurter 1993, 280–82); *Apoc. Paul* 9, 29 (cf. 24 on prideful ascetics); Tertullian, *De ieiunio* and *De monogamia* 3.1, 10–12; Apollonius *apud* Eusebius, *Hist. eccl.* 5.18.2.

37. Among the most important representatives of this position in the study of the Christian "Old Testament Pseudepigrapha" are Kraft (1994; and in Nickelsburg 1972, 121–37, especially 129–37) and de Jonge (1991, 233–43), with Simon 1954.

38. On Egyptian judgment in Christian texts, see, e.g., *T. Abr.* A 11–13, with Nickelsburg, in Nickelsburg 1972, 32–40; and Pearson, in ibid., pp. 243–55. Wis. 4:20–5:1 suggests that the synthesis of a neo–Egyptian judgment scene evidently began already in first-century Alexandrian Judaism. On Egyptian passage of the soul (with emphasis on obstructing deities and passwords to avoid them) in Christian texts, see especially *2 Jeu* 49; *Apoc. Elijah* 1.8–10; *Apoc. Paul* (NHC V, 2); *Apoc. Paul* (Coptic rec.) 14, 16; Origen, *Contra Celsum* 6.31; Irenaeus, *Against Heresies* 1.21.5. See Frankfurter 1993, 35–37, and in VanderKam and Adler 1996, 178–79.

⇌BIBLIOGRAPHY_____

Aune, David E. 1983. *Prophecy in Early Christianity and the Ancient Mediterranean World.* Grand Rapids: Eerdmans. Meticulous study of the language and performance of prophecy, based closely on texts with broad attention to biblical and other Mediterranean traditions.

Bauckham, Richard. 1994. "The *Apocalypse of Peter:* A Jewish Christian Apocalypse from the Time of Bar Kokhba." *Apocrypha* 5:7–111. The most recent and exhaustive study of the text, arguing strongly for a close historical relationship with the Jewish Bar Kokhba revolt of the early second century C.E.

Bergren, Theodore A. 1990. *Fifth Ezra: The Text, Origin and Early History.* Society of Biblical Literature Septuagint and Cognate Studies 25. Atlanta: Scholars Press. A careful study of this short prophetic text, emphasizing the nature of the manuscripts but including valuable observations on cultural context.

Cameron, Ron, and Arthur J. Dewey, eds. 1979. *The Cologne Mani Codex: "Concern-*

ing the Origin of His Body." Society of Biblical Literature Texts and Translations 15. Missoula, Mont.: Scholars Press. Text and translation of the first half of this third-century prophet's autobiography, part of which stresses his affiliation with Jewish apocalyptic tradition.

Charlesworth, James H., ed. 1983–85. *The Old Testament Pseudepigrapha.* Vols. 1–2. Garden City, N.Y.: Doubleday. Many texts included in this collection originated or took substantial form in Christian circles. Offers more elaborate introductions to texts than Sparks 1984, with occasionally idiosyncratic hypotheses or translations.

Collins, John J., ed. 1979. *Apocalypse: The Morphology of a Genre. Semeia* 14. Chico, Calif.: Scholars Press. Articles by A. Yarbro Collins on early Christian apocalypses and F. Fallon on Gnostic apocalypses provide the first synthetic assessments of the literature, while J. Collins's introduction is the first attempt to define the apocalypse as a literary genre.

Cox Miller, Patricia. 1995. *Dreams in Late Antiquity.* Princeton: Princeton University Press. Important study of the role and interpretation of dreams in Mediterranean antiquity, including chapters on the *Shepherd of Hermas* and the *Martyrdom of Perpetua.*

de Jonge, Marinus. 1991. *Jewish Eschatology, Early Christian Christology, and the Testaments of the Twelve Patriarchs.* Leiden: E. J. Brill. Previously published essays, including important discussions of the Christian composition and appropriation of biblical pseudepigrapha.

Frankfurter, David. 1993. *Elijah in Upper Egypt: The Apocalypse of Elijah and Early Egyptian Christianity.* Minneapolis: Fortress Press. Study, with translation, of this third-century Egyptian prophetic tract, reconstructing an apocalyptic Christianity in upper Egypt and examining the native Egyptian legacy in apocalyptic texts.

———. 1997. "Apocalypses Real and Alleged in the Mani Codex." *Numen* 44:60–73. Discusses the third-century prophet Mani's claims to affiliate himself with Jewish apocalypses.

Hall, Robert G. 1990. "The *Ascension of Isaiah:* Community, Situation, Date, and Place in Early Christianity." *Journal of Biblical Literature* 109:289–306. An insightful interpretation of the *Martyrdom of Isaiah's* story as a projection of the conflict among some Christian prophetic cabals.

Harlow, Daniel C. 1996. *The Greek Apocalypse of Baruch (3 Baruch) in Hellenistic Judaism and Early Christianity.* Studia in Veteris Testamenti Pseudepigrapha 12. Leiden: E. J. Brill. Important discussion of a Jewish apocalypse as it was taken over and edited by Christians.

Heine, Ronald E. 1989. *The Montanist Oracles and Testimonia.* North American Patristic Society, Patristic Monograph Series 14. Macon, Ga.: Mercer University Press. The sources for New Prophecy, gathered with text and translation from their authors' works.

Hills, Julian. 1990. *Tradition and Composition in the Epistula Apostolorum.* Harvard

Dissertations in Religion 24. Minneapolis: Fortress Press. Important study of the background and ideological perspectives of the *Epistula Apostolorum.*

Hollander, H. W., and Marinus de Jonge. 1985. *The Testaments of the Twelve Patriarchs: A Commentary.* Studia in Veteris Testamenti Pseudepigrapha 8. Leiden: E. J. Brill. Exhaustive study of the *Testaments of the Twelve Patriarchs,* with special attention (and texts relevant) to the identification of Jewish sources.

Hurst, André, Olivier Reverdin, and Jean Rudhardt. 1984. *Papyrus Bodmer XXIX: Vision de Dorothéos.* Cologne/Geneva: Fondation Martin Bodmer. The first edition of the *Vision of Dorotheos,* including study of language and convincing suggestions for the text's historical origins.

Kessels, A. H. M., and P. W. Van Der Horst. 1987. "The Vision of Dorotheus (Pap. Bodmer 29)." *Vigiliae Christianae* 41:313–59. A second edition of the *Vision,* after further study of the manuscript.

Koenen, Ludwig. 1986. "Manichaean Apocalypticism at the Crossroads of Iranian, Egyptian, Jewish and Christian Thought." In *Codex Manichaicus Coloniensis: Atti del Simposio Internazionale,* edited by Luigi Cirillo, 285–332. Cosenza: Marra Editore. Invaluable discussion of eschatological themes in Manichean literature as well as the interaction of various Mediterranean eschatological traditions in that literature.

Koenen, Ludwig, and Cornelia Römer, eds. 1988. *Der Kölner Mani-Codex: Über das Werden seines Leibes.* Papyrologica Colonensia 14. Opladen: Westdeutscher Verlag. The standard edition (with German translation) of the *Cologne Mani Codex,* including pages not included in Cameron and Dewey 1979.

Kraft, Robert A. 1994. "The Pseudepigrapha in Christianity." In *Tracing the Threads: Studies in the Vitality of Jewish Pseudepigrapha,* edited by John C. Reeves, 55–86. Atlanta: Scholars Press. The most important of a number of essays by Kraft on the Christian revisions, preservation, and inventions of ostensibly Jewish writings.

Lane Fox, Robin. 1987. *Pagans and Christians.* New York: Knopf. Chapters 8–9 provide an important discussion of early Christian visionary activity and martyrological tradition in the context of late antique history in general.

Luttikhuizen, Gerard P. 1985. *The Revelation of Elchasai.* Tübingen: Mohr (Siebeck). Most exhaustive study of the fragments of the *Book of Elchasai,* emphasizing its apocalyptic nature.

McGinn, Bernard. 1979. *Visions of the End: Apocalyptic Literature in the Middle Ages.* New York: Columbia University Press. Useful collection of sources on western apocalypticism (predominantly eschatological), extending from the fourth to the fifteenth century, with astute critical introductions.

Musurillo, Herbert. 1972. *The Acts of the Christian Martyrs.* Oxford: Clarendon Press. Includes the standard edition and translation of the *Martyrdom of Perpetua.*

Nickelsburg, George W. E., Jr., ed. 1972. *Studies in the Testament of Abraham.* Society of Biblical Literature Septuagint and Cognate Studies 6. Missoula, Mont.:

Scholars Press. Various essays examine the *Testament of Abraham*'s possible Jewish affiliations, Egyptian legacy, supernatural themes, and associated Coptic texts.

Norelli, Enrico. 1993. *Ascension d'Isaïe*. Turnhout: Brepols. Short study of the *Ascension of Isaiah*'s sources and prophetic religious culture, in general agreement with Hall 1990.

Pearson, Birger. 1990. *Gnosticism, Judaism, and Egyptian Christianity*. Minneapolis: Fortress Press. Previously published essays, many of which show convincing links between early forms of Gnosticism and Alexandrian Jewish conventicles.

Piovanelli, Pierluigi. 1993. "Les origines de l'*Apocalypse de Paul* reconsidérées." *Apocrypha* 4:25–64. Returns the dating of the *Apocalypse of Paul* to the late fourth century, following its introductory legend but against much twentieth-century scholarship ascribing the text to the mid-third century.

Podemann Sørensen, Jørgen. 1992. "Native Reactions to Foreign Rule and Culture in Religious Literature." In *Ethnicity in Hellenistic Egypt*, edited by Per Bilde, Troels Engberg-Pedersen, Lise Hannestad, and Jan Zahle, 164–81. Studies in Hellenistic Civilization 3. Aarhus: Aarhus University Press. Discusses the apocalyptic traditions of the Egyptian priesthood that contributed to various forms of Gnosticism and Christian apocalypticism.

Potter, David. 1990. *Prophecy and History in the Crisis of the Roman Empire: A Historical Commentary on the Thirteenth Sibylline Oracle*. Oxford: Clarendon Press. Introductory discussions place the Christian Sibyllines in the broader cultural context of the Roman Empire.

Riddle, Donald W. 1931. *The Martyrs: A Study in Social Control*. Chicago: University of Chicago Press. Seminal attempt to comprehend early Christian martyrdom ideology according to sociological and psychological principles, with attention to apocalyptic literature as a means for defining martyrs.

Satran, David. 1995. *Biblical Prophets in Byzantine Palestine: Reassessing the Lives of the Prophets*. Studia in Veteris Testamenti Pseudepigrapha 11. Leiden: E. J. Brill. Important discussion of the *Lives of the Prophets* as an essentially Christian collection meant to ground the Byzantine cult of the saints.

Schneemelcher, Wilhelm, ed. 1991–92. *New Testament Apocrypha*. Vols. 1–2. Trans. and ed. R. McL. Wilson. Rev. ed. Cambridge: James Clarke; Louisville: Westminster/John Knox. Vol. 2 includes the most important collection of translations and introductions to early Christian apocalyptic literature.

Schürer, Emil. 1973–87. *The History of the Jewish People in the Age of Jesus Christ*. Vols. 1–3. Second ed. rev. and ed. by Geza Vermes, Fergus Millar, and Martin Goodman. Edinburgh: T & T Clark. Vol. 3 (parts 1 and 2) incorporates a survey of Jewish communities known in the Greco-Roman world and the best English discussions of ancient Jewish and Christian works written in the names of biblical heroes.

Simon, Marcel. 1954. "Les Saints d'Israël dans la dévotion de l'Église ancienne."

Revue d'Histoire et de Philosophie Religieuses 34:98–127. The most important study of early Christian veneration, in multiple contexts, for biblical figures.

Sparks, H. F. D., ed. 1984. *The Apocryphal Old Testament.* Oxford: Clarendon Press. Many texts included in this collection originated or took substantial form in Christian circles. Some translations are more reliable than those in Charlesworth 1983–85.

Trevett, Christine. 1996. *Montanism: Gender, Authority, and the New Prophecy.* Cambridge: Cambridge University Press. Exhaustive study of the sources for New Prophecy, reconstructing various stages in the development and spread of the movement, with particular attention to the perspectives of the (unsympathetic) witnesses.

VanderKam, James C., and William Adler, eds. 1996. *The Jewish Apocalyptic Heritage in Early Christianity.* Compendia rerum iudaicarum ad novum testamentum III.4. Assen/Maastricht: Van Gorcum; Minneapolis: Fortress Press, 1996. Important essays on the preservation of Jewish apocalypses among early Christian groups, including Adler on the meaning of apocalyptic texts in earliest Christianity and Frankfurter on the diverse uses and legacies to which the Jewish texts were put in Asia Minor and Egypt.

Yarbro Collins, Adela, ed. 1986. *Early Christian Apocalypticism: Genre and Social Setting.* Semeia 36. Decatur, Ga.: Scholars Press. Useful essays on Revelation, *Hermas,* the *Ascension of Isaiah,* and other texts, identifying central themes among these texts and clarifying the nature of the apocalyptic "genre" since its formulation in Collins 1979.

PART 4

Epilogue

13

Apocalyptic Temporality and Politics in the Ancient World

Bruce Lincoln
University of Chicago

Only our concept of Time makes it possible for us to speak of the Day of Judgment by that name; in reality it is a summary court in perpetual session.
—Franz Kafka, "Reflections on Sin, Pain, Hope, and the True Way," Aphorism #38

☙OF TRUTH AND THE LIE

For heuristic purposes, I find it useful to begin with a set of texts that are not normally considered apocalypses, although they share many characteristics of the genre. These are the royal inscriptions of the Achaemenian king Darius the Great at Bisitun and Susa. Bisitun, which means "The Place of the Gods" (Old Persian **Baga-stāna*), is a mountain that rises abruptly over the main east–west thoroughfare of Iranian antiquity. There, some sixty meters above a dramatic point where the route winds between sheer rock and a spring of fresh water, Darius placed an elaborate relief, accompanied by a lengthy tri-lingual inscription (Elamite, Akkadian, and Old Persian, the first written attestation of the last language). Work on this monument was begun in 520 B.C.E., and its purpose was to commemorate events of 522–521, which

457

included Darius's accession to power and a series of rebellions throughout the empire, all of which he managed to quell, thereby securing his kingship (Schmitt 1991).

The relief depicts fourteen figures: twelve human, one royal, and one divine. Reading from left to right, one first encounters a group of three figures, all of whom face right. The first one bears a spear, the second a bow, and together they represent the might of the Persian army; the third is a full head larger than the others, and this is Darius himself. In his left hand, he too holds a bow, and he raises his right hand in a polysemic gesture that is simultaneously a greeting, an assertion of rectitude and power, and a sign of control. Floating above the rest of the composition in a winged circle is the chief deity of the pantheon, the Wise Lord (*Auramazdā*; cf. Avestan *Ahura Mazdā*, Pahlavi *Ohrmazd*), who faces Darius and raises his right hand, mirroring the gesture made by the king. Beneath this god, the composition is completed by ten figures, much smaller and sadder than the Persians. The first of their number lies on his back with arms upraised in supplication, as Darius plants a foot squarely on his chest. Behind him are nine more figures. As a group, they face Darius, their collective identity and fate established by a rope that binds them together at the neck. Their hands are also bound behind them. For all that they share the status of the vanquished, their portraits are individualized to convey ethnic stereotypes. Beneath each one is a formulaic caption:

> This Açina lied. He said thus: "I am King in Elam." (DBc)

> This Nidintu-Bel lied. He said thus: "I am Nebuchadnezzar, son of Nabonidus. I am king in Babylon." (DBd)

> This Fravarti lied. He said thus: "I am Xšaθrita, of the family of Cyaxares. I am King in Media." (DBf)

And so on, seven more times. Together, the picture and captions identify these unfortunate men as pretenders in all senses of the term: people who represented—and perhaps rightly understood—themselves as heirs to a throne, but whom their conqueror perceived and constituted as nothing more than frauds and deceivers.

The phrase "frauds and deceivers" signals a central concern of Old Persian ideology, but it fails to convey the way issues of truth and falsehood are treated within a discourse that is simultaneously ethical, theological, and cosmological. Thus, Old Persian *arta* denotes not just "truth" but the principle of right, order, and coherence on which the universe depends. Speech acts that are true in this broad sense create and maintain proper human relations; they also were understood to have real creative power beyond the social sphere. As a result, true speech—in particular, that of deities, priests, and kings—calls an orderly cosmos into being, advancing the Wise Lord's goals for his creation.[1] Truth is demanded of all righteous persons, and those who fulfill this obligation enjoy a blessed state after death, in which condition they are designated *arta-van-*, the righteous ones or, more literally, "possessors of truth."

Similar ideas are attested in other branches of the Indo-Iranian family, suggesting that this ideology has a deep prehistory. Thus, the cognate term in Avestan (*aša*) not only denotes an abstract principle but is also the name of an important deity: "Truth" personified, who is the foremost assistant of the Wise Lord. In Vedic Sanskrit, the cognate (*rta*) designates not just truth but the subtle cosmic order on which all depends.

Conversely, "the Lie" (Old Persian *drauga;* verbal forms are built on the root *duruj-;* cf. Avestan *drug,* Vedic *druh,* German *Trug,* English *be-tray*) is that most antithetical to truth, order, and the well-being of creation. The Lie encompasses all that corrupts, perverts, beguiles, and deludes; all that leads people into evil and renders them destructive to themselves, others, and the world around them. Just as Truth is the chief instrument of the Wise Lord, so the Lie does similar service for his primordial adversary, the Evil Spirit (Avestan *Angra Mainyu,* Pahlavi *Ahriman*). Ancient Iranian religion is built on the dualistic premise that these forces contend throughout history, but that history has a finite duration, which spans the time from the moment creation assumed material (instead of purely spiritual) form until the world's end, a period which Pahlavi sources tabulate in a series of nine or twelve millennia. During this period, it is the responsibility of humans to choose rightly between the two rival forces, knowing that history is moving toward its cataclysmic finale, at which time the Wise Lord, Truth, and their adherents will triumph decisively over Ahriman and the Lie, establishing a renewed, purified, and perfected creation for all eternity.

KINGS, REBELS, AND IMPOSTORS

Each paragraph of the inscription at Bisitun begins with a formula that announces its narrator and underscores the authority of his voice: "Says Darius the King" (θāti Dārayavauš xšāyaθiya). The first nine paragraphs form a prologue, in which Darius announces his titles (DB 1), his genealogy (DB 2), his family's claim to the throne (DB 3–5), the provinces in his empire (DB 6) and the extent of his power over them (DB 7–8). Most significant is his claim of legitimacy, which could not be based simply on lineage and descent, since neither his father nor grandfather ruled the empire (also, most anomalously, both men were still living when Darius took power).[2] Neither did it derive from proper coronation ritual, there being no indication that such was held. Rather, it rests squarely on divine election and God's continuing favor.

> Says Darius the king: The Wise Lord bestowed this kingdom on me. The Wise Lord bore me aid until I consolidated this kingdom. By the Wise Lord's will I hold[3] this kingdom. (DB 9)

With this as preamble, the Great King commences his narrative at DB 10. The story is complex, and critical responses to it have been varied. Some take it more or less at face value, while others regard it as royal propaganda that covers up some fairly dirty dealings. It begins with Cambyses, son and heir of Cyrus the Great, who ruled the Persian empire from 529 to 522 B.C.E. According to the Bisitun inscription and the relevant Greek sources (which draw on Darius's version but also preserve some independent information), Cambyses secretly murdered his brother Bardiya before departing for the conquest of Egypt.[4] Then, while Cambyses was on that campaign, there were unrest and rebellion in the home provinces. Darius describes the situation in terms that lead one to understand the crisis as not just political but moral, religious, and ultimately cosmic: "The people became disloyal (or: evil)[5] and the Lie (drauga) became great throughout the land" (DB 10).

At this juncture, the text introduces the character depicted supine in the relief, who incarnates all that is evil and whose treacherous actions initiate a long string of woes. This is "Gaumāta the Magus," a man whose title marks him as a Median priest, but whose conduct mocks and perverts the requirements of priestly office. Of him we are told: "He lied [adurujiya] to the people, saying 'I am Bardiya, the son of Cyrus, the brother of Cambyses.' Then the people all became rebellious from Cambyses" (DB 11). After three months of successful impersonation, this audacious deceiver claimed the throne for himself and became undisputed king when Cambyses died under mysterious circumstances (DB 11).[6]

Drawing on traditional Iranian myths, Darius describes Gaumāta first as a demonic figure who threatens the order of the cosmos and then as the victim whose sacrifice restores it.[7] He brands him a thief and usurper (DB 12), then describes how, once enthroned, this false-priest-cum-false-king instituted a reign of terror, killing anyone who threatened to unmask him (DB 13). Silence fell over the land until there arose a savior: a descendant of the Achaemenian line (but not of Cyrus, a fact the text acknowledges but elides).[8] More importantly, this hero was chosen and supported by God himself.

No one dared to say anything about Gaumāta the Magus until I arose. Then I asked the Wise Lord for assistance. The Wise Lord bore me aid. Ten days of the month Bagayadi had passed (29 September 522) when I, with a few men, slew that Gaumāta the Magus and the people who were his foremost followers. . . . By the Wise Lord's will I became king. The Wise Lord bestowed the kingship on me.

Says Darius the king: The kingship that had been usurped from our lineage, I put that in its place. I restored it in place. Just as they had been before, so I made the temples that Gaumāta the Magus destroyed. I restored the pastures and live-stock and servants and houses of the people, of which Gaumāta the Magus had deprived them. I set the people back in place, in Persia and Media and the other lands. Just as it was before, so I brought back that which had been usurped. By the Wise Lord's will I did this. I strove until I restored our (royal) house to its place, just as before. Thus I strove, by the Wise Lord's will, so that Gaumāta the Magus did not usurp our (royal) house. (DB 13-14)

With this account of restoration—social, political, and religious, all accomplished by divine favor—the drama of Gaumāta is brought to a close. Quickly, Darius moves on to speak of the nine rebellions that broke out in Elam, Babylon, and other provinces of the empire over the following months (DB 15–53). In each case, he fleshes out the brief descriptions of the captions on the relief. A given individual represented himself as the heir to a royal line that had seemingly ended when the nation in question was conquered and incorporated as a province of the Persian empire. Although the text treats all such claims as false—that is, inspired by the Lie—it acknowledges that people rallied to the standards of these pretenders and that each of them raised armies for his cause of nationalist revolt. Although embattled and occasionally out-numbered, Darius invariably called on the Wise Lord, from whom he received assistance. In his first year as king, he and his generals fought nine-teen battles, winning victory in all. The text constitutes these victories as incontestable proof that he was and remains God's chosen.

In each of these cases, the rebellion ended with the capture of the pre-tender, who was punished in exemplary fashion. Most striking is the fate of Fravarti and Tritantaxma, the two rebels who claimed descent from Cyaxares and who sought to restore the Median empire, which, from the Persian point of view, would amount to reversing the course of world history. Both these men were bound and taken before Darius, who had their nose, ears, and tongue cut off and an eye put out, after which he placed them on public display and finally had them impaled (DB 32–33). Clearly, such acts were meant to provide an object lesson for other would-be rebels, and they may also be understood as a theater of cruelty, in which the king's power was graphically demonstrated. Beyond this, they echoed Indo-Iranian myths in which creation involved the sacrificial dismemberment of a primordial victim. Above all, they were meant to be read as conclusive judgments, through which Truth was reestablished and the Lie suppressed.

> Says Darius the king: These are the nine kings whom I seized in these battles.

> Says Darius the king: These are the lands that became rebellious. The Lie made them rebellious. These men lied to the people. Then the Wise Lord put them into my hand. As was my desire, so I did unto them.[9]

> Says Darius the king: You who may be king hereafter—Protect yourself boldly from the Lie! The man who is a follower of the Lie, punish him with a good punishment if you would think "Let my land be secure." (DB 53–55; cf. 62–64)

Fittingly, Darius then swears that all he has said is true (DB 56–57) and suggests that he has deliberately understated his accomplishments in order that his readers not be tempted to the mistake of incredulity (DB 58–59). He calls down blessings on whoever reads his story and repeats it to others, with corresponding curses on whoever would conceal or destroy it (DB 60–61, 65–67). He ends by naming the six noble Persians who helped him to kill Gaumāta and asks that their offspring enjoy benefits forever (DB 68–69). The final paragraph of the original inscription states that the king himself has supervised preparation of this text and has had his scribes prepare parchment copies for dissemination throughout the empire (DB 70). A later addition describes events in the second year of Darius's reign (521–520 B.C.E.), which included the suppression of Elamite rebels (DB 71–73) and an expedition against the Scythians (DB 74–75), both of whom are denounced on religious grounds.[10] The text ends with a benediction that underscores its religious nature, the religious nature of its author, and that of the regime that produced it: "Says Darius the King: He who worships the Wise Lord, may there be favor for him, both while living and when dead" (DB 76).

NEW HEAVEN, NEW EARTH

The moral universe described on the rock face at Bisitun is one that initially is in disarray. So prevalent is the Lie that people repeatedly misrepresent themselves as kings, while countless others, unable to discriminate between truth and falsehood, choose to follow the impostors. Kingship, however, is not theorized as an elective office, in which ratification by the populace plays a role of any ultimate consequence. Rather, it is represented as a charisma in the most literal sense, such that true kings enjoy God's favor and triumph over all rivals by the force of that truth. The central proposition of the text, which it never tires of repeating, is that Darius alone acted—and inevitably prevailed—"by the Wise Lord's will" (vašna-Auramazdāhā, on which see Lincoln 1996).

DB thus traces a crisis it takes to be simultaneously dynastic and cosmic, narrating the eruption of evil in the form of a foreign priest, inspired by the Lie, who usurped and perverted the world's foremost empire. The text goes on to describe the heroic intervention of a savior prince, God's chosen, who perceived the Lie, conquered the villain, saw the world and empire through a period of unprecedented woes, then meted out judgment, restored righteous order, and ushered in a new age of perfection. The establishment of that paradisal condition is treated in a second set of texts, which date to a later phase of Darius's reign, ca. 518–512 B.C.E., when he built his great palace at Susa, where these inscriptions are found.[11]

The nineteen inscriptions that have been recovered at Susa were written in mono- and trilingual versions on clay and marble tablets, as well as on statues, columns, bricks, and marble plaques from the palace complex. Many texts exist in multiple copies, including the most extensive one (DSf), which was placed, *inter alia,* on the glazed tiles that formed the frieze of the great hall. All these texts follow a consistent pattern, although individual elements may be lacking in any given variant. Those elements are, in the constant order of their presentation: (1) an account of the cosmogony; (2) a list of the king's titles; (3) a list of the provinces in his empire; (4) a legitimating account of his divine election; (5) an assertion that his deeds were accomplished by the Wise Lord's will; (6) description and praise of his palace at Susa; (7) a benediction. Although no variant realizes this pattern in its totality, DSf comes closest, lacking only one element.

Within this structure, subtle resonances and parallelisms between the first and sixth sections advance an audacious subtext, insinuating that God's purpose in history has now been fulfilled with the erection of Darius's palace. Toward this end, creation is described in two fashions. In several of the longer inscriptions, the Wise Lord is credited with five specific accomplishments. First comes creation of the earth, then sky, humanity, and human happiness, all of which deeds are described with the verb dā-, "to put in place, create." God's last accomplishment, however, is set somewhat apart from the others, while it is also represented as his culminating act. For this, the text uses a different verb: kar-, "to make, build, do."

> A great god is the Wise Lord, who created this earth, who created that sky, who created mankind, who created the happiness of mankind, who made Darius

king: one king over many, one architect over many. (DSe 1 = DSf 1 = DSt 1 = DNa 1, on which see Herrenschmidt 1977)

A second version occurs in a shorter inscription that is limited to a creation account and a benediction.

A great god is the Wise Lord, who makes a wonder (fraša) on this earth, who makes mankind on this earth, who makes the happiness of mankind, who makes good horses and good chariots. On me he bestowed them. May the Wise Lord protect me and what has been built by me. (DSs; cf. DSp and DNb 1)

Several points in this brief text merit attention. First, God's creation of heaven and earth is here summarized in a single term, the significance of which we will shortly consider: fraša, "a wonder." Second, his creative acts are here all denoted with the verb kar-. Third, the same verb occurs in the final benediction, where Darius asks the Wise Lord to protect what he, as king, has made and built (kartam, the past passive participle of kar-). This verbal echo suggests that, like God himself, Darius is a creator; further, that after creating the universe, the Wise Lord consigned it to Darius's care, so that his royal deeds could complete the creation.

The parallelism between divine and royal creativity is further underscored by Darius's use of the term already noted—fraša, "a wonder." Within the Old Persian corpus, only two actors are ever said to have created (dā-), planned (fra-mā-), or built (kar-) such a wonder, and only two items are so designated. In the first instance, as we have seen, the Wise Lord's creation of heaven and earth can be called the making of a fraša (DSs, DNb 1). In the second, Darius repeatedly refers to his palace at Susa with the same term.

Says Darius the king: By the Wise Lord's will, may this palace built [kartam] by me appear a wonder [fraša] to whoever may see it. (DSj 3; cf. DSa 2, DSd 2, DSf 4, DSj 3, DSo, DSz lines 35–37)

From all indications, Susa truly was a marvel, and was so regarded throughout antiquity. In one inscription, Darius details the way each province of his empire contributed the substances for which it was most famous: gold from Bactria, cedars from Lebanon, turquoise from Chorasmia, ivory from India and Ethiopia (DSf 3f–3k). The point was not just conspicuous consumption. Rather, the palace was meant to be a microcosm of the empire, the central point at which all regions of the globe were reconciled and, what is more, the culminating accomplishment of world history, which the Great King built with the finest matter of the Wise Lord's creation. With the completion of Susa, Darius seems to have believed—or at the very least, wished his subjects to believe—that the Lie had been vanquished, Truth restored, the cosmos purified and perfected for the eternity that was just dawning. All this is summarized in his use of Old Persian fraša, a term that in Avestan and Pahlavi texts (i.e., the specifically religious literature of Zoroastrianism) specifically denotes the eschatological perfection of existence, including the coming of a savior, defeat of the Evil Spirit, resurrection of the dead, last judgment, and purification of the cosmos for eternity.[12]

RECALIBRATING THE TEMPORAL SCHEMATA OF POLITICALLY SIGNIFICANT NARRATIVES

Darius's inscriptions closely resemble apocalyptic literature, not only in form but in their core theological content. Both genres thematize dualistic struggles between the embattled forces of a good God and their quasi-demonic adversaries. In both cases, a battle for royal power and legitimacy is understood to be so profound that the fate of the cosmos hangs on it. And in both, after a series of perilous travails, God's chosen hero wins a definitive victory over evil, then undertakes works of reconstruction that found a new age of peace and perfection.

In light of all this, one might well ask: Why are Darius's inscriptions *not* considered an instance of the apocalyptic genre? The answer, I think, is fairly simple, but no less instructive for that. The discourse of the inscriptions is in the first person and the past tense, describing things the author has already accomplished. In contrast, the crucial passages of apocalyptic literature are normally in the third person and the future tense, a future so charged with urgency and intensity that it often borders on the imperative. These grammatical differences reflect different temporal orientations, subject positions, and political agendas.

For his part, Darius imposed a religious pattern on recent events, consistent with his imperial purposes. Accordingly, his account contrasts the turbulence, danger, and immorality of the immediate past to the regime of truth and righteousness he established. Although opinion is not unanimous, most scholars now take this account *cum grano salis,* and read "Gaumāta the Magus" as a convenient fiction of Darius's invention. In their view, the man Darius killed was exactly who he claimed to be: Bardiya, son of Cyrus, brother of Cambyses, and from March until September of 522, reigning king of the Persian empire. Rather than seeing the gaps and implausibilies of Darius's account as the reflection of events Byzantine in their complexity, they take them to have been the instruments through which a new but shrewd monarch attempted to discredit his predecessors and justify himself. Blaming Cambyses for the secret, previously unknown murder of Bardiya and redefining Bardiya as a secret, previously unknown impostor, Darius thus crafted a story line in which he played the role of hero and savior, rather than that of regicide and usurper.[13]

Critical readers have also been prompted to ask what caused the rebellions of 522–521. Here a piece of information omitted from the Bisitun text but preserved elsewhere holds some interest. Herodotus states that during Bardiya's brief reign, "he exhibited great deeds of benevolence [*euergesias megalas*] for all his subjects, so that when he died all the peoples in Asia yearned for him, except the Persians themselves. For the Magus began by sending messages to all the nations of the empire and he proclaimed them exempt from tribute and military service for three years" (Herodotus 3.67; cf. Justinus 1.9.12-13).[14]

Writing shortly, but securely, after the fact—when Bardiya was dead, the rebellions crushed, and tributes reimposed—Darius offered a very different picture, exercising the victor's control over the historic record to brand the rebels followers of the Lie. At Bisitun and Susa, we can observe him shifting from an emergency campaign of military pacification to a long-term project of ideological control. The texts his scribes produced for him at these sites were designed to persuade his subjects—and perhaps to persuade even Darius himself—that with his accession God's plan for history had been fulfilled, and that further change was as unthinkable as it would be undesirable.

All of this contrasts with the standard conventions of apocalyptic literature, although similar incidents figure therein: a time of woes, the coming of a savior, war against the beast, the triumph of good, judgments on the wicked, the creation of a new world order, which culminates in the erection of a glorious new city, palace, or temple. Apocalyptic texts, however, treat these not as *faits accomplis* but as certainties anticipated in the immediate future. Where imperial propaganda constructs an official, sacred history that speaks of the past in order to stabilize the present and foreclose the possibility of any different future, apocalypse constructs a prophetic utterance that speaks of the future in order to destabilize an offensive status quo.

The similarities and differences of the two genres are hardly accidental, and one can observe a complex dialogue and war of position between them. Thus, apocalypses take as their starting point one of the central tenets of imperial propaganda: the equation of an imperial order with the order of the cosmos itself. That granted, however, they strategically reshape another key element of imperial ideology to serve their own, antithetical purposes. For instead of concluding that the empire in question is, like the cosmos, eternal and unchangeable, they assert that the cosmos, like this empire, is fast approaching its violent end.

This is why apocalyptic texts take the form of a future-tense discourse, portraying events that are imminent and inevitable, being parts of a pattern that God has inscribed on historic time and a malleable cosmos. It is their task, moreover, to disclose the true nature of this pattern by speaking of creation, heaven and hell, the course of world history, the succession of empires, and so forth, in order to explain the present degraded state of affairs and to announce the prospect of its violent end. The violence of their eschatological vision thus indexes the severity of the problems they confront and reflects their conviction that these difficulties are irresolvable in any less radical fashion.

In his influential article "Religion as a Cultural System," Clifford Geertz (1973) argued that religion offers both a "model of" and a "model for" existence. In general, it has been assumed that it is one and the same model that simultaneously serves both purposes. In apocalypticism, however, the two models are not just separate but stand in pointed opposition to one another. Thus, the "model of" existence governs the present state of affairs, which is taken to be hopelessly flawed, while the "model for" is set in the future and is used to denounce and correct the perceived failings in the "model of." This tension between an intolerable "is" and an eagerly anticipated "ought, will, and must be" makes religious discourse an instrument not for the reproduction of culture (as in cases where the two models are isomorphic) but for critique and transformation. And when the future is patterned after an ideal set in the past (either recent or primordial), it can become an instrument of reaction and/or restoration.

Along these lines, apocalypses regularly denounce a scandalous world, where wealth, power, royal office, and other advantages belong to foreigners, turncoats, and those judged immoral. Beyond this, they call for cataclysmic change: the humbling of the mighty and exaltation of the meek. This inversionary message reorients people whose situations might otherwise dispose them to feel anxiety, frustration, and impotence, leading them to a new—if often extreme and extremely unrealistic—sense of hope, confidence, and self-righteousness.

Whether or not this will lead to militance and outright insurrection is hard to predict. Many factors influence the ways individuals and groups respond to an apocalyptic message. Quiet waiting is a possibility, as are withdrawal, proselytizing, despair, and rebellion. One variable that has its importance is the way different apocalyptic texts handle the question of agency. Thus, apocalypses that attribute the anticipated salvific acts predominantly or exclusively to a divine actor can console and reassure their audiences, predisposing them to a period of calm, patient waiting. In contrast, texts that ascribe these acts to exceptional, but wholly human subjects—particularly to collective subjects like a nation, sect, band of the righteous, or chosen people—are more prone to foster attitudes of militance and activism.

In general, one can understand apocalypticism as a religious style that gives voice to the interests and latent consciousness of the dispossessed and defensive. By this I mean to indicate sectors of society that have lost power, prestige, wealth, confidence, and/or security within their historic memory, or who feel acutely threatened by such loss in the present. As examples, one could point to displaced elites, marginal intellectuals, those deprived of patrons, peoples in exile, and classes threatened with structural obsolescence. Within the ancient world, however, apocalypses are most frequently associated with those who would extricate conquered nations from the grasp of foreign empires and who, toward that end, seek to recuperate native kingly rule. Along these lines, Jonathan Z. Smith has written insightfully.

> In the Near Eastern context, two elements are crucial: scribalism and kingship. The *situation* of apocalypticism seems to me to be the cessation of native kingship; the *literature* of apocalypticism appears to me to be the expression of archaic, scribal wisdom as it comes to lack a royal patron. . . . [T]he *apocalyptic pattern* [involves the perception] that the wrong king is on the throne, that the cosmos will be thereby destroyed, and that the right god will either restore proper native kingship (his terrestrial counterpart) or will assume kingship himself. . . . (J. Smith 1982, 94)

As we have seen, Darius's inscriptions can be understood as an attempt to freeze both political and historic process by misrepresenting the Great King as God's chosen savior and the perfecter of creation. Apocalyptic texts use the same narrative line and draw on the same repertoire of images and themes as imperial propaganda, but they do so to very different purpose. By recalibrating the temporal schema ever so slightly—putting woes in the present rather than the recent past, salvation in the near future rather than the present—they speak for the nationalist rebels who periodically challenged world empires. Instead of Darius's voice, we hear that of his enemies: Açina, Nidintu-Bel, Fravarti, Tritantaxma, and their brethren. Although such leaders occasionally met with success (Judah Maccabee, for instance), more often they ended their lives nailed to crosses and impaled on stakes, after which they became characters in the victor's self-serving texts. Before that, however, they were heroes and authors in texts of their own, texts we characterize as apocalyptic.

⌒THE SECRET LIFE OF TEXTS _____

While most rebellions fail, the texts rebels produce may linger on, remaining available for revision, redaction, and subsequent reuse of unforeseen sorts. Over the course of their transmission they can gain novel audiences, expanding their range of applicability as they do so. In the process, however, they lose the specificity of their original context and world of reference, while also coming in for some highly creative, not to say tortuous, hermeneutics.

Even victors' texts can follow a similar trajectory, moving into new contexts where they are adapted for purposes quite different from those of their original authors and patrons. So it is with the propaganda employed by Cyrus the Great, founder of the Achaemenian dynasty, who began his career as a rebel against the Median empire, and who triumphed successively over Medians, Lydians, and Babylonians alike. An interesting step in his path to imperial power is preserved in the Akkadian text known as the "Cyrus-cylinder," which was written shortly after his conquest of Babylon (October 12, 539 B.C.E.), with the help of Babylonian priests. The second half of this text is similar to Darius's inscriptions at Susa, as the king speaks in the first person, announcing his titles, lineage, charismatic legitimation; recounting his deeds, especially those of restoration and pacification; and pronouncing a final benediction. The first half of the inscription follows a different pattern, however. Here, Cyrus's scribes told the Babylonian populace that their king, Nabonidus (556–539) had committed a series of cultic offenses, as a result of which their chief god had withdrawn support from him and conferred it on another.

> He scanned and looked through all the countries, searching for a righteous ruler. . . . He pronounced the name of Cyrus, king of Anšan, and declared him to be ruler of all the world. . . . Marduk, the great lord, a protector of his people, beheld with great pleasure Cyrus's good deeds and his upright mind, and ordered him to march against his city Babylon. He made him set out on the road to Babylon, going at his side like a real friend. Without any battle, he made him enter his town Babylon, sparing Babylon any calamity. He delivered into his hands Nabonidus, the king who did not worship Marduk. All the inhabitants of Babylon . . . bowed to Cyrus and kissed his feet, jubilant that he had received the kingship. Happily they greeted him as a master through whose help they had come to life from death and had been spared damage and disaster, and they worshiped his name. (Trans. A. Leo Oppenheim, in Pritchard 1969, 315–16 [slightly modified])

This text, which is shrewdly modeled after certain inscriptions of Aššur-banipal (Harmatta 1971), is designed to smoothe the transition from a native king to a foreign conqueror, to erase the role of force in the conquest, and to attract the support of local elites. Toward those ends, it represents Cyrus as a much more pious and proper ruler than the man he defeated, ventriloquistically placing this conclusion in the mouth of the native God. Not only is the "Marduk" of this text made to select and hail Cyrus as king; he accompanies Cyrus on the march to Babylon, then delivers the city to him as the jubilant locals celebrate their new ruler.

One may be permitted to doubt if the scene enacted by Babylonians upon the loss of their independence was as simple or as unambiguously joyous an affair as Cyrus's script makes it appear.[15] Nationalist and anti-Persian sentiments were strong in Babylon for some time, and they remained focused on the native kingly line. This became clear during the rebellions Darius faced some seventeen years later, two of which were led by men claiming "I am Nebuchadnezzar, son of Nabonidus. I am king in Babylon" (DBd and DBi; cf. DB 16 and 49). Presumably each one claimed Marduk's favor with no less right than did Cyrus.

Cyrus's propaganda seems to have been most effective not in Babylon itself but among peoples he liberated from Babylonian rule, on whom the Persian yoke rested a good deal more lightly than had that of Nabonidus and his predecessors. Nowhere was this truer than in Israel, which had suffered crushing defeats, failed rebellions, the loss of native rule, deportation of large sectors of its population, destruction of Jerusalem and the Temple in the course of the sixth century—all at the hands of the Babylonians. News of Cyrus's triumph carried quickly to Israel, and it seems likely that the Persian monarch established communications with some of the Israelite exile community resident in Babylon. The policies he adopted would fulfill their fondest desires, for he granted permission to return from captivity and rebuild the Temple (2 Chr. 36:22–23; cf. Ezra 1:1–11 and 5:13–6:5). It is in this immediate context that an influential Israelite text used imagery and theology similar to that found in the propaganda of Cyrus and Darius.

> Thus says the Lord, your Redeemer, who formed you from the womb;
> "I am the Lord, who made all things, who stretched out the heavens alone,
>   who spread out the earth . . .
> Who says of Cyrus, 'He is my shepherd, and he shall fulfill all my purpose';
> saying of Jerusalem, 'She shall be built,' and of the temple, 'Your foundations
>   shall be laid.'"
> Thus says the Lord to his anointed, to Cyrus,
>   whose right hand I have grasped,
> to subdue nations before him
>   and ungird the loins of kings,

to open doors before him
    that gates may not be closed:
"I will go before you
    and level the mountains,
I will break in pieces the doors of bronze
    and cut asunder the bars of iron,
I will give you the treasures of darkness
    and the hoards in secret places,
that you may know that it is I, the Lord
    the God of Israel, who call you by your name.
                (Isa. 44:24–45:3)

One should probably understand the authorship of this text as overdetermined, for several ventriloquists adopt the persona of Yahweh (M. Smith 1963). Prime among them are the scribes responsible for Cyrus's propaganda, who persuaded Israel to accept Persian rule with some of the same strategies they had deployed in Babylon: endorsement of Cyrus by the local deity, who calls him by name, takes his hand, and walks alongside him to the lands he delivers unto him. More immediate, however, is an Israelite voice that celebrates liberation from the Babylonians and seeks to reconcile his countrymen to the odd but inescapable fact that God had chosen a foreigner as his instrument for the rebuilding of Jerusalem and the Temple—acts that would set right the cosmos—rather than an heir of the Davidic line. Indeed, Yahweh hails Cyrus portentously, calling him "my anointed" (*māšîaḥ* [whence English *messiah*]; Septuagint *christos*), the only time the Hebrew Bible uses this title for someone outside the covenant community and the first time it expands its sense to denote one not just a king but also a savior.

Tracing the influence of the messianic tradition inaugurated by this passage would require an encyclopedia unto itself (most recently, see Sawyer 1996). In conclusion, I would simply note two of its stranger reverberations in the twentieth century. First, when Woodrow Wilson came to Europe in 1919, promoting his Fourteen Points as the basis for a just and lasting peace, Nathan Söderblom, archbishop of the Swedish National Church, professor of history of religions at Uppsala University, and a leading authority on Iranian religions, sent him a telegram with an elegant allusion. His message consisted of excerpts from Isaiah 45, starting with the phrase "Thus says the Lord to his anointed," but omitting the name of Cyrus. In this fashion, he apparently hoped to suggest that the idealistic American president might play the same role for Europe that the Persian monarch had played for Babylon and Israel: savior, rebuilder, and God's prince of peace. This well-intentioned gesture turned controversial, however, when some Swedes took it more literally than its author intended and polemicized that Wilson could just as well be Antichrist as the Messiah (Melander 1919).

Second, there is the name a certain Vernon Howell (1959–1993) took for himself in 1990, before winning notoriety in Waco's flames. Although Howell stated in his legal petition for a change of name that he wished to use that he desired a name he could use in his work as an entertainer, later events reveal a deeper meaning and purpose. Thus, his new name served to announce his claim that he united within himself the qualities of the two foremost messianic figures of the Hebrew Bible. And if his first name—"David"—made transparent reference to the line of Israelite kings, his surname did similar service for the Achaemenians, since "Koresh" is the standard Hebrew transcription of Old Persian Kuruš, the man known to us as Cyrus and to Isaiah as Yahweh's chosen and anointed (Tabor and Gallagher 1995).

NOTES

1. The high importance Persians accorded to the truth was noted by Greek authors, including Herodotus (1.136 and 138) and Xenophon (*Cyropaedia* 8.8.2).

2. This is established in DSf 3b (Kent 1953, 142–44).

3. Both this and the preceding verb (*dar-* and *ham-dar-*) suggest the possession of something one holds fast (cf. the cognate Latin *fir-mus*). Moreover, they involve wordplay on Darius's name, which literally means "He who holds fast the good" (from participial **dhārayat-vasu-*).

4. The most important of the Greek sources is Herodotus 3.61-79. Others include Aeschylus *Persians* 770 ff., Ctesias, Trogus *apud* Justinus, and several of much lesser value.

5. There is some disagreement over the precise form and significance of this word. Schmitt (1991, 50) reads *arīka-* and compares Vedic *álīka-* "unfaithful, disloyal. " In contrast, Kent (1953, 170) reads *arika-* (with a short *-i-*) and derives it from **asra-*, cognate to Avestan *angra-*, "evil," the defining quality of the "Evil Spirit" (Angra Mainyu) in Zoroastrianism.

6. The text somewhat cryptically states that Cambyses "died his own death" (*Kambujiya uvamṛšiyuš amariyatā*, DB 11). Some have taken this to mean suicide and others, a natural death. Herodotus treats it as a freak accident guided by an inexorable fate (3.64).

7. Although space does not permit me to develop this argument in detail, Darius draws on two bodies of myth. The first is the cosmogonic account of the Evil Spirit's first assault on the world and the ironic way his murder of the first man and first bovine (Gayōmard and Evagdād) redound to the good of creation. The second treats the origins of the social and political order, focusing on the first king (Yima),

who lost his realm to a monstrous usurper (Aži Dahāka), and the hero (Thraētaona) who defeated the latter and restored proper kingship.

8. The Achaemenian genealogy is as follows. Those who ruled over the empire, rather than a single province, appear in capital letters (after Kent 1953, 158). The dynasty was founded by Cyrus the Great, who initially was succeeded by his own descendants. Darius's accession disrupted this dynastic line, and one can view his invocation of Achaemenes (DB 2–3)—the (mythic?) ancestor he shared with Cyrus—as a strategic intervention and perhaps a convenient fiction.

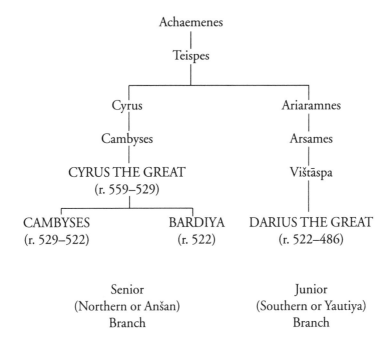

9. This formula occurs elsewhere (DB 72 and 75), also with reference to the punishment of rebels. The diction of the Old Persian texts as a whole makes it clear, however, that they do not wish the king's desire (*kāma*) to be understood as volatile, frivolous, self-indulgent, sadistic, or erotic, for all that a critical reader might perceive such aspects. In most contexts, the king's desire is simply to establish that which is just and good (DNa 4, DNb 8a–e). Moreover, desire is attributed to two subjects only, the king and the Wise Lord, the desire of the one being a reflection and extension of the other's. As Darius states in DSf 3c: "This was the desire of the Wise Lord: In all the earth, he chose me as [his] man. He made me king of all the empire."

10. "Says Darius the King: 'These [people] were evil. The Wise Lord was not worshipped by them'" (DB 72 and 75). This seems to be a new line of propaganda developed when column 5 was added to the Bisitun text (519 B.C.E.), since the charge of nonbelief is not made in the first four columns.

11. Most of the texts are available in Kent 1953, 141–46, with the exception of

DSz, which is found in Steve 1974, 164. On the importance of the palace complex, see Briant 1996, 177–80; Dandamaev and Lukonin 1989, 256–59.

12. On fraša, see Lincoln 1996. For broader discussions of Achaemenid royal propaganda, see Briant 1996, 175–265; Root 1979.

13. A convenient summary of the literature is provided by Herrenschmidt 1982.

14. Herodotus gives Darius's predecessor and victim the name "Smerdis," which is one of several attempts to capture Old Persian *Bardiya* within Greek phonology. Others include Mardos (Aeschylus, *Persians* 773–75), Merphis (scholium to idem, line 770), and Mergis (Trogus *apud* Justinus). Herodotus gives no indication of knowing the name Gaumāta. Rather, he tells that the Magus-impostor had the same name as the prince he impersonated, to whom, as a further coincidence, he bore an uncanny resemblance (Herodotus 3.61).

15. On Cyrus's conquest of Babylon, see Briant 1996, 50–55.

BIBLIOGRAPHY

Abbreviations

DB	Darius, Bisitun inscription (Schmitt 1991, 49–76)
DB a–k	Minor inscriptions at Bisitun (Schmitt 1991, 77–80)
DN a and b	Darius's inscriptions at Naqš-i-Ruštam (Kent 1953, 137–40)
DS a–y	Darius's inscriptions at Susa (Kent 1953, 141–46)
DS z	Additional inscription of Darius at Susa (Steve 1974, 164)
XP a–k	Xerxes' inscriptions at Persepolis (Kent 1953, 147–52)

Briant, Pierre. 1996. *Histoire de l'empire perse de Cyrus à Alexandre.* Vol. 1. Leiden: Nederlands Instituut voor het Nabije Oosten.

Dandamaev, M. A. 1989. *A Political History of the Achaemenid Empire.* Leiden: E. J. Brill.

Dandamaev, Muhammad A., and Vladimir G. Lukonin. 1989. *The Culture and Social Institutions of Ancient Iran.* Cambridge: Cambridge University Press.

Geertz, Clifford. 1973. "Religion as a Cultural System." In *The Interpretation of Cultures,* 87–125. New York: Basic Books.

Harmatta, J. 1971. "The Literary Patterns of the Babylonian Edict of Cyrus." *Antiqua Academiae Scientiarum Hungaricae* 19:217–31.

Herrenschmidt, Clarisse. 1982. "Les historiens de l'empire Achéménide et l'inscription de Bisotun." *Annales Économies Sociétés Civilisations* 37:813–23.

Kent, Roland G. 1953. *Old Persian: Grammar, Texts, Lexicon.* New Haven: American Oriental Society, 1953.

Lincoln, Bruce. 1996. "The Wise Lord's Will and the Making of Wonders: At the

Intersection of Religious and Imperial Ideology." *Indogermanische Forschungen* 101:147–67.

Melander, Henning. 1919. *President Wilson och Cyrus-profetian*. Huddinge: För-fattarens eget Forlag [sc. "The Author's own publishing house"].

Pritchard, James B., ed. 1969. *Ancient Near Eastern Texts relating to the Old Testament*. 3rd ed. Princeton: Princeton University Press.

Root, Margaret Cool. 1979. *The King and Kingship in Achaemenid Art*. Leiden: E. J. Brill.

Sawyer, John F. A. 1996. *The Fifth Gospel: Isaiah in the History of Christianity*. New York: Cambridge University Press.

Schmitt, Rüdiger. 1991. *The Bisitun Inscriptions of Darius the Great: Old Persian Text*. Corpus Inscriptionum Iranicarum, Part I, Volume I. London: School of Oriental and African Studies.

Smith, Morton. 1963. "II Isaiah and the Persians." *Journal of the American Oriental Society* 83:415–21.

Smith, Jonathan Z. 1982. "A Pearl of Great Price and a Cargo of Yams." In *Imagining Religion: From Babylon to Jonestown,* 90–101. Chicago: University of Chicago Press.

Steve, M.-J. 1974. "Inscriptions des Achéménides à Suse." *Studia Iranica* 3:7–28, 135–69.

Tabor, James D., and Eugene V. Gallagher. 1995. *Why Waco? Cults and the Battle for Religious Freedom in America*. Berkeley: University of California Press.

Index of Ancient Sources

Index of Names